Economic Issues:
A Canadian Perspective

Economic Issues:
A Canadian Perspective

C. Michael Fellows
Mount Royal College

Greg Flanagan
Mount Royal College

Stanford Shedd
University of Calgary

Based upon *Economics of Social Issues, Twelfth Edition*

Ansel M. Sharp
Frank W. Wilson, Professor of Political Economy
The University of the South

Charles A. Register
Mississippi State University

Paul W. Grimes
Mississippi State University

Represented in Canada by:
**McGraw-Hill
Ryerson Limited**

IRWIN

Toronto • Chicago • New York • Auckland • Bogotá
Caracas • Lisbon • London • Madrid • Mexico • Milan
New Delhi • San Juan • Singapore • Sydney • Tokyo

McGraw-Hill
   A Division of The McGraw-Hill Companies

Based upon *Economics of Social Issues, Twelfth Edition*

ECONOMIC ISSUES: A CANADIAN PERSPECTIVE

This book is printed on acid-free paper.

1 2 3 4 5 6 7 8 9 DOC/DOC 9 0 9 8 7

ISBN 0-256-20993-6
Library of Congress Catalog Card Number 96-60972

Publisher: *Roderick T. Banister*
Project supervisor: *Robert A. Preskill*
Production supervisor: *Pat Frederickson*
Designer: *Matthew Baldwin*
Prepress Buyer: *Heather Burbridge*
Compositor: *Interactive Composition Corporation*
Typeface: *10/12 Palatino*
Printer: *R.R. Donnelley & Sons Company*

http://www.mhcollege.com

Preface

The main purposes of *Economic Issues: A Canadian Perspective* are (1) to create student interest in the study of economics and (2) to provide students a grounding in the economic theory useful in analyzing real world issues in a Canadian context. This book is adapted from *Economics of Social Issues* by Ansel M. Sharp, Charles A. Register, and Paul W. Grimes, which, through twelve American editions, has successfully provided a well-structured framework of basic and analytical economic tools useful in the analysis of social problems of interest to students. This book endeavours to continue this approach while reformulating the issues in a Canadian context. Most social issues facing modern market economies are very similar, and therefore the proposal to adapt *Economics of Social Issues* for a Canadian market at first seemed relatively straightforward: replace American data with Canadian data, adjust for a few different mannerisms and use of language, and let the universal approach of economic methods shine through. In pursuing this adaptation, however, we quickly found that considerable and significant differences exist between Canadian and American perspectives on similar social issues. Therefore, this book is a major rewrite of *Economics of Social Issues* and includes an additional chapter dealing with resources as well as new material throughout the book. Professors Sharp, Register, and Grimes deserve full credit for the development of this approach to learning economics and for the structure and organization of this book. However, this edition is so substantially changed to incorporate a Canadian perspective, we take full responsibility for any errors, or omissions, in theory or fact.

Structure

Presented here are 16 chapters dealing with specific social issues important to Canadians. In each chapter we raise a particular issue, first outlining some factual information pertinent to that issue. Then we develop the economic concepts and principles useful in analyzing the issue and apply them in order to discover if economics can help us resolve the issue. The topics are arranged to provide a logical development of basic economic concepts and to reinforce understanding of these concepts through repeated use and application. We believe that the issues are interesting to Canadians and will encourage and help students learn the important basic principles of economics. The book will lend itself to a number of uses. It can be used alone as a textbook for an introductory one-semester course when motivating interest in economics is of primary importance. The book can also be used in a two-semester course in conjunction with a traditional theory text when the purpose is to cover economics in greater depth and rigour. The issues discussed here can be used as "case studies" in the application of economic theory in such courses. Alternatively, the book could be used in a one-semester, second-year course in Canadian economic issues when the students have already taken the traditional first-year micro- and macroeconomics theory courses.

Learning Features

Every chapter starts with quotations that express one or more opinions about the issue in that chapter. As this book is about the economics of issues important to Canadians, the opening passages should generate debate. Many of the issues discussed in this book are controversial and have at one time or another been hotly debated. These quotations will encourage the debate about the issues because not everyone will agree with the point of view expressed. Nor should they necessarily agree, as the purpose of the quotes is to stimulate interest in the further analysis of the issue and learn how economics can inform the debate.

Precise use and understanding of the vocabulary of economics is desirable when discussing the economics of social issues and contributes to building and reinforcing the skills used in effective economic analysis. To promote this end, important economic terms are highlighted in italic type in the text when they are first introduced and their accompanying definitions are set in the margin with the terms in boldface type. The "Checklist of Economic Concepts" at the end of each chapter highlights the new terminology presented in the chapter. These terms and concepts along with their definitions also appear in the glossary at the back of the book.

Canadian data from Statistics Canada, government departments and ministries, and other real-world sources are used in the figures, graphs, and tables throughout the text. In some cases hypothetical data are used to illustrate particularly difficult concepts, and in these cases we have indicated that hypothetical data are being employed. The captions describing each graph and figure generally begin with a brief summary statement followed by a reasonably complete description of what is portrayed. Each caption is a more concise presentation of the complete descriptions of the concepts within the figures and graphs to provide another study aid for students.

The "Summary" at the end of each chapter is fairly comprehensive and concisely reinforces the chapter discussion. The summary ties together the main concepts developed in the chapter and alerts the student to areas that may require re-reading.

The "Discussion Questions" section at the end of each chapter encourages students to think about and discuss the issues and concepts raised in the text. A number of these questions are designed to encourage the further advancement of the students' understanding and use of economic analysis at a fairly sophisticated level. Some questions are appropriate for class discussion or essay questions on examinations.

An annotated "Supplementary Reading" list is included at the end of each chapter. This list will help students and instructors extend the discussion and analysis of each issue as they see fit and have the time. The reading list will be of special interest to second-year students who may wish to pursue the issues in greater depth. Rather than rely solely on economic viewpoints, the suggested supplementary reading reflects the range of disciplines that study these social issues.

Acknowledgments

First, we would like to thank the authors of the American edition for trusting us to revise their book in a Canadian context. We also acknowledge former author Richard H. Leftwich's contributions to past American editions of this work. We thank James D. Gaisford and Daniel Gordon of the Department of Economics at the University of Calgary for their detailed comments on particular chapters and all of our colleagues at both the University of Calgary and Mount Royal College who assisted us in various ways. We would like to express appreciation to the reviewers who have provided detailed comments and suggestions to improve and focus this edition as Canadian: Lorne Carmichael, Queen's University; Lionel Ifill, Algonquin College; Marion Jones, University of Regina; Robert Kerton, University of Waterloo; Chris McDonnell, Malaspina University College; and Jack Rink, Red River Community College. The people that reviewed the U.S. edition—*Economics of Social Issues*—and supported the idea of writing a Canadian edition should also be acknowledged: Gordon Holyer, Malaspina University College; Peter Sephton, University of New Brunswick; William Sinkevitch, St. Clair College; Maurice Tugwell, Acadia University; and Marian Weber, University of Alberta. In addition, we would like to thank Robert Preskill of Richard D. Irwin, Inc., June Waldman, and Colin Murcray for their contributions ensuring a consistency of style and making this a better product; and Rod Banister, publisher, for his support and encouragement of the project.

C. Michael Fellows
Gregory L. Flanagan
Stanford Shedd
Calgary, 1997

Contents

Introduction

This book is an application of economic analysis to social issues of common interest to most Canadians. Almost any issue can be seen as an economic issue. The great English economist Alfred Marshall defined economics as "the study of mankind in the everyday business of living."[1] Marshall's definition suggests the wide possible scope of economics. To cover all of the economic issues relevant to Canadians would be impossible; therefore, the issues addressed in this book are only a sample that we believe include some of the most important. Economics is vital to the understanding of the world around us. Most of the day-to-day decisions we all make have economic consequences—costs and benefits. We emphasize in this book the economic aspects of individual decisions and their social implications. It would, however, be a mistake to assume that economics can explain all aspects of the issues that face us daily. Issues have other, often more important, dimensions. The general purposes of this book are to introduce economic concepts through their application to specific social issues while demonstrating the relevance of economic analysis in providing insights to these as well as all important social issues.

Economics is the study of how society chooses to allocate its *scarce* resources among competing goals to best fulfill its unlimited wants.

A standard definition of economics may help you better understand how economics is related to everyday life. *Economics* is the study of how society chooses to allocate its *scarce* resources among competing goals to best fulfill society's unlimited wants.

A resource is **scarce** if there is not enough of it so that everyone can have all they want at a zero price.

Resources are the inputs we use to produce the goods and services we consume. There is a limited amount of resources relative to the infinite purposes we would like to use them for, therefore, resources are scarce. When economists say something is scarce, they do not necessarily mean it is rare or even uncommon. As you read this book, you will find that economists sometimes use specialized, very precise definitions for words that have everyday meanings. The term *scarcity* has a specialized meaning in economics. In everyday English, something is scarce if it is rare or uncommon or at the very least not plentiful. In economics, however, scarcity is a relative term. For example, water covers two-thirds of the

---

[1]Alfred Marshall, *Principles of Economics* 8th ed. (Toronto: Macmillan, 1966), p. 1.

world's surface—in an absolute sense it is one of the most abundant substances in the world—nonetheless water is a scarce resource. Conflicts often develop over how water should be allocated because not everyone can have all the water that he or she wants. Therefore, every society must decide who will have access to water and how much water each person can use; that is, water must be rationed. Water is an *economic good*. An economic good is a good that is both desirable and scarce. Society must allocate scarce resources between competing uses. A resource that is not scarce is a *free good*.

> An **economic good** is one which is both desirable and scarce. A **free good** is one which is not scarce.

The economic problem is that human wants are unlimited while resources are limited. It is possible to have so much of one thing that you get tired of it and want no more. In this case you are satiated with that good or service. However, you are still likely to desire other goods and services. Even if you had all the material things in the world, you would want more time in order to enjoy them. You might want more and better health care services so that you could live longer to enjoy your immense wealth. Or, being altruistic, you might want more food and better health care for those lacking it. That human wants are unlimited implies that the economic problem of scarcity exists in a rich country like Canada just as surely as it does in poor countries.

> **Microeconomics** is the study of individual economic agents and their interaction in the economy.
>
> There are three types of economic agents in our society. They are **households**—individuals and families, **firms**—business enterprises, and **government**.

Economics is often divided into two main branches—microeconomics and macroeconomics. *Microeconomics* is the study of individual economic agents and the way they interact in the economy. There are three types of agents—households, firms, and governments. *Households* include individuals and families who provide the inputs used to produce goods and services. They are also the consumers of goods and services. Households, we assume, generally try to maximize satisfaction. *Firms* are the business enterprises. They hire the inputs and combine them to produce goods and services. Firms, we assume, try to maximize profits. Economists usually speak of *the government* but actually there are many governments. For example, Canada has 1 federal government, 10 provincial governments, 2 (soon to be three) territorial governments, and thousands of local governments, as well as many government agencies, commissions, and enterprises. Whereas we expect households to maximize satisfaction and firms to maximize profits, what we expect governments to maximize is much less clear. In theory, governments exist to maximize the well-being of society.

> **Macroeconomics** is the study of the whole economy or large subdivisions of it.

The other branch of economics is *macroeconomics*. It is the study of the whole economy or large subdivisions of it. Modern macroeconomics dates back to the 1930s and the work of the English economist John Maynard Keynes. Macroeconomics is concerned with issues such as unemployment and inflation. Both microeconomics and macroeconomics are concerned with the overall performance of the economy although from different perspectives. Canada, as most modern economies, is a mixed market system. Therefore, both microeconomics and macroeconomics consider the workings of markets, the appropriate roles for government in a market system, and the efficiency and equity aspects of both market and government operations.

The concept of scarcity—insufficient resources to serve unlimited human wants—leads directly the notion of *efficiency*. To be economically efficient means to optimize, and in economics has two aspects. First, we need to allocate our resources in a manner that maximizes the possible goods and services produced. However, numerous combinations of goods and services meet this first condition—that is, a combination of goods and services when no more could be produced with the given resources and technology. The second condition requires that the combination of goods and services produced provides the society with the maximum satisfaction achievable. This second condition requires some social mechanism for determining the collective value of each combination of goods and services. The question of efficiency is always a dominant theme in economic analysis. Equity issues are also a prominent theme in many of the social issues considered. The concept of *equity* deals with the question of what is a "fair" distribution of the economy's goods and services. Although fairness is an ethical or a normative question (as economists define it), there is considerable agreement that a more equal distribution of income than that which would occur in a pure market economy is desirable or equitable. Society can redistribute income and opportunity in a number of ways: direct money income transfers; government provision of some goods, such as medically necessary health care services and education, according to need and not ability to pay; and the subsidization of the costs of other goods, for example, postsecondary education.

The issues discussed in this book involve both microeconomics and macroeconomics. Some chapters fall mainly into one or the other category, but many economic issues involve both perspectives. In recent years many economists would argue that the division between micro and macro has become relatively unimportant. Most chapters also consider the efficiency and equity aspects of each issue. You will see that every chapter starts with a quote. As you read the book, you may not agree with everything you read in these quotes. The authors of the book do *not* agree with everything in the quotes. Often the quotes express one or more opinions. As this book is about the economics of issues important to Canadians, it should generate debate. By definition an *issue* is a matter of dispute and debate. Many of the issues discussed in this book have at one time or another been hotly debated. For example, the issue of free trade, be it with the United States, Mexico, or other countries, continually raises loud and vigorous discussion. Other examples abound: Do players in the NHL make too much money? Should we change the Medicare program? Is there too much crime? Are interest rates too high? Is unemployment too high? Should postsecondary education students pay the full cost of their education?

Discussion and debate can be productive, leading to correct answers about "what is"—objective scientific fact. For example, in the 16th century

---

Economic efficiency requires the production of the most socially valued maximum combination of goods and services that can be produced with the current resources and technology.

Equity concerns deal with the ethical questions of what is a fair distribution of the economy's goods and services and how to achieve it.

there was considerable debate about whether the sun and the other planets revolved around the earth, or whether the earth and the other planets revolved around the sun. Eventually, astronomers were able to prove that the sun was actually the centre of the solar system, and everyone agreed that the earth and the other planets revolved around the sun. A proposition that can be proven right or wrong is a *positive* proposition. Such knowledge is objective.

In economics many propositions are also objectively verifiable. They can be shown to be true or false. The statement "increased government spending will contribute to lower unemployment rates" is a positive statement. It is subject to verification. Such verification may not be easy, but in theory a positive economic statement is a testable hypothesis. For example, economists could look at historical evidence to determine the validity of this statement, identifying whether past increases in government spending resulted in decreases in unemployment. A different form of testing checks the logic of an explanation of the relationship between government spending and unemployment. It might even be possible to conduct an experiment. For example, Parliament could vote to increase spending and then Statistics Canada (StatCan) could measure the effect on unemployment. The objective investigation of economic relationships is called *positive economics*. It is the economics of what has been, what is, and what can be, helping define the alternatives available to society.

Positive economics is the study of what has been, what is, and what can be. Positive economic propositions can in theory be proven true or false.

Not all debates can be resolved by proving that one position is correct. Often debates involve aspects that are subjective. Subjective knowledge does not lend itself to objective verification. Subjective or normative debate is based on moral and ethical considerations or on personal preferences. Is red a prettier colour than blue? Is it fair that childless households have to pay taxes to support schools? Is unemployment a more serious problem than inflation? Economists refer to questions involving ethics and norms as normative. The discussion of the subjective economic issues is called *normative economics*. It is the economics of what *ought* to be. Normative economics must frequently deal with situations in which an economic decision will make some individuals better off but leave other individuals worse off. Societies that give equal importance to all individual preferences regardless of how many people hold a particular view, can not make a verifiably correct decision on such a problem. Any decision will be based on normative judgments about worth. Subjective, normative debate can, however, lead to agreement about what ought to be. It is agreement on norms that provides social cohesion.

Normative economic propositions arise from the question what ought to be and can not be proven true or false. **Normative economics** considers policy options to correct economic situations perceived to be unfair or unjust to some individuals or groups in society.

Both positive and normative economics play important roles when studying an economic issue. Positive economics can provide society with a list of possible ways of resolving the issue. Economists use *economic theory* to explore the possible answers to an economic question. The real world is too complex to be completely understood. In order to reduce problems to a level were they are tractable, economists build abstract theoretical models.

Economic theory is the aggregation of the models that economists have developed.

In the process of model building, economists make a number of simplifying assumptions. Basic to almost all economic models is the assumption that humans act in their own best interest—human actions are economically motivated. Although there is no way of proving this assumption, it is a valuable assumption that normally leads to useful conclusions. Another common assumption is to limit the number of variables in a model. For the purpose of a model, the economist chooses only the most important variables to the problem and considers how those variables interact while all other possible influences are assumed to remain constant. This simplifying assumption allows economists to logically develop an hypothesis. An hypothesis can explain why economic events occur as they do. In some cases a model may allow economists to predict future events. However, before an hypothesis can be accepted, its validity must be empirically tested and the evidence must support it. If that testing cannot reject the validity of the hypothesis, it becomes a working *economic model*. Economists have developed and tested models to explain most aspects of economic behaviour. Taken together these models form economic theory. This book will introduce readers to a substantial part of the body of economic theory.

An **economic model** is a logically developed and empirically tested explanation of economic events.

Unfortunately, economic theory is not sufficient to resolve economic issues. Theory can guide social action but it can not tell us what we want to do. Society must make subjective choices about what it wants, and these choices become its economic goals. The role of *economic policy* is to help society find ways to reach its economic goals given the constraints of scarce resources and normative differences.

Economic policy is the means society uses to achieve subjective economic goals. To be effective it should be based on economic theory.

Economic Issues:
A Canadian Perspective

Chapter 1

Human Welfare
The Most Important Issue of Them All

The Government's new foreign policy statement "Canada in the World" released on February 7, 1995, provides a clear mandate for Canadian Official Development Assistance (ODA).

"The purpose of Canada's ODA is to support sustainable development in developing countries, in order to reduce poverty and to contribute to a more secure, equitable and prosperous world."

In addressing the objective of poverty reduction, the Government recognizes the vital link with sustainable development and the need for a broad array of programs and policies working together in an integrated fashion.

Poverty results from a lack of human, physical and financial capital needed to sustain livelihoods and from inequities in access to, control of, and benefits from resources, be they political, social or economic. In an interdependent world, poverty in developing countries increasingly affects the economic, social and political welfare of developed countries. Global poverty manifests itself in many forms: drugs, loss of natural resources, terrorism, political instability and large-scale migration.

Poverty reduction is a complex and difficult challenge. Despite considerable poverty programming experience in CIDA [Canadian International Development Agency], there is still much to know and learn about poverty reduction. CIDA's approach to poverty reduction will entail:

- a better understanding of the country-specific and local characteristics of poverty;
- a coordinated use of project, program, institutional support and policy interventions to achieve maximum impact; and
- a clear view of CIDA's role and capabilities.

In this context, the policy will provide a framework for poverty reduction and guide programming in each of the six programming priorities—basic human needs, women in development, environment sustainability, infrastructure services, human rights, democracy and good governance, and private sector development—established for the new ODA.[1]

Some two-thirds of the world's population go to sleep hungry at night. The World Bank estimates that perhaps as much as one-quarter of the world survives on no more than $1 per day. Outright famine regularly occurs in various parts of the world—recent examples being the mass starvation of an estimated 1 million people in Ethiopia during the drought of 1984–85 and the contemporary tragedy of perhaps even

---

[1]Canadian International Development Agency, "CIDA's Policy on Poverty Reduction," June 1995.

greater proportions in Somalia. Most of the hungry have no protection from the summer's heat or the winter's cold. They receive little or no medical care and live in unsanitary surroundings. Infant mortality is high and life expectancy is low. Whereas in Canada about eight infants out of each 1000 live births die before reaching their first birthday, the rate explodes to well over 1 in 10 in places such as Ethiopia, Pakistan, and Tanzania. At the opposite end of life, the typical Ethiopian can expect to die about 30 years earlier than his or her contemporary in Canada.

Recognition that the misery of poverty is the lot of the largest part of the world's population leads us to ask the questions: Why is it so? What are the causes? How can it be alleviated? This in turn leads us directly into the province of economics. An assessment and analysis of human welfare requires an explicit understanding of the very foundations of economic activity. The welfare of a country's people depends on its resources, its technology, the efficiency with which those resources are used, and the way in which the benefits are distributed among the population. In short, how a country chooses to organize its economy most directly and forcefully affects the welfare of its people. In this chapter we introduce the fundamental aspects of these issues, concentrating on the definitions of terms and measures used in economics. The chapters following will expand on economic issues in much greater depth.

Scarcity—The Ultimate Problem

Economic activity springs from human needs, wants, and desires. Human beings need the things necessary to keep them alive—food and protection from the elements of nature. We usually want a great many other things, too, and the fulfillment of these needs and wants is the end toward which economic activity is directed.

Our Insatiable Wants

As nearly as we can tell, human wants in the aggregate are unlimited or insatiable. This is true because once our basic needs are met, we desire variety in the way they are met—variety in foods, in housing, in clothing, and in entertainment. Additionally, as we look around, we see other people enjoying things that we do not have (digital audio equipment and home computers, for example), and we think that our level of well-being would be higher if we had those things, too. But most important, want-satisfying activity itself generates new wants. A new house generates wants for new furnishings—the old ones look shabby in the new setting. A college or university education opens the doors to wants that would never have existed if we had stayed on the farm or in the machine shop. To be sure, any one of us can saturate ourselves—temporarily, at least—with any one kind of good or service (like ice cream or beer), but almost all of us would like to have more than we have of almost everything and higher qualities of purchases than we now can obtain.

Our Limited Means

The fundamental economic problem is that the means available for satisfying needs and wants are scarce or limited relative to the extent of the wants. The amounts and qualities of goods and services per year that an economic system can produce are limited because (1) the resources available to produce them cannot be increased by any great amount in any given year, (2) the technology available for production is subject to a limited degree of annual improvement, and (3) the social institutions and traditions change slowly.

An economy's resources are the ingredients that go into the making of goods (like automobiles) and services (like medical examinations). Production is similar to cooking. Resources (ingredients) are brought together; technology is used to process these resources in certain ways (mixing and cooking them); and finally a good or service results (a cake, perhaps). Some outputs of production processes are used directly to satisfy wants. Others become inputs for additional production processes. The resources available in an economy are usually divided into three broad classifications: (1) labour, (2) capital, and (3) land.

Labour resources refer to the physical and mental efforts of an economy's people that are available to produce goods and services.

Labour resources consist of all the efforts of mind and muscle that can be used in production processes. The ditch digger's output along with that of the heart surgeon and the university professor is included. The main common characteristic of the many kinds and grades of labour resources is that they are human.

Capital resources refer to all the human-produced ingredients of production such as buildings, machinery and equipment, and semifinished materials.

Capital resources consist of all the human-produced ingredients that go into the production of goods and services. Capital resources include bridges and roads, buildings and equipment, and the economy's stock of tools that have been built up over time. In addition, all the semifinished materials that exist in the economy at any given time and that are available for use in production are capital resources. Sheets of steel and grocery store inventories are examples of semifinished materials.

Land resources refer to all the natural resources that are used in production.

Land resources refer to all the natural resources that are used in production. They include land that provides space for production facilities as well as land that is able to grow crops. Land resources include water, forests, oil, gas, and mineral deposits. The characteristic that makes them natural is that they are found in a state of nature, untouched by humans. Land resources are scarce and, in many cases, are rapidly becoming more scarce. An important distinction with regard to land resources is the difference between renewable and non-renewable resources. Renewable resources, although scarce, should be sustainable over time with proper management. Non-renewable resources will be depleted with time, although this problem can be offset with recycling programs. The time pattern of use becomes a critical question in the use of non-renewable resources, while with recycling, energy sources become the vital issue. These special issues relating to land resources are discussed in detail in Chapter 16.

Resources are always scarce relative to the sum total of human wants. Consider the Canadian economy. The Canadian population will reach 30 million in 1996. Most Canadian citizens want more things than they now have. Can the economy increase next year's production enough to fulfill all of these wants? Obviously not. The labour force available from the present population cannot be increased substantially in either quantity or quality very quickly. Both may be increased over time by increasing the size of the population, by increasing the participation rate in the labour force, and through improving the education and training of the general population, but increasing the labour force increases total wants, too. The stocks of buildings, machines, tools, raw and semifinished materials, and usable land are not susceptible to rapid increases either; instead they are accumulated slowly over time.

Technology refers to the known means and methods available for combining resources to produce goods and services. Given the quantities of an economy's labour and capital resources, the better its technology, the greater is the annual volume of goods and services it can turn out. Usually improvements in technology in an economic system result from increasing the scope and depth of its educational processes and from an ample supply of capital that provides a laboratory for experimentation, practice, and the generation of new ideas.

In addition, social institutions and traditions are major factors affecting productivity. Changes in these take place at a slow pace, often requiring a generation and the influence of public education.

The Capacity of the Economy to Produce

Gross Domestic Product and Gross National Product. Given the fundamental problem of scarcity that all societies face, it is essential that we be able to track how well a particular economy translates labour and capital resources into goods and services. In general terms, we wish to be able to quantify the total dollar value of all final goods and services produced. Two measures of the value of production are commonly employed: *gross domestic product*, abbreviated as GDP, and *gross national product*, or GNP.

Although not identical, both measure the economy's annual output of final goods and services. The difference between the two measures is best understood by considering two related questions. When General Motors (U.S. owned) builds the popular Camaro in Canada, should this production be part of Canadian output? Conversely, when Bombardier (Canadian owned) produces light rapid transit (LRT) trains in the United States, should such production be considered part of Canadian output? The an-

---

Technology refers to the know-how and the means and methods of production available within an economy.

Gross domestic product (GDP) measures the market value of all final goods and services produced within an economy during one year. GDP ignores the issue of whether the resources used for the production are domestically or foreign owned.

Gross national product (GNP) measures the market value of all final goods and services produced by domestically owned resources during one year regardless of where the production takes place.

swer to each question is the same: yes and no, depending on whether one is considering GDP or GNP. If the focus is on GDP, who owns the production facilities makes no difference; if the production takes place in Canada, it is counted towards Canadian output. Thus GDP includes the value of the Camaros produced in Ontario and excludes the value of the U.S.-built LRT trains. On the other hand, GNP focuses on the output derived from domestically owned resources and, consequently, would include the value of the LRT trains but not that of the Camaros.

Put simply, then, GDP measures the market value of the annual output of final goods and services produced within an economy, whereas GNP measures the market value of the annual output of final goods and services produced using domestically owned resources. Given this difference, during any particular year GDP may be greater than, less than, or equal to GNP. Each is a valid measure of national production; however, we will follow, where possible, the Canadian government's convention and employ GDP as our measure of production.

Production Possibilities. Given an economy's available stocks of resources and its level of technology, the combinations of goods and services that can compose its GDP are practically limitless. For simplicity, suppose that it produces only two items—bread and milk—and that all of its resources are devoted to the production of these two products. Table 1–1 indicates a number of output combinations that it is possible to produce with the available resources at a point in time. Note that only one combination could actually be achieved at one time.

The production possibilities curve represents the maximum quantities of two goods and/or services that an economy can produce when its resources are used in the most efficient way possible.

The curve *AE* in Figure 1–1 is drawn from the data presented in Table 1–1 and represents all possible combinations of bread and milk that can be produced. It is appropriately called the economy's *production possibilities curve.*

Thus the economy's output may consist of 100,000 loaves of bread per year with no milk as shown by point A, or 100,000 litres of milk per year

Table 1–1	The combinations of bread and milk that a country could produce (hypothetical data)		
Combination		Bread 1000s of Loaves	Milk 1000s of Litres
A		100	0
B		90	40
C		60	80
D		50	88
E		0	100

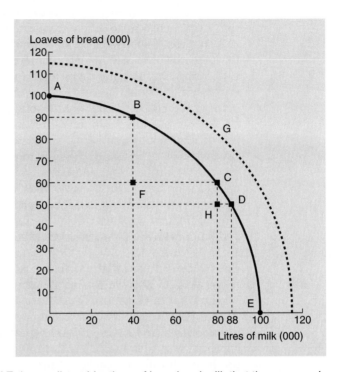

Curve *AE* shows all combinations of bread and milk that the economy's available resources and techniques of production can produce annually. Combinations such as *F* imply unemployment of resources or inefficiency in production. Those such as *G* are not attainable. If the economy were originally producing combination *D* and then moved to combination *C*, the opportunity cost of the additional *HD* of milk is the *HC* of bread that must be given up to produce it.

with no bread as shown by point E. Or it may consist of any combination on the curve, such as B, containing 90,000 loaves of bread and 40,000 litres of milk; or C, containing 60,000 loaves of bread and 80,000 litres of milk; or some combination under the curve such as F, containing 50,000 loaves of bread and 40,000 litres of milk.

If an economy's output is some combination of goods and services like F, which lies inside its production possibilities curve, the economic system is not operating efficiently. Some of its resources may be unemployed, used in the wrong places, or wasted. It also may not be using the best available techniques of production.

Combinations of goods and services, like G, lying above the production possibilities curve, are not currently attainable. The economy does not have sufficient quantities and qualities of resources and/or good enough techniques of production to push its production out to that level. Over time, perhaps, it can accumulate enough resources and/or improve its techniques and press its production possibilities curve outward to the dashed curve. If so, the combination G would become a feasible level of output.

The line AE represents all possible GDP combinations of bread and milk that the economy can produce when it is operating efficiently. For each combination, all of its resources would be employed, and it would be using the best technology available.

The **opportunity cost principle** states that the true cost of producing an additional unit of a good or service is the value of other goods or services that must be given up to obtain it.

The Opportunity Cost Principle. Have you heard the expression "There is no such thing as a free lunch"? Actually this is a simple way of expressing one of the most important concepts in economics, the opportunity cost, or, as it is sometimes called, the alternative cost principle. Suppose the economy is producing combination C, containing 60,000 loaves of bread and 80,000 litres of milk. Now let the output of milk be increased to 88,000 litres. What is the cost of the additional 8,000 litres of milk? The opportunity cost principle embodies the often overlooked obvious point—for society to produce more of one good or service (milk, for example), it must produce less of other goods or services (perhaps bread). In this sense, the reduced production of bread represents the opportunity cost of producing more milk. In the present case, according to the principle, the cost of the additional 8,000 litres of milk is the 10,000 loaves of bread that must be given up to obtain them. An economy cannot produce more than its resources and its technology will allow, so more of one product necessarily means less of others.

Note how costs are measured abstractly in Figure 1–1. The increase in the output of milk and the decrease in the output of bread are represented as a movement from C to D; that is, HD of bread is given up for HC of milk. The ratio HD/HC, which is the approximate slope of the production possibilities curve between C and D, measures the (average) opportunity cost per litre of milk of each of the 8,000 litres making up the additional output of milk. It is 10,000 divided by 8,000, 1 $\frac{1}{4}$ loaves per litre.

Living Standards

Gross domestic product is measured in value terms—the value of the economy's domestically produced annual output—rather than in terms of so many loaves of bread and so many litres of milk. To get the value measure of the economy's production, multiply the number of loaves produced in a given year by the price per loaf; do the same computation for milk; and add the total values together. Consequently, if we look at data for a series of years and find that GDP in dollar terms is increasing, we cannot really be sure that the economy's production is increasing. The increasing numbers may be a result of inflation—rising prices—rather than a result of rising production.

To see the effect of inflation on GDP, consider a very simplistic economy in which only one good, bread, is produced. Suppose that during 1996, the economy produces 1,000 loaves of bread, which are sold for $1.00 each. Calculating GDP for an economy requires multiplying the number of units of each good or service produced within the economy by the price at which each good or service is sold. For 1996, GDP is $1,000 (1,000 loaves times $1.00 per loaf). Now suppose that during 1997 the economy continues to produce 1,000 loaves of bread but, because of inflation, each loaf sells for $2.00. GDP for 1997 is $2,000. Thus between 1996 and 1997, GDP doubles, even though the production of bread remains unchanged at 1,000 loaves. The entire increase in GDP is because of rising prices, that is, inflation.

To correct for inflation, the entire series of GDP numbers at *current* price levels for each year must be converted to a base year price level. Suppose, using the preceding example, that 1996 is the base year and that 1997 GDP is to be converted to the 1996 price level. The relationship between 1996 and 1997 can be depicted with price index numbers. In percentage terms the price index for each year is calculated by dividing each year's price (or average price if more than one good or service is produced) by the price in the base year and then multiplying by 100, as shown in Table 1–2. Thus the price index for 1996 is 100 (1996 price of $1.00 and divided by the base year price, also 1996, of $1.00, and then multiplying by 100). Likewise, the price index for 1997 is 200, indicating that the average price in 1997 is 200 percent of the average 1996, or base year, price. Once the price index is established for each year, the GDP data can be corrected for inflation by dividing each year's GDP in current dollars by that year's price index after converting the index to decimal form.

When GDP in current dollars is corrected for inflation, the resulting GDP values are called **real GDP** or GDP measured in constant dollars. The correction requires dividing each year's GDP in current dollars by that year's price index in decimal form.

That is, 1996's inflation-corrected GDP is equal to its current dollar GDP of $1,000 divided by the 1996 price index (in decimals) of 1.00, or simply $1,000. Inflation-corrected GDP for 1997 is found in the same way and is also $1,000, since GDP in current dollars for 1997 is $2,000, while the price index for 1997 is 2.00 in decimals. When this correction is made, the resulting inflation-corrected GDP values are referred to as *real GDP* or GDP measured in constant dollars. In this example, although GDP in current dollars doubles between 1996 and 1997, real GDP remains the

Table 1–2			Calculating real GDP using a price index (hypothetical data)		
	(1)	(2)	(3) GDP in	(4) Price Index	(5) Real GDP
Year	Production of Bread (Loaves)	Price of Bread	Current Dollars (1) × (2)	Percentage and Decimal Forms	1996 Dollars (3)/(4, in decimals)
1996	1,000	$1.00	$1,000	($1/$1) × 100 = 100 or 1.00	$1,000
1997	1,000	2.00	2,000	(2/1) × 100 = 200 or 2.00	1,000

same, reflecting the fact that actual production is unchanged between the two years. In this way real GDP shows us what is happening over time to the economy's real production—whether it is increasing, decreasing, or remaining constant.

Real gross domestic product data alone indicate little about how well an economy provides for its inhabitants, but if the economy's real GDP is divided by its population for any given year, the result is per capita real GDP. This concept is a rough measure of an economy's performance potential. For any one country, *per capita real GDP* for a series of years is indicative of whether or not the performance of the economy in terms of the average well-being of its inhabitants is improving. Among countries, the comparative per capita real GDPs are indicative of the comparative economic performances of the countries.

Per capita real GDP is the part of real GDP that, on average, accrues to each individual within an economy. Per capita real GDP is found by dividing real GDP by the economy's population.

In Table 1–3 we track the performance of the Canadian economy for the years 1970 through 1994. Current dollar or current price level GDP is listed in column (2). The column (3) implicit price deflator, or price index number, uses 1986 as the base year and is reported in percentages. The real GDP data of column (4) are obtained by dividing each year's current dollar GDP by its price index number after making the adjustment to decimals for the price index. Note that real GDP declines in 1982, 1990, and 1991, even though current dollar GDP appears to indicate that the economy's production increased steadily over the years. Dividing each year's real GDP by population, we obtain per capita real GDP, our best measure of the economy's performance. This column also shows the declines in 1982, 1990, 1991, and 1992. Interestingly, per capita real GDP also declined in 1992, even though real GDP increased. Although this trend may seem unreasonable, in reality it merely indicates that the growth in population that took place during the period outpaced the growth in real GDP, leaving the ratio of the two, or per capita real GDP, lower than it had been in 1991.

Per capita real GDP is one measure of an economy's standard of living, but it is in no sense a perfect measure. We must consider a number of things. For instance, GDP is a monetary measure of market exchange; therefore, it fails to account for such things as home production and voluntary community activity. Nor does it consider the depletion of natural capital. For example, a high growth in GDP driven by the exploitation of non-renewable resources may suggest economic improvement but be unsustainable in the longrun. As GDP is a measure of gross production, it doesn't exclude the capital production necessary to replace the capital used up in current production. Additionally, GDP includes expenditures on such things as pollution cleanup and crime prevention and control—goods that are increasingly needed to offset deteriorating social and environmental conditions. The greater the expenditures of this nature, the more GDP rises.

GDP also fails to take into account the distribution of the economy's GDP among the population. If a few people get the bulk of the GDP while the masses are at a subsistence level, per capita or average figures provide

Table 1–3	Canadian gross domestic product in current and real (1986) dollars, 1970–94				
(1) Year	(2) Current Dollars (billions)	(3) Implicit Price Deflator	(4) Real or 1986 Dollars (billions)	(5) Population (millions)	(6) GDP per Capita 1986 Dollars
1970	89,116	32.8	271,372	21,297	12,742
1971	97,290	33.9	286,998	22,026	13,030
1972	108,629	35.8	303,447	22,285	13,617
1973	127,372	39.0	326,848	22,560	14,488
1974	152,111	44.6	341,235	22,875	14,917
1975	171,540	49.0	350,113	23,209	15,085
1976	197,924	53.3	371,688	23,518	15,804
1977	217,879	56.6	385,122	23,796	16,184
1978	241,604	60.0	402,737	24,036	16,756
1979	276,096	66.0	418,328	24,277	17,231
1980	309,891	73.0	424,537	24,593	17,263
1981	355,994	80.9	440,127	24,900	17,676
1982	374,442	87.9	425,970	25,202	16,902
1983	405,717	92.3	439,448	25,456	17,263
1984	444,735	95.2	467,167	25,702	18,176
1985	477,988	97.7	489,437	25,942	18,867
1986	505,666	100.0	505,666	26,204	19,297
1987	551,597	104.7	526,730	26,550	19,839
1988	605,906	109.6	552,958	26,895	20,560
1989	650,748	114.9	566,486	27,379	20,690
1990	669,467	118.5	565,155	27,791	20,336
1991	674,766	121.6	554,735	28,118	19,729
1992	688,391	123.3	558,165	28,436	19,629
1993	711,658	124.7	570,541	28,753	19,843
1994	747,260	125.6	594,990	29,251	20,341

Note: Discrepancies in calculations are caused by rounding.
Source: Statistics Canada, CANSIM database matrices: 6628, 6841, 0599, & 6840.

a distorted picture of individual well-being. The question of how GDP is distributed among the economy's population is treated later in this chapter.

Other comparative measures of human welfare are being devised. The United Nations has developed what is referred to as a human development index (HDI). The report states: "The real wealth of a nation is its people—both women and men. And the purpose of development is to create an enabling environment for people to enjoy long, healthy and creative

Table 1–4   **United Nations human development index ranking for selected countries, 1992**

1	Canada	.950
2	United States	.938
3	Japan	.937
4	Netherlands	.936
5	Iceland	.933
6	Finland	.934
7	Norway	.933
8	France	.931
9	Spain	.930
10	Sweden	.929
11	Australia	.927
12	Belgium	.926
13	Switzerland	.925
14	Austria	.925
15	Germany	.927
16	Denmark	.920
27	Luxembourg	.893
45	United Arab Emirates	.861
56	Qatar	.838
61	Kuwait	.821
171	Ethiopia	.227
174	Niger	.207
	World average	.759

Source: United Nations Development Programme, *Human Development Report 1995* (New York: Oxford University Press, 1995).

lives. This simple but powerful truth is often forgotten in the pursuit of material and financial wealth."[2] The HDI includes social, political, and environmental conditions as well as personal incomes. It is based on three components: life expectancy at birth; educational attainment, particularly literacy; and incomes. Some selected HDI values are listed in Table 1–4. The index number indicates how far that country has to go to attain certain goals. These goals include an average life span of 85 years, universal access to education, and a reasonable level of income. The closer a country is to a HDI value of 1, the closer it is to attaining these goals.

[2] United Nations Development Programme, *Human Development Report 1995,* (New York: Oxford University Press, 1995).

Canada has placed first for three years running, 1996, 1995, and 1994, as well as having placed first in 1992. Most developed countries, however, all rank very close together. The United Nations does point out, though, that Canada has room for improvements. Canada ranked second when inequality between men and women was considered and only seventh in terms of average per capita purchasing power. Canada could also do better on income redistribution. Canada's unemployment rate exceeded the average by 4 percent. Improving employment, particularly for youth, is cited as a priority for Canada, as is protecting the environment. The most distressing aspect of the report is that the gap between poor countries and developed countries is widening, with 89 countries worse off than a decade ago.

The World Bank is also developing a new measure of well-being that uses average wealth by calculating the value of a country's produced capital, natural resources, and human resources. Produced capital is defined as human-made capital—machines, buildings, and infrastructure. Natural capital includes land, water, timber, minerals, and energy. Human resources are defined as the value of the nation's labour based on education levels, nutrition, and life expectancy. The method is not complete yet, as the Bank is still working on estimating a country's social capital. Table 1–5

Table 1–5		World Bank estimates of average per capita wealth in U.S. dollars, 1990	
	1	Australia	$835,000
	2	Canada	704,000
	3	Luxembourg	658,000
	4	Switzerland	647,000
	5	Japan	565,000
	6	Sweden	496,000
	7	Iceland	486,000
	8	Qatar	473,000
	9	United Arab Emirates	471,000
	10	Denmark	463,000
	11	Norway	424,000
	12	United States	421,000
	13	France	413,000
	14	Kuwait	405,000
	15	Germany	399,000
Poorest		Ethiopia	1,400
World		Average	86,000

Source: World Bank, *Monitoring Environmental Progress, A Report in Progress*, 1995.

indicates that Canada places second on this measure according to 1990 statistics.

The Requisites of Economic Growth

The economic roots of human welfare become reasonably clear from an examination of the foundations of economic activity. To determine why any particular country has the per capita real GDP it does, we should look at (1) the quality of its labour force, (2) its stock of capital and land resources, (3) the state of its technology, and (4) the efficiency with which it employs its resources. If the economy is to provide rising living standards over time, its specific deficiencies in these areas must be determined and corrected. In the last analysis, if living standards are to rise, the rate of growth in the economy's real GDP must exceed the rate of growth in its population.

Quality of the Labour Force

Almost without exception, the poor countries of the world have labour forces that are not very productive compared to those of wealthy countries. Illiteracy rates are high; often 70 to 90 percent of the population is unable to read or write. Whereas the adult literacy rate in Canada approaches 99 percent, Ethiopia and Haiti barely reach the 5 percent level. Their average level of educational attainment is low; expectations and aspirations of the young are low, and malnutrition and disease take their toll on the physical capacities of the labour force.

Education is the key to improvement in the quality of a country's population and its labour force. Literacy rates and average levels of education are closely correlated with living standards. To improve the health and the productivity of the labour force, people must be able to read and to understand the importance of sanitation. As literacy rates increase, so do the possibilities of upgrading the skills of the labour force. A broad-based primary education system is a prerequisite for literacy, and literacy is, in turn, a basic foundation for economic growth.

Beyond the primary level, secondary and higher education is important in improving labour force quality. Both liberal arts and technical education help develop people with higher skill levels who can think and innovate. Rather than being conflicting in purpose, they reinforce each other, contributing importantly to labour productivity. But a comprehensive educational system is hard to establish in a country whose population lives close to or at a subsistence level.

Further complicating matters, often the best educated and trained workers of poor countries abandon their native lands to offer their services in the relatively rich countries of the world where the rewards for their efforts are greatest. This pattern is especially true for those who pursue advanced education in wealthier countries. Such a "skimming of the cream" of the labour forces of poor countries, known as brain drain, greatly inhibits the development of a high-quality labour force in developing countries.

Stock of Capital and Land, and Capital Accumulation

Small amounts of available capital resources and low capital-to-labour ratios in a country mean low labour productivity and poverty. The Masai family in Kenya owns little in the way of property or tools. It may own a few cattle. A farmer in India has a wooden plow and perhaps a couple of oxen to pull it. His grain will be cut and gathered by hand and threshed by the hooves of oxen driven around in a circle over a hard threshing floor instead of by mechanical harvesters. Countries without mineral deposits, tools, machines, factories, means of communication and transportation, and educational facilities usually have low per capita real GDPs.

Capital accumulation is necessary if a country is to break out of a poverty prison. Tools and machines must be accumulated and utilized. Factories and roads must be built. Telephone lines must be strung. Mineral deposits must be systematically mined. Land must be fertilized. River channels must be widened and deepened. Plant and animal life must be subjected to careful, genetically sound breeding methods.

Capital accumulation is more difficult to accomplish in a poor economy than in a wealthy one. It requires that the economy not consume its entire annual output and that some part of that output be in the form of new capital goods or resources. Of this latter part of output, some must replace capital resources used up or worn out in producing the annual output. Any extra capital resources above the amount used to keep the stock of capital intact serve to increase the total amount of capital available. It is not easy for a poor country, where many people suffer from malnutrition and starvation, to divert production effort away from food and basic consumption items toward capital accumulation.

Once again, however, the problem is complicated by the common phenomenon of "capital flight" wherein, in an attempt to maximize and secure their returns, wealthier citizens of poor countries often invest much of their financial resources, not in their home countries, but in the richer economies of the world. While wealthy countries do provide significant financial infusions into poor countries, these infusions may be canceled out by capital flight.

Technology

A trip through the countryside and a visit to the industrial production sites in a poor country will reveal traditional techniques of production in use. In Egypt and India, waterwheels of types used a thousand years ago are still a primary means of bringing water to the surface. Much of the cloth is produced on handlooms. Burros and oxcarts are important means of transportation. Across the country, production techniques require large inputs of human effort relative to the inputs of capital resources.

Technological development goes hand in hand with advancing educational levels and with capital accumulation. Innovative thinking and ideas germinate technological advances. However, for ideas to bear fruit—or even to survive—the means of testing and proving them must be available. The capital resources of an economy provide the laboratory in which the testing and proving take place. High levels of technology are seldom developed in capital-poor countries.

Poor countries do not have to go it alone to improve their techniques. Usually they can borrow technology from economically advanced countries. They can import foreign techniques, as did the Japanese following World War II. In addition, they can send students and scientists, as they do now, to be trained abroad and to bring home with them technological know-how—that is, if they do not succumb to the brain drain.

Efficiency

Given that resources are limited but that at the same time people's wants are unlimited, the problem that any society faces is how to use scarce resources and organize production to maximize society's well-being. Consequently, the available resources must be used efficiently to obtain the maximum output from the resources at hand. Two major problems can prevent a society from achieving *productive efficiency*. The possible sources of inefficiency are unemployment and resource misallocation.

Maximum productive efficiency cannot be achieved if available resources are not fully used. This holds true for both human and nonhuman resources—land and capital. As long as there are workers looking for work and unable to find it, or as long as capital remains idle, productive efficiency cannot be achieved. In addition, if certain available resources are used to do jobs for which other available resources are better suited, a misallocation of resources occurs. For example, if British Columbia's apple orchards were planted with wheat while Saskatchewan's farms were planted with apple trees, the same total land area would provide the country with substantially less of both crops than the current arrangement yields. Resource misallocation also results whenever the best available technology is not used in a production process. Unemployment or misallocation of resources lead to the economy realizing a point inside of the production possibility frontier, for example, combinations F and H in Figure 1–1, and fail to achieve productive efficiency.

In many poor countries, the available resources, both labour and capital, tend not to be either fully or most efficiently employed. Land tenure systems may hold land units to sizes too small for capital intensive production. Traditional ways of doing things often block the adoption of more efficient methods. Workers may be uninformed regarding opportunities for increasing their incomes. Wage systems may make it uneconomical for potential employers to hire the entire labour force, and unemployment may occur. Insufficient capital accumulation to provide new jobs needed by a growing labour force may result in unemployment. This list can be extended on and on.

Whereas improvements in labour force quality, capital accumulation, and technological development all tend to shift the production possibilities curve of Figure 1–1 outward, the achievement of higher levels of efficiency move the economy from some point inside the curve toward the curve itself. If inefficiencies occur, the economy will be at a point such as F. Increases in efficiency will moves the economy toward the curve *AE*.

Population

Are population growth and population densities serious threats to living standards? Have they kept per capita real GDP from rising, or have they been significant in holding down the rate of increase? Is there any evidence that they have caused living standards to deteriorate? Suppose we examine some GDP data to see if any answers to these questions are evident.

In Table 1–6 we classify a sample of countries as lesser developed, or LDC, and developed, or DC. The classification is rough and arbitrary. We have put those with per capita real GDP of less than $3,000 per year in the LDC classification and those with per capita real GDP of $3,000 and above in the DC classification regardless of income distribution within each country.

The sample of LDCs does indeed show substantially higher rates of population growth and lower average per capita real GDP growth rates than does the sample of DCs. In fact, the averages for these two variables indicate that the LDCs are experiencing population growth rates that are three times greater than those of the DCs, while DC per capita real GDP is growing nearly 30 percent faster than in LDCs. However, each classification of countries has some important exceptions. Among the LDCs, Egypt, Kenya, and Thailand show high population growth rates and relatively high per capita real GDP growth rates. Among DCs, Canada, Singapore, and the United States show high population growth rates as well as relatively strong per capita real GDP growth rates. At the very least, we can say that relatively high rates of population growth do not preclude growth in per capita real GDP. It may be a factor impeding growth in some instances but is not in itself the problem.

Comparative population densities yield some information on the issue of whether overcrowding is a serious problem. The data of Table 1–6 may be a little surprising. Ethiopia has the lowest per capita GDP in the

Table 1-6   **Per capita real GDP and population, actual and growth rates;
population density; and life expectancy (selected countries, 1980–90)**

Country	Population Estimate 1990 (millions)	Annual Rate of Population Increase (1980–90)	Population Density per Square Kilometer (1990)	Per Capita GDP* (1990)	Percentage Annual Growth Rate of GDP (constant prices)	Life Expectancy at Birth (most recent information)
Lesser Developed						
Argentina	32.3	1.3	12	$2,887	−0.4	71
Chile	13.2	1.7	17	2,105	3.2	72
Colombia	32.3	2.0	28	1,273	3.7	69
Egypt	52.1	2.4	52	637	5.0	60
El Salvador	5.2	1.4	248	1,038	0.9	64
Ethiopia	51.2	3.1	42	107	1.8	48
India	849.5	2.1	258	300	5.3	59
Indonesia	178.2	1.8	94	602	5.5	62
Kenya	24.2	3.8	42	312	4.2	59
Mexico	86.2	2.0	44	2,758	1.0	70
Nigeria	115.5	3.2	125	301	1.4	52
Peru	21.7	2.3	17	1,684	−0.3	63
Philippines	61.5	2.4	205	713	0.9	64
South Africa	35.9	2.4	29	2,527	1.3	62
Thailand	55.8	1.8	109	1,437	7.6	66
Venezuela	19.7	2.7	22	2,450	1.0	70
Zambia	8.1	3.7	11	385	0.8	50
Average		2.4			2.5	62
Developed						
Canada	26.5	1.0	3	21,515	3.4	77
France	56.4	0.5	102	21,113	2.2	77
Germany[†]	79.9	0.1	224	18,626	2.1	76
Israel	4.7	1.8	224	11,319	3.2	76
Italy	57.7	0.2	192	18,904	2.4	77
Japan	123.5	0.6	327	23,829	4.1	79
Singapore	3.0	2.2	3,000	11,533	6.4	74
Sweden	8.6	0.3	19	26,524	2.2	78
Switzerland	6.7	0.6	163	33,560	2.2	78
United Kingdom	57.4	0.2	234	16,989	3.1	76
United States	250.0	0.9	27	21,569	3.4	76
Average		0.8			3.2	77

*At market prices (U.S. dollars).
[†]Data are for unified Germany, except GDP and growth of GDP, which are for the Federal Republic of Germany before unification.
Source: World Bank, World Development Report, 1992, pp. 218–23, 268–9.

table along with a low GDP growth rate. Yet its population density is a low 42 persons per square kilometer. Singapore's per capita GDP is many times that of Ethiopia, and it shows a relatively high growth rate. Its population density is 3,000 persons per square kilometer. Note that the population densities of such DCs as Japan, the United Kingdom, and Singapore all exceed that of India, one of the major LDCs. Population density as such, or overcrowding, does not seem to be a major impediment to relatively high levels of per capita GDP or to economic growth.

The data of Table 1–6 are consistent with generally accepted demographic theory.[3] In premodern, poor societies, death rates were high, and for such societies to survive it was necessary that their birth rates be high, too. In modern times the lesser developed countries are succeeding—often with the help of the developed countries—in reducing their death rates. Better medical knowledge and health facilities, improvements in sanitation, and higher levels of nutrition are the responsible factors; and these are generally welcomed by the countries in question. But measures to reduce birth rates do not receive the same social approval as those that reduce death rates. Reductions in the birth rate lag behind reductions in the death rate, and it is during the lag period that so-called population explosions occur. However, as the sample of developed countries indicates, the birth rate eventually falls, and the rapid increase in population subsides. Greater affluence and higher education levels help lower the birth rates.

The available evidence does not indicate that world poverty is caused by population pressure—high rates of population growth and/or population density. In some poor countries, population pressure may be a contributing factor to poverty, but we must look elsewhere—to the other factors cited above—for the explanation of why so much of the world's population lives in misery.

Income Distribution

In the preceding sections, evidence is presented concerning the extent of human welfare in the world today. Assuming that the LDCs listed are representative, Table 1–6 indicates that much of the world's population suffers from a degree of misery that is probably unintelligible to those of us in DCs. Yet even the dire circumstances reflected by the data of Table 1–6 understate the true extent of human misery that faces most of those in LDCs. This understatement is caused by the fact that average measures of well-

---

[3] P. Demeny, "The Populations of the Underdeveloped Countries," *The Human Population: A Scientific American Book*, ed. Scientific American (San Francisco: W. H. Freeman, 1974), pp. 105–15.

being such as per capita real GDP fail to take into account the distribution of GDP within a country. Consider Zambia with its per capita real GDP of $385. Clearly, life would amount to mere subsistence for a Zambian earning $385 per year. Yet most Zambians would dearly love to earn this "average" income. In Zambia, with its very limited GDP, the problem of human misery is further complicated by the fact that this very limited GDP is distributed in an extremely unequal fashion. While a fortunate few earn much more than $385, the majority of Zambians have annual incomes much below this average figure. When income is unequally distributed, per capita real GDP, although technically correct, paints a misleadingly rosy picture of the degree of human misery that exists within a country.

Unequal Distribution of GDP

What is meant by the distribution of GDP, or the distribution of income, as it is more commonly known, may be best understood by considering a simple example. Suppose that two economies, Alpha and Omega, are each composed of five families, A through E. Further, suppose that in Alpha each of the families earns $2,000 per year, while in Omega families A through D have no income and family E earns $10,000 per year, as presented in Table 1–7. In each economy, then, the annual income for all families is $10,000, and the average family income is $2,000. Do these facts suggest that the people of each economy are equally well-off? The answer to this question is clearly no. Simply looking at averages is quite misleading in this case because, although the GDP is the same, the distribution of GDP differs so markedly between the two economies.

In the real world, of course, it is unlikely that either the perfectly equal distribution of Alpha or the perfectly unequal distribution of Omega will exist. Nevertheless, Table 1–7, can help us evaluate the distribution of income that exists within a particular economy. For example, the distribution of income in Alpha is considered to be perfectly equal because each family controls the same share of Alpha's income ($2,000). Put differently, each of the five families represents one-fifth or 20 percent of Alpha's population,

Table 1–7	The distribution of income within an economy (hypothetical data)						
	Annual Income Family A	Annual Income Family B	Annual Income Family C	Annual Income Family D	Annual Income Family E	Annual Income of All Families	Average Annual Family Income
Alpha	$2,000	$2,000	$2,000	$2,000	$2,000	$10,000	$2,000
Omega	0	0	0	0	10,000	10,000	2,000

and at the same time, each of the five controls one-fifth or 20 percent of Alpha's GDP ($2,000/$10,000). Thus perfect equality exists when each 20 percent "chunk" of an economy's families controls 20 percent of the economy's income.

How close do existing economies come to perfect equality? Are there systematic differences in income distribution between LDCs and DCs? Answers to these questions are found in Table 1–8, which reports data on income distribution for selected LDCs and DCs. (You will note that, as is customary, Table 1–8 ranks each economy's families from poorest to richest rather than in randomly chosen 20 percent groups.)

To see the impact of the distribution of GDP on individual well-being, again consider Zambia. Recall that Zambia has a per capita real GDP of $385, which was suggested to understate the degree of poverty felt by Zambians. If GDP was equally distributed, that is, if all Zambians earned $385 per year, then each 20 percent chunk of Zambian families would control approximately 20 percent of Zambian GDP. Yet, as Table 1–8 points out, this is not the case. As miserable as their plight would be with a perfectly equal distribution of income yielding a 20 percent share of GDP for the "poorest" families, in reality these families control only 3.4 percent of Zambian GDP. Thus if the meager Zambian GDP were equally distributed, giving meaning to the per capita real GDP value of $385, the families making up the poorest 20 percent grouping would find their income increasing by more than a factor of five (rising from 3.4 to 20 percent). This is not to suggest that all Zambian families earn less than the average of $385. Such cannot be the case if the average is properly calculated. Table 1–8 indicates that while a majority of Zambian families are truly impoverished, some families are relatively rich. Note the share of Zambian GDP controlled by the richest 20 percent of families. The 61 percent share of national income controlled by this group indicates that the degree of human misery brought on by Zambia's extremely limited GDP is greatly worsened by the fact that this limited GDP is very unequally distributed.

Is this situation unique to Zambia? Unfortunately not. As the averages for the shares of GDP controlled by each group of families for the different countries indicate, the degree of income inequality in LDCs is much greater than in DCs. This is not to suggest that the DCs have distributions that approximate perfect equality. In fact, some people believe that the degree of income inequality that exists in DCs is unacceptably high. The importance of Table 1–8 is that the data indicate that the degree of inequality that exists appears to be significantly greater in LDCs than in DCs. Given this information, it may be concluded that the degree of human misery that is reflected by average measures of well-being such as per capita real GDP, as bad as it is, fails to describe accurately the misery suffered by much of the world's population. Such measures of well-being apparently do paint too rosy a scenario.

Table 1–8   **The distribution of income in selected countries***

Country (year of study)	Total Income or GDP Controlled by Each Group of Families				
	Poorest 20 %	Second 20 %	Third 20 %	Fourth 20 %	Richest 20 %
Lesser Developed					
Argentina (1970)	4.4%	9.7%	14.1%	21.5%	50.3%
Chile (1968)	4.0	8.0	13.0	17.5	67.5
Colombia (1988)	4.0	8.7	13.5	20.8	53.0
Egypt (1974)	5.8	10.7	14.7	20.8	48.0
El Salvador (1976–77)	5.5	10.0	14.8	22.4	47.3
India (1983)	8.1	12.3	16.3	22.0	41.4
Indonesia (1987)	8.8	12.4	16.0	21.5	41.3
Kenya (1976)	2.6	6.3	11.5	19.2	60.4
Mexico (1977)	2.9	7.0	12.0	20.4	57.7
Peru (1985)	4.4	8.5	13.7	21.5	51.9
Philippines (1985)	5.5	9.7	14.8	22.0	48.0
South Africa (1965)	1.9	4.3	10.1	25.7	58.0
Thailand (1975–76)	5.6	9.6	13.9	21.1	49.2
Venezuela (1987)	4.7	9.2	14.0	21.5	50.6
Zambia (1974)	3.4	7.4	11.2	16.9	61.1
Average	4.8	8.9	13.6	21.0	51.7
Developed					
Canada (1987)	5.7	11.8	17.7	24.6	40.2
France (1979)	6.3	12.1	17.2	23.5	40.8
Israel (1979–80)	6.0	12.1	17.8	24.5	39.6
Italy (1986)	6.8	12.0	16.7	23.5	41.0
Japan (1979)	8.7	13.2	17.5	23.1	37.5
Singapore (1982–83)	5.1	9.9	14.6	21.4	48.9
Sweden (1981)	8.0	13.2	17.4	24.5	36.9
Switzerland (1982)	5.2	11.7	16.4	22.1	44.6
United Kingdom (1979)	5.8	11.5	18.2	25.0	39.5
United States (1985)	4.7	11.0	17.4	25.0	41.9
West Germany (1984)	6.8	12.7	17.8	24.1	38.7
Average	6.3	11.9	17.2	23.3	40.8

*Ethiopia and Nigeria were omitted because of a lack of data.
Source: World Bank, World Development Report, 1992, pp. 276–7.

Can Governments Help?

What, if anything, can governments do to help solve world poverty problems? Over the last few decades, populations have looked increasingly to their governments to solve their problems for them. Governments, in turn, have accepted more responsibility for solving the economic problems of their populations. Unfortunately, people often expect more of their governments than those governments can provide. And governments promise more than they are able to deliver.

Governments of LDCs

The single most important decision that government must make with respect to economic development concerns the extent to which it will influence economic decision making. The options range from little or no government involvement to decision making based entirely on government dictate. As we will discuss in Chapter 2, the ongoing movement away from extreme government interference in economic decision making that is sweeping through Eastern Europe and, to a lesser but still significant degree, in places such as China, indicates that development may be enhanced by reducing the economic role of government. Although it may seem paradoxical, the governments of many LDCs, rather than being vehicles for economic improvement, are burdens to development. Economic development tends to reach its potential when individuals and communities, rather than government, are allowed to own economic resources and decide the use for those resources. Equally important, resource ownership must be more equitably distributed with owners allowed to reap the benefits of well-made decisions on resource use and deal with the consequences of poorly made decisions. Governments of LDCs then would well serve the development interests of their people by making sure that government involvement in economic activity is limited to those areas where the economy, left to its own devices, clearly fails to achieve desired development goals. In this regard, the governments of LDCs should pursue policies that improve the quality of the labour force, enhance capital accumulation, raise levels of technology, increase efficiency, reduce inequality, and, perhaps, slow population growth. This is a tall order—more easily said than done.

In most countries where literacy rates are high, governments have assumed responsibilities for primary education. In many countries this responsibility has been extended to secondary and even to higher education. Insofar as it can, the government of an LDC would be well advised to emulate these countries. But universal education does not come easily or without cost. The establishment of an educational system is a slow, expensive task. Physical facilities must be built and a corps of teachers must be trained. LDCs find it very difficult to divert resources from the provision of subsistence goods to the provision of education. The immediate opportunity cost of additional education is high for a hungry population.

Government help in the capital accumulation process may be direct or indirect. One of the most positive things governments can do to create new capital resources directly is to press development of *social overhead capital,* commonly referred to as infrastructure. Examples of infrastructure are transportation networks and communications networks, which contribute greatly to efficiency. So do energy or power systems. Governments can also establish an economic climate favourable to capital accumulation. They can pursue monetary and fiscal policies conducive to economic stability. They can enact tax laws that provide special incentives for capital accumulation. They can formulate policies that allow people to reap the rewards for saving and investing in new capital equipment. In many instances, capital accumulation is discouraged because revenue-hungry governments tax away too large a share of the returns that accrue from it.

Social overhead capital refers to capital resources that are shared by the entire economy rather than being used by one firm. Highways and communications networks are examples of social overhead capital, commonly referred to as infrastructure.

Sparked by governmental activities, some positive action concerning population control appears to be under way in certain parts of the world. In India, Thailand, and China, massive government educational efforts for birth control and family planning have been made. In India voluntary sterilization of both men and women has been subsidized. In China families are encouraged to have only one child and are heavily taxed for exceeding that number. During the late 1970s and 1980s trends in world population growth appear to have turned downward, causing population experts to become much more optimistic in their predictions of future population growth.[4]

Governments of DCs

Since World War II, the economically advanced countries of the world have provided some economic assistance to LDCs, partly for humanitarian reasons and partly in hopes of obtaining ideological allegiance from the LDCs. There has been much rivalry between communist countries and those of the Western world. Some aid to LDCs has been channeled through the World Bank, and individual countries have conducted aid programs of their own. Basically, aid takes two forms: (1) loans and grants and (2) technical assistance.

Loans and grants generally are expected to help the recipient countries improve their labour forces, accumulate capital, improve their technological capabilities, and increase the efficiencies of their production processes. They are used to build educational facilities and for sanitary

---

[4]J. van der Tak, C. Haub, and E. Murphy, "A New Look at the Population Problem," *Futurist* 14 (April 1980), pp. 39–46.

engineering purposes. They help construct power plants, cement plants, communications and transportation facilities, agricultural facilities, and the like. They are also used to import such things as fertilizer, raw and semifinished materials, industrial equipment, agricultural equipment, and spare parts.

Technical assistance helps in upgrading labour force skills and in advancing the technologies of the recipient countries. Much technical assistance is turned toward increasing the productivity of agricultural resources, improving educational systems, and raising standards of public health. In addition, advisors from the DCs often assist in getting industrial projects under way.

The World Bank is an organization through which DCs can jointly assist LDCs. It provides both low-interest loans from funds supplied by the DCs and technical assistance to low-income countries. Loans are made for a variety of projects, large and small, public and private. Bank officials require that the projects for which loans are made show every promise of paying off both the principal and the interest. The World Bank has been quite successful in this respect but has often been criticized as being too stingy with its loans and placing too much emphasis on capital projects rather than human resources.

Summary

Human welfare is without question the major issue that the study of economics is concerned with. For example, in order to understand poverty, its causes, and its possible alleviation, we must first understand the nature of economics and economic activity.

Economic activity is generated by the needs and wants of human beings, which seem to be insatiable in the aggregate. The means available in any economy for satisfying the wants of its population are scarce. They consist of the economy's resources—its labour, its land, and its capital—along with its available technology and social institutions. The supplies of resources, together with the level of technology available, determine the maximum GDP that the country can produce to satisfy needs and wants. Dividing a country's real GDP by its population yields its per capita real GDP, which is a rough measure of its standard of living.

The basic elements of economic activity and economic analysis provide insight into human welfare and the causes of poverty. Poverty stems from low levels of education and training, little land and capital resources for labour to work with, low levels of technology, inefficiencies in the use of resources, and, in some instances, excessive rates of population growth. To break out of the poverty trap, a country must successfully attack some or all of the causes. However, a nation is unlikely to make much progress against poverty unless it also achieves a marked degree of political and economic stability.

The simple production possibilities curve helps in understanding the relationship of resources to productive output, unemployment and resource misallocation, and growth in the production over time. Developing countries find it hard to shift some of their resources to the production of capital as they need all of their resources for the production of goods that meet current needs. Developed countries can and do assist LDCs as they strive to improve their economic possibilities. Aid takes two basic forms: (1) loans or grants and (2) technical assistance. Individual DCs have independent aid programs. They also engage in joint aid programs through such organizations as the World Bank. Much more needs to be done, however, if the income gap between developed and undeveloped nations is to be reduced.

Checklist of Economic Concepts

Labour resources	Gross domestic product, real
Capital resources	Gross domestic product, per capita
Land resources	Production possibilities curve
Technology	Living standards
Production	Price index numbers
Opportunity cost	Efficiency
Opportunity cost principle	Lesser developed countries
Gross national product	Developed countries
Gross domestic product	Social overhead capital
current dollar	

Discussion Questions

1. Explain what the study of economics can contribute to understanding human well being.

2. Draw an "input–output" diagram of an economy that shows the relationship among resources, production, and the distribution of goods and services. Where does capital fit in? How do you illustrate semifinished materials? Where do the "bads" (for example, pollution) go? Discuss whether the political orientation of country would affect how the diagram should be drawn for any specific country.

3. Think about the following situation in terms of the concept of opportunity cost. If you choose not to go to college, suppose your best alternative is to drive a truck for $12,000 per year. If you

choose to go to college, suppose that you must pay a tuition fee of $2,000 per year and buy books and other school supplies amounting to $600 per year. Suppose that your other living expenses are the same regardless of which choice you make. Suppose you choose to go to college. What are the opportunity costs of your college diploma per year?

4. Discuss what the opportunity cost of increasing education levels for a poor country, such as Niger, would include. How could Canada best assist Niger attain this investment in "human capital" without Niger having to bear these opportunity costs?

5. A country has a production possibilities for tractors and cars as indicated in the following table:

Production Possibilities (output per year)
(hypothetical data)

	Combination				
Product	A	B	C	D	E
Tractors (in thousands)	0	25	40	50	55
Cars (in thousands)	40	30	20	10	0

a. Plot the production possibilities curve for the economy characterized by this table.

b. Calculate the opportunity cost of tractors for each point from A to E, and the opportunity cost of cars for each point from E to A. Discuss what is happening to these costs as one moves along the curve.

c. Suppose technological progress doubles the productivity of the process for making tractors and also of that for making cars. Plot the new production possibilities curve.

d. Suppose technological progress doubles the productivity of the process for making tractors but there is no change in the process for making cars. Calculate the new production possibilities table. Plot the new production possibilities curve.

e. Suppose technological progress doubles the productivity of the process for making cars but there is no change in the process for making tractors. Calculate the new production possibilities table. Plot the new production possibilities curve.

f. Why is it that, despite the fact that there is no change in the productivity of producing tractors E, it is now possible at any given level of production of cars to have more tractors?

6. Consider a production possibilities curve for consumer goods (good X) and capital goods (good Y).

a. Explain what a point inside the curve indicates. Discuss how the frontier of the curve could be achieved. Is there an opportunity cost of one good for the other when inside the curve? Discuss the implications of this.
b. How would the choice of a point on today's production possibilities curve affect the position of tomorrow's curve? Choose three different points on today's production possibilities curve and indicate the relative location of tomorrow's curve that is associated with each.
c. Discuss the reasons for the different shifts.
d. If the initial point is where the capital output is zero, what do you think would happen to the curve, assuming all other things remain constant?

Supplementary Reading

Brue, S. L. and D. R. Wentworth. "Mr. Malthus." In *Economic Scenes: Theory in Today's World.* Englewood Cliffs, NJ: Prentice Hall, 1988, pp. 256–66.
A novel approach to summarizing the economics of population growth, resource scarcity, and economic growth.

Ehrlich, P. R. *The Population Bomb.* rev. ed. New York: Ballantine Books, 1978.
A scare book written by a biologist with little understanding of economics. It is an important book, however, worthy of the attention of anyone seriously concerned with population problems.

Hancock, G. *Ethiopia: The Challenge of Hunger.* London: Victor Gollancz, Ltd., 1985.
This book provides a thorough analysis of the roots and extent of the Ethiopian famines of the 1980s. Most notable are the first-hand accounts of life and death in the feeding centers.

Heilbroner, R. L. "The Underdeveloped World." In *The Making of Economic Society.* 6th ed. Englewood Cliffs, NJ: Prentice Hall, 1980, chapter 12.
Discusses such diverse third-world problems as social inertia, population growth, hidden labour surpluses, lack of capital equipment, trade problems, foreign aid, social and political unrest, and ecological problems.

"Least Developed Countries." *World Health,* June 1982.
Special edition devoted to health problems of the 31 least developed countries of the world.

Lecaillon, J.; F. Paukert; C. Morrisson; and D. Germidis. *Income Distribution and Economic Development.* Geneva: International Labour Office, 1984.
A very fine treatment of the relationship between income distribution and economic development. Offers an extensive critical analysis of existing studies in the area.

Mellor, J. W. and B. F. Johnston. "The World Food Equation: Interrelations among Development, Employment, and Food Consumption." *Journal of Economic Literature* 22 (June 1984), pp. 53–74.
A high-level scholarly treatment of the economic problems in developing countries, with emphasis on the question of adequacy of food supplies.

United Nations. *World Development Report.* New York: Oxford University Press, annual.

An outstanding source for data on development issues. Includes data on income, population, life expectancy, health status, and educational attainment (as well as other topics) for well over 100 countries.

Van der Tak, J.; C. Haub; and E. Murphy. "A New Look at the Population Problem." *Futurist* 14 (April 1980), pp. 39–48.

An up-to-date report on one of the most critical problems of the late 20th century.

Wong, S. L. "Consequences of China's New Population Policy." *China Quarterly,* no. 98 (June 1984), pp. 220–40.

An excellent discussion of the development of China's one-child-per-couple population control program and of possible side effects of the program.

Chapter 2

Economic Systems, Resource Allocation, and Social Well-Being

Lessons from the Changes in the Former Soviet Union

MOSCOW (CNN)—An elite group of men have been on the road since February, covering tens of thousands of miles within Russia. They listen sympathetically to hundreds of tales of woe, then promise millions of people that they will make it right. This is the Russian presidential campaign.

Although the field is crowded, there are only two strong contenders for Sunday's votes: incumbent President Boris Yeltsin and Gennady Zyuganov, the candidate of the Communist Party. It may come as a surprise that the Communist Party is even in contention, considering that just four-and-a-half years ago, Russians joyously brought down the Communist regime.

But many are already nostalgic about the social guarantees that Communism had to offer. Thirty percent of Russians live below the poverty line, and 10 percent reap almost 50 percent of the country's income. Boris Yeltsin's government cannot deny that it has failed to fulfill many of its promises to the people.

This time, Yeltsin is promising to spend more time on the road and to start listening to the problems of his citizens outside of the Kremlin walls. His government is often accused of being inattentive to the needs of the majority.

"Reforms have to serve someone," said Alexander Yakovlev, a former Gorbachev adviser. "We have still not found a way to balance this, and the result is a great mass of people are unsatisfied."

When he speaks to people outside the Russian capital, Zyuganov plays on their anger at being left behind in the new economy, and paints a rosy picture of the past. His constituents are mainly those on pensions or workers who are finding it impossible to adjust to the harsh realities of capitalism. They are likely to have poor job prospects, or none at all.

The Uralsky Samosvety Perfume Factory is a prime example of the stark realities reform has brought. Still not a successful company financially, it was forced to forego perfume production in favor of cheaper, more competitive items, like toothpaste. Its struggling workers say things were better under Communism, but they are afraid changing the system once again will only make matters worse.

"You can't glue together a broken cup. Now that everything has been broken, we need a new foundation. I think we have to let Yeltsin continue," said one worker.

Even if Yeltsin wins, things will not stay the same. This election has driven home to the government that while Russians may have dreamed of capitalism and democracy, they want to have it Russian-style.[1]

As was noted in Chapter 1, few human decisions influence social well-being more directly and forcefully than choices concerning the way in which we organize our economies. The history of the Union of Soviet

---

[1]E. O'Connor "A Mandate for Change —No Matter Who Wins," Special section—Pivotal Elections: Russia, June 12, 1996, ©1996 Cable News Network, Inc. All rights reserved. Used with permission.

Socialist Republics, or the USSR, during this century clearly bears out this point. Although czarist Russia had taken the initial steps toward industrialization by the turn of the 20th century, the country still lagged significantly behind the United States, Great Britain, and much of Europe. In fact, by the beginning of World War I, Russia, although very rich in economic resources, was the poorest of the European countries as measured by per capita GDP. The economic development of Russia was to be unalterably changed, however, by the political events of the following decade. The Bolshevik revolution of 1917–18, led by Vladimir Lenin, created the new USSR and ushered in an unprecedented period of economic experimentation and change. Most notably, by the end of the 1920s, Soviet strongman Joseph Stalin had essentially eliminated all vestiges of market-based resource allocation in favour of central planning. And this system remained in place, with only relatively minor changes, until the collapse from within of the USSR in 1991.

The Soviet experience causes us to ask first how resources are allocated in differing types of economies. Then, and more important, we will want to know how well each allocation mechanism serves the people of the economy. In doing so, we should be able to shed light on the issue of whether the fall of the USSR was related to its choice of economic organization. In the recent Russian presidential election, Yeltsin ultimately won with 53 percent of the vote; his rival Zyuganov, the candidate of the Communist Party, garnered 40 percent of the vote. As the opening quote indicates, the type of economic system a society chooses affects the well-being of individuals differently.

Economic Systems

Within any country, organizational arrangements develop that serve as a framework within which economic decisions are made. In general terms these organizational arrangements specify who determines what is produced with the country's scarce resources and who benefits from well-made decisions, as well as who suffers from poorly made decisions. The choice of organizational arrangement does not determine whether decision making will occur, but rather how the decisions will be made. Historically, economic organization ranges from private parties to a mix of private parties and the state, or to the state entirely. The extent to which the state is involved in the economy is determined by the choice of an economic system, which can be thought of as falling on a continuum with the pure market economy at one extreme and the pure command economy at the other.

The **pure market economy** is based on private ownership and control of resources, known as private property rights, and coordination of resource-use decisions through markets.

Pure Market Economy

The *pure market economy* has two essential elements: (1) private ownership of the economy's resources, known as private property rights, and (2) decentralized decision making coordinated through markets. Within the pure market, or capitalist, economy, private individuals, businesses, and combinations of the two are allowed, with minor interference, to engage in whatever voluntary exchanges they feel best maximize their well-being. If offered a job for $5 per hour, the individual may choose whether to accept it or turn it down, depending on such factors as the value placed on his or her time and the availability of alternative sources of income. Similarly, a business owner decides whether to hire more or fewer workers, to seek more or less capital, and to increase or reduce production. The key is that within a pure market economy, choices surrounding the use of resources are left to private resource owners who are expected to make decisions that best suit their goals and aspirations.

A **market** is a mechanism by which individuals interact as buyers and sellers of a product and the price and quantity exchanged of the product are determined.

Once this myriad of decisions is made, coordination of the decisions takes place within markets. A *market* is a mechanism by which individuals interact as buyers and sellers of a product and the price and quantity exchanged of the product are determined. A market economy depends primarily on the outcomes of numerous markets to direct the allocation of resources throughout the economy. Note the absence of any discussion of government in this process, with the implicit exception of legal enforcement of property rights.

Pure Command Economy

The **pure command economy** is characterized by state ownership and/or control of resources and centralized resource-use decision making.

At the opposite end of the continuum of economic systems is the *pure command economy.* This economic system is on the other end of the continuum from pure market capitalism. That is, the pure command economy is characterized by state ownership and/or control of economic resources and by centralized planning. Decisions concerning what to produce and how to produce it are made by central authorities through binding directives to producers. Given the centralization of decision making, alternative means of coordination of decisions such as reliance on markets is not necessary. And the resulting extremely expanded role of government should be obvious; who else can play the role of central planner?

Mixed Systems

Although examples of economies at or at least near the two extremes of pure market and pure command have never existed, Britain during the first half of the 1800s approached unfettered capitalism and the USSR tended towards a pure command system during its existence. Most present-day economies lie somewhere between these extremes. Canada, Japan, and the United States, for example, can each be thought of as having mixed-market economies; although private ownership and decentralized decision making are the rule, part of each economy's resources are governmentally owned and/or controlled and certainly part of the national output of each country comes from the public sector. Similarly, although China, Cuba, North Korea, and Vietnam remain near the pure command end given their pervasive public ownership of property, increasingly each is allowing elements of private property rights and decentralized decision making. For this reason, each is better categorized today as having mixed-command economies.

Although present-day economies do not satisfy fully the criteria of either the pure market or pure command economy, these polar cases are useful in analyzing the way in which resources are allocated within existing mixed economies and the impact these differing allocation mechanisms have on social well-being. The extent to which outcomes of this analysis apply to any particular *mixed system* depends on how closely the economy satisfies the conditions of the pure market or pure command classifications. That is, an economy in which individuals own and control most resources and in which most economic decisions are made in a decentralized fashion can be expected to yield results that conform closely to the pure market model. Conversely, when most resources are publicly owned or controlled and most decision making is centralized, we can expect outcomes that closely mimic those of the pure command economy.

Economies that combine elements of both the pure market and pure command economies are known as **mixed systems.**

Resource Allocation in a Market Economy

When the buyers and sellers of a product or service interact with one another and engage in exchange, a market is said to exist. The geographic area of any market is simply the area within which the two parties are able to transfer information about and ownership of whatever is being exchanged. Some markets are local, some national, and still others international. Markets within the capitalist economy serve to coordinate the infinite decisions concerning resource allocation made by the owners of those resources. For example, in the last few decades, the development and application of digital technology has produced a compact disk player that is a cost-effective substitute for phonographic turntables. And consumers' desires for compact disk players, as you are no doubt aware, has been explosive. Left behind, of course, are turntables that are now considered old-fashioned. Clearly, both the existing producers of turntables and the many new compact disk producers were well advised to reallocate their efforts toward the production of compact disk players and away from turntables. How did this happen? As you will see, this and the infinite other decisions about resource allocation and reallocation are brought together through the marketplace.

Market Structure

The quality of market-based resource allocation decisions is in large part determined by the degree of competition that exists within the market economy. At one end of the spectrum, markets fall into the purely competitive classification. At the other, they are classified as purely monopolistic. The markets of any market economy can be found at or near each extreme, but most tend to fall firmly in between.

Purely Competitive Markets. For a market to be *purely competitive*, it must exhibit five important characteristics. First, it must have enough knowledgeable buyers and sellers of the product so that no one of them acting alone can influence its price. To illustrate, consider the individual consumer buying a loaf of bread in a supermarket or an individual farmer selling wheat at a grain elevator. Second, each of the sellers must be offering a standardized product. This condition is met when consumers are as happy to buy the product from one seller as from any other. Third, the product price must be free to move up or down without interference from government or any other party. Fourth, buyers and sellers must be mobile; that is, any buyer is free to move among alternative sellers and buy from whomever will sell at the lowest price. Similarly, sellers must be free to move among all potential buyers and sell to that individual who is willing to pay most for the product. Fifth, sellers must be free to leave the industry if they wish, and potential sellers must be free to enter if they feel they can produce the product more efficiently than existing sellers.

> A **purely competitive** market has a large number of mobile, knowledgeable buyers and sellers of a standardized product. Further, the price of the product is free to move up or down, and firms are free to enter or leave the market at any time.

Few markets in Canada are purely competitive in the sense of rigorously fulfilling all five requirements, but some almost do. Perhaps coming closest to pure competition in Canada are some markets within agriculture. The market for agricultural products certainly satisfies the first, second, and fourth characteristics of the purely competitive market, although it fails to fulfill the third and fifth. Since 1933 the government has often been actively involved in establishing and maintaining prices in agricultural markets, violating the third characteristic of pure competition. And for some agricultural products such as dairy farming, the large amount of money necessary to effectively enter the market probably poses a significant barrier, violating the fifth characteristic.

Purely Monopolistic Markets. A *purely monopolistic* selling market, at the opposite end of the spectrum, exists when there is but one seller of a product. The seller is able to manipulate the product price to his or her advantage. Typically, the monopolist is also able to block potential competitors from entering the market—sometimes with government help. In many parts of Canada, a single electrical power generation system serves an entire province. In these areas, the electricity market is a pure monopoly. Although examples exist, most markets are not pure monopolies in Canada.

> In a **purely monopolistic** market, there is only one seller of a product. The monopolist has substantial control over price and is often able to prevent potential sellers from entering the market.
>
> Markets that fall between the purely competitive and purely monopolistic extremes are said to be **imperfectly competitive** and may exhibit characteristics of either or both of those extremes.

Imperfectly Competitive Markets. Most markets in Canada fall somewhere between the purely competitive and purely monopolistic extremes. These markets are called *imperfectly competitive*, and the performance of such a market depends on the degree to which the market diverges from the extremes. That is, markets that do not fully satisfy the conditions of pure competition but come close to doing so can be expected to perform much the same as those that are purely competitive; those markets that are almost pure monopolies will likely yield outcomes not too dissimilar from those of pure monopoly.

Market Forces

Markets bring together or co-ordinate all of the decisions that economic agents make within the capitalist economy—you may have heard the term the *forces of demand and supply.* To fully understand the market economy, you must have a solid understanding of how demand and supply interact to determine how scarce resources are allocated in a market economy.

The **demand** for a good or service refers to the quantity of the product that consumers are willing and able to purchase at various prices, other things being equal. The other things that must remain equal are (1) the consumers' incomes, (2) the prices of related goods such as complements and substitutes, (3) the consumers' tastes, (4) the consumers' expectations, and (5) the number of consumers.

Demand. The *demand* for a product refers to the quantities of the product that consumers are willing and able to purchase at various prices, other things being equal. Consider the demand for cola at your college or university. Suppose that during one day, the consumers of cola on campus are willing and able to purchase 1,500 units if the price is $.50 per unit; 1,000 units if the price is $1.00; or 500 units if the price is $1.50. Each of these price-quantity combinations is listed in the demand schedule of Table 2–1 and is then plotted as a demand curve in Figure 2–1. The demand schedule and curve each have several characteristics that are vitally important.

First, we are incorrect if we refer to any of the individual price-quantity combinations listed above as demand. The quantity of a product that consumers are willing and able to purchase at a specific price, reflecting one point on a demand curve, is properly referred to as the quantity demanded at that price. That is, demand refers not to a specific price-quantity combination but to all of the price-quantity combinations taken together. In this way the demand for cola on campus is properly reflected in the entire demand curve or schedule.

Table 2–1	A demand schedule for cola	
	Price (dollars)	Quantity (units per day)
	$ .50	1,500
	1.00	1,000
	1.50	500

Figure 2–1   **A demand curve for cola**

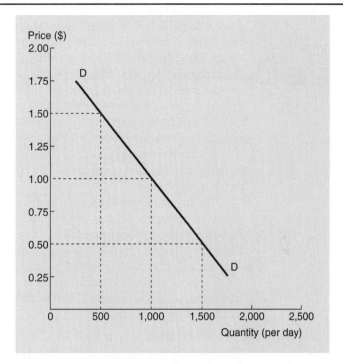

The price-quantity demanded combinations of Table 2–1, plotted graphically, form the demand curve for cola, *DD*. The demand curve shows the quantities of cola that the consumers are willing to purchase at various prices, other things being equal.

Second, demand relates to the quantities of the product that consumers are actually willing and able to purchase at various prices, not merely the quantities of the product that consumers would like to consume. Each of us probably desires an expensive oceanfront home, but unless we are actually willing and able to purchase such a house at its market price, we do not have a demand for it in the economic sense of the term.

Third, demand reflects the quantities of the product that consumers are willing and able to purchase during some specific period of time. For example, the demand schedule and curve presented accurately depict the demand for cola on campus during one day. It makes little sense to discuss the quantity of cola demanded at a specific price unless the period of time in which the purchases may take place is specified.

Fourth, customers will desire more of a product when its price is low than when it is high. Although this concept may seem to be nothing more than common sense, it serves as the often overlooked basis of much that is

The **law of demand** states that the lower the price of the good, the larger will be the quantity demanded; and the higher the price, the smaller will be the quantity demanded, other things being equal.

done in economics. Formally, this inverse price-quantity demanded relationship is called the *law of demand* and states that the lower the price of a product, the larger will be the quantity demanded; and the higher the price, the smaller will be the quantity demanded, other things being equal. Why should price and quantity demanded be inversely related? For one thing, as the price falls current consumers will feel richer and be able to buy more of the good. Secondly, if the price is lower, a greater number of people can afford the product given their incomes. A third reason is that people will likely substitute this product for relatively more expensive similar products when the price is lower. The regularity of this inverse relationship between price and quantity demanded is referred to as the law of demand. This law is illustrated by the downward or negative slope of the demand curve.

The law of demand does not simply state that the quantity demanded is greater when the price is low than when the price is high. The law states that this inverse price-quantity demanded relationship holds only *with other things being equal.* Although many variables could be listed as the other things that must be equal or held constant, the five most important are (1) the consumers' incomes, (2) the prices of goods related in consumption, (3) the consumers' tastes, (4) the consumers' expectations, and (5) the number of consumers.

Changes in the Quantity Demanded versus Changes in Demand. From the information given previously, we know that the consumers are willing and able to purchase 1,000 units of cola per day when its price is $1.00 per unit. This quantity demanded is identified as point A on the original demand curve *DD*, of Figure 2–2.

Should the price of cola increase to $1.50, the consumers would reduce the amount they wish to purchase to 500 units per day. That is, when the price rises to $1.50, the consumers move to the left on their demand curve to point B, which reflects a quantity demanded of 500 units per day. Such a movement along one demand curve, brought about by a change in the price of the product, is called a *change in the quantity demanded*. It is important to understand that this movement is not a change in demand. The consumers are merely moving from one price-quantity combination, or quantity demanded, to another in response to a change in the price of cola.

A **movement along one demand curve, brought about by a change in the price of the product, is called a **change in quantity demanded.**

A shift to an entirely new demand curve, brought about by a change in one or more of the variables assumed to be held constant, is called a **change in demand.**

A *change in demand* is said to occur when the entire demand schedule and curve change. For example, Figure 2–2 includes the original demand curve of Figure 2–1 (labeled *DD*) and two new curves, D_1D_1 and D_2D_2. Along demand curve D_1D_1, consumers desire less cola at each price than is the case along demand *DD*. Thus a shift in demand from *DD* to D_1D_1 is referred to as a decrease in demand. Demand curve D_2D_2 indicates just the opposite, so a shift from *DD* to D_2D_2 is called an increase in demand. In each case the entire demand curve shifts. Shifts in

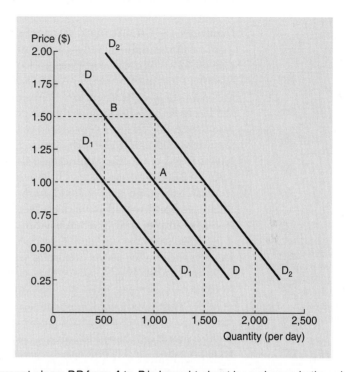

The movement along *DD* from *A* to *B* is brought about by a change in the price of cola and is called a change in the quantity demanded. A shift in the entire demand curve to either D_1D_1 or D_2D_2 is called a change in demand and is brought about by a change in one of the variables assumed to be held constant when the demand curve is drawn.

the demand curve distinguish a change in demand from a change in quantity demanded—a movement along a demand curve.

Changes in demand occur when one or more of the five variables assumed to be held constant changes. Before proceeding to the discussion of how changes in the constants lead to changes in demand, however, you must fully understand the distinction between a change in quantity demanded and a change in demand. If the price of the product rises or falls, consumers will adjust the quantity demanded per unit of time. Graphically, this adjustment is represented by a movement along one demand curve and is called a change in the quantity demanded. By contrast, if one or more of the five variables assumed to be held constant changes, consumers move to an entirely new demand curve, and this adjustment is called a change in demand. It is very important to remember the difference between a change in demand (caused by a change in a variable other than price) and a change in quantity demanded (caused by a change in price).

Changes in Consumers' Incomes. A change in demand may result from a change in the incomes of consumers. Suppose that initially demand curve *DD* of Figure 2–2 applies and the price of cola is $1.00 per unit. At this price the quantity demanded is 1,000 units per day. Now suppose that the incomes of consumers rise. With incomes on the increase, consumers are likely to be willing and able to purchase more cola even if the price remains $1.00. Perhaps now they are willing and able to buy 1,500 units. Similarly, had the initial price been $.50, the increase in incomes might have caused consumers to increase the amount they wished to buy from 1,500 to 2,000 units per day. Thus, when incomes rise, demand increases from *DD* to some higher level such as D_2D_2. Conversely, had incomes fallen, demand would have decreased to some lower level such as D_1D_1.

> If the demand for a good increases as incomes rise and decreases as incomes fall, the good is said to be a **normal good.**
>
> If the demand for a good decreases as incomes rise and increases as incomes fall, the good is said to be an **inferior good.**

In this example, an important assumption is implicitly made. Specifically, it assumes that cola is a *normal good.* A good is said to be a normal good if its demand increases as incomes rise and decreases as incomes fall. Although most goods satisfy this condition and are considered to be normal, for some goods the demand-income relationship is just the reverse. Such goods are known as *inferior goods* and exhibit demands that decrease as incomes rise and increase as incomes fall. Examples of inferior goods might include hot dogs, generic goods of all sorts, public transportation, and rabbit ears for television sets.

Changes in the Prices of Goods Related in Consumption. When considering the demand for a particular good, the prices of two types of related goods are important. First, the prices of *substitute goods* must be considered. In simplest form, goods are considered to be substitutes if they satisfy the same consumer need or desire. More formally, goods are substitutes if an increase in the price of one leads to an increase in the demand for the other. Assuming that cola and ginger ale are substitutes and starting from an initial position at point A in Figure 2–2, how would a doubling in the price of ginger ale affect the demand for cola? Given that the two are substitutes, the rise in the price of ginger ale could be expected to increase the demand for cola to some higher level such as D_2D_2 as consumers substitute cola for the now more expensive ginger ale. Just the opposite would occur if the price of ginger ale were to fall.

> Two goods are said to be **substitute goods** if an increase in the price of one leads to an increase in the demand for the other.

> Two goods are said to be **complementary goods** if an increase in the price of one leads to a decrease in the demand for the other.

Another type of related good whose price must be held constant is *complementary goods.* Complementary goods are used in combination, such as hot dogs and hot dog buns or cars and gasoline. The impact of a change in the price of a complement is just the opposite of that for substitutes. With complementary goods, the demand for the good in question decreases as the price of the complement rises. Again, returning to the campus, suppose that cola and potato chips are complements. A decrease in the demand for cola might be caused by an increase in the price of chips, but why? When the price of chips increases, the quantity of chips demanded will decline. Since consumers use the two products in combination, when they purchase fewer bags of chips, they will demand less cola as well. Just the opposite can be expected when the price of chips falls.

Changes in Consumers' Tastes. When a demand curve is drawn, the consumers' tastes must be held constant. The way in which changes in this factor lead to changes in demand requires little discussion. Put simply, when tastes change in favour of a good, its demand increases, while demand decreases when the reverse occurs. Changes in tastes can occur for a variety of reasons, such as advertising or increased information about the product or its substitutes. Soft drink producers regularly enlist the services of famous recording and film industry stars to advertise their products. To the extent that consumers associate these famous faces with the products, the advertising campaign can be expected to increase demand. At least, this effect is what the makers of cola and ginger ale have in mind.

Changes in Consumers' Expectations. The fourth category of demand variables concerns the consumers' expectations with regard to the future. How would you respond if you believed that the price of cola were to double in the next day? You probably would buy more cola today, that is, increase your demand for cola today, and store it so that you do not have to purchase as much in the next week at its higher price. If other consumers exhibit the same degree of common sense as you do, an increase in the demand for cola such as that from DD to D_2D_2 might accompany an expected future price increase, whereas a decrease in demand can be anticipated when consumers expect future price decreases.

Changes in the Number of Consumers. The final variable that must be held constant concerns the number of consumers in the group being considered. For example, a change in the demand for cola on campus may come about purely because of an increase in the size of the consuming population of the campus. Similarly, a decrease in the demand for cola can be expected each summer as many of the students leave the campus.

The key to this factor, as with each of the others, is that if the factor changes, the entire demand curve shifts. Such a shift is known as a change in demand.

The **supply** of a product refers to the quantity of that product that sellers are willing and able to sell at various prices, other things being equal. The other things that must remain equal are (1) the cost of production, (2) the prices of goods related in production, (3) sellers' expectations, and (4) the number of sellers.

Supply. The *supply* of a product refers to the quantities of the product that sellers are willing and able to sell at various prices, other things being equal. Suppose that the firms that produce and sell cars in the Canadian market are willing to sell 250,000 cars per year when the price of a car is $10,000; 500,000 per year when the price is $20,000; and 750,000 when the price is $30,000. These price-quantity combinations are presented as a supply schedule in Table 2–2 and as a supply curve in Figure 2–3. As was true for demand, the supply schedule and curve have several important characteristics.

First, each of the price-quantity combinations listed in the supply schedule and graphed along the supply curve *SS* is properly referred to as a quantity supplied at a specific price. For example, the quantity supplied is 250,000 cars per year when the price is $10,000. These individual price-quantity combinations do not by themselves represent the supply of cars; rather, the supply of cars is represented by all of these individual price-quantity combinations taken together. Thus the supply of cars is represented by the entire supply schedule of Table 2–2 or the entire supply curve of Figure 2–3.

Second, supply refers to the quantities of the good that sellers are willing and able to sell at various prices during some specified period of time. As was true on the demand side, it makes little sense to identify a specific quantity supplied unless the time period in which the sales are to take place is specified. For this reason the supply information presented here reflects the sellers' intentions during one year.

Third, the positive slope of supply curve *SS* indicates that the quantity of cars offered for sale increases as the price of cars increases. The reason for this change in quantity supplied is simple; as the price increases, it becomes more profitable to sell cars, which encourages existing sellers to produce and sell more cars. This fundamental economic principle is known as the *law of supply*, which states that the higher the price of the product, the larger will be the quantity supplied; and the lower the price, the smaller will be the quantity supplied, *other things being equal*.

The **law of supply** states that the higher the price of the product, the larger will be the quantity supplied; and the lower the price, the smaller will be the quantity supplied, other things being equal.

Once again, the *other things being equal* part of the law is crucial. As was the case with demand, the supply schedule and curve presented above accurately depict the intentions of the car sellers only if certain

Table 2–2	A supply schedule for cars in Canada	
	Price (dollars)	**Quantity (cars per year)**
	$10,000	250,000
	20,000	500,000
	30,000	750,000

Figure 2–3   **A supply curve for cars in Canada**

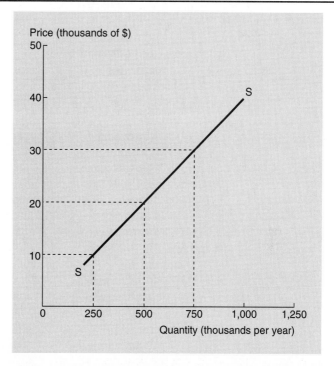

The price-quantity supplied combinations of Table 2–2, plotted graphically, form the supply curve for cars, *SS*. The supply curve shows the quantities of cars that the sellers are willing and able to place on the market at various prices, other things being equal.

other factors are held constant. On the supply side, the other variables that must be equal are (1) the cost of production, (2) the prices of goods related in production, (3) the sellers' expectations, and (4) the number of sellers of the product.

Changes in the Quantity Supplied versus Changes in Supply. Point A on supply curve *SS* in Figure 2–4 indicates that the sellers are willing and able to sell 500,000 cars per year if the price is $20,000 per car. Should the price increase to $30,000, the sellers will move to point B on *SS*, increasing the quantity that they are willing to sell to 750,000 per year. Such a movement along one supply curve due to a change in the price of the product is called a *change in the quantity supplied,* not a change in supply.

A *change in supply* occurs only when one or more of the four supply variables changes. For example, an increase in the supply of cars from *SS* to S_2S_2 or a fall in supply from *SS* to S_1S_1 might be associated with a change

A movement along one supply curve, brought about by a change in the price of the product, is called a **change in the quantity supplied.**

A shift to an entirely new supply curve, brought about by a change in one or more of the variables assumed to be held constant, is called a **change in supply.**

Figure 2–4   **A change in the quantity supplied versus a change in supply**

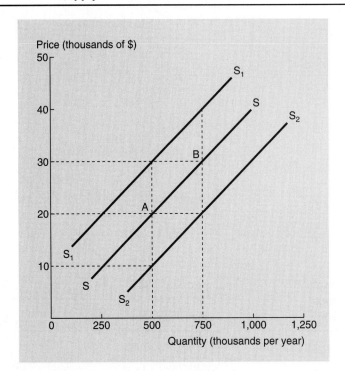

The movement along *SS* from A to B is brought about by a change in the price of cars and is called a change in the quantity supplied. A shift in the entire supply curve from *SS* to either S_1S_1 or S_2S_2 is called a change in supply and is brought about by a change in one of the variables assumed to be held constant when the supply curve is drawn.

in the supply constants. The key is, if the price of the good changes, a change occurs in the quantity supplied, which is depicted as a movement along one supply curve, whereas a movement to an entirely new supply curve is referred to as a change in supply and is brought about by a change in one or more of the four variables assumed to be held constant.

Changes in the Cost of Production. Suppose supply curve *SS* in Figure 2–4 accurately reflects the intentions of car sellers and that the price is initially $20,000. At this price, the sellers are willing and able to sell 500,000 cars per year. What would happen if, for whatever reason, building cars became more expensive? For example, automakers face an increase in the price of steel or the imposition of a tax on autos. Individual sellers would likely find it to be no longer profitable to keep production at previous levels, and some sellers might even choose to cease operations altogether. Nevertheless, we can be certain that when the cost of producing cars increases, the supply of cars will decrease to some lower level such as S_1S_1. Changes in the cost of production can come about in a variety of ways, two of which deserve special note. First, production cost changes are often associated with changes in technology. If a new robot is developed that improves the efficiency of the production process, such an efficiency gain will be translated into a fall in the cost of production. A second common cause of production cost changes is input price changes. When the price of steel, plastic, or labour increases, the cost of producing cars increases.

Changes in the Prices of Goods Related in Production. A change in supply may occur because of a change in the price of a good that is related in production. For example, minivans and cars are related in production because, with some modification, the facilities used to produce cars can be used to produce minivans. Similarly, wheat and barley are related in production, since the land that is used to grow wheat can also be used to raise barley. You should note that the only requirement is for the goods to be produced using similar inputs; the consumer need not view the two goods as being related.

How might a change in the price of minivans influence the supply of cars? When the price of minivans increases, producing minivans becomes relatively more profitable and, consequently, the producers of cars are likely to shift some of their productive capacity to the production of minivans. In other words, an increase in the price of a good that is related in production can be expected to cause a reduction in the supply of the good in question. The reverse holds as well; that is, a fall in the price of minivans will likely result in an increase in the supply of cars.

Changes in Sellers' Expectations. Supply curve SS reflects the intentions of car sellers when they expect the future to be unchanged. If, however, the sellers believe that the price of cars is going to rise in the near future, we will probably witness a decrease in the supply of cars today. Would you sell as many cars today if you felt you could get an additional $1,000 for them next month? Conversely, an expected fall in the price of cars will typically lead to an increase in supply today as sellers attempt to sell the product before its price falls.

Changes in the Number of Sellers. In the last 35 years, a number of new firms have entered the Canadian auto market. All of these firms have been from outside of North America, but their impact has been much the same as it would have been if they were North American.[2] Specifically, the increase in the number of sellers has greatly increased the supply of cars. This is the typical case. When the number of sellers increases, supply increases as well. Were we to witness a fall in the number of firms selling cars in the next 20 years, the result would undoubtedly be a decrease in supply.

The key to this factor, just as with the previous three, is that if the factor changes, there is a movement to an entirely new supply curve; this movement is referred to as a *change in supply*.

Competitive Market Equilibrium and Social Well-Being

Equilibrium Price and Quantity Purchased. The price of a product in a competitive market is determined by the interaction of buyers and sellers. To see how price-setting works, consider the market for pizza at your college or university campus during a typical week, as detailed in Figure 2–5.

At a price of $6, the sellers are willing and able to sell 700 pizzas per week. Why exactly 700 pizzas? The resources used to produce and sell pizza have many other uses. The pizza shops and their equipment might, for example, be used as bakeries, and the employees clearly could offer their employment elsewhere. It can be reasonably assumed that the owners of these resources will offer their resources for employment where they receive the greatest return. The quantity of resources devoted to producing pizza, then, and the resulting number of pizzas offered for sale reflect the value to the resource owner of using his or her resources in the production of pizza, relative to all other possible employments. When the price of pizza is $6 each, the resources necessary to produce and sell 700 pizzas will be drawn away from other production processes because the resources yield a greater return to their owners in producing pizza than in any of their other possible employments. As the supply curve indicates, if the price of pizza rises, new resources will be brought into pizza production from other production processes because those resources now offer their owners an increased return if used to produce pizza, given the rise in the price of pizza.

At the same time, Figure 2–5 indicates that at a price of $6, consumers wish to buy 700 pizzas per week. Once again, the consumers have a nearly

---

[2]Canada does not have an independent market. An agreement between Canada and the United States was made in January 1965 to create a single North American market for passenger cars, trucks, buses, tires, and automotive parts (Canada-U.S. Automotive Products Agreement—Autopact). Canadian producers are subsidiary firms of their U.S. counterparts. The agreement requires that the number of cars produced in Canada equal the number sold (managed trade)

Figure 2–5   **Competitive market price determination**

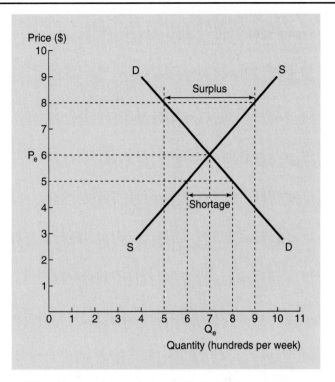

The demand and supply curves together show how the equilibrium price of a product is determined in the market. If the price is above equilibrium, surpluses occur and the sellers undercut each other's prices until the equilibrium price is reached. If the price is below equilibrium, shortages occur and the buyers bid against each other for the available supplies, driving the price up to the equilibrium level. At the equilibrium, neither surpluses nor shortages occur.

infinite number of ways to spend their incomes. When the price of pizza is $6 each, consumers decide that the $4,200 necessary to purchase and consume 700 pizzas ($6 times 700 pizzas) could not be used to purchase anything else that would give them more satisfaction than the pizzas. If this were not true, they would not be willing and able to buy 700 pizzas at this price.

At a price of $6, then, the intentions of the sellers and consumers exactly coincide. That is, the owners of the resources necessary to produce 700 pizzas believe that no other employment of their resources will yield to them a greater return than can be had by producing pizza. And the consumers believe that at this price, the expenditure of $4,200 on pizza yields greater satisfaction than a similar expenditure on any other good or goods. When the

The price at which the sellers of a product are willing and able to sell exactly the same amount as the consumers willing and able to buy is called the **equilibrium price**. As such, the equilibrium price indicates when consumers believe that precisely the correct share of the economy's scarce resources are devoted to producing the product. The quantity of the product that is actually exchanged at the equilibrium price is called the **equilibrium quantity.**

intentions of the sellers and buyers coincide in this fashion, we say that $6 is the *equilibrium price* of pizza and 700 is the *equilibrium quantity* purchased.

This concept of equilibrium price is particularly important. At this price, and only at this price, the consumers of pizza are willing and able to buy exactly the number of pizzas that sellers wish to sell. Put differently, only at this price does the quantity demanded by consumers equal the quantity supplied by producers. If the equilibrium price is a competitive price, then the price reflects the scarcity of the resources used in the production of pizza. Therefore, the interests of consumers coincide with those of the producers. This outcome is of paramount importance in that the goal of any economic system is to minimize the effect of scarce resources, by obtaining the maximum social well-being and ensuring that scarce resources are used where they are most highly valued. An economy based on markets relies on the consuming public to identify the amount of resources that should be used in each production process. Keep in mind, however, that consumer demand depends on the ability to pay as well as the willingness of consumers to buy. Therefore, the distribution of income, discussed in both Chapters 1 and 7, will affect the demand and who can afford a product at the equilibrium price. Typically then, with a given income distribution, an equilibrium price that reflects the costs of producing that quantity of the product indicates when a particular allocation of resources is stable or in equilibrium. To see this more clearly, consider what happens when price is not at its equilibrium.

Effects of a Price Above Equilibrium. If the price is not at the equilibrium level, market forces are set in motion that move the price toward that level. Suppose, for example, that sellers initially priced pizza at $8. As shown in Figure 2–5 the sellers can be expected to offer 900 pizzas per week because pizza now appears relatively more profitable to produce. That is, sellers can be expected to draw additional resources from other production processes and devote them to producing pizza because these resources can now earn a greater return in producing pizza. This change is shown as a movement along *SS* in quantity supplied in Figure 2–5 from 700 to the 900 pizza quantity supplied level.

But how will consumers react to the higher price? At a price of $8, individual consumers can be expected to shift some of their purchasing power from pizza to other goods because these other options are now relatively cheaper. As depicted on the demand curve in Figure 2–5, at the price of $8 per pizza, the consumers are willing and able to purchase only 500 pizzas during a week. Consequently, when pizza is priced at $8 per pizza, the sellers have a surplus of 400 pizzas per week.

From a standpoint of resource allocation, what does a surplus of 400 pizzas imply? Consumers are saying that when the price of a pizza is at $8, the resources necessary to produce the 400 surplus pizzas would be better used (add more to social well-being) in producing some other good or service. A surplus implies that consumers believe that too much of the economy's scarce resources are being devoted to a particular production process and, thus, they would prefer having those resources reallocated to another production process. How will this reallocation take place? When there is a surplus of any product, each seller who is unable to sell all that he or she has produced has an incentive to cut the price a bit below the existing price, because such a price advantage will enable the seller to dispose of his or her own surplus more easily. As long as a surplus exists, each pizza maker is likely to undercut his or her competitors in this fashion. Thus if the price of pizza is above its equilibrium, market forces will cause the price to fall. And the price can be expected to continue falling until the surplus is completely eliminated. Figure 2–5 indicates that the surplus is eliminated when the price again returns to equilibrium ($6). In other words, the price of pizza can be expected to stop falling when the quantity of pizzas that the sellers wish to sell is equal to the quantity the consumers are willing and able to buy. In this way, a competitive market operating on its own ensures that the resources that were used to produce the surplus pizzas are released, to be used in another production process.

Effects of a Price Below Equilibrium. Now consider a price below equilibrium in Figure 2–5. When the price of pizza is $5, consumers desire 800 pizzas per week, while sellers are only willing to sell 600, indicating that a shortage equal to 200 pizzas exists. Shortages of any good or service imply that consumers are willing and able to have a larger share of their economy's scarce resources devoted to producing that product. In this situation, individual consumers have an incentive to offer the seller a bit more than $5 per pizza to increase their chances of actually being able to purchase a pizza. For example, you call the local pizza shop to place an order and are told that the price is $5, but unfortunately, due to a shortage, the pizza cannot be delivered until the next day. How might you respond? Given that you have the ability to pay, you call the pizza shop again and offer to pay $7 if the pizza can be delivered immediately.

Whenever a shortage exists, market forces are put into action that tend to drive up the price of the product. As the price edges upward, the shortage lessens as individual sellers respond to the rise in price by increasing their production of the product. This process continues until the shortage is eliminated, that is, until the market once again reaches its equilibrium price.

In this way, the market operating on its own brings about the reallocation of resources that consumers dictate because the shortage indicated that consumers believed more of the economy's scarce resources should be devoted to producing pizza. In other words, if left alone, the forces of demand and supply tend to ensure that social well-being, as reflected in consumer demands, is maximized.

However, the market-determined outcome does not always maximize social well-being. We have already noted that the distribution of income plays a large role in what the market outcome will determine. In certain other circumstances, which are considered in detail in later chapters, the market fails to maximize well-being on its own. These circumstances are common enough to be properly considered exceptions to the reliance on markets to allocate resources on their own.

Resource Allocation in a Command Economy

As indicated earlier in this chapter, the choice of an economic system is not a choice to have or not have decision making and planning; rather the particular economic system selected simply indicates who will make resource-use decisions and plans. In a market economy, consumer demands largely direct the process. That is, consumers decide what allocation of resources between competing production processes maximizes their well-being. Markets then coordinate this information and bring about any needed re-allocation. In a command economy, as we can see by examining the situation of the former Soviet Union, a bureaucratic process determines resource allocation.

The Soviet Model

On the heels of the Bolshevik revolution of 1917–18, Soviet leader Vladimir Lenin instituted War Communism (1917–20). The key economic features of this system were an aggressive attempt to eliminate all vestiges of the market allocation of resources through the nationalization of important industries and the forced requisition of agricultural output. In other words, Lenin attempted to eliminate private property rights and markets, the defining elements of market economies. The attraction of communism to Lenin and his followers was motivated by the extreme poverty of the peasants amidst the extravagance of the aristocrats. The equity aspects of income distribution in the primitive Russian economy was of uppermost importance to the revolutionary forces; economic efficiency was of secondary importance.

The infant Soviet state was in near economic collapse by 1920. Faced with this, a second phase of Soviet economic policy went into effect, known as the New Economic Policy, which remained until 1928. Under the New Economic Policy, the Soviet Union, in many respects, instituted what we might now call a mixed-command economy by allowing a return of private property rights in certain industries and by introducing the market as a fundamental mechanism for resource allocation. Interestingly, the near collapse of the economy that had occurred during the War Communism period was reversed, or nearly so, during the New Economic Policy.

One might think that the Soviet experiences during War Communism and the New Economic Policy would have led the Soviet leadership to conclude that economic stability and development would be enhanced by reliance on market principles. To the contrary, the lesson Soviet leaders took from this period was that alternative means of resource allocation could be put into place. That is, they believed that War Communism failed not because it eliminated private property rights and the market, but because it did not offer an alternative to market allocation of resources.

Joseph Stalin, in 1928, put this "new learning" into practice by establishing a vast system of centralized economic planning and control that remained in effect until the Soviet Union's collapse. Although overly simplistic in some respects, the Soviet economic system during the period of 1928 to 1991 may be summarized in four words: centralized planning and control.

Planning and control in the Soviet system took place within a rigidly structured hierarchy of ministries, committees, and agencies. In total, by 1990 nearly 100 such groups were promulgating nearly 14,000 pages of *plans* each year concerning the production and distribution of more than 24 million products. The problem for the planners, as mind-numbing as it seems in retrospect, was to determine both the desired quantities of each good or service to be produced and the appropriate production technique to employ. These two questions—what to produce and how to produce it—can, of course, be summarized as one by noting that the problem is to allocate the appropriate quantities of resources to each production process. This determination was made, in broad, general terms, by the ruling political body, the Communist Party of the Soviet Union (CPSU), who would formulate directives on resource use among the competing production processes. These general directives were then fleshed out into precise, although tentative, resource allocations and production targets by the State Planning Commission, known as the *Gosplan*. The production targets were then transmitted down through the ministries, commissions, and agencies responsible for each production process until they reached the actual factory or enterprise level. Then the flow of information changed directions, and the State Planning Commission received feedback on its tentative production targets from those who had to implement its directives. The commission, operating under the authority of only the Communist Party, prepared a final and binding plan that was then carried out through the ministries. In this way resource allocation plans—which carried the force of law—were developed both on an annual basis and on a multiyear basis.

To what extent can we expect that such an allocation mechanism serves to maximize social well-being? This question turns on the answer to another question: Who is the best judge of what will give a person satisfaction—the state or the individual? Within the market economy, it is assumed that the individual is in most cases the best judge. In the Soviet mindset, the state was thought to be the better judge. Which is optimal? Perhaps we can gain some insight by comparing the performance of each system in a *hypothetical example.*

Social Well-Being: Market versus Command

Consider two countries: Utopia—a market economy—and Paradise—a command economy. Suppose that initially citizens of both Utopia and Paradise can purchase a car for the equivalent of $10,000 and that at this price there is neither an obvious shortage nor surplus of cars. That is, suppose each economy initially allocated its resources so that the public is satisfied with the quantity of cars available to them. Now suppose that, for whatever reason (perhaps rising incomes), the public of both countries desires more cars at each price? Put in the terms of this chapter, how well does each economic system respond to an increase in demand for cars?

Market Economy Reaction to Changing Demand

Initially, the demand for cars is DD and the supply is SS, as indicated in Figure 2–6. The interaction of demand and supply yields an equilibrium position with Q_0 cars being produced and sold at a price of $10,000 per car. Now assume that perhaps due to rising incomes, the demand for cars increases to some greater level like D_1D_1. At the existing price of $10,000, a shortage of cars develops equal to $Q_0 - Q_1$ cars. But what does a shortage indicate? Recall that in a competitive free market an equilibrium is said to exist when the consumers' demand indicates that the existing allocation of resources maximizes well-being. By extension, a shortage indicates that the public feels its well-being would be increased if more of the economy's resources were devoted to the production of this specific product.

With this as background, how does the market economy react? In the near term, we can expect the price of cars to rise to $13,000 as each potential purchaser bids the price up a bit in order to increase the chances that he or she will be able to buy a car. But the reaction of suppliers is also of much importance. Specifically, as the price is bid up, each supplier finds it to be in his or her interest to increase the output of cars. This increase in the quantity supplied is depicted as the movement from A to B on supply SS. That is, in response to the rise in price, the quantity supplied increases in the near term to the new equilibrium of Q_2. Already we can conclude that the market is bringing about what the consuming public wants: more cars.

But the market does not stop here. The new equilibrium at $13,000 is in reality only an immediate reaction. Recall that one of the items held constant when supply is considered is the number of firms offering the product. Given the increasing price of cars, we can reasonably expect that

Figure 2–6   **Market economy reaction to a change in demand**

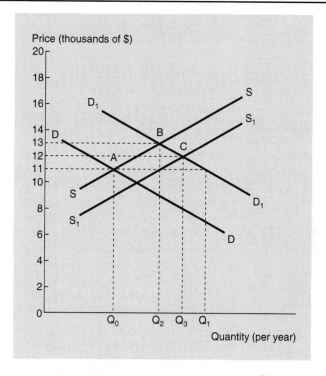

The interaction of the demand for cars *DD,* and the supply of cars *SS,* yields an equilibrium price of $10,000 and equilibrium quantity purchased of Q_0. An increase in demand to D_1D_1 initially causes price to rise to $13,000. In response to this price increase, the quantity supplied and purchased increases to Q_2. In the longer term, the increased profitability of producing cars leads to an increase in supply to S_1S_1. The interaction of D_1D_1 and S_1S_1 yields the final equilibrium price of $12,000 and quantity purchased of Q_3 cars.

in the longer term (long enough to build new facilities, convert factories that were producing tractors, and the like) new firms will enter the car market, leading to an increase in supply to S_1S_1. Given this, a new and final equilibrium is established at point C in which Q_3 cars are being produced and sold at a price of $12,000.

To summarize, the increase in demand for cars indicates that the public desires to devote more of its economy's scarce resources to the production of cars. And the market, operating on its own, causes a reallocation of resources to the production of cars. In this sense the market operated to ensure that social well-being was once again maximized following the increase in demand for cars. And it is essential to note that this reallocation of resources to the production of cars took place without the blessing of government or any other outside party.

Figure 2–7   **Command economy reaction to a change in demand**

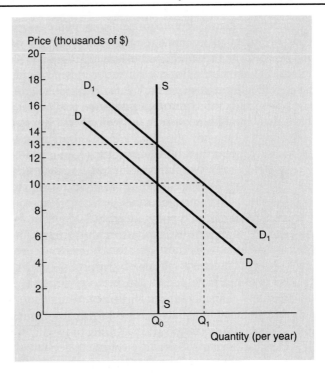

The interaction of demand *DD* and the administratively determined supply *SS* yields the initial price for cars of $10,000. An increase in demand to $D_1 D_1$ leads to a shortage of $Q_0 - Q_1$. This excess demand is either tolerated, leading to long lines, or simply siphoned off by adding a turnover tax of $3,000, raising the price to $13,000 per car.

Command Economy Reaction to Changing Demand

The same situation can be analyzed within a demand and supply context for the command economy, as depicted in Figure 2–7. Demand *DD* is essentially the same as one would find in a market economy. That is, demand *DD* indicates that the people of Paradise would prefer to buy at low prices rather than at high prices, assuming that variables such as income, prices of related goods, and the like are constant, and that these variables are not under the direct control of the central planners. Supply *SS* is, however, different from what would exist in a market economy. Specifically, a particular production level, Q_0, is chosen by the planning commission. Once selected, this production level will remain for the life of the plan. Finally, the planners select a price that they believe will clear the market. At a price of $10,000, the planners decide that neither a shortage nor surplus will exist; thus, $10,000 is chosen as the initial price of cars.

Notice that this price is arrived at administratively. That is, the price indicates little about the cost of producing the product as would be true in a market economy. Suppose, for example, that the actual cost of producing cars in Paradise is $8,000. The $2,000 difference between the cost of production and the administered price is not simply left to the producer as profit. In the command economy, part of the $2,000 may have been left as a "fair" profit, but the remainder was taken by the central authorities in the form of a tax, known as the *turnover tax*. Price determination in a command economy then worked something like this: The central planners estimated the price at which the quantity demanded would be approximately equal to the quantity it wished to supply. Then the cost of producing the good was estimated, allowing for a modest profit. If the cost of producing the good was less than the market clearing price, the difference was taken through the turnover tax. Conversely, for example, with bread and basic foodstuffs, if the cost of producing the good exceeded the market clearing price, central authorities held down the price to the market clearing level and provided a subsidy (or negative turnover tax) equal to the difference between production costs and the market clearing price to the producer.

When shortages of goods and services developed within the Soviet economy, the excess demand was often siphoned off by increasing prices through the addition of, or increase in, the **turnover tax.**

Now, what happens when demand increases? That is, suppose that incomes are rising in Paradise and the public wants more of the economy's resources be devoted to producing cars. This condition is shown as a movement to D_1D_1 in Figure 2–7. As was true in the Utopian market economy, an excess demand or shortage now exists at the $10,000 price level equal to $Q_0 - Q_1$ cars. How do the planners in Paradise respond? Initially, they typically do not. That is, initially, the shortage is tolerated. Long lines form as potential consumers attempt to satisfy their individual needs and desires. In the longer term, if the shortages persist, the planners may simply siphon off the new demand by allowing the price to rise to $13,000 per car. Note, however, that this rising price does not spur an increase in either the quantity supplied from existing producers or an increase in supply from new producers, as would be the case in a market economy. Rather, the increased revenue from the sale of cars simply is taken by the planners in the form of a higher turnover tax. In this way, while shortages and long lines were tolerated in the near term, the planners could ensure that most markets came close to clearing in the longer term by manipulating the turnover tax.

Although markets in some sense clear, does this suggest that social well-being is maximized? A bit of reflection clearly indicates that the answer is no. Assume for the moment that social well-being was at its maximum initially. The public then decided that it wanted to devote more of its economy's scarce resources to the production of cars. That is, well-being was no longer at its peak, but a new higher peak could be reached by having more cars produced. This outcome, although relatively automatic in a market economy, did not occur in the command economy. Rather than responding to the public's increased desire for cars by ordering an increase in production, the planners simply negated the increased demand by pushing up the turnover tax, that is, by increasing the price of cars.

Within a command economy, then, for the public's desires to be taken into account depends on the ability of the planning process to seek and incorporate the desires of the public when resource allocation decisions are made. In the former Soviet Union this process was flawed. The decisions were driven by whatever the central planners viewed as most important, and Soviet central planners had a strong desire not for consumer goods, but for heavy industry and military goods. This situation is depicted in Table 2–3, which reports the position of the Soviet consumer relative to consumers in several selected countries in 1985.

Although it is generally accepted that the USSR, with enormous economic resources at its disposal, developed a military that was second to none, the relatively resource-starved consumer sector of the Soviet economy was incapable of providing its people with the quantities or qualities of products that their counterparts in much of the rest of the world enjoyed. For example, as of 1985, the Soviet Union had developed an inventory of only 36 cars per 1,000 persons compared with 552 cars per 1,000 persons in the United States, and even more telling, compared with 127 cars per 1,000 persons in relatively poor Greece. The second column of Table 2–3 summarizes the standing of the Soviet consumer. It indicates that the quantity of goods available for consumption, per person, in the USSR, was only 28.6 percent of that available to the typical American con-

Table 2–3	The relative position of the Soviet consumer, 1985	
Country	Passenger Cars (per 1,000 persons)	Consumption (per person, United States = 100)
USSR	36	28.6
United States	552	100.0
Germany	412	69.3
France	380	68.1
Japan	226	65.7
United Kingdom	305	65.6
Italy	376	64.6
Finland	315	61.7
Austria	335	59.0
Spain	241	46.1
Ireland	202	37.2
Greece	127	37.0

Source: Abram Bergson, "The USSR Before the Fall: How Poor and Why," *Journal of Economic Perspectives* 5, no. 4, (Fall 1991), pp. 29–44.

sumer and less than the quantity available to citizens of any other country on the list. Does this analysis seem to fit your understanding of the position of the Soviet consumer relative to his or her counterparts in Canada or in other less command-oriented economies?

Summary

One of the most important decisions (if not the most important) a country must make in dealing with the fundamental problem of resource allocation concerns the choice of an economic system. Economic systems range from the pure market economy to the pure command economy. The key differences between the two surround the issues of resource ownership and/or control and the mechanism through which resource allocation decisions are made.

Within a pure market economy, private parties own and control the economy's scarce resources. This situation is referred to as the institution of private property rights. Equally important, within a market economy, private owners make resource allocation decisions and then these decisions are co-ordinated within markets. Within free competitive markets, the forces of demand and supply operate to establish equilibrium prices and quantities at which neither shortages nor surpluses exist. Put differently, markets operating on their own tend to ensure that production is carried to the point where consumer well-being is maximized, given the current distribution of income. The equilibrium reached is one in which the desires of consumers and producers exactly coincide. Should consumer desires change, indicating that they would prefer either more or less of a given good or service, the market reacts to bring about the desired change. Income distribution is considered in Chapter 1 and 7. Other circumstances in which markets fail to maximize social well-being, will be treated in detail in the following chapters. These circumstances occur frequently enough for us to be concerned about using the market as the sole resource allocation mechanism.

A pure command economy is one in which the state owns, or at least directly controls the resources. Further, the state directly makes decisions about resource allocation, and the state's decisions carry the force of law. Put simply, within the command economy, resources are allocated based on the preferences of the planners. Given this, social well-being is maximized only if the planners know better than the public what mix of goods and services yields maximum satisfaction.

The history of the Soviet Union indicates many of the benefits of the market form of economic organization for consumers. In response to rising demands, the Soviet Union's central planners either allowed long lines to exist or siphoned off the new demand with increasing turnover taxes and thus higher prices. Years of such consumer deprivation no doubt played a significant role in the collapse of the Soviet Union. On the other hand, the Soviet state became a tremendous military and industrial force, overcoming its beginning early in the century as a backward agrarian economy.

Modern economies balance the use of the market to direct scarce resources and the imposition of command economy elements. Where the market works well, it is an efficient and responsive means of directing production of goods to serve consumer demands. In some circumstances it fails to work well, particularly in the production of goods that pertain to national developmental goals. The former Soviet nations are now trying to find this balance. The transition to a mixed market economy is not, nor will it be, easy. In fact, for some period of time, the republics of the former Soviet Union are likely to be worse off economically than they would have been had the Soviet state not collapsed.

Checklist of Economic Concepts

Economic systems
Economic systems, mixed
Economy, pure market
Economy, pure command
Market
Market, competitive
Market, monopolistic
Market, imperfectly competitive
Demand
Demand, law of

Demand, changes in
Supply
Supply, law of
Supply, changes in
Price, equilibrium
Surplus
Shortage
Quantity demanded, changes in
Quantity supplied, changes in
Turnover tax

Discussion Questions

1. Compare and contrast the ways in which the two extreme types of economies—pure market and pure command—deal with the three basic questions or problems any economy faces: what goods to produce, how to produce them, and who gets the goods.

2. Choose a number of countries and place them on a continuum from a pure market economy to a pure command economy. Where does Canada place? Explain why you place the countries where you do. What economic factors other than their place on this continuum differentiates the countries?

3. It has been asserted that a pure command economy is characterized by state ownership as well as control of resources and central-

ized resource-use decision making. How necessary do you think state ownership is as a characteristic of a command economy? If a country operated a command economy without state ownership, how would it direct the resources to their end use?

4. List and discuss the five important characteristics a market must exhibit to be purely competitive. Choose a number of industries in Canada and indicate where each industry meets the characteristics and where it fails. Discuss what might be done in order for each industry to be made more competitive.

5. Classify each of the following goods according to whether *in your opinion* it is a normal or inferior good: shoes, beer, leather gloves, life insurance, auto insurance, stereo equipment, pet dog, radial tires, rice, fishing gear. Discuss your answers with a colleague, justifying them with economic arguments.

6. Classify each of the following pairs of goods according to whether you think they are substitutes, complements, or basically unrelated to each other: ham and eggs, meat and potatoes, Neons and BMWs, ice skates and swimsuits, coffee and tea, butter and margarine, apples and oranges, knives and forks, saltshakers and hats, skis and lift tickets, NHL playoff tickets and beer.

7. What do you predict would happen to the market demand curve for oranges in Canada as a result of the following:
   a. A rise in average income.
   b. An increase in the birthrate.
   c. An intensive advertising campaign that convinces most people of the importance of a daily quota of natural vitamin C.
   d. A fall in the price of orange juice.
   e. A fall in the price of grapefruits.

8. If goods that increase human well-being are expensive, why isn't water high priced?

9. What effect do you think an advertising campaign for coffee would have on each of the following, other things constant: the price of coffee, the price of tea, the quantity of sugar bought and sold, the price of doughnuts, the quantity of sleeping pills bought and sold, the price of television advertising time on the late show?

10. Suppose that you read in the paper that the price of gasoline is rising along with increased sales of gasoline. Does this contradict the law of demand or not? Explain.

11. Suppose that a crisis occurs in the Middle East and petroleum supplies are sharply curtailed. Other things remaining the same, what do you predict will happen to the price of gasoline, the price of

natural gas, the quantity sold and the price of automobiles, the price of steel, the price and quantity sold of solar panels, and the price of electricity? At each step of this chain spell out your answer in terms of the relevant shift in a demand or supply curve. What do you think of the characterization of the economy as a chain of interconnected markets?

12. From your results in question 1, you likely found that most economies are "mixed" market systems. If the objective of economic organization is to maximize the well-being of society, discuss the limitations of a pure market system that lead to the introduction of elements of a command economy.

Supplementary Reading

Bornstein, M. *Comparative Economic Systems: Models and Cases.* Homewood, IL: Richard D. Irwin, 1985.

A fine collection of articles on economic systems. Especially note the chapter on Soviet planning.

Carson, R. L. *Comparative Economic Systems.* Armonk, NY: M. E. Sharpe, Inc., 1992.

An excellent and accessible text on the topic of economic systems. This book is especially interesting because of its emphasis on the role of government and the institution of private property rights.

Csaba, L. *Privatization, Liberalization and Destruction: Recreating the Market in Central and Eastern Europe.* Brookfield, VT: Ashgate Publishers, 1994.

In 13 papers, the problems and prospects of transforming the command economies of central and eastern Europe are presented and debated.

Heilbroner, R. L. *Marxism: For and Against.* New York: W. W. Norton & Company, 1980.

The Russian revolution and subsequent development of the Soviet Union was premised on Marxian economic theory. For a balanced view of Marxism as a philisophical foundation for economic organization, this book is a good place to start.

Kern, W. S. *From Socialism to Market Economy: The Transition Problem.* Kalamazoo, MI: W. E. Upjohn Institute, 1992.

This collection of papers presents and analyzes the problems that have plagued the former eastern bloc countries as they have moved toward market reforms.

Leftwich, R. H. *Elementary Analytics of a Market System.* Morristown, NJ: General Learning Press, 1972.

Although somewhat dated, this book provides a thorough discussion of the nature of a market economy.

Remnick, D. *Lenin's Tomb: The Last Days of the Soviet Union.* New York: Random House, 1993.

A journalist who spent the crucial period 1987 through 1991 in Moscow, Mr. Remnick offers a fascinating, first-hand historical account of the fall of the Soviet state.

Stuart, R. C. and P. R. Gregory. *Soviet Economic Structure and Performance*. New York: Harper & Row Publishers, Inc., 1986.

Although dated by the collapse of the Soviet Union, this book remains of great value for those who wish to understand both the way in which the Soviet economy was supposed to work and the way in which it actually worked.

Wolfe, R. D. and S. A. Resnick. *Economics: Marxian versus Neoclassical*. Baltimore: John Hopkins University Press, 1987.

This book compares Marxist theory to the dominant theory of market economics. Students who wish to pursue a more critical approach to society's economic organization may find this book interesting.

Chapter 3

Economics of Higher Education

Who Benefits and Who Pays the Bills?

The importance of higher education in Canada and its central role to the economic well-being of Canadians is evident in many statements made about higher education by academics, politicians, and the media.

- "No advanced society can be competitive without a large portion of its citizenry educated to participate in a global, knowledge-intensive economy."[1]
- "This country leads the OECD countries in the proportion of adults with some post-secondary education."[2]
- Federal government transfer payments to the provinces for postsecondary education exceed $6.5 billion annually.[3]
- The pace of tuition increases has accelerated in the past several years in Canada, and for most of the last half decade it has exceeded the rate of inflation. Newspapers and radio cite Statistics Canada's review of annual tuition and living expenses to inform the public that undergraduates in Canada were paying an average of $2,179 for tuition for the 1993–1994 academic year, 43 percent more than for the 1990–1991 academic year.[4]
- Many academics are concerned about the cost of higher education because "any increase in tuition limits access, and the impact is differentially hurtful for the economically disadvantaged, minorities, and recent immigrant groups."[5]

Problems in Higher Education

In the 1990s Canadian colleges and universities are going through a period of rapid transition. The dominant elements forcing this change are change in the pattern of enrollment as well as reductions and restructuring of government funding to support postsecondary education.

Since World War II, enrollments at colleges and universities have increased greatly, placing chronic pressure on institutions to expand their

---

[1]S. Smith, *Report Commission of Inquiry on Canadian University Education* (Toronto: Association of Universities and Colleges of Canada, 1991), pp. 13–27.

[2]Human Resources Development Canada, *Agenda: Jobs and Growth Improving Social Security in Canada, A Discussion Paper* (Ottawa: Minister of Supply and Services, October 1994), p. 19.

[3]Department of Finance, *Agenda: Jobs and Growth Creating a Healthy Fiscal Climate, The Economic and Fiscal Update* (Ottawa: Minister of Supply and Services, October 1994), p. 76.

[4]*Calgary Herald*, September 16, 1994, p. B1.

[5]J. Evangelauf, "Tuition at Public Colleges Is up 6 Percent This Year, College Board Study Finds," *Chronicle of Higher Education*, October 5, 1994, pp. A41–A49.

personnel and facilities. As you might expect, enrollment grew at uneven rates, echoing the fluctuations in the birthrate over the period. The most rapid growth occurred in the late 1960s and early 1970s as the baby boomers entered the system, but even more recent growth has been impressive. In 1987 486,009 students were enrolled at Canadian universities and another 319,548 were studying in our colleges and technical institutes. By 1991 enrollments at Canadian universities and colleges had grown to 574,314 and 341,161, respectively.[6] Over the same period funding restraints and projections that enrollments may begin to decline slightly by the year 2000 have created an environment in which universities and colleges face financial restraint with its attendant problems of shrinking budgets and labour unrest.

Most institutions face serious financial problems. The problem is especially acute in public colleges and universities where government grants are shrinking or failing to grow as in the past. In response, tuition and fees have risen rapidly. Some say too rapidly. In Canada more than 60 percent of high school graduates proceed directly into some form of postsecondary program of study, and as a nation we add about 174,000 new graduates of degree programs from universities to the labour force each year.[7] We often hear claims that too many degrees are being granted—that there is no room for new college and university graduates to work in the fields of their choice. Although the number of graduates seems large, the percentage of the adult population holding university degrees has remained almost constant at 10 percent for the last 20 years and the new graduates constitute just a little more than 1 percent of the labour force. During the early 1990s the job creation that did occur showed a marked shift in favour of those with higher education. Between 1990 and 1993 the number of employment opportunities for graduates of colleges and technical institutions increased by 8 percent, and the openings for university graduates increased by 17 percent. In contrast, for the same period the openings for those who had ended their education with a high school diploma or who dropped out of postsecondary education before completing their program of study remained constant, but job openings for persons who did not complete high school actually decreased by 19 percent![8] Still others say that colleges and universities are too tradition bound and are not responsive to the needs of society. All of these issues (and more) call for a systematic analysis of the higher education system. The economics of such an analysis center around four interrelated questions: (1) What kinds of higher educational services should be provided? (2) How much

---

[6]Statistics Canada, *CANSIM*. series 008008.1 and 008010.1.

[7]Statistics Canada, op. cit., series 008011.1.

[8]Human Resources Development Canada, op. cit., p. 19.

should be provided? (3) What is the appropriate institutional structure for providing them? (4) Who should pay for them?

What Kinds of Services?

Society expects higher educational institutions to perform multiple roles. Traditionally the institutions have been learning centers, accumulating and transmitting knowledge of all kinds to students. University faculties are expected to engage in research and other creative activities that advance the frontiers of knowledge and to be at the cutting edge of the intellectual, cultural, social, and technological developments of civilization. In addition, society has come to expect colleges and universities to provide both professional and vocational training. These programs range from the preparation of physicians and lawyers to the training of automobile mechanics and administrative assistants. In many if not most cases, these multiple roles of colleges and universities are inextricably bound together and can not be separated.

How Much Service?

The question of how much college and university educational service the society should provide is a very live issue today. Another name for this problem is the *financial crisis* of higher education. Most administrators, faculty members, and students are convinced that a financial crisis exists, that not enough is being spent for educational services.

Over recent years, most provincial governments have reduced government grants to postsecondary institutions as part of provincial restraint programs. They have also made it more difficult for students at the postsecondary level to qualify for remission of fees. The situation is exacerbated by the capping of federal transfers to the provinces and the reorganizing of these federal transfers into a new social transfer program. The new system of federal government transfers to the provincial governments introduced in the 1996 federal budget lumps together most federal transfers to the provinces, eliminating the restriction that specific funds are received to fund education and must be spent on education. Even the wealthy provinces of Alberta, British Columbia, and Ontario have reduced their support for postsecondary institutions by as much as 21 percent causing the withdrawal of hundreds of millions of dollars from the postsecondary system. Tuition fees have increased at a rate five times the increase in the consumer price index in recent years. Do these changes indicate that society is unwilling to support higher education at present levels or that it believes relatively too much is being spent for higher educational services? Alternatively, do the changes mean that society desires the same amount of educational services but wishes to shift the burden of paying for education from the taxpayers who have traditionally covered the cost to the students who receive the education?

What Institutional Structure?

The present system of higher education is almost exclusively made up of large, publicly owned and funded technical institutions, colleges, and universities. In addition, a few much smaller institutions are operated by private firms, religious organizations, and professional accreditting organizations. Is this structure conducive to providing the appropriate kinds and quantities of higher educational services relative to other goods and services desired by the society? Is it flexible? Or is it tradition bound and susceptible to being a political football for politicians?

Who Should Pay?

A related question concerns the extent to which federal and provincial governments (taxpayers) should pay the costs of producing the services of higher education and to what extent the costs should be paid by students and their families. If governments are to bear the burden of paying a substantial part of the cost, how should it go about doing so? Is the government-owned institution, with taxpayer funding for its capital and operating costs, the best solution? Or should the government, instead of making grants to institutions, make funds available to students, allowing them and their parents to choose their schools, while it pays tuition and fees with taxpayer dollars? Should government payments of the costs of higher education favour poor families? These are some of the questions that are of concern to academics, politicians, and members of society.

The Economic Basis of the Problems

The basic issues outlined above are primarily economic problems. The economics of providing higher educational services was largely ignored until the 1960s because such services accounted for a relatively small part of the gross domestic product and used small proportions of the country's resources. In addition, it was somehow thought that education was above mundane things such as analysis of economic benefits and costs. The burgeoning enrollments since World War II changed all that. Those responsible for decision making with regard to higher education—legislators, administrators, faculties, students, and concerned citizens—can no longer ignore the economic consequences of their decisions. The provision of higher educational services requires the use of large quantities of resources, and the resources so used are not available to produce other goods and services. Higher educational services represent one of a great many competing uses for resources. In this chapter we shall construct an economic framework of the higher education "industry" that should be useful in the decision-making processes concerning it. The present system of higher education will be evaluated within the context of this framework.

The Product of Higher Education

Like other producing units in the economy, institutions of higher education use resources to produce something of benefit to individuals and to society. This "something" can probably best be termed as *educational services*. To get at what constitutes educational services, we can pose the question: Why are you attending a college or university? Among the many possible answers to this question are at least three of interest to economists. First, you may expect higher education to improve your capacity to produce and to earn income, that is, to augment the quality of your labour resources. We call this improvement in the quality of your labour the development of *human capital*. Second, quite apart from improving the quality of your labour resources, you may derive direct, immediate satisfaction from your present participation in college or university processes and activities—in this respect education is a direct consumption service. Third, you may expect that the society as a whole will receive some benefits in addition to the benefits that accrue to you from your obtaining higher education. We will look at these facets of educational services in turn.

Human capital refers to that part of the productive power of human or labour resources resulting from investment in education or training.

Later in this chapter we will divide these benefits into direct benefits and indirect benefits. The direct benefits are those that the individual who is receiving the educational services—the student—receives as a result of consuming educational services. The indirect benefits are the benefits to other members of society as a side effect of the student gaining knowledge and skills as a result of becoming educated. The concepts of direct and indirect benefits allow an artificial division between the product of education, which can be thought of as the pleasure of learning new things, and the by-products of education that include a range of diverse benefits such as the increased skills available to society in the future, increased earning due to increased promotion and intellectual development, and decreased risk to the student and to society that the student will be in need of social assistance and employment insurance. Not surprisingly, the direct and indirect benefits of education are inextricably linked, and society engages in much debate over the appropriate proportion of the cost of education that should be paid for by the student. Despite this debate few people would argue that education is just like any other commodity and that students should bear the full cost of "their" education.

Investment in Human Capital

A large part of educational services must consist of the development of human or labour resources, which is called *investment in human capital.* In an economic sense this investment is very much the same as investing in machines, buildings, and other material capital. We invest in additional nonhuman capital whenever we think that it will generate enough additional product output to more than repay the new investment costs. Similarly, it pays an individual to invest in human capital—additional education—if the increase in education increases the earning power of the person being educated by more than the cost of the additional education. Just as investment in nonhuman capital is expected to increase and expand the capacity of capital resources to produce goods, so is a large part of the investment in human capital expected to augment the capacity of labour resources to contribute to gross domestic product.

Investment in human capital is in no sense restricted to the provision of vocational education. A classical education—languages, literature, the humanities, the fine and performing arts, philosophy, and the like—broadens and deepens people's capacities to think, act, and enjoy and thereby increases their productivity in an economic sense. Over many decades Canadian businesses have demonstrated as high an interest in employing graduates of broad liberal arts programs as they have in employing those trained in specific vocational majors. They want to hire bright individuals who know how to think and how to accept responsibility.

Direct Consumption

Some part of the educational services produced by colleges and universities consists of *direct consumption benefits.* Participation in the activities of the institution and interaction with other students in university life yield direct satisfaction to many. Students who have no interest in whether or not their education pays off through increased earning power or through some sense that their knowledge will somehow be of benefit to humankind are the best examples of direct consumers of educational services. To these students the direct benefits can be divided into two subgroups. First are the direct benefits through the direct consumption of educational services. In the same way individuals might enjoy going to a hockey game, they may enjoy the experience of attending a postsecondary educational facility and engaging in learning and campus life as ends in themselves. These students receive a part of their direct benefit through the direct consumption of education. In other words part of their benefit comes from attending class, using the library, and learning to analyze concepts in ways that they could not have done without the educational experience. Their direct consumption is not limited to what they are learning in the classroom or in the library. They may well be gaining some or all of their direct consumption from the conversations with other students over coffee in the student lounge or through attending parties in student residences.

By way of contrast, there are students whose sole purpose in attending college is to enhance their capacities for earning income after graduation. For these students the direct benefits of education, which may include considerably higher lifetime income, are not in the strict sense direct consumption benefits. For example, assume a student enters a program of study hoping only to enhance his or her capacity for earning income. Further assume that the student is not interested in acquiring skills or knowledge as an end in themselves but only as vehicles to certification or accreditation. Students may attend classes or use the library, but only if they see these as easier ways to get satisfactory grades and certification than are embodied in substitute strategies such as correspondence courses. These students gain no enjoyment from listening to a lecture, reading a text, participating in group projects, or researching a topic. They may not participate in any other aspects of postsecondary institutional campus life such as discussion groups, campus politics, intramural sports, student union parties, and campus activities. For a student in this example, the direct consumption benefits of education will be zero. However, even this theoretical student may attain direct benefits from the educational experience. If the student completes certification and if the employment market is such that it rewards the individual with a higher lifetime income, he or she may still be gaining considerable direct benefits of education. Canadian statistics reveal a considerable difference between average income for Canadians who completed high school and for those who received a postsecondary certificate or diploma or university degree. In 1992 average income for Canadians with high school as their highest attained level of education was $12,735 for females and $21,926 for males. By contrast, females who had earned a postsecondary certificate or diploma received an average income of $21,644 while males with certificates or diplomas received $33,501. For those with a university degree, average incomes for females and males were $32,933 and $49,554, respectively.[9]

For most students the consumption benefits are inextricably mixed with the human capital investment elements of educational services. Classes, discussions, and social life combine to provide personal satisfaction as well as to increase the capacities of the human resource to produce goods and services.

---

[9]*The Canadian Encyclopedia Plus* (Toronto, McClelland & Stewart Inc., 1995).

Social Spillovers—Externalities

Sometimes the production or the consumption of a product yields benefits to people who neither produce nor consume it. Suppose my wealthy neighbour hires an orchestra to play at her garden party and I am not invited. She pays for the pleasure of her guests. But who is to stop me, a lover of beautiful music, from listening to its haunting strains from my side of the property line? The production of the music yields what is called *social spillover benefits*, or *external benefits*.

When the production or consumption of a good or service yields benefits to persons other than those doing the producing or consuming, such benefits are referred to as **social spillover benefits** or **external benefits.**

Production or consumption of a product can yield *social spillover costs* or *external costs*, too. These are costs imposed on people not involved in the production or consumption of the good. If one of my neighbours opens a beauty shop at home, there will be a noticeable increase in traffic on our street. It will be necessary to supervise the children on the block more closely to keep them from being run over. This need to use my labour resources to avoid the unintended nuisance and danger caused by my neighbour is a social spillover cost.

When the production or consumption of a good or service imposes costs on persons other than those doing the producing or consuming, such costs are referred to as **social spillover costs or external costs.**

The widespread provision of educational services is generally thought to have social spillover benefits. Many believe that over and above the direct benefits to the individuals who receive them—greater productivity, earning power, and direct consumption benefits—additional benefits accrue to the society as a whole. Some of the spillovers commonly cited are a better functioning democratic process stemming from greater voter literacy, more enlightened citizens who make the society a more pleasant place to live, better government services to the community, and more rapid technological growth. The benefits are as diverse as improved community sanitation techniques and facilities, reduced crime rates, reduced fire hazards, and reduced management costs to private firms.

The Incidence of the Benefits

When individuals obtain college or university educations, to whom do the foregoing benefits accrue? Suppose we look again at the nature of the "product." The direct consumption benefits are easiest to assign. They very clearly add to the level of well-being of the individual student. However, no obvious widespread spillovers of these benefits appear to others in the society as students work their way through a two-year diploma or typical four-year undergraduate degree.

The development of human capital also provides first-order benefits to individuals and their families. Individuals who develop engineering skills, medical skills, legal skills, specialized knowledge, or teaching skills increase their capacities to contribute to gross domestic product; however, at the same time they increase their abilities to earn income. As we will see in more detail in Chapter 11, in a properly working market economy, the extra income that they can earn will be approximately equal to the value of their additional on-the-job productivity. Society as a whole benefits from this additional productivity, since it makes greater supplies of certain goods and services available for consumption, or it may make some available that were previously not available—insulin, for example. Important as these contributions may be, their existence is not sufficient ground to support the argument that they are social spillover benefits. They may represent the same kind of increase in the productivity of the economy's resources that occurs when someone invests in a new, more productive machine. The resource owner is paid for the first-order increases in personal productivity. Then society receives a second-order benefit in the form of a greater gross domestic product.

To the extent that true social spillover benefits occur from higher education, the society, apart from individuals and their families, must receive them. Some of these spillovers involve the increased availability of research provided to local businesses, the increased stable employment opportunities in the region caused by the existence of a postsecondary institution, and the increased market for products used by the employees and students who comprise the institution. In addition the existence of a well-educated population provides benefits to firms wishing to sell products or recruit skilled employees. Identifying, quantifying, and measuring such benefits is very difficult as they may extend to the changes in real estate values adjacent to a campus brought about by the ready market for rental housing coupled with the negative effects of overcrowded parking on the streets. Consequently, people continue to debate and conjecture about how large the net benefits are and the extent to which they exist for higher education.

Many people argue that the social spillover benefits associated with each additional year of education tend to decrease as an individual moves up through the educational system. They believe that the greatest spillovers come from the achievement of literacy—learning to read, write, do arithmetic, and interact with peers. These skills are associated with education at the kindergarten and primary levels. They expect secondary education to develop more complex skills of interacting with others in the society and to provide some measure of sophistication in the administration of the joint affairs of those who constitute the society. They do not believe that higher education provides much more in social spillovers. They believe that higher education benefits society mostly through the benefits it provides to those who obtain its services. Alternatively, recent studies suggest that rapid integration of new technologies coupled with increased globalization in recent years will require much higher education levels to maintain Canada's social infrastructure and standard of living in the future.

In summary, then, first-order benefits of higher educational services accrue to the students and graduates of postsecondary educational facilities. Society receives second-order benefits of higher education from social spillover benefits. The kinds of benefits that accrue to the student as first-order benefits are relatively easy to identify but difficult to quantify. Similarly, the second-order benefits of education that accrue to society as a whole are equally easy to identify but, like the benefits received by the student, difficult to measure. The issue of measuring the first- and second-order benefits with any certainty is further complicated because many of the benefits may be spread out over the lifetime of the person who receives an advanced education and may not show up until years after the student receives the education. These complications about the extent and proportional mix of the first-order and second-order benefits of higher education levels in society foster debate and discussion about what proportion of the cost of higher education should be paid by the student and what proportion should be paid by the government on behalf of society.

Economic Concept of Costs

While some things, such as clean air, clear water, and sunshine are truly free goods in the sense that no one must produce them, one of the most important principles of economics is summed up in the statement, "There is seldom such a thing as a free lunch." We speak glibly of such things as free medical care, free roads, free parks, and free education. What we mean is that those who use these goods and services do not themselves have to pay money directly to use them. All too often our chain of reasoning stops right there. But if we really think that these items are free to the society as a whole, we delude ourselves. The production of these goods is costly to someone—perhaps even partly to their users.

The economic costs of a product may or may not be reflected in the direct money outlays that must be made in producing it. The basic concept underlying economic costs is the *opportunity cost principle*.

The Opportunity Cost Principle Revisited

We defined and discussed the nature of the opportunity cost principle in Chapter 1. The concept is particularly useful in identifying the costs of higher education.

Suppose we start with the production possibilities curve or transformation curve that measures units of educational services along the horizontal axis and composite units of all other goods and services along the vertical axis—all of these in terms of dollars' worths. (See Figure 3–1.) The curve TT_1 shows all alternative combinations of other goods and services and of education that the economy's given resources can produce per year. Suppose that initially combination B, made up of e_2 dollars' worth of education and g_2 dollars' worth of other goods and services, is being produced and the economy's resources are fully employed.

Figure 3–1   The costs of education

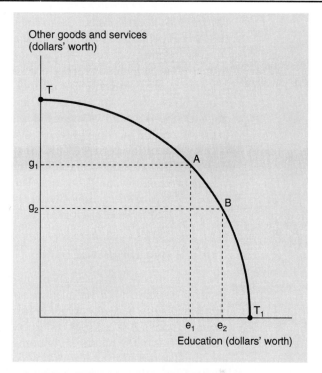

Production possibilities curve TT_1 shows all alternative combinations of other goods and services and education that the economy's resources and technology can produce per year. Two possible alternative combinations are represented by A and B. If the economy is initially producing combination B, it is obtaining g_2 units of other goods and services and e_2 units of education. If e_1e_2 represents one unit of education per year, then g_2g_1 units of other goods and services must have been sacrificed to obtain it. The value of the g_2g_1 units thus measures the cost of a unit of education at the e_2 level of production.

What is the cost to the society of a unit of education when B represents the economy's output mix? *It is the value of the alternative goods and services that must be foregone to produce that unit.* Let the distance e_1e_2 represent one dollar's worth of education. If this unit had not been produced, the society could have had more of other goods and services, equal to the amount g_2g_1. Thus the society had to sacrifice g_2g_1 dollars' worth of other goods and services to produce the one unit of education. The sacrifice of the other goods and services releases just enough resources to produce the additional unit of education. We call the physical amounts of other goods and services sacrificed the *real cost* of producing the unit of education. The value that consumers attach to the goods and services given up is the true *economic money cost*.

Stated in a slightly different way, *the cost of producing a unit of any one good or service is the value of the resources used in producing it in their best alternative use.* A little reflection will show that this statement of the opportunity cost principle is identical to the one developed in Chapter 1.

The opportunity cost principle is capable of general application. In an economy in which resources are fully employed, an increase in the amount of medical services provided draws resources from the production of other goods and services. The value of the goods and services foregone (that is, the value of the resources that were used in their production) is the cost of the increase in medical services. The cost of a tonne of wheat is the value of the corn that must be foregone in order to produce it—if corn production is the best alternative use to which the resources used in wheat production could be put. The cost of a soldier in the Canadian Armed Forces is the value of what that person could have produced as a civilian. Thousands of such examples could be cited.

Explicit and Implicit Costs

The economic costs to a society of producing a good or service do not necessarily coincide with its accounting costs. As an example, consider a small family-owned grocery store for which the labour is provided by the owning family. A large part of the costs of resources used by the store to put groceries in the hands of consumers—costs of grocery stocks, utilities, and the like—is indeed accounting costs, but some resource costs may be omitted from the accounting records. The costs of labour are not likely to be listed. Amortization and depreciation costs on the land, building, furniture, and fixtures also may be omitted. The family may simply take what is left after the out-of-pocket expenses are paid, calling this remainder the *profits.* The costs of resources bought and hired for carrying on the business are called *explicit costs of production.*

The **explicit costs of production** are the costs incurred by the producer to buy or hire the resources required to carry on business. The **implicit costs of production** are the costs incurred by the producer for the use of self-owned, self-employed resources.

These economic costs are the ones most likely to be taken into account by the business, since they are usually actual cost outlays. The costs of self-owned, self-employed resources (like the labour of the family in the example) are called *implicit costs of production.* They tend to be hidden or ignored as costs. Implicit costs of a resource can be identified by using the opportunity cost principle. The worth of the resource in its best alternative use is determined; this amount is its cost to the owner-user. If the family members had used their labour working for someone else, this labour would have produced other goods and services and would have earned income about equal to the value of those other goods and services. So the cost of self-employed labour is what it could have earned in its best alternative employment.

Thus the true cost to society of producing a good or service, what we call the opportunity cost, can be accurately measured only if we take into account both the explicit and implicit costs of the activity. Although accounting costs are often readily available, they are reliable measures of opportunity cost only if an activity involves no implicit costs. And this situation is very unlikely.

The Costs of Higher Educational Services

From the point of view of the society as a whole, the services of higher education are not free. Resources used in their production could have been used to produce other goods and services, and the value of these foregone goods and services is the economic cost of higher education. In this section we shall try to pin down the nature of those costs and identify who pays them.

The Explicit Costs

The explicit costs of the services provided by a college or university are the costs of the resources that it buys and hires to provide those services. These are the costs of capital resources and labour resources. The post-secondary educational institution uses land, buildings, equipment, and supplies. It also uses professors, instructors, researchers, maintenance personnel, administrators, and clerical staff.

The institution's annual budget provides a first approximation of the annual explicit costs of its services. The budget should include amortization costs of major capital outlays, depreciation costs, small-equipment costs, maintenance costs, and the costs of hundreds of kinds of supplies. It should also include the wages and salaries of labour resources used.

The true explicit costs are the values of the resources used by the institution in their best alternative uses. However, this statement should be interpreted with some degree of caution. The economic cost of an educational institution's buildings are not what the value of the buildings would be if the institution were to close its doors. Rather, it is the value of the goods and services that were foregone in order to build and maintain the building. Whether or not the institution's explicit costs are reflected accurately by its accounting records depends upon the accounting procedures it uses.

Additional explicit costs of education to students, apart from the costs of inputs used by colleges and universities in providing educational services, consist of student outlays for various items necessary or desirable in the educational process and unique to it. These items include books, notebooks, calculators, computers, pencils, pens, paper, and the like. They also include clothing, campus parking permits, bus passes, and entertainment costs that would not have been incurred in nonacademic lifestyles.

The Implicit Costs

The costs to a society of producing higher educational services greatly exceed the explicit costs discussed above. To obtain educational services, most students withdraw their labour wholly or partly from the labour force, thus reducing the amounts of other goods and services available to the society. In order to be students, they sacrifice some of what they could have earned as workers, and society sacrifices the value of the goods and services they would have produced had they been working. These foregone earnings, or the equivalent foregone GDP, are implicit costs to the student and to society of the educational services obtained by the student. They do not show up in the institution's budget or books of account.

Sources of Support

One of the economic features in the production and sale of higher educational services in Canada, as in other industrialized nations, is the diversity of the sources tapped to pay the costs. Those who have taken on the responsibility of providing higher educational services have traditionally not been willing—or able—to leave them subject to market forces. Neither public nor the smaller private postsecondary educational institutions charge their customers the full explicit costs of the educational services provided, but the extent to which they approach full costing of those services is a key difference between the two types of institutions.

Public Institutions. Public colleges, technical institutions, and universities depend heavily on government sources to meet their explicit costs. For the fiscal year 1989–1990 governments provided 80 percent of Canadian universities total operating funds.[10] Of approximately $8.8 billion in total spending by Canadian universities in 1989–1990, federal government transfers to the provinces were $5.8 billion.[11] About 60 percent of the funds are in tax credits given to the provincial governments by the federal government, and the remainder consists of cash transfers.[12]

Tuition and *fees* as a means of meeting explicit costs are relatively low at most public educational institutions. Usually public colleges and universities charge higher tuition rates for foreign students than for Canadian students, indicating that government grants are a substitute for tuition to which they believe only the citizens of the country are entitled. About 16.9 percent of university funds came from this source in 1989–1990.[13] To a relatively small extent, public institutions depend on *private donors* to help meet their explicit costs. Funds are received from donors as endowment gifts, cash grants, scholarship gifts, and the like. The donors include foundations, corporations, philanthropists, and alumni who can be convinced that they are contributing to a worthwhile cause. Although this source of funding has increased in recent years, traditionally it tends to be very small, amounting to about 3 percent of public institution funds.[14] Although

---

[10]Smith, op. cit., p. 22.

[11]Ibid.

[12]Department of Finance, op. cit., p. 76.

[13]Smith, op. cit., p. 22.

[14]Ibid.

it has been a very small portion of the overall budgets, this source of funding is significant on some campuses, as it has enabled some institutions to engage in activities that base grants from governments would not have permitted.

In Canadian public colleges and universities, students and their families must pay the implicit costs of educational services. If a student does not work at all, the foregone earnings or foregone goods and services for the society as a whole are implicit costs. If the student works part-time, the implicit costs are the difference between what could have been earned and what is actually earned. If the husband or wife of a student is forced to accept unemployment or less remunerative employment in the vicinity of the college or university than could have been obtained elsewhere, foregone earnings will be larger than those for the student alone.

Private Institutions. Private colleges and universities are a tiny portion of the total enrollment in the Canadian system of postsecondary education, but they are of interest because they provide an alternative way of focusing on how society pays for education.[15] Since they do not receive the same level of support from the government through grants, the private institutions must meet a much higher portion of their explicit costs from the payment of tuition and fees. Contributions from private donors are also likely to serve as a more important source of support—the more the institutions can secure from private donations, the less pressure they have to rely on tuition and the better able they are to compete with the low tuition rates of public institutions. Judging by the experience in the United States, seeking funds from donors is always a major activity of private institutions. In the United States private postsecondary institutions covered about 20 percent of their explicit costs through funds raised from donors in 1991. This amount was about three times the reliance on private donors by government postsecondary institutions. Direct government grants to private educational institutions vary widely among institutions and are lower than those for public institutions. Some institutions receive very little in direct subsidies from government sources. The implicit costs of educational services can be assumed to be about the same for private as for public institutions. They amount to the foregone earnings of students. Tuition fees are generally higher for private institutions than they are for similar programs of study in government run institutions.

---

[15]Illustrative of the public and private enrollment split is the situation in Alberta, where government policy has been generally favourable to the development of private educational alternatives. Enrollment in the public system of the four universities, 11 colleges, three technical institutes, and three vocational training facilities totalled more 115,000 full-time equivalent students in 1992. Enrollment figures for the private institutions are difficult to find and are estimated at less than 5 percent of the total public institution enrollments.

The Incidence of the Costs

Where do the costs of producing the services of higher education finally rest? Table 3–1 shows a rough comparison of the incidence of costs between a public institution and a private institution. We assume that the kinds and qualities of services provided are the same for each institution and that each is equally efficient in providing them. These assumptions are for convenience only, as there may be either economies of scale or diseconomies of scale that favour the typical large public institution over the typical smaller private institution, or vice versa. Because of these assumptions, the total cost is the same regardless of whether we are looking at a public institution or a private institution. Costs are the same in real-world cases but assuming they are allows us to analyze whether the government, the student, or private donors are likely to pay the costs.

Three features of the incidence of costs are significant. First, implicit costs are a very large part of the total costs of the educational services provided a student. They amount to about 54 percent of the total costs. Note that they are the same whether the student attends a public or a private institution.

Second, the major source of support for the explicit costs of public institutions is government grants, whereas for private institutions it is tuition and fees. Except for scholarship holders, the burden of tuition and fees rests on students and their families. Government grants are made from general revenue funds in any given province and consist of money collected from taxpayers of the government; consequently, the incidence of this large part (in our example more than three-fifths) of the explicit

Table 3–1	Estimated per student annual cost of higher education by type of institution and source of support		
		Private	**Public**
Explicit costs			
Tuition and fees (student and family)		$ 5,300	$ 2,200
Government grants and contracts (taxpayers)		2,600	7,000
Private gifts, contracts, and endowment income (donors)		1,800	500
Books and miscellaneous items (student and family)		1,500	1,500
Total explicit costs		$11,500	$11,500
Implicit costs			
Foregone income (student and family)		$13,000	$13,000
Total costs		$24,200	$24,200

Note: We assume equal sizes and qualities of the public and the private institution.

costs of public institutions rests on taxpayers, rather than on students and their families. Public institutions, then, shift the incidence of explicit costs of higher educational services from students and their families to taxpayers. However, a complicating problem reduces the difference in support for public institutions as compared to private institutions. To the extent that students at private institutions pay higher fees, we could say that they bear the increased incidence only to the extent that they or their families bear those increased costs. If a student at a private institution qualifies for government guaranteed student loan programs, the reduced cost of financing the borrowing from the chartered banks is a hidden subsidy from the taxpayers to the students and to the private institutions they attend. Further, to the extent that the students might default on the loans, taxpayers will be required to pick up the losses that would have accrued to the private postsecondary institutions at tuition rates higher than those they would have been forced to pay to fund students in the government run facilities. Similarly, to the extent that students at a private postsecondary institution can use their tuition fees as a deduction when filing their income tax return, the taxpayers may be indirectly subsidizing them at a higher rate than implied by our example.

Third, private institutions rely more heavily on donors as a source of support than do public institutions. To the extent that funds can be obtained from donors and substituted for tuition, the incidence of explicit costs is shifted from students and their families to donors.

Economic Evaluation of the Problems

Although the economic framework established in the preceding sections permits us to approach the problems of higher education in a systematic and logical way, it does not always provide clear-cut, correct solutions. Economic analysis helps determine what causes what, and why. It helps determine, once goals have been set, the most efficient way of reaching those goals. However, economic analysis cannot always provide answers as to what the goals or objectives in higher education or any other activity should be. Equally intelligent people often disagree on the goals that a particular society should seek.

What Kinds of Services?

Are our expectations realistic with respect to the kinds of services higher education should produce? The industry can produce whatever mix of services we as a society want it to produce. The important economic problem is concerned with how well institutions respond to the society's desires or demands for those services.

Economic analysis generates questions as to how responsive the current structure of higher educational institutions permits them to be in meeting societal demands. By and large, throughout the economic system consumers register their demands for goods and services by the ways in which they dispose of or spend their purchasing power. Suppliers respond to the array of prices that result. Is this the way in which the mix of programs that are offered by postsecondary educational institutions is determined? Obviously not.

Colleges, technical institutions, and universities make little or no use of the price-rationing or market forces in determining what programs they will offer. Their officials usually try to offer what they think the society wants—business, engineering, computer science, and the like. Of course, the desires of students and their families must be taken into consideration; otherwise, the enrollments would not be forthcoming. In addition, in public institutions the desires of the provincial government department responsible for the administration of postsecondary education and career development are of great importance. The provincial legislatures can reduce funding for programs that the legislature no longer deems to be sufficiently important to the public good to warrant the support of public funds. Alternatively, the government may offer to provide postsecondary institutions with *project funding* or *supplemental funding* if the institution introduces a program or method of instructional delivery that is consistent with government initiatives not covered by base grant funds. Private institutions face the danger that major donors may try to influence the choice of programs. A firm acting as a donor may provide funds for a program only on condition that the program meets criteria set out by that firm and is useful to it in its immediate short-term hiring requirements. The interests of students and their families are likely to receive prime consideration only to the extent that they provide the major source of revenue to the institutions, whether those institutions are public or private. In short the old saying, "He who pays the piper can call the tune," is as relevant to the delivery of postsecondary educational services as it is to most other things that society produces.

The reasons that the price system is so completely ignored or snubbed in determining program priorities are probably varied. At the undergraduate level most colleges and universities charge almost the same price (tuition) to all students, regardless of the program of study pursued. College and university administrators and faculties, government bureaucrats, elected officials, the public, and students themselves seem to believe that a single tuition rate is the equitable way for the system to promote equality of access to qualified students. It is not our intention to claim that the solution that society has chosen is not the most desirable solution given the ethical value system of society. As we pointed out in earlier chapters, economics has limited ability to deal with issues involving ethics. However, economics does deal effectively with issues of efficiency and scarcity.

In the next section of the chapter, we will attempt to provide a guide to using economic tools to reflect on potential inefficiencies in the present system of delivering postsecondary education in Canada.

Differential Pricing Based on Differences in Demand. Consider two possible undergraduate programs, say business administration and agriculture. Suppose that initial student demand for agricultural programs is represented by $D_{a1}D_{a1}$ in Figure 3–2a.

The price per person per year is a composite of all costs except implicit costs to the student for a year of the program. The demand curve for agricultural programs would be expected to slope downward to the right as do most demand curves—the lower the price of the program, the more education-years of it students will demand. The supply curve $S_{a1}S_{a1}$ of agricultural programs would be expected to slope upward to the right. The more money per year postsecondary institutions can obtain from the sale of such programs, the more resources they can attract and use to expand them. The demand curve $D_{b1}D_{b1}$ and the supply curve $S_{b1}S_{b1}$, for business administration programs (Figure 3–2b) are conceptually the same as those for agricultural programs. Ignore $D_{b2}D_{b2}$ for the time being. Suppose that by some great coincidence, the initial supply and demand curves for both programs are such that the prices are the same for each; that is, p_{a1} equals p_{b1}. The program sizes are s_{a1} and s_{b1}, respectively.

Now, let student demand for business administration programs increase relative to that for agricultural programs. The business administration demand curve shifts to $D_{b2}D_{b2}$, and the agricultural demand curve shifts to $D_{a2}D_{a2}$. What are the effects of maintaining equal prices for the two programs as colleges and universities now tend to do? At price p_{b1}, the institutions cannot expand business administration programs and cover the costs of doing so. A shortage of business administration faculty and facilities will result. Classes will be larger and rooms will be more crowded. The quality of instruction will likely deteriorate. In agriculture programs, at price p_{a1} class sizes will decrease and facilities will be less fully utilized, producing a relative surplus of faculty and facilities. Shortages and surpluses of these types are common today in postsecondary institutions throughout Canada. They represent inefficiencies in the production of educational services as the institution fails to allow the price system to allocate resources efficiently.

If postsecondary institutions were to use a differential pricing scheme for different programs, they could increase both efficiency and responsiveness to adjust their provision of various programs to the expected enrollments. Let tuition and fees in business administration rise to p_{b2}. Additional revenue is obtained to expand to s_{b2}, taking care of the increased demand. The price increase also serves to reduce the pressure on facilities by reducing enrollment from s_{b3} to s_{b2}. Let tuition and fees in agriculture fall to p_{a2}. Postsecondary educational institutions have an incentive to cut programs

Figure 3–2   **Effects of changes in demand for educational services**

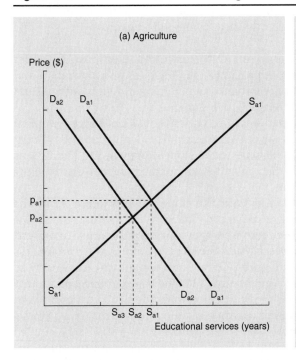
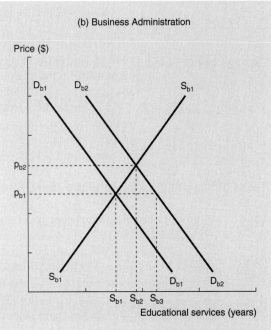

$D_{a1}D_{a1}$ and $S_{a1}S_{a1}$ are the initial demand and supply curves for years of agricultural education, whereas in business administration they are $D_{b1}D_{b1}$ and $S_{b1}S_{b1}$. Now, suppose that demand for business administration increases to $D_{b2}D_{b2}$ and demand for agriculture falls to $D_{a2}D_{a2}$. Maintaining explicit costs (tuition and fees) at p_{b1} and p_{a1} results in a surplus of agricultural educational capacity and a shortage of business administration capacity. Letting the tuition and fees for business administration rise to p_{b2} and those for agriculture fall to p_{a2} will result in increasing the efficiency with which both are utilized.

back to s_{a2}, at which they are once more just covering costs. Additionally, the decrease in the price in agriculture from p_{a1} to p_{a2} will increase the enrollment in agriculture from s_{a3} to s_{a2}.

To make the preceding economic analysis more general, suppose that in universities a demand arises for a program that has previously not existed—say, for ecology studies. Costs of supplying different numbers of years of the program can be determined, and the supply curve can then be matched up with the demand curve. The resulting equilibrium price will reflect the costs of the program and the values of the program to students. It will also generate the correct program capacity, reflecting neither a shortage nor a surplus.

Increases in Tuition and the Price Elasticity of Demand. Differential pricing schemes in response to differing levels of demand for alternative academic programs clearly would encourage school administrations to operate both more efficiently and responsively to the demonstrated demand of students and donors. As noted in the introduction to this chapter, and something that you are undoubtedly aware of, many public school systems are increasing tuition and fees rapidly in the face of reduced infusions of money from traditional government sources. Even before the large reductions of government support to postsecondary institutions in the mid-1990s, institutions had begun increasing tuition fees in an apparent attempt to increase revenue. Between 1981 and 1991, tuition and fees rose by 112 percent at Canadian postsecondary institutions, while the consumer price index increased by only two-thirds this amount over the same period.[16] The rationale is clear—to maintain revenues at the levels perceived to be necessary to fulfill their missions in the face of budget cuts from government grants, the students of public colleges and universities are being forced to carry more of the burden.

But will this strategy work? That is, will the institutions actually take in more revenue from tuition and fees when they increase tuition rates? The answer would seem to be an obvious yes, but recall that the law of demand is not suspended simply because we are discussing higher education. Reconsider Figure 3–2. The law of demand, as expressed through any of the various demand curves of this figure, clearly indicates that, other things being equal, as tuition rises, enrollment falls. That is, if other things remain the same, increases in tuition at public institutions will cause some individuals to choose alternative sources of education (private, trade, or whatever) and others to simply discontinue their educations. The amount of tuition revenue taken in is determined not just by the tuition rate but also by enrollment. Whether tuition revenues rise, fall, or remain unchanged in response to a tuition increase is determined by the relative strengths of the changes in the two key variables: tuition rate and enrollment. The economic term for the relationship between these two variables is the *price elasticity of demand*, which is defined as the percentage change that occurs in the quantity demanded of a good or service given a percentage change in its price. Suppose that tuition increased by 10 percent and in response enrollment fell by 5 percent. The price elasticity of demand for educational services would have a coefficient of $-\frac{1}{2}$, which would imply that for each 1 percent increase in tuition, enrollment could be expected to fall by one-half of 1 percent.

The law of demand indicates that as tuition rises, enrollment will fall. But will the fall in enrollment be sufficient to offset the tuition increase and actually leave the college or university in a position of taking in less revenue than it had prior to the tuition increase? A good estimate of the price elasticity of demand for higher educational services answers the question.

Price elasticity of demand is a measure of the relative responsiveness of the amount consumers want to purchase to price changes. It is equal to the percentage change in the quantity demanded divided by the percentage change in the price of the product. The elasticity of demand is represented by the symbol η, (the Greek letter *eta*) and has two methods of calculation, the *point method* and the *arc method*. Each calculation method has its own formula shown as

Point method:
$$\eta_{(point)} = \frac{\frac{\Delta Q}{Q_1}}{\frac{\Delta P}{P_1}}$$

Arc method:
$$\eta_{(arc)} = \frac{\frac{Q_2 - Q_1}{Q_1 + Q_2}}{\frac{P_2 - P_1}{P_1 + P_2}}$$

The choice of which calcuation to use in a given circumstance is not relevant to our discussion here. You only need to know that for small changes in price both methods usually produce similar results.

[16]Statistics Canada, op. cit., series P490471 and P49470.

Consider the two possible situations detailed in Table 3–2. In each we start with an initial enrollment of 5,000 students and tuition of $2,000 per year, yielding tuition revenues to the institution of $10 million per year. Now suppose, in response to cuts in other support, the administration increases tuition by 10 percent to $2,200. In situation 1 enrollment falls by 5 percent to 4,750, and in situation 2 enrollment falls by 15 percent to 4,250. What happened to tuition revenues? The bottom row shows tuition revenues rising in the first case by $450,000 and falling in the second by $650,000. What is the reasoning behind these very different outcomes? The answer is found in differing price elasticities of demand. Specifically, the price elasticity of demand in the first situation was $-\frac{1}{2}$, while in the second it was three times as great, $-1\frac{1}{2}$. (You should confirm these calculations by substituting the relevant figures into the equation for calculating price elasticity of demand using the point elasticity method $\eta_{(point)} = \Delta Q/Q_1 / \Delta P/P_1$.) Put in less technical terms, the consumers responded much more negatively to the tuition increase in the second situation than in the first, leaving tuition revenues actually lower after the tuition increase than before.

Whether tuition revenues increase, remain the same, or fall in response to a tuition rate increase, then, is determined by how responsive students are to that tuition increase. In general terms, if the coefficient of price elasticity exceeds 1 in absolute value, we say that demand is relatively elastic at the current price; a tuition rise will actually leave the school taking in less revenue than it would without the tuition increase. Intuitively, what is happening in this case is that the revenue-enhancing effect of the tuition increase is more than offset by the revenue-draining effect of the enrollment decrease. Such was the case in situation 2. Alternatively, when the coefficient is less than 1 in absolute terms, demand is said to be relatively inelastic at the current price and a tuition increase does lead to the desired increase in revenues from tuition. Completing the picture, a situation might exist where, at a specific price, the coefficient is equal to 1 in absolute terms. Then a tuition increase will bring about an

Table 3–2   **Tuition rates, revenues, and the price elasticity of demand**

	Situation 1		Situation 2	
	Before	After	Before	After
Tuition	$ 2,000	$ 2,200	$ 2,000	$ 2,200
Enrollment	5,000	4,750	5,000	4,250
Tuition revenue	$10,000,000	$10,450,000	$10,000,000	$9,350,000

offsetting enrollment fall that leads to no change in the school's tuition revenue. In this case, we say that the price elasticity of demand is unitary.

How could educational institutions use this information? Clearly, tuition increases in the face of relatively elastic demand make little sense if the goal is to increase tuition revenue. A more interesting implication, however, couples the notion of price elasticity with differential tuitions as discussed above. Experience with public institutions over the past decade indicates that administrators believe that the most effective means of increasing tuition is simple across-the-board increases. Although this approach is, no doubt, based on notions of equity, an alternative method could be more sensitive to the relative desires of students to study different programs.

Differential Pricing and the Price Elasticity of Demand. Consider a school or university with a strong clinical technician program (from any of the biological/medical fields) and also a strong accounting program. Further suppose that, in response to cuts in government funding, the administration is planning to impose a substantial tuition increase. Suppose further that, from past experience, the administration knows that tuition, at its current level, is relatively price inelastic overall; thus the proposed tuition increase would achieve the goal of increasing tuition revenue. Does it follow that the most effective method of increasing tuition is the across-the-board method preferred by most administrations? The answer depends on the relative price elasticities of demand for the two programs, clinical technician and accounting. That is, while the overall price elasticity for all of the school's students might be relatively inelastic, extreme differences may exist between the elasticity for accounting students versus clinical technician students.

Although many factors influence the degree of price elasticity of any good or service, three tend to be very important with respect to higher education: (1) the proportion of the consumer's income taken by the good or service, (2) the availability of substitutes, and (3) the extent to which the product is considered a necessity by the consumer. Although we have evidence that the children of those from professional schools such as medicine and law are more likely to enroll in those programs than the children of people who have not attended such programs, no strong reason for elasticity differences based on the first criterion between accounting and the clinical technician programs is immediately apparent. That is, given our tendency toward uniform tuition rates, the proportion of income taken by tuition is roughly the same for the accounting student as it is for the clinical technician student. The availability of substitutes is quite a different matter, however. If one wishes to be a professionally chartered accountant, the only avenue is a formal, accredited accounting program. In fact, certification into the profession explicitly requires a carefully specified course of study. In this type of situation in which no good substitutes exist, the price elasticity of demand tends to be very inelastic and any tuition increase would likely lead to a significant increase in tuition revenues.

Compare the previous example with the situation for a student with a clinical technician major. Although an academic technician program is an excellent entree into the profession, it is by no means necessary. Numerous vocational and technical institutions offer programs that are, more or less, substitutes for the clinical technician programs offered by colleges and universities. When substitutes abound, demand tends to be relatively price elastic and any tuition increase would likely lead to a significant fall in tuition revenues.

Given this, what could an administration do if its goal is to maximize tuition revenue through a tuition increase? It must identify the programs for which demand tends to be highly inelastic and require them to bear the brunt of the tuition increase, leaving programs with relatively elastic demands less affected. Can you come up with a list of programs that might fall into the two camps? In any case, the point to be made is that the use of the price system could aid not only in responsiveness to consumer demands but also in funding decisions. It remains remarkable that this valuable tool is often neglected.

How Much Service?

Economic analysis provides a conceptual model to explore how much educational service the economy should produce relative to other goods and services. The resources used in producing educational services can be used to produce other goods and services, and, from the opportunity cost principle, the costs of educational services are the values of those resources in their best alternative uses. Consequently, if the value to society of a unit of educational services is greater than its costs—the resources used in producing it are more valuable in the production of education than in alternative ones—then the output of educational services should be expanded. On the other hand, if the value of a unit of educational services is worth less to the society than it costs to produce it, the output should be reduced.

In terms of demand-supply analysis, let DD represent the demand curve for higher educational services and SS be the supply curve for them, as shown in Figure 3–3. If the economy is presently providing a quantity of s_1 years, the value of a unit to demanders (students) is v_1, but the cost of a unit to the society is c_1. The excess of the value of a year's education over its cost indicates that resources needed to produce a year of education are more valuable if they are so used than they would be in their best alternative uses. Educational services should be expanded relative to the production of other goods and services in the economy. The correct amount of educational services for the society is s_2 priced at p_2 per year. What can you say about quantity s_3?

Figure 3–3   **Determination of the correct quantity of educational services**

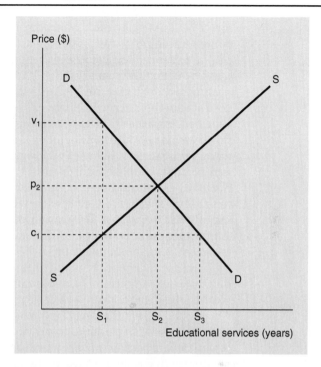

If s_1 years of educational services are provided in the society, the value of a year exceeds its cost, indicating that an expansion of services is in order. At the s_2 level of services, the value of a year is equal to the costs of providing it. The correct amount of services for the society is s_2.

The value of higher education services in relation to their costs is obscured by several complicating factors. Higher educational services are not priced in the marketplace in a way that will cause the quantity supplied to be adjusted to the quantity demanded. In the case of most products traded through the market, the benefits from direct consumption constitute the major portion of the total benefits on the demand side. Therefore, in the case of most commodities, if society allows the consumer to decide what they are willing to pay for various quantities and allows suppliers to respond, an efficient equilibrium can be established. We saw how allowing the market to set the price brings about a condition where social benefit equals social cost in Chapter 2. So why not just use supply and demand to solve the outcome in higher education as Figure 3–2 suggests? The reason is that it is difficult, if not impossible, for society to establish an accurate demand curve for postsecondary education through standard demand theory. The reasons for this difficulty are varied but include two major points worth discussion. First, students themselves have difficulties in determining the amount they would be willing to pay for their education. As we indicated above, students receive two types of direct benefits as a result of acquiring a postsecondary education. Students receive immediate direct consumption benefits, but they also expect to enhance their income in the future. The difference in the nature of these two benefits makes it difficult for students to assess the value of education to them today. While the student can identify with some certainty the value of their immediate direct consumption benefits, the value of the expected increase in lifetime income is uncertain. In addition, because postsecondary education includes significant spillover benefits to other members of society, many of which are not readily quantifiable, we must face an unavoidable ethical issue of what share of the cost of their education students should be expected to pay. These complications have contributed to the present system in which the government picks up the major share of the cost. The combination of public and private sources of support on the supply side compounds the difficulties of valuing educational services and of determining how much should be produced.

In order to explore how the difference in elasticities might be used to fine-tune the composition of programs within the general level of service, we wish to abstract from some of the difficulties discussed above. Again we emphasize that the decision of how much postsecondary education to provide and the share of the cost to be paid by the student is ultimately an ethical debate because of the nature of the extent of the spillovers involved in education. For the purpose of the present analysis, we will assume that the spillover benefits to society are the same regardless of whether a student studies accounting or a medical field. In addition, we will assume that the expected income of students graduating from accounting may differ from the expected income of those graduating in medicine, but graduates from all programs face the same uncertainty about what their income will be. These assumptions may not be realistic, but they allow us to explore how differential fees based on different elasticity of demand may assist in making the allocation of education institutional resources more responsive to the desires of students.

On the demand side, consider potential students who want educational services in some specific field—say medical training. In medical schools throughout the country, the annual number of openings for students is limited. At current levels of costs per student, many more students want training than can be accepted into medical school; that is, a shortage of medical training services exists. Put another way, the shortage means that potential medical students would be willing and able to pay more for the services of medical schools than they are now required to pay. However, students are not permitted to bid up the price at which these educational services are offered, and hence the price system cannot express the public's valuations of them. The same kind of analysis holds true for many other fields of specialization.

The supply of educational services made available by public higher education institutions is not a direct response to student demands. The amounts supplied are determined primarily by the grants public institutions receive from governments, rather than by what students are willing to pay. Colleges and universities compete with a number of other government activities for the dollars that governments have available, and because government funds are limited, educational administrators will seldom, if ever, receive as much as they think they ought to have. At the same time, such public institutions are reluctant to supplement the funds received from the government with tuition receipts. Tuition is supposed to be kept low because of government grants—keeping tuition low is the purpose of the government transfers. The higher the tuition rates set by the public institutions, the less will be their bargaining power against the government for a share of public funds.

Public colleges and universities can expect to encounter a continuous financial crisis. The services they can supply are limited by the always inadequate grants they receive from the government, while the demands for their services are augmented as they succumb to the pressure to keep their tuition rates low. At the same time, the relatively low tuition rates of the public institutions enable them to draw students away from private institutions that offer comparable programs. The competition of public institutions limits the services that private institutions can provide. It also sets upper limits on the tuition rates that private institutions can charge and still remain in business. Pressure on private institutions to obtain gifts, grants, and the like increases. Competition from public institutions makes it very difficult for private colleges and universities to stay solvent.

Who Should Pay?

The controversy over who should pay for higher educational services is undoubtedly the key problem faced by higher education. If this problem could be resolved, answers to the questions *What kind?* and *How much?* would be much easier to determine. At one extreme of the controversy are those who maintain that educational services should be above market forces. At the other extreme are those who believe that each student and family should bear the full costs of that student's education.

To understand how these two differing views come about, consider some of the more obvious benefits that occur when a postsecondary institution is established in a city. Having a university or college in a community is often seen as a very important thing to the local residents and business leaders. It is an indication that the youth in the area will not have to move to another region in order to gain a higher education and the job opportunities that such education implies. Most economic forecasts agree that the changing structure of the economy will require much higher educational levels on average to prepare students for the emerging high-technology jobs. Studies suggest that Canada's changing industrial structure requires increased retraining to help people maintain or regain employment, and the existence of a postsecondary institution makes retraining easier to accomplish.[17] While some proponents argue that private firms will be willing and able to pay the costs of retraining workers, this argument overlooks the problem that skills and education have significant spillover benefits and that profit-maximizing firms may attempt to free ride on the training expenses of competitors. We could argue that if a public institution provides the training at taxpayer expense, it signals firms that a supply of well-skilled labour will be available in the community and that the costs to the firm for recruiting skilled labour will be lower. A post-secondary educational institution serves as a source of culture and research that contributes to making the community better known, enhancing local pride, and making it a more pleasant place in which to live. Because the postsecondary institutions have been relatively large, well-funded, labour-intensive employers, they are often seen as a way of adding a large non-cyclical employer of relatively well-paid labour to a region. Since the funds for postsecondary education have come largely from the federal government, there is a tendency to see the institutions as a means of accessing federal transfer funds for the local economy. Education is seen as the great equalizer, providing opportunities for self-development and self-realization. Many Canadians believe that everyone is entitled to equal opportunity in acquiring as much education as her or his inherent abilities and efforts make possible. These people believe that, like primary school and secondary school, Canada should make postsecondary educational free for those with the willingness and ability to learn. For all these reasons politicians and local interest groups lobby to have the provincial government build institutions of higher learning in their communities.

Despite these benefits critics argue that not every city and region can support a postsecondary educational facility any more than they can all support a local automobile manufacturing industry. They point out that the benefits to one community come at the expense of other communities that must support the university or college with taxes that could have been used in their own communities. Finally the existence of a publicly funded postsecondary institution counters some people's notion of equity. They claim that the direct benefits of higher education received by the student far exceed the indirect spillovers to the community. On these grounds they fail to see why taxpayers, many of whom did not receive postsecondary educations, should be expected to pay for someone else to get one.

---

[17]Human Resources Development Canada, op. cit., pp. 15–27.

"Free" Education. What does "free" education mean? The economic aspects of higher education discussed in this chapter make it clear that there is no such thing from society's point of view. Neither is education free from the individual student's point of view—unless, of course, both explicit and implicit costs are covered by the government or through scholarships. Ordinarily education is said to be free if government grants to public colleges and universities are large enough so that no tuition is charged. In Canada, public colleges and universities are not tuition free; government grants simply permit these institutions to charge substantially lower tuition than if the public support were not forthcoming. The differences in costs between what is generally called a free education in a government college or university and what is called a private education of the type charged by a private college or university modeled on the lines of institutions in the United States are not as great as tuition differentials would lead us to believe. In the example in Table 3–1, the annual costs borne by the student and family in a public institution would be about $16,000, while in the private institution they would be about $19,000.

Government Support of Higher Education. In terms of economic analysis, government support of higher education means that some portion of the costs of obtaining educational services is shifted from the student who receives the services to taxpayers. Federal transfer payments and provincial grants to colleges or universities decrease tuition that students are required to pay. Government grants to the institutions are obtained from taxpayers. Thus government support constitutes a *transfer* of purchasing power from taxpayers to college and university administrations on behalf of students.

Under what circumstances do such transfers seem to be in order? They appear to be defencible (1) to the extent the social spillover benefits are generated by higher education, (2) as a means of enabling children of the poor to develop their human resources, and (3) to the extent that the evolving nature of the industrial structure of Canada's economy necessitate increasing levels of skill and education to maintain our productivity relative to other nations.

When the consumption or utilization of some good or service by one or more people results in spillover benefits to others, those who receive the spillover benefits are in a good position to be *free riders*. Direct consumers of an item pay for the direct benefits they receive; otherwise, they will not be able to obtain whatever it is they want to consume. Those who receive the spillover benefits receive them whether they pay anything or not; their tendency is to be free riders and pay nothing. Direct consumers are in no position to force the free riders to pay, but what they cannot do as individual private citizens, they may be able to accomplish collectively through their government. As we will see in Chapter 5 on pollution, strategies for dealing with the ethical issues resulting from spillover benefits and costs

Those who receive the benefits of a good or service without paying the costs of production are said to be **free riders**. Thus free riders are those who receive social spillover benefits.

involve using the power of government to intervene directly in the production and distribution of the product creating the spillovers. The government can levy taxes on the free riders, thus coercing them to pay for the spillover benefits they receive. The government is a unique and logical agency to accomplish this purpose.

If social spillover benefits from higher educational services exist, the use of taxing powers and government support of higher education sufficient to pay for those benefits would seem to be reasonable. Several major points arise. The most important one is whether or not significant social spillover benefits are generated in the provision of higher educational services. Although society generally agrees that spillover benefits do exist and are significant, they are ambiguous and very difficult to quantify.

The other major argument for public support of higher education is that it enables capable, low-income students to obtain a college or university education. Education serves to increase the capacities of human resources to produce and to earn income. Since poor families do not have the means to pay for higher education for their children, a condition that is not the fault of the children, the government can do much to enable these young people to escape from poverty by providing them with the same kind of educational opportunities that are available to the children of middle- and high-income families.

The case has much merit. One of the generally recognized functions of government in Canada and throughout the industrialized world is that of mitigating poverty. In Canada very substantial parts of both provincial and federal budgets are designated for this purpose. Welfare programs, along with income taxes that are intended to take larger proportions of the incomes of the rich than of the poor, provide examples. It seems reasonable that state support of higher education for the poor should be an integral and important part of any antipoverty program.

Although government support looms large in meeting the explicit costs of educational services in public institutions, the implicit costs that the student and the student's family must meet are a very substantial part of the total costs. The inability of a poor family to meet the implicit costs—the need for children to go to work and earn income—discourages the children of the poor from attending postsecondary educational institutions of any type. For the most part, public colleges and universities are not devices for transferring purchasing power from taxpayers to children of the poor. Most college and university students do not come from poor families; they come from middle- and upper-income families. Most of the transfer, then, is from taxpayers in the middle-income and upper-income groups to the children of middle- and upper-income families.

Student Self-Support. Some people believe that students and their families, rather than the government, should bear the costs of higher education. This idea does not necessarily mean abandonment of government owned and operated postsecondary facilities. A government public college or university can recover the full costs of education through tuition and fees levied on students just as a private one could. The two main arguments for why students should pay for their own education are (1) those who benefit are the ones who should pay and (2) economic resources would be used more efficiently; that is, some waste would be avoided.

The argument that those who benefit should pay is an equity argument. It asks why one group—taxpayers—should be forced to pay a portion of the educational costs of another group—students and their families. To be sure, the two groups will have some overlap; students and other members of their families are also taxpayers. However, a large proportion of taxpayers are not college and university students or graduates of postsecondary education. Further, since enrollment at postsecondary education institutions comprises about one-third of the adult population between the ages 18 and 24 in Canada, we can argue that the majority of taxpayers and their families will not graduate from colleges and universities. Many of these families have a lower income on average than the families of the people who do attend postsecondary institutions. Is it equitable for governments to levy taxes on the rest of society to help pay for the education of children from middle-income and wealthy families?

One argument for students paying for their own education maintains further that investment in human capital is essentially comparable to investment in material capital. Suppose a high school graduate has a choice of investing in an education or investing in a business. One considers the payoff of each in terms of future well-being and makes the choice that one (and one's family) thinks will yield the highest return on the investment. This is the way that most private sector investment decisions are made. In the absence of clearly significant spillover benefits to the economy, we do not expect taxpayers to bear part of the investments of high school graduates starting their businesses. However, Canada does have a long tradition of using subsidies and loan guarantees to private entrepreneurs to reduce the effective risks of creating businesses that are believed to bring significant social spillover benefits. Examples include subsidies or direct government participation in all our transportation industries as well as subsidies and tax reductions to mega-projects such as Syncrude and Hybernia. The same standard that government has used to support private investment in transportation or the energy sector also suggests that even if higher education were nothing more than an investment in human capital with significant longrun spillover benefits, it should be subsidized by government.

Another argument for student self-support is that people tend to overuse whatever is free to them and to economize or conserve whatever they have to pay for. The greater the cost of a purchase relative to one's income, the more incentive one has to use the item carefully in order to increase the possible returns from it. This is said to be the premise underlying high charges made by tax accountants for their services. The argument is used extensively by those who think students should pay for their own education.

If higher educational services are provided at reduced or free tuition costs to students, the incentive to economize on or make the best possible use of the resources providing those services is weakened—so the argument runs. Low tuition induces students who have no interest in learning to attend college or university, whereas higher tuition charges would make them think more carefully about whether or not they should do so. Further, those who do attend would be inclined to make more of their opportunities if they cost more.

Which Way? Which of the arguments is correct? If students and their families reap most of the benefits of higher education—that is, if the benefits of higher education are primarily private human capital development—then a strong case can be made that students and their families should pay its full cost. If substantial social spillover benefits result from putting some part of the population through the processes of higher education, or if higher education is used effectively as a campaign against poverty, a strong case can be made for shifting a part of its cost to taxpayers.

An Alternative Institutional Structure

The possibility that the institutional structure of higher education in Canada can be improved by employing some of the features of the market system are worth considering. The rationale for the government-supported system is that (1) it makes higher education available to the children of poor families and (2) it increases the social spillover benefits of higher education by encouraging large enrollments. Critics of the present system argue that it does not necessarily serve either of these purposes better than other alternative systems might serve these goals. The implicit costs of higher education are so great that even with the low tuition rates of public institutions, few children of the poor find it possible to attend. The present system with its low and largely uniform tuition rates in public institutions produces two chronic problems that may be of interest. The artificially low tuition fees reduce the opportunity for private institutions to earn sufficient returns to provide credible alternatives. These low tuition fees also reduce the ability of the existing public institutions to adjust the resources they would employ to respond to changing student demand. In other words, the present system does not enable society to place accurate demand values on the services desired by students and employers because funding for postsecondary education reflects the priorities of the provincial governments, rather than the priorities of students.

One alternative to the present higher education institutional structure is that it would make greater use of price rationing and market forces in the provision of higher educational services. A key feature of such an alternative is that the demand of students and employers interacting with the supply of educational services be used to set tuition to the colleges and universities at a level sufficient to cover the full explicit costs of educational services. This approach would shift much of the responsibility for determining which programs to provide and how much postsecondary education to produce away from government departments in favour of students and employers.

If society desires to help the low-income students to obtain educational services, it could do so easily and directly. Instead of direct grants to public or private colleges and universities, governments could make grants directly to students of families with incomes below a certain level. If direct grants are to work in alleviating poverty, the grants must be large enough not only to cover the explicit costs of education but also to pay at least some of the implicit costs. Lost income to poor families from having a family member enrolled in an institution of higher education, rather than being a fully employed contributor to the family income, often constitutes a major barrier to poor families that prevents their members from acquiring the benefits of a higher education. Direct grants would enable poor families to overcome the opportunity cost that prevents a family member from entering postsecondary study. Direct grants would have the added advantage of allowing students to choose the institutions they would attend. Presumably they would attend the institutions that they feel will best meet their needs. The antipoverty aspects of government support could be realized directly and efficiently. If the government wishes to provide equality of access, as opposed to treating all citizens the same, the proposed system would have an added benefit. The government would not be supporting those who are not in need. By contrast, the present system supports all students equally, regardless of their ability to pay. In sum, the system would evolve from one in which the taxpayers subsidize all students—the high-income student as well as the low-income student—into one in which only low income students are subsidized.

If, because of spillover benefits, the government desires to encourage larger enrollments than would occur if all students paid the full costs of their education, it could do so directly. For example, raising the minimum income standards used to define which students qualified for subsidies, the government could increase the number of students eligible for public support. The exact nature of the public support could range from tuition vouchers to access to student loans to creation of part-time employment opportunities in crown corporations reserved for qualifying students and the like.

Note that relying more heavily on market forces to set tuition rates does not preclude using the system of higher education as a part of an antipoverty program or regional equalization program nor does it preclude government (taxpayer) support of higher education. Government support would contribute directly and efficiently to making higher education available to the students from low-income families. Government support of higher educational services—whatever the amount of support the society desires—would be provided to students and more directly determined by students than it is under the present system.

Further, a more market oriented system would tend to induce postsecondary educational institutions to supply the quantity of educational services that students and employers want relative to the quantities of other goods and services produced in the economy. Tuition would be the main source of revenue for institutions; it would cover the full explicit costs of services supplied. Colleges and universities would supply services to as many persons as are willing to pay that tuition. This change would constitute both benefits and costs relative to the present system.

The proponents of a more market-sensitive tuition system point out that the system would be responsive to its clientele—students and sponsoring employers. The critics of the proposed system point to this result as the most significant problem inherent in such a system. They argue that the role of postsecondary educational institutions is not limited to the provision of education instruction. Traditionally, postsecondary institutions have had a major role as institutions of social criticism. Universities and colleges grant tenure to faculty largely to protect the independence of academic research and to promote freedom of academic debate to challenge society's conventional views. The critics claim that students and employers may well withdraw financial support from the institutions that are the most active in challenging conventional wisdom. In addition, those critical of the proposed system point out that students are not and should not be regarded as customers or clients. They argue that students who see themselves as customers may well think that the more they pay the more they are entitled to a high grade. The critics point out that education is not so much a product and a process. In the same way that a patient is often in a position of trust relative to a health care provider—owing to the patient's ignorance of medical knowledge in assessing the seriousness of a condition or the appropriateness of various treatments—a student may not be in a position to evaluate the appropriateness or depth of a program of postsecondary study. Finally, a market-driven system to determine what should be provided would place the responsibility of ensuring the academic integrity of the postsecondary system in potential conflict with the institutional need to generate revenue. In sum, the implementation of a more market-sensitive system of funding postsecondary education highlights the opportunities and problems of relying on supply and demand to allocate resources in an activity that includes significant amounts of spillover benefits and involves society's ethical desire to ensure equal opportunity of access to all regardless of their economic condition.

Summary

Colleges and universities face many problems, most of them stemming from four fundamental issues: (1) the kinds of services they should provide, (2) how much service they should provide, (3) the appropriate institutional structure, and (4) who should pay for education services. Economic analysis has much to say about these issues.

Institutions of higher education use resources to produce educational services. These services provide (1) investment in human capital, (2) direct consumption benefits, and (3) social spillover benefits. There is much controversy over the extent and importance of the social spillover benefits provided by postsecondary education. The first-order benefits of educational services accrue mainly to the student who obtains them, although society gains from secondary benefits.

Higher educational services, like all endeavours that employ society's scarce productive resources, have economic costs. All economic costs are measured by the opportunity cost principle. Some costs are explicit in nature, while others are implicit. The explicit costs of higher education services are the costs of the capital and labour resources used by colleges and universities. Most people view these as the total costs. However, students and their families also incur the implicit costs associated with acquiring a postsecondary education. Most important of these are the foregone earnings of students and their families. Structurally, the Canadian system of postsecondary education consists primarily of large public institutions, which receive the bulk of their revenues in the form of government grants, and a few relatively specialized, small, private institutions, which receive the bulk of their revenues from tuition. The implicit costs to students do not enter into college and university budgets. The incidence of the costs of higher educational services rests most heavily on the student and his or her family, despite the relatively low tuition levels achieved through government subsidization of the explicit costs.

Postsecondary education is often seen as a vehicle for increasing social mobility and alleviating poverty. It is a complex activity that embodies providing education and training to students while serving the larger community as a focal point for informed debate and research about a wide range of social issues. Under the present system, tuition fees are largely the same for all programs; the amounts of services provided are almost entirely determined by government grants to government-owned and -operated institutions. An economic evaluation of the fundamental problems involved in the provision of higher instruction to students highlights several areas in which market forces might be incorporated to make postsecondary education more responsive to the needs of students and employers. As a device for making educational opportunities available to students from low-income families, incorporating elements of demand and supply theory might be accomplished without compromising the government's desire to ensure equality of opportunity.

Like all changes in allocation, a move away from the present system of funding and tuition to a more market-sensitive system would involve challenges. Under a supply-and-demand–sensitive system of funding, the role of educational facilities as institutions of social criticism and sponsors of research not linked to profitability in the private sector might be jeopardized.

Checklist of Economic Concepts

Human capital
Spillover benefits, social
Spillover costs, social
Opportunity costs
Production possibilities curve
Explicit costs
Implicit costs
Demand

Supply
Price, equilibrium
Price elasticity of demand
Surplus
Shortage
Transfer payments
Free riders

Discussion Questions

1. Explain the differences between the direct benefits of postsecondary education and the indirect benefits of postsecondary education. Why might it be argued that the government should expect taxpayers to bear the costs for providing the indirect benefits of postsecondary education?

2. Construct a list of the explicit costs and the implicit costs of postsecondary education. Why might implicit costs constitute more of a barrier to obtaining a postsecondary education for students from lower-income families than for students from middle- or high-income families?

3. Explain the concept of price elasticity of demand. If a college administration knew that a particular program faced an elastic demand, how might it adjust tuition fees to increase revenue? What is the relationship between the consumer's elasticity response to a price increase and the availability of substitutes?

4. Construct a production possibility frontier for postsecondary education and other goods and services. Use your graph to explain how an increase in the production of educational services is similar to an increase in the production of capital goods.

5. Why might the present system of government grants to postsecondary educational institutions lead to the provision of too many "course seats" in cultural ethics and too few course seats in accounting? Why might a market-driven system for determining tuition fees for postsecondary education result in too many course seats in accounting and too few in cultural ethics?

6. Why might critics of a system of market-determined tuition fees argue that it will turn institutions of "higher learning" into institutions of "hire learning"?

Supplementary Reading

Bowen, H. R. *The Costs of Higher Education: How Much Do Colleges and Universities Spend per Student and How Much Should They Spend?* San Francisco: Jossey-Bass, 1980.

Addresses the questions raised in the title. Carefully differentiates between monetary expenditures and real costs.

Bowen, H. R., ed. *Investment in Learning: The Individual and Social Value of American Higher Education.* San Francisco: Jossey-Bass, 1977.

Chapter 9, "Social Outcomes from Education," is particularly interesting. Bowen emphasizes the role of higher education in promoting social change and argues that higher education entails social spillover benefits even though he presents little or no empirical evidence to that effect.

Government of Canada. *Agenda: Jobs and Growth, Improving Social Security in Canada, A Discussion Paper.* Ottawa: Minister of Supply and Services, 1994.

Chapter 3 of this discussion paper provides an insight into the extent of government support for postsecondary education in Canada. The discussion paper also proposes changes to the system to increase reliance on student loans and higher user fees to support the system. The plan would shift the burden away from taxpayers and place greater reliance on private sources of funding for research and on tuition to cover the direct costs of instruction.

Dennison, J. D. and P. Gallagher. *Canada's Community Colleges: A Critical Analysis* Vancouver, BC: University of British Columbia Press, 1986.

A thorough discussion of the role of community colleges in Canada.

Douglass, G. K. "Economic Returns to Investment in Higher Education." In *Investment in Learning: The Individual and Social Value of American Higher Education.* ed. H. R. Bowen. San Francisco: Jossey-Bass, 1977.

Describes the decision to acquire a college education as an investment in human capital and presents estimates of the return on investment from empirical research.

Douglas, R. "Unfinished Business." Aukland: Random House New Zealand Ltd., 1993.

Chapter 5 describes the plan by the former Minister of Finance of New Zealand to change the delivery of educational services in a way that would have relied more heavily on market forces and price-rationing.

Doyle, D. P. "The Federal Student-Aid Mess." *The Wall Street Journal*, May 19, 1982, p. 30.

Reviews the Reagan administration's position on federal aid for college students and summarizes Milton Friedman's view and recommendations on the role of government in education.

Psacharopoulos, G., ed. *Economics of Education: Research and Studies.* New York: Pergamon Press, 1987.

An excellent and thorough treatment of the issues raised in this chapter. Especially interesting are the essays concerning the benefit-cost analysis of investment in higher education.

Smith, S. L. *REPORT, Commission of Inquiry on Canadian University Education.* Ottawa: Association of Universities and Colleges of Canada, 1991.

The commission explored the performance of Canadian universities in meeting the sometimes conflicting goals of providing for the research needs of the country as well as delivering educational services directly to students. This comprehensive report deals with such diverse aspects of postsecondary education as the appropriateness of the tenure system for the appointment of academic staff and the ease with which students can transfer credits and gain recognition for study between institutions.

Windham, D. M. "The Public Responsibility for Higher Education: Policy Issues and Research Directions." In *Subsidies to Higher Education.* ed. H. P. Tuckman and E. Whalen. New York: Praeger Publishers, 1980.

A careful, thoughtful discussion of whether or not social spillovers exist in undergraduate education.

Chapter 4

Economics of Crime and Its Prevention

How Much Is Too Much?

Sensational killings punctuated 1995, from grisly slayings of elderly couples in both Montreal and Toronto to the terror campaign of a serial attacker in Abbotsford, British Columbia.

But the number of slayings in Canadian cities remained stable over the past year—a sharp contrast to the United States.

Toronto dropped from 85 to 74 in 1995, Montreal from 75 to 60, Vancouver from 48 to 30, Edmonton from 24 to 19, and Winnipeg from 18 to 16. Slayings in the Ottawa region rose slightly from 17 to 23, and Calgary recorded 18 for the second year in a row.

"In Canada generally the overall homicide rate has remained stable," said Rosemary Gartner, a professor of criminal law at the University of Toronto. "And the characteristics of those killing have remained stable as well—strangers still only make up 10 to 15 percent of murders."

Ms. Gartner, who compares Canadian crime with that of other countries, said homicide statistics are a reliable way of drawing a distinction between Canada and the United States, since they are usually reported accurately.

Data for 1994 showed an average of 2.04 people per 100,000 citizens were killed in Canada, compared with 9.03 in the United States. In Gary, Indiana, a city of only 116,000, 130 killings were reported in 1995.

"Canada has stable cultural attributes which are only likely to change in the long run," Ms. Gartner said. "If we were to become more like the United States, with a stronger violent subculture, then maybe our murder rate would increase."

While gun control and antidrug programs were embraced in 1995 as means of curtailing crime in the long run, Ms. Gartner said doom-and-gloom predictions of the safety of Canadians are rarely well grounded.

"There is a lot of incentive for politicians, police forces and special-interest groups to create a moral panic about crime," she said. "But studies show that public statements about crime are more related to economics climate than the actual crime rate."[1]

Criminal activities create an important set of social problems in Canada. They affect our general well-being by threatening the loss of money and property and by generating concern for physical safety. Yet, for most of us, crime is something we read about in the papers—something that usually affects other people but has the potential of affecting us. We seldom look at crime from a systematic, analytical point of view, but if we

---

[1]Canadian Press. *The Globe and Mail*, January 3, 1996, p. A7. Reprinted with permission.

are to do anything about the problem, we must look at crime in this objective way.

What Is Crime?

It seems almost silly to raise the question, What is crime? However, if we are to look at crime analytically, we must have a solid base from which to work. The concept of what constitutes criminal activity is often not clear in the mind of any one person and may be ambiguous from one person to another. Some people think of crime in terms of that which is immoral; others think of it in terms of that which is illegal.

Immorality?

Are immoral acts criminal? Answering this question is not easy. In the first place, many acts do not fall clearly into a moral–immoral classification. In modern societies some acts are generally considered to be immoral—murder and most kinds of theft, for example. But the morality of many other acts depends on what group in the society is evaluating them. Examples of such acts include marijuana smoking, drinking alcoholic beverages, betting on horse races, homosexual activities, and adultery. These simple examples demonstrate that the moral–immoral classification helps little in determining whether or not specific acts are criminal.

Illegality?

A definition that seems to be meaningful and useful analytically is that a criminal act is one the society (or one of its subdivisions) has decided to outlaw because the society would prefer for that activity not to take place. The activity may or may not be immoral. For example, is it immoral to drive 50 kilometers an hour along a deserted street that is posted for 30 kilometers an hour or to run a stop sign at an intersection where there are no other cars or to catch a fish in a mountain stream before you have obtained a fishing licence? As you quickly discover when you are caught, these acts may very well be criminal in nature. On the other hand, if gambling, drinking, and prostitution are immoral, in many places they are not considered illegal and are, therefore, not criminal. Acts that are illegal or criminal are designated as such by legislative bodies, such as city councils, provincial legislatures, and Parliament. Society offers a number of reasons for making certain acts illegal. Some acts may indeed be offensive to the moral standards of a majority of legislators and their constituents. Murder, sexual assault, and theft are cases in point. Others may lead to consequences (in the minds of legislators, at least) of which the doer is ignorant. The consumption of alcohol, cocaine, or heroin thus may be made illegal because legislators fear that those who try them may become addicted, with disastrous consequences to the users. Still other acts are designated illegal in order to prevent chaos or to promote order—violation of established traffic rules, for example. Further, some acts may carry no taint of immorality but may be made illegal because they are considered contrary to the general welfare of the society. Acts of pollution, such as burning your trash within the city limits, illustrate the point.

Classification of Criminal Acts

In Canada three types of criminal offences are defined. More serious crimes, such as murder or robbery, are indictable offences. Less serious crimes, such as parking tickets and disturbing the peace, are summary conviction offences. Conviction for a summary offence usually is punished by a fine, though it can lead to up to six months in jail. Some offences are referred to as hybrid offences. These crimes may be prosecuted as either summary or indictable at the discretion of the crown. For crime rate reporting purposes, StatCan classifies offences as violent offences, property offences, other criminal code offences, federal statutes (non-drug) and federal statutes (drug), provincial statutes, and municipal bylaws.

Violent crimes are crimes against persons. They include murder, rape, assault, and robbery. Crimes against property include such things as fraud, break and enter, theft, and possession of stolen goods. Other criminal code offences include mischief, disturbing the peace, prostitution, and arson. Crime is generally thought to be a serious problem in Canada. In parts of every large city, and in some smaller ones, many people are reluctant to go out at night for fear of being robbed, raped, beaten, or even murdered.

As can be seen from Table 4–1, crime rates in Canada have risen substantially since 1976. The one clear exception is murder. The murder rate remained relatively constant during the period. The highest murder rate—2.7 per 100,000 persons—occurred in only two years, 1976 and 1991. The lowest rate—2.2 per 100,000—occurred in three years including 1993. The murder rate fell to just over 2 per 100,000 in 1994. It may seem that the murder rate varies considerably. For example, between 1988 and 1991 the rate increased by 28.6 percent. However, because the number of murders is very small, a relatively small increase in actual murders can appear to be a "crime wave." For the same reason, the drop in the murder rate since 1992 does not necessarily indicate a trend to less violence. Nevertheless, we have some reason to believe that we may be heading toward less crime. Table 4–1 does indicate a decline in 1992 and 1993. Preliminary figures indicate that crime rates in general were even lower in 1994.

While the crime rates in general have been rising, some ups and downs have occurred. Notice that all crime rates including murder rose during the recessions of the early 80s and early 90s and then fell. Still

Table 4–1		Crime rate per 100,000, 1976–1993		
Year	Murder	Violent Crimes	Property Crimes	Total Criminal Code Offences
1976	2.7	593	4,600	7,087
1977	2.6	583	4,550	7,102
1978	2.4	592	4,673	7,301
1979	2.5	623	5,013	7,838
1980	2.1	652	5,581	8,553
1981	2.5	666	5,873	8,907
1982	2.5	685	5,955	8,946
1983	2.5	692	5,717	8,634
1984	2.4	714	5,607	8,548
1985	2.6	749	5,555	8,574
1986	2.1	808	5,714	8,984
1987	2.3	856	5,733	9,247
1988	2.1	898	5,630	9,233
1989	2.4	908	5,271	8,860
1990	2.3	970	5,593	9,454
1991	2.7	1,056	6,141	10,310
1992	2.6	1,081	5,890	10,016
1993	2.2	1,079	5,562	9,516

Note: The total crime rate is greater than the sum of the first three columns because many lesser offences are not included in the first three categories.
Source: Statistics Canada, *Canadian Crime Statistics* (various years) (Ottawa: 85–205).

overall crime rates are much higher now than they were in 1976. The higher crime rates may be in part due to higher reporting rates. Almost no one would argue that actual crime rates are falling, but at least some of the apparent increase is likely due to better reporting. Victims sometimes do not report crimes, particularly victims of sexual assault and domestic violence. Changes in police attitudes and legislation to protect victims may have increased the ratio of reported offences, thereby making crime rates appear to have risen more than they actually have.

Causes of Crime

Criminal activity stems from many sources. Some are economic in nature and others are not. Different kinds of crime may have their roots in different sources. The problem of the causes of crime is a hard one to attack; it is like asking what causes a society to be what it is. We can, however, identify some broad factors that tend to result in criminal activities.

Unrestrained passions or emotions are an important factor in many violent crimes. Most murders, for example, result from deep-seated, intense feelings of some sort between the murderer and the victim. In 1991 of the 582 homicides for which the accused was identified, over 33 percent were related to the victim and only 13 percent were strangers to the victim. The level of the murderer's emotion pushes aside the constraints of conscience and the law that the society has established. Even if murders are usually not economic crimes, murder rates tend to go up during periods of high unemployment. Possibly the increase is related to the frustration and hopelessness that some people feel when they lose a job. Sexual and physical assaults are also unlikely to be economic crimes.

On the other hand property crimes and robbery are much more likely to be economic crimes, where the criminal sees the possibility of monetary gain from the commission of the offence. When poverty is coupled with high levels of economic and social aspirations, the stage is set for criminal activities—particularly robbery and dealing in illegal goods and services. People who are thwarted in attaining desired social and economic goals legally may seek to obtain them illegally. In addition, the *opportunity cost* of being apprehended and convicted of a crime are less for those living in poverty than for persons from middle- and upper-income groups. The latter certainly have more to lose in terms of income—if not in terms of social status. Thus we find that poverty produces a disproportionate share of criminals. The problem is made even worse if the poor are members of groups that are marginalized by economic and social discrimination.

The standards and social values of a society are an important determinant of criminal activities. Society's attitudes toward cheating on one's income tax, stealing from one's employer, embezzling, wiretapping, and interfering with the right to privacy help set the stage for acts that may be considered criminal. One of the most serious costs of corruption by government officials is its effect on citizens' view of right and wrong.

The Costs of Crime

That crime has economic costs is certain. The measurement of those costs, however, is at present very inaccurate. In the first place, many criminal activities go unreported. In the second place, an accurate dollar value cannot be attached to the cost of those crimes that are reported. Nevertheless, if economic analysis is to assist society in the reduction and amelioration of criminal activities, the costs of crime must be estimated. The better the estimates, the better the decisions that can be made.

The basis for measuring the cost of crime is the opportunity cost principle. One way to measure the net economic cost of crime to the society is to take the difference between what GDP would be in the absence of both criminal and crime prevention activities and what GDP currently is, given present criminal and crime prevention activities. Remember that the cost of crime prevention activity must be subtracted from actual GDP. GDP includes expenditures on police, courts, and prisons, which would be unnecessary if crime did not exist. Although society may be better off because of these expenditures, if there were no crimes, the expenditures would not be required and those resources could be used to produce other goods and services that society would rather have. For example, imagine that you have decided to buy a home theatre system. You really like one that costs $5,000. However, a friend warns you that home theatre is a popular item with house breakers. As a result of your friend's advice, you decide to buy a less desirable $4,000 system and a $1,000 home security system. Your contribution to GDP is the same, but you would have been better off if you have not needed the home security system and could have had your first choice theatre system.

Current reports on crime are concerned solely with the number of crimes committed and not with dollar estimates of their costs. To estimate correctly the cost of violent crime, we would start with the loss of earnings (or value of production services rendered) of the victims and of those close to the victims. We also must consider pain and suffering costs. Although these costs are hard to quantify, they are real. Courts sometimes award damages for pain and suffering in liability cases. In the case of some victims, the pain and suffering may be emotional. It still represents a cost. If we assume that the victim has substantial resources, we could determine that individual's pain and suffering costs by determining how much he or she would pay to have avoided the incidence. This approach is *not* to suggest that the victims of an assault should have to pay to avoid the offence, but only that the amount that they would have paid to avoid it would indicate the costs that they were forced to bear.

Other costs are associated with violent crime. If a woman, who would like to jog in the evening in a park near her home, does not do so because of fear of assault—she bears a cost. The cost is the utility she gives up because she cannot do what she would be able to do in a low-crime society. Similarly if parents drive their children to school out of fear of teenage gangs, sexual molestation, or drug use, they bear a cost.

Obvious costs of crimes against property are the values of property destroyed or damaged. However, a comparable direct cost to society from traffic in illegal goods and services is not as clear. The production and sale adds to the well-being or satisfaction of their consumers but may at the same time impose spillover costs on the society as a whole. Thus traffic in illegal goods and services imposes a direct cost on society whenever the production and social spillover costs exceed the addition to consumer satisfaction, whereas the reverse would indicate that such traffic actually provides a direct benefit to society. Additional costs of the whole range of criminal activities consist of the costs of prevention, apprehension, and correction, since resources used for these purposes could have been used to produce alternative goods and services valuable to consumers. Many items thought to be costs are really transfers of purchasing power to the perpetrators of the crimes from their victims. In the case of theft, the thief is made better off at the same time that the person from whom the item is stolen is made worse off. Reprehensible as theft may be, concluding that it represents a large net economic cost to society is difficult. Theft may, however, represent sizable costs to the individual victims. Criminal activities in the aggregate lower GDP below what it would be without them. Crime prevention activities should, if effective, raise GDP above the level that it would be in their absence. Crime prevention activities can thus be considered an economic good or service, since GDP is higher with them than it would be without them. We can think of crime prevention activities as using productive resources—labour and capital. The costs of these services are measured by applying the opportunity cost principle: The costs of resources used in crime prevention are equal to the value these resources would have had in their best alternative uses. In 1991 Canada spent over $5 billion on federal, provincial, and local police forces. Nearly $2 billion more were spent on adult correctional services. In addition, there were the costs of the courts, young offenders correctional services, and private policing services and security systems. A recent study by Paul Brantingham and Stephen Easton estimated the cost of crime in Canada for 1993 as between $16.7 billion (their conservative estimate) and $26.2 billion (their more extensive estimate). Additionally, they attempt to estimate the cost of pain and suffering or as they refer to it—the costs associated with "shattered lives." With this cost included the total rose to $37.3 billion.[2]

In summary, while it is possible to estimate the cost of crime, a satisfactory measure of the costs of crime, in terms of GDP lost because of it, have not yet been devised. The costs of crime prevention activities can be estimated with a fair degree of accuracy; however, these leave out a substantial part of the total costs of crime.

Public and Private Goods

Would a 5 percent increase in the police force of your city be worth anything to you personally? Would an increase or a decrease in the number of patrol cars on the city's streets affect you directly? Would you benefit from an increase or decrease in the number of courts and judges in the system of justice? Your answers to these questions will be no, I don't know, or possibly.

Such questions lead us logically to a useful threefold classification of the economy's goods and services. The first includes *privately consumed goods and services*. The second includes *public goods*, that is, goods (or

---

[2]P. Brantingham and S. Easton, *The Crime Bill: Who Pays and How Much?* (Vancouver: The Fraser Institute, 1996).

services) that are consumed collectively. The third is made up of *semipublic goods*, that is, goods (or services) that have some of the characteristics of public goods.

Private Goods

Any good or service that benefits only the consumer of it is said to be a **private good.**

The concept of private goods and services is straightforward. It includes items that directly benefit the person who consumes them. Much of what we consume is of this nature—hamburgers, suntan lotion, pencils, and the like. The person doing the consuming is able to identify the benefits received. For example, eating a hamburger gives pleasure to the eater and reduces hunger pangs. Finally, private goods and services are said to be exclusive in that once they are consumed by one person, they are unavailable for others to consume.

Public Goods

Public goods and services yield benefits to each person within a group, and no one person in the group can identify the specific part of the benefit he or she receives. In addition, once provided, the benefits of a public good or service cannot be excluded from any member of the group.

Public goods lie at the opposite extreme from those that are private goods; in this case, the individual is not able to isolate or identify a specific personal benefit. Consider national defence services. What part of the total defence services provided by the economy can you identify as being consumed by you, and what is your estimate of the resulting increase in your well-being? Services like these contribute to the welfare of the group to which we belong, but we cannot pick out the part of the benefit that accrues specifically to any one person. An additional characteristic of a public good is that once it is provided, no individual can be excluded from its benefits. Can the government exclude you from the benefits of national defence?

Many kinds of services produced and consumed by a society are collectively consumed. They include national defence, crime prevention, space exploration, some aspects of public health, and most antipollution measures.

Semipublic Goods

Semipublic goods and services yield benefits to both the individual doing the consuming and, to a lesser degree, others.

Semipublic goods and services yield identifiable benefits to the one who consumes them, but their consumption by one person yields *spillover benefits* to other persons. My neighbours' consumption of the various items that lead to beautiful landscaping on their property benefits me as well as them. When other people in a democratic society consume the services of primary education—learn to read, write, and do arithmetic—they benefit directly; I benefit, too, because a literate population improves the functioning of the democratic processes. When other people purchase sufficient medical care to avoid epidemics, I benefit from their purchases of health care. For instance, polio is rare today. When the polio vaccine was developed, most people were inoculated. Today even those who do not receive the vaccine are relatively safe from the disease.

A great many items that people consume and that yield direct benefits to them also yield benefits to others as the consumption occurs. These benefits to persons other than the direct consumers were identified in Chapter 3 as social spillover benefits. We also noted that the consumption of some semipublic goods may yield *social spillover costs* to persons other than the direct consumers. Cigarette smoking in a restaurant or workplace in which nonsmokers are present may be a case in point.

The 'Free Rider' Problem

A society may have difficulty in producing public goods because of a tendency for some of the beneficiaries of the goods to be *free riders* (See discussion in Chapter 3). The nature of the free rider problem can be illustrated by an example. Imagine that your economics classroom has no natural light. Today you have an important test in economics, but when you arrive the lights in the classroom are off. Your instructor announces that because of budget cuts, the university is on a pay-as-you-go basis with the electric utility. She admits that she has no power to force anyone to pay, but if everyone donates a penny or two, the class can have light for the exam. She takes a collection, quickly raises enough money to pay for the lights, and the exam proceeds. After a few exams everyone adjusts to the new fiscal realities. Soon students start to notice that some of their classmates never pay. Enough money is raised before the instructor can collect from everyone. However, even though some class members do not pay, the light still comes on for all to use. Collecting the money starts to become more difficult. Everyone starts waiting for others to pay. After all, once the electric bill is paid and the lights come on, everyone can see—even those who did not pay. Each student has an incentive to withdraw support from the group and to become a free rider, since no student, even one who did not pay a part of the costs of providing light, could be excluded from its benefits.

Government Production of Public Goods

The economics class example may seem relatively trivial. However, the ability to be a free rider makes it difficult for the market to provide collectively consumed goods. A lighthouse is often cited as the classic example of a public good. Imagine a town on a harbour where all the residents earn a living by fishing. Often they go out to sea before sunrise or return after sundown. The harbour has some dangerous rocks that cannot be seen in the dark. Because of the hazard, insurance for the fishing boats is very expensive. The community has 100 fishing boats. The boat owners each pay $1,000 a month for insurance. If the harbour had a lighthouse however, the boat owners would have to pay only $300 a month for insurance. A lighthouse could be built and operated for $10,000 a month. Obviously, it is not in the economic interest of any one boat owner to pay $10,000 a month to run the lighthouse. It would be far cheaper to pay $1,000 a month for insurance. On the other hand, if each owner would pay $100 toward the lighthouse, everyone would be much better off. Each owner would now have to pay $300 for insurance plus $100 for the lighthouse for a total of only $400, as opposed to the previous $1,000 for insurance in the unprotected harbour. However, the free rider problem could sabotage the project. What if half of the boat owners refused to pay for the lighthouse. At first glance building a lighthouse would still seem to make economic sense. The remaining 50 boat owners could each subscribe $200 a month to the lighthouse. They would still be better off because $200 plus $300 is only $500—still only half as much as the insurance without a lighthouse. However, the other 50 boat owners would also benefit from the lighthouse and only have to pay $300. In a competitive market the free riders could sell their fish cheaper than the boat owners who supported the lighthouse. Unless everyone could be certain that all boat owners would pay for the lighthouse, the project might never be undertaken. The subscribing boat owners would have no way to force all the others to pay. Only the government has the power to force all boat owners to pay by taxing them. Historically, groups of people have found that in banding together they can do things collectively that they are not able to do as individuals. One of the first things discovered was that groups can provide better protection from outsiders than individuals can provide on their own. In addition, group action is well-suited to protecting the members of the group from predators in their midst.

Group action on a voluntary basis is technically possible, of course. The boat owners provide a good example. But voluntary associations to provide public goods have a tendency to fall apart because of the incentives that induce some people to become free riders and because free riders cannot be excluded from the benefits of the good. Thus the voluntary association is a tenuous mechanism for this purpose.

Supplanting the voluntary association with the coercive association that we call government can effectively remedy the free rider problem. A coercive government unit (and the power of coercion is an essential feature of government) simply requires that all who receive the benefits of a public good or the service it provides should pay appropriate taxes for it. Thus the provision of national defence, crime prevention, pollution prevention and cleanup, and other public goods and services becomes a government function. These items are often referred to as *collectively consumed goods*.

Most modern governments do not confine their production of goods and services to public goods. Name any good or service, and a government somewhere probably produces it. As pointed out in Chapter 2, a

Public goods and services are sometimes referred to as **collectively consumed goods.** Private goods and services are sometimes referred to as individually consumed goods and services.

major difference between the market and command economic systems is that the government of the latter is responsible for the production of private goods as well as public and semipublic goods. The government of the former leaves the bulk of private goods to private business, although it may play a relatively important role in the provision of such semipublic goods as education and health care. Crime prevention is also a semipublic good. If the police protect you from robbery, they also protect your neighbour. If you were a thief breaking into a house and the private police drove up, would you wait to see if the house owner had paid for private police protection?

The Economics of Crime Prevention Activities

The "Correct" Level

Cost-benefit analysis is a technique for determining the optimal level of an economic activity by considering the relationship between the costs and benefits of the activity. In general, an economic activity should be expanded as long as the resulting increase in benefits is at least as great as the resulting increase in costs.

What is the appropriate level of expenditures on crime prevention activities by any government unit? Is a $5 billion level more or less "correct" for the policing in Canada? The same question can be asked appropriately about any category of government activity and expenditure. To find the answer, *cost-benefit analysis* should be used. In this type of analysis, we must estimate the benefits of the activity, determine its costs, and look for the level at which costs of an increase in the activity begin to exceed the benefits of that increase. The framework for such a problem is set up in Table 4–2.

Suppose the annual benefits and costs of crime prevention at various levels have been investigated thoroughly and the estimates have been recorded in columns (1), (2), and (4). A "unit" of crime prevention is a nebulous concept, a composite of police personnel, patrol cars, courthouses, crown prosecutors, judges' services, prison costs, and the like. We avoid the problem of defining physical units by using arbitrary $60,000 units of crime prevention, assuming that each $60,000 chunk is spent in the best possible way.

The money expense of crime prevention to the community is met by levying taxes. The *economic cost* is the value of the goods and services that resources used for crime prevention activities could have produced if they had not been used for crime prevention. The *benefits* of crime prevention are the community's best estimates of how much better off the suppression of crime will make them—the value of the extra days they can work as a result of not being a victim of violent crime, plus the value of property protected, plus the value of the greater personal security the members of the community feel, and so on. Obviously, the benefits will be much more difficult to estimate than the costs. In fact, the most difficult and vexing part of the problem is the estimation of the benefits that ensue from various kinds of crime prevention activities.

Table 4–2		**Benefits and costs of crime prevention, typical Canadian community* (Hypothetical data)**			
(1) Units of Crime Prevention	**(2)** Total Benefit	**(3)** Marginal Benefits	**(4)** Total Costs	**(5)** Marginal Costs	**(6)** Total Net Benefits
per Year					
0	$ 0*		$ 0		$ 0
		$200		$60	
1	200		60		140
		180		60	
2	380		120		260
		160		60	
3	540		180		360
		140		60	
4	680		240		440
		120		60	
5	800		300		500
		100		60	
6	900		360		540
		80		60	
7	980		420		560
		60		60	
8	1,040		480		560
		40		60	
9	1,080		540		540
		20		60	
10	1,110		600		500

*All dollar values in thousands.

If the benefits and costs are known, and we assume in Table 4–2 that they are, determination of the correct level of crime prevention is relatively simple. Consider first whether there should be no crime prevention at all or whether one unit would be worthwhile. One unit of prevention yields benefits to the community of $200,000—keeps $200,000 worth of GDP from being destroyed by criminal activities—and its cost is only $60,000. Obviously, one unit is better than no prevention; the net benefits (total benefits minus total costs) are $140,000.

Now consider two units of prevention versus one unit. The total benefits yielded are $380,000. But note that the increase in total benefits yielded in moving from one to two units is $180,000, somewhat less than the increase in total benefits resulting from a movement from zero to one

The increase in total benefits due to a one-unit increase in an economic activity is referred to as the **marginal benefit** of the activity.

The increase in total costs due to a one-unit increase in an economic activity is referred to as the **marginal cost** of the activity.

unit. The increase in total benefits resulting from a one-unit increase in the amount of crime prevention is called the *marginal benefit* of crime prevention. As the number of units of prevention is increased, the marginal benefits would be expected to decline because each one-unit increase would be used to suppress the most serious crimes outstanding. The more units of prevention used, the less serious the crimes to which they are applied and, therefore, the less the increase in the benefits from each one-unit increase in prevention.

It pays the community to move from the one-unit level to the two-unit level of prevention because the marginal benefits yielded by the second unit exceed the *marginal costs* of the increase. Marginal costs of crime prevention are defined in much the same way as marginal benefits—they are the increase in total costs resulting from a one-unit increase in prevention. Marginal costs of prevention are constant in the example because we are measuring units of prevention in terms of $60,000 chunks. Therefore, the total net benefits will be increased by $120,000 ($180,000 − $60,000) if the community increases the prevention level from one to two units. (Make sure you understand this concept before you go any further.)

Using the same kind of logic, we can determine that it is worthwhile for the community to use three, four, five, six, and seven units of crime prevention. For each of these increases, the marginal benefits are greater than the marginal costs—that is, each adds more to total benefits than it adds to total costs. Therefore, each brings about an increase in total net benefits. Total net benefits reach a maximum of $560,000 at the seven-unit level. If the level of prevention is raised to eight units, no harm is done. Marginal benefits equal marginal costs, and total net benefits remain the same. But if the level is raised to nine units, total net benefits will fall to $540,000.

As citizens, we must understand the logic underlying determination of the correct amount of government activity in crime prevention—or in anything else. It is very simple, very important, and usually overlooked. If a small increase in the level of an activity yields additional benefits worth more than the additional costs of providing it, it should be expanded. On the other hand, if its marginal benefits are less than its marginal costs, it should be contracted. Therefore, the correct level is the level at which marginal benefits of an activity are equal to marginal costs of that activity. (Study Table 4–2 until you understand this concept thoroughly.) The foregoing economic analysis suggests something about dealing with increasing crime rates. If, when crime prevention activities are stepped up, the cost of an increase in prevention is less than the benefits it realizes, we ought to engage in more crime prevention activities. We are irrational if we do not. However, if a unit of prevention is not worth to us what it costs, then to attempt to suppress crime at present levels of crime prevention activities is irrational. Complete suppression of crime is not likely to be economically justified. At some level of crime prevention, the benefits of an additional unit of prevention are simply not worth what they cost. (What about 10 units of prevention in Table 4–2?)[3] The economic analysis developed above, as important as it is, fails to touch on a very large part of the problems of crime. It does not consider, for example, such questions as: What gives rise to crime in the first place? What causes children to become delinquent and to grow up to be criminals? What causes adults to turn to criminal activities? Can criminals be rehabilitated, or should they simply be punished? These and many other questions are psychological, social, and political in nature. Given the social milieu in which crime takes place, however, economic analysis is valuable in determining the level at which prevention activities should be pursued.

Allocation of the Crime Prevention Budget

Economic analysis also has something to contribute in determining the efficiency of different facets of crime prevention activities. Any well-balanced government crime prevention program has several facets. Ideally, it should deter people from engaging in criminal activities. Failing in this—and it is very unlikely that society will ever deter all criminal activity—a prevention program must first detect and apprehend those engaging in criminal activities. This activity is primarily a police function. To determine the guilt or innocence of those charged with criminal acts, the legal system utilizes courts, lawyers, judges, and juries. Those convicted are fined, put in prison, or both. Prisons have three functions. In all cases they are intended to punish wrong doers. This punishment serves a deterrent effect both for those in jail and others who might consider committing future crimes. Punishment may also provide many in society the satisfaction of knowing that "justice" has been done. Prisoners who will return to society may also receive training aimed at rehabilitating them. If that training can increase the individual's earning power in a legitimate job, it may reduce the incentive to commit a subsequent crime. A prison system is often referred to as a corrections system, indicating that the system will attempt to rehabilitate those incarcerated thereby reducing the likelihood that they will engage in further criminal activities. Finally the prison system protects society from individuals who are dangerous.

How much of a governmental unit's crime prevention budget should be allocated to police departments? How much for courts, judges, and prosecutors? How much for jails—rehabilitation, and punishment? Detection and apprehension of persons thought to be committing criminal acts

---

[3]Society can insure against crimes that are uneconomic to prevent. Most individuals carry insurance against theft, and many political jurisdictions provide crime compensation for victims. Even in the case of violent crimes, it would make no sense to spend so much on eliminating the last murder that no resources were left to provide for any health care, construction of safe highways, and so forth.

are of little value unless adequate court facilities exist for trying them. Trying persons apprehended and sentencing those convicted presuppose an adequate system of corrections or punishment. No one facet of crime prevention can contribute efficiently unless the others are available to back it up. The most efficient mix of the different facets of crime prevention is determined logically by what economists call the *equimarginal principle*. The crime budget should be allocated among police, courts, and corrections so that the last dollar spent on any one facet yields the same addition to the benefits of crime prevention as the last dollar spent on the others. In other words, the budget should be allocated so that the marginal benefits from a dollar's worth of police efforts will equal the marginal benefits of a dollar's worth of judicial effort and a dollar's worth of corrective effort in the overall suppression of crime.

The **equimarginal principle** states that an efficient allocation of a budget exists when the last dollar spent on any one facet of the budget yields the same marginal benefits as the last dollar spent on any other facet of the budget.

As an example, suppose that the crime prevention system is relatively overloaded in the area of detection and apprehension. The courts cannot handle all those who are being arrested, so many of them must be set free without trial or, in the case of plea bargaining, sentenced for a lesser crime than the one committed. The mere fact of arrest will have some crime-deterring effects, but the deterrent effect will be much less than would be the case if the system had adequate court facilities to try the persons apprehended. The contribution to crime prevention of an additional dollar's worth of police activity at this point is low. On the other hand, an expansion of court facilities would increase the likelihood of trial and conviction of those apprehended. We would expect the crime-deterring effect of a dollar's worth of such an expansion to be greater than that of a dollar spent on detection, apprehension, and subsequent freeing of those apprehended. Suppose that taking $1 away from police work brings about enough of a crime increase to cause a $.75 loss in GDP to the community. Now suppose that court activity was increased by $1's worth, and the increased activity deters criminal activity enough to make the community better off by $3. Under these circumstances, the community will experience a net gain of $2.25 in GDP by a transfer of $1 from police activities to court activities. Such net gains are possible for any dollar transfer among police activities, court activities, and corrections activities when the marginal benefits of a dollar spent on one are less than the marginal benefits of a dollar spent on either of the others. No further gains are possible when the crime prevention budget is so allocated that the marginal benefits of a dollar spent on any one activity equal the marginal benefits of a dollar spent on any one of the other activities.

Changing the Legal Status of Goods and Services

Economic analysis also provides information that is useful in determining whether or not certain activities should be considered illegal. Historically there has been much controversy over legalizing the purchase, sale, and consumption of alcohol. More recently, other drugs have come into the picture—especially marijuana and cocaine. Legalized abortion has also been a source of heated debate. Various forms of gambling also figure in arguments as to what should and should not be illegal.

In 1992, according to a United Nations report, Canada had the highest level of drug crimes of 60 industrialized countries. It is sometimes suggested that drug use be legalized. Some proponents of legalization argue that all narcotics should be legal. Others argue that only cannabis (marijuana and hashish) should be legal, while the possession of drugs like cocaine and heroin would remain a criminal code offence. Economics cannot tell us whether or not society ought to legalize drugs. That issue is complex, and ultimately any drug policy involves a number of normative questions. However, economic analysis can help us understand some of the issues involved in the decision to legalize drugs.

The possible legalization of hard drugs such as heroin and cocaine provides an example of the contribution economic analysis can make to a discussion of whether or not a particular good or service should be legalized. In Figure 4–1 suppose that D_cD_c and S_cS_c represent the present demand and supply for cocaine. D_1D_1 and S_1S_1 represent the demand and supply curves for cocaine if its use was legal.

As long as the sale of cocaine is illegal, the supply is sharply reduced. Sellers will only be willing to sell any good if the price is high enough to cover the cost. When a good is illegal, those costs are much higher. Consider the transportation costs of legally bringing 100 kilograms of coffee from Colombia compared to the transportation costs of smuggling 100 kilograms of cocaine from the same place. Similarly, distribution costs within Canada are much higher for cocaine than they are for coffee. Substantial proportions of the cocaine brought into Canada will be discovered by the police and confiscated. If two coffee bars operate in the same market, they might have a price war. The costs of a war between rival drug dealers is likely to be much higher. Even the cost of banking the profits are higher. Finally, those in the cocaine business face the possibility of long prison terms if convicted of trafficking in drugs. To compensate for this risk, profits will have to be far higher than they are in the coffee business.

The demand for cocaine is also affected by its illegality. Cocaine addicts are not likely be deterred by the threat of criminal prosecution. However, not all buyers are addicts; for example, some occasional users are not addicts, and novice users have not yet become addicted. If cocaine was legal, more recreational and novice users might buy it. Many of these potential users might eventually become addicts. Legalizing cocaine might shift the demand for it from D_cD_c to D_1D_1.

As an illegal (criminal) substance, the equilibrium price (p_c) is higher than its equilibrium price as a legal substance (p_1). On the other hand, the equilibrium quantity (q_c) for illegal cocaine is much lower than it would be for legal cocaine (q_1). In effect the legalization of cocaine would lower its

Figure 4–1   **The market for legal and illegal cocaine**

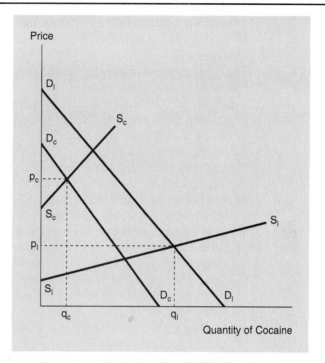

The figure shows the market for cocaine both as a legal and illegal (criminal) good. D_cD_c is the demand curve for cocaine and S_cS_c the supply curve in an illegal market. D_lD_l and S_lS_l are demand and supply curves for cocaine in legal market.

price and increase its availability. Would this change be beneficial? The answer to that question is far beyond the scope of this brief discussion. In fact, it is far beyond the scope of economics. However, some people believe that there are good economic reasons for legalizing (possibly with strict regulations) hard drugs such as cocaine.

A number of crimes are considered to be victimless crimes. These include gambling, prostitution, and drug use. Those who take this point of view would argue that one cannot make a victim of oneself. (Many would dispute the appropriateness of this description.)[4] A general principle of a market economy is that each individual is the best judge of his or her own welfare. Therefore, if individuals choose to eat spinach or liver,

---

[4]Some people argue that individuals can make victims of themselves. Particularly in the case of addictive drugs, some individuals may not be capable of making rational choices. The consequences of their choices may extend to others. For example, some costs of legalized prostitution in Holland may extend beyond the red light district of Amsterdam.

it must be right for them. Similarly if individuals choose to use cocaine, they are affecting their own lives. They are responsible adults and must suffer the consequences of their own decisions. Those who accept this view would argue that the criminalization of drugs creates "innocent" victims.

A frequent suggestion is that drugs and crime are closely linked. Addicts often turn to crime to support their habit. They have little choice. The high prices of illegal drugs make it impossible to earn sufficient income to pay the high prices for drugs by legitimate means. Much cheaper legal drugs would allow many addicts to pay for their habit with even a low-paying legitimate job. It would bring many of them out of a drug underworld and not only reduce crime but also reduce the spread of AIDS and other diseases.

The crime committed by addicts is not the only effect that illegal drugs have on the crime rate. The high risks associated with drug dealing mean high profits for the criminals that are successful. Those high profits have led to conflict among rival drug dealers. Innocent bystanders have fallen victim to the resulting violence. Profits from illegal drugs also strengthen organized crime and can have a corrupting influence on society. Finally, if laws are widely flaunted, one result may be a general lessening of respect for the law.

The legalization of hard drugs might well reduce some of the problems associated with drug use. It was also likely create some new problems. After all, high social costs are also associated with legal drugs—consider the cases of alcohol and nicotine.

An Economic Analysis of Criminal Behaviour

So far this chapter has dealt with crime from the viewpoint of society. Another useful exercise is to look at crime from the economic standpoint of the criminal. Certainly such analysis has its limitation. Often criminal acts are not rational. The motives of criminals are multifacetted, and to suggest that criminal behaviour can be explained by economic analysis is at best moot. However, economics can provide some insight into why many crimes are committed.

We can think of many criminal activities as business activities. They generate revenue and they have costs. If the revenue from a crime is greater than the cost of committing that crime, we might say that "crime does pay." As an example, consider a hypothetical firm Acme Removals, operated by Buster Badguy. Mr. Badguy specializes in housebreaking. The firm's revenues are relatively easy to estimate. Mr. Badguy occasionally finds loose cash that his "clients" leave around their houses. Mainly he steals televisions, VCRs, jewelry, and other items of value. He sells these items at a considerable discount to a fence.

As you will recall from Chapter 3, economists measure costs in terms of opportunity cost. Costs include both implicit and explicit costs. Many of the costs that a criminal incurs are normal operating costs similar to those of a legitimate firm, for example, the tools for break and enter and a van to transport the stolen property. These are explicit costs. However, criminals also have implicit costs. If Mr. Badguy operated a home security consulting firm, he could not at the same time work for a local dry cleaner. He would have an opportunity cost equal to the wage he could have earned at the dry cleaner—or whatever job would have been his best alternative to operating the security service. Similarly, if he operates a break-and-enter firm, he cannot at the same time operate a security service. The income he could have earned in that job is an opportunity cost of break and enter.

An understanding of opportunity costs is important in explaining criminal behaviour. The opportunity cost of committing a crime is much lower for someone who is unemployed than for someone who is employed. The difference in cost becomes even greater if the unemployed person sees little hope of a job in the future. This difference does not mean that the poor will all become criminals or that those in high-paying jobs will never engage in criminal acts. However the opportunity cost—particularly the opportunity costs of getting caught and sent to prison—is much higher for someone with a good job than for someone who is unemployed or who has a low-paying dead-end job. If the potential revenue is high enough—as it often is with white collar crime—even those in the highest income groups may be tempted to commit criminal acts. It also implies that job creation may be a form of crime prevention and that the public provision of good recreational opportunities for youth may be effective in reducing juvenile crime. From a personal standpoint, understanding the role of opportunity costs and revenues in the criminal's decision-making process is useful. An individual can reduce his or her chance of being the victim of a break and enter by taking steps to increase the criminal's costs—better locks or alarms system may lead the criminal to look for a lower-cost job down the street. By the same token, marking valuables for easy identification reduces their value on the black market, thereby making the crime less profitable.

It sounds like choosing a life of crime is not that different from choosing a life in any other line of work. However, two important concepts are relevant to the decision to commit a crime. These concepts are relevant in all economic decision making, but they are particularly clear in the case of criminal activity. The first of these is the concept of *psychic income (costs)*. For example, a couple may choose to operate a family farm even though their opportunity costs are greater than the revenue from the farm's operation. This behaviour would be rational if they enjoyed the lifestyle associated with farming enough so that it compensated them for the lower

An individual receives **psychic income** when he or she gains personal satisfaction rather than money income. An individual can also bear **psychic costs** in the form of personal negative satisfaction (disutility) rather than money costs.

money income. On the other hand, the psychic costs associated with being a criminal may outweigh the "benefits" of a life a crime. Most individuals regard social condemnation as a significant cost of criminal behavior. Also many individuals have a sense of conscience that would result in significant psychic costs if they committed a crime. Economists recognize the existence of psychic costs and benefits in all areas of economic activity. It helps to explain why we have poor-but-honest citizens and rich crooks. However, economists are not particularly trained to understand psychic costs and benefits. The psychic costs and benefits of criminal behavior are better left to sociologists, psychologists, and religious leaders.

The other important concept in economics that the analysis of crime illustrates is the role of *risk and uncertainty* in economic decision making.[5] In textbook examples we can easily say that projected costs and revenues look like those in a hypothetical table. In real life, projected costs and revenues are uncertain. When farmers plant wheat in the spring, they do not know whether the weather will be favourable or the price at harvest will be high. One of the greatest potential costs for a criminal is the cost of punishment. Most criminals would find other work if they knew for certain that they would be caught and sent to prison. Different individuals have different attitudes towards risk and uncertainty. People who are risk adverse avoid taking chances. Others are more willing to take chances. In a normal context they can be valued members of society. In fact, their risk-taking behaviour leads to the entrepreneurial activity that creates economic growth. People who commit crimes are also likely to be risk takers. The more swift and certain the punishment is, the less likely that such individuals will undertake criminal acts. This fact implies that an effective policy to deal with crime is to put more resources into the quick arrest and conviction of criminals, as opposed to spending money on longer (but less certain) prison terms.

We make economic decisions on the basis of the best information available. When unknown factors can affect the outcome, economists say that there is **risk and/or uncertainty.**

Summary

Criminal activities are defined as activities that are illegal. They may or may not be immoral. They are usually classified as (1) violent offences, (2) property offences, (3) other criminal code offences, (4) federal statutes (non-drug), (5) federal statutes (drug), (6) provincial statutes, and (7) municipal bylaws. Crime constitutes a serious problem in Canada; crime rates generally have been increasing over the years. Some of the underlying causes of crime are (1) unrestrained passions or emotions, (2) poverty coupled with high levels of economic and social aspiration, and (3) low standards of social values.

---

[5]Economists often distinguish between *risk* and *uncertainty*. In this book we will lump them together.

Good information on the costs of crime is not available because many criminal activities go unreported and because placing dollar values on the results of some kinds of these activities is difficult. Some reported "costs" of crime are not really economic costs to the society as a whole but are transfers of income from the victim of the crime to its perpetrator. In an economic analysis of crime, we can classify goods and services into three categories: (1) private, (2) public, and (3) semipublic goods. Governments, with their coercive powers, are in a unique position to efficiently produce such public goods as crime prevention. Consequently, public goods of this type are usually provided by governments.

Cost-benefit analysis may be used to advantage in determining the optimal level of crime prevention activities in a society. The costs of crime prevention can be determined easily, but the benefits—many of which are intangible—are hard to estimate. Conceptually, they are the difference between what GDP would be with crime prevention and what it would be without such activities. On the basis of the best estimates that can be made, the society should seek that level of crime prevention at which the total net benefits are greatest. This level will be the one at which the marginal benefits of crime prevention are equal to its marginal costs of prevention. Economists use cost-benefit analysis to investigate a number of areas of social policy. It is important to understand that the estimates of both costs and benefits often involve the economist in making value judgments. While cost-benefit analysis is a valuable tool in the evaluation of public policy decisions, it is never an entirely objective tool.

Once the level of the government's crime prevention budget is determined, it should be efficiently allocated among the different facets of crime prevention activities. These include detection and apprehension of violators, determination of their guilt or innocence, and corrections. The most efficient allocation of the crime prevention budget among these facets is determined by applying the equimarginal principle. The most efficient allocation will be such that the marginal benefits from a dollar's worth of detection and apprehension are equal to the marginal benefits from a dollar's worth of each of the other two facets of crime prevention.

Economic analysis is also helpful in determining whether goods or services should be considered illegal. Typically, when an illegal activity is made legal, both supply and demand increase, although in most cases the increase in supply can be expected to be greater in degree than the increase in demand, leading to a fall in the equilibrium price of the activity and an increase in the equilibrium quantity purchased. Additionally, we can expect the quality of the good or service to increase. In each case, just the reverse may be anticipated if a currently legal activity is made illegal.

While economic analysis is limited in its ability to explain criminal behaviour, it can provide some insights into why criminals break the law. A rational criminal will not undertake a crime unless the expected revenue from the crime exceeds the expected costs of committing the crime. These benefits and costs included psychic income and psychic costs. A great amount of uncertainty is associated with undertaking a criminal act. Therefore, individuals can protect themselves from crime by increasing the cost to the criminal or by decreasing the revenue. Society can protect itself by increasing the opportunity costs of crime—particularly by increasing the certainty of punishment.

Checklist of Economic Concepts

Opportunity costs

Private goods

Public goods

Semipublic goods

"Free rider" problem

Marginal benefits

Marginal costs

Cost-benefit analysis

Equimarginal principle

Spillover costs

Spillover benefits

Risk and uncertainty

Psychic income and costs

Discussion Questions

1. If you were the head of a private investigations agency, you could easily measure the performance of your company—just look at the firm's profits. You are chief of police in a large Canadian city. Consider how you would evaluate the success of your department. (Hint: You might want to consider statistics like the number of crimes cleared by arrest or changes in the crime rate.) You should be able to think of several such measures. You should also think how each measure is flawed.

2. Your neighbour has a valuable stamp collection. He hires a private police service to regularly patrol his house. How do you benefit? What economic principle is involved?

3. There is political pressure for longer jail terms for convicted criminals. In light of the equimarginal principle, what are the possible consequences of an increase in jail terms?

4. A professional thief can break in to almost any house. Explain, from a thief's point of view, why better locks deter crime.

5. Many people suggest that Canada should legalize the possession of small amounts of cannabis (marijuana and hashish). In economic terms, what would be the benefits of legalization?

6. Alcohol and tobacco are legal. In economic terms, what costs are associated with the use of these drugs?

Supplementary Reading

Avio, K. L. and C. S. Clark. *Property Crime in Canada: An Econometric Study.* Toronto: Ontario Economic Council-University of Toronto Press, 1976.

Statistical material is completely out of date, but the economic model of crime (Chapter 2) is of interest. The methodology may also be of interest to students with an econometric background.

Boaz, David, ed. *The Crisis in Drug Prohibition.* Washington, DC: The Cato Institute, 1990.

Taken together, the essays in this text offer an in-depth, thoughtful, and balanced analysis of the question of legalizing drugs.

Brantingham, P. and S. Easton, *The Crime Bill: Who Pays and How Much?* Vancouver: The Fraser Institute, February, 1996.

A short monograph discussing the cost of crime in Canada. It provides some statistical background on crime in Canada and makes some useful international comparisons.

Caputo, T. C. "The Young Offenders Act: Children's Rights, Children's Wrongs." *Canadian Public Policy* 13, no. 2 (June 1987), pp. 125–143.

An overview of one of the most controversial areas within the Canadian criminal justice system.

Fleming, T. and L. A. Visano. *Crime, Law and Deviance in Canada.* Toronto: Butterworth & Co., (Canada), Ltd., 1983.

Something for everyone but relatively little economic content.

Hatt, K.; T. Caputo; and B. Perry. "Criminal Justice Policy Under Mulroney, 1984–90: Neo-Conservatism, Eh?" *Canadian Public Policy* 18, no. 3 (Sept. 1992), pp. 245–260 .

Discussion of changes to criminal justice policy under the Mulroney government.

Hofler, R. A. and A. D. White. "Benefit-Cost Analysis of the Sentencing Decision: The Case of Homicide." In *The Cost of Crime.* ed. C. M. Gray. Beverly Hills, CA. Sage Publications, 1979.

A step-by-step description of applying benefit-cost analysis to a criminal justice problem. Read it for the flavour rather than for the details.

Klein, J. F. *Let's Make a Deal.* Toronto: Lexington Books, 1976.

The deal under negotiation is a plea bargain. The book provides an interesting background on how the criminal justice system really works.

North, D. C. and R. L. Miller. *The Economics of Public Issues.* 5th ed. New York: Harper & Row, 1983.

Chapter 3 discusses the economic gains from legalizing prostitution. Chapter 28 stresses the economic nature of criminal activity. The authors argue that to reduce crime, the price paid (punishment) by the criminal must be increased.

Chapter 5

Pollution Problems
Must We Foul Our Own Nest?

Is Canada's environment in as good a state as we received it from the generation before us? Yes and No. In many ways the environment we pass on to our sons and daughters is healthier, as many of the worst instances of pollution have been improved. But many long-standing environmental problems remain inadequately resolved, and new problem areas and polluting substances continue to be discovered. What we don't know can surprise or even hurt us, and we continue to find major gaps in our knowledge base.

Are our actions sustainable? Not yet, although there are signs of progress. Although we are successfully reducing the levels of most pollutants that we measure, many hot spots remain to be cleaned up. Despite improvements in resource management, in many areas more is harvested than can be sustained or replenished.

Canadians continue to place greater stresses on the environment than individuals in most of the rest of the world. Progress is evident in the reduction, reuse, and recycling of some materials, but our lifestyle continues to be based on high levels of consumption.

There are signs of progress as Canadians begin to respond to the challenge of sustainable development. Canada has been an active international player, addressing global problems such as ozone depletion, acid rain, and climatic change. Canada's Green Plan is now in place. All provinces and territories have established round tables. As well, many industries are adopting environmental policies and codes of practice. Many communities and individuals have taken action at the local level. Nevertheless, despite these initiatives, it is evident that environmental factors are not yet central to the decisions and actions of most Canadians.

Major gaps remain in the information needed to report to Canadians on the state of the environment and the impacts of our actions. For many environmental problems there is no consistent monitoring. As a result, Canadians often do not receive the integrated information needed to support informed decisions regarding the environment.

In many respects we are taking better care of our environment than we did 25 years ago. But many problem areas remain, and our attitudes and actions need to change greatly if we are to successfully build a sustainable Canada for future generations. We will have to become not only better stewards of the environment, but better managers of our own actions and their impacts on the Ecosphere. We are at a crossroads—a sustainable path is evident, but we have not yet clearly chosen that path, and we are far from our ultimate destination.[1]

Most of us are concerned about environmental problems, but we are not quite sure what we can do about them. As individuals, we seem to

---

[1]From the conclusion of the *The State of Canada's Environment* (Ottawa: Government of Canada, 1991), p. 27–1.

believe that we can do little. In fact, we are likely to add to the problems by thinking that our own bit of pollution is just a drop in the bucket.

Public reaction to pollution varies a great deal. At one extreme are people who object to everything that decreases the purity of the air and water or that mars the natural beauty of the landscape. At the other extreme are those who seem not to value at all clean air, water, and natural beauty. Most of us are somewhere in between these two positions.

Economic analysis along with inputs from other disciplines—especially the natural sciences—can provide a framework for developing solutions to many pollution problems. In particular, economic analysis may help us (1) determine why and under what circumstances economic agents pollute, (2) determine the extent to which pollution control should be exercised, and (3) evaluate alternative antipollution activities of the government.

What Is Pollution?

We will not make much progress in an economic analysis of pollution until we are familiar with both the nature of the environment in which we live and what constitutes pollution of that environment. We shall consider these two concepts in turn.

The Environment and Its Services

The environment is easily defined. It consists of the air, water, and land around us. These components provide us with a variety of important services, including a habitat in which to live and resources with which to produce goods and services. The environment sustains and enriches us. In using the environment, however, both renewable and non-renewable resources may be depleted, affecting profoundly all life on the planet.

The services of the environment are used by producers and consumers as they engage in activities of various kinds. Producers lay heavy claims on the environment's resources, but they may also make use of its habitat and amenity characteristics.

As producers engage in the process of transforming raw and semifinished materials into goods and services that will satisfy human wants, they affect the environment in at least three ways. First, some of the environment's stocks of exhaustible resources may be diminished. These include coal, petroleum, and many mineral deposits. Second, it is called upon for replaceable resources like fish, timber, grassland, oxygen, and nitrogen. Third, it is used as a place to dispose of the wastes of the production and consumption processes—as a gigantic garbage disposal.

Recycling of Wastes and the Concept of Pollution

The pollution problem arises primarily from the use of the environment by producers and consumers as a dumping ground for wastes. We litter the countryside with cans, paper, and the other residues of consumption and production. We dump the emissions from our automobiles and factories into the atmosphere. We empty sewage and residue from production directly and indirectly into streams, rivers, and lakes.

As wastes from production and consumption are dumped into the environment, nature sets recycling processes in motion. Animals use oxygen, giving off carbon dioxide wastes. But plants use carbon dioxide, giving off oxygen wastes. Dead plant and animal life are attacked by chemical elements that decompose them, restoring to the soil elements that the living organisms had withdrawn from it. Living organisms frequently contribute to the decomposition process. Iron and steel objects rust and disintegrate over time. So does wood and other matter decompose. Wastes that can be decomposed in air, water, and soil are said to be biodegradable, but some wastes are not biodegradable. Aluminum containers such as beer cans are a case in point.

Recycling—the transformation of wastes into raw materials that are again usable—requires variable lengths of time, depending on what is being recycled. For example, it takes many years for a steel pipe to rust away. The time required for the complete disintegration of wood varies a great deal, but many plant and animal products decompose quickly.

Pollution consists of loading the environment with wastes that are not completely recycled, are not recycled fast enough, or are not recycled at all. It involves a diminution of the capacity of the environment to yield environmental services. Pollution occurs when recycling processes fail to prevent wastes from accumulating in the environment.

Common Forms of Pollution

Pollution is as old as civilization itself. Wherever people have congregated, their wastes have tended to pile up more rapidly than the forces of nature can digest them. As long as the world was sparsely populated and few permanent cities existed, no great problems were created. When the extent of pollution in one locale imposed costs on the people living there that outweighed the costs associated with moving, the residents simply moved away. Then, given time, natural recycling processes could in many cases take over and restore the excess wastes to usable form.

When towns and cities came into existence, pollution raised more serious problems. How could body wastes from humans and animals, as well as refuse from the daily round of living, be disposed of? Until fairly recent times, wastes were not disposed of in many instances—levels of sanitation were unbelievably low, and levels of stench were unbelievably high. As the density of the world's population has increased and as it has become more difficult to move away from pollution problems, the human race has turned its attention more and more toward the development of control measures. But in order to control pollution, it must be identified as accurately as possible in its various forms.

Air Pollution. In the processes of production and consumption, five major kinds of wastes are dumped into the atmosphere. Most result from combustion and have caused local problems for a long time, dating back to the 1800s in Britain. Since millions of cubic miles of atmosphere are able to absorb these wastes, however, air pollution did not cause great global concern until the last few decades. Additionally, indoor air pollution is becoming an increasing concern. Sources of this pollution include factory dust, cigarette smoke, and gases emitted by modern construction materials.

In 1969, the Canadian government introduced the *Clean Air Act* to address the problem of air pollution. National Ambient Air Quality Objectives were established by the federal government in the early 1970s to protect human health and the environment. They set limits for the following common air pollutants: carbon monoxide, sulphur oxides, nitrogen oxides, ozone, and total suspended particulates. All of these pollutants are measured under the National Air Pollution Surveillance program.

Carbon monoxide, an odourless, colourless gas, makes the atmosphere a less hospitable habitat for animal life. In concentrated amounts, it causes dizziness, headaches, and nausea in humans. Exposure to a sufficiently high concentration for a few hours can be fatal. Automobiles and other forms of transportation account for 29 percent of Canada's end-use energy demand and produce millions of tonnes of carbon monoxide, as well as carbon dioxide and various other pollutants. Retail sales of gasoline for motor vehicles account for 54 percent of these emissions, or 16 percent of end-use energy demand.[2] Emissions from energy use contribute to smog that plagues many Canadian communities. For example, in Vancouver, Calgary, Toronto, Ottawa, Montreal, and Quebec City air pollution from transportation has a major influence on air quality.

Sulfur oxides constitute a second major source of atmospheric pollution. Where they are heavily concentrated, they cause damage to both plant and animal life. Oxides result largely from the production and combustion of fuel oils and coal. Consequently, high levels of concentration are most likely to occur where these fuels are used for the generation of electricity and for residential heating.

---

[2]Statistics Canada, *Quarterly Report on Energy Supply-Demand in Canada*, 1990-IV, Catalogue No. 57–003 (Ottawa: 1990).

A third atmospheric pollutant is nitrogen oxides. These compounds can cause lung damage in human beings and may also retard plant growth. The main sources of this pollutant are automobiles and stationary combustion processes such as those used in generating electric power.

Ground-level ozone constitutes a fourth kind of air pollution. Ground-level ozone is created from chemical reactions in the air between volatile organic compounds (hydrocarbons) and nitrogen oxides and ultraviolet rays of the sun to form petrochemical smog. High ozone concentrations tend to occur under conditions of bright sunlight, high temperature, and a stable air mass and are therefore strongly influenced by weather conditions. The smog may produce breathing difficulties and eye irritation for human beings. The most serious recorded air-pollution episode in Canada was the "Grey Cup smog" of November 1962, which lasted five days. It caused an increase in hospital admissions throughout southern Ontario and forced the postponement of a football game in Toronto because of poor visibility.[3] In addition, ozone speeds up the oxidation processes to which paints and metals are subject, resulting in substantial damages to industrial plants and equipment. Almost 50 percent of hydrocarbon emissions behind ground-level ozone comes from industrial sources, and another 40 percent comes from automobiles. The highest smog concentrations are normally found in the Windsor–Quebec City corridor, the Saint John area of the Southern Atlantic region, and the Lower Fraser Valley in British Columbia.

A fifth air pollutant consists of a heterogeneous mixture of suspended solids and liquids called particulates. These are largely dust and ash, along with lead from automobile exhausts. The major source of particulates, however, is fuel combustion in stationary sources and in industrial processes and mining. Particulates reduce visibility. Open fires used to burn trash and garbage also make their contributions, although such fires have largely been banned in urban areas. Some particulates, such as lead from automobile exhausts, may be directly harmful to human beings, although lead too has been banned for use in gasoline.

Water Pollution. Water pollution is ordinarily measured in terms of the capacity of water to support aquatic life. This capacity depends on (1) the level of dissolved oxygen in the water and (2) the presence of matters or materials injurious to plant and animal life.

The level of dissolved oxygen is built up through aeration of water and through the photosynthetic processes of plant life living in the water. It is destroyed in the decomposition of organic matter that originates in or is dumped into the water. The oxygen needed for decomposition purposes is referred to as biochemical oxygen demand, or BOD. The level of dissolved oxygen available for supporting aquatic life, then, depends on

---

[3] *The Canadian Encyclopedia Plus* (Toronto, McClelland & Stewart Inc., 1995).

the balance between aeration and photosynthesis on the one hand and on BOD on the other.

Several factors affect the level of dissolved oxygen. First, it tends to be higher when the amount of a given volume of water exposed to the atmosphere is greater. In nature, fast-running streams, rapids, and waterfalls contribute to aeration. Artificial aeration is frequently accomplished by shooting streams of water through the air. Second, it tends to be higher when the amount of photosynthesis that occurs in the water is greater. In some instances, the amount of photosynthesis that occurs in aquatic plant life may be reduced by air pollution. In this way, air pollution may be a source of water pollution. Third, dissolved oxygen tends to be higher when the temperature of the water is lower. Use of the water for cooling by steel mills, oil refineries, and electricity-generating plants raises the temperature of the water, which lowers its capacity to hold dissolved oxygen. Fourth, organic wastes, from both domestic and industrial sources, create BOD so the level of dissolved oxygen varies inversely with the amounts of these wastes that are dumped. The decomposition of such wastes can be greatly facilitated, and BOD can be correspondingly reduced, by chemical treatment of such wastes before they are discharged into streams, rivers, lakes, or oceans.

The capacity of water to support aquatic life is reduced when various kinds of materials are dumped into it. Among these pollutants are toxins that do not settle out of the water and are not easily broken down by biological means. Mercury is a toxin that has created problems of contamination in various types of fish. Phenols, herbicides, and pesticides have also contributed greatly to the water pollution problem. Heated discussions in recent years have considered the propriety of using these substances in large quantities. Acid rain resulting from air pollution, specifically nitrogen oxide and sulphur dioxide, changes the pH factor of lakes, resulting in water pollution. Questions have been raised also as to whether the oceans should be used for the dumping of nuclear wastes and for undersea nuclear explosions.

Land Pollution. Land pollution results from the dumping of a wide variety of wastes on the terrain and from tearing up the earth's surface through such activities as strip-mining. Highways are littered with refuse thrown from passing automobiles. Junkyards grow as we scrap prodigious amounts of junked automobiles and other machinery and appliances that are retired from use. Garbage dumps and landfills grow as towns and cities dispose of the solid wastes they collect and accumulate. The disposal of tires illustrates the problem. About 20 million vehicle tires are discarded every year in Canada. Many are stockpiled, as there is no economic way to recycle them. This waste poses a blight on the land, as well as a significant hazard. One of the most dramatic cases was the fire that broke out near Hagersville, Ontario, in February 1990. The dump containing millions of used tires burned for 16 days, spewing oil and toxic smoke. The cost to put out the fire was $1.5 million, and it caused untold economic damage. Even more troubling are hazardous waste sites, many of which are located in densely populated parts of Ontario and Quebec. All of these dumps reduce the capacity of the terrain to render environmental services.

The growing emphasis on coal as an energy source creates mounting concern over the effects of mining on the landscape. Strip-mining has typically left unsightly blemishes on the countryside. Can and should the mined area be restored? In pit-mining areas, can and should steps be taken to make slag and rock piles more attractive?

The extensive cropping of the vast grasslands of the Canadian prairies is contributing to soil loss and desertification through wind and water erosion. Estimates suggest that as much as 50 percent of the original organic matter has been lost.

Economics of Pollution

No one likes pollution. Almost everyone would like to see something done about it. Toward this end, we consider in this section the fundamental economics of the pollution problem. We shall examine the reasons pollution occurs, analyze the effects of pollution on resource allocation, look at the costs of pollution control, and identify its benefits. We shall attempt to establish criteria for determining the appropriate level of control.

Why Polluters Pollute

Why is it that pollution occurs? What characteristics of environmental services cause consumers and producers to use the environment as a dumping ground? Ordinarily, pollution results from one or both of two basic factors: (1) the fact that no one has property rights or enforces them in the environment being polluted and (2) the public goods characteristics of the environment being polluted. Or, in more personal terms, inconsiderate individuals think only of the shortrun benefits to themselves (ease and cost of disposal), rather than of the longrun costs to the environment and the economy.

If no one owns a portion of the environment or if an owner cannot police it or have it policed, then it becomes possible for people to use a river, a lake, the air, or an area of land as a wastebasket without being charged for doing so. Because no one owns the air above city streets and highways, automobile owners can dump combustion gases into it without paying for the privilege of doing so. Similarly, a paper mill can dump its wastes into a river without charge because no one owns the river. But even ownership of the environment may not be enough to keep pollution from occurring. How many times have you seen litter accumulate on a vacant lot or junk dumped in a ditch in a pasture away from town because the owner was absent or did not take steps to prevent the dumping? And how many owners of land hold little appreciation for the indigenous flora and fauna or the public attributes of their land's aesthetic value?

In addition, many environmental services are public goods; that is, they are collectively consumed or used. It is hard to single out and determine the value of the air that one person—or an automobile—uses. Similarly, it is often difficult to attach a value to the water deterioration caused by one industrial plant when thousands dump their wastes into a river. Would any one person be willing to pay someone not to take an action that would destroy a beautiful view across the countryside? When values cannot be placed on the amounts of environmental services used by any one person, it is difficult to induce people not to pollute by charging them for doing so.

Pollution and Resource Allocation

In the process of polluting the environment, polluters impose *spillover costs* or *external diseconomies* on others. Polluters' costs are thus reduced below what they would be in the absence of pollution. On the other hand, costs to others (non-polluters) of using environmental services are greater than they would be in the absence of pollution. Polluters, then, are induced to overuse environmental services at the expense of other users, and other users of the polluted environment are induced to underuse them. Thus, pollution involves inefficient use or misallocation of environmental resources among those who use them.

Suppose, for example, that two industries are located along a river-bank. An industry producing paper is located upstream, using the river as a place to discharge its wastes. Downstream is a power-generating industry that requires large amounts of clean water for cooling purposes. If the paper industry were not there, the water from the river would be clean enough for the power industry to use. However, since the paper industry is there—just upstream—the firms in the power industry must clean the water before using it.

Since the use of the river by one set of parties as a dumping place for wastes may reduce the value of the river's services to other users, a transfer or spillover of costs may be incurred by the dumping. If recycling of the dumped wastes occurs fast enough, or if the environment is large enough relative to the wastes dumped into it so that no one is injured by the dumping, no cost or pollution problems occur.

The use of the river for waste disposal by the paper industry decreases the value of the river's services for power production in the example, so cost spillovers are involved in that dumping. In effect, the paper industry shifts some of its costs of production to the power industry—the power industry must pay to clean the water that the paper industry pollutes.

Figure 5–1   Effects of water pollution on water users

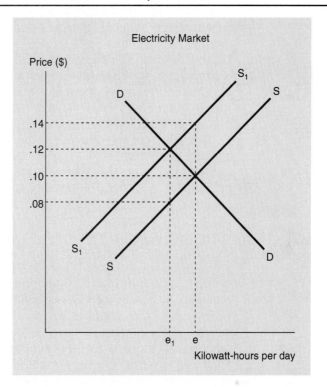

The demand curve for the output of the power industry is *DD*. Its supply curve, when it can obtain clean water, is *SS*. Consequently, it will produce and sell *e* kilowatt-hours per day at a price of 10 cents per kilowatt-hour. However, if a paper industry located upstream pollutes the water, costs of cleaning the water before using it move the supply curve to the left to $S_1 S_1$. The power industry accordingly reduces its output to e_1 and raises its price to 12 cents per kilowatt-hour. Both the power industry and its customers pay the costs of cleaning the paper industry's wastes from the water.

Consider first the power industry situation if there were no pollution by the paper industry. In Figure 5–1, the demand curve for power is *DD*, and the supply curve in the absence of pollution is *SS*. The equilibrium output is e, and the equilibrium price is 10 cents per kilowatt-hour. The cost of producing a kilowatt-hour at output level e is also 10 cents.

Suppose, now, that the power industry must clean the water before using it. Since it must cover its costs, the price that it must receive in order to induce it to produce any specific quantity of electricity will be higher by an amount equal to the costs per kilowatt-hour of cleaning the water. This is simply an application of the law of supply. Recall from Chapter 2 that supply decreases as the cost of production rises. Having to clean the water before use increases costs and thus reduces supply to S_1S_1. If the output of the power industry were e_1 kilowatt-hours, the price necessary to bring forth that output in the absence of pollution is 8 cents. With pollution occurring, the necessary price is 12 cents, with 4 cents being the cost per kilowatt-hour of cleaning the water. Similarly, for an output level of e, the required price in the absence of pollution is 10 cents; with pollution it is 14 cents, and the cost per kilowatt-hour of cleaning is also 4 cents. So the supply of electricity is decreased by the pollution of the paper industry from what it would be in the absence of pollution.

The effects of the decrease in the supply of electricity are a smaller quantity bought and sold, a higher price paid by consumers, and a lower return to producers than would be the case without the paper industry's pollution of the water. The quantity exchanged is reduced to e_1, the price paid by consumers goes up to 12 cents, and the return to producers after paying the cleaning costs for water decreases from 10 cents to 8 cents per kilowatt-hour. Thus we see that both the consumers and the producers of electricity bear the costs of pollution by the paper industry.

In addition, the power industry is induced to underproduce. The supply curve SS shows the opportunity costs per kilowatt-hour to the economy of producing various quantities of power when unpolluted water is used. For example, at output level e, the power industry must pay 10 cents for the resources necessary to produce 1 kilowatt-hour. Ten cents is what those resources could earn in alternative employments; it is what they are worth in those other employments, and it represents the opportunity cost to the economy of a kilowatt-hour of electricity. Similarly, at output level e_1, the opportunity cost of producing a kilowatt-hour is 8 cents. With the paper industry polluting the river, however, consumers pay 12 cents per kilowatt-hour, which is more than the costs of production. Whenever consumers are willing to pay more for an item than the cost to produce it, output usually expands. In this case, however, the power industry will not produce more electricity because, in addition to the production costs, it must incur an additional outlay, 4 cents per kilowatt-hour, to clean the water; that is, the power industry must pay to undo what the paper industry has done.

The supply of the paper industry is increased by its access to the river for waste disposal. In Figure 5–2, let SS be the paper industry's supply curve, assuming that the river is not available as a "free" dumping space. The supply curve shows the alternative prices that the paper industry must receive to induce it to produce and sell various quantities of paper. To induce it to produce and sell r reams, the price per ream must be $11. To induce it to place r_1 reams on the market, the price must be $13. Suppose now that the river is made available to the paper industry as a free dumping ground for wastes. The costs of producing a ream of paper are now reduced, and for an output level of r reams per day, the price need not be higher than $7—if the cost saving per ream is $4. Similarly, for r_1 reams

Figure 5–2   **Effects of water pollution on the polluter**

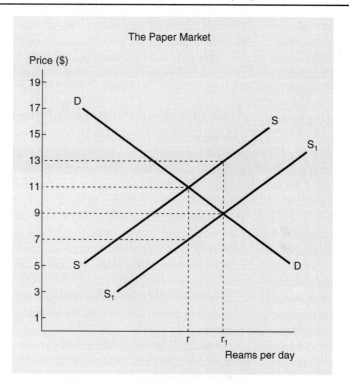

The Paper Market

The demand curve for the output of the paper industry is *DD*. When it must clean its own wastes, its supply curve is *SS* and its output level will be *r* reams of paper per day. If it can dump its wastes into the river, cleaning costs are saved and its supply curve shifts to the right to S_1S_1. Its output will increase to r_1, and it is able to shift a part of its costs to downstream users of the water.

and a cost saving of $4, the necessary price is $9. The supply curve of paper is thus shifted to the right due to the fall in the cost of production brought about by the accessibility of the river as a free place to dispose of its wastes.

The same type of reasoning that tells us the power industry under-produces because of the paper industry's pollution also tells us the paper industry overproduces. In Figure 5–2 *DD* is the demand curve for paper. If the paper industry were to bear the costs of its dumping of wastes by leaving clean water for the power plant, its supply curve would be *SS*, its price would be $11, and its output level would be *r*. However, since the paper industry is able to use the river for waste disposal, its supply curve becomes S_1S_1, it produces r_1 reams of paper per day, and, it sells its product for $9 per ream. The evidence of overproduction is that opportunity costs per ream of paper exceed what consumers pay to get it. The opportunity cost per ream is $13. Of this amount, $9 is the cost to the paper industry of resources other than waste disposal used in the production of a ream of paper at output level r_1, and $4 is the cost of waste disposal that is transferred to the power industry per ream of paper produced. This latter amount is not taken into account by the paper industry, so the true cost of a ream of paper exceeds what it is worth to consumers.

The Costs of Controlling Pollution

Our reactions to pollution often motivate us to say, "Let's wipe it out." We feel we are entitled to clean air, clean water, and clean land. But how clean is clean? Cleanliness, like goodness, is a relative, rather than an absolute, quality. To determine the amount of pollution, if any, that should be allowed, we must first consider the costs of keeping the environment clean. Pollution control is not without cost. An industrial plant that scrubs or cleans its combustion gases before discharging them into the air must use resources in the process. labour and capital go into the making and operation of antipollution devices, and resources so used are not available to produce other goods and services. The value of the goods and services that must be given up is the cost of the plant's pollution control activities. The cost of pollution control is a straightforward application of the opportunity cost principle.

The costs of pollution control to society are illustrated graphically by the production possibilities curve of Figure 5–3. The worth in dollars of all goods and services other than pollution control are measured on the vertical axis, and the worth of pollution control is measured on the horizontal axis. At point A_1, the labour and capital of the economy are producing q_1 dollars' worth of goods and services and c_1 dollars' worth of antipollution activities. If still more pollution control—a cleaner environment—is desired, some value of goods and services must be sacrificed. By giving up $q_2 q_1$ dollars' worth of goods and services, pollution control can be increased by $c_1 c_2$ dollars' worth. Thus $q_2 q_1$ dollars' worth of goods and services is the economic cost of an additional $c_1 c_2$ dollars' worth of control or of a cleaner environment.

The Benefits of Controlling Pollution

The benefits of pollution control consist of the increase in the well-being of the members of the society that results from having a cleaner environment in which to live. To measure the benefits of a pollution control activity, we must determine the value of the increase in wellbeing that it generates. Suppose, for example, that smog permeates a particular metropolitan area but that pollution control activities can reduce or perhaps even eliminate it. To determine the benefits of, say, a 50 percent reduction in smog, we can ask each individual living in the area how much such a reduction would

Figure 5–3   The costs of pollution control

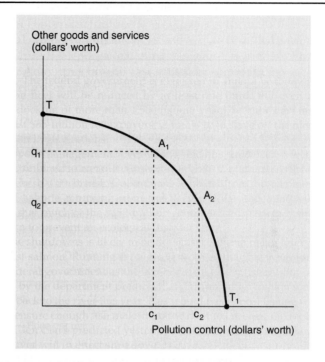

The combinations of other goods and services and pollution control that the resources of the economy can support are shown by the production possibilities curve TT_1. By giving up q_1T dollars' worth of other goods and services, the economy can have c_1 dollars' worth of pollution control, as shown at point A_1. If c_1c_2 more dollars' worth of pollution control are to be obtained, the cost will be q_2q_1 additional dollars' worth of other goods and services.

be worth personally. By totalling all the replies, we would arrive at the dollar value of the expected benefits.

The Appropriate Level of Pollution Control

Since pollution control—a cleaner environment—has costs, society must make a choice between the level of goods and services its resources will be used to produce and the degree of cleanliness of its environment. If the society experiences a level of pollution that is distasteful, the society will be willing to sacrifice some quantities of goods and services for some level of pollution control.

The appropriate level of pollution control is determined by weighing its benefits against its costs. If the benefits of additional control—what cleaner air is worth to the citizens of the society—exceed the costs of the additional

Table 5–1			Annual costs and benefits of pollution control (hypothetical data)			
(1)	(2)	(3)	(4)	(5) Community	(6)	(7)
Pollution Control or Eliminated Stench	Total Cost of Control ($000)	Marginal Cost of Control ($000)	Per Person Marginal Benefits of Control	Community Marginal Benefits of Control ($000)	Total Benefits of Control ($000)	Net Benefits of Control ($000)
1st 10%	$10	$10	$10.00	$100	$100	$ 90
2nd 10	20	10	8.00	80	180	160
3rd 10	30	10	6.00	60	240	210
4th 10	40	10	4.00	40	280	240
5th 10	50	10	2.00	20	300	250
6th 10	60	10	1.60	16	316	256
7th 10	70	10	1.20	12	328	258
8th 10	80	10	0.80	8	336	256
9th 10	90	10	0.40	4	340	250
10th 10	100	10	0.20	1	341	241

control, then pollution control should be increased. However, if the benefits of additional control are less than their costs in terms of sacrificed goods and services, the additional control is unwarranted. You should recognize this logic as another application of cost-benefit analysis, which was presented in Chapter 4 in the context of the appropriate level of crime prevention.

As an illustration, consider a community of 10,000 persons that is pervaded by a nauseating stench from an incinerator used to dispose of the community's garbage. Suppose that the odour can be completely eliminated by an expenditure of $100,000 per year for an alternate method of garbage disposal (carrying it away and burying it in a landfill outside the town) and that it can be partially controlled by using various combinations of burning and burying.

Suppose that the costs of different levels of partial control are those of columns (1), (2), and (3) of Table 5–1. By spending $10,000 on carrying and burying, the community can eliminate 10 percent of the stench; each additional $10,000 expenditure eliminates another 10 percent of the original total stench until a $100,000 expenditure entirely eliminates the pollution.

Column (3) of Table 5–1 lists the marginal costs of pollution control. The concept is essentially the same as the marginal costs of crime prevention—it shows the change in total costs per unit change in the amount of pollution control. Since each increment in pollution control (an increment is defined as 10 percent of the control needed to eliminate the odour) adds

$10,000 to the total cost of pollution control, the marginal cost of pollution control at each control level is $10,000. The assumption of constant marginal cost of pollution control is used here merely to facilitate the analysis. The more typical case is for marginal cost to rise as pollution control is expanded. This case will be discussed later in this chapter.

The benefits of pollution control to the community are shown in columns (4), (5), and (6). Before any control is undertaken, each person in the community is asked for an opinion of what a 10 percent reduction in the stench is worth. If each person indicates a willingness to pay $10, we conclude that $100,000 measures the total benefits yielded by the first 10 percent reduction. Since the benefits exceed the costs by $90,000, the first 10 percent reduction is clearly warranted.

The question now arises as to whether a second 10 percent reduction in the stench is worthwhile. Since the pollution is not as intense as it was with no control, a second 10 percent reduction is of less value than was the first one. If each person values the move from 10 percent control to 20 percent control at $8, the community valuation of the extra control—or the marginal benefit of it—is $80,000. Since the marginal costs of the additional control are only $10,000, putting it into effect adds $70,000 more to the total net benefits of control and is therefore a good investment for the community.

Column (5) shows the community's marginal benefits at different levels of control. We define the marginal benefits of pollution control, like the marginal benefits of crime prevention, as the change in total benefits per unit change in whatever element yields the benefits. Note that the total benefits at any given level of control are obtained by adding up the marginal benefits as the level of control is increased unit by unit up to that level.

Marginal benefits, as shown in Table 5–1, decline as the level of pollution control is increased (the level of the stench decreases), which is what we would expect to happen in this case. The greater the amount of control, or the lower the level of the stench, the less urgent additional control becomes. Falling marginal benefits as pollution control is increased will be the usual situation in controlling pollution.

The level of pollution control yielding the maximum net benefits to the people of the community is the level at which the marginal benefits just cease to exceed the marginal costs. The marginal benefits of the first two 10 percent increments in the total amount of control needed to eliminate the stench exceed the marginal costs of making them. Thus net benefits are increased by increasing control at least to the 20 percent level. The third, fourth, fifth, sixth, and seventh 10 percent increments also yield marginal benefits exceeding their marginal costs, and they increase the net benefits of control to the community. Now consider the eighth 10 percent increment. Marginal benefits are $8,000, and marginal costs are $10,000. Extending pollution control from the 70 percent level to the 80 percent level reduces the net benefits by $2,000. The eighth 10 percent increment is not worth to the community what it costs.

The principle is perfectly general. Net benefits will always increase by increasing control if the marginal benefits of the increase are greater than its marginal costs. Net benefits will decrease from an increase in the control level if the marginal benefits of that increase are less than its marginal costs. The appropriate level of control is the one that approaches as closely as possible the level where the marginal benefits equal the marginal costs.

What Can We Do about Pollution?

Typical recommendations call for direct control of pollution by the government. But this avenue is only one of the possible ways to reduce pollution problems. Others include indirect government control through a system of incentives encouraging potential polluters not to pollute or to limit their pollution and government creation of markets for the right to pollute.

Direct Controls

An appealing, simple way to control pollution is to have the government ban polluting activities or materials. If phosphates contaminate water, then ban the use of phosphates in detergents. If DDT pollutes water and land, ban the use of DDT. If the burning of fuel oil and coal increases the sulfur oxide content of the atmosphere, prohibit their use. Require industrial plants to clean the pollutants from whatever they discharge into the atmosphere or water. The method is straightforward and, on the face of it, seems eminently fair.

Government agencies, notably Environment Canada at the federal level, use direct controls to reduce many kinds of polluting activities. They set and attempt to enforce emission standards for such polluters as automobiles, power plants, and steel mills. Environment Canada enforces legislation that protects the environment, ensuring compliance with federal laws and regulations aimed at reducing pollution and protecting wildlife. These acts include the *Canadian Environmental Protection Act* (CEPA), the pollution prevention provisions of the *Fisheries Act*, the *Canada Wildlife Act*, the *Migratory Birds Convention Act*, and the *Wild Animal and Plant Protection and Regulation of International and Interprovincial Trade Act*.

Environment Canada supervises most provincial regulation of polluters, to the extent that it is accomplished. "The roles of the federal and provincial governments in ensuring compliance are being defined through separate agreements with each province and territory. The agreements will ensure consistent environmental and wildlife protection across Canada, while minimizing overlap and duplication between the activities of the different levels of government. Each level will have full authority for enforcement within its own area of jurisdiction."[4]

The case of the city with the terrible stench shows that complete prohibition of pollutants is not likely to be worth its costs. Pollution control uses resources that could have produced goods and services, and the value of the goods and services forgone is the opportunity cost to society of controlling the pollution. If the damage done by an additional unit of pollution is less than the costs of preventing it from occurring, community welfare is greater if it is allowed to occur. Consequently, direct controls usually aim at a less idealistic goal than a pollution-free environment. They may take the form of controlling the level of pollution by such devices as setting emissions standards or limits for industrial plants, automobiles, and other polluters.

One problem raised by the use of direct controls to limit the amount of pollution is that it presupposes the regulatory body can determine the economically desirable levels of pollution. This problem is not insurmountable. Tolerance limits on the amount of pollution to be allowed can be reasonably well established. Within those limits, overall costs can be weighed continually against benefits to establish an approximation of the desirable levels of pollution.

A second problem is the difficulty facing a regulatory body in achieving an efficient allocation of the permissible pollution among different polluters. For example, eliminating a unit of sulfur dioxide from its emissions may be more costly for a steel mill than it is for a power plant. In the interests of economic efficiency, the best solution is to eliminate pollution where it is least costly to do so. Thus the power plant should be required to reduce its sulfur dioxide emission before the steel mill is required to do so. Making this kind of decision is difficult for a regulatory body because it is responsible to a political body for which economic efficiency is not a primary goal.

In addition, a third problem is the inability to obtain perfect information. It is unrealistic to suppose that the regulatory body has a working knowledge of the economic damage of each pollutant and of the nature of costs of every polluter. Also, it is unreasonable to assume the relevant information is easily available.

A fourth problem is that of enforcing the standards of emissions once those standards have been determined. Direct controls fail to provide polluters with an economic incentive not to pollute. In fact, polluters will benefit by seeking ways and means to evade the pollution standards set for them. But we should not overstate the enforcement problem. Almost any prohibition of activities that individuals and business firms want to engage in creates enforcement problems.

---

[4]Enforcement Bulletin, Environmental Protection Service, Environment Canada, February 27, 1995.

Indirect Controls

The government can control many types of pollution by placing taxes on polluting activities. When the amounts of polluting discharges can be measured for individual polluters, a tax can be placed directly on each unit of discharge. This tax will induce the polluter to reduce the amount of pollution it discharges. In some cases when measurement is not possible, polluters may be taxed indirectly—for example, automobiles not equipped with pollution control devices can be subjected to a tax on a mileage basis. This tax would induce the vehicle owners either to install pollution control devices or to drive less. At this time, not much use has been made of this method of control.

Figure 5–4 illustrates the use of a tax to control the amount of pollutants discharged into the environment. Consider an industrial concern

Figure 5–4   Pollution control by means of a tax on polluting discharges

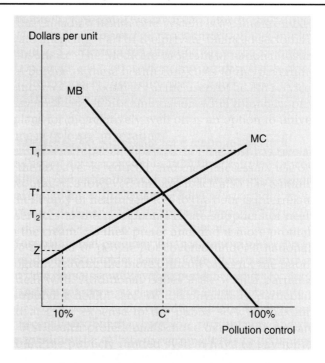

When the tax exceeds the marginal cost of control, a firm will choose to eliminate its polluting discharge and avoid the tax. If the cost and benefits of pollution control can be accurately estimated, a tax can be established that will cause the firm to voluntarily produce the appropriate level of pollution control. In this case, a tax of T^* per unit of polluting discharge will bring about the optimal level of pollution control C^*.

that discharges its polluting wastes into a river. Processes for cleaning the wastes to control the extent of pollution are available, but they are not free. As shown in Figure 5–4, as more of the pollution is suppressed, that is, as we approach 100 percent control, the marginal cost of additional control rises. For example, suppose that the polluting discharge is a composite of a number of chemical wastes. If the firm is left on its own to clean up the discharge, what strategy will it follow? Given that a number of chemical wastes are involved, the rational firm will first eliminate those wastes that it can eliminate most cheaply. The waste that can only be eliminated with extreme cost will be saved until last. This approach is simply the rational firm's response to the problem of eliminating its discharge. In other cases, the polluting discharge may involve only one offending substance, and we can expect the marginal cost of control to rise as control is pressed toward 100 percent. For example, minor adjustments in the production process might yield modest increases in pollution control, while complete elimination of the polluting discharge may only be brought about by a complete overhaul of the production process.

Regardless of the exact reasoning, the marginal cost of pollution control can be expected to rise as the degree of control increases, giving the positively sloped marginal cost curve of Figure 5–4. From the opposite perspective, as we have already discussed, the marginal benefits of pollution control to society are likely to fall as the degree of control is increased, giving the negatively sloped marginal benefits curve of Figure 5–4.

As discussed earlier in this chapter, we can identify the appropriate level of pollution control in this situation as C^*, that is, that level at which the benefits of additional control just cease to outweigh the cost of additional control. If C^* is the desired level of pollution control, how can it be achieved through taxation? As you have probably already guessed, a tax of T^* per unit of polluting discharge will bring about the desired degree of pollution control C^*. The reason for this is clear: For units of pollution control below C^*, the firm will eliminate its discharge and avoid the tax because the marginal cost of control is less than the tax. For example, the marginal cost of the first 10 percent unit of pollution control is Z dollars. Put differently, the firm can eliminate 10 percent of its polluting discharge if it incurs a cost of Z dollars. In doing so, the firm avoids paying the tax of T^*. Consequently, the firm can save $T^* - Z$ dollars by eliminating the first unit of pollution. Savings of this nature to the firm exist for each unit of pollution control up to the C^* level. Beyond this level, the firm will choose to pay the tax because the tax is less than the cost of control.

It is equally important to realize that such a tax regimen can lead to less than optimal outcomes. For example, a tax of T_1 per unit will result in too much pollution control effort and, thus, too much of the economy's scarce resources devoted to pollution control, whereas a tax of T_2 per unit will result in too little control and too little of the economy's resources devoted to this purpose. Can you explain why?

The use of taxes to control pollution has advantages. A major one is that the tax provides an incentive to the polluter to seek improved ways and means of avoiding or cleaning up its discharge. Another advantage is that the tax prevents the polluter from shifting some of its production costs (pollution costs) to others; it reduces the incentive to overproduce.

This type of tax also has disadvantages. First, determining the benefits—total and marginal—to society of cleaning the discharge is usually difficult. The criticism should not be carried too far, however, since it applies to any attempt to control pollution. Second, enforcement of such a tax is not easy. Policing is necessary to determine that the discharge is indeed properly cleaned. Third, taxes are levied by political rather than economic bodies, and politics may well get in the way of the enactment of appropriate tax levels.

The federal government has also used subsidies—the opposite of taxes—extensively as a pollution control measure. These consist primarily of grants made to provinces and local governments for the construction of sewage treatment facilities.

Creation of Pollution Rights Markets

The absence of well-defined property rights to the use of the environment's services is the primary source of pollution problems. Recall the example of the upstream paper industry and the downstream power industry. Since neither owns the river, that is, since neither has a property right to use the river, the paper industry is able to use the river as a sewer for its polluting wastes and the cost of cleaning the wastes falls on the power industry.

In many such instances, government can bring about the optimal level of pollution control in a cost-efficient manner through the establishment of a *pollution rights market* in which firms buy and sell government-issued licences to pollute. Specifically, the government can determine how much discharge it wishes to allow based on marginal benefit and marginal cost analysis, print licences or permits that in total grant the holders the right to discharge the optimal amount, and then allocate to the polluting firms a share of these licences.

When firms are allowed to buy and sell government-issued licences granting the holder the right to create a certain amount of pollution, the resulting market is called a **pollution rights market.**

To see how this system might work, suppose that after the market for pollution rights on the river has been in operation for some time, an equilibrium price is established—a firm can purchase the right to dump 100,000 gallons of discharge into the river for $1,000. Any paper producer capable of making a 100,000-gallon reduction in its discharge for less than $1,000 could increase its profits by making the reduction and then selling a licence to dump 100,000 gallons of waste that it holds to another firm. Any firm that could only reduce its discharge by 100,000 gallons at a cost greater than $1,000 would be happy to purchase this licence because the difference between the licence price of $1,000 and the cost of the reduction in discharge would be directly added to profits. If the government wants to reduce the overall level of pollution, it could buy back some of the licences it had previously made available to the market. In this way, the government can achieve any particular level of pollution control it wishes, and it can be sure that any needed reductions in pollution will be made where it is cheapest to do so. Put differently, through the establishment of a pollution rights market, the government can accomplish any desired level of pollution control in a way that places the least burden on the economy's scarce resources.

Interestingly, the use of pollution rights licences and the resulting creation of a pollution rights market is not just an academic exercise. Although this method has been applied in Canada, Chile, and other countries, the United States Environmental Protection Agency (EPA) is in the forefront in the use of property rights to control pollution.[5] A major problem in North America is acid rain, and one of the main contributors is sulphur dioxide emissions. To address this problem, the EPA has set a target for total U.S. emissions from stationary sources of some 9 million tonnes a year. In the *Clean Air Act* of 1990, the US federal government took its initial steps in this direction by allowing electric companies to trade in sulfur dioxide licences. Specifically, the act allowed roughly 100 utilities operating principally in the Midwest to produce a certain amount of sulfur dioxide discharge each year. Firms that could reduce their discharge cheaply were allowed to sell their licences to others. Those that could not reduce their discharge as cheaply could then purchase the right to continue to pollute. The reduction will be achieved in two phases. Phase I began in January 1995 and is designed to achieve a 5-million tonne reduction in SO_2, relative to baseline levels, while phase II is scheduled to begin on January 1, 2000, and imposes further reductions. Estimates are that this approach should bring about the desired reduction in overall pollution at a savings of $1 billion per year when compared to a direct control such as requiring equal reductions in discharge from all firms.

International Agreements

A number of environmental problems go beyond national borders. Many even have adverse global effects, for example, the deterioration of the ozone layer, global warming, and the loss of biodiversity. Thus, in addition to the problems associated with implementing domestic environmental policies, a further complication arises whenever countries must grapple with international pollution effects. Pollution does not recognize national

---

[5]For a review of the control of air pollution in the United States, See N. Kete, "Air Pollution Control in the United States: A Mixed Portfolio Approach," in *Economic Instruments for Air Pollution Control*, ed. by G. Klaasen and F. R. Forsund (Dordrecht: Kluwer Academic Publishers, 1994).

boundaries. Without international cooperation, many pollution problems cannot be addressed.

Using multilateral agreements to reduce emissions is complicated by a number of factors. (1) Countries may not join an agreement, choosing to free ride, especially when the cost of complying with the agreements is large. This problem is especially difficult in the case of greenhouse gas emissions where the total costs of stabilizing carbon emissions to 1990 levels is estimated to be about 4 percent of world gross domestic product per year.[6] (2) Even if countries sign international agreements, the problem of verification and enforcement between countries remains. (3) Designing a mechanism for pollution control perceived by all countries as "fair" can also be difficult, particularly when the costs and benefits of pollution control are not evenly distributed across countries. For example, should the developing world be expected to reduce its emissions in the same proportion as the United States? (4) The planning horizon and the weight placed on the present generation relative to future generations may vary across countries, leading to different preferences in terms of when and how emissions should be reduced. (5) Scientific opinions about the expected impacts on the environment may vary.

Despite the potential difficulties of establishing successful international agreements to protect the environment, some notable successes include the protocols to reduce and eliminate chlorofluorcarbons (CFCs), the U.N. Law of the Sea Conference on Marine Resources, the International Convention for the Regulation of Whaling, and the Convention on International Trade in Endangered Species of Wild Fauna and Flora, among others. Successful agreements require compromise among countries, a promotion of scientific exchange, and some sharing of either the benefits or costs among countries affected.

The reasons for the successes and failures of international co-operation may be illustrated by comparing the agreements on the elimination on CFCs and the climate convention on greenhouse gases. In the case of CFCs, a number of countries took unilateral action in the 1970s and early 1980s to reduce their use because of the belief that CFCs may damage stratospheric ozone. In 1985 British scientists published the discovery of a large atmospheric ozone hole in Antarctica, and in 1988 a significant loss of ozone was found in the Arctic and temperate latitudes. By this time, the evidence that CFCs caused the ozone layer depletion was overwhelming. Given that an average ozone loss of 1 percent may cause a 2 percent increase in skin cancers as well as other problems, many governments became alarmed. As a

---

[6]The information in this section is taken from Quentin, G.R., G. L. Flanagan, and R. A. Devlin, "The Environment and Pollution: An Economic Perspective of Regulation" (Ottawa: working paper 1996). The information about international pollution agreements is expanded and documented in this paper.

direct result of this concern, the 1987 Montreal Protocol specified 50 percent reductions in the principal CFCs by 1999. Similarly, the 1990 London amendments agreed to phase out CFCs by the year 2000. The London amendments also set up a fund for technology transfer and assistance to help developing countries to meet their obligations. To meet the agreement most countries have used standards and controls, although a major producer, the United States, has also instituted a permit system for producers of CFCs and imposed taxes on ozone depleting chemicals.

The 1992 Framework Convention on Climate Change (CCC) to control greenhouse gases has as its goal to keep emissions to their 1990 level. Unlike the Montreal Protocol, the CCC lacks specific commitments to developing countries. It exempts countries from complying with the guidelines if other social and economic goals are of greater priority. Furthermore, unlike the targets for CFC reductions, which are being met, several important members of the agreement, such as the European Union, are projected to increase their emissions well into the next century. And, as yet, there is no agreement about imposing a uniform carbon tax in Europe. The CCC does have some innovative features and allows countries to offset their reductions by either paying to reduce emissions in other nations or by funding "carbon sinks." However, only in countries with land suitable for forests, such as Canada, Russia, and Brazil, will carbon sinks in the form of forestation be a viable option. Achieving the guidelines of the Convention is left to individual countries who may employ direct and indirect controls. International carbon permits were initially allocated on a per capita basis. They have also been proposed as a means for achieving the guidelines of the Convention simultaneously with a transfer of resources from the developed to developing countries.

Several factors may explain both the poor reception accorded the CCC as well as the success of the Montreal Protocol. First, the problem of CFC emissions is well accepted while the potential impact of greenhouse gases is less certain and will take generations to measure. Second, and most importantly, CFCs represent only a tiny fraction of the world economy and commercially available substitutes exist (although they are more expensive). Some estimates place the cost of meeting just the U.S. carbon dioxide emission guidelines to be between US$800 billion and US$3.6 trillion. Given that fossil fuels are a primary input to industry and transportation, the opposition to increases in their costs is formidable in industrialized countries. In addition, a significant increase in energy costs is likely to reduce economic growth rates, further reducing the incentive for their adoption.

In 1992 the United Nations Conference on Environment and Development (UNCED), "Earth Summit," was held in Rio de Janeiro. The 178 countries represented adopted Agenda 21—a blueprint for sustainable development. Agenda 21 was a statement of 27 non-binding principles and globally coordinated plans for action on environmental concerns and economic development. This plan was extended in Copenhagen and Cairo in 1994, in Beijing in 1995, and in Istanbul in 1996 where more detailed plans of action were produced as part of Agenda 21. The jury is still out on whether anything concrete was achieved by this summit. The conference was useful, however, by bringing so many countries together at once in order to consider common global environmental issues. UNCED also increased the realization that the environment and the economy cannot be treated as separate issues. The nations agreed on the principles to guide environment and development policy and endorsed an 800-page action plan. Additionally the conference helped generate a broad-based interest in environmental and development issues.

Whatever the difficulties in ensuring international co-operation, international agreements are necessary to deal with global environmental problems. Successfully implementing such agreements requires an innovative mix of institution building and regulations that may include legal liability, permits, environmental taxes, and standards and controls. The goal of these agreements is not so much to achieve an "efficient" outcome, which is not possible, but to form sustainable coalitions that make all participants collectively better off. Inevitably, this result must involve political and economic trade-offs.

Summary

The environment provides environmental services that are used by both consumers and producers, and in the processes of consumption and production wastes are generated. If the ecological system cannot recycle these wastes as fast as they are generated, wastes accumulate. Accumulated waste constitutes pollution.

Economic analysis of pollution provides a perspective on its causes and its effects, along with the costs and benefits of controlling it. Incentives to pollute stem from (1) an absence of property rights in the environment and (2) the collectively consumed nature of whatever is being polluted. Polluters, by polluting, transfer a part of their costs to others. Cost-benefit analysis is useful in determining how much pollution should be allowed and indicates that it is seldom in the common interest to forbid pollution altogether.

There are three main avenues that government pollution control policies can take. First, certain polluting activities may be controlled directly through prohibitions or limitations on polluting activities. Second, they may be controlled indirectly by providing polluters with incentives not to pollute—say through taxation of polluting activities. Third, some cases of pollution may be efficiently controlled by the creation of markets for pollution rights in which firms buy and sell government-issued licences to pollute.

Many pollution problems go beyond national boundaries. The global nature of pollution creates the need for international agreements that implement environmental policies. Without international cooperation, many pollution problems cannot be addressed. To date, the experience with international agreements has been mixed. For agreements to be successful, the countries must have a common appreciation of the problem, agree to share the costs and efforts needed to address the problem, and also receive a fair share of the benefits that their efforts achieve.

As a final note, the use of economics can shed a great deal of light on environmental problems, but in the final analysis economics depends on the estimation of costs and benefits, which in many cases must remain subjective.

Checklist of Economic Concepts

Public goods and services	Marginal costs
Demand	Marginal benefits
Supply	Spillover costs, social
Opportunity costs	Efficiency, economic
Production possibilities curve	Pollution rights markets
Cost-benefit analysis	

Discussion Questions

1. Humans use both renewable and non-renewable resources for their needs. Describe policies for an appropriate use of these types of resources. Explain how and why these policies need to change.

2. Cigarette smoking increases the incidence of sickness and death. Relatively recent research has shown that non-smokers who are exposed to second-hand smoke also face an increased risk of disease and a reduced life expectancy. Use demand and supply analysis to explain how this spillover cost results in an inefficient market outcome. Many Canadian cities are banning cigarette smoking in public places, including restaurants. Comment on how this ban changes the analysis.

3. Explain what direct pollution controls are and discuss the problems in their application.

4. Pulp and paper mills are located near lakes, rivers, or oceans because they use large amounts of water in their production processes. By-products of paper production reduce the quality of the water and have an adverse effect on fish and other wildlife. Often, the cost imposed by this pollution is not taken into account in the

market. Illustrate how the government could use indirect controls in order to improve upon the unregulated market outcome.

5. What policies could address the spillover costs associated with the emissions of sulphur dioxide and the problems of acid rain migrating across the Canada–U.S. border?

6. Lawrence Summers, formerly chief economist at the World Bank, suggested in a memo to his staff that the Bank should be encouraging the migration of "dirty" industries to the Third World. He argued the following:

   • The value of a deterioration in the environment can be measured in increased illness and death. Consequently, health-impairing pollution with lost days at work and reduced life expectancy should mean that the cost to the environment for an equivalent level of pollution will be less in low-wage economies than in high-wage economies.

   • The marginal cost curve from pollution is likely to be gently sloped for low levels of pollution but be very steeply sloped at high levels of pollution because of "threshold" effects. Thus a transfer of pollution from relatively highly polluted developed countries to relatively unpolluted developing countries should be beneficial to both parties.

   • The demand for a clean environment is likely to have a high and positive income elasticity.

   Critically discuss these arguments including analysis from an economic perspective.

Supplementary Reading

Anderson, F. J. *Natural Resources in Canada, Economic Theory and Policy.* Scarborough, ON: Nelson, 1991.
Chapter 3, pp. 70–102 gives a more thorough discussion of the pollution control model.

Baumol, W. J. and W. E. Oates. *Economics, Environmental Policy, and the Quality of Life.* Englewood Cliffs, NJ: Prentice Hall, 1979.
An excellent and very readable exposition of the environmental dilemma. Includes topics such as the absence of property rights in causing problems, the incidence of the costs and benefits of pollution control, the appropriate level of pollution, and the pros and cons of various environmental policies.

Carson, R. B. *Economic Issues Today.* New York: St. Martin's Press, 1987, pp. 70–86.
Analyzes the acid rain problem by considering both conservative and liberal arguments.

Dorfman, R. and N. S. Dorfman. *Economics of the Environment.* New York: W. W. Norton & Company, 1993.

A classic set of papers including works by the most influential authors working on environmental problems. A must for any serious student of the environment.

Field, B. C. and N. Olewiler. *Environmental Economics. 1st Canadian Ed.* Toronto: McGraw-Hill, 1995.

A textbook treatment of environmental economics that goes well beyond the introductory material in this chapter. See pages 481–483 for a list of selected international agreements.

Garbage: The Practical Journal for the Environment. Various issues, monthly.

Offers a wealth of well-balanced information about the various problems and proposed solutions of pollution. Sample articles of interest include W. L. Rathue. "The History of Garbage." September 1990, pp. 32–42; Janet Marinelli. "After the Flush." January 1990, pp. 24–36; and R. Kourik. "What's So Great about Seattle." November 1990, pp. 24–32.

Levy, M. A.; R. O. Keohane; and P. M. Hass, eds., *Institutions for the Earth: Sources of Effective International Environmental Protection.* Cambridge, MA: MIT Press, 1993.

An article by the editors discusses how to improve the effectiveness of international environmental institutions. The book also includes an excellent review of the agreements to protect the ozone layer: "Protecting the Ozone Layer" by E. T. Parson.

McKenzie, R. B. *Economic Issues in Public Policies.* New York: McGraw-Hill, 1980, pp. 158–69.

Describes in some detail the market answer to reducing pollution.

Millert, R. B. "Do We Owe Anything to Future Generations?" *Futurist* 16 (December 1982), pp. 52–59.

A philosopher looks at conservation and environmental issues, among other things. Can you find any economic fallacies among the excellent points he makes?

Taylor, J. "Smog Swapping: New Rules Harness Power of Free Markets to Curb Air Pollution." *The Wall Street Journal*, April 14, 1992, p. 1.

Describes ways in which many companies are beginning to acquire and trade pollution rights following the *Clean Air Act* of 1990.

Taylor, R. A. "Do Environmentalists Care about Poor People?" *U.S. News and World Report*, April 2, 1984, pp. 51–52.

A set of examples in which conservation interests conflict with the use of resources to advance the interests of the poor. How active are the poor in the conservation movement?

Victor, P. *Economics of Pollution.* London: Macmillan, 1972.

An early comprehensive work on the economics of pollution in Canada.

Chapter 6

Health Issues
Is It Worth What It Costs?

Ever since universal health insurance was first proposed by William Lyon Mackenzie King back in 1919, Canadians have been witness to an ongoing debate about how health services should be organized and funded. Over the course of some twenty-five years, starting with Saskatchewan in 1946, Canadians made a series of democratic and deliberate decisions that gave Canada its system of universal hospital and medical care—Medicare. The obstacles were formidable and at times seemed insurmountable, but we succeeded.

Canadians have become accustomed to the notion of a perpetual health care "crisis." Health care systems are prone to emotional debates because they involve two things that we care a lot about: health and money—in fact, a great deal of money. Mix this with the mostly single-payer, publicly funded approach that Canada has adopted, and you have a ready-made recipe for an ongoing debate among governments, health providers and the general public. There is also something distinctively Canadian in all of this: Medicare is more than a health care system—it reflects a shared commitment to fairness and compassion.

Yet we are told by some that the demise of Medicare is just a matter of time—unless we allow more private money into the system. Others claim that there are no fundamental problems with the system; rather, better management is what is needed. Conflicting messages about funding, costs and "tiers" are making their way into newspaper editorials, talk shows, and everyday discussions. For many Canadians, it is difficult to see through all the confusion and know whom to believe—governments, health providers, health policy experts, private entrepreneurs, patients or the media. How is it possible for the system to be underfunded when Canada has one of the most expensive systems in the world? What is the difference between a one-tier system and a two-tier system? If there is waste and inefficiency in the system, why are some people talking about rationing services?

There is widespread support for Medicare and for the values and principles embodied in the Canada Health Act. But we recognize that the first step in preserving what we think is valuable is to debate how best to do it.[1]

The Nature of Health Services in Canada

Canada's health care system is a complex set of programs provided by the various levels of government (federal, provincial, and municipal) and services delivered by private health care providers. The responsibilities for health care services were set out in the *British North America Act* (1867) and its successor *the Constitution Act* (1982), which gives primary jurisdiction

---

[1]*The Public and Private Financing of Canada's Health System* (Ottawa: National Forum on Health, 1995).

over health care to the provinces. The federal government, however, has had significant impact on health care policy through financial support and leverage. For example, in 1994, federal health transfers accounted for 33 percent of provincial government health expenditures.[2]

Canadians received rather inconsistent and chaotic health services prior to World War II. These services were largely financed by private out-of-pocket expenditures or offered to the indigent as charitable services. A bewildering array of private insurance plans was also available, but none protected the average citizen from a financial disaster resulting from serious illness. The wealthy could afford to pay for health services, where they were available. Either charitable organizations served the poor or doctors and health nurses provided their services for free, personally bearing the costs. Health care was a haphazard affair at best. With rising incomes in the post war years, Canadians demanded increases in health care services.

Saskatchewan led the way in public provision of health services with the introduction of a universal insurance program (1946), providing hospital care to all residents regardless of ability to pay. Newfoundland, British Columbia, and Alberta soon followed with similar plans. The federal government entered the arena (after two unsuccessful attempts in 1919 and 1945) with the *Hospital Insurance and Diagnostic Services Act* (1957). This legislation gave federal monies to any province where hospital services were delivered under uniform terms and conditions to all residents regardless of their ability to pay. All provinces had joined this plan by 1961. This act covered hospital care; however, physician services were excluded. The result of this bias was an overemphasis on hospital construction and acute care. Canadians were using hospitals for routine medicine, as it was publicly funded while physician services outside hospitals were not.

To address this problem and extend the principle of public-funded health care, Saskatchewan passed the *Medical Insurance Act* (1962), which added coverage for doctors' services. A Royal Commission (1964) headed by Justice Emmett Hall (often called the father of Medicare) recommended universal health care for all Canadians. Following the recommendations of this commission, the federal government enacted the *Medical Care Insurance Act* (1966). This legislation provided for 50/50 cost sharing to any province that agreed to adopt the five basic principles of the program. These principles are (1) public administration, (2) comprehensiveness, (3) universality, (4) portability, and (5) accessibility. Public administration requires that the health insurance plan of each province be operated by a non-profit public authority accountable to the government. Comprehensiveness requires that the health insurance plan insure all health services provided by hospitals and physicians, and any

---

[2]*Highlights*, (Ottawa: Health Canada, 1996).

other health care practitioners where the province permits. Universality requires that all insured persons have equal access—uniform terms and conditions—to the insured health services. Portability assures coverage when moving or traveling across the country. It restricts residency requirements to a maximum period of three months for eligibility while guaranteeing coverage by one's previous plan during this residency. Accessibility ensures reasonable access to services by all insured persons with no direct or indirect barriers (user fees). By 1972 all the provinces and territories had accepted these principles and had joined the program—popularly known as Medicare.

The Canada Health Act (1984) reconfirmed the principles set out in the *Medical Care Insurance Act* and included the ability to impose financial penalties on any province failing to abide by these principles. Although physicians can opt out of the Medicare entirely if they wish to charge fees (very few do), extra billing for "medically necessary" services was expressly forbidden under this act. It gives the federal government the power to reduce the amount of its grants to the provinces by an amount equal to the extra billing or user fees collected in a province. In 1996 Alberta was losing $400,000 a month under this provision, as it was allowing private clinics to charge "facility" fees in addition to collecting the set fees for service established under the Medicare program. When the issue was finally settled, Alberta had lost a total of $3.6 million of federal financing.

The Financing of Health Services

Canada's current health care system offers a diverse array of services and includes a mixture of public and private funding. The provision and funding of health care both have public and private elements. (1) Financing of most services and facilities is publicly funded or insured; however, some services are paid for through private insurance or individual payments. (2) Delivery of health services is provided by both public and private organizations. It is important to be clear on the distinctions between delivery and financing when discussing the issues regarding public versus private. Canada's system has sometimes been inappropriately termed "socialized medicine" by its critics. However, as health care is primarily delivered by private organizations and individuals, the system is much more appropriately termed private medicine with socialized funding. Table 6–1 shows the types of health care services delivered in Canada and the type—public or private—of financing and delivery. This table illustrates that Canada is essentially a health care system with private delivery and public financing for medically necessary services with a system of other health services privately delivered and privately funded or insured.

Table 6–1	Health services—type, financing, and delivery	
Hospitals	100% public for "medically necessary" services	mixed public/private; highly regulated
Physicians	100% public for medically necessary services	predominantly private; professional association; (self) regulated
Clinics	public for medically necessary; some charge additional "facility" fees; private for other services	private; little regulation
Dental/orthodontic Optometry (eye)	mostly private; some public for medically necessary; some provinces provide public for children and seniors	private with professional association; (self) regulated
Prescription drugs	mixed public/private; some public for seniors and welfare recipients; public if dispensed in hospital or by public health nurses	private prescription by physician; dispensing by pharmacist or hospital
Non-prescription drugs	mostly private except hospitals	private
Long-term care	mixed public/private; public covers health services; private covers room and board	mixed public/private
Home care	partial public coverage	mixed public/private
Public health programs	public	public
Ambulance	mixed public/private	mostly private, but some public (municipal)
Services to status Indian and Inuit	public	mixed public/private; some services directly from federal government
Other professional services*	private	private

*These include psychologists, physiotherapists, chiropractors, midwives, private duty nurses, naturopaths, homeopaths, and alternative medical practices.

Source: Adopted from *The Public and Private Financing of Canada's Health System* (Ottawa: National Forum on Health, 1995).

National Health Care Dollars—Where They Came from and Where They Went

National expenditures on health care have grown at a rapid pace in the past decades. In 1975 the average provincial per capita expenditure was $507; it was $915 in 1980, $1,763 in 1987, and by 1994 it had reached over $2,400. Table 6–2 shows these averages and how they break down by each province. For example, per capita total health expenditures were the highest in British Columbia ($2,631) and the lowest in Nova Scotia ($2,231) in 1994. More important, Table 6–2 and Figure 6–1 shows that these expenditures have grown faster over the decades than the gross domestic product has grown.

Table 6–2   **Total health expenditures**

Expenditure	per Capita				as % of GDP			
Province	1975	1980	1987	1994	1975	1980	1987	1994
Newfoundland	$435	$ 795	$1,473	$2,264	10.73	11.03	11.72	13.55
Prince Edward Island	470	939	1,534	2,293	11.97	13.64	12.15	12.71
Nova Scotia	481	795	1,772	2,231	10.13	10.68	11.64	11.34
New Brunswick	413	794	1,601	2,399	8.83	11.01	10.78	12.14
Quebec	532	932	1,770	2,286	8.03	8.25	8.86	9.96
Ontario	559	924	1,985	2,665	6.71	6.89	8.20	9.64
Manitoba	536	948	1,852	2,536	7.86	8.69	9.97	11.43
Saskatchewan	511	898	1,871	2,348	6.73	6.96	10.99	10.29
Alberta	570	1,018	1,906	2,379	5.46	5.07	7.69	7.86
British Columbia	565	1,098	1,869	2,631	7.06	7.67	8.88	9.66
Mean	$507	$ 915	$1,763	$2,403	8.35	8.99	10.09	10.85

Source: Adapted from *Regulatory Mechanisms in the Health Care Systems Canada and Other Industrialized Countries: Description and Assessment,* Queen's—University of Ottawa Economic Projects: 1993, and Health Canada, (Ottawa: Government of Canada, 1996).

National health care dollars come from three major sources—the government through provincial health insurance plans, private health insurance, and the consumer or patient. In 1994 the share the patient paid directly or through private health insurance was 28 percent, and the part paid by governments was 72 percent with a third of this amount coming from the federal government. Governments obtain the funds for health care from general revenues, with Alberta, British Columbia, and the Northwest Territories levying specific health care premiums. Ontario has had a health care payroll tax. In 1994 the government monies were spent on the following services: hospitals 48.4 percent, other institutions 10.1 percent, physicians 20.9 percent, other professionals 1.43 percent, drugs 5.68 percent, capital 2.27 percent, other expenditures 11.25 percent.[3] Figure 6–2 shows these shares of total expenditures.

During the 1970s national health expenditures represented less than 8 percent spent on the final goods and services produced in the country. Over this period the federal and provincial governments shared these expenses equally. In the late 1970s the *Established Programs Financing Act* (1977) replaced this financing formula for health care, education, and other social programs with block transfers and tax points to the provinces. This change has allowed for decreased federal funding of these programs.

---

[3]*Government Health Expenditures by Category, 1994,* Health Canada (Ottawa: Minister of Supply and Services, 1996).

Figure 6–1   **Health care expenditures**

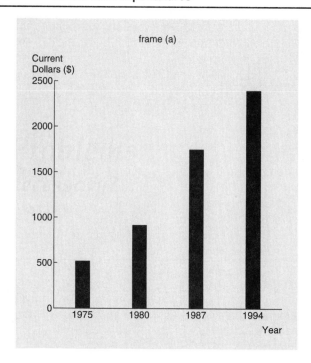

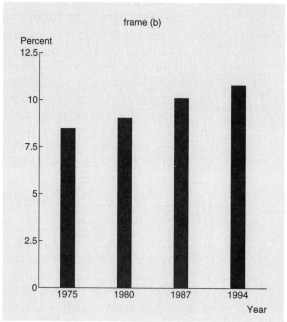

Frame (a) shows the average provincial expenditures on health care per capita for selected years. Frame (b) shows these same expenditures as a percentage of gross domestic product.

Figure 6–2   **Government health expenditures by category, 1994**

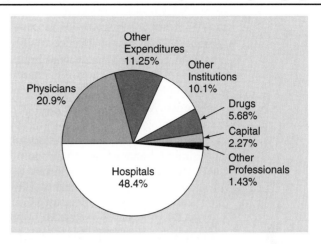

This chart shows the share of government expenditures on various components of of health care services.

Source: *Government Health Expenditures by Category*, 1994, Health Canada (Ottawa: Minister of Supply and Services, 1996).

By the end of 1994, health expenditures represented more than 10 percent of the gross domestic product. At the same time the federal share of financing was decreased again. The *Canada Health and Social Transfer Act* (1995) consolidates the separate block transfers and grants for each program into one grant and further reduces the amount of federal financing of health care as well as other social programs. As the federal transfers diminish, there are people who fear that the federal presence in the funding and therefore control of health care policy will diminish to the point that Canada will have 10 separate health systems and the principles set out in the *The Canada Health Act* will become meaningless.

Factors Explaining the Growth in Expenditures for Hospital Care and Physician Services

A number of factors explain the growth in health care expenditures generally, and more specifically, the growth in expenditures for the two major personal health care services, hospital care and physician services. These factors are population growth, changes in the demographic features of the population, inflation in the economy, increases in medical care prices in excess of general price inflation, and other factors related to underlying forces operating in the market for health care services, such as changes in consumer tastes and preferences and changes in the techniques of supply.

Population Growth and Demographic Change. Population growth accounts for much of the growth in total expenditures on hospital care and physician services. More people generally means more spending for most goods, and more spending on personal health care services will be no exception. However, the average annual growth rate in the population has been 1 to 1.5 percent in recent years, and population growth as a factor explaining the growth in health care services is declining in relative importance. More important than population growth per se is the rise in the average age of the population. Older people need more health care, and most of their needs are translated into effective demands through government-financed health programs. Figure 6–3 shows the population trends over the last 25 years. Frame (a) shows the total population. Frame (b) shows the increase in the percentage of seniors (65 years of age or older) relative to the total population, while frame (c) indicates the rising median age of the population. As health care needs increase with age, this demographic shift explains a good portion of the rise in health care expenditures over time. For example, in 1994 seniors (65 years or older)

Figure 6–3   **Population trends**

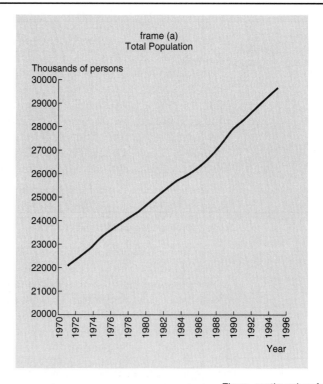

Figure continued on facing page.

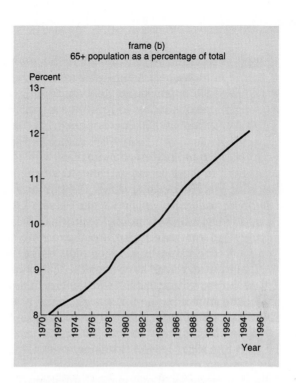

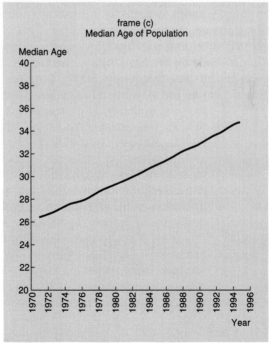

The increase in the total population of Canada is shown in frame (a). Frame (b) indicates the increase in the percentage of Canadians 65 years of age or older. The increase in the median age of Canadians is shown in frame (c).

165

represented 11.9 percent of the population and accounted for 38.7 percent of total health expenditures in Canada. We spent on health an average of $1,156 per capita for children younger than 15 years old, $1,663 for persons in the 15 to 44 age group, $2,432 for persons in the 45 to 64 age group, and $8,068 for persons aged 65 years and over.[4]

Price Inflation. Much of the growth in spending on health care services is attributable to price increases. First, is the economywide inflation that reduces the purchasing power of the dollar in general so that a person needs more dollars to buy a given quantity of goods and services, including health care services. Second, price increases in the health care sector are in excess of the general inflation rate. Figure 6–4 compares the inflation rates for health services to the general rate. Health care prices have increased at a higher rate than prices for all items, increasing more than general inflation for 15 of the last 20 years.[5] By mid-1996 the CPI for all items was 134.9 while the CPI for health was 143.6 (1986 = 100).[6] What do these figures mean? General price inflation is causing the cost of health care services to rise—as it is for most goods. However, rising prices specifically related to the health care industry are responsible for a 25 percent increase in the cost of these services above general inflation. This rise indicates the *real* or constant dollar cost of health services is increasing with increases in demand for these services.

All other Factors. Other factors account for some of the increase in expenditures for health care and physician services. As mentioned previously, these other factors include forces in the market that influence demand and supply of health care services. On the demand side of the market, per capita consumption and the "intensity" of consumption for health care services are increasing, reflecting changes in tastes, income, and the pattern of consumer spending. On the supply side of the market, more resources are used in a given medical care treatment, which gives rise to higher real cost in the supply of a given unit of service. These forces operating on the demand and supply of personal health care services will be discussed in more detail in the next section.

There is nothing special or unusual about the rising cost of personal health care services, generally, including hospital care and physician services. Price increases, population growth, and greater quantity and quality of services explain the rise in costs of most, if not all, goods and services. The reason people are so nervous about the rising cost of medical

---

[4]*Highlights* (Ottawa: Health Canada, 1996).

[5]The exceptions are for the years 1975, 1976, 1981, 1991, and 1995.

[6]Consumer price indexes for Canada, CANSIM. Note: For details concerning concepts, methods and sources, consult "The Consumer Price Index," reference paper, updating based on 1992 expenditures, cat. 62-553, occasional.

Figure 6–4   Inflation rates

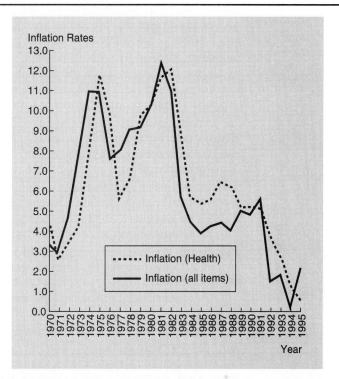

The graphs compare inflation rates for all items and health care expenses. Health care prices increased at a higher rate than prices for all items increased between 1974 and 1993 except for the years 1975, 1976, 1981, 1991, and 1995.

care services lies, in part, in the special characteristics of the demand and supply of these services.

Special Characteristics of Health Services

Is health care just another good or service? Health care, along with some other goods, is a basic human need. Some people believe that the interaction of supply and demand in free markets will efficiently meet this need in the same way other needs are met. They believe that the provision of health care services is just another large and complex industry. However, the provision of health services has some special characteristics. Additionally, many people believe that unlike most goods, the ability to pay should not determine access to basic health services.

The Role of the Physician. A special characteristic of health services involves the role of the physician, who operates on both sides of the market. The physician is both a supplier and a demander of health services. It is the physician who provides the consumer directly with services and determines the service she or he needs from other suppliers—hospitals and suppliers of drugs and medicines. Decisions about medications, getting well at home or in the hospital, number of days spent in the hospital, and special medical services required are all influenced by the physician. Consumers usually do not even determine where they will receive hospital care. The selection of a hospital depends largely on where their physician happens to have admitting privileges.

Consumer Ignorance. Consumers are probably less informed about medical services than they are about anything else they buy. They usually can shop around, look, try, and compare goods and services they wish to buy. Consumer magazines such as *Consumer Reports* publish the results of testing certain products and provide valuable information that can help customers make rational purchasing decisions. Almost no objective information is available concerning the quality of health services, however. Physicians are reluctant to evaluate of the work of other physicians. Hospitals' and physicians' services generally are not subject to quality controls. Human errors, mistakes, and incompetencies in the supply of medical service may go undetected until it is too late for the individual user.

It is not a usual practice in the health field to disclose a list of prices for services. In many instances, consumers do not inquire about and do not know the prices of medical services unless they are provided in the private sector, such as dentistry services, but even in this case the common use of insurance distances the user from price information. The prices, quantities, and qualities of medical services are unknown to most consumers. The suppliers of health services have done little to change this situation.

Spillover Benefits. In Chapter 3, on education, we noted that benefits that flow to the specific users of goods and services are called direct benefits. As people use the goods and services, there may be indirect or social spillover benefits to other individuals.

Social spillover benefits are indirect benefits that flow to other members of society and add to the direct benefits resulting from the provision of health care to a particular patient.

The best illustration of social spillover benefits in health services involves communicable diseases. The use of medical services to get well from a disease that may spread to others directly benefits the user of the service and indirectly benefits others. Immunization shots benefit not only the person receiving the immunity from a disease, but the benefit extends beyond the individual user to others in society. A healthy society is also a more productive society—sick leave is an expense to employers.

However, benefits from many medical services flow to the individual users of these services. A heart or kidney transplant benefits primarily the individual receiving the transplant. The increased quantity and quality of medical services from the use of new equipment and intensive care hospital rooms increases the chances of survival to the individual patients making use of these services.

A Right to Good Health. Most Canadians regard good health as a "right," to be treated the same as access to defence, police, or the judicial system. They believe that a sick or injured person should have access to medical services regardless of his or her income. This is why people are appalled when they hear that in the United States a person in a serious accident or with a serious illness could be refused medical treatment because he or she did not have either money or health insurance to pay for the services needed. The basic idea that health services are essential needs and that people have a right to receive them is in direct conflict with the idea that money prices should be the determinant of the distribution of health care services.

Unpredictability of Illness. Individuals and families, through budgeting, may carefully plan what goods and services they will buy, the quantities of each, and how much they will save. Some medical and health services can be planned for in this way, and others cannot. A family may plan for medical and health needs that are predictable, such as physical examinations or immunization shots, but to plan for illnesses or accidents is difficult. For one thing, people do not usually like to consider the prospects of illness. Second, and more critical from the viewpoint of family financial planning, the incidence of illness is uneven and unpredictable for a family.

On the other hand, the incidence of illness is predictable, and therefore insurable, for large numbers of people or the population as a whole. Voluntary private health insurance could provide a way for individuals and families, with the desire and ability to pay for it, to plan for an cover some the risks of illness or injury. Private health insurance companies, however, cannot provide full protection against exceptional or extremely high-cost illnesses. The consumer remains, in general, unprotected against prolonged and catastrophic illnesses or injuries.

Public health insurance provides a way for all individuals and families, regardless of their ability to pay, to be covered for all risks of illness or injury. The risk is socialized under a public system of health insurance, reducing the risk and expense for any individual in the group.

Health Care Problems

The special characteristics of health services provide a good background for an understanding of the nature of health services. They do not, however, give rise to a unique set of problems. The major economic problems in the health care industry are those of efficiency in the supply of health services and equity in their distribution.

The Public View

Most people seem to view the rising cost of health care as the major health care problem. It is certainly true that the costs of treatment of a given illness—hospital room and board, routine office visits, and other health care services—have risen significantly, much faster than other goods and services in general. But are rising prices and costs necessarily the major problem? Rising costs for health care services may be only the symptom of a problem and, therefore, may not be the real problem at all.

The Economist's View

Economists in general do not look upon the rising costs of any good or service as necessarily a problem. Changes in prices and quantities of individual goods and services bought and sold may reflect changes in demand and supply in the market. The total amount of money spent for individual goods and services increases when the demand and supply for these goods or services rise. There is no problem here. This condition is what is expected in a market economy.

However, the rising costs of health care may indicate or be a symptom of factors economists are concerned about, such as the restrictions on entry into the health care industry, the response of supply to demand changes, and the impact of government finance on the demand for health care services. A central economic problem as seen by economists involves the efficient use of scarce resources in the health care industry. The analysis of demand for and supply of health care services that follows provides a framework for an evaluation of the health care industry in terms of economic efficiency.

Analysis of Demand for Health Care Services

Price Elasticity of Demand

Consumers of certain health care services, such as hospitals' and physicians' services, are not generally very responsive to price changes. An increase in price will not reduce the quantity demanded very much, and a decrease in price will not increase the quantity demanded very much. As we explained in Chapter 3, the price elasticity of demand in this instance is low or inelastic. However, the price elasticity of demand for specific medical care services may vary from one service to another. For example, the demand for a critical surgery may be almost totally inelastic (a price of zero would have almost no more takers than a price of $10,000). On the other hand, the demand for a physical examination is likely to be more elastic.

To be more specific and to review the calculation of price elasticity of demand, suppose that the price of an office visit to see a dentist increases from $20 to $30 and that as a result the number of office visits per day decreases from 20 to 15. What is the price elasticity of demand for office visits? Do you remember from Chapter 3 the arc price elasticity formula? You first calculate the change in quantity demanded and divide this change by the average or midpoint of the two quantities. The change in the quantity demanded in our illustration is 5 office visits, and the midpoint between 20 and 15 office visits is 17.5. The percentage change in office visits, then, is equal to 28.6 percent (5/17.5). Then you calculate the change in price and divide this change by the midpoint of average of the two prices. The change in price is $10, and the midpoint between $20 and $30 is $25. The percentage change in price, then, is 40 percent (10/25). Finally, the price elasticity of demand is equal to the percentage change in quantity demanded (28.6 percent) divided by the percentage change in price (40 percent), which equals .715. Consequently, for every 1 percent increase in price, quantity demanded decreases less than 1 percent—exactly .715 percent.

The price inelastic demand for health care services in general explains why private health care providers may have strong incentives to increase prices. The reason now is clear. As discussed in Chapter 3, when demand is price inelastic, the seller's total revenues increase when the price of the service is increased. Let's take the example above and prove this statement. Total revenues are $400 per day when the price of an office visit is $20 and the number of office visits is 20. However, total revenues are $450 per day when the price of an office visit is $30 and the number of office visits is 15. If the demand for office visits had been price elastic (greater than 1), just the opposite would have occurred—the increase in the price of office visits would have led to a fall in the dentist's income. Can you prove this?

Factors Changing the Demand for Health Services

Price elasticity of demand explains the shape of the demand curve for health services. In addition, the demand for health services, both those publicly and privately financed, has increased. We will first consider the demand for health care services using the analysis developed in Chapter 2. We will modify this analysis later in order to account for the situation that results from public financing of hospital and physician care for medically necessary services.

Changes in the incomes of consumers is a variable that affects demand. Rising incomes of consumers in Canada have been one cause for the demand curve for health care services to shift to the right. Health care is, in general, a normal good; therefore, as incomes increase demand increases. The increase in demand from D_1D_1 to D_2D_2 in Figure 6–5 illustrates this type of shift. The demand for many health care services is likely to be highly responsive to increases in income.

A greater health consciousness of the general population implies changes in tastes and preferences. Changes in consumer tastes and preferences also change demand. An increase in tastes and preferences for medical services increases demand for these services, which means that consumers are willing to buy larger quantities of medical services at every possible price. This is particularly true for elective procedures. It cannot be said for certain, but an increase in tastes and preferences for medical care appears to have played at least a small part in stimulating the demand for health care services. This change in preference for health care results at least in part from the development of new techniques and procedures. If a cure or relief from a medical condition is discovered, sufferers will demand it.

Increases in the population also add to the increase in demand. In addition, the changed demographics with greater a percentage of elderly in the population increases demand, as medical use tends to increase with age.

Changes in the price of goods and services that they may be substituted for medical services also change the demand for these services. Because many medical services have only a limited number of substitutes, the demand for medical services is probably not appreciably affected by changes in the price of substitutes—another reason why demand for health care is inelastic. However, staying in good health by exercising and adhering to good eating habits is the lowest cost substitute to personal health care services.

Less than full-cost pricing means that consumers of health care services can buy a dollar's worth of services for less than a dollar out of their own pockets.

An important reason for the increase in demand for medical care and the rise in medical care costs has been the development since 1966 of government-financed Medicare. Consumers do not directly pay the full costs of health care services. As mentioned previously, direct consumer payments represents only a small percentage of all health costs. The impact of *less than full-cost pricing* is to increase the demand for health services. Consumers may view medical services as a "good buy," since a dollar's worth of services may be bought for little or no cost out of their own pockets. Of course, consumers have to pay the cost in the form of taxes and health insurance premiums. But an individual consumer may not see any connection between spending on health care services and taxes, and insurance premiums are a fixed cost and have to be paid regardless of one's consumption of health services. A higher rate of consumption of goods and services will likely ensue when they are priced at less than full cost to the user. However, even if medical services are fully paid for by government or insurance, they still have a cost to the user—in time lost from work or other activities, transportation, and out-of-pocket expenses.

Analysis of Supply of Health Services

Supply Characteristics: Physicians

The number of professionally active physicians in Canada in 1992 was 61,649,[7] Prior to the introduction of Medicare in 1966, there was a perceived shortage of physicians in Canada. As part of Medicare four new medical schools were created. Most (81 percent) of these physicians received their medical training and education in the 16 Canadian medical schools, and the rest were trained in foreign medical schools and allowed to practice in Canada. The number of doctors in this country rose by 14,000, or 30 percent, between 1982 and 1992. The increase in supply outpaced the increase in population, and the ratio of the population per doctor decreased during the period from 535 to 464. Some economists suggest that part of the increase in the cost of health care services may be a result of the increase in the supply of physicians, however, this relationship has not been clearly established.[8]

The average income of physicians after business expenses were deducted was reported to be $129,000 in 1991.[9] This relatively high income attracts foreign-trained physicians to this country to practice medicine and encourages more qualified people in the country to select medicine as a profession. Also, since physicians don't pay the full cost of their own training, the supply of physicians increases more than it would if they bore the full cost. Supply, then, has responded to the rising demand for physicians, but not fast enough to prevent rapidly rising costs for physicians' services. There are restrictions to entry into the field of medicine, and it takes time to train physicians. The admission practices of medical schools check the supply of physicians and work to keep supply from catching up with the demand. Medical schools reject a high number of qualified applicants. To the extent that the high rejection rate of medical schools has been caused by limited capacity, a lowering of the rejection rate will require an expansion in medical school facilities. Admissions to Canadian medical schools have recently been curtailed by 10 to 15 percent, and the immigration of foreign-trained doctors has been limited.[10]

Physicians cannot practice in any province solely by virtue of having completed their medical education. With the support of medical associations, provinces require that physicians be examined and licensed before practicing medicine. Licencing and examining procedures can be an effective way of

---

[7]*Health Personnel in Canada,* (Ottawa: Minister of Supply and Services, 1992).

[8]See R. G. Evans, "Models, Markets and Medicalcare," In *Issues in Canadian Economics,* L. H. Officer and L. B. Smith (Toronto: McGraw-Hill Ryerson, 1974).

[9]Revenue Canada, as reported in J. R. Columbo, ed., *The Canadian Global Almanac* (Toronto: Macmillan, 1995).

[10]D. M. Wilson, *The Canadian Health Care System* (Edmonton: 1995), p. 40

controlling the supply of physicians coming from abroad. Foreign-trained physicians and other medical personnel may be encouraged or discouraged from practicing medicine in this country by changes in the difficulty of the examinations and other costs associated with getting a licence.

Supply Characteristics: Hospitals

The shortrun supply of hospital services consists of the quantities of hospital services that will be supplied holding constant the number of hospitals and hospital equipment, technology, and costs of hospital inputs. The longrun supply curve differs from the shortrun curve in that hospital investment (hospital facilities and equipment) may vary in the longrun. Changes in hospital investment, technology, and costs of inputs cause shifts in shortrun supply.

The principle of **diminishing marginal returns** states that given the quantity of fixed inputs (plant and equipment), increases in variable inputs (doctors, nurses, supplies) will eventually result in declining increases in output

The shortrun supply curve of hospital services tends to be upward sloping, indicating that the greater quantities supplied are associated with higher costs. These higher quantities result in higher costs per unit of output because of the principle of *diminishing marginal returns*. Chapter 9 develops the concept of diminishing marginal returns in greater detail. Given the fixed sizes and facilities of the hospitals, the application of more and more variable resources (nurses, medical personnel, supplies) will eventually result in smaller and smaller increases in output. These smaller increases in output associated with given increases in variable resources or inputs mean higher costs per unit. Higher costs of hospital services may eventually be encountered, also, if hospital size increases. A wide range of services and, thus, more costly services are often associated with large hospitals. In addition, diseconomies may be connected with larger outputs due to increasing complexities of management.

Factors Affecting the Supply of Hospital Services

Investment. An increase in hospital investment, that is, the construction of new hospitals, the expansion of existing hospitals, and the purchase of new equipment increases the capacity of the hospital industry to provide hospital services. Hospital investment is a way to increase the supply of hospital services to meet the growing demand for these services. This is not to suggest that more hospital investment is needed at this time, for, in general, there appears to have been excessive investment in the 1980s as evidenced by excess hospital bed capacity and in the underutilization of hospital equipment in the early 1990s.

Technology. Technology advancements increase the quantity and quality of hospital services. As a result of new technology, a greater quantity of the same services may be provided at lower costs or new and better services may be provided. New medical technology such as open-heart surgery, cobalt therapy, intensive care, and other new procedures and techniques usually result in both improved hospital care and higher hospital costs. In fact, technological changes in the industry were a major cause for increases in the three specific sector factors (admissions per capita, input prices, and intensity per admission) that explain the growth in hospital costs.

Wages and Other Costs. Hospitals are buying greater quantities of labour and medical supplies and are having to pay higher prices for these inputs. Unless higher wages and prices paid by hospitals are offset by increases in productivity, these increases represent the added cost incurred in producing the same amount of hospital services.

Evaluation of the Canadian Health Care System

In terms of outcomes, the Canadian health care system is one of the best systems in the world.[11] However, this is not to say that the system can not be improved by changes and reforms. Although our system is particularly good at equitable distribution of services, it has shortcomings with respect to the efficient supply of services. As a matter of fact, the health care industry is presently undergoing some fundamental changes, many of which appear to be changes in the right direction. But further changes and reforms are needed in order to overcome the weaknesses that still remain in our health care system and to continue to ameliorate the delivery of health care services.

In this section, the discussion centers on the issues behind the reforms that are contemplated in regard to the delivery of health care services. Then we consider the way the performance of the health care system may be improved.

Medicare

The national health insurance program—Medicare—is regarded as sacrosanct at one extreme; nothing should be changed, and governments should provide all the funding necessary to meet demand. At the other extreme, it is regarded as bad "socialized medicine" full of abuse and inefficiency because users don't have to pay and providers are not disciplined

---

[11]The two most frequently used gross indicators of health care outcomes are life expectancies and infant mortality rates. Canada ranks in the top six countries and significantly better than the United States, which spends much more of its GDP on health care. See the comparisons for 1990 in *Regulatory Mechanisms in the Health Care Systems Canada and Other Industrialized Countries: Description and Assessment*, Queen's—University of Ottawa Economic Projects: 1993, p. 151.

by market competition. Canada's experience with Medicare over the last three decades has raised many issues, and many health care problems have not been completely solved by it.

The goals envisioned by proponents of Medicare can be summarized as follows: (1) to ensure comprehensive and portable access to "necessary" health care for every citizen, (2) to eliminate the personal financial burden connected with the acquisition of health services, and (3) to control and limit health care costs through public financing and administration. How to fulfill these goals simultaneously is not clear. The goals may very well be in conflict. For example, it appears difficult, if not impossible, to limit the annual increases in health care costs while at the same time providing comprehensive and universal care. Several basic issues arise.

Basic Issues

Many issues are involved in our national health care system. Among the important interrelated issues are these:

- Medical necessity—who and what will be covered?
- Financing—what is the balance between public and private financing?
- Cost containment—how do we keep Medicare affordable?
- Efficiency—how do we get the most value for health care expenditures?
- Reform—how do we use the system to promote health rather than merely treat illness?

Medical Necessity—Who and What Should Be Covered Under Medicare? There is a wide range of health services and it is difficult to draw the line as to the kinds of health services that are essential to good health and therefore should be covered under national health insurance. Comprehensive coverage might include almost all of them. Most provincial plans cover a wide range of services; however, the *Canada Health Act* refers to medically necessary services only. The interpretation of this term has varied across the country. Provinces have at different times included such items as eyecare, prescription drugs, and dentistry services to some or all groups in society.

Universal coverage means that the entire population is supposed to be covered under the national health insurance program. The current program provides incomplete coverage and leaves a part of the population without access or much access to many health care services. Only those services deemed medically necessary must be provided without cost to the user. Most Canadians have government health insurance coverage that will pay for almost all of the cost of medically necessary services. Nursing home care, prescription drugs, most dental work, eyecare and glasses, ambulance services, cosmetic surgery, private nurse or room, experimental treatments, hearing aids, rehabilitation services, and complete health care in the home are examples of medical care services that may not be covered by Medicare. Private health insurance supplements many of the health expenses not covered by public insurance. Most of these services remain in the privately financed sector of health care, and many people are not covered by employer benefits plans or insurance. The segment of the population that is of major concern is the part that cannot afford to pay for excluded health services, either because of generally low incomes or because of the financial hardships health care expenses can create.

One of the current directions, in an effort at cost containment by cash-strapped governments, is to delist various services previously covered under Medicare. Some provinces have asked Ottawa for a clear definition of the term *medically necessary* in order to determine what services must be covered.

How Is Health Care Financed? As mentioned earlier in the chapter, the share of health care expenses patients paid directly or through private health insurance was about 30 percent, and the part paid by governments was 70 percent. A third of the public money comes from the federal government. The public portion is financed from health premiums, payroll taxes, and general tax revenues. Premium payments, where they are currently levied, do not vary directly with income and are therefore regressive; that is, they are a smaller fraction of the income of high-income Canadians than they are of low-income Canadians. Payroll taxes, where they are levied, are less regressive than a fixed-premium payment, but they are still regressive on income groups above a certain income level. Financing Medicare from provincial and federal general tax revenues is slightly progressive. In all of these financing schemes, the connection between individual benefits and costs is broken. Equity considerations would discourage the use of regressive methods of finance.

Standard efficiency considerations would encourage the use of methods of finance that maintain a relationship between individual benefits and costs. The 30 percent of all health care costs paid by the users of certain services makes this direct linkage between user demand and cost. Some segments of society wish to see more services fall into this area where prices act as a rationing mechanism. The goals of equity and efficiency often come into conflict with health care provision under Medicare.

How Much Should Patients Pay? Many health care services uninsured by Medicare vary in regard to direct payments by patients. Under private health insurance schemes, direct payments by patients are generally in the form of deductibles and co-insurance provisions. A deductible is the amount that the patient pays of the cost up to some figure, and co-insurance is the fraction of the cost above the deductible that the patient pays. For example, if we assume the deductible is $100 and co-insurance is 10 percent, the total cost of a health care service of $400 would be divided between the patient and insurance as follows:

Paid by		
Patient	Deductible ($100)	
	Co-insurance (.1 × 300) = $30	
		$130
	Insurance	$270
	Total cost	$400

The disadvantage is that deductibles and co-insurance provisions could prevent people from receiving necessary care. Or they may postpone seeking care until their condition becomes more serious and more expensive to treat. This disadvantage could be essentially removed by scaling the patient's share to the income of the patient. Also, cost ceilings could be established. In a given year, for example, a patient's out-of-pocket expense could be limited to a given amount, say $500.

What is the balance between public and private financing? As we have seen, the Canadian health care system is a complex mixture of public and private financing. Part of the private-financed sector is also served by private insurance. The Medicare program of national insurance shifts the financial burden of these health care costs to the government and redistributes income from taxpayers to the users of health services. Limiting coverage, say, to the poor, in combination with voluntary private health insurance plans for the relatively well off is an option to universal coverage that some people are advocating.

A system in which patients pay part of the cost has two advantages. The cost to the taxpayer is reduced, and the unnecessary use of health services is discouraged. However, this approach also has a number of difficulties, as the supply of health services to the poor is interrelated with the supply of services to the non-poor. Private suppliers of health services may "skim the cream" as they prefer and find it more profitable to meet the effective demand of people not covered under a national health insurance program, leaving the more difficult cases for the publicly funded system to deal with. Additional issues arise with a partial market approach to supplying health care. Would physicians, particularly specialists, trained at great expense to the public seek to maximize profits? Would the best health professionals move over to the privately funded system? Would the publicly funded system have to pay for any complications arising from procedures carried out by privately funded facilities? Would taxpayer support for the public system erode if they did not receive the direct benefits of the public system?[12] Many people believe

---

[12]See issue 5 in *The Public and Private Financing of Canada's Health System*, (Ottawa: National Forum on Health, 1995).

that the answers to these questions are yes and therefore reject this "two tier" approach to health care provision.

Efficiency

Figure 6–5 on the following page illustrates the economic aspects of private or public finance of health services. If all health care services were left up to a market solution, the equilibrium "price" per unit of health services would be at p_1 and the equilibrium quantity would occur at q_1. If the market were competitive and free of externalities, then this equilibrium would be considered to be "efficient." The marginal benefits of the services as indicated by the demand curve D_1D_1 would just equal the marginal costs of providing the services as indicated by the supply curve SS. The total costs of health services would be the product $p_1 \times q_1$.

This equilibrium outcome is not considered "equitable," as the demand curve depends on the ability to pay. If we wish to achieve equity by removing the ability to pay from the determination of the quantity demanded, health services would have to be provided without cost to the user. The quantity demanded, then, would be at q_2 in Figure 6–5. In order to induce private providers to supply this quantity, the fee for service would need to set at p_2. The government would pay the sum indicated by the area $p_2 \times q_2$.

What if the appropriate fee p_2 was not achieved through negotiations. If medical associations are able to negotiate a fee at p_3, it would be in physicians' interest to provide total services of q_3. The only way they can achieve this output level is to generate an increase in demand to D_2D_2, where the quantity demanded at zero price to the users is equal to q_3. On the other hand, if the association was only able to negotiate a fee of p_0, physicians would only supply q_0. A shortage of $q_3 - q_0$ would occur, generating a waiting list for the service.

We should note that although p_2 brings about the correct supply response to the demand quantity q_2 so that the goal of equity is achieved, the output-price combination is not efficient from an economic perspective. The marginal cost of producing q_2 is higher than the marginal benefit to consumer-patients as indicated from their demand curve. If any fee other than p_2 occurs, even greater distortions of efficiency occur.

Cost Containment. Cost containment of health care is the main issue most provinces are trying to grapple with today. The rise in health care costs per capita and in constant dollars is of concern. Costs, however, are not increasing any faster than in the past. What has occurred has been a decline in the growth of the economy overall, and therefore health costs are rising faster than GDP is rising. In addition all governments in Canada have been accumulating debts and wish to reduce expenditures. Health care is the greatest area of expenditure by provincial governments, and the

Figure 6–5   **Supply and demand for health services**

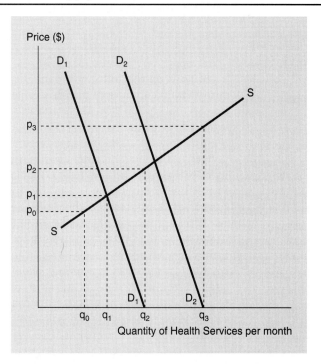

The demand curve D_1D_1 indicates consumer willingness and ability to pay for health services. The supply curve SS indicates the willingness and ability of physicians to provide health services. If health care services are left to market forces the equilibrium will occur at p_1, q_1. If health care services are free to the user, then q_2 is demanded and a fee of p_2 needs to be paid to providers in order to induce q_2 to be supplied. If p_3 is the fee, there is an incentive for physicians to increase demand to D_2D_2. If the fee is p_0, providers will supply only q_0 and a shortage or excess demand of $q_2 - q_0$ will exist, creating waiting lists for the service.

federal government has reduced its financial commitment to health. The combination of low growth and increasing public debt not the rise in costs is driving the reductions in health care funding.

A study initiated by the Economic Council of Canada has looked at the ability of various countries to restrain costs. Their findings, based on an overall indicator measuring cost control capacity, indicate that Denmark, Ireland, and Sweden performed best in cost containment; the United States had the worst record, while Canada falls into a group with mediocre performance.[13] However, cost containment in Canada has likely

---

[13]*Regulatory Mechanisms in the Health Care Systems Canada and Other Industrialized Countries: Description and Assessment*, Queen's—University of Ottawa Economic Projects: 1993.

improved since the study was completed. For example, the annual rate of increase of total health expenditures in Canada has slowed to 1.0 percent in 1994, down from 2.5 percent in 1993 and 5.6 percent in 1992.[14] Most provinces have in the past few years implemented major spending reductions and reforms in the way they pay for Medicare.

Reforms in the Delivery of Health Care Services

Increasing Efficiency. Given that equity is the paramount concern of Canadians, efficiency in the sense of a competitive equilibrium price where the marginal cost of the services is equal to their marginal benefits is not achievable. What follows then are proposals that would increase the efficiency of supplying a given quantity of services in order that the cost be as low as possible for this output. The efficiency of the present health care system could be greatly improved. This goal could be accomplished through the increased use of paramedical personnel, group practices and health centers, and the implementation of some internal competitive practices. The survival of the system of health care as we know it today may depend on the improvements we can make in the supply and cost of health services.

Paramedical Personnel. Medical personnel who have had less training than doctors, perhaps nurses, could be used more frequently to do some of the work that doctors now usually perform. This can save the time of doctors, increase their productivity, reduce costs, and increase the supply of medical services.

Although progress has been made in the use of auxiliary personnel, the idea of a lesser trained and lower paid assistants is not generally accepted. Many patients prefer the expertise and the bedside manner of the licenced physician and nurse. This attitude could be changed by an education program pointing out to the public the savings and the more efficient use of the physicians' and nurses' time. Health service jobs would have to be redefined and new training programs devised so that assistants could perform certain jobs as competently as the more qualified, and higher paid, personnel could perform them. The use of paramedical personnel could increase the productivity of more highly trained and more costly medical personnel where possible.

Group Practice. The usual way of providing doctors' services is through a solo practice. A doctor receives an M.D. degree; obtains a licence to practice medicine; rents office space; buys furniture, supplies, and equipment; puts up a sign; and goes to work. The chances are that business

---

[14]*Highlights,* (Ottawa: Health Canada, 1996).

will be thriving in a short time. In some instances, a young physician may join an established practice.

More and more young physicians are joining a group practice, for solo practices are not usually efficient. Modern medical equipment may not be available and, if available, may not be fully utilized. A solo practice does not favour the maximum use of paramedical personnel and does not permit the pooling of human and capital resources or the productivity gains from specialization and division of labour.

Group practices vary in size, type of legal organization (partnership, corporation), services provided, method of pricing, and method of financing. In a group practice, physicians share in the costs and revenues. A type of group practice that has attracted substantial support is a prepaid plan called a comprehensive health organization (CHO), similar to the health maintenance organization (HMO) found in the United States.[15] Medical services are supplied for people in a certain area at fixed fees contracted for in advance. These organizations have an incentive to provide medical services at the lowest possible cost, since the net income of the organization varies inversely with the cost of providing medical services. This same incentive, however, may contribute to inadequate care as a means of keeping costs down.

Community Health Center. An extension of the concept of a group practice is the community health center. In the health-center concept, patients are tested, classified, and distributed to the area of the center that is best staffed and equipped to treat and cure them. Diagnostic tests could be handled by paramedical personnel. A computer could be used to classify patients as to the type of medical care needed and distribute them to center areas in accordance with their respective health needs. An important part of this concept is that doctors would be on a salary rather than on a fee-for-service payment system.

A logical way to develop health centers is around the modern hospital, since the hospital is the focal point of health activities today. A hospital-based health center could contain many hospitals under a single management system, and each hospital could provide specialized health services. Local health centers, nursing homes, first-aid stations, and clinics would be a part of the organizational structure of the hospital-based health center. The center could have mobile health teams to provide advice and assistance to local health units and supply health services to areas that are without adequate health care personnel and facilities.

Internal Competition. Chapter 2 discussed the efficiency obtained through the interaction of supply and demand in a competitive market. The special characteristics of the supply and demand for health services and the

---

[15]See M. Rachlis and C. Kushner, *Strong Medicine* (Toronto: HarperCollins, 1994).

general desire of Canadians to not ration health care through markets limit the effectiveness of competition in the medical system. Therefore, the concept of creating "internal" markets is being considered. The idea is to achieve some of the efficiencies generated in a competitive market setting by creating markets internal to the general government-financing framework without recourse to charging users directly, which would threaten universal access. Competition among health care providers would be established by having various providers bid to provide the services required of various units, for example, a hospital.[16] Competitive bidding can achieve the efficiencies of a competitive market under the right conditions.[17] One way to approximate this outcome is to require sealed bid tenders from the competing providers. It will be apparent to each provider to submit a bid for the contract at their cost of production, that is, where the price bid is equal to their average cost of producing a unit of the service. For example, if the price bid were higher than the average cost, a competitor could obtain the contract by bidding a lower price. If this competitor's bid were still higher than the average cost of production, another competitor could bid an even lower price, and so on, until the provider that bids the price equal to the average cost gets the contract. The logic of this competive bidding process compells each provider to bid an initial price just equal to their average cost. They can not provide the service at a price lower than this and they will not likely gain the contract at a higher price.

Cost Containment

It is one thing to generate the efficient cost of a given level of health services but quite another to restrict the overall cost of the system. Reforms in health care are attempting to achieve both these goals. Cost containment implies putting a cap, or at least a cap on growth, on overall health expenditures by government. A number of policies have been implemented in various provinces to reduce overall expenditures on health care.

Regional Health Authorities. Health care is a provincial responsibility that was generally delegated to lower level local authorities—municipal and county government—and hospitals. In many provinces regional authorities were created to administer programs that overlap a number of local authorities. The provision of health care is one program that extends over local governments. Hospitals were largely administered autonomously. In many provinces regional health authorities are being

---

[16]M. Jérôme-Forget; J. White; and J. M. Wiener; eds., *Health Care Reform Through Internal Markets* (Montreal: The Institute for Research on Public Policy, 1995).

[17]Joseph Bertrand made the argument in book reviews of *Théorie Mathématique de la Richesse Sociale and Recherches sur les Principes Mathématiques de la Théorie des Richesses. Journal des Savants* (1883), pp. 499–508.

drastically reduced in number and the hospitals are coming under their domain. This amalgamation, it is hoped, has the effect of reducing the administrative overhead and allowing for the rationalization of hospitals. Previously, hospitals tended to compete with each other in offering a complete range of services and incurring duplication of some costly services. For example, if one hospital obtained some new diagnostic machine, all other hospitals' administrators wanted one too. Each machine might be underused, leading to expensive excess capacity.

Hospital Closures. Most provinces have been closing hospitals. In many cases such closures are an appropriate reaction to the development of less invasive surgical procedures that require far fewer days recuperating in hospital. In other cases closures are a recognition that hospital stays were generally longer than required—and perhaps not even healthy. For example, the hospital stay after giving birth has been drastically reduced.[18] As the need for hospital beds diminished hospitals closed whole wards, nevertheless, the hospitals were still operating with the same very high fixed costs. There are two aspects to this issue: Too many hospitals operating with excess capacity, and too many small, inefficient hospitals. Figure 6–6 illustrates the different average costs associated with hospitals of different sizes. If the average cost curve for a small hospital is AC_s and the hospital operates at its lowest possible cost, it would provide q_1 at a cost of AC_1. If this same hospital operates at less-than-optimum quantity owing to reduced patient days, then cost per patient would rise to AC_2. Fewer of these hospitals would be required in order to reduce the average cost to AC_1.

Economies of scale refer to situations in which the larger the level of output, the lower the per unit cost to provide it. There may be large economies of scale in hospital care. In Figure 6–6, the average cost per patient in a large hospital is shown as the curve AC_L. If demand warrants, a large hospital could replace a number of smaller hospitals and lower the average cost even if the system were operating at full capacity. For example, costs could be lowered to AC_3 if one large hospital providing $4 \times q_1$ patient days replaced four small hospitals each providing q_1.

Hospital closures are occurring across Canada. This trend may be a short-term solution to costs that will be regretted in the future as the population continues to grow and the senior population—the greater users of hospitals—grows as a percentage of the population.[19] It should also be noted that much of the hospital-care costs are only shifted. If hospital care is reduced only to be replaced by home care, the burden of the care (and its costs) are shifted to family and friends of the ill or to home care nurses and

---

[18]The reduction in hospital time for birthing may have gone too far. We are hearing reports of increased postpartum complications and increased infant mortality as a result.

[19]D. K. Foot and D. Stoffman, *Boom, Bust & Echo: How to Profit from the Coming Demographic Shift* (Toronto: Mcfarlane Walter & Ross, 1996).

Figure 6–6   **Cost comparisons between large and small hospitals**

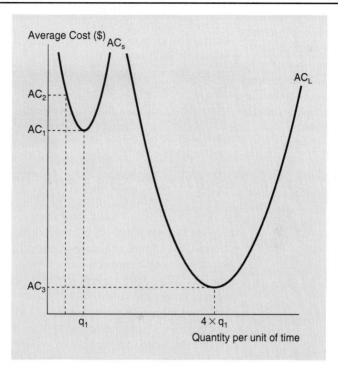

The average cost per patient day in a small hospital is shown as AC_s. If the hospital were to operate at its lowest possible cost, it would provide q_1 at a cost of AC_1. If this same hospital were to operate at less than optimum quantity due to reduced output, then cost per patient would rise to AC_2. Fewer of these hospitals would be required in order to bring the average cost back down to AC_1. The average cost per patient day in a large hospital is shown as AC_L. A large hospital could replace a number of smaller hospitals and lower the average cost to AC_3.

other home care providers. The closing of hospitals may reduce hospital-care costs, but will not necessarily reduce health care costs only shifting the costs on to others. Reducing hospital costs through closures poses other problems with respect to access. As hospitals become larger and more centralized, access becomes more difficult. Increasingly, people have to travel greater distances for care. Additionally, large hospitals are more daunting and make it more difficult for people to move through the system.

Physicians' Fees. The expenditures on physicians is the product of price times quantity. Provincial governments have determined on the whole how physicians are going to be paid. They rely on fee schedules, and most physicians are paid on a fee-for-service basis. This system has supported increases in costs in two ways. First, the fees negotiated by governments and physicians' groups have increased at a rate greater than overall inflation. Therefore, the real dollar costs of health services have increased. Second, the number of physicians has increased at a rate greater than the population as a whole. When fees were negotiated the number of services offered was not constrained. More physicians mean increased billings; therefore, the quantity of services has also increased. Fee-for-service payment provides a financial incentive for physicians to provide a larger number of services. Recently governments have started negotiating "caps" in spending in addition to the fee schedule. In this way the total expenditure on physicians will remain within a budget set for health care.

A Final Look at Rising Health Care Costs

The issue of rising health care costs needs to be reexamined in light of what we have learned about the health care industry and the role of government. Rising health care costs reflect the increasing quantities and qualities of health care services supplied and demanded. Increasing prices for a unit of health care suggest that demand is rising faster than supply. The real issues are not that health care costs are rising, but why they are rising and what should be done, if anything, to slow down costs.

One choice is to leave the health system as it is and contribute more government funds to health care as the growth in demand, primarily driven by demographics, continues. As was discussed in Chapter 1, all choices have opportunity costs. Given the current levels of government deficits and debt loads, if we continue spending more on health care we will need to increase taxes to pay for it, reduce government expenditures on other public services, or a combination of both. Many health care analysts argue against this choice:

> It is both well known and documented that the level of the health of the population is not associated with the overall level of per capita spending on health. The most significant determinations of a population's health are found outside of the health care system. Policies intended to raise health levels should be aimed at educating and supporting young children, providing employment, achieving reductions in income disparities, raising overall educational achievement, and promoting a healthy lifestyle. Under those conditions a responsible government must keep the costs of health care under control so as to maintain the capacity to intervene in other areas that affect the population's health.[20]

Supply and demand analyses reveal two other choices for containing health care costs. Choice 1 is to increase the efficiency and reduce the costs

---

[20]*Regulatory Mechanisms in the Health Care Systems Canada and Other Industrialized Countries: Description and Assessment*, Queen's—University of Ottawa Economic Projects: 1993, pp. 1–2.

of the supply of health care services, and choice 2 is to reduce demand. Although these courses of action are clear, pursuing them creates other issues. We shall consider a reform approach.

Supply Approach

Suppose the health care industry were a highly competitive unregulated industry. Many sellers would be competing with one another, each striving to combine resources so that any given output would be produced at the lowest cost. Each competitive seller would select an output that would maximize its profits. Above-normal profits in the industry would attract more competitive sellers, thereby increasing the supply of health care services and lowering prices.

The health care industry does not fit this description of a competitive industry. Hospitals are not organized on a profit basis and often are controlled by another supplier, the government. When several hospitals serve a market—with some exceptions—they do not compete on a price basis; instead they compete for physicians and for the latest capital equipment. In contrast to hospitals, physicians probably do behave in a profit-maximizing way. But because the supplies of physicians and other medical personnel are controlled largely by monopolistic devices and fees are set by the government, little competition exists among the sellers of health care services.

Some health economists believe that a privatized health care industry would not perform very well even if the industry were a competitive one. Certain problems would not be resolved by a highly competitive health care industry; for example, the problems pertaining to externalities in the consumption of health care services, equity in the distribution of services, third-party payments, and high-price inelasticity of demand and supply. Thus a realistic assessment of the industry seems to preclude the likelihood that the issue of rising health care costs can be or will be resolved by fundamental changes in the structure of the health care industry. On the other hand, there is room for progress in increasing the efficiency of supplying health care and reducing the costs of delivering a given quantity of services through the rationalization of hospitals and the introduction of internal competition in some service delivery.

Demand Approach

If the real issue were rising health care costs, the problem would be rather easy to resolve, at least in part, by reducing demand for health care services through eliminating or reducing government financing under the Medicare program. However, these programs were based on the desire for equity in the distribution of health care services, and, therefore, the matter of efficiency was considered to be of secondary importance. Even if Medicare were cut or eliminated and the health care industry became more competitive, inefficiencies would continue in the form of "excess" consumption of health care services because of private health insurance coverage. Both government and health insurance stimulate increased demands for health care services.

The Effect of Health Insurance on Demand. Recognizing the high price inelasticity of demand for health services, the effect of health insurance is to move consumers down their respective individual demand curves, resulting in an increase in market quantity demanded. Also, at the quantity q_2 demanded and supplied (see in Figure 6–5), the consumer's marginal benefits are less than marginal costs, indicating an inefficient quantity.

Increase the Price Paid by the User? One way to slow down rising health care costs is to reduce quantity demanded by increasing the price that users have to pay for health care services. We know that if the consumer-user pays the full price, "excess" consumption disappears. The quantity of health care services provided could be regulated by changing the price paid by the users under these programs. Of course, this plan is tantamount to introducing the price system as the way to allocate resources. People who could not afford to pay the prices would be eliminated from the market, which is the purpose of increasing the price to the user. As we have discussed, this option is not desirable, and most Canadians prefer that the ability to pay not be the rationing device for health care services. Also, the experience in the United States suggests that private insurance would be offered for the user-paid portion, thereby increasing the administration costs.[21]

Reform in the Payment and Delivery System

The **fee-for-service principle** is in effect when a seller is paid an amount based on the price and the actual quantity of services provided.

Health economists generally agree that little progress will be made in the improvement of the economic performance of the health care industry until the payment and delivery system is reformed. The traditional scheme is based on the *fee-for-service principle*. Hospitals, physicians, and other providers are paid by users and third parties for services rendered. This scheme works well in most markets. However, this scheme is highly inefficient in a market where there are restrictions to entry, where demand is heavily subsidized, where there are large externalities, where sellers (primarily physicians) determine demand, and where users generally pay directly only a small part of the cost of services.

An alternative to the traditional system is a prepayment plan based on a negotiated schedule of fixed fees. Hospitals' and physicians' services

---

[21]R. G. Evans, "Less Is More: Contrasting Styles in Health Care," in *Canada and the United States, Differences that Count*, David Thomas, ed. (Peterborough, Ontario: Broadview Press, 1993).

could be provided under a contract with the government, private organizations, and health insurance companies that specifies the services to be provided and the cost. These arrangements would provide an incentive for services to be supplied in an efficient manner, for the net income of hospitals and physicians would depend on supplying services at a cost below the cost agreed on in the contract. Under the present system, suppliers have an incentive to provide more services, and often more services than are needed, because they are paid for the amount of services supplied whatever the amount may be.

Summary

The recent rise in the cost of medical care reflects growth in demand, slow response of supply, improvements in the quality of medical services, and inefficiencies in the delivery of the health care services. The growth in demand for health services is primarily a result of the rise in the average age of the population, in per capita income, and the development of third-party payments. More people with more income desire greater quantities of health care services. Third-party payments, that is, payments for health care made by government and private health insurance companies on behalf of people, have extended health care to more people and have encouraged the utilization of health services. Government payments for medical services have increased demand by providing the means of payment for services covered under Medicare. Prepaid voluntary health insurance for other services reduces the out-of-pocket costs of medical care to the consumer and, consequently, increases the use of health services.

It is difficult to achieve all of the goals envisioned by the proponents of Medicare, ensuring everyone access to adequate health care, and also to control and limit the rise in health care costs. The impact of more people, higher income, better information, and third-party payments on the prices of health services would be minimized if the supply of health services responded quickly to the rise in demand. However, supply has not responded by keeping costs and prices down. It takes time to restructure health care, improve efficiencies, and create the right incentives for health care delivery. Increases in productivity can offset in part or entirely an increase in cost. Although the health care systems have had some increases in productivity, the system in general has inefficiencies. A great deal of progress can be made toward increasing the efficiency with which health services are supplied with major changes in the organization and structure of the health care system. A hospital-based health center is one type of organization within which health services may be supplied more efficiently.

Medical services have improved in quality. New and better medical equipment has been introduced. New medical procedures and treatments are being used. A part of the rising cost of medical care, then, is a response to more sophisticated products and improved technology. The ability to provide better and more varied services has raised many issues with the provision of health services under Medicare. Who should be covered? What should be covered? How should it be financed? How much will patients pay? The maintenance of the Medicare principle will depend upon the success of current changes in the health care system and the implementation of proposed changes.

A final look at rising health care costs reveals that the promising ways to slow down health care costs are to reform the payment and delivery system. A change in the payment and delivery system to the prepayment system based on fixed fees may encourage providers to be more efficient. Even more basic reforms in the health care industry will be necessary in order to reach the goals of cost containment while maintaining universal health insurance coverage.

In conclusion, real problems are associated with the supply and demand of health care services—a very complex "industry." These problems are not going to disappear automatically. Although they are only symptomatic of the problem, rising health care costs will remain an important issue in the 1990s.

Checklist of Economic Concepts

Equity principle	Changes in supply
Social spillover benefits	Principle of diminishing marginal
Price elasticity of demand	returns
Changes in demand	Investment
Per capita income	Technology
Tastes and preferences	Catastrophic health insurance
Substitution effects	Entry barriers
Less than full-cost pricing	Fee-for-service principle
Elasticity of supply	

Discussion Questions

1. Medicare guarantees public payment for "medically necessary" health services. Make a list of the services you consider to be medically necessary and another list for those you consider not necessary. What criteria determines which service goes on which list? Discuss the problems you encountered in placing a service on one list or the other.

2. List a number of factors that explain the growth in health care expenditures in Canada. Discuss whether the increase in expenditures is reasonable and expected or excessive and unexpected. Why do you think the growth in expenditures is reasonable or excessive?

3. The chapter states that consumer ignorance is a special characteristic of the demand for health services. Do you think that consumers are more or less ignorant when they obtain health services than when they purchase other commodities, for example, automobiles? If so, explain why. Discuss ways to improve consumer information about health care services and options.

4. Physicians are generally paid on a fee-for-service basis. Explain how the incentives of this method of payment may undermine the achievement of the efficient level of health services. Discuss the advantages and disadvantages of alternate payment schemes.

5. Health care services have public goods characteristics. Explain the difference between a public good and a private good. What makes health care a public good? How is health care like a private good?

6. Medical services are extremely important to people's well-being, but so are many other goods. Like all goods, health care has opportunity costs. What are the opportunity costs of health care in Canada? Draw a graph showing the opportunity cost principal with health care on one axis and the other goods you have identified on the other axis.

Supplementary Reading

Armstrong, P. et al. *Take Care, Warning Signals for Canada's Health System*, Toronto: Garramond Press, 1994.
A well-documented critical appraisal of the current reforms going on in Medicare and its delivery. The book shows how cuts to medical budgets affect hospital patients and workers, in particular how health care delivery reforms affect women.

Brown, M. C. *Health Economics and Policy*. Toronto: McClelland & Stewart Inc., 1991.
An advanced analytical textbook approach to the economics of the health care industry.

Holahan, J. F., and L. M. Etheredge, eds. *Medicare Physician Payment Reform*. Washington, DC: The Urban Institute, 1986.
Many issues are examined in a group of essays dealing with the Medicare physician payment system, such as adjusting fees for location and quality, setting fee levels, and controlling the volume of services.

Jérôme-Forget, M.; J. White; and J. M. Wiener, eds. *Health Care Reform Through Internal Markets*. Montreal: The Institute for Research on Public Policy, 1995.
This book takes an international approach to health care issues, focussing on the common problems of cost containment and efficiency in delivery. "Internal" markets are proposed as a means of creating competition among health care providers without recourse to charging users directly, which would threaten universal access. Four of the 11 papers deal with reform in Canada in the context of the experiences of other countries.

Lindsay, C. M., ed. *New Directions in Public Health Care: A Prescription for the 1980s.* San Francisco: Institute for Contemporary Studies, 1980.

A collection of excellent essays concerning health care issues in the 1980s. Of special interest are essays written by Cotton M. Lindsay and Arthur Seldon on the health care systems in Britain and Canada and the essay by Congressman W. Philip Gramm and David Stockman, former director of the U.S. Office of Management and Budget, on the Reagan administration's position concerning hospital cost containment.

Rachlis, M., and C. Kushner. *Strong Medicine.* Toronto: HarperCollins, 1994.

This book is comprehensive and compassionate treatment of the health care system in Canada and what ails it. It provides a strong perspective on not confusing the equity and efficiency issues and is a passionate proponent of the public financing of the health care system on equity grounds while recognizing the problems with efficient delivery and the need for cost containment. Numerous suggestions for improving the efficiency of delivery of health services are included. It proposes that the health system put more emphasis on primary care in place of acute care and deliver this care through community health clinics with group physician practice working in a team with other health care providers.

Russell, L. B. *Is Prevention Better Than Cure?* Washington, DC: Brookings Institution, 1986.

Examines preventive health measures pertaining to smallpox and measles vaccination, screening and drug therapy for hypertension, and exercise. Although preventive measures may improve health, they are not without cost and risks and rarely reduce health care expenditures.

Chapter 7

Poverty Problems
Is Poverty Necessary?

Economic and social conditions in Canada have undergone a profound transformation in recent decades. Although some of these changes have been for the better, others have placed increasing stress on the safety net designed to protect the incomes of needy Canadians. In the face of mounting cost and huge government deficits, some observers have called for program reductions that could seriously imperil the income security of many Canadians. Indeed, a number of the more recent changes to the system have already resulted in lower benefits levels.

Income security, as provided by government programs, is part of the daily lives of Canadians. Today, senior citizens are much better off than were their parents when *they* retired. Workers who experience interruptions in employment are more financially secure than the unemployed of 30 and 40 years ago. Families with children have a variety of income supplements available to them. All citizens also have access to basic-education and health-care services, and when they are in need, to other social services—generally without charge.

While Canadians can be proud of their social support system and of the progress that has been achieved, they must not be complacent on the subject of income security; the system is being strained—almost to the limit. Growing numbers of people are unemployed or have low incomes. As a result of these demands on resources, many of the anti-poverty programs are subjected to financial stress.[1]

"Poverty amidst plenty" is a striking feature of the Canadian scene. Our nation is one of the richest countries in the world, yet millions of people are poor; millions more who do not live in absolute poverty are poor relative to others. The existence of poverty amidst affluence is a paradox. Poverty may be a more serious problem in our society than it is in societies with much less income and wealth. Poverty amidst poverty is easier to understand and even condone. But in a land of abundance, it is difficult to comprehend why some people are inadequately fed, clothed, and sheltered. In rich countries such as Canada, poverty is essentially an issue of the distribution of income. Enough income is earned in Canada so that no one need have a low income, but it is not distributed equally. Poverty is a reality that needs to be studied, understood, appreciated, and many believe eradicated. It is a much more complex issue than many people believe. Some critics take the view that the poor are lazy leeches who simply want a handout. Others see the poor as individuals who are poor because of unfortunate circumstances, who therefore deserve society's unquestioning support. If we are to deal with the problem of poverty effectively,

---

[1]Economic Council of Canada, *The New Face of Poverty* (Ottawa: Minister of Supply and Services Canada, 1992), p. 1.

objective analysis must replace such stereotypes . Poverty, in fact, has been studied in Canada and other countries. In the 1960s, Lyndon Johnson declared a "war on poverty" in the United States. In 1968 the Canadian Senate established a Special Senate Committee on Poverty. That committee under David Croll issued a major report, *Poverty in Canada*. The report highlighted the seriousness of the problem of poverty in Canada.

Poverty can be approached in two ways. First, we examine poverty in reference to *absolute* income level. This approach permits the identification of people who live below a designated level of income. That level of income could be established by pricing a basket of essential goods. The problem with this approach is establishing what is essential in a rich country such as Canada. Alternatively, that level of income could be based on a percentage of average income. Second, we could study income in terms of *relative* incomes, that is, the share or percentage of national income that people receive. For example, we could use the share of income earned by the poorest 20 percent of the population.

Poverty in Terms of Absolute Income Levels

Statistics Canada publishes **low-income cut-offs.** They are often referred to as *poverty lines* and can be useful for formulating policies to redistribute income.

For a number of years Statistics Canada (StatCan) has published a set of *low-income cut-offs.* These cut-offs are often referred to as *poverty lines.* The method StatCan uses to determine these cut-offs is simple but arbitrary. Over the years the definition of the low-income cut-offs has changed. These low-income cut-offs are based on a Survey of Consumer Finances. Generally, when StatCan does a new survey, it redefines the low-income cut-offs. The low-income cut-offs are based on the proportion of gross income an average family spends on food, shelter, and clothing. In the 1969 survey, the average Canadian family spent 42 percent of its gross income on these three groups of goods. The low-income cut-offs were set so that any family that had to spend more than 20 percent more of its income on these goods was below the low-income cut-off. In other words, if a family had to spend more than 62 percent of its gross income to buy food, shelter, and clothing, that family was "poor." In the 1978 survey, the average Canadian family spent 38.5 percent of its gross income on the three groups of goods. Therefore, the low-income cut-offs were set at 58.5 percent. New surveys were conducted in 1986 and 1992, and the bases were set at 56.2 and 54.7, respectively. Once the base is determined, StatCan prices a typical basket of food, shelter, and clothing. Obviously, the basket will cost more for a family of four than for a single person. It also will cost more in a large city where housing costs tend to be higher. To see how StatCan set a low-income cut-off, let us assume that it costs a family of four who live in a large city $16,797 to buy their essential goods. The low-income cut-off would then be $16,797 divided by .547 or $30,708. StatCan publishes 35 different low-income cut-offs. They vary depending upon household size:

from single individual through families of seven or more. And they vary depending upon the population of the center in which the household lives: from rural to cities of 500,000 or more. While the bases change only when StatCan does a new Survey of Consumer Finances, the low-income cut-offs change every year to reflect inflation. Table 7–1 gives the low-income cut-offs (1986 base) for 1994.

Figure 7–1 shows the trends in the incidence of low income in Canada from 1971 to 1993. Notice that the graph has four lines that correspond to the four different cut-off bases. Notice also while more recent bases are always higher than earlier bases, the lines move up and down in almost perfect harmony. While StatCan has used four different bases since 1971, they are in a sense the same base. In each case any individual or family that must spend 20 percent more of its income than the average family spends to buy the essentials is considered to have low income. Therefore, we can make meaningful comparisons over the entire period. In 1971 a little more than 20 percent of Canadian residents had low income. The proportion of low-income persons declined rapidly during the early 1970s. It then remained relatively constant for three years before declining again. It rose sharply during the recession of the early 1980s and then fell with the recovery. The proportion of low-income persons began to rise at the end of that decade and continued to rise with the recession of the early 1990s. In 1993 the proportion of families who had to spend 20 percent more of their income than the Canadian average to buy essentials was back up to 18 percent—not that much lower than it was in 1971. That 18 percent of the population translates into about 5 million persons. More than 1 million families with about 1.5 million children had incomes below the low-income cut-offs. Unattached individuals had an even higher incidence of

Table 7–1	1994 Statistics Canada low-income cut-offs (1986 base)				
Family Size	500,000 or More	100,000– 499,999	30,000– 99,999	Less Than 30,000	Rural Area
1 person	$15,479	$13,596	$13,282	$12,108	$10,538
2 persons	20,981	18,430	18,004	16,411	14,286
3 persons	26,670	23,426	22,884	20,860	18,157
4 persons	30,708	26,969	26,348	24,019	20,905
5 persons	33,550	29,467	28,787	26,242	22,841
6 persons	36,419	31,983	31,246	28,483	24,792
7 or more	39,169	34,403	33,609	30,638	26,666

Source: National Council of Welfare (1995), *Poverty Profile 1993*, Ottawa.

Figure 7–1   **The incidence of low income**

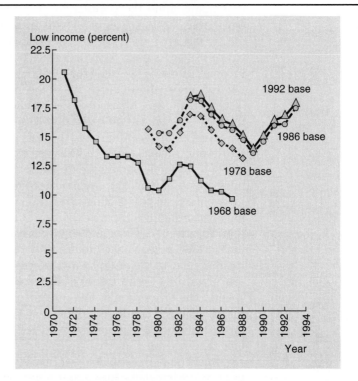

The figure shows the trend in the incidence of low income since 1971. Note that Stat-Can has used four different bases for the low-income cut-offs during that period.

low-income. More than 40 percent of one-person families lived below the cut-offs.

What Is Poverty?

StatCan does not refer to its low-income cut-offs as poverty lines because poverty is not easily defined. Poverty is subjective. The StatCan low-income cut-offs are based on the idea of needs. Clearly everyone needs food, shelter, and clothing. However, needs are not easy to identify. A sick person may need drugs, but a healthy person does not. Should drugs be included in a basket of essential goods? A healthy 65-year-old widow who owns her own house and has a supportive family close by may live comfortably on $1,200 a month. On the other hand, a disabled 45-year-old man who must rent and has no family to help out may be hard pressed to get by on $2,400 a month. A medical school student may live happily on $1,000 month, while an unskilled labourer with the same income but little chance of improvement feels hopelessness. Any dollar value we choose to set as a poverty line is subject to debate. In fact, since 1990 StatCan has also published another set of low-income measures. They vary according to the number of adults and children in a family, but not place of residence. This set is not based on the cost of buying a basket of essentials. These low-income measures are based on one-half the median family income in Canada. For a family of two adults and two children in 1992, the low-income measure was $18,700. The 1992 StatCan low-income cut-off for a family of four was between $20,494 and $30,105, depending on the place of residence. The 1992 poverty threshold level for a family of four for the United States was $16,428 Canadian. All these poverty lines are different. None are wrong. They simply reflect different value judgments. We can define poverty in many different ways. Some individuals who have low incomes are happy, and some individuals with high incomes are sad. Unfortunately, we have no way to measure happiness, but we can measure income, so we use it as our yardstick. Just as a meter is longer than a yard, one index can be different from another. We have to choose one that we find useful. For this discussion we will use the StatCan low-income cut-offs (1986 base) because they will allow us to make a number of comparisons. For convenience we will refer to anyone with an income below the low-income cut-offs as "poor."

Who Are the Poor?

In 1993, StatCan reported that 1,116,000 families and 1,306,000 unattached individuals in Canada were poor. Altogether that amounted to 4,775,000 people or 17.4 percent of Canada's population. We have to have a policy to deal with these poor people. (Even if we decide that the government should not intervene to help, we have a policy.) Whether or not we want the government to intervene probably depends upon who the poor are. How the government should intervene also depends on who the poor are. In 1971, for example, 34.8 percent of all families whose head was 65 or older were poor. The incidence of poverty was far higher among the elderly than among any other age group. The government increased assistance to the elderly, and by 1980 the incidence of poverty among families with an aged head was only 8.1 percent. Clearly the first thing we need to know is who are the poor. Table 7–2 gives the incidence of poverty by different characteristics. For families the characteristic refers to the head.

As you can see from the table, unattached individuals are much more likely to be poor than members of a family. Families in Quebec and Newfoundland are more likely to be poor than families elsewhere in Canada. Similarly unattached individuals in Quebec, Newfoundland, and New Brunswick have the highest incidence of poverty. In a market economy, we might assume that either out migration would occur by those living in Newfoundland and Quebec or employers would move into the area in hopes of low labour costs. However, barriers may impede this market

Table 7–2 The incidence of poverty in 1993

Characteristics	Families	Individuals
By Province		
Newfoundland	16.1%	41.4%
Prince Edward Island	7.0	32.2
Nova Scotia	14.5	32.4
New Brunswick	11.9	41.3
Quebec	17.6	45.0
Ontario	13.4	32.7
Manitoba	14.4	36.7
Saskatchewan	13.8	31.2
Alberta	15.0	38.6
British Columbia	14.0	34.4
By Age		
<25 years	42.8%	59.1%
25–34 years	21.5	29.3
35–44 years	13.9	26.5
45–54 years	9.5	51.4
55–64 years	12.8	38.5
>64 years	10.8	43.2
By Age and Sex		
Males < 65	10.9%	32.3%
Males > 64	10.1	32.1
All males	10.8	32.2
Females < 65	45.6	37.9
Females > 64	16.0	32.1
All females	41.5	41.7
By Employment Status		
Worked full-time–full year	5.2%	8.8%
Other workers	23.8	49.5
Did not work	29.5	56.0
By Education		
0–8 years	19.9%	57.8%
Some secondary	19.6	44.7
Completed high school	15.3	33.2
Some postsecondary	16.5	43.3
Postsecondary diploma	12.0	27.1
University degree	7.8	20.1

Source: Statistics Canada (1993), *Income Distribution by Size in Canada*, Ottawa (13-207).

adjustment. Newfoundland has an isolated location, and language and cultural barriers exist between Quebec and English Canada. We may also find some discrimination against French-speaking workers in English Canada.

Young families and individuals have a markedly higher incidence of poverty than any other age group. Many of this group have not completed their education and are not yet in the labour force. Those out of school lack job experience and consequently earn lower wages. In recent years the members of this cohort have been fighting to enter the labour market at a time when job creation has been low. As a result many of this group are unemployed or underemployed.

The incidence of poverty among families headed by females is much higher than the incidence of poverty among families headed by males. In part, this figure is a statistical illusion. If a male and a female adult live in a family, the family will tend to identify the male as the head. Therefore, most families headed by a female have only one wage earner, while many families headed by a male have two wage earners. However, unattached females have a substantially higher incidence of poverty than unattached males have. A number of factors explain the lower income of women. Many observers feel that a substantial proportion of the gender gap can be explained in terms of discrimination. The issue of discrimination is discussed in the next chapter. They would argue that the low income of female-headed families is one of the more important social issues facing our economy.

Poverty is comparatively rare among families where the head works the entire year. The same is true for unattached individuals. However, the incidence of poverty soars for all other families and individuals. Part-time workers, even if they work the entire year, are far more likely to be poor than are full-time workers. So are workers who have seasonal jobs or who are laid off for any significant period during the year. Canada's "poverty problem" would be greatly lessened if we could lower unemployment. The issue of unemployment is discussed in Chapter 13.

The last important factor in poverty is education. The incidence of poverty declines as the level of education increases. If the head of the family has less than a grade-eight education, the probability that the family will live in poverty is more than 2.5 times greater than if the head has a university degree. One curious fact that someone who starts a postsecondary program but then drops out is more likely to be poor than someone who completes only high school. Quitting is not rewarded. Of all the factors that contributed to poverty, education is the one that society can most easily change.

The Upward Struggle of the Poor

It is often stated that a person living in poverty today will likely live in poverty in the future. The main argument is that a poor person becomes "trapped" and has little chance of breaking out of the economic conditions that put him or her there in the first place. Furthermore, some believe that a poor person does not have the motivation to advance and is even encouraged to retain a low economic status by low-income support programs of the government. Others believe that the poor do not have the opportunity to lift themselves or their children out of poverty. As you read in the last section, lack of education is highly correlated with poverty. In many cases a vicious circle exists. Families are poor because they lack education. Their poverty begets a lack of education in the next generation, which may in part be because poor families do not value education. They pass that attitude on to their children. However, even if poor families understand the need for education, they cannot afford the cost of books and supplies or the cost of tuition if a child is to go beyond high school. Still more important is the opportunity cost. Even 20 hours a week at minimum wage is a significant sum of money to a family on a subpoverty line income. Lack of education is not the only possible reason for the vicious circle of poverty. A poor diet for young children can affect their development and their ability to become functional adults. Poor prenatal diet, inadequate prenatal medical care, and prenatal alcohol and drug abuse can destine the child to a marginalized life. Some commentators believe that living on welfare eventually suppresses the will to try to improve one's situation.

We have very little research on the upward mobility of the poor, but an Economic Council of Canada Study (1992) does provide some information.[2] Its research indicated that between 1982 and 1986 about 27 percent of those who were poor in any given year escaped poverty the next year. A slightly smaller number enter into poverty each year, so the overall poverty rate did not decline that much. However, many of those who escaped became poor again in a later year. Nevertheless, only 5.9 percent of the Canadian population were poor in all five years of the study. An American study also indicates that the proportion of the "permanent" poor is a minority.[3]

Poverty in Terms of Income Distribution

The second approach to poverty considers the distribution of income in Canada. We have said that the poverty problem in this country is mainly one of income distribution. Therefore, the level of income in our country is high enough so that a more equal distribution of income should mitigate if not eliminate the poverty problem.

---

[2]Economic Council of Canada, *The New Face of Poverty* (Ottawa: Minister of Supply and Services Canada, 1992).

[3]G. J. Duncan, *Years of Poverty, Years of Plenty* (Ann Arbor, MI: Institute for Social Research, University of Michigan, 1984).

Income Equality

A **Lorenz curve** is one way to measure the distribution of income. A Lorenz curve can be drawn by ordering families (or individuals) from the lowest income to the highest income and then graphing the cumulative proportion of income received against the cumulative proportion of families (or individuals).

Economists sometimes explain income equality and income inequality by reference to a curve called a *Lorenz curve*, after M. O. Lorenz. Income equality among families means that any given percentage of families receives an equal percentage of family income: 10 percent of families receives 10 percent of income, 20 percent of families receives 20 percent of income, and 100 percent of families receives 100 percent of income. In Figure 7–2, equal percentages of families and incomes can be measured along the two axes. Income equality is shown by a 45-degree line starting at the origin. At any point on the 45-degree line, the percentage of families shown receives an equal percentage of total family income.

Income Inequality

Income inequality can be illustrated graphically by lines that deviate from the line of income equality. A Lorenz curve derived from actual data on income distribution will lie to the right of the line of income equality (the 45-degree line). The farther to the right of the 45-degree line it lies, the greater the inequality in income distribution. Lorenz curves are useful in illustrating income distribution comparisons in a given year among different countries or in the same country over time.

Table 7–3 divides families into five numerically equal groups, or quintiles, and indicates the distribution of personal income among these groups. You can see that income is distributed very unequally. The highest 20 percent of families received 39.9 percent of income in 1993, and the lowest 20 percent received 6.4 percent. For reference the quintiles are also given for 1971 and 1981. The 1993 data on income inequality was used to draw the Lorenz curve in Figure 7–2. Income shares are before taxes; however, they include any cash transfers. For comparison the last column (1993AT) shows the after-tax share of income for 1993. As you can see, the after-tax distribution of income is slightly more equal than the before-tax distribution. The effects of taxation on the distribution of income will be discussed later in this chapter and again in Chapter 15.

Income inequality was reduced during the 1930s and the years of World War II. The share of income received by the highest 20 percent of families decreased dramatically between 1929 and 1944, while the share received by the lowest 20 percent of families increased. Economists generally agree that the two main reasons for this trend toward greater income equality are that property income fell drastically during the Great Depression of the 1930s and that the gap between low-paid and high-paid workers was reduced when full employment was reached during World War II.

During the 1980s, income inequality increased slightly. The share of income going to the top 20 percent income class increased from 38.4 percent

Figure 7–2 **The Lorenz curve for Canada for 1993**

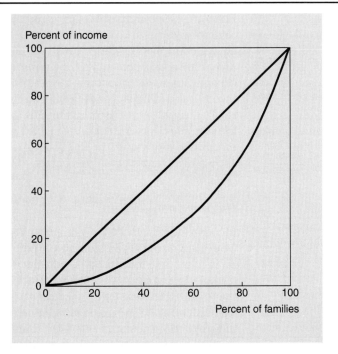

The Lorenz curve shows the degree of inequality in income distribution among families in Canada in 1993. The horizontal axis measures the percentage of families, starting with the poorest. Thus, 20 percent represents the lowest fifth of the families. In 1993 the lowest 20 percent earned 6.4 percent of the total income, and the lowest 40 percent earned 18.4 percent. If perfect income equality existed, the Lorenz curve would be a 45-degree line.

Source: Statistics Canada (various years), *Income Distribution by Size in Canada*, Ottawa (13-207).

Table 7–3 **Income distribution among families for Canada (by quintiles)**

Quintile	1971	1981	1993	1993AT
Lowest	5.6	6.4	6.4	7.7
Second	12.6	12.9	12.0	13.2
Third	18.0	18.3	17.6	18.1
Fourth	23.7	24.1	24.1	23.8
Highest	40.0	38.4	39.9	37.2

Note: Total may not sum to 100 percent because of rounding.

Source: Statistics Canada (various years), *Income Distribution by Size in Canada* and *Income After Tax, Distribution by Size in Canada*, Ottawa (13-207 and 13-210).

to 39.9 percent between 1981 and 1983, a percentage increase of 7.5 percent. All of the income classes by quintiles with the exception of the lowest and the highest 20 percent received a smaller share of income in 1993 as compared to 1981.

The Economic Causes of Poverty

Determinants of Resource Prices and Employment

Family incomes depend on the quantities of resources that families can place in the market and the prices received for those resources. To understand poverty, then, we need to understand what determines the prices paid for human, capital, and natural resources and what determines the quantities that can be employed.

Wage Rate Determination. Under competitive market conditions, the basic principle of wage rate determination is that units (person-hours) of any kind of labour tend to be paid a price equal to any one worker's (hourly) contribution to an employer's total receipts. In other words, workers are paid about what they are worth to employers. Economists refer to what a worker is worth to an employer as the *marginal revenue product of labour (MRP$_l$)*. MRP_l is the change in the firm's total revenue resulting from adding or subtracting the last unit of labour, say, adding an hour of work or adding another worker. Thus it indicates the value of a unit of labour to the firm. The concept of marginal revenue product will be thoroughly developed in the next chapter but, because of its relevance to the causes of poverty will be briefly outlined here.

The **marginal revenue product of labour** *(MRP$_l$)* is the change in total revenue resulting from the addition of an extra worker.

Suppose the marginal revenue product of the worker is $11 per hour; that is, an hour of labour is contributing $11 to the receipts of the employer. Then the worker is worth $11 an hour to the employer and would be paid that amount under competitive conditions. If a worker is paid less than what she or he is worth to an employer, the worker would also be paid less than she or he would be worth to other employers. Consequently, other employers would bid for the worker's services, driving up the worker's wage rate (hourly wages) to what she or he is worth. On the other hand, rather than pay $12 an hour, an employer would lay off a worker.

This principle can be seen more clearly with reference to Figure 7–3. The demand curve for labour shows what employers are willing to pay at different quantities of labour (person-hours per month), or alternatively, how much a unit of labour is worth at different possible employment levels. The supply curve for labour shows the quantity of labor that will be placed on the market at different wage rates. If labour is paid less than $11 per hour, the hours workers want to supply is less than the hours employees want to hire. If the wage rate is more than $11 per hour, the amount of

Figure 7–3   **Wage rate determination in a competitive market**

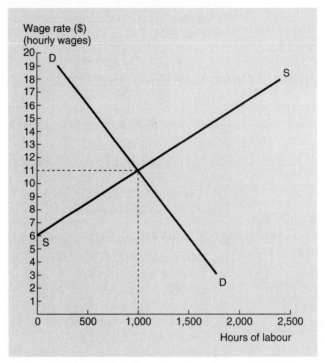

Notice that there is only one wage rate—$11—where the market is in equilibrium.

labour employers want to hire is less than the number of hours workers want of work. Only at $11 per hour is the quantity of labor supplied equal to the quantity of labour demanded. Thus in a competitive market the wage rate will move to $11 per hour.

The Price of Capital and Natural Resources. In a competitive market the price of a unit of capital, say a machine, is determined in a way similar to the price of a unit of labour. The price of any kind of capital depends on the demand for and supply of units of capital, and at market equilibrium, the price of capital equals what that capital is worth to its employer. The same principle holds for natural resources.

Determination of Individual or Family Income

The income of a person depends on the *price* he or she receives for his or her resources and the *quantities* of resources he or she can place in employment. For example, the monthly family income from labour equals the quantity of its labour employed multiplied by the wage rate. From capital, its income equals the quantity of capital employed multiplied by the price of each unit of capital. Total monthly family income, then, is a summation of all monthly income flows.

Determinants of Income Distribution

The distribution of income among individuals and families depends on the distribution of resource ownership and the prices paid for resources of different kinds in different employments. The ownership pattern of resources is unequally distributed among individuals and families. This unequal ownership pattern of resources gives rise to an unequal distribution of income in our society. People at the bottom of the income ladder own a small share of the nation's resources on which the market places a high value.

Causes of Differences in Labour Resource Ownership

Brains and Brawn. The inheritance of mental and physical talents is not equally distributed among people. Some people have greater capabilities than others. Some families have exceptional learning abilities; others have special labour resources—talents such as acting, singing, playing hockey or baseball. Other families are not so fortunately endowed.

Skill Levels. Skill levels vary among individuals. Differences in skills among people are primarily due to differences in inherited capabilities, training opportunities, and discrimination. Some people inherit specific abilities to do certain tasks better than other workers. Most often people with high skill levels have acquired them from their training and education. In some instances, people have low skill levels because they have been discriminated against and have not had equal opportunities for training and education. Even with the same training, certain groups, say women and visible minorities, may not receive the same pay as others, although they perform the same tasks. In general, those with highly developed skills are worth more and, therefore, are paid more in the market than are unskilled or semiskilled workers.

Capacity Utilization Rate. The capacity utilization rate is the ratio of actual earnings to earnings capacity. Utilization rates differ among people for many reasons, including their individual difference with respect to their preferences for income and leisure and with respect to their responsiveness to changes in their income due to, say, taxes and government transfer payments. Also, some people, such as working wives, may have low utilization rates because of certain labour supply barriers. In general, the variation in earnings capacity seems to be far more important in explaining income inequality than is the variation in capacity utilization rates. Moreover, involuntary unemployment plays a significant role in the variation of capacity utilization.

Causes of Differences in Capital Resource Ownership

Inheritance. Some individuals and families inherit real property and claims on real property such as stocks, bonds, real estate, and other assets. These people have a head start over people who do not begin with inherited capital resources.

Luck. Luck is not evenly distributed among the population. Some families may be at or near the bottom of the income pyramid because of bad luck. A business failure caused by a depression, a prolonged illness, a fatal or disabling accident, or a natural disaster may leave persons and families without income or the ability to earn an adequate income. Others may do very well because they were in the right place at the right time. One might even argue that those born before the baby boom were born at the right time, while those in "generation X" were much less lucky.

Propensities to Accumulate. People vary as to their propensities or tendencies to save and accumulate capital resources. Those who are strongly motivated are willing to forego consumption today in order to enjoy greater income in the future. Others are more concerned about their current consumption standards. They do not save and do not accumulate capital resources. Those who accumulate a large amount of capital may then find it very much easier to accumulate still more.

Summary of the Causes of Poverty

Several things are clear about the poor and about low-income families. They have small quantities and low qualities of resources. The market places a low value on the services they provide in the market. The low productivity and, therefore, the low pay of the poor may be due to low levels of training and education, misfortune, relatively small inheritances, and discrimination. The poor are in a vicious circle that is difficult to escape. What they need in order to move out of poverty, they do not have and cannot afford to acquire. So they remain poor.

Government Attempts to Alleviate Poverty

The first question is not, How does the government alleviate poverty? but Ought the government alleviate poverty? This is a normative question, so it has no "right" answer. Nevertheless, the question is important. Virtually all governments provide some form of social assistance. Table 7–4 shows the level of social-assistance spending in several countries. Amounts do not include spending on health or education.

Societies choose to provide social assistance for a number of reasons. Probably the most important is altruism. Most of the world's major religions teach that some form of sharing is good. Many people, even those not particularly religious, tend to feel some concern for their fellows. An individual may actually gain satisfaction from helping others, or may gain satisfaction from seeing those less fortunate become better off. Economists often refer to satisfaction as utility. Alternatively, individuals may feel guilt if they do not share. Societies may share for reasons other than altruism. No individual can ever be completely sure about the future. Social assistance can be regarded as part of a social contract. If I do well, I will pay more taxes in order to help those who do less well. If I do not do well, I will be entitled to collect benefits. In this context, social assistance becomes social insurance. Some of Canada's assistance programs are actually run more or less like insurance programs. The last possible reason for social assistance might be called the bread-and-circus approach. It is a response to the fear among those who have that the have-nots will revolt and simply take what they want. While a "revolution of the proletariat" seems unlikely in Canada today, many of our social programs date back to the Great Depression when that fear was far greater.

Society also has reasons for not providing social assistance. The most obvious is that some individuals may not receive any utility from giving or seeing those less fortunate better off. A second reason has to do with the

Table 7–4	Level of social spending as a percentage of GDP in selected countries for 1985			
Country	Pensions Spending	Unemployment Programs	Other Programs	Total Social Programs
Denmark	8.5	3.2	9.8	21.5
France	12.7	2.8	5.8	21.3
Netherlands	10.5	3.3	4.8	18.6
Italy	15.6	0.8	. . .	15.4
United Kingdom	6.7	1.8	2.2	10.7
Canada	5.4	3.3	1.6	10.3
United States	7.2	0.4	0.9	8.5
Australia	(for 1984) 4.9	1.3	. . .	7.1
Japan	5.3	0.4	1.4	7.1

Source: Economic Council of Canada (1992), *The New Face of Poverty*, Ottawa.

need for incentives in a market economy. Social assistance is often seen as reducing the incentive to work or to save, thereby reducing society's total output and making us all worse off. Whether one gains utility from the welfare of others is an ethical or moral question, and economics cannot answer moral questions. Whether or not inequality will breed revolution or Canada's Unemployment Insurance Plan Program will create disincentives to work are empirical questions. Economics can objectively answer such questions. Unfortunately, they are very difficult questions and to date definitive answers have not been found. Still, Canada like all other industrial countries has a complex social safety net. We will look at Canada's system of social security.

Two approaches to poverty are suggested by the foregoing analysis. First, we can try to remedy the symptoms of poverty. The main symptom of poverty is low-income. To remedy low income we have simply to transfer income to the poor. Some people, such as the very young, the very old, the disabled, and the ill, cannot earn income. For such individuals all society can do to assist them is provide income-support programs because they either are unproductive or at best their productivity is too low to allow them to support themselves. Second, we can try to remedy the causes of poverty. For example, we can increase the productivity of the employable poor through subsidized education for the children of the poor, adult training and education programs, counselling and guidance, job-placement programs, and elimination of discrimination. Clearly, remedying the causes, rather than treating the symptoms, is the better approach.

Programs for the Aged

The *Old Age Pension Act* was passed in 1927. Over the years, income support for the aged has changed and become considerably more generous. Today three federal programs assist seniors: *Old Age Security (OAS), Guaranteed Income Supplement (GIS),* and *Canada (Quebec) Pension Plan (CPP or QPP).*

OAS. OAS is a universal program, financed out of general revenue. Most Canadian residents 65 or older receive OAS. It is taxable income so the government recovers some of the benefits paid to higher-income Canadians. In 1994 seniors who earned $53,215 or more had to repay all or part of their OAS pension. Universal programs have frequently been criticized in recent years, but they have some advantages. They are easy and inexpensive to administer. All the government has to do is determine that the applicant is a Canadian resident and is at least 65 years old. As we will see later, universal programs also tend to have less disincentive effect. Finally, no one attaches a stigma to cashing on OAS cheque. Because most seniors get an OAS cheque, there is no presumption of "laziness." However, the government must collect more taxes to pay seniors, even those with substantial other income, OAS. The benefit is indexed, so payments increase with inflation. As of April 1994 the maximum OAS payment was $387.74 per month for an individual and $775.48 for a couple.

GIS. GIS is not a universal program; it is means tested. GIS is a type of negative income tax plan. (We will discuss negative income tax plans in general later in this chapter.) Although all Canadian seniors are eligible, only about half have a low enough income to actually receive GIS benefits. If a senior had no income except for OAS, he or she would qualify for full GIS. As of April 1994 full benefits were about $460 per month for an individual and about $590 for a couple. Benefits are indexed in the same way as OAS. GIS is not subject to regular income tax. However, each additional dollar of income earned reduces the GIS benefit by 50 cents. OAS is not considered income for this purpose. Now you can see why a universal program has less disincentive effect than other types of income assistance plans. Assume that a elderly widow, whose only income was OAS and GIS, was offered a part-time baby-sitting job. If the job paid $200 a month, it would have no effect on her OAS; she would still collect full benefits. However, she would lose $100 (.5 × $200) of her GIS. In effect, she would net only $100 for baby sitting. Still the situation could be worse. Many income-assistance plans would be reduced by the entire amount of the earnings, entirely removing the incentive to work.

CPP and QPP. These two plans are essentially the same. QPP covers workers in Quebec and is controlled by the Quebec government. CPP covers workers in the rest of Canada. Unlike GIS and OAS, CPP (QPP) are not, strictly speaking, a form of income assistance. Workers and their employers pay premiums during the individual's working years. The benefits retirees receive depend upon the amount they paid into the plan. In 1994 employees had to pay 2.6 percent of their income in CPP. The first $3,400 of income was exempted. The year's maximum pensionable earnings (YMPE) was $34,400. No premium was collected on income above that amount. An individual earning the YMPE or more in 1994 would have paid $806 in premiums. His or her employer would have paid the same amount. Self-employed workers have to pay both the employee and employer contributions.

The maximum benefit that an individual can receive at age 65 is 25 percent of the YMPE. For 1994 that would have been $694.44 monthly. Individuals who earned less than the YMPE or who were not employed for a sufficient number of years receive less. The plan also provides benefits for surviving spouses and in some cases children and for disabled workers. CPP (QPP) benefits are taxable and fully indexed to inflation.

In the best of all worlds the contributions would have been large enough and invested well enough so that the plan would always have sufficient funds to pay all benefits. In the political world in which we live, the contributions were not large enough and the funds were not invested. For many years funding benefits was not a problem. Benefits were far less than the current revenue, and the plan was run on a pay-as-you-go basis. In recent years, however, concerns have been raised about the future of CPP (QPP). As the population, particularly the baby boom, ages, the fund is in danger of going broke. Premiums are being increased. By 2011 the combined premiums are scheduled to increase to 9.1 percent. At some point benefits may be decreased or the retirement age increased. Alternatively, the extra funds will have to come out of general revenue. Many younger workers believe that CPP will disappear completely by the time that they retire.

Several provinces have their own income-assistance programs for the elderly, but the benefits are relatively modest and not likely to have much influence on anyone's decision to retire.

Some people believe that everyone should provide for his or her own retirement, and many Canadians do save in order to be able to enjoy a more comfortable retirement. However, the government provides many savers with a form of income assistance, too. Subject to certain regulation, the government allows taxpayers to shelter income from taxes in registered retirement savings plans (RRSP) and registered pension plans (RPP). While that income will eventually be taxed, it is likely to be taxed at a lower rate and at a much later time. The ability to tax shelter retirement saving represents a significant tax loss to the government.

Employment Insurance

Most Canadian workers are covered by employment insurance (EI). At the end of 1995, the federal government proposed a number of changes to unemployment insurance (UI). Its name was changed to employment insurance (EI). Under the changes, hourly and salaried workers have to work between 420 and 700 hours to be eligible to collect EI benefits. The qualifying period depends upon the regional unemployment rate. Normally, workers must be laid off to collect benefits. Those who are dismissed for cause (fired) or quit are not eligible for benefits. Those who qualified received 55 percent of their salary. In 1996, the maximum benefit was $413 per week. Families with annual incomes below $26,000 would be eligible for supplemental benefits. Individuals with incomes over $48,750 are subject to a partial tax on benefits. Benefits can last up to 45 weeks depending upon the regional unemployment rate and the number of weeks worked. Benefits may decrease for repeat users.

EI is an insurance plan. In theory the premiums paid by employees and employers fund the program. However, the unemployment rate has been higher than anticipated when the plan was established and EI has required funds from general tax revenue. The 1996 rates for employees are $2.95 per $100 of insured earnings and for employers $4.13 per $100. Only about $39,000 of income is insured.

Some other benefits are also available under EI. It will provide up to 15 weeks of sickness benefits. New mothers receive 15 weeks of maternity benefits. Ten weeks of parental benefit are also available. Finally a number of training programs are available to unemployed workers. They will be discussed later.

EI has been very controversial. Unemployment insurance in the United States varies from state to state but is generally less generous than the Canadian plan. (New York state actually has an even more generous plan than Canada.) The ease with which workers can qualify and the high level of support has led many to conclude that EI is a partial cause of the relatively high rates of unemployment in this country. Some critics claim that EI is a subsidy to seasonal industries such as fishing. Some labour leaders have implied that some employers use EI to reduce their labour costs by laying off workers quickly in slack time, secure in the knowledge that their former employees are not so likely to take other jobs if they are on EI. These problems influenced the federal government to tighten up EI and more changes are possible.

Training and Employment. A high proportion of the unemployed are young, relatively inexperienced and often poorly trained. Therefore, EI offers a number of training and retraining programs. The provinces also offer assistance with training, but since those programs vary depending upon the province we will look at the federal programs.

In some cases the unemployed can be helped through employment counselling. Job seekers may simply need information on available employment. Counsellors can advise job seekers (clients) on possible career choices and try to ensure that the job seeker has realistic goals. If appropriate, a training program may be considered.

Training can range from two day courses on job-search strategies to multiyear training programs. Most of the training is vocationally oriented. Project-based training combines classroom and on-site training. It is intended to provide technical job skills as well as life and interpersonal relation skills. Much of the training undertaken by EI recipients is purchased either by EI or by the client. The type of training depends upon the client and the labour market requirements. Eligible programs include vocational and skills training, academic upgrading (generally high school completion), language courses for students not able to function well enough in French or English, and apprenticeship training programs. EI assisted trainees receive benefits while in training. In rare cases, benefits could extend up to three years, but more than one year is uncommon. EI may pay all or part of the cost of training, but in some cases the client must pay the costs. All training programs must be approved by EI.

Canada Assistance Plan

Social assistance or welfare is a provincial responsibility; however, the federal government shares the cost of social assistance under the Canada Assistance Plan (CAP). The February 27, 1995, budget speech proposed dismantling CAP and replacing it with block grants. Federal funding of medicare and postsecondary education was changed to block grants in 1977 under an arrangement referred to as Established Program Financing (EPF). Under EPF the federal government transfers funds to the provincial governments partly in the form of cash grants and partly in the form of tax points. The transfer of tax points means that the federal government decreases its tax rates and the provincial government increases its tax rate. Two significant differences exist between the cost-sharing and EPF approaches. First, the federal contribution decreases. Second, the degree of federal control decreases. Under CAP the federal government has, under the threat of decreased funding, been able to impose three conditions upon the provinces. First, the provinces must provide assistance to all persons judged to be in need. Second, they must implement an appeal procedure against welfare rulings. Last, they cannot impose any residence requirements. The first two of these conditions will disappear with CAP. The formal repeal of CAP will not come before March 31, 2000, so CAP is still relevant for our discussion.

Who Is Eligible for CAP?   While the federal government is involved in sharing the cost of welfare, the administration of welfare is left to the lower levels of government. As a result welfare varies from province to province and even from locality to locality within provinces. However, some common qualifying conditions generally exist across Canada. Obviously, those with adequate income do not qualify. Usually, only those between 18 and 65 are eligible. People 65 or older should qualify for OAS and GIS, and those under 18 would normally be expected to live at home, although they may qualify for assistance in special cases. Generally, students do not qualify, but often those who otherwise qualify are allowed to undertake training in order to improve their employability and get them off the welfare rolls. CAP limits the assets a recipient can hold, but some fixed assets are usually allowed. These assets could include a house, possibly a car, and tools required to work. Liquid assets such as a bank account, over a set maximum, must be cashed in and used before a person can qualify for assistance. Provinces impose their own standards with regard to liquid assets, but they may not exceed the federal maximums, which are $2,500 for individuals ($3,000 if disabled or aged) and $5,000 for a couple or individual with a dependent. Each additional dependent increases the limit by $500. The system also defines limits on the amount of income that an individual or family can have and still qualify. Income from some sources (federal GST rebate and child tax benefit) is not usually included in the calculation. If the applicants' needs exceed their ability to pay, they qualify for assistance. Only assistance to those deemed in need qualifies for federal cost sharing. Obviously, the process of determining need is somewhat subjective.

Determination of the Rate of Assistance. Each province determines its own rates of assistance. Generally, the costs of essentials, food, clothing, shelter, utilities, and household and personal needs are included. Special needs such as medicines are included when required. Households that live in larger centers usually receive a greater shelter allowance to cover the higher rent they must pay. Similarly, those who live in remote areas may receive extra funds to reflect the higher cost of transportation. In some provinces employable recipients receive lower benefits than unemployable recipients receive.

Rates of Assistance. Actual rates of assistance vary considerably from province to province. Table 7–5 gives the basic social assistance rates by province for 1994. Four cases are given for each province.

Residents of the two territories are also eligible for social assistance. The rates in the Yukon and the Northwest Territories are relatively high, reflecting the high cost of living in the North.

Welfare is in a state of change. Alberta has already dramatically changed its social-assistance program by reducing its welfare rolls by about 50 percent between 1993 and 1995. Most of the people dropped were employables; some of them have moved into jobs, while others have entered training programs. The Alberta Minister of Family and Social Services announced plans to get all employables off welfare. The province of New Brunswick has reformed its welfare by moving to "workfare" for its employable recipients. The newly elected Harris government in Ontario has announced major cuts in welfare funding. Other provinces may follow suit, particularly as CAP funding is reduced.

Income Tax

Taxes can be used to redistribute income. Most individuals in Canada pay a variety of taxes. We will consider only some of the taxes that individuals pay. Individuals pay *federal* income tax and the goods and services tax. (GST): they pay the *provincial* income tax and except for Alberta the provincial sales tax (PST); individuals also pay local property taxes. Taxes can be progressive, proportional, or regressive. A proportional tax takes the same percentage of income from each taxpayer. A regressive tax takes a higher proportion of income from those with low incomes and a lower proportion from those with high incomes. A progressive tax takes a higher proportion of income from those with high income and a lower proportion from those with low income. Canadian income tax is progressive. In 1994 there were three tax rates. Those with very low income paid no tax. The exact threshold at which an individual has to pay tax depends upon her or his tax deductions and tax credits. Those with taxable income less than $29,590 paid 17 percent federal income tax. On taxable income between $29,590 and $59,180, the federal tax rate was 26 percent. Federally, all income over

Table 7–5	Basic social assistance rates for 1994 by province			
Province	**Single Employment**	**Disabled Person**	**1 Parent; 1 Child**	**2 Parents; 2 Children**
Newfoundland	$4,326	$6,810 +1,500	$11,262	$12,186
Prince Edward Island	7,160	7,860 +1,092	10,860	16,008 +175
Nova Scotia	5,904	8,568	10,560	12,432
New Brunswick	.3,084	6,296 +1,800	8,844	9,876
Quebec	6,000	8,088	10,200 +1,080	12,000 +1,219
Ontario	7,956	11,160	14,652 +105	18,723 +407
Manitoba	5,914	7,157 +840	9,636	16,103
Saskatchewan	5,760	7,500 +780	10,381	14,640 +160
Alberta	4,728	6,348 220	9,192	14,472
British Columbia	6,530	9,220	11,746	14,818

Note: Amounts indicated in the partial rows represent additional benefits to all or some of the recipients in that category for the province in the row above. In a few cases, other minor additional benefits may be given. For example, British Columbia gives a Christmas "bonus" to all recipients.

Source: National Council of Welfare (1995), *Welfare Incomes 1994*, Ottawa.

$59,180 was taxed at 29 percent. In addition to federal income tax, individuals must pay provincial tax for the province in which she or he lives. Provincial taxes are a proportion of federal taxes. The proportion depends upon the province in which one lives. Provinces' taxes range from about 45 percent to about 60 percent of federal taxes. For the sake of our discussion, let us assume that provincial income tax rate is 50 percent of federal tax. Under that assumption, an individual with a taxable income of $100,000 would pay $.435 in taxes on each additional dollar of income, an individual with a taxable income of $50,000 would pay $.39 on each additional dollar of income, and an individual with a taxable income of $20,000 would pay $.255.

The Canadian income tax system allows two ways for expenses to be written off an individual's income tax. One is a tax deduction. The other is a tax credit. Tax deductions include contributions to RRSP and RPP, child care expenses, union and professional dues, and alimony and maintenance payments. Most other allowable expenditures can be claimed as tax credits. Credits include the basic personal amount, CPP and EI premiums, charitable donations, donations to political parties, and educational fees.

Tax credits are relatively new. Until recently all write-offs came in the form of tax deductions. The shift from deductions to credits was made to make the income tax more progressive. When individuals claim tax deductions, they subtract the deduction from their income and then pay taxes on the net income. A $1,000 deduction would reduce taxes by $255 for the individual with $20,000 income. It would reduce taxes by $390 for the individual with the $50,000 income and by $435 for the $100,000 income. The higher income individual benefits the most from the tax deduction. A tax credit is subtracted at a specified rate from the individual's taxes. Most tax credits are calculated at the 17 percent rate against the federal tax. For our hypothetical province with a 50 percent tax rate, the tax credit would reduce the taxes on all three individuals by $255. The rich individual would no longer gain more than the low-income individual.

GST Credit. Sales taxes such as the GST and the PST can be progressive, proportional, or regressive. Generally sales taxes tend to be regressive. By excluding food and including services, the degree of regressiveness is decreased. Property taxes also tend to be regressive. Generally renters "pay" the property tax in the form of higher rents. When the GST was first introduced, one of the criticisms of it was that it would be regressive. To offset this situation, the federal government refunds GST to low-income Canadians. The amount of the GST rebate depends upon one's income and the number of dependents. In 1994 the basic credit for an individual was $199, and for a family of three, it was $503. A family of three should have applied for the GST credit if its income did not exceed $36,000.

Child Tax Benefit. In 1944 the federal government introduced family allowances or, as they were popularly called, "baby bonuses." Over the years family allowances evolved into a universal program for all Canadian families with children. During the 1980s the government considered changing this program so that only lower-income families would be eligible, but at first any move away from universality met strong opposition. Eventually the opposition was overcome, and family allowances were completely phased out by January 1, 1993. The new program was the child tax benefit, which replaced family allowances; the refundable child tax credit; and the non-refundable child tax credit. In order to receive the benefit, the family must file a tax return. The program is federal, but the provinces have some input. In 1994 the maximum benefit in most provinces for a single parent with one child was $1,020 plus $213 if the child was less than seven years old. Quebec varies the payment depending upon the age of the child and the number of children. In Alberta the benefit varies with the age of the child.

Income in Kind

Income in kind refers to the transfer of goods or services instead of money. For example, in the United States, the federal government provides food stamps to low-income families. Economists generally regard the redistribution of income in kind as inefficient. Each individual is the best judge of his or her own needs. If the government provides goods or services instead of money, the individual will generally be less well-off than if she or he had been given money and allowed to choose among the available alternatives. Another argument is that income in kind is degrading to recipients because it treats them as unable to make responsible choices on their own. One argument for redistribution of income in kind is that it provides external benefits. For example, postsecondary education in Canada is heavily subsidized by the government. One reason for this subsidy is that a well-educated labour force benefits not only those who receive the education but also society in general. The total social benefits are greater than the private benefits to the students. Similarly the government provides Medicare, which can be justified in part on the grounds of external benefits and in part on the grounds of internal economies of scale.

An important form of redistribution of income in kind is government-subsidized housing for low-income families. Most Canadian cities have some subsidized housing, generally provided by local government. Subsidized housing falls under the external benefits argument. Slums are unsightly, and therefore their elimination benefits the general population by making the city more attractive. Some would also argue that slums breed crime, and therefore public housing is good.

Private Charity

You may wonder why private charity is being discussed in a section on government programs to redistribute income. The reason is that most private charity actually costs the government money. Charitable donations frequently earn a tax credit. Individuals earn a 17 percent credit against the federal income tax on the first $200 of donations and a 29 percent credit on the balance of their donation to a maximum of 20 percent of their income. Since provincial income tax is a proportion of an individual's federal tax, many donations earn about a 50 percent credit. In other words giving an additional $100 to charity only costs the individual about $50. The other $50 comes from the government in the form of a tax expenditure. A *tax expenditure* is the term economists use to refer to tax revenue lost by the government because of tax credits or deductions. Similarly, charitable donations by businesses reduce their corporate tax.

A **tax expenditure** is the tax revenue lost to the government because of a tax credit or tax deduction.

Canadians are not particularly generous. Americans donate about 2 percent of their income to charity. Germans donate about 1.7 percent. Canadians donate only about 0.5 percent, and the British donate only about 0.2 percent.[4] Still 0.5 percent of total Canadian income is a lot of money. When an individual gives to a food bank and claims a tax credit, every other taxpayer in Canada has to pay a part of that donation. In effect, that part of

---

[4]M. L. Katz and H. S. Rosen, *Microeconomics* (Burr Ridge, IL: Irwin, 1994), p. 75.

the donation becomes part of the government's redistribution policy. The same is true when an individual gives to the local opera. Only in that case, very few poor people will benefit from the government subsidy.

Price Floors and Ceilings

In addition to governmental programs specifically designed to alleviate poverty, the government has also intervened in the marketplace to assist the working poor. This intervention comes in the form of price controls—the legal imposition of prices either above or below the market-established equilibrium.

A **floor price** is a legislated minimum price. To have any effect, it must be set above the equilibrium price. In a free market, a floor price will result in a surplus. A minimum-wage law is an example of a floor price.

A *floor price* is a minimum allowable price for a good or service. Price floors, or minimum prices, are set by government for particular items. The intent of the government usually is to increase the incomes of those who sell the items. A classic example is that of minimum-wage legislation. All Canadian provinces have minimum-wage legislation. In 1994 they range from a low of $4.75 in Newfoundland and Prince Edward Island to $6.70 in Ontario. In addition, a federal minimum wage of $4.00 applies to work under federal jurisdiction. Governments can also pass a floor price for a particular commodity to increase the income of those who produce that commodity. For example, the government could enact a minimum price of wheat in a effort to increase the income of wheat farmers. Floor prices are an attempt to increase the incomes of the poor (and the not so poor) by increasing income without providing welfare.

A **ceiling price** is a legislated maximum price. To have any effect, it must be set below the equilibrium price. In a free market, a ceiling price will result in a shortage. Rent controls are an example of a ceiling price.

Ceiling prices are legislated maximum prices. Ceiling prices have been used as a means of controlling inflation. Massive inflation occurred during World War I. Therefore, when World War II started, the Canadian government established price controls on almost everything. The control prevented prices from increasing and in effect became ceiling prices. Price controls were combined with rationing. In order to buy a rationed good, the consumer had to have a ration coupon as well as the purchase price. During the war, price controls were effective largely because Canadians saw the controls as part of the war effort. In 1975 the Canadian government again tried to use price controls to limit inflation, but this time the controls were not very successful.

Ceiling prices can also be applied to a single good or service. For example, the government could decide that the price of milk is too high for low-income families and legislate a ceiling price on milk. In practice the most common ceiling price of this type has been rent controls.

Minimum Wages

Many people in our society favour minimum wages, which are often seen as a way of helping low-income families. Other people believe that minimum wages interfere with the market and increase unemployment, thereby actually hurting some low-income families. The exact effects of minimum wages are difficult to know for a variety of reasons.

The Effects of a Minimum Wage. Starting from the equilibrium wage of $5.00 in Figure 7–4, suppose a provincial legislature, concerned with the low incomes of unskilled workers, enacts a minimum wage of $5.50 per hour. What is the impact of the program? Consider the impact of the program on the demand for and supply of labour separately. Employers must now pay $5.50 for each unit of labour hired. Given that a rational employer will hire a worker only if the worker's marginal revenue product is greater than or equal to the wage, then the quantity of labour demanded will fall in response to the wage increase. Recalling that the demand for labour represents the marginal revenue product of labour, Figure 7–4 indicates that the quantity of labour demanded will fall to 700 hours when the wage rises to $5.50. The reason for this change is clear. For each unit of labour between the 800-hour and 700-hour levels of employment, the wage rate is greater than the marginal revenue product of labour.

The supply reaction to the minimum wage further complicates this situation. Specifically, the effect of the minimum is to increase the quantity

Figure 7–4   **The effects of a minimum wage law on a competitive market**

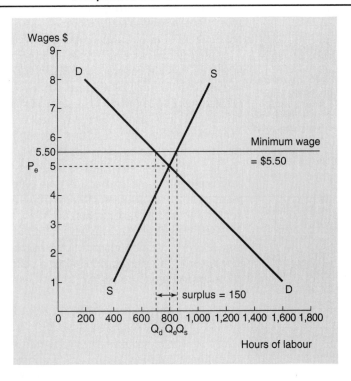

of labour supplied from 800 hours to 850 hours. This added labour is attracted into the labour market by the possibility of higher wages.

At the minimum wage of $5.50, then, we have a surplus of labour equal to 150 hours. That is, at this wage, workers wish to provide 150 hours of employment that no one wants. Notice that a minimum wage of $4.50 would have had no effect. A minimum wage below the equilibrium wage is said to be *non-binding*. For most workers even the $5.50 minimum wage is non-binding. However, for very young and inexperienced workers, or for workers with very little in the way of training or skills, minimum wages often are binding. In a competitive labour market, minimum wage laws can cause unemployment. If the labour market is not competitive—for example, there is only one employer, leaving the workers in a "take it or leave it" position—minimum wage legislation may not cause unemployment even if the minimum is binding. In theory, the establishment of a minimum wage can lead to some unemployment, but what about increases in an existing minimum wage? A bit of insight suggests that the analysis just presented is equally applicable to a minimum-wage increase as it is to the initial establishment of a minimum. For example, suppose that the existing minimum of $5.50 was increased to $6.00. What would be the result of such a policy? The quantity of labour demanded would fall further; the quantity of labour supplied would increase further; and the two taken together would lead to even more unemployment.

Given the unemployment effect of the minimum, we might conclude that minimum wages fail to make economic sense. Such a decision must rely on an analysis of the benefits and costs of the program. The costs are clear, but what are the benefits? Returning to Figure 7–4, we note that the minimum generated a good deal of unemployment, yet not all workers lost their jobs. In fact, 700 hours of labour remained employed. These workers clearly benefited from the establishment of the minimum, given that they earn more for their labour. Further, if these workers are from the lower end of the income distribution, the fact that they are earning more suggests that the minimum may tend to improve the distribution of earnings in the economy as a whole. It is also possible that if a worker can only hope for a very low paying job, that worker is more likely try to get social assistance. Some proponents of increased minimum wages argue that a higher minimum wage tends to stimulate the aggregate demand for goods and services and thereby create jobs.

Given that the minimum wage involves costs and benefits, to properly evaluate the minimum wage or increases in the minimum, we must answer three questions: How many people gain, and by how much do they gain when a minimum is established or increased? By how much does the unemployment rate rise when the minimum wage is increased? To what extent does the minimum improve the distribution of income in the economy? Relatively little research has been conducted on the first of these questions. An exception is the study by the United States Department of Labor concerning the 1981 increase in the minimum from $3.10 to $3.35 per hour. Its estimates suggest that 5.5 million workers stood to gain from the increase in the minimum. Further, the study indicates that the increase in the minimum added about $2 billion to the incomes of workers in the economy.

In contrast, a considerable amount of research has been done in a number countries directed toward analyzing the unemployment impact of increasing the minimum wage. Although the outcomes of these studies differ in some regards, two results are commonly found. First, in terms of increased unemployment, teenagers appear to be more vulnerable to harm by the minimum than any other group of workers, since they work in disproportionate numbers for the minimum wage. In fact, increases in the minimum appear to have little or no effect on the unemployment rate of adult workers. Beyond this, the research suggests that a 10 percent increase in the minimum is associated with an increase in the teenage unemployment rate of about 1/2 of 1 percent. For example, if the teenage unemployment rate is initially 18 percent and the minimum wage is increased by 10 percent, teenage unemployment can be expected to rise to about 18.5 percent.[5]

Research into the third question is also quite informative. Specifically, the evidence suggests that the minimum wage has little impact on the distribution of income in our society.[6] The primary reason for this outcome is that many of the individuals benefitting from the minimum wage are teenagers from middle- and upper-income families. As a policy designed to help the working poor, then, the minimum wage may be poorly targeted.

What may we now conclude about the minimum wage? First, some individuals clearly benefit from the minimum. The primary beneficiaries are those who remain employed and have their earnings increased in response to the minimum. Second, however, we know that other individuals lose when a minimum wage is established or increased. Especially hard hit are the many teenagers who lose their jobs in response to the minimum. Third, the minimum wage appears to be a poor means of improving the distribution of income in the economy, since many of its recipients are not poor. At this point, a final decision concerning the desirability of the minimum wage must be left to each of us. Clearly, however, these outcomes are not exactly what government had in mind when it enacted the minimum wage.

Rent Controls

The cost of housing in many of Canada's large cities is very high. Obviously, rent is a major part of a low-income family's budget, so high rents are a very real burden to the poor. Just as some advocates believe

---

[5]Charles. C. Gilroy, and A. Kohn, "The Effects of Minimum Wages on Employment and Unemployment," *Journal of Economic Literature*, June 1982, p. 487.

[6]W. Johnson and E. Browning, "The Distributional Effects of Increasing the Minimum Wage," *American Economic Review*, March 1983, p. 204.

that poverty can be lessened by legislating minimum wages, others believe that the poor can be helped by passing a ceiling price on rental accommodations.

The Effects of Rent Controls. In a free market, supply and demand will determine the rent on an apartment. Of course, if all the apartments in a city are owned by one landlord, the market would not be free and the following analysis would not be relevant. Figure 7–5 illustrates a market for apartments. The price (rent) of an apartment is on the vertical axis; the quantity of apartments is on the horizontal axis. The problem is that what we mean by the "quantity of apartments" is not clear. For example, saying that at $1,000 I will buy one television and at $700 I will buy two televisions makes sense, but usually a family wants to rent only one apartment regardless of the price. Moreover, although televisions vary, talking about a particular model is simple enough. Talking about apartments is harder because any number of features make one apartment worth more than another—its size, location and condition; the appliances included; and so forth. Therefore, we will use the quantity of apartments to refer to an index of quantity and quality. All other things being the same, a larger apartment would have a higher index number than a smaller apartment,

Figure 7–5   **The effects of rent controls on a competitive market**

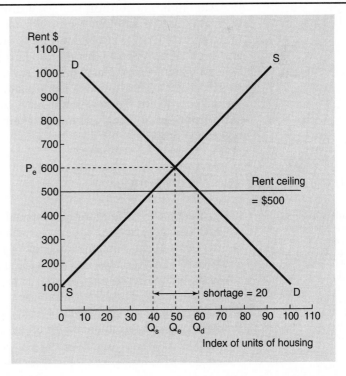

a better-finished apartment would have a higher number than an unattractive apartment, and a better-maintained apartment will have a higher number than a dilapidated apartment.

If the market is allowed to operate, equilibrium in Figure 7–5 would occur at a rent of $600 for 50 units of housing. Now assume that a ceiling price is placed on the market at $500. At $500 a month, tenants would want to rent 60 units of housing, while landlords would want to rent only 40 units of housing, producing a shortage of housing. Part of the shortage would be caused by the fact that tenants want an extra 10 units of housing at the rent control price. The other part of the shortage would occur because landlords want to rent 10 units less housing with the rent controls. We can see why the landlords would not build extra housing units to accommodate the increase in the quantity demanded. But how they would suddenly produce fewer units is not so obvious. Housing is not like eggs. If a farmer is faced with a too-low price for eggs, he can sell his chicken to the local soup company and stop producing eggs. It is true that in some cases apartments could be converted into offices or retail stores, but usually only at a high cost. The decrease in the quantity supplied would occur slowly as landlords reduce the amount they spend on maintenance. Remember that we measured quantity with an index of units of housing. That index included not only the size but also the quality of housing. As landlords put less money into renovations, the apartments become less and less desirable. Some units might eventually become slums.

Although rent controls still exist, they are much less common than they were before. Usually, high rents are a signal to the market to build more apartments. In effect, high rents are caused by shortage of units, and high rents mean high profits. High profits lead to the building of new units, which eliminates the shortage. Rent controls simply make the shortage worse, and can also lead to slums. If housing is too expensive for the poor to afford, it would be far better for the government to either subsidize their housing or increase their welfare payments than to impose rent controls.

Negative Income Tax Proposals

A **negative income tax (NIT)** is a form of income transfer. An NIT transfers income to all families and individuals who have income below a guaranteed minimum level. As the family or individual earns income, the transfer is taxed back at a predetermined rate.

In this final section, we examine proposals for a *negative income tax* (NIT). An NIT is a government subsidy or cash payment to households who qualify because their income falls below a minimum or guaranteed level of income. Many groups and individuals have suggested that Canada adopt an NIT to replace its present system of welfare. The first serious recommendation of an NIT for Canada dates back to the 1971 Croll committee's report *Poverty in Canada*. We will present the essential features of this reform proposal, followed by an evaluation of the negative income tax proposal.

The Negative Income Tax

Every negative income tax scheme has three variables: the guaranteed level of income, the tax rate on earned income, and the break-even level of income. In the example in Table 7–6, the guaranteed level of income is $12,000, and the tax rate on earned income is 50 percent. The break-even level of income, that is, the level of earned income at which the negative tax payment or cash payment is zero, is $24,000.

The relationship among these variables may be seen from the following formulas:

$$Y = rB$$

$$r = Y/B$$

$$B = Y/r$$

where Y = Guaranteed annual income
r = Tax rate on earned income
B = Break-even level of income

In Table 7–6 the negative tax payment varies inversely with earned income. A family with earned income of $6,000 receives a cash payment from the government of $9,000, a family with earned income of $12,000 receives a cash payment of $6,000, and so on. The cash payment or negative

Table 7–6	Negative income tax plan for a family of four		
Guaranteed Income	Earned Income	Negative Tax	Total Income
$12,000	$0	$12,000	$12,000
12,000	2,000	11,000	13,000
12,000	4,000	10,000	14,000
12,000	6,000	9,000	15,000
12,000	8,000	8,000	16,000
12,000	10,000	7,000	17,000
12,000	12,000	6,000	18,000
12,000	14,000	5,000	19,000
12,000	16,000	4,000	20,000
12,000	18,000	3,000	21,000
12,000	20,000	2,000	22,000
12,000	22,000	1,000	23,000
12,000	24,000	0	24,000

tax payment is equal to the guaranteed income ($12,000) minus the tax on earned income (0.5 × earned income). The total income of the family is the earned income of the family plus the cash payment from the government. Thus the family with earned income of $6,000 has total income of $15,000 ($6,000 + $9,000), and the family with earned income of $12,000 has total income of $18,000 ($12,000 + $6,000).

Evaluation of the Negative Income Tax Scheme

The NIT scheme has many attractive features. It is based on the idea that when a household has income above a certain threshold, the household pays positive taxes; and when a household has income below that threshold, the government pays the household (negative taxes). The scheme is designed for individuals and families that have one and only one characteristic, they live in poverty. It is not necessary to be old and poor or blind and poor. To be eligible, you need only be poor. An NIT program is simpler and therefore less costly to administer than most of the current programs for the poor, since the only consideration is money income. Under this reform proposal, people are always better off if they earn income than they are if they do not earn it; the more they earn, the better off they will be. This latter feature means that an NIT is less likely to create a disincentive to work.

The cost of a negative income tax plan will depend upon the number of eligible households, the earned income of each eligible household, the minimum annual income level guaranteed, and the negative tax rate. Given the first two variables, the cost of the plan will vary directly with the guaranteed level of income and inversely with the negative income tax rate. In the illustration presented in Table 7–5, the minimum guaranteed income is $12,000 for a household of four, and the tax rate on earned income is 50 percent. A negative tax payment or cash payment would be made to these households until their earned income reached $24,000. Of course, an appropriate guaranteed income would have to be established for individuals and for families of different sizes.

Any income transfer program generates two costs to society. One cost is the cost of administering the program. That cost should be relatively low with an NIT. A universal NIT would replace EI, CPP, OAS, GSI, CAP, and all the other programs to provide assistance to low-income Canadians, thereby replacing several programs with one simple plan. The other cost is the output lost because of any disincentive to work or save that results from the program. That cost is difficult to predict. Some people presently collecting benefits under existing programs may be discouraged from working because they lose all or almost all of their benefits if they work. As they entered the labour force, GDP would go up. On the other hand, given the generosity of the program outlined in Table 7–6, some individuals presently working might decide to quit and live on the guaranteed income. As they left the labour force, GDP would go down. We cannot know a priori whether an NIT would increase or decrease the supply of labour. A number of experiments have been done in the United States and more recently in Canada. The two Canadian experiments were the Mincome project in Manitoba and the WIN project in Ontario. Unfortunately, none of these programs have yielded conclusive results.

In addition to the two costs to society of an income transfer program, we must also consider a third cost. Assume a society has only two individuals, Ms. A and Mr. B. If A gives B $100, society is no better or worse off. Ms. A is $100 poorer and Mr. B is $100 richer, but the transfer cancels out for society as a whole. However, there was a $100 cost for Ms. A. Similarly, the implementation of an NIT would increase taxes for most Canadians. For those Canadians the NIT would have a cost. Whether or not imposing the extra taxes on some Canadians to help other Canadians is good is a normative question.

Summary

The Proportion of Canadians living below the StatCan low-income cut-offs has declined from 20.6 (1969 base) in 1971 to 17.9 (1992 base) in 1993. The decline would have been greater if StatCan did not change its base as the proportion of income that the average Canadian family spent on food, shelter, and clothing declined. While the long-term trend is falling, we noted a number of cyclical increases and decreases in the proportion of Canadians who are poor. Also, because the population of Canada is growing, the total number of poor is not declining.

Certain characteristics increase the probability of being poor in Canada. Those who live in some parts of the country are more likely than the average Canadian to be poor. Young individuals and families headed by a young person are more likely than the average Canadian to be poor. Females and families headed by females have a high incidence of poverty. Those who are poorly educated are disproportionately poor. Finally those who are not full-time employees are more likely than the average Canadian to have low incomes.

A number of programs in Canada aid people with low income. OAS, GIS, and CPP (QPP) have substantially reduced poverty among seniors. EI assists those who are temporarily out of work. CAP helps those who cannot work or who are not eligible for EI. The child tax benefit aids low-income families with children.

Changes and improvements are needed in the current provincial and federal programs for the poor. Many programs have developed in a piecemeal fashion, and many were not designed strictly for the poor. A guaranteed annual income plan in the form of a negative income tax scheme appears to be more efficient than the current in-kind and cash payment programs or price controls.

Checklist of Economic Concepts

Income inequality	Ownership pattern of resources
Demand for labour	Price floors
Marginal revenue product of labour	Price ceilings
Supply of labour	Unemployment
Wage rate determination	Negative income tax
Determinants of income distribution	Lorenz curve

Discussion Questions

1. What are the main causes of poverty in Canada?

2. Which of the following do you see as the most important issue relating to the distribution of income in Canada? Consider the implication of your answers for government policy.

    a. The fact that Canadians have considerable variation in incomes.

    b. The fact that a few individuals and families have very high incomes.

    c. The fact that some individuals and families have very low incomes.

3. Many economists and policy analysts have recommended an NIT as a way to reform welfare. Why is it so hard to get governments to implement an NIT?

4. Why have minimum wage laws had so little effect on poverty?

5. Rent controls are intended to aid the poor. Can you suggest a more effective policy to provide adequate housing for low-income Canadians.

6. Discuss the factors that determine the distribution of income. Which factors do you think are the most important?

Supplementary Reading

Bruce, C. J. *Economics of Employment and Earning*. 2nd ed. Scarborough, ON: Nelson Canada, 1995.
Chapter 17 provides a theoretical discussion of Canadian minimum-wages legislation and income-support schemes.

Dooley, M. D. "Women, Children and Poverty in Canada." *Canadian Public Policy*, December 1994, pp. 430–43.

Attempts to determine whether poverty has become a women's and children's issue.

Economic Council of Canada. *The New Face of Poverty*. Ottawa: Minister of Supply and Services Canada, 1992.

Discussion of trends in poverty during the 1980s and the realities of deficit reduction in the 1990s.

National Council of Welfare. *The 1995 Budget and Block Funding*. Ottawa: Minister of Supply and Services Canada, 1995.

A social-activist view of the proposed changes in the federal funding of social assistance.

Senate Committee. *Poverty in Canada*. Ottawa: Queen's Printer, 1971.

While long out-of-date, the report of the Croll Committee on Poverty is still interesting. It advocated the introduction of an NIT.

Chapter 8

Discrimination
The High Cost of Prejudice

OTTAWA—The Canadian Human Rights Commission castigated the federal government yesterday for failing to live up to its promise to outlaw discrimination against homosexuals.

"In my view this is unworthy—and I underline that word—of a government that has told Canadians this is a priority that they will deal with," Chief Commissioner Maxwell Yalden said at a press conference after submitting his annual report to Parliament.

"I remind the government, this one and any other in this country, that the universal declaration of the United Nations on human rights and indeed the Canadian Human Rights Act says that all human beings are equal in their rights—all. . . ."

The situation of Canada's aboriginal peoples continues to be the country's most serious problem, Mr. Yalden said.

"That will continue to be true until native Canadians have proper control over their own affairs and fair and equal access to benefits of Canadian life, like education, employment and economic development."

The annual report commends the government for making some progress toward self-government for aboriginal peoples. It also praises Ottawa for strengthening the federal Employment Equity Act.

But it notes that the wage gap between men and women in Canada still exists, citing a Statistics Canada study that found men earn more than women in 513 of 524 occupations. Another study found that the average wage of women is 70 percent that of men, a drop of 2 percentage points from the year before. . . .

Mr. Yalden said he doesn't like to use the word racism, but the potential for racial, ethnic and religious intolerance is considerable in a country of immigrants like Canada. . . .

"There is a marked impression that the tide of positive changes in human-rights matters in Canada could be on the turn, unless we are prepared to be more vigilant in their defense than many have been these past 12 months."[1]

No discussion of poverty in Canada can avoid making reference to the Indian, Eskimo, and Metis members of our society. A few simple statistics tell a brutal story. One is that the average life expectancy of an Indian woman in Canada is 25 years. Another is that the infant mortality rate among Eskimos is about 293 deaths per thousand live births, more than 10 times the infant death rate for the population as a whole.[2]

---

[1]A. McIlroy, "Yalden Flunks Liberals on Gay Rights," *Globe and Mail,* March 20, 1996, pp. A1 and A8.

[2]Economic Council of Canada, *Fifth Annual Review: The Challenge of Growth and Change* (Ottawa: Queen's Printer 1968), pp. 121–2.

What Is Discrimination?

The Public View

Most people relate discrimination to what they consider to be unfair treatment of some sort. Discrimination is viewed as the opposite of social justice. A person who is discriminated against is one who is treated unjustly.

There is nothing wrong in relating discrimination to unfair treatment. The shortcoming of this view is that it does not go far enough. It leaves unanswered the vital question, What is unfair treatment? The problem with defining discrimination in terms of fairness is that fairness is normative. No one would suggest that it is unfair that the NHL does not hire out-of-shape middle-age men to play hockey or that a business hires a Queen's MBA with 10-years experience over the recent "business college" graduate to manage its finance department. Certainly you have the right to insist that your open heart surgery be performed by an M.D. and not a chicken plucker. A newspaper ought to hire a person with "discriminating" tastes as its arts editor. Not one of these examples qualifies as discrimination in the sense that we are using the word in this chapter. In fact, all the examples represent "fair" choices. On the other hand, almost all individuals would accept that the treatment of aboriginal peoples discussed in the second quote was unfair. We would find less of a consensus over discrimination on the basis of sexual orientation. Economics can not establish what is fair. However, if society can agree on what is fair, economists, along with other social scientists, can help us understand some of the consequences of discrimination. For example, we can estimate the wage differentials between genders that result from discrimination. We can also demonstrate the economic cost to society of discrimination. When an employer refuses to hire the "best man" for the job simply because *she* is a woman, society bears a cost. Resources are being allocated in an inefficient way, and society will operate inside its production possibilities curve. Society as a whole will have a lower standard of living than would be the case in the absence of discrimination.

A Working Definition

Discrimination exists when equals are treated unequally or when unequals are treated equally.

Discrimination as we use it means that equals are treated unequally or that unequals are treated equally. More specifically, discrimination exists in a labour market when people with equal productivity are paid different wages or when people with differences in productivity are paid equal wages. Discrimination also exists in the product market when consumers pay different prices for the same product. Such discrimination, known as market discrimination, is different from product differentiation. In that case a seller charges a higher (or lower) price for a product that is different or at least made to seem different from a similar product. For example, brand-name products cost more than similar generic products.

Market discrimination exists, then, when the terms on which market transactions are based are not the same for all. A seller who charges different prices to different consumers for essentially the same product or service is practising price discrimination. (It is not price discrimination when there are cost differences. For example, if a department store chain charges a higher price to buyers in a remote location to cover the extra shipping cost.) An employer who pays different wages for identical labour services provides another illustration. Sellers who cannot sell in a certain market and buyers who cannot buy in a certain market for reasons other than price provide examples of complete market discrimination.

Economic Analysis of Discrimination

Sources of Market Discrimination

There are two conditions that must exist if there is to be market discrimination—the power to discriminate in the market and the desire to discriminate.

Monopoly Power. Monopoly power may exist on the selling and buying sides of markets. A monopolistic market is one in which the seller is able to manipulate the product price to his or her own advantage and can keep potential competitors out of the market. A similar problem exists on the buying side of the market when one firm or a group of firms acting as a cartel hires all or most of the available labour in a particular area and of a particular type. An example might be a mining town in a remote part of the Canada or, as discussed in Chapter 11, professional sports leagues. In this case the firm or firms are said to be labour market monopolists or simply monopsonists. A *monopsonist* has the power to influence the price at which labour is hired. The existence of monopoly power on the buying and selling sides of the market makes it possible for consumers and workers to be exploited. Consumers are exploited when the price of a product is above the unit cost of producing it, and workers are exploited when the wage rates paid are below their marginal revenue product, that is, below their contributions to the receipts of their employer.

Exploitation may exist without discrimination. For example, both males and females with the same productivity may be paid equal wages that are below their productivity. However, monopoly power is a source of discrimination. In the exercise of monopoly power, a seller may segregate the market and charge consumers different prices for the same product. A monopsonistic buyer may segregate the job market and practice discrimination by paying workers on a basis other than merit or productivity.

Desire to Discriminate. Some people have a taste for discrimination and strive to satisfy this taste or desire. An employer who desires to discriminate acts as if non-monetary costs were connected with hiring those whose skin colour, religion, age, gender, or sexual orientation, among other factors, differ from the employer's subjective ideal. Alternatively, an employer may discriminate because his or her customers or the majority of his or her employees have a taste for discrimination. The result is that resources are allocated on a basis other than productivity, and the employment opportunities and incomes of the affected groups are distorted. When discrimination is based on an individual's taste for discrimination, it is known as *deliberate discrimination*.

> **Deliberate discrimination** exists because individuals have a taste for discrimination. Such individuals have a preference to associate with a particular group or to avoid associating with a particular group. If necessary, these individuals will pay to discriminate.

Labour Market Discrimination

Market discrimination can take different forms and can occur in a variety of situations. Three major types of discrimination are found in labour markets. These are wage, employment, and occupational discrimination. Labour market discrimination may create significant economic costs for those who experience it and, in some cases, for those who practice it. In order to understand the effects of labour market discrimination, we must first understand how wages and employment are determined in competitive labour markets. As we will see, an employer in a competitive labour market will treat workers of equal productivity equally.

Market Demand for Labour. The demand for unskilled labour by the employers of the economy is given in Figure 8–1. The quantity of labour is measured on the horizontal axis, and the price of labour, or the wage rate, is measured on the vertical axis. The wage rate is the price of labour per hour. An important difference exists, however, between the demand for labour by employers and the demand for a good or service by consumers. Specifically, consumers demand a good such as orange juice because they receive satisfaction directly from consuming the product. Employers do not demand labour for this reason. Employers demand labour not because they directly receive satisfaction from labour but because they indirectly receive satisfaction from labour, in the form of increased revenues, when they sell the products that are produced by labour. For this reason, the demand for labour, or any other input used in production, is said to be an indirect or *derived demand*. In other words, the demand for labour is derived from the demand for the product being produced.

> The demand for any other factor of production is said to be dependent on, or derived from, the demand for the product being produced by that factor. In this sense, the demand for labour is a **derived demand**.

The demand curve for labour in Figure 8–1 is downward sloping, just as the demand for a good such as orange juice would be. Such a negatively

Figure 8–1   The market demand for unskilled labour

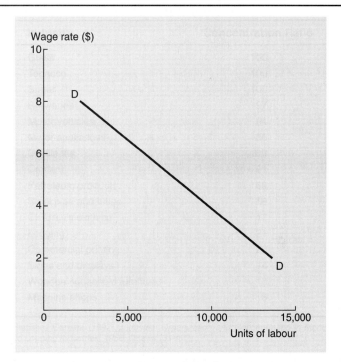

The market demand for unskilled labour shows the quantities of labour that employers in the economy are willing to hire at various wage rates. It is important to note that the law of demand holds for labour. That is, the quantity of labour demanded by employers falls as the wage increases, other things being equal.

sloped demand curve for orange juice suggests that the value placed on an additional unit of orange juice by the consumer declines as more orange juice is consumed. The demand for labour is downward sloping for exactly the same reason. The negative slope of the demand for labour indicates that, in terms of increased revenues, the value of an additional worker to the employer declines as more labour is hired.

We can reasonably argue that the fifth litre of orange juice consumed during a week yields less satisfaction than the fourth, but why would the same be true for units of labour? That is, why would a fourth unit of labour add less to the revenues (satisfaction) of the employer than the third? To answer this question, we must give detailed consideration to the way in which a firm's revenues change as the firm's employment level changes. Thus we must move away from the demand for unskilled labour by all employers, as presented in Figure 8–1, and consider the demand for unskilled labour by one employer.

The Demand for Labour by One Employer. When a firm hires a unit of labour that unit produces a certain amount of additional output, which is converted into additional revenue for the firm once it is sold. The increase in revenue due to hiring one additional unit of labour is called the *marginal revenue product of labour (MRP$_l$)* and, as such, indicates the value of the worker to the firm. Our goal, then, is to determine why the marginal revenue product of labour declines as more labour is hired. The marginal revenue product of labour has two parts: (1) the increase in output due to hiring the additional unit of labour called the *marginal product of labour (MP$_l$)* and (2) the increase in revenue for the firm when each of the additional units of output is sold called the *marginal revenue (MR)*.[3] Given this, if the marginal revenue product of labour is to decline as additional labour is hired, at least one of these two components must be declining. Consider first the marginal revenue. Marginal revenue indicates the amount of revenue the firm brings in when it sells each additional unit of its product. If the firm is purely competitive, marginal revenue is simply the market-determined price of the good. A characteristic of the purely competitive market structure is that no single firm has any influence over the market price. Thus the marginal revenue of a purely competitive firm does not change as it sells additional units of its product. Consequently, if the marginal revenue product of labour is to decline, the decline must be due to a declining marginal product of labour. The answer is now found. Economists are so confident that the marginal product of labour declines as additional units of labour are hired that they refer to this phenomenon as the *law of diminishing returns.* This law states that as additional units of a variable input such as labour are added to a given amount of a fixed input such as capital, the resulting increases in output (the marginal product of labour) will eventually decline. A simple example should help readers understand this law.

Table 8–1 details a typical situation for a firm that sells hamburgers when various numbers of workers are hired to work during a one-hour period. (If you think about it, there is a difference between hiring two workers to work together for one hour and hiring one worker to work two hours.) Labour is the variable input for this firm, and its capital consists of its building, tools, equipment, and in this case for simplicity, raw materials such as the meat, buns, and so forth. When the firm hires no workers, total production is, of course, zero hamburgers, as given in column (2). When the first worker is hired, total production rises to five hamburgers per hour. Thus the first worker contributes five units of production, which

> The increase in revenue that accrues to the firm when an additional worker is hired is called the **marginal revenue product of labour** (MRP$_l$) and, as such, indicates the value of the worker to the firm.
>
> The increase in output due to hiring an additional worker is called the **marginal product of labour** (MP$_l$).
>
> The increase in revenue from selling an additional unit of the product is called the **marginal revenue** (MR).
>
> The **law of diminishing returns** states that as additional units of a variable input are added to a given amount of a fixed input, the resulting increases in output eventually will decline.

---

[3]Mathematically the *MP*, *MR*, and *MRP* of an input can be defined. The marginal product of any input (*MP$_i$*) is the change in output (*Q*) divided by the change in the input (i) or $MP_i = \frac{\Delta Q}{\Delta i}$. Marginal revenue is the change in total revenue (*TR*) divided by the change in output or $MR = \frac{\Delta TR}{\Delta Q}$. The marginal revenue product for any input is the $MRP_i = MP_i \times MR$. Alternatively $MRP_i = \frac{\Delta TR}{\Delta i}$.

Table 8–1	Total production, marginal product, marginal revenue, and marginal revenue product for a hypothetical hamburger shop			

(1) Number of Workers	(2) Total Product	(3) MP	(4) MR	(5) MPR
0	0			
		5	$.50	$ 2.50
1	5			
		20	.50	10.00
2	25			
		25	.50	12.50
3	50			
		20	.50	10.00
4	70			
		10	.50	5.00
5	80			
		5	.50	2.50
6	85			
		1	.50	.50
7	86			

is given as that worker's marginal product in column (3). The firm operates in a purely competitive market so the marginal revenue or price is constant at $.50 per burger, as indicated in column (4). Finally, column (5) reports the marginal revenue product of each unit of labour. The first worker increased production by five units, each of which sold for $.50. Thus the first worker's marginal revenue product is $2.50.

Suppose now that a second worker is hired. Total production rises to 25 burgers, indicating that the second worker's marginal product is 20 units. Why does the second worker add more to production than the first? Think about the way in which the firm would have to operate with only one employee. This worker would have to be a jack-of-all-trades, first taking a customer's order, then scrambling to the supply area for the needed ingredients, and then scrambling to the preparation area and to the grill. Once the meat patty is cooked, the worker must assemble the burger and scramble (now short of breath) back to the counter to serve the customer. Health laws require that each time the worker handles money he or she would have to stop to wash hands. Put simply, with only one worker (or perhaps only a few workers), too little labour exists for the amount of capital that the firm has at its disposal. In other words, the firm's capital is underutilized. When the second worker is hired, the available capital can be used much more efficiently through the specialization of labour. For example, perhaps one worker concentrates on taking customers' orders and collecting the money while the other worker actually prepares the burger. Such specialization of labour often yields increasing returns to labour initially and serves as the justification for modern assembly-line processes. Adam Smith, sometimes called the father of economics, first explained the importance of the specialization of labour in his book *The Wealth of Nations* published in 1776.

Returning to Table 8–1, you see that the same situation holds true for the third worker. Eventually, however, just the opposite occurs. Experience teaches that just as capital can be underutilized, leading to the possibility of increasing marginal returns to labour, capital eventually becomes overutilized. When this occurs, diminishing returns to labour follow. For the hamburger shop, this occurs with the addition of the fourth worker. When this worker is hired, total production rises from 50 burgers per hour to 70. The marginal product of the fourth worker is 20 units, which is 5 less than the marginal product of the third worker. Diminishing returns of this nature come about for a variety of reasons, the most obvious being that the hamburger shop itself is only large enough to accommodate a certain number of workers. Common sense dictates that regardless of the size of the firm, if additional workers are continually hired, eventually a new worker will do little more than get in the way. Just as the old expression says, "Too many cooks spoil the broth."

Diminishing returns for labour may also come about because of the overspecialization of labour. Although requiring each worker to be a jack-of-all-trades is clearly inefficient, specialization can go too far. If specialization goes to the point where the extent of a particular worker's job is squirting ketchup on buns all day, the worker will likely become bored, easily distracted, and perhaps even a bit resentful. The result is clear—reduced efficiency or, in other words, diminishing returns to labour.

Regardless of the exact cause of the fall in efficiency, experience has taught us it will eventually occur. The outcome of diminishing returns is equally clear. The value to the firm of additional units of labour falls. Consider the hamburger shop. The third worker has a marginal revenue product of $12.50; thus this worker is worth $12.50 to the firm. When the fourth worker is hired, the marginal revenue product and, therefore, the value of the fourth worker falls to $10. The same will be true for each unit of labour hired beyond the third. As additional units of labour are hired by a firm, the value placed on each new worker eventually declines owing to the law of diminishing returns.

Now that we have answered the question of why an additional unit of labour may be valued less highly by the firm than a previously hired unit, the firm-level discussion of the demand for labour must be tied into the discussion of the demand for labour by all employers as presented in

Figure 8–1. This requires two steps. First, as you have probably guessed, the marginal revenue product of labour is the firm's demand for labour. A demand curve simply indicates the value placed on each unit of a good or service by the purchaser. Marginal revenue product is the firm's valuation of labour; thus it is the firm's demand curve for labour. Plotting the data on the marginal revenue product of labour from Table 8–1 gives the demand for unskilled labour for the hamburger shop in Figure 8–2. Figure 8–2 includes the data for only the third through the seventh worker because if the hamburger shop is managed rationally, it would never hire fewer than three workers. Why? The third worker is more valuable than either of the first two workers. Thus, if it is rational to hire the first and second workers, it must be rational to hire at least three.

The second step requires a tie between one firm's demand for labour and the demand by all firms. That is, 100 or even 1,000 firms may be similar to the hamburger shop. In such a case, how is the demand for labour by one firm linked to the demand for labour by all firms? If your common sense suggests that all that must be done is to sum the individual firms' demands,

Figure 8–2   **The demand for unskilled labour by one firm**

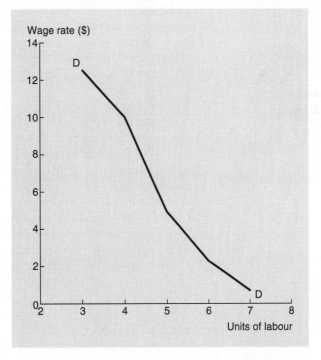

The demand for labour for an individual firm is given by the marginal revenue product of labour, which measures the increase in firm revenues due to hiring additional units of labour.

then you are right. The procedure is quite simple; for each wage, each individual firm's quantity demanded is added to the quantity demanded by all of the other firms to form the quantity demanded of labour by all firms. In this way, the demand for labour by all employers, as represented by Figure 8–1, may be thought of as the summation of the individual demands for labour by the individual employers in the economy. Of course, in the real world it is not as simple for individual employers to estimate the *MRP* of labour as it was in our hypothetical example.

Market Supply of Labour. The supply of labour refers to the quantities of labour that workers are willing to offer at various wage rates, other things being equal. As such, the supply of labour curve indicates what happens to the units of work offered by an economy's workers when a change in the wage occurs. For example, suppose there is a general wage increase. In such a situation, what will happen to the number of hours that workers are willing to work? The temptation is to conclude that the number of hours increases as the wage increases, but this temptation should be resisted. In fact, the number of hours offered by workers may increase, decrease, or remain the same as the wage increases. The reason for the uncertainty is that a wage change puts two offsetting effects into action.

The **substitution effect** of a wage change refers to the change in the hours of work that occurs in response to a wage change, other things being equal.

The first is called the *substitution effect* and is defined as the change in the hours of work that occurs in response to a wage change, other things being equal. The substitution effect takes into account the fact that people have numerous ways in which to spend their time other than working. For simplicity, suppose that we group all of these alternative uses of time into a category called leisure. Thus, the individual can spend his or her time working or consuming leisure. The only other point needed for an understanding of the substitution effect is the realization that the wage rate is the opportunity cost of leisure time. For example, if the wage is $5 per hour and a worker chooses to work one hour less than normal—that is, if the worker chooses to consume one additional hour of leisure—the worker must give up, or pay, $5 to do so. Now consider the substitution effect of a wage increase. A wage increase amounts to an increase in the price of leisure and, as such, leads to a reduction in the quantity of leisure demanded by the individual. Since less leisure is being consumed, the individual of necessity is choosing to work more. Consequently, the substitution effect causes the hours of work offered to increase as the wage increases and would, on its own, give a positively sloped supply of labour curve.

The **income effect** measures the change in the hours of work that occurs in response to a change in income, other things being equal.

Before drawing the conclusion that the supply of labour is positively sloped, however, recall that a wage change puts a second and offsetting effect into action. This effect is called the *income effect* and is defined as the change in hours of work that occurs in response to a change in income, other things being equal. We will assume leisure is a normal good. Recall that a normal good is one for which demand rises as income rises. Given a wage increase and the accompanying income increase, the demand for leisure can be expected to increase. With the demand for leisure increasing, the hours of work offered tend to decline in response to the income effect of a wage increase. Thus the income effect of a wage increase, on its own, gives a negatively sloped supply of labour curve.

Which of the two effects dominates? If the substitution effect is dominant, the supply of labour is positively sloped, while a dominant income effect gives a negatively sloped supply. Clearly, this question cannot be answered theoretically; it must be answered empirically. We know that historically the average number of hours worked has declined as hourly wages have risen. At much lower wages Canadians worked longer hours. One hundred years ago real wages were much lower, and work weeks of over 50 hours were not uncommon. Gradually we saw a 48-hour work week and then a 44- and 40-hour week. Today the average full-time work week is less than 40 hours.

There is another factor to consider. We have been discussing the demand for labour in the hamburger industry. Workers in that industry could work for other types of fast-food restaurants or any other industry requiring relatively little job training. Workers could also move from other industries into the hamburger industry. Whether or not they move will depend on the wages in the different industries in which they can work. Higher wages in one labour market will attract workers from other labour markets. The supply in each market will be upward sloping. Such a supply of labour curve is drawn in Figure 8–3.

The Labour Market. Figure 8–4 brings together the demand for and supply of unskilled labour in the economy. Once this is done, it becomes clear that the labour market behaves much like any other market. For example, if *DD* and *SS* are the initial demand and supply curves, there is an equilibrium wage and quantity hired of $6.00 and 6,000 units of labour, respectively. Note that at this wage neither a surplus of labour (unemployment) nor a shortage of labour occurs. Just as in any other market, the equilibrium indicates that the intentions of the buyers (firms) are the same as the intentions of the sellers (workers). In other words, at this wage the firms are willing to hire exactly the number of units of labour that the workers desire to offer.

Before continuing, it is important to understand why the employers desire 6,000 units of labour at the equilibrium wage of $6.00 per hour. A rational employer will hire a worker only if the worker adds at least as much to revenue as to cost. The addition to revenue is given by the marginal revenue product or the demand for labour curve. The addition to cost, on the other hand, is given by the wage rate. Thus the rational firm increases employment up to the point at which the wage rate equals the demand for labour. Figure 8–4 indicates that this point occurs at the 6,000-hour level of employment. For each unit of labour up to the 6,000-hour level, the marginal revenue product is greater than the wage, indicating that these

Figure 8–3   **The supply of labour for the entire economy**

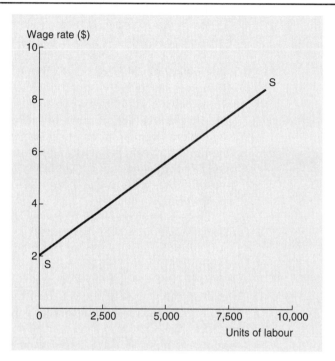

The supply of labour shows the number of units of labour that individuals are willing to offer at various wage rates.

workers are profitably hired. Were employment to be carried even one unit beyond 6,000, however, the firm would be losing money on the additional worker, since the worker would be adding more to cost than to revenue.

Wage Differentials. In our complex, market-oriented, mixed economy the wages of workers vary widely among industries and firms. Even workers hired by the same employer to perform similar jobs are often paid different wage rates. Given what we have learned about how wages are determined, we can easily see why wage differentials exist. Remember, the demand for labour reflects a worker's productivity and the ability to generate revenue for the employing firm. More productive workers can command higher wages because they are more valuable to employers than less productive workers are. Workers who differ in skill and ability will not be treated as equals by the labour market. Thus it is not surprising that the average university graduate earns approximately 67 percent more than the average high school graduate. Wage differentials among workers that result from different levels of productivity should not be labeled as discrimination.

Figure 8–4   **A competitive labour market**

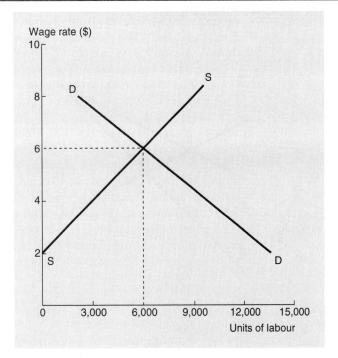

A competitive labour market without discrimination will result in a market wage equal to the workers' marginal revenue product. In this case marginal revenue product is $6.00 per hour, and 6,000 units of labour will be hired.

Another important point to recall is that labour is a derived demand. Consumer demand for the product or service that workers produce influences the employer's demand for labour. Everything else being the same, product markets with relatively strong demand will result in higher prices than product markets with relatively weak demand. Higher product prices, in turn, imply higher wages for the workers who produce the product. This pattern is true because higher product prices, which increase revenue, make each worker more valuable to the employer. Thus wage differentials may exist among industries or firms because of differences in the demand for their products. Once again, when workers vary in their contribution to a firm's revenue, non-discriminatory wage differences may result.

In Canada wages also vary substantially from region to region. Areas that have rapid economic growth often have labour shortages. These shortages result in higher wages as employers try to hire relatively scarce workers. Areas that are economically stagnant tend to have labour surpluses, and these surpluses result in depressed wages. If labour markets worked perfectly, the wage differentials between the have and have-not regions would tend to cause workers to migrate from the low-wage to the high-wage areas. Unfortunately, markets are not perfect, and barriers to migration exist. Workers prefer to live in the area where their friends and family live, they do not have the money to move, they fear the unknown, or having grown up in a poor region, they may lack the education to seek work in a rich region. While many Canadians regard the regional disparities as unfair and worthy of government efforts to correct, these wage differentials are not the result of discrimination.

Wage Discrimination. In 1993 full-time working women earned, on average, about 72 percent of what full-time working men earned.[4] The situation appears better for aboriginal males. In 1993 full-time working aboriginal males earned about 90 percent of the earnings of full-time white working males. However, aboriginal females earned only 63 percent of white male incomes. Workers who belong to other visible minorities—blacks, Asians, and others—also earn less than whites. Other visible minority males earned only about 94 percent of white males. Female workers from visible minorities earned 71 percent of white males. Disabled workers earned 96 percent (male) and 71 percent (female).[5] While the wage gap between white and visible minority males seems modest, an earlier study indicated that visible minority male workers earned lower wages in spite of the fact that they tended to be better educated than their white counterparts.[6] These statistics understate the difference in earning by gender and race because they represent only one source—the variation in wages—of the total variation in earnings. Still to understand the difference in earnings between groups, we need a better understanding of what constitutes wage discrimination.

The meaning of wage discrimination can be elucidated by the slogan "equal pay for equal work." Suppose a man and woman complete their accounting degrees at the same time and place, have identical grades in the same courses and equally good recommendations, are hired by the same accounting firm as entry-level staff accountants, and differ in only one respect—the man is paid $35,000 a year and the woman is paid $30,000 a year. This situation is a case of discrimination. Two workers contribute equally to their employing firm, but are paid unequal wages.

It is often difficult to be sure that wage discrimination exists. The person who discriminates typically denies it, and the relative productivities of labour may be difficult to measure. A discriminator may say that qualified females cannot be found or that females are paid less than males because females are less productive than men. In some instances

---

[4]Statistics Canada, *Earnings of Men and Women in 1993*, Ottawa (13–217).

[5]J. D. Leck, S. St. Onge, and I. Lalancette, "Wage Gap Changes among Organizations Subject to the Employment Equity Act," *Canadian Public Policy* 21, no. 4 (December 1995), pp. 387–400.

[6]J. Moreau, "Employment Equity," *Canadian Social Trends*, Autumn 1991, pp. 26–8.

these statements may be right; in others they may only be made to hide discriminatory behaviour.

The meaning of wage discrimination is clear enough—unequal pay for equal contributions. But proving discrimination depends on being able to distinguish among individuals on the basis of individual efforts and productivity. Generally speaking, in a competitive economy human resources, like any other resources, are paid approximately what they are worth. Thus wage differences where competition exists imply differences in labour productivity. Wage discrimination that does exist in the economy means that the market is not working properly in allocating resources among alternative uses. We need to understand that a labour market is not competitive if most employers or workers have prejudices. For example, the presence of a large number of employers generally means that the labour market is competitive. However, if the vast majority of employers are men who believe that all females are less productive than all males, then the market would not behave competitively. Similarly, if the majority of employers are white and have a taste to discriminate against natives, the market would not be competitive.

What can we conclude with regard to the importance of discrimination in explaining the existence of the earnings gap by gender? Some part of the gap may be due to "legitimate" factors such as differences in education, experience, absenteeism, and voluntary occupational choice. If we were able to determine the part of the earnings gap that is due to these and similar factors that affect productivity, the part of the gap that remained might serve as a rough estimate of the degree of discrimination in earnings.[7] Researchers have spent much time doing just this and the general conclusion of this research is that legitimate factors explain only part of the earnings gap between genders. In general, studies done in Canada have explained less than 50 percent of the gender gap.[8]

Employment Discrimination. Employment discrimination means that some people are not hired because of non-economic characteristics such as race or gender. Two individuals with the same training, education, and experience apply for a job. One is Francophone and one is Anglophone, but both can function in either language. If both do not have the same chance of getting the job, discrimination has entered into the decision-making process.

Employment discrimination, like wage discrimination, is difficult to identify positively. Differences in unemployment rates among whites and

---

[7]Actually, the part that cannot be explained by known factors such as educational differences is just that—unexplained. Still most economists believe that the unexplained variation in income is, at least in part, due to discrimination.

[8]A thorough summary of Canadian studies on the gender gap can be found in C. J. Bruce, *Economics of Employment and Earnings* (Scarborough, ON: Nelson Canada, 1995), pp. 436–41.

minority groups and between males and females may suggest discrimination, but do not prove that it exists. Much higher unemployment rates among aboriginal people than among whites may indicate evidence of employment discrimination. For example, in 1986 the unemployment rate of aboriginal males was 24 percent. It was slightly lower for aboriginal females at 22 percent. These figures were more than twice the level of unemployment for whites. Moreover, aboriginal males were substantially more likely to be employed in manual labour than whites.[9] Unemployment is even more of a problem for aboriginal people living off reserves. In 1986 29 percent of aboriginal men and 27 percent of aboriginal women were unemployed. Moreover, their labour participation rate was substantially lower than that for whites. In 1986 the participation rate for aboriginal males was 66 percent compared to 77 percent for all Canadians. The rate for aboriginal females was 45 percent compared to 55 percent for all females.[10] A 1991 survey of aboriginal people found that over 67 percent of them identified unemployment as a problem.[11] Although not conclusive, evidence of this nature certainly is suggestive of employment discrimination. Unemployment rates for other visible minorities were only slightly higher than the national average. Curiously, for the population in general, unemployment rates among females tend to be slightly lower than among males.

Occupational Segregation. One possible explanation of how women (and visual minorities) are discriminated against is the theory of occupational segregation. This theory holds that women are crowded into certain jobs. Most women work in occupations that are mainly filled by women. Examples of "women's jobs" includes nurses, bank tellers, and secretaries. While women are not excluded from other jobs, entry is more difficult. As a consequence women are crowed into "pink ghettos." This crowding increases supply in these areas and lowers wages. While labour market segregation may be decreasing, many economists believe that it is a significant factor in explaining differences in pay, especially gender differences in pay.

Why do women fail to enter higher paid male-dominated occupations? Some employers place barriers to females who try to enter male occupations. In addition, some women may be socialized into roles that minimize the importance of establishing a career. The lack of female role models in many occupations may enforce the traditional view. In the past, women were frequently taught from an early age that their primary roles were as housewives and mothers. The division of labour within households often left women at home to produce domestic services, such as rais-

---

[9]Joanne Moreau, ibid.

[10]R. J. McDonald, "Canada's Off-Reserve Aboriginal Population," *Canadian Social Trends*, Winter 1991, pp. 2–7.

[11]Statistics Canada, *Language, Tradition, Health Lifestyle and Social Issues: 1991 Aboriginal Peoples Survey* (Ottawa, 1991).

ing children, whereas men pursue work in the marketplace to provide income for the family. Even though the traditional economic roles of men and women have changed dramatically during the latter part this century, many men and even some women continue to view gender roles in the traditional way. Even today some possibly well-meaning people advise female high school students to take typing or to train as a nurse rather than as a doctor. Today two-income households are the norm, but the woman's job is still most often considered "secondary."

Some evidence suggests that women have made major gains in several male-dominated occupations in the recent decades. For example, the proportion of female graduates in dentistry has increased from only 9.6 percent in 1975 to 35.8 percent in 1990. Table 8–2 shows the increase in the female share of first degrees (including first professional degrees) of a number of disciplines between 1975 and 1990. As you can see, women have made dramatic inroads into many male-dominated fields.

However, such dramatic changes have not occurred in all occupations. For example, during the same period women graduating in engineering increased from 1.8 percent to 11.7 percent. While this represents a significant change, the profession is still heavily dominated by men. Moreover, there has been very little movement of males into the female-dominated jobs. Registered nurses, secretaries, and child care workers continue to be mainly female. Clearly, a large degree of occupational segregation still exists in our economy. Moreover, it should be obvious that change will be slow. The 1975 graduates are still relatively young. Many of them will be in the labour force well into the 21st century. Even if we reach complete

Table 8–2	A comparison of the proportion of bachelor's degree recipients who were female for selected disciplines for 1975 and 1990 (percentage)		
	Discipline	**1975**	**1990**
	Law	28.2	47.2
	Medicine	23.9	45.9
	Commerce	13.3	45.8
	Agriculture	22.0	41.3
	Mathematics	30.9	39.7
	Chemistry	19.3	36.7
	Architecture	10.7	32.5
	Economics	16.6	32.5

Source: C. W. Stout, "A Degree of Change," *Perspectives*, Winter 1992 (Ottawa: Statistics Canada, 75-001E).

equality in training in the year 2001, the entire labour force would not reflect the change in gender balance for more than 40 years.

Product Market Discrimination

Price Discrimination. In 1990 a shopping study in Chicago revealed that white males were systematically offered new cars at lower prices than were blacks and females.[12] The study involved 90 new-car dealerships and nearly 200 "customers" who had been trained to bargain in the same fashion so as to minimize differences in offered prices that might simply be due to differences in bargaining abilities. The author reports that white females on average had to pay about $150 more than white males to purchase identical cars. The situation was even worse for blacks. Black males on average could purchase the vehicle only if they were willing to pay an additional $425, while the premium for black females averaged $950. Although this study was done in the United States, we have reason to believe that similar discrimination may exist in Canada.

In other cases, price discrimination may take the form of preventing a person, because of race, from having access to a given market. The housing market is a market in which some sellers may not sell at any price to certain buyers. Another illustration is the refusal to allow aboriginal people equal access to the capital or credit markets. The purchase of real capital—equipment, machinery, buildings—is usually financed from borrowed money. The complete or partial barring of aboriginal people from the credit market may result in low ratios of capital to labour for aboriginal peoples and, consequently, low productivity and incomes. Their production efforts are thus limited to products and services that require high ratios of labour to capital.

Economic Costs of Discrimination

The economic costs of discrimination are both individual and social in nature. The individual costs of discrimination are those imposed on individuals or groups who lose one way or another because of discrimination. The social cost of discrimination is in the form of a reduction in total output in the economy due to discrimination.

Individual Losses and Gains. Individual losses and gains flow from discrimination. Individuals discriminated against, the victims, suffer losses in the form of reduced living standards. They tend to be paid less for what they sell, to pay higher prices for what they buy, to have fewer employment opportunities, and to be segregated in low-paying occupations. Individuals who discriminate, the discriminators, may gain and may

---

[12]I. Ayers, "Fair Driving: Gender and Race Discrimination in Retail Car Negotiations," *Harvard Law Review*, February 1991, pp. 817–74.

lose. An employer-discriminator may gain if a female worker can be hired at a lower wage than a male worker, assuming both are equally productive. The wages of whites may be kept artificially above aboriginal peoples if aboriginal people are shut off from jobs and occupations because of race. Discriminators, however, may lose by having to forfeit income in order to satisfy their taste for discrimination. For example, an individual who refuses to sell a house to a Asian may end up selling the house at a lower price to a white, or an individual who refuses to hire a woman may end up paying a higher wage to a man with the same productivity.

Output Reduction. We have said that the cost to society of discrimination is the reduction in the nation's output of goods and services (GDP) resulting from discrimination. In this way, discrimination causes a dead-weight welfare loss much like that attributed to monopoly in Chapter 9. Placing a value on the cost of discrimination is difficult. How can one measure the hurt and possibly fear that some Jews feel because their synagogue is defaced by neo-nazis or the enjoyment millions of baseball fans would have lost if Jackie Robinson had not broken the colour barrier in major league baseball? What has 300 years of abuse and neglect cost the aboriginal people of Canada? If you did not buy 100 shares of a particular stock issue last year, you can easily check the price today and determine your loss. How do we know the cost to society if last year a bank promoted a less-qualified male rather than a more-qualified female to be a bank manager? One American study places the cost of gender discrimination in the United States at about 3 percent of GDP per year.[13] The male–female wage differential is about the same in Canada and the United States, so that figure provides a rough estimate of the cost here. When discrimination against aboriginals, other visible minorities, the disabled, Francophones in English Canada and Anglophones and allophones in Quebec, gays, and other groups is added to that 3 percent, discrimination probably costs Canadians billions of dollars each year.

Discrimination causes losses of goods and services to society because it results in unnecessarily low levels of economic efficiency. Without discrimination, resources would tend to be allocated on the basis of their productivities. Units of any given resource would tend to be used where their productivity is the greatest. Consider the following rather absurd example. A metal working company needs two new drill presses, and the shop manager, a white man, is charged with the responsibility of deciding which brand of drill press to buy. Brand A is white. Brand B is black. One of the drills will be used in an application that requires a press that can automatically align a metal plate and drill a number of holes in an exact pattern. If any plate has a hole that is more than .01 of a millimeter out of alignment, quality control requires that it be discarded. The other press does not need

---

[13]E. James, "Income and Employment Effects of Women's Liberation," in *Sex, Discrimination, and the Division of Labour,* ed. C. B. Lloyd (New York: Columbia University Press, 1975), p. 406.

to be as accurate, but it will receive much heavier use. The black drill is more accurate, but the white one is more durable. The shop manager is prejudiced and does not like black drill presses. His prejudice leads him to assume that the white drill is better for precision drilling and that the black one will be satisfactory for the utility drill. The company ends up with an 8 percent rejection rate on the plates instead of a 3 percent rate, and the utility drill is down for repairs 6 percent of the time instead of 2 percent. It is simple to see how that decision would cost the firm. Most shop managers do not believe that the colour of a machine tool is relevant, so the example is trivial. However, some managers do believe that the race, age, or gender of a worker is relevant in hiring workers. If a firm hires workers on the basis of race, age, or gender it will be inefficient. If the firm with prejudiced management operates in a competitive market, it would be driven out of business by its more efficient competitors. However, if it is an oligopoly or a monopoly or if it operates in a market in which all management is prejudiced, it will be able to continue to discriminate even though it is an inefficient user of resources.

The production possibilities curve shown in Figure 8–5 illustrates the impact of discrimination on the production of goods and services in the economy. Point D represents the combination of goods X and Y produced

Figure 8–5   **Production possibilities with and without discrimination**

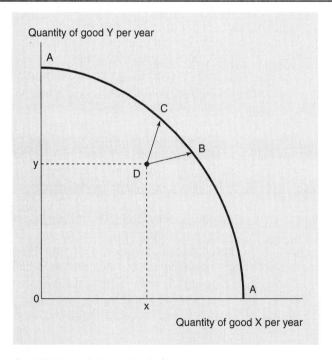

Point D = Combination of X and Y with discrimination. Points B and C = Combination of X and Y without discrimination. Line AA = Production possibilities curve.

in the economy when discrimination exists, with its resultant inefficiency. Without discrimination, the quantities of goods X and Y may be expanded to such points as B and C.

Discrimination prevents the efficient use of resources, causing the combination of goods and services that is produced to lie below the production possibilities curve. The elimination of discrimination makes possible the production of those combinations of goods and services that lie on the curve. The social cost of discrimination is equal to the difference between the gross domestic product represented at point D and that represented by points on the production possibilities curve, such as points B and C.

Non-Market Discrimination

Social Discrimination

Social tastes and attitudes, customs, and laws are the bases for social discrimination. Social discrimination may take the extreme form of preventing certain individuals or groups from engaging in social interaction. A baseball Little League or a Midget Hockey League rule that prohibits girls from playing in games provides an illustration. Fraternities and sororities that have rules, probably unwritten, excluding blacks, aboriginals, or Jews provide another. Societies such as South Africa while it was still under apartheid are structured along lines of social discrimination. Under these arrangements, discrimination by race is a way of life, sanctioned by custom and frequently enforceable by law. Deviations from the legal segregated manner of behaviour are crimes, and severe punishment may be handed out to offenders. Often social discrimination can have economic costs. In the past many private clubs such as Calgary's Petroleum Club denied women memberships. (A few clubs still do.) Women argued that business was often transacted at such clubs. In effect the denial of membership affected women's ability to make deals or find jobs.

Social discrimination is difficult to root out, since it is based on deep-seated beliefs and customs often supported by law. In contrast to market discrimination, it is difficult to associate monetary costs with social discrimination. Members who may with joy vote to keep certain people from joining their country club often with the same joy sell products to them in the market. Although the source of much market discrimination is social discrimination, the self-interest motive in the market tends to overcome and reduce the effectiveness of discrimination in the marketplace.

Educational Discrimination

A great many people believe that if everyone had equal access and opportunity to training and education, many of the major issues in our society, such as poverty and extreme income inequality, would be significantly alleviated, perhaps even eliminated. Even those who do not accept that society needs equality of outcome often believe that everyone ought to have equal opportunity. Unfortunately, however, inequality and discrimination exist even in our public school system.

Historically public education for Canada's aboriginal peoples has been underfunded and often misdirected. Aboriginal people have substantially less education than Canadians in general. In 1986, for example, 26 percent of the aboriginal population age 15 or older had less than a grade 9 education compared with 17 percent for the overall population. Forty-two percent of Canadians had at least some postsecondary education compared to 32 percent of aboriginal peoples.[14]

What Can We Do about Discrimination?

Markets and humans are not perfect. Perfection may be beyond reach; however, movement in the direction of perfection is possible. What courses of action can we take to move in the right direction? What policy implications can we draw from our analysis?

Reduce Tastes for Discrimination

If tastes for discrimination are to be reduced, people must be persuaded that they should alter their views and behaviours. These tastes may be reduced by education, by legislation, and by the use of government penalties or subsidies to discourage discrimination.

Education. A task of education is to teach people to understand one another so they will not be prejudiced. Some prejudice is based on stereotypes. Usually these stereotypes have little or no basis in fact. If society in general believes that all individuals from Mars are dirty, then society will behave as if it were true. Obviously, we do not want dirty individuals to handle food in restaurants; therefore, Martians should be banned from jobs where they have to handle food. However, if Martians are not really any more likely to be dirty than anyone else, then the regulation discriminates against Martians. This type of discrimination is known as *erroneous discrimination*. Education can be effective in eliminating this type of discrimination.

Erroneous discrimination exists when those who discriminate honestly believe untrue stereotypes, which suggest that the discrimination is based on objectively valid criteria.

Legislation. Changing the tastes of people by coercion, that is, by passing laws is difficult. In fact, laws are usually effective only when they are supported by or coincide with people's beliefs. However, laws can establish the framework for reducing tastes for discrimination. A

---

[14]Moreau, ibid.

substantial body of legislation that is intended to prevent discrimination exists in Canada. Most basic is the Canadian Charter of Rights. In addition, we have provincial charters to protect human rights and federal and provincial legislation that deals with wage and employment discrimination. On the federal level, the *Canadian Human Rights Act*, together with *Section 182* of the *Canada Labour Code*, requires "equal pay for work of equal value." This legislation applies to only certain workers—employees working for the federal government, in industries regulated by the federal government, and federal crown corporations. Other employees are covered by provincial laws; however, these vary from province to province.

While legislation cannot force people to change their prejudices, it can have substantial effects on the way they behave. As suggested earlier, some individuals have a taste for discrimination. If one has a taste for something, one is willing to pay for it. Legislation can reduce this deliberate discrimination if the law increases the cost of discriminating above the amount that the individual is willing to pay. The penalties could include fines or loss of government contracts.

Legislation can also help eliminate discrimination in another way. Sometimes an employer discriminates not because of personal prejudice, but because of the desire of his or her customers to discriminate. If a substantial proportion of restaurant patrons have a taste to be served by white staff, restauranteurs will refuse to hire servers of colour, because such action could cost them customers. If the law requires all restaurants to stop discriminating, then the prejudiced customer has no place to turn. Restaurant and hotel associations in the American South actually lobbied for civil rights legislation so that they could hire and serve blacks without fear of customer backlash.

Government Subsidies. If the sole goal of society is to eliminate discrimination, government subsidy payments to employers may be used to encourage them not to discriminate. Subsidy payments would be made to employers who do not practice discrimination in hiring, wages, and promotions. Employers who discriminate would be sacrificing subsidy payments. Thus an incentive is provided not to discriminate. The opportunity cost of discrimination is equal to the subsidy payment. Government subsidy payments will reduce discrimination if the subsidy payments are equal to or greater than the nonmonetary gain the discriminator receives from discrimination. Many readers might reject this suggestion as inappropriate. Certainly no one would suggest that we could reduce bank robberies by paying robbers not to steal. However, it may have some merit in some cases. Just as some workers may be discriminated against because of customer and not employer prejudice, some workers are the victims of past discrimination. An aboriginal worker who was discriminated against in the educational system is passed over for a promotion because he or she lacks the training to do the job. The worker is still a victim of discrimination; however, society cannot expect the employer to train someone when other workers already have the training to do the job. The government might "correct" the problem by paying the employer the cost of on-the-job training for the worker.

Reduce Market Imperfections

Market defects such as scarce labour market information, imperfect competition, and immobility of labour constitute a major source of market discrimination. Some people receive low wages, that is, wages below what they could earn in alternative employments, because they are unaware of other job openings. Better access to job information would reduce the chances for a person to receive income below what he or she would be paid on a similar job.

The market for goods and the market for resources may not work well at all if little competition exists in these markets. In imperfect markets, discrimination may be prevalent. A seller or a buyer has control over the price of what he or she sells or buys in highly monopolized markets. Other potential sellers or buyers are shut out of the market. Price, wage, employment, and occupational discrimination may remain unchallenged in the absence of competitive forces and in the presence of monopolistic controls. Competition policies to reduce barriers to entry into markets would be an important way to eliminate or at least lessen discriminatory market behaviour.

Reduce Discrimination in Development of Human Capital

Investment in human capital, that is, spending on education, training, and health, provides a high rate of return in the form of increased productivity and income. Blacks and some other minority groups generally do not and cannot invest enough in human capital, and public investment in human capital is unequally distributed. The elimination of human capital discrimination would tend to make most forms of market discrimination, such as wage and employment discrimination, less effective. The reason is that it is difficult to treat human resources unequally if they are productive and have access to other jobs. Lester Thurow, who believes human capital investment holds the key to non-discrimination, states, "Attacking human capital discrimination will not raise Negro incomes by itself, since wage, employment, and occupational discrimination would also have to be eliminated, but eliminating human capital discrimination would make the enforcement of these other types difficult in the absence of government discrimination."[15]

---

[15]L. C. Thurow, *Poverty and Discrimination* (Washington, DC: Brookings Institution, 1969), p. 138.

Reduce Occupational Segregation

Women, aboriginal people, and other minority groups have been pushed into low-wage occupations. The effect of segregation by occupations is twofold. First, the supply of labour is increased in occupations restricted to minority groups, depressing wages in those occupations. Second, the supply of labour is decreased in occupations closed off to minority groups, thus increasing wages in those occupations. The result of these effects is to create a wider gap between low- and high-wage occupations.

In addition, if a member of the minority group crosses over into segregated occupations usually closed to members of the group, he or she has typically not received equal pay for equal work. For example, a black male with a PhD in chemistry who works as a research chemist for an oil company may be discriminated against in wages and opportunities for advancement because he has a position typically reserved for whites. In recent years this situation has been reversed in many cases by the application (or threat of the application of) federal and/or provincial human rights legislation. In some cases employers have actively bid for minority group personnel. The small supply of these workers who are qualified has in some cases been a barrier to hiring them. However, this practice does not mean that the problem of discrimination against women and visible minorities is solved. Affirmative action programs encourage the employment of groups who have historically been discriminated against. In some cases such programs can result in "reverse discrimination." Proponents of such policies claim it is justified as a counterbalance to existing discrimination. They also believe that it can provide valuable role models for the young. For example, a female professor of engineering would serve to encourage female students to enter the profession or an aboriginal medical doctor might induce other natives to enter medicine. Opponents to such programs believe that reverse discrimination is still discrimination and therefore is unfair.

Still segregation by occupations will be difficult to maintain if minority groups become relatively well-educated and well-trained. Education and training open up job opportunities. Those who have job opportunities cannot easily be forced into designated occupations; they are more mobile and can cut across occupations. Providing improved job opportunities for minority groups is one way to break up segregation by occupations.

Pay Equity Controversy

Frustration over the slow progress toward equality that women have experienced has led to a call for more aggressive approaches to reducing discrimination. One such proposal is to replace market determination of

Pay equity is sometimes referred to as equal pay for work of equal value. Pay equity legislation is stronger than equal pay legislation, which only requires equal pay for equal (the same) work. Pay equity (or comparable worth pay) would replace market determination of wages with a pay system based on the skill, effort, and responsibility requirements of individual jobs.

wages with *pay equity.* The essence of pay equity or comparable worth pay systems is a realization that women and men do not do the same work. As mentioned earlier in this chapter, women are concentrated into a relatively few low-paying occupations, while men are disproportionately represented in the higher paying occupations. Given this situation, equal pay laws—which require paying the same wage to all workers, regardless of gender, race, or other stated characteristics, who work in jobs that are substantially similar—do not adequately address the problem. Such legislation can deal with only a limited number of cases. As an example, consider a hospital that employs males as orderlies and females as nurses' aides. Basically they do the same work, but orderlies are paid more. Equal pay legislation would require that the two jobs pay the same.

However, equal pay laws cannot deal with an employer who employs male and female workers in very different jobs. To deal with this situation, most provinces have passed laws similar to the Manitoba Pay Equity Act. Instead of simply requiring "equal pay for equal work," pay equity is extended to provide for "equal pay for work of equal (comparable) value." Is such an approach desirable? Strong arguments are made on each side of the debate.

Proponents

Pay equity advocates argue that the low pay in occupations dominated by women (nursing, clerical, and so on) is *not* due to "free market forces," but is the result, at least in part, of women having been crowded into these occupations by employment discrimination. Some would argue that in a male-dominated society, the work done by women is of necessity valued less than comparable work done by men. A logical extension of this argument suggests that if a job currently dominated by females (such as nursing) switches and becomes primarily male, the average pay of nurses would increase substantially. Consistent with this view, pay equity advocates often cite Margaret Mead, who once wrote, "There are villages in which men fish and women weave and in which women fish and men weave, but in either type of village the work done by men is valued higher than the work done by women."[16]

The remedy proposed is to require employers not only to pay equal wages for equal work but also to require equal wages for jobs of comparable worth, where the comparability of jobs is determined by factors such as the skill, effort, and responsibility requirements of the jobs. For example, suppose that a pay equity investigation determines that secretaries (primarily female) and plumbers (primarily male) who work for the same employer do jobs that are comparable in terms of skill, effort,

---

[16]J. O'Neill, "Issues Surrounding Comparable Worth: Introduction," *Contemporary Policy Issues,* April 1986, p. 1.

and responsibility. The comparable-worth doctrine would require that the firm pay its secretaries and plumbers the same salaries. Although comparable worth pay systems have not made significant inroads in the private sector, the federal and a number of provincial and municipal governments have started the process of evaluating jobs, determining their "intrinsic value," and paying workers accordingly.

Opponents

Although the arguments of the comparable worth adherents are logical and to some extent consistent with evidence concerning occupational segregation and the pay of women, comparable worth may not be the panacea its advocates hope for. A number of fundamental policy questions have been raised in regard to comparable worth. The opponents of pay equity offer counter arguments. Overlooking the difficulties involved with determining the intrinsic value of a job, opponents suggest three shortcomings of comparable worth. First, the essence of comparable worth is to increase the pay of women relative to men. To the extent that the program is successful, the outcome may be to reduce the employment of women relative to men. This argument is directly parallel to the argument raised with reference to the minimum wage in Chapter 7 of this book. While some women will gain (those who remain employed), other women may lose. Second, opponents suggest that the best solution is for women to move into the higher paying male occupations and that pay equity, by making the female occupations more attractive, will do just the opposite. "Pay equity will encourage women to stay in female jobs." According to this logic, the policy would serve to reinforce occupational segregation, rather than to reduce it. Finally, opponents argue that pay equity treats a symptom of a disease, rather than the disease itself. Specifically, opponents argue that women are low paid because they work in low-paying jobs, and to the extent that this occupational segregation is due to discriminatory hiring and promotion factors, the appropriate remedy is more strict enforcement of existing laws rather than pay equity legislation.

Pay Equity: A Definitive Conclusion?

Although no definitive conclusion may be reached with regard to the pay equity controversy, the debate points out several important issues with regard to discrimination and attempts to deal with it. First, even when problems of discrimination are perceived, the development of remedial actions that generate widespread support is very difficult. Second, before policy actions are undertaken, careful consideration must be made of all the possible effects of the policy. In many cases, those we wish to help most may end up being harmed. Advocates of pay equity believe that discrimination represents a market failure. They believe that administrated wages would be fairer than wages determined in an imperfect market that allows discrimination. Opponents of pay equity fall into two groups—those who deny that a market failure exists and those who admit that a failure exists but believe that administered wages will be even more imperfect than wages determined in the market. We can be sure that the pay equity controversy will continue and may intensify.

Summary

Market discrimination means that people with the same economic characteristics are not treated equally. For example, workers who have the same productivity receive different wages, and consumers are charged different prices for the same product.

Discrimination comes from two sources—market imperfections and human imperfections. Market imperfections are due to imperfect knowledge, immobility of resources, and imperfect competition. Human imperfections are revealed in the tastes and preferences that some people have for discrimination.

Competitive labour markets will result in workers of equal ability being treated equally by an employer. The demand for labour is determined by the workers' marginal revenue product. Workers who contribute more to their employer's output and revenues will command higher wages than those who contribute little. Wage differentials in competitive markets reflect differences in worker productivity. Such wage differentials should not be confused with labour market discrimination. Labour market discrimination exists in the form of wage, employment, and occupational differentials due to factors unrelated to differences in worker productivity.

Discrimination is costly both to individuals and to society. There are individual welfare gains and losses from discrimination, we cannot always say who gains and who loses. Sometimes the discriminator can lose. One certain loss to society from discrimination is a reduction in output.

The economic analysis of market discrimination stresses two related points: (1) the observed differences in wages and prices may reflect differences in productivity, and (2) market discrimination exists only to the extent that wage and price differences cannot be explained on the basis of productivity. Competitive markets tend to minimize the extent and degree of discrimination. Occupational segregation explains to a large extent differences in wages and income between the genders. Discrimination is sometimes deliberate, based on a taste to discriminate, and sometimes erroneous, based on stereotypes. Several policy conclusions may be drawn from our analysis. First, tastes for discrimination have to be reduced. This can be done by changing the tastes of people concerning discrimination through education, preventing by law the fulfillment of tastes for discrimination, and encouraging people not to discriminate by the payment of subsidies to employers who refrain from discrimination. Second, the source of exploitation and much discrimination—the exercise of monopoly power—has to be reduced. The way to reduce the use of monopoly power is to reduce that power itself through vigorous enforcement of competition policies. A great deal of market discrimination is primarily a result of human capital discrimination. If there were no discrimination in regard to investment in human capital (education, training, and health), segregation by occupations would be dealt a serious blow. Employers would be less able to discriminate against people who are productive and have job choices.

Checklist of Economic Concepts

Labour market discrimination	Employment discrimination
Product market discrimination	Occupational segregation
Derived demand	Price discrimination
Marginal revenue product	Non-market discrimination
Law of diminishing returns	Monopoly power
Substitution effect	Exploitation
Income effect	Pay Equity
Wage discrimination	

Discussion Questions

1. What do economists mean by a "taste for discrimination"? How can government reduce this type of discrimination?

2. At the beginning of this chapter, we pointed out that society discriminates in a number of ways, and that discrimination becomes a social issue only when the grounds are inappropriate. Do you believe that the following examples represent unfair discrimination? What part of your opinion is based on objective facts and what part is normative?

   a. Mandatory retirement at age 65.

   b. Higher car insurance rates for males under 25.

   c. Benefits for same sex couples.

3. Would it be fair if the owner of a cafe refused to hire minority workers because his or her customers preferred white servers? What could the government do to prevent such indirect discrimination?

4. Why is an equal pay for equal work policy ineffective if occupational segregation exists?

5. Explain why discrimination imposes a cost on society.

6. Explain why the wages of workers in a fountain-pen factory would go up if fountain pens became more popular.

7. How does a free market protect against discrimination?

Supplementary Reading

Bruce, C. J. *Economics of Employment and Earnings: A Canadian Perspective.* 2nd ed. Toronto: Nelson Canada, 1995.

Chapter 15, "Wage Discrimination," provides a through discussion of Canadian literature on gender discrimination.

Christofides, L. N. and R. Swidinsky. "Wage Determination by Gender and Visible Minority Status: Evidence from the 1989 LMAS." *Canadian Public Policy* 20, no. 1 (March 1994), pp. 34–51.

A statistical study of wage differentials based on the 1989 Labour Market Activity Survey. It covers women, aboriginal peoples, the disabled, and other visible minorities.

Drost, H. "Schooling, Vocational Training and Unemployment: The Case of Canadian Aboriginals." *Canadian Public Policy* 20, no. 1 (March 1994), pp. 52–65.

This article examines the impact of the level and type of education on the unemployment of aboriginal peoples in Canada.

England P. *Comparable Worth: Theories and Evidence.* New York: Aldine DeGruyter, 1992.

Perhaps the most thorough treatment of the economic problems faced by women and the proposed comparable worth remedies available today.

Flanagan. T. "Equal Pay for Work of Equal Value: Some Theoretical Criticisms." *Canadian Public Policy* 13, no. 4 (December 1987), pp. 435–44.

The view from an opponent of pay equity. It is paired with the Robb article cited below.

Jain, H. C. and P. J. Sloane. *Equal Employment Issues: Race and Sex Discrimination in the United States, Canada, and Britain.* New York: Praeger Publishers, 1981.

Examines the complex human resources problems faced by policy makers regarding minority employment. Uses economic analysis to point out where we might expect discrimination to be more extensive.

Lavioie, M.; G. Grenier; and S. Coulombe. "Discrimination and Performance in the National Hockey League." *Canadian Public Policy* 13, no. 4 (December 1987), pp. 407–22.

Is our beloved NHL a hotbed of discrimination? If you are interested, this article is the first of a number of papers on the topic in *Canadian Public Policy*.

Leck, J. D.; S. St Onge; and I. Lalancette. "Wage Gap Changes among Organizations Subject to the Employment Equity Act." *Canadian Public Policy* 21, no. 4 (December 1995), pp. 387–400.

An evaluation of the effectiveness of the federal Employment Equity Act. If you wish that we would tell whether the J in J. D. Leck stands for Joseph or Joanne, maybe you are part of the problem.

Robb, R. E. "Equal Pay for Work of Equal Value: Issues and Policies." *Canadian Public Policy* 13, no. 4 (December 1987), pp. 445–61.

The pro side of the paired articles on pay equity.

Thurow, L. C. *Poverty and Discrimination*. Washington, DC: Brookings Institution, 1969.

Covers the economic theories of discrimination. In Chapter 7, various kinds of market discrimination are presented and analyzed.

Weiner, N. and M. Gunderson. *Pay Equity*. Toronto: Butterworths, 1990.

This book discusses both the principles and application of pay equity.

Chapter 9

The Economics of Big Business
Who Does What to Whom?

The Acquisitors[1] and *The Canadian Corporate Elite*[2] examine the power of giant corporations in Canada, and the ways they erode the role of law and ethical precepts. These massive institutions create serious adverse consequences for consumers, workers, shareholders, taxpayers, small businesses, and community residents; they operate without effective internal and external accountability to those persons so harmed. The growing damage—often latent, diffuse, or deferred—compounds the need to rethink and reshape the political economy away from these many forms of injustice.

Large corporations, commanding immense political, economic, and technological power, are different in kind and in degree from their smaller counterparts. They advance their control of political units by transcending the jurisdictions of these units, provincially, nationally and multinationally, and by financing or otherwise nourishing the political process. These corporations possess decisive market power, sometimes collusively with their giant brethren and sometimes unilaterally. Where smaller firms might have to face the bankruptcy option, these companies, controlling major resources, are considered too big to fail, despite their own mismanagement or corruption. Governments are thereby forced to socialize their losses and guarantee their tenure.

The nonmarket impacts of giant corporations have become institutionalized in Canada as they have in other industrialized economies. Pollution of the human environment is rationalized as an economic necessity. Subsidies have become an entrenched corporate welfare system including inefficiencies and political rewards. Such corporate excesses align big government and big business against public interests. Critics of the close relationship between government and business argue that power begets power, resulting in large corporations being able to pursue their activities beyond the law, or against the law—a state of affairs clearly incompatible with democracy.[3]

The Public View of Big Businesses

While most Canadians and Canadian politicians have often viewed large corporations with their vast resources to transform the nation as engines of growth and regional development, there is an attendant suspicion of

[1]P. C. Newman, *The Acquisitors, The Canadian Establishment, Vol. 2* (Toronto: McClelland and Stewart, 1981).

[2]J. Porter, *The Canadian Corporate Elite, An Analysis of Economic Power* (Toronto: McClelland and Stewart, 1975).

[3]R. Nader, M. Green, and J. Seligman, *Taming the Giant Corporation* (New York: W. W. Norton, 1976), pp. 7–8.

how big business enterprises behave. Public concern with big business can be traced back to Charles Dickens's fictional characters striving for human dignity in the brutal capitalism of Victorian England and to the era of the robber barons in the last half of the 1800s in Canada and the United States. This mixed record of seeing big business as a vehicle of growth and at the same time as a potential source of abuse has shaped Canadian experience through much of our history. Examples of the complex mix of views that big business is at the same time the vehicle upon which to build the country and a potential source of abusive economic and political power appear throughout our history books. The construction of the Canadian Pacific Railway opened the western provinces and truly established Canada as a country that stretched from sea to sea. At the same time the allegations of corrupt business practices that surrounded its construction and allegations of political impropriety connected to it contributed to the fall of John A. MacDonald's government. More recently, concern over the influence that big business had in shaping the policies of former Prime Minister Brian Mulroney's decision to support the Free Trade Agreement has caused much discussion over why the government supported the agreement.[4] What are the reasons for public concern toward big businesses? There are several possible answers—all of them related.

First, some people believe that economic activity is dominated by a few gigantic firms. They think that families and individuals have little or nothing to say about their own economic destinies or about the paths that economic events take over time. They feel impotent and frustrated, sensing that it is big business that wields the economic power.

Second, they suspect that big businesses deliberately hold back output, especially whenever there are shortages. They attribute housing shortages in some cities in the early 1980s to land development companies being able to hold back on land development, and many people believe that the energy crises of the 1970s were contrived by the major oil companies. More recently there have been concerns expressed that the takeovers in the communications industry may give dominant firms in the industry, such as Shaw Communications and the Southam and Thompson newspaper chains, too great an ability to influence public opinion and to realize profits from noncompetitive circumstances.

Third, some Canadians believe that big businesses can charge whatever prices they please for their products. Steel companies, automobile companies, oil companies, and even the makers of breakfast cereals are believed to have the power to set prices in blatant disregard of consumer interests. In fact, many people believe that inflation is often caused by the exercise of such power.

Fourth, the general public and some politicians express concern that big businesses earn exorbitant profits—"monopoly rip-offs." These profits

---

[4]L. McQuaig, *Behind Closed Doors* (Markam, ON: Viking, 1987).

presumably are made at the expense of (1) consumers, who are charged prices that are far higher than they need to be to give firms a fair return for producing the products, and (2) employees, who are paid wages and salaries that are too low. The relationship of presumed excessive profits to the other three beliefs about bigness is obvious.

Finally, and somewhat contradictory to the four points above, is the belief held by many academics and much of the business community itself that big business is necessary to the health and development of the Canadian economy. They argue that because the Canadian market is so much smaller than that of the United States, Canada may not provide the opportunities for firms in some industries to compete while still maintaining the low costs per unit that result from large volumes and economies of scale. This argument is often made in connection with industries such as the manufacturing of automobiles and in the transportation and communications industries. Our laws governing monopoly power have generally been more liberal toward big business compared with similar laws in the United States. In Canada it is not illegal to be a monopoly or to be a firm in an industry that is dominated by only a few very powerful firms, but Canadian law makes it an offence for a firm to abuse its dominant position to the detriment of the general public or potential competitors.

The Economics of Monopoly Power

In a nutshell, although the public and academics are generally supportive of big business, they are wary of abuses that result from the exercise of monopoly power by big businesses. To think in a systematic way about the problem and to understand what kind of threat, if any, big businesses pose, we look first at what constitutes monopoly power. Then we analyze its impact on outputs and prices. Next, we examine the profit issue. Finally, we turn to the effects that monopoly power can have on the operation of the economy.

What Is Monopoly Power?

As we noted in Chapter 2, *monopoly* in its strictest sense means a single seller of a good or service exists in a marketplace. Not many big businesses, however, fit the full condition of this definition. Most large enterprises operate in markets in which several other firms are also producing and selling the same product. In Chapter 2, we labeled such a market structure one of *imperfect competition*. It is the monopoly power exercised by firms in imperfectly competitive as well as monopolistic markets that people worry about and to which we address ourselves in this chapter.

The monopoly power of a firm refers to the extent of its control over the supply of the product that is produced by the industry of which it is a part. The more firms there are producing and selling a given product, the less control any one of the firms can exercise over industry supply. If enough firms exist in an industry so that one firm's output and its control over industry supply are insignificant, we have a market that should tend to be competitive. On the other hand, if only one firm is producing and selling the product, we have a market of pure monopoly. The monopoly power of a firm in an imperfectly competitive market is greater the larger the firm's output is relative to the output of the industry as a whole. It is less the smaller the firm's output is relative to the output of the entire industry.

In order to measure the degree of monopoly power in imperfectly competitive markets, we often use *concentration ratios.*

Concentration ratios, or the percentage of industry sales accounted for by the four (or eight) largest firms in an industry, provide a measure of monopoly power.

The most common measure is the four-firm concentration ratio, which indicates the percentage of industry sales controlled by the four largest firms in an industry. An imperfectly competitive industry with four or fewer than four firms would have a concentration ratio of 100 percent and would be thought to have a very high degree of monopoly power. However, an industry with a large number of small firms might have a concentration ratio of 10 or 20 percent and would be thought to have very little monopoly power. Typically, one might suspect a significant degree of monopoly power when the concentration ratio reaches 70 or 80 percent.

Table 9–1 shows four-firm concentration ratios for selected industries. As an example, consider the major appliance industry. The concentration ratio of 86 percent indicates that 86 percent of the sales of major appliances is controlled by the four largest firms. Consequently, this industry probably resembles the pure monopoly model more closely than the pure competition model.

The rather high degrees of concentration indicated in Table 9–1 might suggest that the economy is composed of highly monopolistic markets. However, we should be careful before drawing such a conclusion. Although concentration ratios are valuable and do indicate the potential for monopoly power, they have some limitations. Consider the motor vehicles industry. The concentration ratio for this industry is 94 percent. In reality, however, the industry is not quite so concentrated because the ratio does not take into account the sales of imported cars. With the sales of imports included, this industry might have a four-firm concentration ratio of about 70 percent. As an example of an opposite limitation, consider the cement industry. The concentration ratio is 83 percent, indicating that 83 percent of cement sales nationally is controlled by the four largest cement firms. The problem with this number is that because of the product's inherent characteristics, cement producers compete only with other cement producers who are located in the same geographic area. That is, for cement, we should be interested in the percent of cement sales in one geographic area controlled by the four largest cement producers in that area. If this were done, the cement industry would appear much more concentrated than Table 9–1 suggests.

Table 9–1	Selected four-firm concentration ratios
Industry	**Concentration Ratio**
Glass	100
Tobacco	100
Sugar	100
Breweries	97
Motor vehicles	94
Major appliances	86
Distilleries	83
Cement	81
Petroleum products	69
Steel pipe and tubes	58
Children's clothing	17
Logging	21
Commercial printing	20
Signs and displays	14
Wooden household furniture	13
Machine shops	8

Source: Statistics Canada (1992), *Industrial Organization and Concentration in Manufacturing, Mining and Logging Industries, 1986*, Ottawa (31-402).

How then should we interpret the data in Table 9–1? Bearing in mind the limitations of concentration ratios, a reasonable conclusion is that some evidence of monopoly power exists in the economy.

Outputs and Prices

What impact does monopoly power have on the price a firm charges and on the output level it produces and sells? A useful approach to this question is to contrast the price and output of a firm that exercises monopoly power with those of a competitive firm.

Demand. We look first at demand for the product being sold. Figure 9–1 illustrates a typical market demand curve. We know that with any market structure—competitive, monopolized, or imperfectly competitive—sellers must take into account what buyers will do. For quantity x_1 per unit of time, buyers will pay a price not higher than p_1. If sellers try to raise the price above p_1, say to p_2, they cannot sell quantity x_1. At the higher price they can sell quantity x_2 only. Consequently, we conclude that the price that sellers are able to charge is always limited by what buyers are willing and able to pay. Sellers cannot escape the law of *demand*.

The law of **demand** holds that the price sellers are able to charge is always limited by what buyers are willing and able to pay.

Figure 9–1   **A market demand curve**

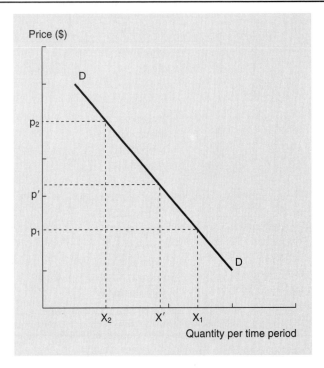

A market demand curve is downward sloping to the right like *DD*. Consumers will not pay more than p_1 per unit for an output of x_1 per unit of time. In order to sell at a price of p_2 the total sales level must be reduced to x_2 per unit of time. If four firms of equal size were producing output level x_1, one of the four could cause the product price to rise to p' only by cutting its output and sales to zero.

When more sellers are in the market for a product, any one seller has less control over the price that it can charge. Suppose, for example, that in Figure 9–1 four sellers of approximately equal size are selling quantity x_1. By how much can any one of the four raise product price? If one firm reduces its output and sales to zero, the other three firms would be selling a total of approximately x' per unit of time, and the price would be p'. Price p', then, is the highest level to which any one of the four firms acting independently can force the price, and it can do this only if it ceases to produce the product. To stay in business it must of necessity charge less than price p'.

Using the same reasoning, if there were 100 sellers of similar size in the market, the power of one seller to raise the price would be much less. If 1,000 sellers of similar size existed, one seller would not be able to affect the market price of the product at all. If it were to drop out of the market, the total amount sold would decrease by only $1/1000$ of x_1 which is not enough to cause the price to rise perceptibly. This latter case is typical of a competitive selling market.

Profit Maximization. Economic agents, such as consumers, resource owners, and business firms, like to do the best they can with what they have. Consumers like to get as much satisfaction as possible from spending their annual incomes. As resource owners, we like to get as much income as possible from selling or hiring out the labour and the capital we own. Similarly, firms try to set prices and output levels so as to make as much profit as possible. The profit maximization principle is simply the business manifestation of a principle that affects most of us—we prefer more to less.

Profit maximization is not a goal peculiar to firms that have monopoly power. It tends to be a major objective of firms in all types of market structures. It is simply the logical conclusion that economic agents reach because they too prefer more to less and make their choices accordingly. Although profit maximization is undoubtedly a major goal of businesses, it is not necessarily the only goal. Firms may also want to build up goodwill in a community, act honourably toward their employees, control large amounts of financial resources, or be known for a quality product. They may also want to get rid of their rivals, collude to raise prices, or block entry into the industry. In any case, prices and outputs tend to be set so as to maximize profits (or minimize losses) regardless of whether firms producing and selling the product are competitive or have monopoly power. But monopoly power, as we shall see, has important implications for what those prices and outputs will be. Finally, we should recognize that modern corporations, whether they operate under competitive or noncompetitive conditions, are generally run by professional managers who may find themselves in conflict between their own economic interests and the firm's goal of profit maximization. Modern corporations are sometimes immensely powerful economic units buying billions of dollars worth of supplies on an annual basis. Even a relatively minor decision that subtracts only a tiny percentage from the return to stockholders can generate millions of dollars to a subcontractor supplying a component to the firm. This reality coupled with the ability of professional managers to invest in firms acting as suppliers to the firms they manage can create sufficient inducements for some managers to put their own personal interests ahead of those of the firms they manage.

Price and Output in a Competitive Market. How does a firm in a competitive market determine what price to charge and what output to produce? Consider the ordinary market demand and supply diagram in Figure 9–2. The market price is p_x and the market output is X. But one individual firm selling this product has *no price-setting capabilities whatsoever*, since it supplies an insignificant part of the total market supply. The

Figure 9–2   **Price and output determination in a competitive market**

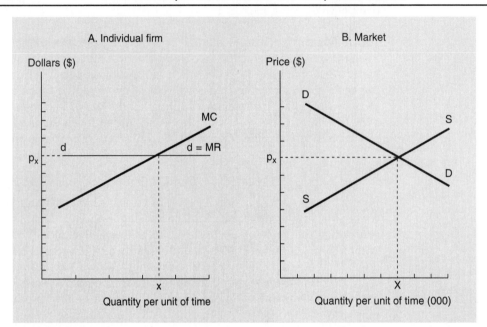

Product price p_x is determined in the market by the interaction of all buyers and all sellers. The individual firm faces the horizontal demand curve *DD*, which is also the firm's *MR* curve. The firm maximizes profits by producing output level *x*. Altogether the many firms in the market produce output *X* in the market diagram. The market quantity scale is highly compressed relative to the firm quantity scale. The price scale is the same in both diagrams.

individual competitive firm can determine only the quantity per unit of time to sell at the market price p_x.

The competitive firm thus faces the horizontal demand curve *dd* for its possible outputs. Its level is determined by the market price of the product. Suppose the market price is $14. In Table 9–2 columns (1) and (4) represent the demand schedule facing the firm, and column (5) shows the firm's total revenue (*TR*) at output levels up to 10 units per day. Although the numbers in column (6) are the same as those in column (4), the concept of marginal revenue for the firm differs from the concept of price. *Marginal revenue (MR)* is defined as the change in total revenue resulting from a one-unit change in the output level. The significance of this concept will become apparent shortly.

On the cost side, column (2) in Table 9–2 represents the firm's total costs (*TC*) at different daily output levels. Marginal cost (*MC*), a concept used in Chapter 4, is the change in the firm's total cost as a result of a one-unit change in the output level.

The increase in revenue accruing to the firm from selling an additional unit of its product is called **marginal revenue.**

Table 9–2   **Outputs, revenues, costs, and profits for a competitive firm**

(1) Output (X per day) (000)	(2) Total Cost ($000)	(3) Marginal Cost (MC)	(4) Price (P_x)	(5) Total Revenue ($000)	(6) Marginal Revenue (MR)	(7) Profit ($000)	(8) Marginal Profit ($)
1	8	$ 8	14	14	$14	6	6
2	17	9	14	28	14	11	5
3	27	10	14	42	14	15	4
4	38	11	14	56	14	18	3
5	50	12	14	70	14	20	2
6	63	13	14	84	14	21	1
7	77	14	14	98	14	21	0
8	92	15	14	112	14	20	−1
9	108	16	14	126	14	18	−2

Profits, equal the difference between total revenue and total cost, are maximized by producing the output at which marginal revenue equals marginal cost. Stated differently, profit is maximized when the **marginal profit** of selling an extra unit of product is zero.

Determination of the output level that maximizes the firm's profits is easy once we know its TC and its TR at each possible output. *Profits* are the difference between TR and TC at any given output level and are listed in column (7). Profits are maximum at either six or seven units of output per day.

An alternative means of identifying the firm's profit-maximizing output is to find the output at which MR equals MC. Consider any output below the six-unit level, say three units. A one-unit increase in output would increase TR by $14, or by the amount of MR. It would increase TC by $11, or by the amount of MC. Therefore, a one-unit increase in output would increase profits by $3, the difference between the MR and the MC of the fourth unit of output. In other words, the *marginal profit* of this unit of output would be $3. We have discovered an important principle: When MR is greater than MC, an increase in the output level will increase profits, since marginal profit is greater than zero. Further increases in output through five and six units also increase profits, since MR is greater than MC for each of the increases. The marginal profit shown in column (8) is positive over the range of output where MR is greater than MC. An increase in output from six to seven units per day adds nothing to profits, the marginal profit becomes zero, since MR = MC = 14. However, it does not cause profits to decrease. If output is increased from seven to eight or more units per day, MR is less than MC, the marginal profit is negative, and profits decrease—another important principle. But the most important principle is that profits are maximized by producing the output level at which MR equals MC. In Table 9–2 profits are maximum at an output level of seven units per day. To be sure, profits are also maximum at six units of product per day, but it will be easier to remember—and always correct—to settle on the output level at which MR equals MC, where marginal profit is zero.

The individual firm diagram of Figure 9–2 shows output x as the firm's profit-maximizing output. Note from Table 9–2 that if a firm's MR is plotted for each output, it will be a horizontal line coinciding with the firm's demand curve dd. Think of the firm's MC curve as column (3) of Table 9–2 plotted against output. The output level at which profits are maximum is the one at which MR equals MC.

The MC curve of the firm is the *firm's supply curve* for x, showing how much the firm will be willing and able to offer for sale at alternative possible prices, other things being equal. In Figure 9–3 ignore for the present the market diagram and consider the individual firm diagram only. At a price of $14, seven units per day will be produced and sold by the firm. What would the firm do if the price were $10 instead of $14? The firm's demand curve and MR curve become d_1d_1 and MR_1, respectively. The profit-maximizing output level falls to three units per day. Since the firm seeks to maximize its profits, whatever the market price happens to be, the firm will try to produce the output at which MC equals MR—where the marginal profit is zero. For a competitive firm, MR and p_x are always equal to each other, so in producing the output level at which MC equals MR, the firm is also producing the output level at which MC equals p_x. Thus, the outputs that will be produced at alternative price levels are shown by the MC curve, making it the firm's supply curve for the product.

By adding the quantities that all firms in the market will place on the market at each possible price, we get the *market supply curve*. For example, in Figure 9–3 if 1 of 1,000 identical firms in the market will place seven units of product per day on the market at a price of $14, all firms together will place 7,000 units per day on the market. In Figure 9–3 at the $14 price, the firm would be at point a on its supply curve. The market as a whole would be at point A. Similarly, at a $10 price level the firm would be at point b, and the market as a whole would be at point B. The market SS curve is said to be the *horizontal summation* of the individual firm MC or ss curves. It is really a market marginal cost curve for all firms together.

The simultaneous determination of the market price of a product, the individual firm level of output, and the market level of output for a competitive market now fall neatly into place. In Figure 9–3 let the market demand curve be DD and the market supply curve be SS. The price of $14 is determined by the interaction of buyers and sellers in the market as a whole. Any one firm in the market takes this price as given and cannot change it. To maximize profits, the firm chooses the output level at which MC equals MR—seven units in this case. The market output level of 7,000 units is, of course, the sum of the output levels of all firms producing the product when they are confronted with a $14 product price.

Figure 9–3   Marginal costs and supply in competitive industry

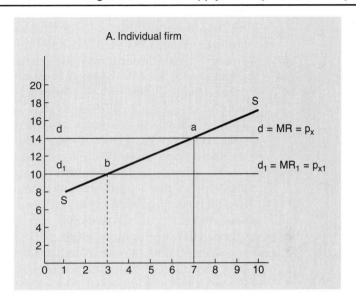

A. Individual firm

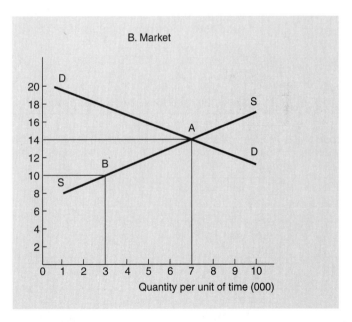

B. Market

Quantity per unit of time (000)

Since an individual firm produces the output at which $MC = MR = p_x$ in order to maximize profits, the firm's MC curve shows how much product it will place on the market at alternative price levels like $10 and $14. The market supply curve shows the combined quantities that all firms in the market will supply at each alternative price. It is the horizontal summation of the MC curves of all the individual firms and is thus an MC curve for the market as a whole.

Pricing and Output in a Monopolized Market. To show the effects of monopoly power on the price and the quantity produced of a product, we will suppose that the purely competitive market just discussed becomes monopolized. Consider first the competitive market. The market demand curve DD of Figure 9–3 is listed as a demand schedule in columns (1) and (4) of Table 9–3. Similarly, the horizontal summation of the MC curves of the 1,000 individual competitive firms, which comprises the supply curve SS in Figure 9–3, is listed in columns (1) and (3) of Table 9–3. This information is presented again as DD and SS in Figure 9–4. As we noted in the preceding section, the market price of producing X is \$14, and the quantity produced and sold is 7,000 units per day.

Now let the 1,000 competitive firms merge into one gigantic monopoly. Suppose that all the production facilities of the 1,000 firms are taken over in their entireties and that they can be operated by the monopolistic firm with no change in efficiency. What happens to the output of the industry and the price of the product?

Keep in mind the quantities the competitive firms were producing as they maximized their profits. Each firm found itself looking at a \$14 product price that it could not change. Each firm saw a horizontal demand curve for its own output at the \$14 level. Each firm viewed marginal revenue as constant at the \$14 level—equal to the product price. Each firm produced an output level at which its MC was equal to MR and product

Table 9–3				Outputs, revenues, costs, and profits for a monopolized firm			
(1) Output (X per day) (000)	(2) Total Cost (\$000)	(3) Marginal Cost (MC)	(4) Price (P_x)	(5) Total Revenue (\$000)	(6) Marginal Revenue (MR)	(7) Profit (\$000)	(8) Marginal Profit (\$)
1	8	\$ 8	20	20	\$20	12	12
2	17	9	19	38	18	21	9
3	27	10	18	54	16	27	6
4	38	11	17	68	14	30	3
5	50	12	16	80	12	30	0
6	63	13	15	90	10	27	−3
7	77	14	14	98	8	21	−6
8	92	15	13	104	6	12	−9
9	108	16	12	108	4	0	−12

Figure 9–4   **Comparison of pricing and output in competitive and monopolized markets**

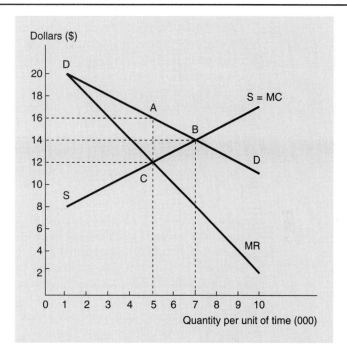

If the market is competitive, the market price will be $14 and the output will be 7,000 units. Each of the 1,000 firms in the market faces a horizontal demand curve and marginal revenue curve at the $14 level and maximizes profits by producing the output at which its *MR* equals *MC*. Monopolization of the market causes the firm to see *DD* as the demand curve it faces. Since *DD* slopes downward to the right, *MR* lies below *DD*. The profit-maximizing output for the monopolistic firm becomes 5,000 units, which will be sold at a price of $16 per unit.

price. Each firm's output level was seven units per day, and the total industry output was 7,000 units per day.

All of that is changed by monopolization of the industry. The monopolist faces the market demand curve *DD*, which is downward sloping to the right instead of horizontal. This fact has important implications for marginal revenue. Any firm that faces a demand curve that is sloping downward to the right will find that its marginal revenue is less than product price at any given output level. We demonstrate this principle in Table 9–3. If the monopolist were selling 2,000 units of product per day and were to increase sales from 2,000 to 3,000 per day, total revenue of the firm would increase from $38,000 ($19 × 2,000) to $54,000 ($18 × 3,000). Since the 1,000-unit addition to output increases total receipts by $16,000, each one-unit increase in output has increased TR by $16. So marginal revenue for the firm in moving from the 2,000-unit to the 3,000-unit level of output is $16 and is less than the price of $18 at which each of the 3,000 units is sold. Marginal revenue in column (6) is computed in the same way for each output level listed in column (1). Compare price and marginal revenue at each level of output. Marginal revenue is plotted as the MR curve in Figure 9–4.

If you were the monopolist what output would you produce and at what price would you sell if your objective were to maximize profits? You would reduce output and sales from 7,000 units per day to 5,000 units per day. You would raise the price from $14 to $16, which would increase your profits from $21,000 per day to $30,000 per day as column (7) indicates. At the 5,000-unit output level, MC equals MR—marginal profit equals zero—for the monopolist.

To recapitulate the analysis, in a monopolized market the price of the product tends to be higher and output tends to be less than it would be if the industry could be and were competitive. This is not because the managements of monopolized firms are inherently evil, while those of competitive firms are not. The managements of firms in both types of markets seek the same general goal of maximizing profits. The monopolistic firm restricts output and charges a higher price because its managers see a different relationship between marginal revenue and price than do the managers of competitive firms.

Referring back to Figures 9–3 and 9–4, the managers of competitive firms face demand curves that are horizontal at the market price of the product. Consequently, they see marginal revenue curves that are also horizontal and that coincide with the demand curves. To maximize its profits, the competitive firm chooses the output level at which $MC = MR = p_x$. In the diagrams this relationship occurs at the seven-unit output level for each firm. Since all firms in the market maximize profits in the same way, the market output is 7,000 units.

If the market is monopolized and the monopolist continues with the 7,000-unit output level, the monopolist's MC would be equal to the product price of $14. But MR for the monopolist at that output level is only $8 because the monopolist faces a downward sloping demand curve. To maximize profits the monopolist cuts the output back to 5,000 units per day and raises the product price to $16. The monopolist's $MC = MR = $12 at that output level.

By reducing output and increasing the product price, the monopolist imposes a significant economic cost on society in the form of reduced welfare. To see the cost to society, we must have a thorough understanding of Figure 9–4. Consider the demand curve. This curve indicates the maximum prices consumers would be willing to pay for particular quantities of the good. The fact that consumers are willing to pay a price equal to the marginal benefit they expect to receive from consuming additional units of the good indicates that the demand curve may be thought of as

The **marginal social benefit curve,** or demand curve, indicates the additional satisfaction that society anticipates from consuming successive units of the product.

The **marginal social cost curve,** or supply curve, indicates the opportunity cost of producing various units of a product in terms of the resources required.

the *marginal social benefit curve.* That is, the demand curve shows the additional satisfaction, or benefit, that society expects from successive units of the good. The marginal cost curve indicates the alternative cost or opportunity cost of the resources used to produce the good. Since we are considering only one firm, a monopolist, the firm's marginal cost is also the *marginal social cost* of producing the good.

We now have curves in Figure 9–4 depicting the marginal social benefit and marginal social cost of producing the good. What quantity of the good should be produced? The method for answering this question was presented in Chapter 5. In that analysis, it was argued that pollution control (the good) should be produced up to the point where net benefits to society are maximized. Net benefits are increased by increasing output whenever marginal social benefits exceed marginal social cost; thus, production of a good should be carried out to the point where marginal social benefits are just equal to marginal social cost. In Figure 9–4, this logic suggests that the socially optimal level of production is 7,000 units (where marginal social benefits *DD* are just equal to marginal social cost *MC*). As has been pointed out, a competitive industry would produce this quantity. However, if the industry is monopolized, production is reduced to 5,000 units. In Figure 9–4, we see that when production is reduced from 7,000 to 5,000 units, net social benefits are reduced because, for the lost units, marginal social benefits (*DD*) are greater than marginal social cost (*MC*). Adding together the lost net benefits for each of the units between 7,000 and 5,000 yields the lost welfare for society due to the monopoly. Graphically, this loss is equal to the area of the triangle ABC in Figure 9–4 and is known as the *dead-weight welfare loss due to monopoly.*

The exercise of monopoly power generates a reduction in social welfare known as the **dead-weight welfare loss due to monopoly.**

Entry Restrictions

Prices, costs, profits, and losses in a market economy provide the incentives for a continuous reallocation of resources from uses where they contribute less to uses where they contribute more to consumer satisfaction. In industries where demand is falling or costs are rising, investors will eventually receive less-than-average returns on their investments. Firms in these industries are said to be incurring *economic losses.* As it becomes possible for them to do so, investors and the firms producing those products will leave the industry, reducing supplies and raising prices relative to costs, until the returns to remaining investors are average for the economy as a whole.

In areas where demand is increasing or costs are falling, investors receive higher-than-average returns, or *economic profits.* New investment and new firms have incentives to enter the industry. If they are successful in doing so, product supplies increase and prices fall relative to costs until the return on investment is again average. The profit and loss mechanism is thus the prime force for contracting productive capacity and output where these are not so urgently desired and for expanding them where they are more urgently desired.

Monopoly power tends to throw sand in the gears of the reallocation mechanism. Over time, firms with monopoly power in profitable industries, those that yield higher-than-average rates of return to investors, may be able to impede or block the entry of new investment and new firms into those industries. To the extent that the firms are able to do so, outputs will be lower, prices will be higher, and profits will be greater than they would be if entry were open, free, and easy. When a monopoly is successful in restricting output and raising prices, purchasing power is continually shifted away from other members of society in favour of the owners and employees of the monopoly. Such *barriers to entry* can be classified conveniently into private barriers and government barriers.

Monopolists are often able to protect their favoured positions from potential competitors through establishing or maintaining **barriers to entry** such as product differentiation, economies of scale, and government licencing.

Private Barriers. Private entry barriers arise from the nature of markets themselves or from marketplace actions of the firms that enjoy their fruits. There are many privately imposed restrictions on entry into specific industries. We shall list some of the more important ones—not necessarily in the order of their importance. First, consider a situation in which a firm or the firms already in a market own or control most of some key raw material needed for making the product. All they must do to restrict entry is deny potential entrants access to it. Second, suppose that when new firms are in the process of entering, the existing firms threaten to lower prices to the extent that the newcomers would experience substantial losses. This threat tends to discourage entry. It is also difficult on those already in the market, but they may be able to withstand temporary losses better than the potential entrants can. Third, product differentiation may be successful in retarding entry in some instances. *Product differentiation* refers to the well-known practice on the part of each firm in an industry of making its own brand of the product slightly different from that of the other firms. Then it tries to convince consumers that its brand of the product is superior to any other brand. Consumers tend to prefer the old tried-and-true brands and to be skeptical of purchasing the brands of new entrants. This consumer trait is undoubtedly one of the many factors discouraging entry into the automobile industry. Fourth, if the production process used to produce the product involves substantial *economies of scale*—a concept more fully discussed in Chapter 10—a market may not be large enough to support more than one or a few firms of a size large enough to be efficient. Although one or a few firms may be able to make higher-than-average returns for investors, the entry of a newcomer may increase supply, reduce prices, and increase the average cost to each of the firms in the industry so much that none makes an average return or normal profit. The list of private entry barriers could go on and on, but the ones we have mentioned should be sufficient for illustrative purposes.

Government Barriers. The firms already in specific industries have difficulty in policing and enforcing restrictions on entry. Consequently, they frequently turn to the government for help. They lobby city councils, provincial governments, and Parliament to pass legislation restricting entry into their markets. Nor is the practice of lobbying the government to limit the entry of new firms into an industry restricted to existing firms. There are many examples in Canadian economic history when consumers or well-meaning interest groups from the Canadian Medical Association to anti-smoking groups to the Consumers' Association of Canada, have lobbied the government to restrict the production or sale of some product. As a part of these lobbying efforts, special interest groups will sometimes request control and regulation of the existing firms in the industry. In acceding to these requests, whether they come from the firms or the interest groups, governments seem not at all reluctant to take actions that confer monopoly power on existing firms and help them to maintain it over time.

First, in some industries such as airlines, banking, communications, forestry, nuclear electrical power generation, railroads, tourism inside the national parks, and trucking, regulatory authorities have established entry-blocking rules that have all the force of law. Regulatory commissions such as Atomic Energy of Canada, the National Transportation Authority, and the Canadian Radio and Television Commission were established in part to protect customers from certain practices of monopolistic firms or the dangers of unsafe practices by firms that might try to operate in the regulated industry. The range of the commissions' activities have often included control of entry into the industries they are regulating. Because of the potential profits or monopoly rents that a firm can earn, even in the longrun, if it is not pressed by the competitive behaviour of rivals, significant financial incentives motivate a firm to work to preserve its monopoly status. Naturally, government agencies acting in the public interest are unlikely to create or preserve monopolies for the purpose of generating monopoly profits, but government agencies will defend a monopoly's right to exist for a variety of reasons, and monopolies are sometimes adept at exploiting these. Existing monopolies often expend large sums of money on legal actions to prove that a potential competitor might reduce safety standards or may not act in the "Canadian interest." Similarly, existing monopolies often resort to advertising campaigns in the media to raise public awareness of some alleged danger to the public by having a new firm enter the industry. If successful, an advertising campaign may encourage the public to lobby elected and appointed officials on the firm's behalf to reduce competition. Sometimes one suspects that the regulatory board's primary function has evolved to "protect" the existing firms from consumers or potential competitors.

Second, many occupational licencing laws are on the books of individual provinces licencing accountants, barbers, electricians, lawyers, midwives, nurses, physicians, plumbers, real-estate agents, teachers, truckers, undertakers, and a host of other occupations. Whatever else such laws may do, one thing is certain—they restrict entry into the licenced occupations.

Licencing standards and licencing examinations usually are controlled by licenced members of the occupation concerned, that is, by those who are already in it and who may have a vested interest in keeping the number of new entrants relatively low.

A number of other forms of government-imposed entry barriers exist. Import duties and import restrictions limit the entry of foreign firms into many of our markets. Patent and copyright laws impede entry. Exclusive franchises to taxicab companies and cable television operators block the entry of new firms. Zoning ordinances and building codes are used to restrict entry into certain housing markets. Like that of private barriers, the list of government-imposed barriers to entry is a lengthy one.

Nonprice Competition

In industries containing only a few firms, it is common practice for firms to compete on grounds other than price. Each such firm in a given industry can increase its profits if it can increase its monopoly power at the expense of its rivals—that is, if it can increase its own share of the total market for the product. One very obvious way for a firm to increase its market share is to reduce the price at which it sells its brand of the product relative to the prices charged by the other firms in the industry. But price-cutting presents dangers to the firm that does it. The other firms can cut their prices, too, thus preventing the firm from accomplishing what it set out to do. Worse yet, all firms could end up with lower prices, a larger industry output, and smaller profits. So firms in imperfectly competitive markets are reluctant to use price-cutting to increase their individual market shares. Usually they attempt to increase their degrees of monopoly power through nonprice competition.

Advertising is a major form of nonprice competition. In 1986 two firms, Procter and Gamble and John Labatt, each spent over $80 million a year on advertising and promotion in Canada.[5] While these were the two largest corporate budgets for advertising and promotion, they are indicative of amounts spent by firms on advertising. Although these expenditures may provide consumers with important information about a firm's product, often the major objective of advertising is to increase the market share or monopoly power of the firm that does it. Unlike a price cut by the firm, a successful advertising campaign is hard for other firms to duplicate. Other firms will try to duplicate or match the advertising campaign of the first firm, but it takes time for them to do so. Meanwhile, the first firm reaps the rewards of its efforts. Eventually, if other firms succeed with effective campaigns of their own, all may end up with approximately the same market shares they had before. Much of the advertising effort will have been

---

[5]*The 1996 Canadian Encyclopedia Plus,* (Toronto: McClelland and Stewart, 1996).

wasted, and since the resources used for advertising purposes are not available to produce other goods and services, consumers receive a smaller total output from the economy as a whole.

Periodic change in the design and quality of the product is another major form of nonprice competition. Annual model changes fall in this category. Model changes may incorporate new technological developments, and to the extent that they do so, they enable given quantities of resources to make greater contributions to consumer satisfaction. But they may also simply rearrange or change the colour and the shape, making old models obsolete and new models no better. Successful design and quality innovations by one firm, like successful advertising, may be hard for other firms to imitate immediately and may increase the market share and monopoly power of the firm for a time. However, if other firms are successful over time with their own designs and quality changes, all may again end up with approximately the same market shares or with some rearrangement of market shares.

Should We Fear Monopoly?

Does the existence of monopoly enterprise put our economic future in jeopardy? Does monopoly power exist even in relatively small firms and how does it represent a threat to the economic well-being of other members of society? The economic analysis that we have just completed leads to the conclusion that in industries in which monopoly power is exercised, outputs will be lower and prices will be higher than they would be if the industries were more competitive. Monopoly power also may impede the entry of additional investment and firms into industries in which profits are made. Thus monopoly power may cause the resources or productive capabilities of the economy to be allocated poorly among alternative uses, with too little of the economy's resources allocated to the production of products made by industries in which monopoly power exists and too much allocated to products that are produced competitively. Monopoly power in imperfectly competitive markets may result in some waste of resources on nonprice competition. Finally, monopoly power can lead to hidden permanent distortions in income by transferring purchasing power from lower-income groups in society to upper-income groups.

Differences between Bigness and Monopoly Power

Surprisingly enough, a business enterprise that is big in terms of the value of its assets or the value of its sales does not necessarily have a high degree of monopoly power. On the other hand, a relatively small firm may have a great deal of monopoly power. The degree of monopoly power all depends on the position of the firm in the market in which it operates. Chrysler

Corporation is a very large firm in terms of its assets and annual sales volume, yet it may have little monopoly power. If it drops out of the market, other firms will easily take up the slack. If it raises its prices relative to those of other firms in the auto industry, it will very quickly price itself out of the market. It has much actual and potential competition. On the other hand, for many years Edmonton Telephone of Edmonton, Alberta, was a small firm in terms of assets and annual sales volume, but it came very close to being a pure monopoly. It had no direct rivals in the provision of local residential telephone service in Edmonton, with the exception of cellular telephone service. We must therefore be careful not to confuse bigness with monopoly power. In assessing the monopoly power of firms, we must look at specific industries and at individual firms within each industry to see whether or not they are able to have a significant effect on market outputs, prices, and buyers' access to the kind of product produced and sold by the industry. The distinction is that a firm may have a very large amount of capital and labour and produce a large absolute volume of product, but it may still account for only a small share of the total industry output—bigness may not indicate monopoly power. In such cases bigness may be an indicator of the need for large-scale production to keep unit cost low and allow a firm to compete against other firms in an industry. On the other hand, a firm may seem small in terms of the number of employees and the amount of invested capital when, in fact, it is the dominant firm in its industry and able to influence industry output and prices to its own benefit. Geographic dispersion or the technical sophistication of a product may permit even a relatively small firm to account for a very large portion of the production or sales in a particular industry. If strong barriers to entry exist, the threat of entry by potential competitors will be low and the existing firm may be able to exercise considerable monopoly power.

Outputs and Prices

When imperfectly competitive firms restrict output and increase prices, they impose an economic cost on society in the form of reduced social welfare. This reduction in welfare is the dead-weight welfare loss due to monopoly. We could better understand the issue of "fearing bigness" if we have a definitive estimate of this loss. While no definitive estimate exists, and while concentration ratios are higher in most industries in Canada than in the same industries in the United States, one fairly respected estimate places the loss in the United States at about 1 percent of gross domestic product per year.[6] That is, monopolistic elements within the economy serve to reduce economic welfare, as measured by GDP, by about 1 percent of GDP per year.

---

[6]F. M. Scherer, *Industrial Market Structure and Economic Performance* (Chicago: Rand McNally, 1980), p. 464.

Is this a significant loss in welfare? This decision is for each of us to make. However, we must bear in mind two points while making the decision. First, a basic economic truth is that while the economy's ability to produce is limited, society's desires for goods and services are unlimited. Consequently, any economic factor that tends to reduce the economy's ability to produce goods and services must be viewed as making an already difficult situation worse. Second, although 1 percent of GDP may not seem significant, 1 percent of Canada's GDP amounted to nearly $7.8 billion in 1996.

In other words, if all vestiges of monopoly power had been eliminated prior to 1996, during that year society could have consumed $7.8 billion in additional goods and services. For example, if the increased production due to the elimination of monopoly were equally distributed, during 1996 each individual in Canada would have received about $300 worth of additional goods and services.

Entry Restrictions and Resource Allocation

Economywide evidence of longrun misallocation of the economy's resources because of private entry barriers is rather difficult to find. In recent years we have seen many examples of easy entry. Personal computers are a case in point. Simple, early models commanded relatively high prices and were produced by a very few firms. But the success of the new product and the profits that were generated soon attracted new producers into the field. Supplies increased, prices fell, and the quality and sophistication of the units increased. The same sort of thing happened with compact disk players. Quite often, private entry barriers to markets break down rather easily.

Where entry to markets is blocked by law, it is easier to find evidence of resource misallocation. One of the more glaring instances of resources being used in quantities that are relatively too small is the medical profession. The average net income of physicians is at the top of the list for professions or occupations. Although the situation has changed in recent years, for many years with their tight legal control of entry into medical-training programs and into the profession itself, medical doctors could deter a large percentage of qualified applicants to medical schools from entering training. Similar entry restrictions and limitations on graduates to register as practitioners in their fields exist in accounting and law. Nor is the ability to limit entry restricted to the professions; among the building trades and the transportation workers, we can find many examples. In many local building markets, especially in the commercial construction end of the market, prices have soared, and profits to commercial contractors have been high because building codes have inhibited the introduction and use of new technology and prefabrication. The Canadian transportation industry hears many complaints regarding the derth of scheduled passenger and freight service (by rail, truck, and air) to regional markets because of the ability of dominant firms to limit the supply.

Nonprice Competition

The impact of nonprice competition on the public is far from clear. Although estimates of the total expenditure on advertising in industrialized countries vary, one study in the United States places the cost as equal to about 2.2 percent of GDP for 1993.[7] Statistics Canada *CANSIM* data indicate that almost 3 percent of Canada's gross domestic product on a factor-cost basis is used in travel, promotion, and advertising.[8]

Some share of the money spent on advertising—regardless of whether the medium of communication is point-of-sale posters, advertisements in magazines and newspapers, or radio and television promotions—provides useful information to potential consumers about the availability and price of a product. In most cases the money collected by the newspaper or television network pays part of the cost of producing the newspaper or providing the range of programming available to the public. Media firms often argue that the cost of service would be prohibitively high if the people reading a newspaper or watching the television programs had to pay the full cost of the service. In a sense advertising is payment—some might say an overpayment—for the "inexpensive newspapers" and the "free" radio and television programs that we enjoy.

We also cannot be sure whether or how much the public loses from product design and quality changes. Many useful innovations are introduced in this way—the self-starter on the automobile, no-frost freezers and refrigerators, word processors, and thousands of other items that make our lives more comfortable. But the only purpose of many other innnovations seems to be to make the previous years' models obsolete.

Income Distribution

How does monopoly power in the sale of products affect the distribution of income among economic units in the economy? The initial impression is that because entry into imperfectly competitive industries is restricted and because greater-than-average returns on investment may be obtained over time by firms in those industries, income is redistributed away from consumers toward those firms. But on further investigation

---

[7]U.S. Department of Commerce, Bureau of the Census, *Statistical Abstract of the United States, 1992.* p. 559.

[8]Statistics Canada *CANSIM* series I325033, I326013, I334513, I324233 and various issues of *The Daily.*

this outcome becomes somewhat less clear. Most monopolies and firms operating with some monopoly power are corporations; some are owned by only a small group of individuals, but many have thousands of stockholders who are actually the owners of the business. The monopolistic enterprise itself provides a legal framework that enables many individuals to own stock in the firm either directly or through such diverse investment options as company pension funds and the mutual funds offered by financial intermediaries. In this way the stockholders or investors can get together for purposes of production and participate in the profits from production and the change in the asset value of successfully run companies. To the extent that the enterprise yields above-average rates of return, it may pay higher wages and provide higher levels of benefits to some or all of its employees than are given to people employed in more competitive sectors. To the extent that above average returns are paid out in dividends, those returns accrue to people who own stock in the company. Consequently, we can be sure that monopoly power carries with it a transfer of income from other members of society to those involved in owning and operating the monopolies. This transfer is from consumers to the workers, management, and stockholders of the monopolistic firms. If one assumes, as seems reasonable, that those who tend to own stock tend also to be predominantly middle- and upper-income earners, then it may be concluded that monopoly power leads to income redistribution from those who, on average, have less—the consuming public—to those who, on average, have higher incomes—the workers, managers, and stockholders of the monopolistic firms.

At the same time, when a corporation yields higher-than-average returns on investment to its stockholders, its stock becomes attractive for people to buy. Increased demand for its stock drives the stock price up. This increase in the capital value of the stock increases the return to the existing stockholders and thus constitutes a second redistribution of purchasing power from other members of society to those who owned shares in the monopoly. Further, only those stockholders who owned the stock at the time when the higher-than-average returns were made stand to gain because the increasing price of the stock reduces the real returns to anyone who buys shares after the price has increased.

Some economists have suggested that this monopoly transfer of purchasing power can be viewed as a form of permanent taxation on low-income groups to increase the income of high-income groups. When monopoly profits are viewed in this way, it is evident that unlike real forms of taxation levied by elected governments, monopoly profits are not democratically determined and the consumers who pay these "privately levied taxes" are not involved in determining how the revenues raised might be used to contribute to the public good.

Summary

Many members of the general public tend to believe that big businesses are in a position to exploit them. Many people believe that a few business firms control the economy and that these firms restrict product outputs and charge higher prices than they should. They also believe that big firms make unjustifiable monopoly profits. At the same time most members of society agree that the Canadian market is small enough that monopoly may be the only way some industries can realize the economies of scale necessary to achieve low cost. In addition, throughout our history, Canadians have often seen large firms as the only ones that could undertake the high risks that accompany the building of new industries in remote areas.

To the extent that an individual firm produces a significant part of an industry's output, it can exercise some degree of monopoly power. Monopoly power induces firms to produce smaller outputs and charge higher prices than would be the case if the markets in which they operate were competitive. Firms with monopoly power are frequently able to restrict entry into their industries, thus compounding their output restrictions and higher prices and inhibiting movement of resources from less valuable to more valuable uses. They also engage in nonprice competition that may result in the waste of some of the economy's scarce resources.

We have some evidence that monopolistic elements within the Canadian economy have imposed, and continue to impose, an economic cost on society in terms of reduced social welfare. Although this is true, it is important to realize that bigness does not necessarily imply monopoly power. To identify monopoly power requires considering the size of the firm relative to the market in which it operates. Thus when we speak of the welfare loss due to monopoly, we should not immediately think just in terms of large firms. Much of the loss in welfare may come from rather small firms. Estimates of the dead-weight welfare loss due to monopoly place it at about 1 percent of GDP per year. In terms of 1996 GDP, this figure implies that monopolistic elements within the economy were responsible for a $7.8 billion reduction in GDP during that year. Consequently, it is important to keep a close watch on existing and potential monopoly problems. The more competition the market economy can sustain, the better the price mechanism will operate in allocating the economy's scarce resources among their many uses.

Checklist of Economic Concepts

Market, monopolistic
Market, imperfectly competitive
Market, competitive
Concentration ratio

Demand
Demand curve facing a firm
Marginal revenue
Marginal cost

Profit-maximizing output
Supply
Supply curve of a firm
Marginal social benefit

Marginal social cost
Dead-weight welfare loss
Entry barriers
Nonprice competition

Discussion Questions

1. Explain what a concentration ratio measures and how it can be used to indicate whether a firm is operating in a competitive industry or a noncompetitive industry. Why might high transportation costs reduce the effectiveness of using concentration ratios to identify monopoly industries in Canada?

2. Explain the concept of marginal revenue. Why is marginal revenue equal to the price of the product for a firm operating under competitive conditions but marginal revenue is less than price for a monopoly?

3. Discuss whether or not a monopoly firm would tend to produce and charge more than a similar firm with the same cost structure operating under competitive conditions?

4. Describe the barriers to entry that can create or sustain monopoly power in a particular industry.

5. Explain the distinction between bigness and monopoly power. Why might a large firm not possess monopoly power? Identify a local firm that you believe has monopoly power and discuss the sources and consequences of that power?

6. Use a graph for a firm operating in a monopoly situation to illustrate the dead-weight welfare loss of monopoly. Why does this dead-weight welfare loss reduce employment opportunities?

7. Explain why some economists regard monopoly profits as a "permanent private tax on the poor." What specific groups in society might benefit from this monopoly profit?

Supplementary Reading

Adams, W. and J. Brock. *The Bigness Complex*. New York: Pantheon Books, 1986.
    Provides the most thorough analysis of bigness available today. Includes a thoughtful critique of both conservative and liberal approaches to bigness.

Alpert, G. "Is Market Structure Proof of Market Power?" *Mergers and Acquisitions*, 19 (Summer 1984), pp. 47–51.

An excellent discussion of the loose linkage between market structure and market power. Several case studies are cited.

Carson, R. A. "Monopoly Power: What Should Be Our Policy Toward Big Business?" In *Economic Issues Today: Alternative Approaches*. 4th ed. New York: St. Martin's Press, 1987, chapter 4.

Presents the liberal, the conservative, and the radical answer to the question posed in the chapter title.

Friedman, M. "Monopoly and the Social Responsibility of Business and Labor." In *Capitalism and Freedom*. Chicago: University of Chicago Press, 1962, pp. 119–36.

A penetrating analysis of market structures with emphasis on the sources of monopoly power in the United States.

Galbraith, J. K. *Economics and the Public Purpose*. New York: Houghton Mifflin, 1976.

John Kenneth Galbraith has written many works during his 50-year career at Harvard. Many of his works deal with the role of professional managers as a force for influencing public economic decision making and as a group that has motives quite separate from those of the owners of the corporations for which they work.

Gorecki, P. K. and W. T. Stanbury. *Objectives of Competition Policy 1888–1983*. Montreal: Institute for Research on Public Policy, 1984.

A comprehensive study of Canadian laws and public policy concerning competition.

Leiss, W.; S. Kline; and S. Jhally. *Social Communication in Advertising*. Toronto: Meuthen, 1986.

An insightful and comprehensive study of the influence and extent of advertising in society.

Newman, P. C., *The Canadian Establishment*. Vol 2. Toronto: McClelland and Stewart, 1977.

Newman, P. C., *The Acquisitors, The Canadian Establishment*. Vol. 2. Toronto: McClelland and Stewart, 1981.

Peter Newman's works investigate the influence of corporate concentration on many facets of Canadian society and commerce. He looks at the regional and national effects of concentration of everything from direction and control of some of the nation's key industrial sectors to the influences that affect political decision making.

Porter, J. *The Canadian Corporate Elite, An Analysis of Economic Power*. Toronto: McClelland and Stewart, 1975.

Porter's study of the degree of corporate concentration in Canada and the prevalence and influence of oligopoly throughout the Canadian economy is a readable and concise investigation of the subject. It has been widely used as a starting point by other writers interested in this topic.

"Review of the Top 500." *Financial Post: Summer Supplement*. Toronto: 1996.

Each summer the *Financial Post* issues a special edition that reviews the assets, sales, number of employees, and profits of Canada's largest businesses. The magazine does not specifically identify monopolies, but it does give some indications in select industries, such as banking, of industry activity accounted for by the largest firms.

Chapter 10

Airline Regulation and Deregulation:

Economic Issues of Government Regulation

Today people in Atlanta can fly nonstop across the Atlantic to Amsterdam, Brussels, Frankfurt, London, Munich, Paris, Shannon and Zurich as well as to Bermuda, Mexico City and other destinations in the western hemisphere. But they cannot fly nonstop to any Canadian city.[1]

We recommend that the passenger transportation system be guided by the following objectives;

(a) safety,
(b) protection of the environment,
(c) fairness to taxpayers, travelers and carriers and
(d) efficiency, so that services are provided where benefits to the individual traveler equal or exceed the cost, and given levels of service, are provided at the lowest possible cost.

We believe that national passenger transportation policy should not be guided by objectives of nation-building and regional development.[2]

As the two quotations indicate, the regulation of airline passenger service in Canada is a complex multifaceted balancing act among often conflicting goals. In addition, we learn that regulation affects transborder traffic as well as purely domestic air travel. In fact, transborder traffic between Canada and the United States accounts for almost as many passenger-kilometres per year as all scheduled service within Canada accounts for.

The Problems of Regulation and the Promise of Deregulation

From the middle of the 1700s to the 1800s, what would become the central Canadian industrial heartland was composed of a collection of small firms in relatively isolated communities. Between the 1880s and the 1920s, this landscape underwent great change. Rather than industries being composed of numerous small firms, many industries in central Canada became increasingly dominated by corporate giants in concentrated urban centers that were linked to the expansive rural hinterland by a transportation grid,

---

[1]M. Dresner, "Regulation of U.S.–Canada Air Transportation: Past, Present and Future," *Canadian-American Public Policy*, March 1992, N. 9, p. 20.

[2]Government of Canada, *Directions: The Final Report of the Royal Commission on National Passenger Transportation; Summary* (Ottawa: Minister of Supply and Services, 1992), pp. 6–7.

it too, controlled by huge corporations. This growth of big business in the industrial heartland of Ontario and in our transportation sector is one of the defining features of the political economy of Canada.[3] It increased the country's productive capabilities, led to a significant improvement in living standards, brought about the modern system of international standard-time measurement, and made possible a Canada stretching from sea to sea to sea. It also brought with it increasing concern in the regional hinterlands that the best interests of the regions did not always coincide with the economic interests of the large transportation firms or the corporate giants of central Canada. Many Canadians and especially those in the regional hinterlands felt that the concentrated economic power of these huge corporate enterprises should be kept in check through government intervention. The *British North America Act* of 1867 and the later *Canada Act* of 1982 established transportation by all modes as industries that fall within the jurisdiction of the federal government. With the establishment of the Railway Committee of the Privy Council in 1888, the government entered an unprecedented era of regulation of private business that would last almost exactly 100 years. During this period, in many industries and particularly in the transportation sector, the federal government regulated prices, production levels, research and development, capital expenditures, entry into and exit from industries, product quality, and safety as it affected employees and the general public. Between 1888 and the present, the changes to the transportation and communications sector have resulted in whole new industries falling within this area of government regulation. The growth of inland shipping on the Great Lakes and elsewhere, highway motor transport, airline passenger and freight traffic, pipelines, radio, television, cable television, digital data transfer, and cellular communication have all led to the creation of new responsibilities for the federal government. These developments required changes to existing legislation and to the regulatory framework for administering and regulating transportation and communication to the benefit of investors operating firms in these sectors, the employees working in these industries, the customers, and the general public.

There have been many successes along the way. Sometimes, however, the regulatory agencies have had difficulty balancing the commercial interests of the firms in the regulated industry with the interests of the general public. Some critics would argue that the regulatory agencies have sometimes forgotten who they were established to protect. That is, in some instances regulatory agencies seemed to have acted almost exclusively to protect the interests of one group to the exclusion of the legitimate interests of the others. On occasions they appear to act in the interests of the customers purchasing the regulated product, sometimes to the detriment of the taxpayer who may end up paying the bills by having

---

[3]K. W. Studnicki-Gizbert, *Issues in Canadian Transportation Policy* (Toronto, ON: Macmillan, 1974), Ch. 1.

to provide subsidies to firms made unprofitable because of low regulated prices. Alternatively, the commercial interests of firms may take precedence over the collective public need for regional development and nation building. For this reason, government regulation has often been viewed by firms as a legal means of protecting themselves from competition. At other times the same firms have blamed the government for preventing them from providing some service they deem necessary to their profitability and financial survival.

Even in cases where the regulatory agency has maintained and communicated its focus on serving the public interest, the outcomes have often been less than ideal, simply tending to replace an imperfect unregulated market outcome with an imperfect governmentally regulated outcome. As a result of these difficulties, public opposition to government regulation has increased in the 1990s. The opponents of regulation argue that the interests of consumers and taxpayers might be better served through a general deregulation of many industries. In Canada, as in other western countries, this trend is illustrated by deregulation in many industries including airline passenger service, banking, broadcasting, cellular communication, courier services, electrical utilities, home heating fuels, garbage collection and disposal of hazardous waste, issuance of fishing permits and licences, liquor sales, marketing of petroleum, telephone services, and trucking. In this chapter, we consider the case of regulation and deregulation by focussing on the airline industry. The first step in the process is to consider the economically justifiable circumstances for government regulation.

When Should Government Regulate Business?

Numerous justifications have been offered for government regulation of business. While most of these have economic aspects, they are often primarily an outgrowth of social and political factors. Experience has taught that regulation works best, and is most likely to be successful, when it is limited to cases in which its primary justification is economic. In general terms, government regulation may be called for when three conditions are met. First, there must be market failure, that is, a situation in which the market operating on its own fails to lead to an efficient allocation of resources. Second, and equally important, there must be reason to believe that the market outcome may be improved through some degree of government control over the production process. Third, the constituents being regulated—the firms, their customers, the taxpayers who may be called upon to provide subsidies, and the general public—have a fairly clear sense of the purpose of the regulation and understand what it entails.

The three circumstances that most clearly meet these criteria are natural monopoly, cases of deficient information, and cases of poorly defined property rights. These circumstances are often present in public goods and cases in which equity issues and externalities are important in the provision of the product. However, regulation is not always appropriate when one of these circumstances exists. That determination requires a consideration of the relative benefits and costs of the regulation. If regulation is successful, the benefits are clear—increased social welfare due to a reduction in resource misallocation. The costs are, however, equally clear and include not just the costs of administering the regulation from the government's perspective but also the costs that the firms must bear in attempting to comply with the regulations. In some cases one of the three justifications for regulation may clearly exist, yet the appropriate policy for government to follow is to not regulate, since the expected costs outweigh the expected benefits. Thus the existence of one of the three justifications for regulation should be viewed as providing only a circumstance in which regulation may be economically justified, but not ensuring the desirability of regulation.

Natural Monopoly

The **average cost** of production, sometimes called the per unit cost, is found by dividing total costs by the number of units being produced.

In Chapter 9, two concepts of a firm's costs were presented, total costs and marginal cost. A third important concept of cost is *average cost*, which is simply the firm's total costs divided by the number of units being produced. Thus if a firm is incurring total costs of $500 to produce 50 units of its good, then its average cost is $10 per unit ($500/50 = $10).

Assuming that both of the firm's inputs, labour and capital, may be varied, Figure 10–1 presents a typical longrun average cost curve (AC) for a firm.

Minimum efficient scale for a firm occurs at the output level where the firm's longrun average cost is at its lowest level.

When longrun average cost can be reduced simply by increasing the firm's size and producing more of the product, the firm is said to be enjoying **economies of scale**. Such economies of scale are often the result of being able to use better technology to ensure the efficient use of resources when the scale of production increases.

The most important characteristic of a longrun average cost curve is its U-shape, which indicates that average cost declines initially as output per unit of time increases but eventually turns and increases. At the output level Q_0, where the average total cost is at its minimum, the firm is operating at its *minimum efficient scale* (MES). When the firm is on the downward sloping portion of the curve (production levels less than Q_0), we say it is enjoying *economies of scale*. In this situation, the average cost of production may be reduced simply by increasing the firm's size or scale and producing more of the product until MES is reached at Q_0. Suppose, for example, that General Motors was constrained to produce only 1,000 cars per year, rather than the 3 to 4 million cars it now produces. In such a circumstance assembly lines would be out of the question. Each car would have to be produced essentially by hand.

Also ruled out would be bulk-buying discounts for inputs and any benefits that might be derived from the division and specialization of labour. That is, as Sam and George McLaughlin of Oshawa, Ontario, realized, producing such a small number of cars rules out the use of numerous production techniques that are capable of radically reducing average cost. It was partly this realization in 1918 that caused them to sell

Figure 10–1   **Long-run average cost of production for a typical firm**

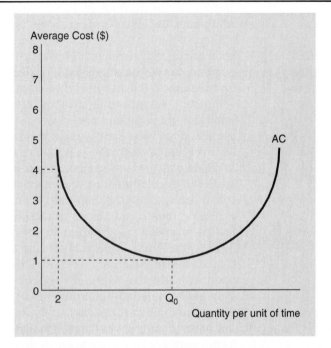

The long-run average cost of production for a typical firm is U-shaped. For production levels less than Q_0, an increase in production lowers average cost. This range is the range of economies of scale. Production increases beyond Q_0 lead to an increasing average cost; thus this range is referred to as the range of diseconomies of scale.

their McLaughlin Carriage Company, makers of the McLaughin-Buick, to General Motors. Thus a GM producing only 1,000 cars per year is clearly operating at a much smaller output level than Q_0. It can enjoy significantly reduced average cost simply by increasing the scale of its operation.

The factors leading to economies vary from one industry to another and may be more pronounced in one industry than in another. They are usually the result of some combination of the division of labour and specialization, an ability to make use of by-products, the growth of supporting facilities, or the ability to negotiate volume discounts from suppliers. If the volume of output is high enough, individual workers and machines can be organized to perform and repeat one task thousands of times per day, lowering the cost per unit of output. In addition, the division of tasks may result in the need for specialized equipment or highly specialized skills, neither of which is used in other industries. Patents on specialized machinery and the development of training procedures to get workers to learn specialized skills may create barriers to the entry of potential competitors.

The introduction of the automotive assembly line provided many examples of the division of labour and the development of specialized equipment and skills, bringing with it both lower cost per unit output and higher barriers to the entry of new firms. A second source of economies of scale occurs if firms have high enough production levels to create an opportunity to recycle some or all of their own waste products to produce by-products. A third source of economies of scale can be found in the development of supporting facilities. When a firm grows, it is often worthwhile for its suppliers and even governments to provide it with the services it requires. For example, to win a contract to transport coal mined by a very large coal mine, a railway may decide to build special loading facilities and to develop specialized marshalling services to handle the coal. The development of these facilities may reduce the cost of selling coal in foreign markets. Similarly, the desire to reduce the cost per unit of exporting bulk commodities to world markets was an important reason for government participation in the construction of the St. Lawrence Seaway, the Trans-Canada Highway, and the major pipeline systems in Canada. Once these large scale facilities and support systems are developed, they are often cheaper to operate than the small scale systems that they replaced. Finally, economies may result from a firm becoming large enough to force its suppliers to offer it volume discounts. As we explained in Chapter 9 and as we will explore again in Chapter 11, in some situations a firm may not be a price taker. A firm may possess sufficient monopoly power as a buyer of inputs to force its suppliers to reduce its cost of production—even at the expense of some other groups in society.

Such economies of large-scale production do not continue over the entire range of output possibilities. As certain as we are that economies of scale exist over some range of output in many industries, we are equally certain that if the scale of operation continues to grow, longrun average cost will eventually turn and go up. When average cost starts increasing (output levels greater than Q_0,) we say the firm is encountering *diseconomies of scale*. The most obvious explanation for this phenomenon is that the firm simply becomes too large to be effectively managed, with each increase in size adding an additional layer of bureaucracy to the production process. Elliott Estes, former president of General Motors, said it best: "Chevrolet is such a big monster that you twist its tail and nothing happens at the other end for months and months. It is so gigantic that there isn't any way to really run it."[4]

Another factor that might lead to diseconomies of scale is worker boredom. The division and specialization of labour inherent in modern production processes narrows the scope of each worker's job so that the worker is capable of becoming very adept, that is, very efficient at the job.

Beyond a certain size and production level, average cost can be expected to rise as production is increased. This outcome is caused by **diseconomies of scale.**

---

[4]P. Wright, *On A Clear Day You Can See General Motors* (Grosse Pointe, MI: Wright Enterprises, 1979), pp. 114–5.

This sort of job narrowing can go too far, however. When it does, boredom is likely to set in and the output is reduced productivity.

A typical situation for a firm, then, is to initially enjoy falling average cost as its size and production level are increased due to economies of scale. Beyond some production level, however, diseconomies of scale arise, which cause average cost to turn and go up. These forces taken together give the longrun average cost curve its U-shape.

Now back to the case of natural monopoly. The average cost curve of Figure 10–1 shows that the average cost of producing the product reaches a minimum of $1 per unit when the level of production is Q_0 per unit of time. Suppose that this level of production is 10 units per week. Now consider three separate cases. In the first case, the market for the product is such that 1,000 units may be sold during a week. Here, the market could support 100 firms (1,000/10 = 100), each producing at the minimum possible average cost of $1. In this market we could expect a high level of competition among a large number of firms, each of which is small relative to the market.

As a second case, suppose that the market is such that only 100 units of the product may be sold per week. Here, only 10 efficient firms could be supported. In terms of the vocabulary of Chapter 9, we would say that the concentration and thus the potential for monopoly power is greater in this case than the first case.

When the industry's average cost of production is minimized by having only one firm produce the product, the industry is a **natural monopoly.**

Now consider an extreme third case in which only 10 units per week may be sold in the market. In this case, only one efficient firm, a *natural monopolist,* could be supported. This case is referred to as a natural monopoly because no matter how many firms are initially in operation in this market, the largest will have an undeniable average cost advantage over the smaller firms and should eventually push each of the smaller rivals out of business. That is, when the cost structure of an industry is such that the average cost of production is minimized when only one firm operates, the industry is a natural monopoly.

As discussed in Chapter 9, society's interests are well served when markets are composed of many relatively small firms in competition with one another. When natural monopoly is present, this is not the case. To see this point, return to Figure 10–1 and assume that output level Q_0 occurs at 10 units of production per week. Would society be better served by having the 10 units of output produced by one firm or by five firms? With one firm, a natural monopolist, the average cost of production is $1. With five firms, each producing two units per week, the average cost is $4 per unit. Thus, requiring "competition," that is, insisting on the existence of five firms, rather than a monopolist, causes the product to be produced at an average cost four times greater than necessary. In an opportunity cost sense, this implies that it takes four times the value of resources to produce 10 units of the good when production is distributed among five firms than when production is concentrated in the natural monopolist. In this case, there are clear benefits to society in allowing the monopolist to exist.

Although these benefits are undeniable, as noted in Chapter 9, unregulated monopolists tend to impose costs on society as well in the form of reduced output and increased prices. Thus, resource misallocation appears to be inevitable under free market conditions. If we allow the natural monopolist to exist, we reap a dead-weight welfare loss of the type explained in Chapter 9. The dead-weight welfare loss is due to the monopolist's tendency to reduce output and increase price, whereas if we require numerous firms to exist, we cause the product to be produced at an average cost above that which is possible. This is the trade-off that justifies government regulation. In the case of natural monopoly, government regulation is designed to allow the monopolist to exist (yielding the benefits of a low average cost of production) but avoiding the dead-weight cost of unregulated monopoly. The regulation attempts to force the monopolist to produce a higher output than it would under unregulated conditions and charge a price equal to its average cost, simulating the price that would exist if competitive conditions existed at that output level. Although relatively few markets have cost structures that yield economies of scale sufficient to justify them being viewed as natural monopolies, a few examples exist, including local distribution of natural gas and electricity and, perhaps, local telephone service and cable television. Suffice it to say that although the existence of natural monopoly is quite rare, it does provide an economically justifiable case for government regulation.

Deficient Information

The fact that consumers often lack complete and reliable information about the products they purchase provides government with another economically justifiable case for regulation. To see the impact of deficient information, consider a case in which a somewhat unsafe car is sold. Perhaps the safety defect is in the form of a transmission that causes the car to shift into the drive position without input from the driver. Suppose that when consumers are unaware of this defect, the interaction of the supply of the car (SS) and the demand for the car (D_1D_1) yields an equilibrium in which 100,000 cars are being sold per year at a price of $18,000 per car, as is depicted in Figure 10–2. Government regulation could impose a requirement that the firm make public disclosure of the defect to make the public aware of the frequency and the consequences of the defect's occurrence. Once the consuming public is made aware of the defect, what is likely to occur? It can be reasonably expected that the demand for the car will fall to some lower level. In light of the new information about the defect, some people may decide not to purchase the product under any conditions. It is quite likely that some other people, upon receiving the new information, will have a reduced willingness to purchase the product but would still be willing to buy it. Thus the demand curve is likely to shift left to some position such as D_2D_2, resulting in a new equilibrium being established in which

Figure 10–2   **The effect of deficient information on the market for cars**

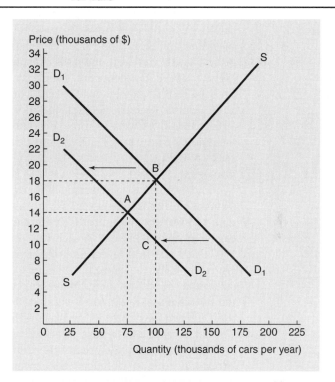

Because consumers lack information concerning the safety defect, an equilibrium is reached with 100,000 cars being purchased each year for $18,000 per car. When the safety defect is made known to consumers, their expectations about the car change for the worse, resulting in a fall in demand to D_2D_2. A new equilibrium is established in which 75,000 cars are sold each year for $14,000 each.

75,000 cars sold for $14,000 per car. You may recall this as a simple application of the law of demand as presented in Chapter 2. That is, the law of demand indicates that the original demand D_1D_1 is valid only under the assumption that other things, including the consumers' expectations about the product, remain constant. With the new information about the product, the consumers' expectations clearly change for the worse; thus demand falls to the new level D_2D_2.

Now consider the two outcomes. Prior to the new information, consumers purchased 100,000 cars, whereas afterward, they chose to purchase only 75,000. The deficient information, therefore, caused consumers to "overconsume" the product. In other words, the resources that had been used to produce the 25,000 cars that are no longer being purchased were misallocated in the sense that consumers, when given complete information, preferred to have the resources used elsewhere. To see the resource misallocation more clearly, recall from Chapter 9 that the supply curve of an industry may be thought of as the marginal social cost of producing successive units of a product. That is, supply curve SS indicates the value that would be placed on the resources necessary to produce any given quantity of cars had those resources been used in their next most highly valued employment. Similarly, the demand curve D_2D_2 of Figure 10–2, which exists when full information is present, may be thought of as a marginal social benefit curve, since it indicates the benefit that society anticipates from consuming successive quantities of cars. Given this terminology, how many cars should be produced? Or, in other words, how much of the economy's scarce resources should be devoted to the production of cars?

The answer is, of course, that production should be carried to the point where marginal social benefits and marginal social costs are just equal. Returning to Figure 10–2, we see that this point occurs when 75,000 cars are produced and sold each year. For each car between the 75,000 and 100,000 production levels, the marginal cost to society (SS) of production is greater than the marginal benefit to society (D_2D_2) derived from consumption. In other words, the resources used to produce these 25,000 cars would have yielded greater satisfaction to society had they been used in their next most highly valued use rather than in the production of cars. The total value of the loss in social welfare due to this resource misallocation is given by the area of the triangle ABC in Figure 10–2. This misallocation due to deficient information provides the justification for government regulation that might, in this case, take the form of requiring public disclosure. This has been done in the case of some products, such as tobacco, by requiring manufacturers to label the product with warnings as to the effects of its use and by the government providing public service information bulletins about the negative effects of using the product. Just as some consumers have continued to purchase cigarettes and other tobacco products after the imposition of government labeling regulations requiring tobacco manufacturers to warn the public that "This product can cause cancer," some consumers might well purchase automobiles that had warnings that driving the vehicle under certain conditions could result in vehicle failure endangering the lives of the occupants.

In other cases of deficient information, appropriate regulatory tools might include health and safety codes for products and workplaces, government product testing, or in some cases, the outlawing of items deemed too unsafe to be available for general consumption. In the case of government safety codes, the benefit to society is that the demand curve remains in the same place and that the producer must alter the nature of the product to comply with the safety code. The disadvantage of using public disclosure is that the firms and the government must try to inform 30 million consumers of potential problems with the product. In the case of durable products this information must be repeated many times so that when a present owner of the product decides to sell the product at a garage sale, the purchaser is aware of the defect. With each new generation of consumers, the information must be repeated, and because people forget the details or severity of the defect, the information must be repeated over and over. This public information program requires the use of society's scarce resources and adds to the profits of the mass media. In many cases the public can be protected at very little cost to the producers by making regulations and codes specifying the product must meet certain standards at the time of manufacture or else it cannot be sold. For example, most people would agree that it would not be satisfactory or efficient for meat-processing plants to sell diseased or rotting meat even if they included a label to the effect that eating the meat might kill the consumer. Instead, at very little cost the government's and the firms' meat grading and inspection at the processing plants ensure that potentially dangerous products are not sold. Plants that package substandard meat are ordered to conform to standards, or they will face severe penalties. In the same way, an alternative to labelling in the car example would be to require standards to which each car must conform at the time of manufacture. Today we take for granted that all new cars must have headlights, brakes, and safety belts—and that these safety devices are in working order. We do not leave it up to the tastes of the public or misguided notions of adventure or frugality that some of members of society may wish to buy a car more cheaply because it is manufactured with defective brakes!

Poorly Defined Property Rights

The problem posed by poorly defined property rights is best exemplified in the case of pollution that was treated in detail in Chapter 5. To refresh your memory, recall that in Chapter 5 we saw that in the absence of well-defined property rights, pollution causes polluting firms to "overproduce" while causing the firms that must clean up the pollution to "underproduce." This situation occurs because the polluting firm is able to push some of its costs of production onto other firms. These outcomes are a simple application of the law of supply as presented in Chapter 2. You will recall from Chapter 2 that as production costs fall, supply increases. That is, overproduction on the part of the polluter is simply a rational response to the fall in production costs that comes about when the firm is allowed to use natural resources without paying for them. Just the reverse causes the firm that must clean up the pollution to underproduce—its costs of production are artificially increased, and thus its supply falls. Here again we find an inefficient allocation of resources, which provides a justification for government regulation. The exact nature of the regulation is not, however, clearly prescribed. In Chapter 5, it was suggested that government regulation for pollution control might take the form of taxes, direct controls on emissions, outright prohibitions on the use of particular substances, or in some cases, the establishment of markets for pollution rights.

Other examples of regulation being prompted by poorly defined property rights might require a different mix of regulatory cures. In the case of airwave communications, for example, the government pursues policies that allocate specific frequencies to individual users. That is, the Canadian Radio and Television Commission (CRTC) gives radio stations, television broadcasters, and cable television suppliers what amounts to property rights to broadcast on particular frequencies and serve specific geographic markets. Regardless of the exact nature of the property rights problem and the resulting regulation, the key is that poorly defined property rights often lead to circumstances in which government regulation may be viewed as an economically justifiable means of improving the existing allocation of resources.

The History of Airline Regulation and Deregulation

The history of scheduled airline regulation in Canada has been characterized by three major themes: an ongoing desire to ensure the safety of the flying public, a desire to ensure the financial health and stability of the firms developing domestic routes, and a desire to see that the flying public and the scheduled carriers have convenient access to a growing number of domestic and international destinations. These desires have sometimes been in harmony with each other, and on other occasions conflicts among them have complicated the regulation of air transportation.

In the early 1920s the air transport industry in Canada was characterized by a large number of small "bush operators" serving the mining industry and remote northern communities. By the 1930s the development of the mining industry in remote areas coupled with the federal government's desire to assert sovereignty in areas not served by road or rail produced a need for regular, scheduled air service by larger and more complex aircraft. As a way of satisfying these perceived needs, the government moved into airline regulation with the passage of the Transport Act of 1938, which placed the control of routes and the approval of rate schedules into the hands of the Board of Transport Commissioners.[5] The essence of the policy was substantially a repetition of the type of regulation that had proved successful during the evolution of the country's railroads over the previous half century. The government envisioned a regulated monopoly to be created out of a Winnipeg-based firm, Canadian Airways. The proposed new monopoly would be a three-way joint venture with

---

[5]H. L. Purdy, *Transport Competition and Public Policy In Canada* (Vancouver: University of British Columbia Press, 1972), p. 38.

ownership divided among the Canadian Pacific Railway, the government-owned Canadian National Railway, and the existing owners of Canadian Airways. Within a very short time, the conflicting goals of the parent firms resulted in Canadian National Railways buying out Canadian Pacific's interest. Canadian Airways withdrew from the venture. The resulting government owned firm was renamed Trans-Canada Airlines in 1937 and operated as an independent subsidiary of Canadian National Railways. In 1964 the name was changed to Air Canada. Canadian Pacific and Canadian Airways retained an interest in creating a scheduled air carrier, and they formed Canadian Pacific Air Lines. This airline evolved into a regional carrier, concentrating on north-south routes complementing the transcontinental routes and international routes being developed by Trans-Canada Airlines. The dominant theme in the early stage of Canadian regulation, as far as domestic traffic is concerned, was an attempt to develop an infrastructure of transcontinental routes through a regulated monopoly. The accepted view that the airline industry in Canada was a natural monopoly seems well stated in the words of James Richardson, the former owner of Canadian Airways, that "there was no room for two large aviation companies in Canada."[6]

In the development of international traffic, the presence of the United States and the ease with which aircraft could penetrate the border made transborder flight a reality from an early stage. In 1929 Canada and the United States signed their first agreement to grant reciprocal permission to air carriers of both countries to serve destinations in each other's territory—in effect, Canada and the United States had an "open skies policy."[7] Beginning in the 1930s, restrictions were imposed on Canadian carriers entering the United States and on American airlines entering Canada because both countries were concerned about the effects of international competition on the financial health of domestic carriers offering scheduled service. In 1934 the United States instituted the *Air Mail Act* that developed a system of monopoly routes with government subsidies. The rapid development of government-subsidized monopoly routes in the United States, coupled with possible economies of scale in the United States, contributed to the view in Canada that American air carriers had unfair advantages compared to Canadian carriers. By 1959 Canadian Pacific had received permission to operate a second domestic transcontinental scheduled service. The problem was that Canada was now concerned that the two Canadian transcontinental carriers would not be economically viable if Americans were carrying some of Canada's domestic traffic. Canada moved to further restrict access to Canadian destinations served by American carriers. This trend toward restricted access to each other's

---

[6]W. Skene, *Turbulence: How Deregulation Destroyed Canada's Airlines* (Vancouver: Douglas and McIntyre, 1994), p. 54.

[7]Dresner, op. cit., pp. 1–34.

routes between Canada and the United States continued well into the 1960s. Both countries were aware that any easing of restrictions might ultimately have to be shared with the carriers of other nations, and as technology advanced after 1960, with the introduction of long-range, wide-bodied jet aircraft, that threat meant potential competition with major Asian and European carriers.

Between 1979 and 1995, Canada and the United States have been attempting to renegotiate bilateral agreements to increase access to each other's air transport markets. By 1989 scheduled passenger service between Canada and the United States was nearly as large as the total domestic Canadian market.[8] In addition, the transborder traffic between Canada and the United States and American domestic traffic had grown much more rapidly than the domestic market in Canada. This resulted in Canadian carriers increasing pressure on the Canadian government to negotiate a new arrangement with the United States for less restricted access to the destinations in the United States. Negotiations of this type are complex, involving the interests of two sovereign governments, as well as the business interests of the airlines being represented by the negotiating governments and the interests of the traveling public. Understandably, on several occasions treaties unraveled because of the possibility that if the United States granted a concession to Canada, the precedent might compel the United States to offer the same access to other nations.

American carriers had 60 percent of the scheduled transborder service. Canada also recognized that the real advantage to more open skies for Canadian carriers would lie in opening up a portion of the huge American domestic traffic to Canadian scheduled carriers. Canadian carriers wanted an agreement that would give them the right to pick up passengers and carry them between U.S. destinations along their routes between Canadian and American destinations—so-called *cabotage* traffic. The danger to Canadian firms was that the major carriers in the United States each had fleets of aircraft that were multiples of the fleets owned by Air Canada and the smaller Canadian airlines. Canadian carriers had a concern that in order to get cabotage in the United States for Canadian carriers, the Canadian government would have to agree to cabotage for American carriers entering Canadian air space.

The Canadian Transport Commission and National Transportation Authority

Canada developed a system of airline regulation that separated the safety concerns of the industry from the economic aspects. The first, dealing with safety and certification of flight crews and aircraft, was placed

---

[8]Ibid., p. 25

under Transport Canada's National Transportation Safety Board (NTSB). The second, dealing with economic concerns and the development of a national infrastructure of air transport to supplement the existing transportation infrastructure of the rail, highway, and shipping systems, was placed under the Canadian Transport Commission (CTC), which later evolved into the National Transportation Agency (NTA). In short, the CTC was part of the tradition of using the influence of government regulation in the transportation and communications industries to foster nation building.

The system appeared well conceived and functioned well for many years, developing economically viable service on a reliable and safe basis. However, it was not designed to create an industry with large numbers of competitive carriers offering low fares. In most regions of the country, the north-south feeder routes were developed by small regional carriers such as Eastern Provincial Airways, Pacific Western Airlines, Quebecair, and Transair, complementing the transcontinental and international service of Air Canada and Canadian Pacific. Several successful charter services including, Nordair, Nation Air, and Wardair, also developed. These charter operators, along with others, offered discount-fare charter services to Asia, the United States, and Europe. Collectively, Canadian charter operators accounted for 96 percent of the low-fare transborder flights between Canada and the United States by 1989.[9]

In 1978 the Carter administration in the United States passed legislation to deregulate domestic and international air service as a way of breaking the monopoly power of some airlines on domestic routes in the United States and bringing about a lower rate structure.[10] By 1979 the United States had renegotiated 20 new bilateral international treaties on airline service but had failed to get agreement with Canada. The sticking point was cabotage on the United States portion of flights to and from Canada. In Europe, deregulation and changing technology were also forcing change. The Liberal government in Canada responded to the the changing international and technological environment by introducing the New Canadian Air Policy of 1984. This policy effectively deregulated the domestic airways, allowing scheduled carriers to set their own fares and choose their own destinations on southern routes. It also allowed charter carriers like Wardair to enter the domestic transcontinental scheduled routes. In 1987 the move to deregulation was completed when the Conservative government of Brian Mulroney passed the National Transportation Act, which came into force in 1988. The last recommendation of the 1992 Royal Commission on National Passenger Transportation, quoted at the beginning of the chapter, shows how far thinking has evolved from the position that transportation policy was part of the nation-building function

---

[9]Ibid., p. 3.

[10]Ibid., pp. 12–7.

of the government so prevalent from 1888 to 1987. At this juncture the government's official position was that the industry was mature and that the market was large enough to support a number of competitive firms. In short, the belief seems to have been that the industry was no longer in danger of evolving into a natural monopoly and the appropriate role for the government was to foster competition.

Airline Industry Performance: The Impact of Deregulation

Proponents of deregulation in Canada, as elsewhere, point to what they believe are the benefits of relying on competitive market forces to drive the economic decisions about what to produce, how much to produce, what price to charge, how many firms should supply the product, and to whom product should be supplied. Their initial assumption usually includes a belief that the regulators are protecting the firms in the industry rather than acting in the interest of consumers. They claim that under regulated conditions the market will have evolved to a point where prices are too high, services are scarce, and firms make abnormally high profits. They argue that deregulation will lead to new firms entering the industry, offering a wider variety of product and increased volumes of product, which will lower prices and reduce profits. To the extent that these arguments applied to airline regulation in Canada prior to 1988, we should be able to see if deregulation brought with it lower air fares, more frequency of service, more choice in the kinds of services, more firms providing the service, and reduced but adequate profit levels. Alternatively, some critics of regulation argue that government regulators tend to pander to the concerns of consumers with little or no regard for the firms in the industry. If regulation had worked to the benefit of consumers at the expense of the firms, the result should have been too many firms, prices would have been held artificially low, and profits would have been low compared to other industries. If this were the situation in Canada's airline industry, deregulation should have resulted in a reduction in the number of firms, an increase in the prices charged to customers, and an increase in profit levels for the firms that remained in the industry after deregulation.

Fares and Frequency

The impact of deregulation on fares may be considered in two ways. The first method is to compare the price of a ticket on a particular type of service between two centers (a city-pair) before deregulation with the price on the same route for the same service after deregulation. Once the rate of increase on the price of the service is known, it can then be compared to factors such as the general rate of inflation or the increases in the costs faced by the industry supplying the product. If the price is rising more slowly than other prices or than the industry costs or if the rate of growth in prices slows in the period following deregulation, then it may indicate that deregulation has contributed to a downward pressure on prices. Another method, used fairly widely by experts who study transportation issues, is to try to identify the kinds of services and the types of discount fares that may have resulted from deregulation and to estimate the percentage of the passengers taking advantage of these discount fares. An example of the first method reveals that a regular non-stop return fare from Calgary to Victoria was $586.00 in December 1989 and $680.00 in March 1996. The use of any one particular route and particular carrier raises the concern that the airline or route chosen may not be typical of the overall performance of the industry. Statistics Canada reviews the average fares paid by the consumers per passenger-kilometre on all scheduled city-pairs to eliminate the chance of choosing a route that is not representative of the general trend. According to Statistics Canada, the average fare (all types) paid on all city-pairs increased by 3 percent in 1994 and increased by 16.5 percent between 1992 and 1993.[11] Over the same period airline workers had taken wage rollbacks, the price of fuel had not risen significantly, and worker layoffs had resulted in productivity gains. These three factors suggest that operating costs (excluding the debt-servicing cost of aircraft) had actually decreased slightly. The general level of inflation over this period was below 3 percent per year. Thus in the period after deregulation, airfares rose more quickly than did other prices, and this increase cannot be attributed to increased costs faced by suppliers in the industry.

Using the second method to assess what share of the traffic flew on discount fares, to check the frequency and convenience of service and the number of carriers serving various routes is also interesting. While the discussion above indicated that the regular return fare was $680.00 from Calgary to Victoria, the same airline offers a seven-day, advance-booking, discount return fare at $138.00. As deregulation progressed, the percentage of the travelers paying full fare decreased. By 1992 more than 72 percent of the passenger-kilometres flown between Canadian destinations were receiving discounted fares.[12] More recently, this phenomenon has increased as firms have instituted travel policies to ensure that employees flying on business stay over the weekend to get seven-day excursion discounts rather than paying full business-class fares. In reviewing the convenience of service, Canadian carriers are more aggressive in advertising their schedules and increasing the frequency of flights. For example, the three Canadian scheduled carriers offering Calgary-to-Vancouver daily service were running more than 60 flights per day in the spring of 1996. This frequency amounts to more than one flight per half hour per carrier or, between the three carriers, the equivalent of one flight every

---

[11]Statistics Canada, *Daily*, March 24, 1995.

[12]Ibid.

12 minutes. The pattern was evident on domestic routes, where aircraft movements have grown by 10 percent, as well as on international routes, where aircraft movements have grown by 50 percent since 1992.[13] On this basis, deregulation appears to have succeeded in increasing both the availability and variety of service. A larger portion of the flying public were able to qualify for reduced fares, and service was more frequent than before deregulation.

Competition and deregulation should have led to increased service levels and increased choice *if* the previous industry structure was providing too little choice or too little service relative to market demand. Proponents of deregulation in the airline industry often seem to have assumed that the level of service must have been too low and the price must have been too high simply because regulation existed. They forget that the competitive market model suggests that if an industry has more resources than are warranted by demand, then some firms will be forced out of business and levels of service will decrease. The information in the previous paragraph shows that the number of flights and capacity were increasing and the effective fares for passengers were increasing, but it does not necessarily mean the market had too few resources prior to deregulation. By the mid-1980s Canada already had the highest per capita destination linkages in the world and the lowest air fares outside the Communist bloc.[14] Whether the level of service could have been considered too low depends on more than the number of flights and the number of seats offered. It is useful to look at how many passenger-kilometres were being flown and how full the aircraft were when they left the ground. If Canadians had experienced a shortage of flights and service prior to deregulation, then as deregulation allowed new flights to be inaugurated, the number of passenger-kilometres should have increased and the number of passengers per flight (load factors) should have remained the same or increased. A review of the facts shows that as deregulation progressed, the number of flights did increase and the number of passenger-kilometres also increased, but load factors actually declined significantly. The load factors reached an all-time low of 60.8 percent in February 1995 before rising to 65.7 percent by September 1995.[15] Between 1990 and 1993, the number of seats exceeded the number of passengers by a factor of three to two on average—on many routes it was two to one, and on a few routes, like Calgary to Ottawa, it was a staggering six seats per passenger.[16] Clearly, deregulation had not led to a increase in needed capacity to address a shortage of seats caused by unmet demand. Instead it had led to

---

[13]Statistics Canada, op. cit., February 8, 1995.

[14]Skene, op. cit., p. 138.

[15]Statistics Canada, op. cit., November 7, 1995.

[16]Skene, op. cit., p. 49.

aircraft regularly flying half empty and in some cases flying two-thirds empty, implying a misallocation of society's resources and the creation of overcapacity.

Mergers

The proponents of deregulation also suggested that regulators protected inefficient firms, particularly the government-owned Air Canada, from competition from supposedly more efficient private firms. If there had not been enough good-quality service, as the market was deregulated, new firms should have had an opportunity to enter the industry. Expanded competition would have forced fares lower and increased service levels, resulting in higher profits. One way to assess the effectiveness of the deregulation, then, is to compare the number of firms in the industry before deregulation with the number of firms after deregulation and to see how these firms are faring in terms of their profits and the rate of return to their owners.

The decade from 1984 to 1994 was a decade marked by a concentration of scheduled and charter service into fewer and fewer larger firms. The first contributing factor causing increased concentration came when relatively successful regional feeder lines could not find financing to replace aging fleets of aircraft. Pacific Western Airlines out of Vancouver, a major regional carrier and the most important scheduled service to northern Alberta, British Columbia, and the Yukon, announced that it would have to shut down if it could not find a suitable merger. Because of the importance of the airline to the transportation infrastructure of western Canada and particularly its vital role for the development of the petroleum and tourist industries of the region, the Alberta government purchased controlling interest in the airline. On January 1, 1987, for the second time in 60 years Canadian Pacific Corporation withdrew from the airline industry, selling its subsidiary, the nation's second-largest scheduled carrier, to Pacific Western. The new firm, renamed Canadian Airlines International, subsequently took over the largest charter carrier in Canada, Wardair, in 1989. Over the same period, the federal government sold its interest in Air Canada, transforming the company into a private, profit-seeking company. Air Canada, like Canadian Airlines, launched into a series of mergers and takeovers of small regional airlines and charter carriers. By the beginning of the 1990s, Air Canada, Canadian Airlines International, and their regional affiliates accounted for almost 100 percent of the domestic scheduled air service in Canada.[17] This reduction in the number of firms suggests that the factor preventing an increase in the number of carriers was neither regulation nor regulators who were protecting large, inefficient carriers from smaller, more efficient firms.

---

[17]Dresner, op. cit., p. 18.

By 1992 Air Canada and Canadian Airlines International had accumulated a combined debt of approximately $7 billion, as they had worked to modernize their fleets, acquire regional subsidiaries, and expand capacity. Their acquisitions left them with a combined debt/equity ratio estimated at 3.65 to 1.[18] By 1994 Air Canada had 19,000 employees and assets of $4.5 billion, while Canadian Airlines International Limited had 16,000 employees and assets of $2.4 billion.[19] As large as these numbers may appear, the airline industry had lost approximately 6,000 jobs while increasing the size and dominant position of the two main carriers. In addition, and surprisingly, the two carriers had both slipped, compared to their previous rank among the world's commercial carriers, in terms of numbers of passengers.[20] The two dominant domestic airlines each had fleets less than one-fifth the size of the largest potential competitor south of the border.[21] They also were less financially secure than their potential competitors. Air Canada was experiencing losses of $1.8 million a day, and Canadian Airlines International had losses of $0.8 million per day. Their costs per passenger-kilometre ranged from 15 cents to 18 cents.[22] Transportation experts who studied the comparative costs of Canadian and American carriers concluded that Air Canada and Canadian International Airlines were within the operating range of the largest six airlines in the United States.[23] The cost per passenger-kilometre were however estimated to be 30 to 50 percent higher on Canadian carriers than for the most cost-efficient large American carriers.[24]

Air Canada and Canadian Airlines International had combined losses of $173 million in 1995. This loss continued the unbroken string of losses for both airlines dating back to the deregulation of 1988.[25] Put another way, for the 16 years prior to deregulation, Canadian carriers had provided profits for the investors in the industry while charging the travelers low fares. By contrast, at least in the first decade following deregulation, despite markedly higher fares, reduced numbers of suppliers, and increases in the passenger-kilometres carried, the industry has suffered chronic losses totalling $2 billion. While we can not be certain that the losses are attributable solely to the deregulation, they do suggest that regulation contributed to a better environment for earning profits through providing air services in Canada.

---

[18]Skene, op. cit., p. 18.

[19]*Compact Disclosure* (Digital Library Systems, Inc., July 1994).

[20]Skene, op. cit., p. 214.

[21]A. Willis, "Open Season in the Air," *Macleans*, March 6, 1995, p. 38.

[22]Skene, op. cit., pp. 30–40.

[23]Dresner, op. cit., p. 23.

[24]Skene, op. cit., p. 40.

[25]Statistics Canada, op. cit., March 6, 1996.

Safety Concerns

Fears have existed, and still exist, concerning the relationship between deregulation and airline safety. Many opponents of deregulation of airlines in Canada and elsewhere have argued that deregulation would lead to higher rates of "occurrences"—accidents endangering the public. What these opponents of deregulation forget is that the New Canadian Air Policy of 1984 and the National Transportation Act of 1987 changed only the authority of the government to set air fares and to prevent the entry of qualified carriers into commercial service. The changes did not reduce the power of the National Transportation Safety Board or the National Transportation Agency to suspend licences when safety was an issue. In other words, the legislative changes did not change the laws governing the regulation of airline safety. If airline safety has deteriorated since 1984, this deterioration would have to be a result of deterioration in administration and enforcement of the existing regulation, rather than as a consequence of deregulation.

Even some of the harshest critics of deregulation have been quick to point out that the major Canadian carriers are among the safest airlines in the world. Canadian Airlines International was recently ranked as being one of the five safest mid-sized scheduled carriers in the world. Air Canada missed being classed in the top category only because of a death caused by a fire in a washroom in 1983—the year before Canadian deregulation started.[26] Over the years technological improvement in a maturing industry have made commercial air travel less dangerous, until today it is safer than any other mode of transportation. Safety fears associated with deregulation seem to be unfounded.

Airline Deregulation: What Went Wrong?

It has been said that we learn more from our failures than from our successes. If this is true, the government's experience in regulating and deregulating the airline industry should teach us much that we need to know about regulation. The case of airline regulation suggests some important lessons: (1) regulation is most easily enforced and economically justifiable when the characteristics leading to natural monopoly exist in the industry, (2) regulation is most likely to succeed when the constituents being regulated, the passengers, the firms in the industry, the public, and the taxpayers share a common view of the purpose of the regulation; (3) regulation is likely to be economically inefficient in the circumstances in which it can

---

[26]Skene, op. cit., p. 49.

not influence the entire industry; and (4) if great care is not taken, the regulatory body is likely to end up serving the interests of one of the constituents being regulated at the expense of the others it was established to regulate.

Was Airline Regulation Economically Justified?

Earlier in this chapter, three economically sound justifications for regulation were presented. These cases for regulation are the existence of natural monopoly, deficient information, and poorly defined property rights. To what extent do any of these exist in the airline industry? The question of the existence of natural monopoly is handled by stating that the production of international airline service is not naturally monopolistic. That is to say, the large markets of the United States and the international routes between Asia, Europe and the Americas provide sufficient traffic to support co-existing competitive service. However, we have much less evidence that this situation is true of domestic service in a geographically dispersed, low-density population country like Canada. Recall that natural monopoly exists when an industry's average cost is minimized by having only one firm provide the product. When an industry is naturally monopolistic, larger firms have an undeniable cost advantage over their smaller counterparts. The immense capital cost of acquiring machinery to operate in the industry provides a barrier for smaller firms to remain competitive. The absence of any evidence of successful entry of a large number of new, relatively small airlines since deregulation, and the takeover and merging of relatively successful regional carriers and charter services by the two dominant carriers, suggest the existence of significant barriers and relative advantages enjoyed only by large firms. Conversely, the absence of such evidence tends to dispel the notion that government regulation was protecting large, inefficient firms from the competition of smaller, more competitive, and cost-efficient firms. While the industry has not become a monopoly in the aftermath of deregulation, evidence shows that it came very close to becoming one in the summer of 1993.

Between 1991 and 1993 mounting losses of Canadian Airlines International had forced the company to seek a merger with a larger carrier as a way of ensuring its survival. In July the federal government accepted that the only way of maintaining Canadian control and ownership of the Canadian airline industry was through a merger between Canadian Airlines and Air Canada to create a monopoly air carrier.[27] Canadian Airlines International managed to avoid a merger with Air Canada by arranging an alliance with American Airlines that involved American Airlines gaining effective control of the smaller Canadian firm.[28] Air Canada was also suffering losses and formed alliances with two American carriers. Air

---

[27]Skene, op. cit., p. 33.
[28]Ibid., p. 221.

Canada arranged a formal marketing agreement with United Airlines. Subsequently, it effectively rescued the fifth-largest American carrier, Continental Airlines, from bankruptcy by acquiring 20 percent of Continental's shares.[29]

Although the existence of mergers and the reduction of the number of small firms in the industry may point to a tendency toward natural monopoly, there is much disagreement about this point. Many experts who have studied the airline industry, both in Canada and around the world, conclude that the airline industry is inherently competitive, with apparently very limited evidence of economies of scale. Perhaps the clearest statement of this situation was given by Thomas Kauper, assistant attorney general for antitrust, in testimony before the United States Senate Subcommittee on Administrative Practice and Procedure: "Evidence is quite abundant that there are no important economies of scale in air transportation; that is, larger firms are not more efficient or less costly simply because of their size. In fact, other things being equal, the largest air carriers tend to have a higher level of unit costs, and there are some indications that these increased costs are caused by the difficulties of managing an airline of very large size."[30] As pointed out earlier, Air Canada and Canadian Airlines conform to this pattern. The larger firm, operating at over 18 cents per passenger-kilometre is not quite as cost efficient as Canadian Airlines, which was operating at 15 cents per passenger-kilometre for the same period.

Along with the mixed evidence about the existence or lack of existence of economies of scale, how should the issue of possible deficient information be handled? Airline travel seems to be a case where consumers lack a great deal of important information about the service being provided. Most important, consumers may lack information about the safety performance of individual carriers and probably lack the technical skills to know what to look for in areas such as servicing schedules. This lack of information does provide government with an economically sound rationale for regulation. In this case appropriate regulation has taken the form of establishing safety requirements for the airlines, which cover items such as service and maintenance schedules and pilot certification. Does this suggest that airline regulation should lead to a wider scope of regulation, including reducing the number of firms or creating a crown corporation as a monopoly? Not necessarily. While the National Transportation Agency can suspend a licence when safety is an issue, its primary functions focus on economic issues such as fares, route structures, and entry into and exit from the market. The National Transportation Safety Board, on the other hand, has been in charge of airline safety.[31] Thus the information deficiencies that exist in the provision of airline service do allow for

---

[29]Ibid., pp. 65–8.

[30]W. Adams and J. W. Brock, *The Bigness Complex* (New York: Pantheon Books, 1986), p. 220.

[31]In September of 1996 Westjet of Calgary did voluntarily suspend all scheduled service for three weeks because of concerns raised by NTSB officials over maintenance practices.

regulation by government, whether the industry is to be structured as a competitive industry or a regulated monopoly.

Finally, we must consider the question of property rights. When property rights are poorly defined, government can have a positive impact on the performance of an industry through regulation. Poorly defined property rights do exist in one important respect in the airline industry—the use of navigable airspace. Clearly, no airline has a well-defined property right for any particular airspace unless there is a system of national and international regulation to set out the air routes, landing rights, cabotage, general rules of service, and fare structure. In the early part of this century, poorly defined property rights in air transportation posed little problem given the sparse nature of air transportation. The enormous growth in air transportation that has taken place since the 1930s has brought the lack of well-defined property rights to airspace into prominence. Imagine the chaos of an airline system in which pilots were free to fly wherever they wished. While governments must establish and police the property nature of the air transport, this requirement may be seen as no different from the role of government in establishing the appropriate property relations for the conduct of business in general—at least on domestic routes. It is not by itself an argument for economic regulation. The only complicating factor is that the international transborder nature of airline competition and aspirations to serve growing foreign markets require the government to negotiate reciprocal agreements with foreign governments on the industry's behalf. This situation also is not very different from other international businesses requiring government consultation; by itself, it does not imply a need for economic regulation to limit the number of firms in the industry.

The Capture Theory of Regulation

The belief that regulatory agencies, regardless of their intentions, eventually come to serve the interests of the firms being regulated, rather than the general public, is called the **capture theory** of regulation.

The government's regulation of the economic aspects of airline service has been controversial and at times may have been based on the desire for nation building instead of on economic principles. Numerous analysts of regulation have come to the conclusion that the typical case of government regulation entails a regulatory agency being taken captive by the industry it was established to control. The reasons for this conclusion are unclear. Perhaps the firms are able to use political influence to have "friendly" regulators appointed, or maybe it occurs simply as an outgrowth of the fact that regulatory bodies have to rely on the firms being regulated to provide the data the regulatory bodies need to carry out their tasks. In some cases regulatory agencies in their search for highly specialized people to staff the agency, end up hiring people who gained their expertise by working for the firms that they are being hired to regulate. These experts may have a biased perspective that regards what is good for the firms in the industry as good for the industry as a whole. Regardless, the outcome of the capture theory, as it is called, is that the regulatory agency decides on policy based on the interests of the firms in the regulated industry, rather than on the interests of the consumers.

If capture theory is valid, we would expect that firms would desire and actually seek to be regulated by government. Evidence suggests that this is, in fact, sometimes the case. For example, during the industry restructuring that came in the aftermath of deregulation, Canadian Airlines president Rhys Etyon delivered a speech to the Canadian Club of Vancouver, claiming that the federal government must "enforce a competitive airline policy and prevent a monopoly emerging by default."[32] Significantly, this speech came within several weeks of his firm seeking loan guarantees totalling several hundreds of millions of dollars from two provincial governments and the federal government, as well as arranging a deal with the Department of National Defense to purchase several surplus aircraft from Canadian Airlines. Similarly, Hollis Harris, the president of Air Canada, made public statements during the post-regulation period to the effect that the government must allow Air Canada to take control of Canadian Airlines to prevent the Canadian airline industry from falling into foreign hands where it might not serve the interests of Canada. At the time, Air Canada was already forming alliances with two American partners, arranging a financial rescue for the fifth-biggest American carrier, and appeared more interested in establishing cabotage service on transborder routes to Atlanta, Georgia, than in developing a Canadian domestic service. The protestations for protecting sovereignty by Mr. Harris had an ironically humourous twist in view of the fact that he had once been the president of Continental Airlines and Delta Airlines and was an American citizen.

There are then cases in which the firms of an industry feel as if government regulation is in their interest. But does the capture theory usually apply in the case of Canada's airline regulation? The answer to this question is probably no. The best we can do is to attempt to offer evidence that is inconsistent with the theory. The reason for suggesting that the capture theory does not apply in the airline case is that some of the airlines themselves were among the most vocal proponents of deregulation in the period leading up to deregulation. Firms as diverse as Air Canada, Canadian Pacific Airlines, Pacific Western Airlines, and Wardair all pushed to have the government deregulate and open the skies to more competition. Apparently, they felt they had much to gain by eliminating regulation. The reasons for this behaviour may be found by considering the economic life of a firm in a regulated industry versus an unregulated environment. In a regulated environment in which economies of scale may be present, a firm is constantly tempted to expand its service in order to use the low-cost extra capacity of its capital. If the industry has rules to restrict firms from direct competition with each other, as the Canadian domestic scheduled service did from the 1930s to the 1980s, then individual firms may be

---

[32]Skene, op. cit., p. 191.

frustrated by not being able to find customers to make use of their excess capacity. Airlines like Wardair undoubtedly believed that if they could just gain a share of Air Canada's domestic business, they could lower their own costs per passenger-kilometre and increase their load factors. As the law of demand states, the lower the price, the higher will be sales, other things being equal. Thus, if one firm lowers its price relative to others, it is likely to gain sales at the expense of its rivals. If a firm could lower its cost per passenger-kilometre by increasing its load factor, it could charge a lower price in an unregulated market and would, so the thinking goes, attract more customers. However, if all firms in an industry experiencing economies of scale decrease their prices at the same time, they may saturate the market. In such a price war, the largest firm will likely improve its financial position relative to its smaller rivals. Some analysts and industry players may have forgotten to consider the last part of this theory.

In countries like the United States and Japan where the market for air service is very large relative to the optimal size of an airline, the fear that the industry might capture the regulators may be a real and present danger to the public interest. We have more difficulty seeing that capture theory applies to the same extent in countries where the minimum amount of capital needed to run an airline requires expenditures of billions of dollars on aircraft that ply the skies half full. Preventing multiple carriers from serving the same routes may be in the public interest as well as in the interests of the investors. In Canada the argument that the CTC or the NTA were "captured" by the airlines could make sense only after the public agenda abandoned the goals of ensuring safe, reliable, low-cost service to a wide range of destinations while ensuring reasonable returns to the airlines. As official policy changed to fostering lower fares on competitive routes, the regulators were freed from acting in a larger public interest. In the post-deregulation era, the proliferation of discount fares would have suggested that airlines had captured the regulators before deregulation if the lower fares had led to increased competition. Instead deregulation was accompanied by a reduction in the number of firms and increased concentration. Similarly, capture theory could be suggested if returns in the industry moved from abnormally high levels relative to other industries down to more normal rates of return. Airline profits were reduced in the wake of deregulation, but the devastation does not reflect a move to normal levels. Most regional carriers were eliminated, and the remaining dominant firms were running at losses. In short, rather than deregulation leading to financial stability, the industry became financially unstable after deregulation.

What the Future Holds

Evidence indicates that, through the first half of the 1990s, the open skies policy has resulted in benefits and costs to the economy. The benefits include improved convenience of scheduling and routing. Consumers now have a much wider range of fares, depending on whether they book in advance or fly at a regular fare. While this is a benefit to the consumer, the bottom line is that the actual fare per passenger-kilometre has risen significantly.

The application of economic theory to a particular industry always brings with it the problem that industries are not static; they evolve, and the circumstances surrounding the market change over time. Several potentially important developments may change the nature of the airline industry in Canada over the next half decade. Two of these developments deserve discussion—increased concentration and financial instability of the remaining firms.

Increasing Concentration and Financial Instability

Chapter 9 taught a valuable lesson about monopoly—if a competitive market becomes an unregulated monopoly, consumers can expect a reduction in the quantity of the product or service being offered and a corresponding increase in the price. When the CTC regulated fares and entry, the domestic airline industry was actually a number of regulated monopolies servicing geographically separate markets or offering differentiated service to the same destinations (regular, scheduled daily service versus advance-booking charters). The regulatory framework helped ensure that each carrier was able to generate revenues that provided reasonable profits to investors, whether those were private interests, as in the case of Wardair and Canadian Pacific, or taxpayers as in the case of Air Canada and later Pacific Western. With deregulation this picture quickly changed. Intense rivalry, especially between the nation's two dominant firms, moved the market toward a more monopolistic outcome with increased fares and lowered returns to the two remaining players. The smaller firms were forced to merge or withdraw from the industry.

The same pattern seems to be emerging in the United States. When deregulation began in the United States, with its much larger market and denser concentration of population, the initial results were very encouraging. However, the economies of scale were less evident—as noted above some analysts even claimed that they were non-existent. Initially more firms entered the industry, fares fell, and the frequency of service increased. By 1986 the situation changed. Whether as a result of economies of scale or for some other reason, the American airline industry experienced a wave of mergers and concentration ratios began to rise. By late 1990, TWA, Midway Airlines, Eastern Airlines, and Pan Am Corporation were each at one stage or another of selling off assets. Eastern and Pan Am have actually ceased operations. The impact of this activity on market concentration, coupled with the merger wave, is clear. The four-firm concentration ratio in the airline industry rose from 43 percent in 1985 to 65 percent in 1992. That is, the industry's four largest carriers controlled 65 percent of all air travel in the United States. This concentration ratio is far lower than the 100 percent controlled by the two dominant carriers in Canada, but the American market is more than 10 times the size of the Canadian market. Chapter 9 indicated that significant monopoly problems may be anticipated when the concentration ratio reaches, perhaps, 70 percent. Thus, it is not surprising that the dual monopoly problems of increasing fares and falling service began to appear in the unregulated American market. The folding of Eastern Airlines in 1991 created an opportunity for less competitive pricing by its former rivals on the Florida routes. United Airlines—Air Canada's future affiliate—raised its Chicago-to-Miami weekday fare by 91 percent and Continental Airlines—Air Canada's other American affiliate—increased the fare on the same route by 79 percent.[33] In March 1994 the six largest American air carriers including Air Canada's affiliate, Continental, and Canadian Airlines' affiliate, American Airlines, accepted the United States Justice Department's position that their price-fixing arrangements between 1988 and 1990 had cost American travellers in excess of $2 billion.[34] Even some of the most respected advocates of deregulation concede that deregulation has taken far longer and involved far more difficulties in terms of financial volatility and structural adjustment than they expected.[35] Other American analysts are now arguing that halting the growth in concentration that has been taking place is clearly in the interest of the consuming public. They are exhorting their government to enforce existing antitrust guidelines in the airline industry. The American view seems to be that the situation for consumers will improve only in a competitive environment. Proponents of reregulation argue that consumers are likely to be even more poorly served by an unregulated shared monopoly due to mergers and bankruptcy than they were with a regulated shared monopoly—even if the capture theory arguments were accurate.

Economic theory contradicts the idea that government regulation is necessary or desirable whenever the concentration ratio is high. Even though only one firm may be supplying a commodity or service, if that firm believes that it faces a credible threat from new firms entering the industry and competing with it, government regulation may be neither necessary nor desirable. The *theory of contestable markets* suggests that when only one firm exists in an industry and that firm believes that the entry of potential competitors is likely, it will keep its price low and maintain production levels high enough to prevent the entry of new competitors. In other words, even a monopoly firm or highly concentrated industry that fears potential competition will have few of the undesirable dead-weight

The **theory of contestable markets** states that if a monopolist faces a credible threat of entry by new competitors, it will reduce its price and increase production until the price equals the average cost of production.

---

[33]Q. N. Asra "Air Fares Rising Sharply in Wake of Eastern Exit," *Wall Street Journal*, January 23, 1991, p. B1.

[34]Skene, op. cit., p. 206.

[35]S. Morrison and C. Winston, *The Evolution of the Airline Industry* (Washington, DC: Brookings Institution, 1995), p. 162.

loss characteristics normally expected to accompany unregulated monopoly. If firms in a highly concentrated market become aware that potential competitors are unwilling or unable to enter the industry, for whatever reason, the firms in the industry are likely to exhibit all the undesirable behaviours of charging high prices and restricting output. In industries with high concentration ratios in which the entry of new competitors does not pose a credible threat to the firms already in the industry, government regulation can improve the allocation of resources and provide a needed check on the abusive power of the existing firms.

It would be nice to believe that the financial instability discussed earlier in the chapter is over, but several factors suggest this is not the case. In 1996 a new scheduled carrier, Westjet Airlines, entered service on several regional routes in western Canada. In July 1996 Greyhound Air, a joint venture of Greyhound Lines of Calgary and Kelona Flightcraft Air Charter Limited inaugurated service on several routes in southern Canada. It is still too early to tell whether either of these attempts to break into scheduled air service will be successful in the longrun. In the shortrun, however, the entry of new carriers may reduce fares and increase service, reducing the opportunity to earn normal profits for an industry already staggering under the burden of a decade of losses. Another major factor that may ultimately threaten the financial health of all scheduled carriers is the decision in July 1996 to privatize air traffic control in Canada. Nav Canada, which is to operate the system, will have a privately owned monopoly operating the air traffic control system in Canada. The aim is to provide the service on a cost-recovery, non-profit basis, which implies that the airlines will have to provide the revenue to support the operation and capital investment for air traffic control. In the past the government provided these funds as part of the public commitment to transportation infrastructure. This change may increase airline costs, causing further financial uncertainty for the firms operating in the industry.

Summary

The government's regulation of the airline industry began as a logical extension of the regulation of transportation infrastructure from the railway era. The primary provision of this regulation was to promote development of a reliable, financially stable industry that provided safe, efficient service to the public at the lowest cost possible. In the formative period the regulation of safety and the economic regulation were effectively divided between the Canadian Transport Commission (more recently the National Transportation Agency) and the National Transportation Safety Board. The National Transportation Act of 1987 led to the effective deregulation of the industry, reducing the government's control over the economic aspects of fares, scheduling, and the entry and exit of airlines.

The history of the airline industry while under government regulation and since deregulation teaches several important lessons about government regulation in general. First, there are economically justified instances for regulation. When a solid economic rationale exists for regulation, properly structured regulation may serve to improve industry performance. If this economic justification is missing, regulation is likely to seriously inhibit industry performance. Even where regulation is warranted, it is often misunderstood by the consumers in the industry as well as the firms being regulated and the general public.

In general, government regulation is advisable when a natural monopoly exists, when consumers operate without complete information about products, or when property rights are poorly defined. In the airline industry, some evidence suggests that economies of scale may exist in relatively small-market countries like Canada, which can result in high levels of concentration if regulation is relaxed and the possible emergence of natural monopoly. The lack of consumer information, especially as it concerns safety, and poorly defined property rights concerning the use of airspace support government regulation. Certainly the justification exists for government involvement in establishing and enforcing safety standards and air routes.

The second lesson to be learned from airline regulation is that even when regulation seems firmly founded in economic principles, it is likely to lead to less than ideal results. In Canada the law covering regulation charged the regulatory authority with the multiple responsibilities of ensuring orderly development of the transportation infrastructure to promote nation building and promoting the financial viability of the suppliers of air services. In such circumstances the regulating agency must balance the interests of the consumers, the general public, the taxpayers, the firms involved in the industry, and the government. The danger is that the regulator may become captive of the industry it was designed to control. Alternatively, the regulator may forsake the interests of the employees and investors in the industry and promote competition because it seems to promote lower prices for consumers and increased service even when this competition may jeopardize the financial viability of suppliers and the jobs of people in the industry . The fact that following deregulation air fares rose, the number of independent carriers declined, and the remaining firms were financially less secure implies that the regulators were able to juggle the competing demands of the various constituents prior to deregulation. The result does not mean that regulation was a perfect solution, but it suggests that during the period of regulation the regulators appear to have avoided sinking too far into the pattern described by capture theory.

Given an outcome of this nature, consumers in general would be well served by a thorough analysis of the growing reliance by governments on using market forces at the federal and provincial level as the primary means of regulating economic behaviour and fostering the appropriate allocation of society's scarce resources. In those areas where clear economic justification exists for the regulation, or when the regulation appears to be generating more benefits than costs, regulation may reduce some of the unexpected problems that were experienced as a result of deregulation of the airlines.

Checklist of Economic Concepts

Average cost
Economies of scale
Minimum efficient scale
Diseconomies of scale

Natural monopoly
Concentration
Capture theory
Contestable markets

Discussion Questions

1. Discuss the statement: "Because of economies of scale, incomplete property rights, and incomplete information, politics will dictate that government regulation will always be with us—just like death and taxes."

2. Identify and discuss three sources of economies of scale. In most firms why do diseconomies of scale eventually replace economies of scale at very high scales of operation?

3. Identify an industry that is a major employer in your region of Canada and suggest the factors that might be generating economies of scale or diseconomies of scale in that industry. What externalities are created by this industry?

4. Describe when a firm might be a natural monopoly. What characteristics must be present for a firm to operate as a natural monopoly?

5. Explain the elements of the so-called capture theory of government regulation.

6. The recommendations of the Royal Commission on National Passenger Transportation were that regulation should be guided by concerns for safety; protection of the environment; fairness to taxpayers, traveler and carriers; and efficiency. How might these recommendations contribute to an environment in which capture theory can explain the behaviour of regulators?

7. How might capture theory explain why a regulated industry would charge a higher price and produce a lower volume of product than if it were left unregulated?

8. Some critics of airline regulation in Canada used capture theory to argue that, among other things, deregulation should lead to lower airfares, an increase in the number of airlines, and an increase in industry profits. Discuss how capture theory can suggest these seemingly conflicting outcomes. Does the Canadian airline industry experience in the first decade following deregulation support the conclusions of these critics?

9. Briefly explain the theory of contestable markets.

10. Why might a proponent of the theory of contestable markets argue that even in an industry in which one firm supplies all the output, government regulation may not be necessary?

Supplementary Reading

Adams, W. and J. W. Brock. *The Bigness Complex.* New York: Pantheon Books, 1986.

Part 5 offers an excellent and readily accessible treatment of government regulation in general. Of particular interest is Chapter 16, which deals specifically with airline deregulation.

Dresner, M. "The Regulation of US-Canada Air Transportation: Past, Present and Future." *Canadian-American Public,* no. 9 (March 1992), pp. 1–34.

A comprehensive investigation of the nature and importance of the transborder market to Canadian carriers. Dresner discusses the dual nature of the presence of the American market on the development and aspirations of the Canadian airline industry. The American presence exerts pressures for Canadian regulators and airlines to harmonize Canadian regulation and costs to American norms and also creates a real financial danger to Canadian carriers who risk having large U.S. carriers seek entry and cabotage in the Canadian market.

Kahn, A. E. "I Would Do It Again." *Regulation* 12, no. 2 (March–April 1988), pp. 22–8.

A very provocative treatment of airline deregulation in that Professor Kahn was a driving force behind the introduction of the Airline Deregulation Act of 1978 in the United States, especially because he was, at the time, the chairman of the Civil Aeronautics Board.

Morrison, S. and C. Winston. *The Economic Effects of Airline Deregulation.* Washington, DC: Brookings Institution, 1986.

Provides a very thorough treatment of airline deregulation in its entirety. Further, the authors question whether the outcomes enjoyed to date are as good as possible.

Morrison, S. and C. Winston. *The Evolution of the Airline Industry.* Washington, DC: Brookings Institution, 1995.

A follow-up to the previous investigation of the effects of airline deregulation in the United States by Morrison and Winston. The scope is comprehensive, dealing with the effects of 20 years of deregulation on travel time, pricing, scheduling, and related matters. The study includes clear and readable discussions of the statistical methods used to establish causality that will be of interest to students wishing to see how statistical methods can be competently employed in studying social phenomena.

Purdy, H. L. *Transport Competition and Public Policy in Canada.* Vancouver: University of British Columbia Press, 1972.

Provides a thorough, although dated, perspective of the role of regulated monopoly and government equity interest in the development of Canada's transportation industry. The book also reviews the political forces that led to Canada relying more heavily on government intervention and regulation of its industry than was the case in other countries.

Skene, W. *Turbulence: How Deregulation Destroyed Canada's Airlines.* Vancouver: Douglas and McIntyre, 1994.

A very thorough review of the evolution and effects of deregulation in Canada's airline industry. Skene has included a wealth of facts not easily accessible elsewhere and written in a thoroughly readable style. The book is provocative and controversial, but it provides a refreshing point of departure for consideration of the broader issues surrounding regulation and deregulation.

Studnicki-Gizbert, K. W. *Issues in Canadian Transportation Policy.* Toronto: Macmillan, 1972.

A collection of papers and discussions from the Conference on Canadian National Transportation Policy in May 1972 that sheds a great deal of light on the factors influencing Canada's transportation policy. Section IV in particular deals with the institutions and mechanisms for defining common goals and balancing conflicting agendas of various interest groups that are involved in setting a national transportation policy.

Chapter 11

The Economics of Professional Sports
What Is the Real Score?

Wayne Gretzky is one of the most recognized faces and names on three continents. By 1994 he had broken almost every offensive record in the history of professional hockey. Children from all across North America idolize him and wish to use the same type of hockey stick or skates as "the Great One." Like Gordie Howe, Bobby Orr, and Maurice ('The Rocket') Richard before him, he is a Canadian sports hero. His career in many ways symbolizes the breadth and complexity of economic issues embodied in professional sports.

The following comments and quotations, which are from an article about Gretzky by James Deacon, illustrate many of the economic issues surrounding professional sports that will be explored in this chapter:

- Gretzky's first endorsement contract was in 1979 for $5,000 per year with Titan Hockey Sticks.
- "Wayne was responsible for us building that factory in Canada ... he made Titan hockey-sticks—no one in our company would dispute that." Bob Leeder, sales director, Titan.
- "I was 18 years old, I got to travel, meet people, play in golf outings, shoot some local TV commercials—it was great." Gretzky speaking about his first endorsement contract.
- By 1989 Gretzky received $150,000 annually from the Titan endorsement.
- In 1989 Gretzky signed a four-year, fee-plus-royalty deal with Easton to endorse an aluminum handled stick. Industry sources estimate Easton's hockey sales increased by $26 million in the five years after the deal.
- "Even today his voice takes on a hard edge when he talks about Oilers owner, Peter Pocklington, selling (him) out of Edmonton." James Deacon.
- Gretzky was paid $11.6 million a season by Los Angeles—the highest salary in professional sports at that time.
- In 1994, in addition to his salary, he received $12 million from endorsements and promotions.
- Endorsement income combined with his salary totalled $23 million for 1994, making Gretzky the fourth-highest paid professional athlete in North America—behind Michael Jordan, Jack Nicklaus, and Arnold Palmer.
- "I want the league to prosper but when push comes to shove, I am part of a union and I am not going to back off that." Gretzky speaking on the NHL lockout in 1994.[1]

---

[1] J. Deacon, "Gretzky Inc.," *Maclean's*, Dec. 5, 1994, pp. 50–8.

The Professional Sports Business

Does the sports page in your favourite newspaper often resemble the business section? Articles concerning labour disputes, ticket prices, television contracts, team relocations, changes in ownership and management, and, of course, player salaries can easily outnumber reports concerning the latest games and scores. Why do the happenings in the boardroom gather as much attention as the happenings in the arena or on the field? Examination of the economics of professional team sports reveals why following the business of athletics has itself become a major spectator sport for many people.

Alan Eagleson is the former agent for many professional athletes and the often controversial former head of the National Hockey League Players Association. Eagleson's testimony before the Banking, Trade and Commerce Tribunal of Canada's Senate summarizes many of the issues surrounding professional sports in North America: "Professional sports is a business. This fact is indisputable, as witness the commercial contracts negotiated, the people employed, the profit and loss statements calculated, the advertising sold and the general economic structures of professional teams and leagues; but sport is unique, and therefore could not draw on other businesses for ideas in organization and structure. Instead, it had to develop its own system."[2]

The statement is only partly correct. All professional sports are businesses and do involve commercial contracts, leagues, advertising, and large numbers of spectators paying to attend and witness athletic achievement. Despite these similarities, professional sports can be divided into two broad categories that are quite different. Not all professional sports involve competition between teams, and not all leagues behave in the same way from the point of view of economic theory. Many professional sports, among them such diverse activities as boxing, figure skating, free-style skiing, golf, and tennis, do not involve teams that compete against each other. These sports form a group of professional sports in which individual athletes use their talents and training to entertain the paying public to earn their income. In many ways the economic issues surrounding the individual-centered sports are similar to those that arise in other industries that involve individuals earning their incomes through exploiting their unique talents or training such as acting, architecture, being comedians, providing specialized legal and medical services, painting, professional writing, singing, and sculpturing. By contrast, a second group of professional sports, including such activities as baseball, basketball, cricket, football, hockey, and soccer, is organized around small numbers of teams that hire athletes as employees to play for the team. In these professional team sports, the role of the teams as businesses and their economic relationships with their employers and the

---

[2]D. Clayton, *Eagle: The Life and Times of Alan R. Eagleson* (Toronto: Lester and Orpen Dennys, 1982) p. 137.

other teams in the same league create quite different economic behaviour from that found in individual-centered sports. As we will see later in the chapter, the income and working conditions of the athletes in professional team sports is jointly determined by the teams and the players. The major focus of this chapter will be on the economics of professional team sports and especially the National Hockey League.

Like all businesses, professional sports teams face a myriad of economic decisions in their quest to earn profits. And many sports clubs in North America are very profitable. For example, the Edmonton Oilers of the National Hockey League earned more than $3.5 million annually in the mid-1980s.[3] In addition to the annual profits from gate receipts and broadcast rights, the owner of the Oilers, Peter Pocklington, earned a capital gain by selling off the rights to the Oilers top player—Wayne Gretzky. Pocklington is quoted as saying that he traded Gretzky when he did because Gretzky would have become a free agent and therefore "an asset worth zero in four years."[4] Teams in small-market cities regularly budget for a return on equity of between 3 percent and 5 percent amounting to profits of over $1 million annually.[5] Even a relatively short strike or lockout can have profound financial consequences that reach far from the arena or the playing field. The potential loss in advertising revenues to Canadian television broadcasters from the 1994 labour dispute in the NHL was estimated to be $74 million.[6] However, professional sports clubs are unlike most other businesses in at least two important ways: The organizational structure of the professional team sports industry and the unique relationship between the sports clubs and their most important employees, the players, have created a number of economic and social issues that have captured public attention.

In recent decades, a number of scholars have moved the study of sports beyond the domain of departments of physical education and physiology. Sports is now studied in the humanities, social sciences, and in faculties of business. Today more than 100 interdisciplinary programs in sports studies are to be found on college and university campuses, along with numerous specialized journals and book series.

Organizational Structure

Today four major team sports are played professionally in Canada: baseball, basketball, football, and hockey. Each of these sports has a long and colourful history. In addition to these team sports, a number of individual

---

[3]P. Staudohar and J. A. Mangan, *The Business of Professional Sports* (Urbana: University of Illinois Press, 1991), p. 191.

[4]Ibid., p. 192.

[5]M. Miller, "On Solid Ground," *Calgary Sun*, May 5, 1996, pp. 8–9.

[6]"NHL Lockout Threatens $74M in Ad Revenue Chill," *Advertising Age* 65, no. 44 (October 17, 1994), p. 37.

sports, such as golf and tennis, are played professionally. Although the details vary somewhat among sports, a similar organizational structure has evolved within each of the four professional team sports.

In most cases individual teams, or clubs, are owned and operated for profit by private individuals or partnerships. The team owners are entrepreneurs who hire and fire the managers, coaches, and players; rent or build the stadiums; sell the tickets and broadcast rights to games; and market a vast array of team souvenirs. The owners of a sports club are ultimately responsible for the economic decisions necessary to the daily operation of the organization.

The spirit of all team sports is competition.[7] To attract ticket-buying fans, a sports club must compete on the field or the ice against other teams. Thus sports clubs cannot operate independently, but must co-operate with each other in order to sell their entertainment services to the public. The necessary co-operation between teams is institutionalized through the professional sports leagues—the American League (AL) and National League (NL) in baseball (collectively known as Major League Baseball (MLB), the National Basketball Association (NBA), the Canadian Football League (CFL), and the National Hockey League (NHL).[8] The leagues are formal organizations of individual clubs.

In three of the four North American professional team sports, baseball, basketball, and hockey, Canadian teams comprise only a small portion of the overall international leagues in which they operate. All of the major sports leagues in these sports currently have fewer than three dozen member clubs in each league, a situation that fosters intense rivalry and also great interdependence. Sports clubs are located in major metropolitan areas scattered across Canada and the United States. In professional team sports the leagues serve as the mechanism for the co-operation that is necessary between the geographically dispersed teams.

Teams that are members of a professional sports league are contractually obligated to one another. Member clubs agree to abide by the rules and guidelines of the league. Among other things the league determines the annual schedule of games, makes and enforces the game rules, and sets the guidelines for hiring new players. Because the league also determines when a new team will be admitted to the league and allowed to compete with its members, clubs are often referred to as *league franchises*. In general the professional sports leagues are controlled by the club owners who hire an outside (non-owner) "commissioner" and staff to oversee

---

[7]For an interesting discussion of the transformation of Canadian team sports from amateur activity played for social reasons to professional businesses organized around competition with a focus on profits, see A. Hall, T. Slack, G. Smith, and D. Whitson, *Sport in Canadian Society* (Toronto: McClelland and Stewart, 1991), chapters 2 and 3.

[8]Examples of this institutionalized co-operation operating outside Canada are common in other professional leagues such as the National Football League (NFL) in the United States and the governing bodies for cricket and soccer in other parts of the world.

the league's operations. The decisions made by the commissioner of a professional sports league are intended to be made in the best interest of the sport, not to favour any individual owner or group of owners.

The rules and guidelines adopted by a professional sports league have important economic implications for the individual member clubs. In general the rules that govern the relationship between the teams and their players have the greatest consequences on operating costs and revenues.

Teams and Players

The relationship between professional sports clubs and their players is perhaps unlike any other employer–employee relationship in our economy. Nowhere else is a worker's productivity so visible to so many and so easily measured. Productive workers in most firms do not receive the cheers of tens of thousands for a job well done or have the quality of their work publicly reviewed in the press. Likewise, most workers who make a mistake on the job (and who hasn't made a mistake?) do not hear the boos and catcalls of an upset crowd. The productivity of a professional athlete is constantly monitored by fans through a myriad of statistics—runs batted in, pass-completions, goals and assists, and so on. Although the performance of professional athletes may be objectively measured and compared by the vast quantities of statistics compiled by sports analysts, controversy still surrounds whether their individual efforts justify their salaries.

The general public is still shocked when a star player signs a multi-million dollar contract to play baseball or hockey, yet many professional athletes claim they are underpaid by the team's owners. Further, it is not uncommon for one player to earn 10 or even 20 times more than other players on the same team. Ironically, rules imposed by each of the major sports leagues to promote competition on the playing field contribute to the seemingly inconsistent economics of players' salaries.

Each of the major professional sports leagues has very specific and detailed rules that govern the employment of players by the member clubs. Competition on the field would diminish if any club had the ability to hoard the best athletic talent. Thus league rules are designed to ensure that each club has the opportunity to employ and retain quality players. In essence, the leagues establish the procedures whereby member clubs acquire the "property rights" to contract with specific players. Because specific clubs may hold the exclusive right to contract with a player, athletes are not always free to work for the highest bidder.

Economic Analysis and Professional Team Sports

Economic analysis provides a means of understanding the issues and controversies surrounding the business of professional team sports. Likewise, professional team sports can serve as an example of how market structures and institutional arrangements can influence the economic behaviour of firms in an industry.

The preceding discussion suggests that professional sports teams operate in imperfect markets. In fact, sports clubs sell their services in an imperfect product market and hire their players in an imperfect resource market. A *product market* exists when buyers and sellers engage in the exchange of final goods and services. When a sports team sells you a ticket for a game or a jacket emblazoned with the team logo, the transaction takes place in a product market. On the other hand, a *resource market* exists when buyers and sellers engage in the exchange of the factors of production. Thus when a sports team hires a new player or builds a new arena, the transaction takes place in a resource market. (Later, in Chapter 13, we will explain how product and resource markets are related in the overall aggregate economy.)

A closer examination of the product and resource markets in professional team sports can help us to better understand many of the economic issues discussed daily in sports columns across the country. But perhaps even more important, our study of professional sports will provide us with general conclusions about how imperfect markets affect consumers and employees.

> **Product markets** exist when buyers and sellers engage in the exchange of final goods and services.
>
> **Resource markets** exist when buyers and sellers engage in the exchange of the factors of production.

The Product Market

Co-operation among Teams

As we noted earlier, the essence of professional team sports is competition. However, it is in the best interest of the leagues in professional team sports that most of this competition occurs in the arena and not in the marketplace. The reason is easily observable. Imagine that professional hockey teams competed for fans in purely competitive markets. The more successful teams would sell more tickets and team merchandise and would naturally earn higher profits, which, in turn, would allow these franchises to attract the best players through higher salaries. Over time, these teams would become so much stronger than the less successful teams that competition on the ice would deteriorate and become boring for spectators. Weak teams would eventually be forced into bankruptcy, and strong teams would lose fans. Thus a professional sports team's economic decisions are inherently interdependent with those of its rivals.

In order to remain in business and earn profits for their owners, professional sports teams must avoid the above scenario. How are they able to do this? The answer is through co-ordination of economic decisions through league rules and guidelines. The alliance of teams through league organizations co-ordinates and restrains economic competition among member teams. In many ways professional sports leagues resemble market cartels. A *cartel* is a group of firms that formally agrees to co-ordinate

> A **cartel** is a group of firms that formally agrees to co-ordinate its production and pricing decisions in a manner that maximizes joint profits.

its production and pricing decisions in a manner that maximizes joint profits. Thus a cartel can be viewed as a group of firms behaving as if they were one firm—a shared monopoly.

In Canada the Competition Act makes it illegal, in most cases, for firms to monopolize an industry through the formation of a cartel. In most industries the formation of a formal cartel is illegal if it is felt that it restricts trade and damages the public. Operating an illegal cartel is punishable under the Competition Act. The provisions of the act allow for criminal prosecution of the individuals suspected of conspiring against the public, and the penalties, if convicted, can be lengthy jail sentences and fines up to $10 million. The business of professional sports is a unique exception. Until relatively recently hockey was legally considered a sport, not a business, and as such not subject to the normal laws covering business.[9] In 1969 J. C. H. Jones, an economist at the University of Victoria, investigated the economic issues in the National Hockey League and concluded: "The NHL clearly possesses monopoly and monopsony power and, if market power is enough to warrant application of the Combines Act, then the NHL is liable."[10] Jones went on to point out that there could be problems in trying to bring professional sports under competition laws because the law, at that time, covered only physical goods and did not extend to services, and sport was considered a service. Half a decade passed before the government attempted to include professional sports under the provisions of competition legislation. At that time even those with much to gain by having the NHL covered by the law offered testimony to support a cautious partial application of the law to professional sport. Alan Eagleson, in a submission to the Senate, urged the government to remember that it was necessary for professional hockey to combine into a monopoly and that it should be exempted from the law. Eagelson also argued that because the league was a monopsony—the only employer of professional hockey players—its treatment of players should be covered by the law.[11] As a result of the hearings The Competition Act now covers professional sports but recognizes that a professional sports team can profitably survive only as long as its league survives.

Cartels

The unique status of the professional sports leagues helps them avoid many of the problems faced by cartels in other industries. Professional sports leagues have been able to maintain economic co-operation between member teams over long periods of time. For any cartel to be successful, several requirements must be met.

---

[9]D. Clayton, op. cit., p. 136.

[10]J. C. H. Jones, "The Economics of the National Hockey League," *Canadian Journal of Economics* 2, no. 1 (February 1969), p. 20.

[11]D. Clayton, op. cit., p. 136.

First, the cartel members must be responsible for most of the output produced in their market. The greater the proportion of total market output generated by the cartel members as a group, the greater the cartel's degree of monopoly power. Further, in order to maintain monopoly power, the cartel must be able to prevent new competitors from entering the market or be able to integrate new competitors into the cartel. Each of the major sports leagues has been successful in eliminating competition from teams outside its cartel. By controlling the contracts of star players and holding exclusive contracts to play in major stadiums and arenas, the existing leagues have restricted the ability of newly formed rival leagues to compete for the fans' attention. In several instances new competitors have been driven out of the market. A recent example was the demise or relocation back to Canada of the American expansion teams in the Canadian Football League—including the league's 1995 Grey Cup champions. In other cases, rival leagues were successful in finding new market territories that had been overlooked by the established leagues. When this occurred, the established leagues found it beneficial to invite the upstarts to join their cartel. Over the past 25 years, we have witnessed the mergers of the World Hockey Association (WHA) with the NHL, the American Football League (AFL) with the NFL, and the American Basketball Association (ABA) with the NBA. These mergers helped the leagues maintain their shared monopoly power in their respective sports.

A second requirement of a successful cartel is the production of fairly homogeneous outputs by the member firms. That is, each firm in a cartel should produce outputs that are substitutes for the outputs produced by the other member firms. Pricing and output agreements are easier to enforce and maintain if all member firms are producing the same goods and services. If each cartel firm produced different products, special agreements would have to be made for each output. Within a professional sports league, all teams do produce the same primary output—entertainment for fans who watch the games. The league structures ensure that all the games played by member teams are fairly homogeneous. All teams must follow a common set of game rules and regulations enforced by referees and umpires hired by the league. Further, some leagues like the NFL determine the schedule of games whereby each club plays other clubs based on the competitive strength of the teams. This desire to maintain a homogeneous product among the teams in the leagues even extends to three of the major sports having extensive networks of farm teams and affiliations and sponsorships with amateur leagues and educational athletic programs. Thus common game rules and league-determined schedules help reinforce the appeal of sports and help the leagues maintain their cartel arrangements.

A third requirement for a successful cartel is the ability to divide the market into territories controlled by each member and to establish production quotas. In essence, the cartel members must agree on how to share their combined monopoly power among themselves. In professional sports the market territories and output quotas are determined through the league structure. Each franchise's territory is protected from inside competition by the league. The location of new expansion teams and the ability of established teams to relocate are determined through league rules and normally require the agreement of a majority of the teams' owners. Likewise, the production of games is controlled by the league offices, which set the schedule for each season. All teams are given an equal share of the total output during normal seasons by playing an equal number of games. These actions by the professional sports leagues grant local monopoly power to each team and help maintain the shared monopoly of the cartel.

Fourth, in order to succeed, the cartel must have the power to prevent "cheating" by member clubs. In many cartel situations an incentive to cheat on the agreement exists for member firms. Some firms may find it profitable to break production quotas or enter another member's sales territory in an effort to capture more than the agreed-upon share of the monopoly. Because most non-sports cartel arrangements are illegal, it is virtually impossible for members to enforce their agreements. However, in professional sports the league offices have the contractual power to enforce league rules and guidelines. In each of the major sports, the league's commissioner is empowered to sanction and levy fines against member teams that do not adhere to the rules. Again, the unique legal status of professional sports leagues reinforces the ability of teams to maintain monopoly power through the enforcement of cartel agreement.

Co-ordinated Behaviour

The most obvious forms of cartel behaviour among a league's member teams involve various methods of joint marketing and revenue sharing. A professional sports team receives revenue from three major sources: ticket and concession sales, merchandising rights for team souvenirs and novelties, and radio and television broadcast rights. Professional sports teams co-operate with one another in each of these three areas through their respective league organizations.

Each of the sports leagues has specific rules for dividing the revenue generated through ticket sales between the host home team and the visiting team. For example, in the NFL the home team receives 60 percent, and the visiting team receives 40 percent of ticket sales. By contrast, the NHL does not split gate receipts from regular season games, but does have gate-receipt sharing for play-off games.

The league organizations also regulate the business of merchandising products that carry team logos and trademarks. One reason for doing so is to discourage counterfeiters, but it also allows the league to promote entire lines of merchandise for all the member teams and to minimize interteam competition in this area. If you look hard enough, you can find almost anything from T-shirts to toilet-bowl lids in your favourite team's colours with its name and logo on it. The revenues from the sale of merchandice is considerable. A spokesperson for the NHL Players Association suggested that 1995 gross retail sales of products exceeded $1 billion.[12]

In recent years, the primary source of revenue for most sports franchises has been the sale of broadcast rights to television and radio. Broadcast rights is the area in which sports teams have been relatively successful in jointly selling their entertainment services through their respective leagues. Each league sells the North American television and radio broadcast rights to all the games played by its members as "package deals" to the highest bidder. The revenue from nationwide, or international, broadcast of regular season games is then shared on an equalization formula between the teams in the league. By contrast with the league's nationwide contracts, the revenues from local area broadcast are often sold separately by the local franchise to individual stations serving the local market with receipts remaining with the individual team. While there are similarities between all the professional sports with respect to media broadcast rights, each has a different formula for equalization and different rules for designating local area markets, nationwide coverage of regular season games, international coverage, and exhibition and play-off game coverage.

In the NHL the revenue from broadcast rights is complex. Broadcast revenues for local markets remain with the local franchise, and the local teams often arrange separate contracts for radio and television with individual stations serving their local broadcast areas. Revenues from broadcasting is divided equally among all teams for nationwide broadcasting of regular season games. Canadian network television rights to regular season games have been sold by the league for a five-year period to Molstar Communications as "Molson's Hockey Night." Molson in turn has signed package deals with the CBC and with 12 Global Television Network stations in southern Ontario for broadcast to the public. In the United States, television broadcasting rights to NHL regular season games were leased in 1994 for five years to Fox at a price of $155 million (U.S.). In addition to the Fox deal, the NHL arranged a separate package to ESPN for $80 million (U.S.) to broadcast a package of regular and play-off games.

The previous review makes clear that although the leagues attempt to equalize revenue between teams, teams with large and lucrative local markets have a revenue advantage. Generally speaking, the professional sports with financially successful teams and with stable ownership have the least difficulty sharing revenue across the league. The professional sports that have the greatest difficulty in working out effective equalization are leagues undergoing rapid expansion or contraction and those with a wide mix of large-market and small-market teams. The NHL and CFL have been less successful than the NFL or MLB in working out

---

[12]S. McTavish, NHL Players Association, interview, May 8, 1996.

equalized revenue to prevent large-market teams from exploiting their local-market advantage in broadcast revenue. Later in the chapter we will explore whether the inability of the NHL to work out stable revenue sharing arrangements among teams may affect the ability of small-market teams to attract and retain some of the more talented players and threaten the league's ability to serve and earn profits in so-called small markets.

Pricing and Output for Broadcast Rights

To see the effect of cartel behaviour on the pricing and output of broadcast rights to professional sporting events, consider Table 11–1.

The hypothetical data reflect the output, revenue, and cost figures a sports league faces in the provision of broadcast rights over a period of

Table 11–1			Monthly broadcast output, costs, revenues, and profits for a professional sports league			
(1) Units of Output	(2) Total Costs ($000)	(3) Marginal Costs ($000)	(4) Price ($000)	(5) Total Revenue ($000)	(6) Marginal Revenue ($000)	(7) Profit ($000)
0	$ 0		$100	$ 0		$ 0
		$40			$100	
1	40		100	100		60
		45			90	
2	85		95	190		105
		50			80	
3	135		90	270		135
		55			70	
4	190		85	340		150
		60			60	
5	250		80	400		150
		65			50	
6	315		75	450		135
		70			40	
7	385		70	490		105
		75			30	
8	460		65	520		60
		80			20	
9	540		60	540		0
		85			10	
10	625		55	550		−75

time, in this case, one month. The league faces the demand schedule reported in columns (1) and (4) of Table 11–1, which is shown as demand curve *DD* in Figure 11–1. *DD* represents the summation of the downward sloping demand curves for broadcast rights faced by each team in the league. Given its monopoly power, the league's marginal revenue curve *MR* lies below the league's demand curve. The league's marginal cost

Figure 11–1   Pricing and output for a cartel

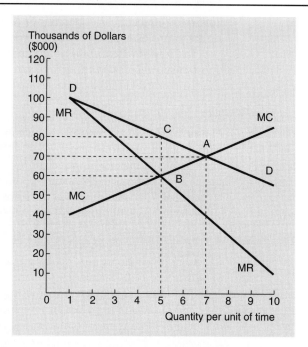

As a shared monopoly, cartel members collectively face demand *DD* and marginal revenue *MR*. Just like a single monopoly firm, the cartel can maximize market profits by producing output such that marginal cost *MC* equals *MR*. In this case, the cartel output is 5 with a price of $80,000. If cartel members competed with each other, the market would reach equilibrium at an output of 7 and an average price of $70,000.

Note: You may notice a slight difference between the graph and the data it represents. In Table 11–1 the marginal cost and marginal revenue are shifted to the midpoint of the range over which they occur. For example, as output increases from 0 to 1 unit, *MC* is $40 and *MR* is $100; similarly, as output increases from 4 units to 5 units, *MC* and *MR* are both $70. In the table we emphasize that *MC* and *MR* take place between output level 0 and 1, and between output level 4 and 5, by showing *MC* and *MR* occurring at outputs of .5 and 4.5, respectively. Because we assume that the league will produce whole games (it makes little sense to offer the fans half a game), we show the *MC* and *MR* curves graphed at output of 1 unit, 2 units, and so on. Because of this difference, on the graph *MC* equals *MR* at an output of 5.

As an exercise, you might try graphing the data as it appears in Table 11–1. At what output does *MC* equal *MR*? At what output does *MC* equal *DD*?

curve *MC* is the horizontal summation of the marginal cost schedules each team would face if it individually and competitively provided broadcast rights to its games. Thus columns (1) and (3) in Table 11–1 list the total marginal cost schedule for the league as a whole.

If a cartel agreement did not exist and teams competed against each other in the market for broadcast rights, each team would maximize its profits by selling up to the point where its own marginal cost equaled its own marginal revenue. Because each individual team is a local monopoly facing its own unique demand and costs schedules, it is likely that the profit-maximizing level of output will vary among teams. But how many total games would be broadcast across all teams without a cartel agreement? Recall from Chapter 9 that the *MC* curve can be considered the supply curve for an individual competitive firm. Thus in Figure 11–1, because *MC* represents the summation of marginal costs across all clubs, *MC* can be thought of as the competitive market supply schedule. Likewise, *DD* represents the market demand schedule. Without a cartel agreement, the market would reach equilibrium at point A where *DD* intersects with *MC*. The market equilibrium price for the rights to broadcast a game would be $70,000, and seven games would be broadcast in total each month. On average, each broadcast would generate marginal revenue of $70,000 for the team selling the game. Examination of Table 11–1 reveals that the competitive solution would result in $490,000 of total revenue and $105,000 in average profits each month for the clubs that sold games.

Note that this analysis does not indicate how the profits would be distributed among the clubs in the absence of a cartel agreement. In the short-run, teams of poorer quality may find it difficult or impossible to sell the broadcast rights for their games. In this case the quality of athletic competition would decline as teams that were successful in selling their broadcast rights earned more profits and could afford to hire the best players. Thus in the longrun, less successful teams would be forced to shut down, leaving the league with fewer teams.

By agreeing to collectively sell their broadcast rights as a league, and not as individual firms, the teams effectively enter an agreement to share their monopoly power and behave as if they were one firm. Each team would no longer examine its own demand and costs schedules to determine its profit-maximizing output, but would accept a share of the overall market profits. As a cartel the teams in the league collectively face demand curve *DD* and marginal revenue curve *MR* in Figure 11–1. Just like a single monopolistic firm, the cartel can maximize profits by producing the level of output where marginal revenues equal marginal costs. Table 11–1 reveals that marginal revenue is equal to marginal cost when the broadcast rights to five games are provided each month. Marginal revenue and marginal cost are $60,000 at this level of output. This level can be seen in Figure 11–1 as point B where the *MR* curve intersects with the *MC* curve. The demand schedule in Table 11–1 indicates that buyers will pay $ 80,000 per game for five games (point C in Figure 11–1). Profit maximization can therefore be achieved by selling the rights to five games each month for $80,000 per game. This conclusion is verified in column (7) of Table 11–1, which shows that this output and price combination maximizes the cartel's collective profit at $150,000 per month.

The cartel agreement to sell broadcast rights as a league affects both price and quantity. In this example the cartel will provide five games for broadcast at $80,000 per game, whereas individual teams in competition with each other will provide seven games for $70,000 each. Given the costs of producing additional games for broadcast, the cartel agreement increases total profits for all the league members from $105,000 to $150,000. Without the cartel agreement, the distribution of profits favours the teams of relatively greater athletic success. With the cartel agreement, the distribution of profits is determined by the league's rules and guidelines. Today most revenue from the sale of broadcast rights is equally divided among a league's member teams. Even teams that rarely appear on national television or radio receive the same share of revenues from the sale of the league's broadcast rights.

Through the formation of a cartel, professional sports teams have found it in their best economic interest to co-operate in the competition for the fans' dollars. By restricting output below competitive levels and raising price, overall profits for cartel members can be increased and a degree of stability in the number of teams can be achieved.

The Resource Market

The Employment of Players

Perhaps the most controversial economic aspect of professional team sports involves the leagues' rules that govern the hiring and employment of players. Each of the major professional leagues strictly controls the methods by which teams hire and fire their player–employees. The employment contracts between teams and players must meet the very specific guidelines imposed by the league. The rules are designed to ensure that no team can gain a competitive athletic advantage due to its employment practices.

The most visible of a league's employment rules involve the procedures used to allocate new players among the league's member teams. In an effort to generate a competitive playing balance among teams (sometimes referred to as parity) and to prevent any single team from hoarding quality players, each sport conducts an annual "draft" of the new players who enter the market. Although the specific procedures are different in each sport, the basic design of each league's draft is the same. In a predetermined order, teams take turns choosing (drafting) players from the available pool of new players. The drafting order is normally determined by the previous season's league standings. In general teams with relatively poor records choose first and relatively strong teams choose last. Under league rules, when a team drafts a player, that team has exclusive rights to sign the player to a contract. No team can hire a player drafted by another team unless that team first sells or trades away its exclusive rights to hire the player. In most cases league rules dictate that once a drafted player signs a contract with a team, that team maintains its exclusive right to the player's services for a specified number of seasons. Thus new players become the "property" of their employing franchise and do not have an open opportunity to offer their skills to the highest bidder. League rules also forbid a team from "tampering" with a rival team's players by offering them employment opportunities while they are still under contract.

For decades professional athletes who were drafted had virtually no ability to choose the team for which they played. Until 1974 the general rule was that once signed to a professional team in the NHL, a player had quite literally signed away his right to negotiate a contract with any other team in the league for the rest of his life![13] Players could change teams only if their employing franchise chose to trade their contract for the contract of a player whose rights were owned by another franchise or if another team purchased their contract. If an athlete wished to play professional sports, he had to agree to these terms as imposed by the leagues. Thus players had little, if any, real bargaining power when salaries were determined. Obviously, this situation provided owners with the opportunity to pay their players relatively low wages.

Even though professional sports league employment rules are designed to increase the quality of competition on the ice or in the field, it is clear from the description above that drafts and hiring restrictions reduce the quality of competition in the market for players. When league rules allow the member clubs to own the property rights to new player contracts, an imperfect factor market called a monopsony is created.

Monopsony

A **monopsony** is a market with only one buyer, or employer.

A *monopsony* is a market with only one buyer, or employer. When only one team, according to league rules, has the right to contract with a specific player, that team becomes a pure monopsony from the player's perspective. In an even broader sense, the leagues themselves can be considered joint monopsonies. For example, if you want to play professional hockey in Canada, you must play in the NHL or one of its affiliated minor leagues. Through affiliation arrangements, the NHL draft provisions apply to junior

---

[13]P. Staudohar and J. A. Mangan, op. cit., p. 136.

and amateur levels. No other buyers wish to purchase the specific athletic talents of professional hockey players. A league's draft and employment rules reinforce and strengthen the monopsony powers collectively held by its member clubs.

Two major factors create monopsony power for professional sports teams and leagues. The first of these is the immobility of new players who have been drafted. New draftees who wish to play professional sports are required to sign contracts that bind them to their teams for a specified number of years as determined by league rules. Once a player has entered the league and signed a contract, he does not have the option of negotiating with other teams.[14] In fact, because of the draft structures, new players who are drafted often never have the option of offering their services to the highest bidder. Thus from a legal perspective, the mobility of players is severely limited. New players become "locked in" to their teams for the period specified in the contracts sanctioned by the leagues. Because new players are contractually obligated, the employing clubs become the only potential buyer of the players' athletic talents in the league.

The second factor that generates monopsony power in professional sports is the highly specialized athletic talents and skills possessed by the players. Athletes who are qualified to play a professional sport have invested many years in training and instruction to learn their craft. The athletic skills and knowledge acquired during this preparation by a professional athlete are in most cases very specific to their sport and are not readily transferable to other sports or employment situations. Very few athletes have the training and ability to excel at more than one professional sport. (Deion Sanders and Bo Jackson are rare exceptions.) Players who possess only very specialized skills have limited employment opportunities, only a few employers require such skills. The talents of a player who has trained and studied to be a professional quarterback are demanded by only nine CFL clubs in Canada and 30 NFL clubs in the United States. Since each club employs only three or four quarterbacks, fewer than 30 individuals in Canada and only 150 individuals in North America earn their living in the professional leagues in this highly specialized occupation. Compare this with the nearly 4 million people who are school teachers or even the 127,000 people who are professional economists throughout North America! Teachers and economists are more generally trained than quarterbacks and have many more options in the labour mar-

---

[14]*He* is used not because the text is being inadvertently sexist, but rather to emphasize the reality that the four professional team sports are male dominated. For example, in professional hockey only one women has played, and she was employed in an exhibition game on an expansion team! Students interested in the factors that contributed to professional team sport being a male enclave can find insightful discussions in A. Hall, T. Slack, G. Smith, and D. Whitson, op. cit., chapters 3, 5 and 7.

ket. The specialized talents of professional athletes clearly contribute to the monopsony power of their employers.

Wages and Employment in a Monopsony

The effects of monopsony power on wages and employment are illustrated in Table 11–2. Because a monopsony is the single buyer of labour in its market, it faces a positively sloped market supply curve of labour. (The market supply curve of labour was previously discussed in Chapter 8.) We will make a simplifying assumption that the monopsony must pay the same wage rate to workers of equal skill who are doing the same job. This assumption may not be perfectly applicable to the employment of professional hockey players, but it eliminates the need to analyze the motivation issues of paying different workers at different wage rates. Thus in order to attract additional workers, a monopsony must increase its wage offer as it hires additional employees. This situation is shown in column (2) of Table 11–2. The monopsony hockey team in this example can hire two left wingers for an average wage of $400,000 each, but to hire three left

Table 11–2		Hypothetical wages, costs, and the marginal revenue product of NHL left winsgers		
(1) Number of Players	(2) Wages ($000)	(3) Total Cost of Labour ($000)	(4) Marginal Cost of Labour ($000)	(5) Marginal Revenue Product ($000)
0	$ 0	$ 0		
			$ 300	$1,500
1	300	300		
			500	1,300
2	400	800		
			700	1,100
3	500	1,500		
			900	900
4	600	2,400		
			1,100	700
5	700	3,500		
			1,300	500
6	800	4,800		

wingers it must pay a wage of $500,000 each. Columns (1) and (2) are plotted in Figure 11–2 as the market supply curve *SS*.

Because a monopsony firm must raise the wage along the market supply of labour schedule in order to hire additional workers, the monopsony firm will experience a change in its total labour costs that is in excess of the wage. This fact can be seen in Table 11–2. Columns (2) and (3) report that when two left wingers are hired at $400,000 each, the total cost of labour is $800,000. However, in order to hire a third left winger, the wage of $500,000 must be paid to each, which raises the total cost of labour to $1.5 million. By hiring a third left winger, the club experiences a change in its total labour cost of $700,000. The change in the total labour cost of a firm due to hiring an additional worker is known as the *marginal cost of labour (MCL)*. The *MCL* is reported in column (4) of the table. Notice that the *MCL* is

The **marginal cost of labour** is the change that occurs in a firm's total labour costs due to hiring an additional worker, per unit of time.

Figure 11–2   Wage and employment determination for a monopsonist

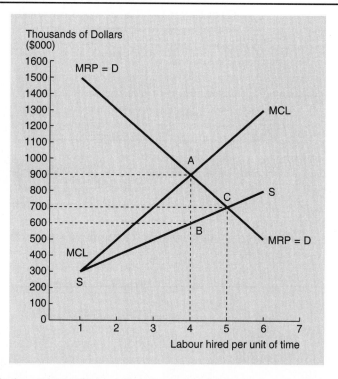

As the single employer of labour, the monopsony faces the market supply of labour curve *SS*. The marginal cost of labour curve *MCL* reflects the addition to costs the firm experiences by hiring an additional worker. The monopsonist will hire workers up to the point where *MCL* equals *MRP*. In this case, the firm will hire four workers at a wage of $600,000.

greater than the wage beyond the first player hired because a monopsony must pay a higher wage to the additional worker as well as all workers previously hired. The *MCL* curve is plotted in Figure 11–2 using the numbers from columns (1) and (4) of Table 11–2. Graphically, the *MCL* curve lies above and is more steeply sloped than the supply of labour curve.

Column (5) of Table 11–2 reports the marginal revenue product (*MRP*) for the left wingers hired by the hockey team. Recall that *MRP* is the change in revenue experienced by a firm when it employs an additional worker. As the hockey team hires additional left wingers, the team can produce more games and other entertainment services that generate revenue for the franchise. However, just like any other firm, the hockey team experiences diminishing returns from hiring additional workers. Thus as more left wingers are added to the team's roster, team output and revenue increase at a declining rate. Column (5) shows *MRP* falling as the number of left wingers hired increases. Recall from Chapter 8 that the *MRP* schedule represents the demand for workers.

How many left wingers will the hockey team's management decide to hire, and what wage will they be paid? To answer this question, first compare columns (4) and (5) of Table 11–2. When the *MCL* in column (4) is less than the *MRP* in column (5), the hockey team adds less to its labour costs by hiring an additional left winger than it adds to its revenues. In this case, the hockey team would increase its hiring. However, when the *MCL* in column (4) is greater than the *MRP* in column (5), the hockey team adds more to its labour costs by hiring an additional left winger than it adds to its revenues. In this case the hockey team would reduce its profits by hiring. Thus the team will continue to hire left wingers up to the point where *MCL* = *MRP*. In our example this point occurs when four left wingers are hired and *MCL* and *MRP* are both equal to $900,000. Note that if the hockey team hired more than four left wingers, *MCL* is greater than *MRP* and the club would experience a loss of profitability.

As our example illustrates, for a monopsony the optimum quantity of labour to hire is found at the point where *MCL* = *MRP*. This is shown in Figure 11–2 as point A where the *MCL* curve intersects with the *MRP* curve. Point A indicates that *MCL* and *MRP* are equal at $900,000 when four left wingers are hired. However, according to the market supply schedule, the hockey team can attract and hire four left wingers for a wage of $600,000 each. This situation occurs at point B on the supply curve *SS* in Figure 11–2. Thus even though a left winger contributes $900,000 to the team's revenues (*MRP*), each left winger will be paid a wage of only $600,000. In a monopsony, the difference between a worker's contribution to the firm's receipts and the wage is known as *monopsonistic surplus*. In our example the hockey team earns a monopsonistic surplus of $300,000 for each of the four left wingers hired for a total of $1.2 million. This surplus is the additional revenue received by the hockey team because of its monopsony power.

Monopsonistic surplus is the difference between the workers' contribution to a monopsonistic firm's receipts and their wages.

Recall from Chapter 8 that in competitive labour markets additional workers are hired up to the point where the wage is equal to *MRP*. If the hockey team in our example operated in a competitive labour market, it would hire more than four left wingers. According to Table 11–2, the wage rate is equal to *MRP* when five left wingers are hired, which is seen in Figure 11–2 as point C where the supply curve *SS* intersects with the *MRP* curve. If the labour market was competitive, five workers would be hired for $700,000 each and their *MRP* would also be $700,000. Thus in a competitive labour market, a firm does not earn a monopsonistic surplus.

As our example illustrates, a monopsony hires fewer workers than a competitive firm and pays a lower wage than a competitive firm. Because of these two economic outcomes, it is often said that monopsonies "exploit" their workers. If firms with monopsony power are made to purchase labour under more competitive conditions, we should expect to see more workers hired and wages rise. In fact, in recent years professional sports leagues have been forced to give up some of their monopsony powers because of the growing power of players, unions and changes to Canadian and American competition laws. Partly as a result of these changes we have seen dramatic increases in players' salaries.

Free Agency

For many years a professional athlete was asked to sign a contract that reserved the right of the employing team to hold exclusive rights to the athlete's services for the major portion of the athlete's expected career. As in the matter of broadcast rights, each professional sport is slightly different in the area of determining the rights of a team to the services of an athlete. In professional baseball, for example, the basic contract's reserve clause extended in perpetuity. A baseball player could change teams only if his employer traded or sold the rights to his contract to another team. By contrast, a professional hockey player was bound to the first team that contracted for his services for the first 10 years that he played professionally. At the end of 10 years, a professional hockey player could become a free agent if he was being paid less than the league average. Regardless of the slight differences between the professional sports, the clauses covering the rights to a player's services gave franchises monopsony power over the players they hired.

Realizing that the reserve clause kept salaries below what could be obtained in a competitive market, baseball players organized and fought the owners in court using American antitrust laws. In 1975 an independent arbitrator overturned the reserve clause in Major League Baseball. The players and owners eventually reached a compromise whereby the employing teams can hold exclusive rights to a player's contract for a specified number of years after which the player can declare "free agency" and sell his services to the highest bidder. A free agent is a player whose contract is no longer exclusively held by one club.

Each of the major professional team sport leagues has very specific rules concerning when a player can declare free agency. In baseball a player must have at least six years of playing experience and not be under contract with any ball club. In 1993 football players in the NFL entered into an agreement with the owners that gives unrestricted free-agency status to uncontracted players with five years of experience. In the NHL, after a bitter lockout in 1994, the free-agency provisions were broadened. Arcane rules still cover players from Europe and some other minor conditions exist, but the major change was that players will become free agents at an age of 31 or after 10 years in the league, whichever comes first. In all professional leagues, some team owners have openly opposed free agency, and players have accused team owners of secretly agreeing not to hire certain free agents. However, the advent of free agency has greatly reduced the degree of monopsonistic exploitation in professional sports.

The impact of free agency on player salaries has been dramatic. In 1975 the average NHL hockey player earned $73,000. By 1995 the average player was earning more than $732,000! Wages and prices in the overall economy also increased during this time, but not to the same extent. For example, the average weekly earnings of a full-time worker in Canada roughly tripled over the same period that the average salary of an NHL hockey player increased more than 10-fold.

As another point of comparison, consider the "plight" of professional hockey players. Until 1994 hockey players had very limited access to free-agency status. For example, in 1983, before the new free agency rules, the Calgary Flames spent 22.1 percent of its $15.8 million budget on players' salaries. After free agency was expanded, the Flames spent 57.6 percent of its $40.3 million 1995 budget for players' salaries.[15] This increase implies that the teams were forced to pay a larger portion of their revenues to players as the general level of wages rose throughout the industry. This increase in the share of budget going to the Flames players was also accompanied by the team losing key veterans to other teams that outbid it for players reaching free-agent status. The situation for the Flames is not an isolated case. In 1996 the Los Angeles Kings traded Gretzky to the St. Louis Blues at midseason even though Wayne Gretzky was undoubtedly the most valuable player on the Kings. In return for the rights to Gretzky's services, the Kings received the the rights to Craig Johnson (left wing), Roman Vopat (center), Patrice Tradif (right wing), plus a fifth-round draft pick for 1996 and a first-round draft pick for 1997.[16] It is significant that Gretzky had only one year to run on his contract with the Kings and would have been old enough to qualify for free agency by July 1, 1996. For Los Angeles to capitalize on its property rights to the services of Wayne Gretzky, the team had to trade him before he became a free agent. Free agency clearly reduces the

---

[15]M. Miller, op. cit.

[16]Knight-Ridder/Tribune News Service, February 28, 1996.

degree of monopsonistic exploitation in professional sports, and the threat of players becoming free agents forces teams to change their behaviour. Free agency also appears to increase the threat that only large-market teams will be able to employ the best talent in the league. In 1996 the St. Louis Blues outbid the rest of the league to gain the services of three veteran players, two free agents and one, Wayne Gretzky, who would reach free agency within six months. The Blues agreed to employ Grant Fuhr, Dale Hawerchuk, and Wayne Gretzky at a combined annual salary of over $20 million per year.[17] Despite the attractive compensation for Gretzky's services in St. Louis, upon reaching free agency in July 1996, Wayne Gretzky accepted a two-year contract to play for the New York Rangers. To the extent that the reforms to free agency have increased the earnings of exceptional players like Gretzky, in a league unable or unwilling to reform the equalization system of distributing advertising revenues, small-market teams may face an increased risk of being unable to attract enough good talent to remain competitive.

Labour Disputes

Professional athletes have fought for many years against monopsonistic employment rules, such as the reserve clause, enforced by the leagues. In opposing the restrictive employment practices of team owners, players in all four major sports have united to form labour unions. A *labour union* is a formal organization of workers that bargains on behalf of its members over the terms and conditions of employment. Players' unions and players' associations negotiate with team owners to determine the standards that are applied to all player contracts.

A **labour union** or **professional association** is a formal organization of workers that bargains on behalf of its members over the terms and conditions of employment.

Disagreements between the team owners and the players' associations have resulted in a number of labour disputes in the last several years. In 1994 the Major League Baseball Players Association (the players' union that represents baseball players in both the American and National Leagues) called a *strike* that forced the cancellation of hundreds of games, including the World Series. Later in the same year, the team owners of the NHL cancelled half a season by enforcing a *lockout* against professional hockey players. In both cases the major points of disagreement concerned the mechanics of how players would be paid and the conditions necessary for players to become free agents.

A **strike** is a work stoppage initiated by labour; a **lockout** is a work stoppage initiated by management.

The shortened baseball and hockey seasons of 1994 resulted from the players' resistance to the owners' proposed "salary caps." A salary cap is a rule that limits the amount of money that any team can spend on player compensation. The owners argued that player salaries were too high for them to make a "fair profit" on their investments and limits needed to be placed on their spending to ensure parity. However, a salary cap also

---

[17] S. McAllister, op. cit.

prevents owners from bidding against each other for the services of talented players. As Wayne Gretzky put it during the 1994 NHL lockout, "Who is scared of who? The owners are scared of their partners, that's who."[18] Therefore, baseball and hockey players argued that a salary cap would keep their salaries artificially low.

In terms of the analysis presented in this chapter, a salary cap can be viewed as a mechanism for owners to enforce the monopsonistic employment of players leaguewide. In other words, a salary cap is just another cartel rule, which is intended to maximize the joint profits of the leagues. The CFL, NFL, and NBA currently enforce salary caps among their member teams. In these cases players have actively spoken out against the rules. Future labour disputes are likely to occur in these sports unless the players and owners can agree among themselves on how profits should be divided.

Do Professional Athletes Earn Their Pay?

The competition among teams for free agents and the insistence by owners on salary caps have caused many people to wonder why professional athletes command such lofty salaries. The premier players in each sport can easily earn several million dollars a year. How can someone earn millions of dollars playing a game when the average household income in Canada is only about $53,000?[19]

Recall that as long as an employer experiences an increase in revenue that is greater than the increase in costs due to hiring an additional worker, the employer can increase profits with each additional hiring. Stated another way, profits increase as long as the marginal revenue product is greater than the marginal cost of labour. Therefore, a team can make a profit and pay its players millions of dollars if those players generate even more millions of dollars in revenues. For example, in 1988 the Los Angeles Kings of the NHL paid $15 million to Peter Pocklington and the Edmonton Oilers for the right to hire Wayne Gretzky. The Kings then signed Gretzky to an eight-year agreement. By 1994 the Kings were paying Gretzky $11.6 million per season for playing—the highest salary in professional sports at the time.[20] Was this a good deal? Analysts estimate that Gretzky increased the Kings' revenues over the eight years by as much as $52.15 million through increases in season ticket sales, game attendance, and cable television rights.[21] Because of Gretzky's contract, the Kings experienced a change in total costs of $35 million, but revenues were expected to increase even more. Gretzky, wishing to play on a team

---

[18]J. Deacon, op. cit., p. 58.

[19]*The Daily*, Statistics Canada, May 10, 1996.

[20]J. Deacon, op. cit., p. 51.

[21]R. J. Downs and P. M. Sommers, "Is the Great One Slipping? Not on the Ice," *Journal of Recreational Mathematics* 23, no. 1 (1991), pp. 1–5.

that had a real chance to win the Stanley Cup in 1996, pushed for a trade to the St. Louis Blues. Depending on the performance of the new additions to the Kings roster in return for trading Gretzky, the Kings could go on earning monopsony surpluses from its original deal with Gretzky well into the next century.

The salaries of professional athletes reflect their contribution to the team's revenue. The same is true for all workers in a market economy. The more a worker contributes to his or her employer's revenues, the more that worker will be paid. Workers with relatively large *MRP*s will command higher wages, and those with relatively small *MRP*s will command lower wages. Why doesn't the average doctor or teacher have a multimillion dollar contract? Because he or she does not generate millions of dollars in revenues for an employer. Salaries in a market system are not determined by a worker's contribution to the public's health or overall well-being, but by the worker's contribution to his or her employer's revenues. Professional athletes earn their salaries because fans are willing to pay to enjoy their performances.

Summary

The business of professional team sports provides an example of imperfect market structures. A unique characteristic of professional sports is the interdependence of teams. A professional team can be successful only if its competitors are successful. Each team must have rivals to play games and attract fans. To ensure their mutual success, hockey teams are organized into a professional league. The league has important economic implications in both the product and resource markets.

Professional sports leagues are economic cartels. Through the leagues, teams formally agree to behave as if they were a single firm—a shared monopoly. By forming cartels, sports teams can increase the joint profits for all members of the league by restricting output and increasing price relative to a competitive market. By sharing the joint profits from the sale of their output, leagues can ensure the longrun survival of member teams.

In the resource market, professional sports leagues enforce employment rules that grant member teams exclusive rights to player contracts. When a team holds the exclusive rights to contract with an athlete, the sports franchise is a monopsony—the single buyer of labour in the market. A monopsony is able to employ workers at wages below what would be observed in a competitive market. In recent years professional athletes have won the right to free agency, which reduces the monopsony power of the teams. In response to free agency, the average salaries of professional athletes have dramatically increased. The size of a professional athlete's paycheck reflects the player's contribution to his club's revenue.

Checklist of Economic Concepts

Markets, imperfectly competitive
Product markets
Resource markets
Cartel
Competition Act
Demand and supply
Marginal revenue

Marginal costs
Monopsony
Supply of labour
Marginal cost of labour
Marginal revenue product
Monopsonistic surplus
Profit maximization

Discussion Questions

1. Define the term *cartel*. What characteristics must be present in an industry for it to operate as a cartel?

2. Explain why all the teams in a professional team sport league must cooperate in order for any one team to have a competitive product?

3. Why might there be more similarity between the factors that determine the income of a popular singer like Celine Dion and a professional golfer like Arnold Palmer than there is between Arnold Palmer and a professional hockey player like Roman Vopat?

4. Discuss the activities used by a league to prevent large-market teams from dominating the competition on and off the field? What is one strategy employed by the NFL that makes it more successful than the NHL in balancing competition?

5. Why has the reform of free agency weakened the ability of the team owners to exploit players?

6. Define the term *monopsony*. Explain how a monopsony can keep employee compensation below the level that would evolve in a free competitive factor market.

7. Would it be fair to reply to Peter Pocklington's statement that Wayne Gretzky "was an asset worth zero in four years" by countering that free agency did not change the value of Wayne Gretzky the asset; it just changed who received the income from that asset?

8. What is the difference between a *strike* and a *lockout*?

9. Explain what a *monopsonist surplus* is. Would you agree with the allegation that professional hockey players on a team were overpaid if the team owner was receiving a monopsonist surplus?

10. In a monopsony situation why is there a difference between the wage paid to a worker and the marginal cost of labour to hire that worker?

Supplementary Reading

Clayton, D. *Eagle: The Life and Times of Alan R. Eagleson.* Toronto: Lester and Opren Dennys, 1982.

A biography of the most influential and controversial man to challenge the monopsony power of the National Hockey League. Eagleson acted as director of the National Hockey League Players Association in the mid-1960s. He worked to divert the monopoly rents of the league away from the club owners. Clayton is detailed in her descriptions of the events that weakened the monopsony control by the league.

Cooper, R. M., ed. *Sports: Win, Place, or Show.* Cincinnati: South-Western Publishing, 1981.

A collection of essays concerning the role of sports in the U.S. economy.

Dryden, K. *The Game: A Thoughtful and Provocative Look at a Life in Hockey.* Toronto: MacMillan, 1983.

As the title states this book provides insight into both the human and business sides of professional hockey.

Dryden, K. and R. MacGregor. *Home Game: Hockey and Life in Canada.* Toronto: McClelland and Stewart, 1989.

The book provides a biographical view of the life of a professional hockey player in the NHL. After retiring from playing professionally in the NHL, Dryden became a lawyer and successful author.

Gruneau, R. and D. Whitson. *Hockey Night in Canada: Sport, Identities, and Cultural Politics.* Toronto: Garamond Press, 1993.

A study concentrating on the political and sociological development of professional hockey in Canada.

Hill, A.; T. Slack; S. Smith; and D. Whitson. *Sport in Canadian Society.* Toronto: McClelland & Stewart, 1992.

A comprehensive study of the legal, political, and sociological role of amateur and professional sports in Canada.

Lineberry, W. P. *The Business of Sports.* New York: W. H. Wilson, 1973.

A collection of articles emphasizing business decision making in professional sports.

Jones, J. C. H. "The Economics of the National Hockey League," *Canadian Journal of Economics* 2, no. 1 February (1969).

This article provides a clear analysis of the conditions of monopoly and monopsony and demonstrates the degree to which the National Hockey League satisfied those conditions between its founding in 1917 and the end of the 1960s.

Quirk, J. and R. D. Fort. *Pay Dirt: The Business of Professional Team Sports.* Princeton: Princeton University Press, 1992.

An inside look at the modern business of professional sports. Includes a detailed bibliography.

Scully, G. W. *The Business of Major League Baseball.* Chicago: University of Chicago Press, 1989.

An in-depth economic analysis of the many facets of major league baseball.

Staudohar, P. D. and J. A. Mangan. *The Business of Professional Sports*. Urbana, IL: University of Illinois Press, 1991.

An examination of the relationship between players' unions and team owners. Chapters 5 through 10 are especially relevant to the examination of the economic issues of monopoly and monopsony in professional sports in North America.

Weistart, J. C. and C. H. Lowell. *The Law of Sports*. Indianapolis, IN: Bobbs-Merrill, 1979.

Provides a detailed historical analysis of the antitrust controversy in professional sports.

Chapter 12

Protectionism versus Free Trade
Who Wins from Trade?

Five years ago [in 1988], we were in the midst of vigorous debate about the economic future of this country. We debated whether we should open our economy to greater competition and secure a new set of rules to govern our trade relations with the United States. Canadians put forward their views with great passion and conviction. In the end, Canadians wisely chose free trade.

Five years later [in 1993], the debate flared up again. There is, however, a fundamental difference in its substance. Five years ago, we staked our faith on what might be; today we can talk about what is. Despite the problems generated by a tough global recession and a spate of difficult disputes with the United States, there is now clear evidence that the Canada-U.S. Free Trade Agreement (FTA) is working. It is laying the foundation for a stronger, more prosperous, more resilient and more confident Canada, a Canada that is a vibrant part of the global economy.

As Canadian companies become more competitive and more confident exporters as a result of their U.S. experience, they are turning to opportunities beyond our borders. In fact, our trade commissioners around the world are reporting an upsurge in inquires from Canadian companies that want to compete in new markets. At the same time, overseas exporters and investors are increasingly finding Canada a good place to do business.

We live by trade and are critically dependent on rules that ensure a fair basis for all our partners. Because our future depends on it, we have been at the forefront in every major trade negotiation. We know that we remain burdened by protectionists—at home and abroad—and we know that the only effective weapon against them is a good rule book, premised on open markets; a rule book that is constantly updated and improved. We are a nation with many advantages—an educated workforce, abundant resources and an efficient infrastructure. We need to reward private initiative and encourage entrepreneurs to approach the future with the confidence necessary to exploit new opportunities. . . .

One of the most telling votes of confidence in the FTA came from the people of Mexico. They looked at the Canada-U.S. FTA and, in large measure, asked to be part of it. The NAFTA looks to the rules of the FTA, and extends them to Mexico. That is why much of the onus in these negotiations was on Mexico. Canada and the United States had already adjusted to the rules of the FTA. Now it is Mexico's turn. . . .

The successful conclusion of the NAFTA means that Canadians have gained vastly improved access for goods, services and investment to a growing market of more than 85 million people on the same basis as our American competitors. In this case, the past is not a good indicator of the future. Unlike Canada, Mexico was a closed economy. Our exports to Mexico have been modest; until now they could sell to us, but we could not sell to them. The NAFTA will open the Mexican economy to Canadian and U.S. firms and provide significant scope for new business.

The NAFTA negotiations encouraged Canada and the United States to take advantage of their experience over the past four years to strengthen the FTA.

Improvements have been made to the rules of origin, customs administration, financial services, and much more. These changes provide Canadian-based firms with even more stable and predictable framework within which to pursue new opportunities, now extended to an integrated market of 360 million consumers.[1]

Canada is a nation of traders. A large part of our history is a record of trading fish, furs, timber, and other staples to England in exchange for manufactured products. Today Canada's trade is very different. Most of our exports are manufactured products. In 1995 Canada's merchandise export had a value of $253.6 billion. That figure is just over 32.5 percent of our GDP. Roughly one-third of all Canadian workers are employed to produce goods or services for buyers in other countries. Industrial goods, machines and equipment, and automobile products accounted for about 65 percent of total exports. Agriculture and fish products, energy products, and forest products made up only a little more than 30 percent of our exports. As we will see, trade is a two-way street. Canadians also buy products from other countries. In 1995 Canada's merchandise imports had a total value of $225.3 billion.

A Description of Canadian International Trade

We often hear that Canada and the United States have the longest unguarded border in the world. We might refer to that border as the longest sales counter in the world. In 1995 Americans bought almost $201.8 billion worth of Canadian goods, and Canadians bought just over $168.9 billion worth of American goods.[2] Canada and the United States have the greatest value of bilateral trade of any two countries in the world. Living next to the largest market in the world has been a great benefit to Canadian producers. It is also the source of considerable concern. At various times in our history, many Canadians have felt less than comfortable with so powerful an economy next to our own. Since before Confederation, Canadians have been divided over whether to seek closer trading relations with the United States or to build a protective wall to reduce the volume of trade with Americans. Canadians who favour freer trade with the Americans claim that freer trade allows our standard of living to rise. Opponents of freer trade fear increased American domination of our economy. They

---

[1]M. Wilson, (Wilson was writing as minister of Industry, Science and Technology and minister of International Trade.) "Forward" in *NAFTA What's It All About?*, External Affairs and International Trade Canada (Ottawa: Government of Canada, 1993).

[2]In this chapter we will refer to both Canadian and American dollars. $ will refer to Canadian dollars. US$ will be used to refer to American dollars.

often argue that we should diversify and trade less with the Americans and more with the rest of the world.

Canada does in fact trade with the rest of the world, but that trade is on a much smaller scale than our American trade. In 1995 we exported $3.8 billion to the United Kingdom, $12.2 billion to all the other countries in the European Community (EC), $11.4 billion to Japan, and $24.3 billion to all other countries. In total just over 20 percent of our exports go to countries other than the United States. Canada imports $56.4 billion or just under 25 percent of our total imports from countries other than the United States.

While most of Canada's international trade is with one country, our trade is relatively diversified in terms of the goods and services traded. Our most important export is automobile products. We also export a substantial volume of machines and equipment and industrial goods. Forest, agricultural, fish, and energy products are also important exports. Most of our imports are manufactured products. The graphs in Figures 12–1 and 12–2 will help you get a picture of Canadian international trade.

Figure 12–1   Canadian trade by country

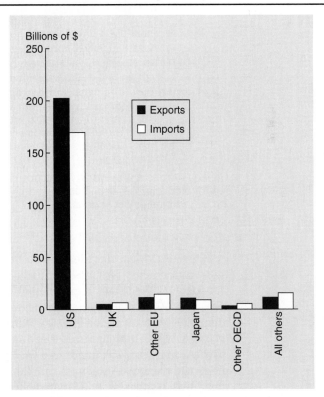

Canada trades with a number of countries. By a wide margin Canada's most important trading partner is the United States.

Figure 12–2   Canadian trade by category of goods

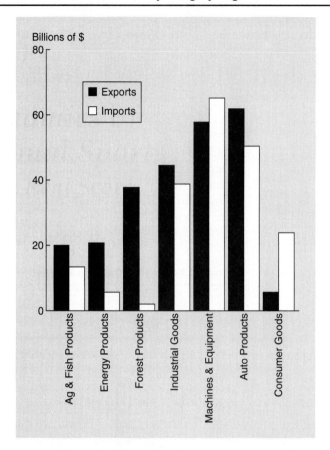

Canada exports a wide variety of goods. The largest category of exports is auto-mobile products. We also import a variety of goods. Machinery and equipment is the largest category of imports.

During the last decade Canada has entered into two very important trade agreements. In 1988 Canada and the United States signed a Canada–U.S. Free Trade Agreement (FTA). It went into effect on January 1, 1989. In 1991 formal negotiation began to allow Mexico to join the agreement. Five years after the FTA, the North American Free Trade Agreement (NAFTA) was implemented. Negotiations are ongoing to add Chile to NAFTA. In addition, Canada is a member of a multinational trade agreement, the General Agreement on Tariffs and Trade (GATT). That agreement was regularly renegotiated. The most recent GATT negotiations were the Uruguay Round. This set of negotiations, which began in Uruguay, further reduced trade barriers between member nations.

The Controversy over International Trade

During the 1981–83 and 1990–91 recessions, we saw a growing tide of resentment against the importation and sale of foreign goods in Canada. Actually, the resentment was nothing new. Foreign trade issues have been hotly debated throughout Canadian history. The FTA and NAFTA were strongly opposed by a substantial proportion of the Canadian population. The controversy was merely augmented, as it often is, by recession. Historically, since the human race has organized itself into geographic groups and engaged in trade among those groups, conflict has emerged between those wanting to suppress trade relationships and those wanting to promote them. The Canadian government severely restricted merchandise importation for most of our history as a nation. In fact, protection for Canadian industry was a vital part of Sir John A. MacDonald's National Policy. Since 1936, when Canada and the United States signed the first of a long series of bilateral trade pacts, import restrictions have tended to fall slowly but steadily. The pace of the reduction of import restrictions by Canada and the rest of the world has recently increased with the enactment of various multinational trade accords, such as the NAFTA and the GATT. Opposition still remains keen, however. What underlies the conflict between *protectionists* and *free traders*? It is useful to consider the polar positions, recognizing that within the Canadian population one finds all shades of intermediate positions—people who are free traders in some respects and protectionists in others.

The Protectionist Viewpoint

First, protectionists want to reduce foreign competition against Canadian goods and services. They see the importation and sale of foreign goods as crowding Canadian goods out of markets in such areas as apples, automobiles, steel, footwear, and textiles. They argue that shrinking markets for Canadian goods means less demand for Canadian labour and higher domestic unemployment rates. Our industries cannot compete successfully, in the protectionists' view, against those in other countries that pay only a fraction of the wage rates that Canadian producers pay. Some even argue that American producers have an advantage because they pay lower wages. This argument usually gains force during recession periods as unemployment increases. It also received much attention during the debates surrounding the NAFTA because that accord leads to the elimination of tariffs on imports from the substantially lower-wage economy of Mexico.

Still another protectionist argument is that certain key industries in Canada are vital to our security and to our economic welfare. Among such industries we find automobiles, aerospace, steel, petroleum energy, and nuclear energy. We cannot depend on foreign suppliers during times of war. To be able to be competitive with other countries in the technology of key industries, we must encourage their development and growth by restricting imports of those products from other countries. In recent years this argument has changed. We have been more fearful of the importation of foreign culture than of the importation of foreign steel. While the concern with foreign culture can be seen as simply an attempt to protect Canadian actors, writers, musicians, and other producers of culture, many regard Canadian television, radio, books, and other outputs of the cultural industry as vital to our national identity.

Finally, many of those that are concerned with trade liberalization see FTA and NAFTA as a threat to our political independence. They believe that these agreements create pressure on the Canadian government to reduce or eliminate Canadian social programs such as Medicare, unemployment insurance, agricultural supports, and regional development policies.

The Free Trade Viewpoint

Free traders generally maintain that it is in the best interests of consumers worldwide if economic agents in all countries are free to engage in whatever voluntary exchanges they believe will be advantageous to all countries. They see trade among nations conferring the same benefits on the exchanging parties as trade among individuals within any one country. If all parties to a potential voluntary exchange fail to see gain for themselves in it, then it will never be consummated. So they argue, why inhibit economic activity—voluntary exchange—that takes place only if all participants gain? We are all made better off, they argue, through specialization and voluntary exchange.

The Economics of International Trade

What can economic theory contribute toward resolving the conflict of viewpoints? It is useful to learn and apply to the problem (1) the underlying mechanics of international trade, (2) the production and consumption possibilities of a country, without trade and with trade, (3) the principle of comparative advantage, and (4) the financing of international trade.

Why Trade Takes Place

It takes two to tango. A country cannot unilaterally import unless it also exports goods. Neither can it export unless it also imports goods.

Suppose the *only* potential international transaction that exists, now and forever, between Canada and the rest of the world is the importation by a Canadian of a German Mercedes. Where would the Canadian get

German marks[3] to make the purchase? The answer is obvious. There are and will be none available. Or, looking at the question from the other side of the water, if the Canadian wants to pay in dollars, what would the Germans do with dollars? They would have no use for dollars and, consequently, would not accept them. The transaction would never take place.

Suppose now that the Canadian wants to import a Mercedes, and Bombardier wants to export Ski-Doos to German citizens who wish to take up snowmobiling. If Bombardier can sell the Ski-Doos for marks, then the Canadian car buyer can purchase marks from Bombardier for dollars, using the marks in turn to purchase the Mercedes. In order for people in one country to import, it is also necessary that they export or sell domestic assets. There is no escape from this fundamental proposition.

Production and Consumption Possibilities

In general, why do people in different countries want to engage in exchange? The underlying reason is that it enables them to increase the levels of well-being they can get from their resources. Recall from Chapter 1 that an economy's production possibilities curve shows the maximum quantities of goods and services that can be produced when the economy's resources are used efficiently. The production possibilities curve may also be thought of as a *consumption possibilities curve* because, in the absence of trade, the economy can consume no more than what it produces. With trade, however, it becomes possible to consume more goods and services than is produced domestically. That is, trade can cause the consumption possibilities curve to shift outward, beyond the production possibilities curve. Thus trade enables the totality of consumers in each country to achieve higher levels of economic well-being with the complement of labour, capital, natural resources, and technology available to them.

> The **consumption possibilities curve** represents the maximum quantities of two goods and/or services that can be consumed in an economy when its resources are used efficiently.

To make our example simple, we will assume a world that has only two countries and only two goods. Naturally, there are many countries and many goods, but the same principle will hold in a multi-country multi-goods world. Let's see how the arrangement works for two countries, Canada and Mexico, that can engage in trade with each other. We will assume that the only goods are cellular phones and cowboy boots.

Without Trade. Consider a hypothetical production and consumption possibilities curve for Canada in the absence of international trade. Given Canada's resources and techniques, suppose it can produce either 50,000 pairs of cowboy boots or 100,000 cellular phones per day. Assuming that its resources are not specialized to either product, the trade-off between the two products is one pair of boots for two phones. By giving up two phones,

---

[3]The mark is the German unit of currency.

Canada can always produce one more pair of boots. Put another way, the opportunity cost of a cell phone is one-half pair of boots, or the opportunity cost of a pair of boots is two phones. If we used a cell phone as our unit of currency, the price of a pair of boots would be two phones. (If this sounds strange remember that for part of our history we actually used beaver pelts as money. Hudson Bay blankets still have their price in beaver pelts marked right on the blanket.) Canada alone can produce and consume any combination of boots and cell phones on line *AB* in Figure 12–3. Thus *AB* is both Canada's daily production possibilities curve and its consumption possibilities curve in the absence of trade. Suppose Canadians select combination C, containing 25,000 pairs of boots and 50,000 cell phones.

Figure 12–3   **Canada's hypothetical production possibilities curve with and without trade**

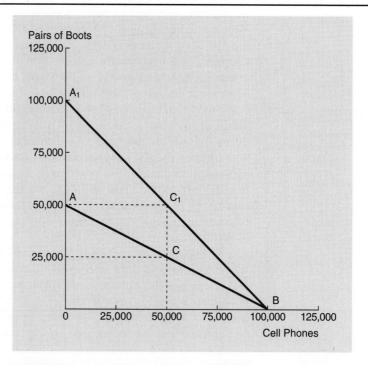

Boots are measured in pairs per day, and cell phones in units per day.
In the absence of trade, Canada's resources will produce 50,000 pairs of boots or 100,000 cell phones or any combination of the two products as shown by AB. Given this, *AB* is both the production and consumption possibilities curve for Canada when there is no trade.
    If trade started and the terms of trade were one for one, Canada's production possibilities curve would remain *AB*, but its consumption possibilities curve would rotate outward to *A₁B*. Canada could concentrate on cell-phone production and trade for boots at less than its own cost of production.

Let Mexico's resources differ somewhat from those of Canada, but consider that they, too, are not specialized. Suppose hypothetically that Mexico's economy can produce, without trade, either 100,000 pairs of boots or 50,000 cell phones per day. The trade-off in production between the two products is 100,000 pairs of boots for 50,000 cell phones. The opportunity cost of a cell phone in Mexico would be two pairs of boots. Conversely, the opportunity cost of a pair of boots would be one-half cell phone. Mexico's production possibilities curve is *MN* in Figure 12–4. Likewise, since there is no trade, *MN* is also Mexico's consumption possibilities curve. Suppose its population settles on combination P, containing 50,000 pairs of boots and 25,000 cell phones.

Figure 12–4   **Mexico's hypothetical production and consumption possibilities with and without trade**

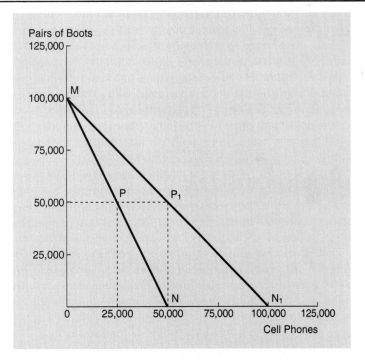

Boots are measured in pairs per day, and cell phones in units per day.
In the absence of trade, Mexico's resources could produce 100,000 pairs of boots or 50,000 cell phones or any combination of the two products as shown by *MN*. Given this, *MN* is both the production and consumption possibilities curve for Mexico when there is no trade.
    If trade started and the terms of trade were one for one, Mexico's production possibilities curve would remain *MN*, but its consumption possibilities curve would rotate outward to *MN₁*. Mexico could concentrate on boot production and trade for cell phones at less than its own cost of production.

With Trade. What would happen if Mexico and Canada were now able to enter into international trade relationships? Under what circumstances would Canada and Mexico be willing to trade boots for phones? Or phones for boots? We will assume that transportation costs are zero and that no other barriers to trade exist. First, we determine the limits within which the terms of trade must fall if the countries are to engage in trade. The *terms of trade* are the price a country pays for its imports in terms of its exports. Second, we show what trade within the terms of trade limits will do for each country.

The **terms of trade** are the cost, in terms of the home country's exports of goods and services, of a unit of imported goods and services.

Canada would refuse to enter into any trade relationships in which the cost of importing a pair of boots exceeds two cell phones or in which the cost of importing a phone exceeds one-half pair of boots. A pair of boots produced domestically costs Canada only two phones. Why import them if the cost per pair of the imports is greater than the cost of domestic boots? A cell phone produced domestically costs one-half pair of boots, so Canada would not be willing to pay more to import it. We summarize these results in Table 12–1.

Mexico would not voluntarily engage in trade if the price of a pair of boots was more than one-half cell phone or if the price of a cell phone was more than two pairs of boots. These limits are shown in Table 12–1.

Suppose now that the countries engage in trade. If you think about it, cell phones are cheaper in Canada. A phone costs only one-half pair of boots in Canada. On the other hand, boots are cheaper in Mexico. Where the cost of a pair of boots is one-half cell phone. Therefore, a profitable trade can develop with Mexico trading boots to Canada in exchange for cell phones. In this case the ratio of boots for phones at which trade will occur is the terms of trade. The exact terms of trade cannot be determined from the limited information we have; however, they must be between two pairs and one-half pair of boots for one cell phone. Assume that the terms of trade work out at one pair of boots for one cell phone. (There is no reason to assume that the terms of trade would be at one for one. It would depend on the market equilibrium that applies between the trading partners.) With these terms of trade, both Canada and Mexico can gain from trade. Canada can get a pair of boots from Mexico cheaper after trade. Before trade, a pair of boots cost two cell phones in Canada; with

Table 12–1	Limits to terms of trade in boots and cell phones, between Canada and Mexico	
	Canada	**Mexico**
Pair of boots	2 cell phones	0.5 cell phone
Cell phone	0.5 pair of boots	2 pairs of boots

trade Canadians will have to pay only one cell phone for a pair of cowboy boots. Mexico will get cell phones cheaper from Canada after trade. Before trade, a cell phone cost two pairs of boots; after trade, the price drops to one pair of boots. The reason each can gain is that while trade leaves each country's production possibilities curve unchanged, trade causes their consumption possibilities curves to rotate outward. If Canada produces only cell phones and trades some of its phones for boots, the population of the country can import one pair of boots for each cell phone it is willing to export. If it were to export all its cell phones, it could import 100,000 pairs of boots. While the production possibilities curve remains AB, Canada's consumption possibilities curve rotates outward to A_1B in Figure 12–3. Thus the impact of trade is to allow Canadians to consume more than they can produce domestically, given their resources and technology.

If Mexico concentrates all of its resources on bootmaking and trades for cell phones, it can import a cell phone for every pair of boots it produces and exports. If it exports 100,000 pairs of boots, it could import 100,000 cell phones. Thus, with trade Mexico's production possibilities curve remains MN, but its consumption possibilities curve becomes MN_1 in Figure 12–4. As was true for Canadians, trade allows Mexicans to consume more than they can produce domestically, given their resources and technology.

Canada will concentrate on the production of cell phones, and Mexico will produce boots. Producing phones only, Canadians are not limited to combination C of cell phones and boots, which contains 25,000 pairs of boots and 50,000 cell phones. Canadians can produce 100,000 cell phones and trade 50,000 of them for 50,000 pairs of boots, leaving themselves with combination C_1, containing 50,000 cell phones and 50,000 pairs of boots. Canadians are 25,000 pairs of boots better off than they were before the trade. Of course, Canadians would not have to take all their gains from trade in boots. The could choose some other combination on A_1B— probably one which represented more boots and more cell phones than the original combination C.

Mexicans will be better off producing only boots and trading for cell phones. Before trade they chose combination P, containing 50,000 pairs of boots and 25,000 cell phones. By specializing in boots, they can produce 100,000 pairs of boots, trade 50,000 pairs of boots for 50,000 phones, and end up with combination P_1, containing 50,000 pairs of boots and 50,000 cell phones. Trade enables the Mexicans to obtain a net gain of 25,000 cell phones. Again it is not necessary that Mexico take its gain only in cell phones. With trade it could have more of both goods.

The Principle of Comparative Advantage

Clearly, specialization and exchange help Canada and Mexico to increase the volumes of goods and services available for their people to consume. It pays any country to specialize in producing those things in which it has a comparative advantage and to trade for goods in which it experiences a comparative disadvantage. If cell phones and boots are the only two goods and Mexico and Canada are the only two countries in the world, then the total production of boots and phones is the world's GDP. Before trade the world produced 75,000 cell phones (25,000 in Mexico and 50,000 in Canada) and 75,000 pairs of boots (50,000 in Mexico and 25,000 in Canada. After trade the world's GDP was clearly higher—100,000 cell phones (all produced in Canada) and 100,000 pairs of boots (all produced in Mexico). Even if we allow for some transportation cost, both Mexico and Canada are better off after trade.

A country has a *comparative advantage* in the production of any good that it can produce with a smaller sacrifice of some alternative good or goods, that is, at a lower opportunity cost, than can the rest of the trading world. Note that there is no presumption that the country can produce that good at a lower *absolute* cost than other countries can. In terms of the number of units of labour and capital necessary to produce a cell phone, Canada may use 3 times (or 10 times) more of each than other countries. By the same token, it may use less resources. Yet if Canada must give up two cell phones to produce one pair of boots and can trade one cell phone for one pair of boots, Canadians are better off by trading. Using the same reasoning, Mexico is also better off by trading.

Symmetrically, a country has a *comparative disadvantage* in the production of any good that requires a greater sacrifice of some alternative good or goods, that is, it produces at a higher opportunity cost, than is required in the rest of the trading world. Canada in our example has a comparative disadvantage in the production of boots. It must sacrifice two phones for a pair of boots if it produces boots domestically. But it can import a pair of boots by giving up only one cell phone to the international market. In which product does Mexico have a comparative disadvantage?

Look again at the complete examples of Mexico and Canada, without and with trade. Note that if a country has a comparative advantage in the production of one good (and it most certainly will have in the real world), it must have a comparative disadvantage in the production of some other good or goods. Usually a country will have comparative advantages in the production of several goods and comparative disadvantages in the production of several others.

The reasons that every country has comparative advantages in the production of some goods and comparative disadvantages in the production of others is that countries differ in their respective resource endowments and in their states of technology. Some countries are short on certain mineral deposits such as oil, coal, and copper, but they may have relatively large quantities of good capital equipment and high levels of technological know-how. Such a country, Japan, for example, will likely have comparative advantages in the production and sale of goods embodying high technology and good stocks of capital with which to work.

A country has a **comparative advantage** in the production of a good when it has a lower opportunity cost of producing the good than any other country has.

A country has a **comparative disadvantage** in the production of a good when it has a higher opportunity cost of producing the good than another country has.

Some countries have vast quantities of good agricultural land, while others do not. Some are particularly well-suited in terms of climate, terrain, and soil to grow outstanding wine grapes. Some excel in coffee production and others in growing tea. A beef industry seldom thrives in densely populated, mountainous countries. Some countries have high literacy rates. In others the bulk of the population may be illiterate. All of these differences, and many more, confer on each country or region of a country certain comparative advantages and disadvantages that make specialization and exchange worthwhile.

The principle of comparative advantage is not hard to understand; however, it is sometimes hard to believe. Wages are much lower in Mexico than in Canada. Many Canadians believe that lower wages mean lower cost of production and therefore free trade with Mexico will mean that all production will eventually move there because of the low wages. On the other hand, many Mexicans believe that their economy has no chance of competing with the much higher productivity of Canadian and American workers. If low wages determined trade, all production would have long since moved to the third world. (The opposite viewpoint is probably closer to reality. Third-world countries have more problems selling to the developed countries than developed countries have selling in the third world. In fact most of the world's trade occurs between highly developed countries.) Even if low wages were the only source of advantage in international trade, how would the developed countries pay for all their cheap imports from the low-wage countries. Obviously, the developed countries would have to export something in exchange for their imports. What could we export? The wages are high in all sectors of a developed economy. But if the developed economies cannot export, how can they pay for imports? No country has wages that are low enough to give its exports away.

To make absolutely certain that you understand the principle of comparative advantage, let us consider one more example. Again assume a world with only two goods and only two places. (Trade exists within countries as well as between countries. Trade takes place between a city in a province and the hinterland around that city or between two provinces within Canada. The same principle that applies to international trade also applies to interregional trade.) Again the example is hypothetical. We assume that *within* each country resources are not specialized in the production of one or the other good. In this case assume that the two goods are bread and cars and the two countries are called Alpha and Beta. Both countries have the same size labour force. Table 12–2 summarizes their daily outputs of bread and cars.

Alpha is less productive than Beta is. Even though both countries have the same number of workers, Beta can produce more of either good than can Alpha. Accordingly Alpha will be the lower-wage country. Beta has an *absolute advantage* in the production of both cars and bread. Alpha's workers can produce only 5 million kilos of bread a day or 500 cars a day. Beta can

An **absolute advantage** is based on the absolute cost of production as opposed to the relative cost of production. Absolute advantage does not determine trade.

Table 12–2   Hypothetical production possibilities for Alpha and Beta

	Alpha	Beta
Bread (kilos)	5,000,000	10,000,000
Cars	500	2,000

produce more cars (2,000) and more bread(10 million kilos) a day. However, the opportunity costs of a car in Alpha and Beta are different. In Alpha a car will cost 10,000 kilos of bread. In Beta a car will cost only 5,000 kilos of bread. Similarly, the opportunity costs of bread are different. In Alpha a kilo of bread will cost 0.0001 of a car, and in Beta a kilo of bread will cost .0002 of a car. Cars are cheaper in Beta, but bread is cheaper in Alpha. Both sides could gain by trade. Let us assume that before trade each country consumes 2.5 million kilos of bread. If Alpha produces 2.5 million kilos of bread, it will have half its resources left to produce cars. Therefore, it can produce only 250 cars a day. Beta will need to use only one-quarter of its resources to produce 2.5 million kilos of bread, leaving enough resources to produce 1,500 cars. Total production between the two countries will be 5 million kilos of bread and 1,750 cars.

With trade Alpha can specialize in the production of bread and Beta can specialize in the production of cars. As long as the terms of trade fall between 5,000 kilos of bread for one car and 10,000 kilos per car, trade will be mutually beneficial. Again the exact terms of trade will depend on the circumstances. Let us assume that the trade takes place at 8,000 kilos of bread for one car. Alpha is better off trading 8,000 kilos of bread to import a car than giving up 10,000 kilos of bread to produce the car domestically. If the price of a car is 8,000 kilos of bread, then the price of a kilo of bread in international trade is .000125 cars. Clearly Beta is better off buying bread from Alpha at that price than producing it domestically at of cost of .0002 cars.

If Alpha specializes in producing bread, it can produce 5 million kilos per day. It can trade the extra 2.5 million kilos for 312.5 cars. It will gain 72.5 cars. Beta can now specialize in the production of cars. It can produce 2,000 cars per day. It must trade 312.5 cars to buy the 2.5 million kilos of bread it needs. That leaves Beta with an extra a 187.5 cars—its gain from trade. Notice than Beta gained more from trade than Alpha gained. It is common for one country to gain more from trade than the other country. The exact gains for each partner depend on the terms of trade, which we already know depend on the circumstances that exist in the market. However, both countries do gain from trade. If both countries did not gain, there would be no basis for trade.

The Principle of Comparative Advantage—Some Practical Considerations

In the real world transportation and other costs are associated with trade. For trade to actually occur, the gains from trade must be greater than these costs. If Ontario has a comparative advantage in gravel and Saskatchewan has a comparative advantage in top soil, trade is unlikely to develop because transportation costs would be far greater than the possible gains.

Assuming away transportation and other transactions costs was not the only simplifying assumption we made in the previous discussion. We also assumed that the resources in each country were not specialized in the production of either product. If inputs are not specialized, they are perfectly substitutable in production. Workers, machines, and other inputs could be shifted from the production of cars to bread or bread to cars with no reduction in output. This assumption explains why the production possibilities curves were straight lines. In Chapter 1 we explained that production possibilities curves usually bow out, as in Figure 1–1. A production possibilities curve normally bows out because different resources tend to be better suited for the production of different outputs. If resources between two countries tend to be specialized, then resources within a country are also likely to demonstrate some tendency toward specialization.

A straight-line production possibilities curve means that resources within the economy are not specialized. If that is the case, the opportunity cost of one good in terms of the other is constant. The production possibilities curve between wheat and oats is probably very near to a straight line. Resources (land, farm equipment, and worker's skills) needed to produce wheat are very like the resources needed to produce oats. A bowed-out production possibilities curve means that some resources are better suited for the production of one good than for the production of the other. For example, if there are two goods—bread and wine—the resources in the Canadian prairies are better suited for producing bread and the resources in the Okanogan are better suited to producing wine. If limited amounts of bread and wine were desired, production would take place initially using the best-suited resources. As an economy moves along its production possibilities curve and produces more and more wine, it would have to move into less and less suitable resources. The less suitable resources would mean higher and higher opportunity costs for wine in terms of bread. Eventually producers would be forced to grow grapes in hot houses on the prairies, and the cost of the extra wine in terms of bread would be very high. Similarly, if more and more bread were demanded, eventually wheat would have to be grown on the steep slopes along the Okanogan valley. Again the opportunity cost of bread in terms of wine would become very high. A bowed-out production possibilities curve means that costs are increasing. Increasing costs can affect comparative advantage. Initially one country may have a lower opportunity cost for one good, and another country may have a lower opportunity cost for the other good. As a result, trade takes place. As one country exports, its production increases and it starts to experience increasing costs. The other country will also experience increased costs for the good it is exporting. Eventually further trade becomes impossible because the level of production in each country has risen to the point that both countries have the same opportunity costs for the production of both goods. Increasing costs help to explain why a country will import some of a good it consumes and also produce the same good domestically. It imports the good up to the point that further imports would cost more than domestically produced units.

The fact the most resources are specialized creates another problem. You will remember from Chapter 7 that individuals and families earn their incomes by selling the resources that they own. The prairie farmer can earn money by using her land to grow wheat. The factory worker can earn income by selling his labour to produce cars. The factory owner can earn a living by using her capital to produce cell phones. If the land the farmer owns, the labour of the worker, and the machinery owned in the plant are better at producing certain goods or services, the owner of those resources will be affected by the demand for the goods they produce.

In our first example Mexico ended up specializing in the production of cowboy boots, and Canada specialized in the production of cell phones. Both countries gained from the trade. Total production went up because both countries used their resources more efficiently. Once again, both countries benefited from the trade. However, the fact that both countries gained overall does not mean that every individual in the two countries gained. Some individuals would almost certainly lose. The workers in Mexican cell-phone factories would initially be out of a job. The owners of those factories would have machinery that could no longer be used to make cell phones. Similarly the resources of those in the cowboy-boot industry in Canada would suffer. Thus opening up trade would benefit some and hurt others. Whenever some people are made better off and others are hurt, the issue becomes normative. However, some objective observations can be made about the opening of trade. Given sufficient time, individuals could adjust to the new situation. Jobs would open in the cell-phone industry in Canada and in the boot-making industry in Mexico. Workers could retrain and move into these new jobs, but some short-term unemployment would occur in both countries. Some capital could be shifted for one industry to another, but some capital would have to be written off. With no worthwhile options, older workers might be forced into early retirement. In some ways the real world is not as flexible as a hypothetical example. The real costs are incurred by real people.

In other ways the real world is more flexible than our hypothetical model. The real world has far more than two products. If the Canadian cowboy-boot industry was eliminated by more efficient production (*note we did not say by lower wages*) in Mexico, the boot industry does not have to change over to cell-phone production. It could move into product lines much more similar to cowboy boots. The workers and machinery might move into the production of winter boots—a product in which Mexico is not likely to have any expertise. An old boot factory might move into the production of leather holsters and carrying cases for cell phones. Similarly the Mexican cell-phone industry might move into some other area of consumer electronics. When countries agree to lower trade barriers so that freer trade can take place, they generally phase in the changes over a period of time to allow for retraining and plant conversion. The time also allows older workers to retire from the industry gradually as it contracts. Many of the tariffs eliminated by NAFTA are being reduced to zero in steps over 5 or 10 years.

One important point remains: Although freer international trade creates winners and losers, it also produces net positive gains. Part of these gains can be used to compensate the losers by subsidizing retraining, factory conversions, and earlier retirements.

How International Trade Is Financed

International trade has two important characteristics that set it apart from trade within the boundaries of any given country. First, each country has its own currency. Producers in any given country want to be paid in that currency, and buyers want to use it to pay for goods and services. Second, nationalism and political objectives are invariably injected into trade relationships among nations. Governments enact all sorts of impediments to trade to further their political ends, even though the trade, if allowed, would have been in the best economic interests of the trading parties. Remember that voluntary exchange will occur only if *all* parties to the exchange expect to gain. In this section we concentrate mostly on the problems arising from the different currency units used by different countries.

An **exchange rate** is the cost of one country's currency in terms of the currency of another country. Each pair of currencies has two exchange rates, for example, the Canadian dollar price of the American dollar and the American dollar price of the Canadian dollar.

The link between the currencies of any two trading countries is the *exchange rate.* An exchange rate is the price of one country's currency in terms of the monetary units of another. We can think of the exchange rate as the dollar price of another country's currency. We list a recent sample of such exchange rates in Table 12–3. The dollar exchange rate for the British pound of $2.1225 is the highest rate listed. The lowest exchange rate listed is $0.0009 for the Italian lira, which amounts to 9/100 of a cent.

Exchange rates, in the absence of government intervention, are determined in exchange markets that arise from millions of such transactions as the importation of a Mercedes into Canada or the export of a Ski-Doo to Germany. The existence of exchange markets makes the pairing of individual import transactions with individual export transactions unnecessary. Anyone in Canada can buy foreign currency with dollars and can use it to import that country's goods. Similarly, anyone with excess amounts

Table 12–3   **Canadian dollar exchange rates of selected foreign currencies, July 10, 1996**

Country	Dollar Price	Foreign Currency Unit
Australia	1.0927	Australian dollar
Denmark	0.2329	krone
France	0.2651	franc
Germany	0.8971	mark
Italy	0.0009	lira
Japan	0.0124	yen
Mexico	0.1796	new peso
United Kingdom	2.1225	pound
United States	1.3689	American dollar

Source: Bank of Montreal Treasury Group as reported in the *Globe and Mail*, July 11, 1996, p. B17.

of a foreign currency on hand from selling goods abroad, or for any other reason, can sell that currency for dollars in the foreign exchange market.

In a free market, the exchange rate of any country's currency for a foreign currency is determined, like any other price, by the forces of demand for and supply of the foreign currency. Again, for simplicity assume a world with only two countries—Canada and the United Kingdom. To assist you in understanding the foreign exchange market we will explain what determines the demand for and supply of foreign currency. Demand for foreign exchange, pounds sterling (£), is created when a Canadian purchases goods or services from the United Kingdom. It is also created if a Canadian wishes to invest in the United Kingdom or make a payment, for example a dividend payment, to a resident of the United Kingdom. British residents supply pounds through their demand for goods and services produced in Canada, when they invest in Canada, or make a payment to a Canadian. The demand curve for pounds is essentially the same as the demand curve for anything else. That is, it slopes downward to the right, like DD in Figure 12–5, since it is derived mainly from the demand for British produced goods, which is itself negatively sloped. Similarly, the supply curve SS in Figure 12–5 usually slopes upward to the right because it is derived mainly from the British demand for goods produced in Canada. The exchange rate r is the equilibrium price. It is the dollar price of a pound. Quantity q is the equilibrium quantity exchanged of pounds. The horizontal axis measures the quantities of pounds, and the vertical axis measures the price per pound in dollars. Another way of thinking is to consider the market for Canadian dollars in terms of United Kingdom pounds. For each currency there are two exchanges rates. In Table 12–3, £1.00 has a Canadian currency price of $2.1225. We could also price the Canadian dollar in terms of

Figure 12–5   **The Canadian supply, demand, and
                          exchange rate for pounds**

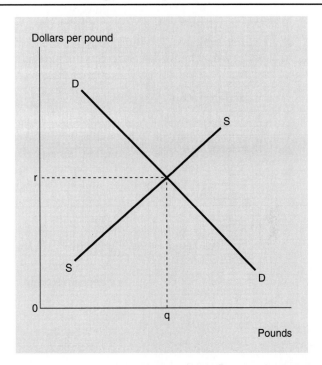

Demand for pounds per day is represented by *DD* and supply is *SS*. The equilibrium
exchange rate is *r* dollars per pound and the equilibrium quantity of pounds is *q*.

the pound. If £1.00 costs $2.1225, then $1.00 is worth $1.00 ÷ 2.1225 =
£.4711. In practice there is a margin between the price at which banks buy
and sell currencies so that they can make a profit, but the Canadian dollar
price of any foreign currency is the approximate reciprocal of that foreign
currency price of the Canadian dollar.

The fact that in the real world more than two countries exchange currency does not alter the way exchange rates are determined. Consider the
case with three countries: Canada, the United Kingdom, and the United
States. There is a market for Canadian dollars in terms of American dollars
and a market in terms of pounds. There is also a market for pounds in terms
of American and Canadian dollars. Finally there is a market for American
dollars in terms of Canadian dollars and British pounds. Each of these
markets will work exactly as explained above in the two-country case.

Moreover, all these markets must be consistent. If the pound cost $2.00
and the American dollar costs $1.3333, then the pound must cost US$1.50
($2.00 ÷ 1.3333 = 1.50). If £1 was worth $2.00, US$1.00 was worth
$1.3333, and £1 was worth only US$1.40, then one could make a profit by

Arbitrage is the simultaneous buying and selling in two or more markets to profit from inconsistent prices in the different markets. This practice occurs in commodity markets such as wheat or gold as well as currency markets.

buying American dollars with Canadian dollars and then buying pounds with the American dollars and converting the pounds back to Canadian dollars. $1,333.33 would buy US$1,000; US$1,000 would buy £714.285; and £714.285 would buy $1,428.57. Clearly as soon as any such inconsistency developed, it would be profitable to buy and sell currencies until the rates were consistent. Such buying and selling is called *arbitrage*.

The Canadian Balance of Payments

In order to discuss the demand for and supply of foreign currency more formally, consider the summary of Canadian international transactions for 1995, which is presented in Table 12–4. As noted above, our demand for foreign currency arises from our desire for foreign goods, services, and investments. Thus our demand for foreign currency may be determined by

Table 12–4	Canadian international transaction for 1995 (in millions of dollars)		
Transaction Type	**Demand for Foreign Currency**	**Supply of Foreign Currency**	**Balance**
Current Account			
Merchandise exports		$253,536	
Merchandise imports	$225,251		
Merchandise balance			$28,285
Service exports		35,005	
Service imports	43,924		
Investment income receipts		16,347	
Investment income payments	49,224		
Transfers receipts		4,467	
Transfers payments	4,028		
Balance on current account			−13,123
Capital Account			
Canadian claims on non-residents net flows	16,176		
Canadian liabilities to non-residents net flows		23,260	
Total balance on capital account net flows			7,064
Statistical discrepancy		6,039	

Source: Statistics Canada, *Canadian Economic Observer*, Catalogue No. 11-010 (Ottawa: May 1996).

identifying any payments that we want to make abroad. The largest part of our demand for foreign currencies in 1995 arose from imports of merchandise. This demand source is straightforward. The second largest demand for foreign currency arises from the importation of services. This item includes travel by Canadians to foreign countries. When "snow birds" go to Florida, they are importing other services including shipping charges and insurance. The third source of demand for foreign currency is the payment of investment income to foreigners. When foreigners receive interest, dividends, or other investment income from a Canadian source, they want to convert it to their own currency, thereby creating a demand for foreign currency. The last current account item is transfers. This item includes gifts to foreign individuals and organizations. Another source of demand for foreign currency arises when Canadians wish to invest in a foreign country. If Canadians buy a foreign firm, they will have to pay for that firm with foreign currency. The same is true if a Canadian wishes to buy shares of stock in a foreign firm or foreign bonds. When a foreigner buys a factory, a farm, or other real asset, it is called direct investment. Direct investment carries with it control of the asset. When a foreigner buys a share of stock or a bond, it is called portfolio investment. Portfolio investment does not give the foreign investor any control of the asset. Both direct and portfolio investment are included in the capital account.

Supplies of foreign currencies, as one would expect, arise from transactions reciprocal to those generating demand. The largest supply source in 1995 was the merchandise exports. When foreigners wish to buy Canadian goods, they supply their own (foreign) currency. Canada also exports services to foreigners and receives investment income and transfer payments from foreign sources. These payments contribute to the supply of foreign currency. If we look at only the trade in merchandise, Canada exports more than it imports. Therefore, the supply of foreign currency is greater than the demand for foreign currency. We say we have a positive balance in merchandise trade.[4] In 1995 Canada's balance on merchandise trade was $28,285 million. However, when we add trade in services, investment income, and transfers, Canada has a negative balance on its current account. In 1995 Canada's current account balance was −$13.123 million. In other words, the quantity demanded of foreign currency is greater than the quantity supplied of foreign currency. However, we know in a free market that the interaction of supply and demand ensures an equilibrium price (in this case an equilibrium exchange rate) where the quantity supplied equals the quantity demanded. The excess demand for foreign currency is offset in the capital account. Foreigners

---

[4]Historically, economists have called a positive balance "favourable" and a negative balance "unfavourable." This terminology is useful as long as you remember that favourable and unfavourable have only that meaning. An unfavourable balance of payments is not necessarily bad (and a favourable balance of payments is not necessarily good.)

invested more in Canada than Canadians invested in foreign countries. In 1995 Canada had a capital account balance of +$7,084. This amount does not exactly offset the current account deficit. Keeping track of all the international transactions that occur is impossible, so the difference is corrected by the statistical discrepancy.

The separation of transactions in Table 12–4 into current account and capital account is simply a classification convenience. Current account items are more or less immediate and short term in character. A transaction is consummated, and that is the end of it. Others of a similar nature are occurring concurrently and over time. Capital account items are long-term transactions that will persist into the future and yield continuing influence on the demand for and supply of foreign exchange. For example, when a German holds a Canadian government bond, he or she will receive interest payments until the bond matures. Similarly, if an American buys a Canadian firm, he or she hopes to receive profits for as long as he or she owes that firm. Thus a positive balance on the capital account implies a future flow of payments out of the country.

Alternative Exchange Rate Systems

When a country's exchange rates are determined in a free market, they are called **floating** or **flexible exchange rates**.

Under a **gold standard,** a country defines the value of its currency in terms of gold and freely exchanges its currency for gold. International payment deficits are also paid in gold.

Exchange rates that are determined by supply and demand in a free market are called *floating* or *flexible exchange rates*. Exchange rates are not always determined in a free market. Canada and most other industrial countries were on a gold standard for most of the period 1879 to 1934. Under a *gold standard*, a country defines the price of its currency in terms of gold and makes its currency redeemable in gold. If a country's international payment debits exceed its international payment credits, it pays the difference in gold. While a few people still wish to return to the gold standard, it is unlikely to happen.

The demise of the gold standard occurred during the Great Depression. The birth of a new "standard" to replace it had to wait until the end of World War II. In 1944 a number of the world's industrial countries sent representatives to Bretton Woods, New Hampshire, to establish a new system for dealing with international exchange. Under the Bretton Woods system, the United States agreed to buy and sell gold at US$35 an ounce. Other countries agreed to fix or "peg" their exchange rate to the American dollar. Such a system is called a *fixed* or *pegged exchange rate system*. For much of the 1960s, the Canadian dollar was pegged at US$.925 an ounce.

Under a **pegged** or **fixed exchange rate system**, each country defines the value of its currency in terms of an agreed currency (US$). Each country buys or sells its currency to maintain its pegged value.

The period of the Great Depression and World War II was a time of extreme instability. It is not surprising that the leaders of the major industrial powers wanted stability in the postwar period. Fixed exchange rates seemed to offer stability. Imagine that you have saved enough money to take a vacation at Disney World next winter. In order to get the cheapest possible flight, you must book early. At the time you book your flight, US$1.00 costs $1.37. At that exchange rate you have enough money to afford the trip. However, before you leave, the Canadian dollar depreciates (falls in value). It now costs you $1.42 to buy US$1.00. You can no longer afford your winter holiday. If exchange rates were fixed, then the price of US$1.00 would not have changed and you could plan ahead with reasonable certainty.

While Bretton Woods seemed to promise stability, problems developed. There was still a supply of and a demand for foreign exchange and supply and demand still determined an equilibrium price, as explained above. If that equilibrium price stays very near the pegged price, there is no problem. Toward the end of the 1960s, Canadian receipts from exports and investment in Canada rose faster than Canadian payments to foreigners. That is to say, the the demand for Canadian dollars rose more rapidly than the supply of Canadian dollars. The result was upward pressure on the Canadian dollar. However, the Canadian government was bound to maintain the pegged value of US$.925. To hold the Canadian dollar to the pegged price, the Bank of Canada had to increase the supply of Canadian dollars, which it did by selling Canadian dollars for foreign currency or gold. Eventually this policy started to have negative effects on domestic economic policy, and Canada abandoned fixed exchange rates for floating exchange rates. The opposite problem can also occur.

If a country's exports stagnate, there can be downward pressure on its currency. This problem occurred repeatedly to Britain in the postwar years. In such a case the supply of a country's currency is growing faster than the demand for it. The central bank of the country must buy its own currency to increase demand and hold it to the pegged value. It buys its own currency by selling its reserves of other currencies or gold. If these reserves become depleted, it has no choice but to *devalue* its currency. Britain devalued its currency a number of times in the 1950s and 1960s. When a currency is devalued, its price falls suddenly by a substantial amount instead of gradually over a period of time. So much for the desired certainty of pegged exchange rates. Pegged exchange rates were eventually dropped because the American dollar came under increasing pressure in the 1970s and 1980s. As long as the American dollar was used to define the value of other currencies, the United States could not devalue its currency. If you are still worried about next winter's vacation, you can buy futures on American dollars. A future is a contract to buy currency (or other assets) at a determined future time at a presently agreed upon price.

Analysis of the Controversy

In the light of this brief survey of the economics of international trade, what light is shed on the controversy between protectionists and free traders? Should we protect ourselves from imports of Japanese and European automobiles and steel? Is it wise to limit textile imports from South Korea,

Taiwan, Hong Kong, and China? Does the FTA mean that the Americans will buy all our natural resources or all our factories? Is free trade with the United States a threat to the existence of our social programs or even our existence as an independent country? Will American television and movies subvert our cultural identity? Does the NAFTA mean that Canada will be flooded with goods produced by low-wage workers in Mexico? Will it increase unemployment in Canada? Does the last round of GATT mean that we will will be flooded with cheap foreign textiles?

Barriers to Trade

Before discussing the arguments for imposing barriers to trade, we will briefly outline the tools that countries can use to block international trade.

A **tariff** is a tax on imported goods.

The most common barrier to trade is a tariff. Tariffs are also referred to as duties. A *tariff* is a tax on an imported good that is not applied to domestic production. Since they apply only to foreign production, tariffs give domestic producers a cost advantage over imports. In the early 1930s Canada imposed average tariffs of over 20 percent on imported goods. By 1989 when the FTA went into effect, average tariffs in Canada were less than 4 percent. Today most goods enter Canada duty free. Tariffs affect buyers because tariffs increase the cost of imports directly and allow domestic producers to charge higher prices. Tariffs do, however, provide tax revenue for the government. Historically they were an important source of revenue to many governments, but today tariffs are too low to raise much revenue.

A **quota** is a quantitative limit on the amount of a good that can be imported.

A second common barrier to trade is a quota. A *quota* establishes a maximum level of imports that will be allowed. Protectionists often prefer quotas to tariffs because they put a fixed limit on imports. Since they reduce supply, quotas also increase the price that domestic consumers pay. However, they do not normally provide any revenue for the government unless it auctions off the quotas. Sometimes exporting nations voluntarily agree to quotas. Canada uses a quota system to limit the importation of foreign television programs.

A **subsidy** is a government payment to a firm based on its production of a particular good. It may or may not be intended to influence international trade.

Subsidies can sometimes be used to affect foreign trade. A *subsidy* is a government payment to a producer of a good or service. Of the various barriers to free trade, subsidies have probably caused the most controversy and been the most difficult issue on which to reach agreements. Subsidies may be instituted for reasons that have nothing to do with foreign trade. For example, a government might want to subsidize the manufacture of thermal insulation to encourage energy conservation and to reduce greenhouse emissions. Governments sometimes use subsidies to increase the income of certain producers. Many countries use subsidies to support agriculture. Canada and other countries have used subsidies to attract firms into areas of high unemployment. While the intent of such subsidies is not to interfere with international trade, they may do so inadvertently.

Even when subsidies do not have a significant effect on international trade, other countries may claim that these payments are unfair barriers to trade.

Sometimes subsidies are intended as trade barriers. Subsidies can be used to protect infant industries until they are productive enough to compete on their own. Mature but unprofitable industries with political influence may also receive this type of protection. Finally, some countries may pay firms export subsidies. In this case firms receive the subsidy only on the production that they export. Because subsidies can be a tool of both domestic and international economic policy, they are one of the most controversial trade topics at bilateral and multinational trade negotiations.

Finally, administrative controls can affect international trade. Governments often pass legislation controlling the quality of products. For example, almost all countries require that meat be inspected to ensure that it is safe to eat. Such controls are generally in the public interest and have nothing to do with trade. However, regulations can be written or administrated so that they become trade barriers. Canadians have often complained that one American meat inspector at a Montana port of entry is unreasonable in his inspection of Canadian meat exports. Such controls are also used as a barrier to interprovincial trade within Canada. For example, the use of provincial regulation to reduce competition from out-of-province tradespersons.

Protection from Cheap Foreign Goods

The principle of comparative advantage and the economic gains ensuing from specialization and exchange make it reasonably clear that a country's population as a whole will lose from import restrictions. It will have less of all goods and services to consume. Real per capita income and living standards will be lower than they would be if all potential international voluntary exchanges were allowed to be consummated. Foreign goods cannot displace all or even a large part of the domestic production and sale of goods. A country cannot import unless, by selling domestic goods and services or other kinds of domestic assets to foreigners, it earns foreign exchange with which to buy those imports. International trade is a two-way street, enabling those countries that engage in it to shift their consumption possibilities curves outward. It serves to *increase* real per capita income and living standards in the trading countries.

Free trade may indeed injure segments of a country's economy. In fact, concern for that part of the population investing in and working in the injured segments prompts most protectionist efforts. For example, import quotas on dairy products keep the demands for the outputs of the domestic dairy industry higher than they would otherwise be, thus supporting higher profits, wages, and employment in this industry. Conversely, free trade enables foreign competitors to invade the domestic producers' markets, resulting in lower domestic profits, wages, and employment levels in those industries.

Consequently, the imposition of import restrictions leads to winners (investors and workers in the protected sector) and losers (consumers who must pay higher prices for the protected good). But do the winners "win" by more than the losers "lose"? In other words, do the benefits of the import restrictions outweigh the costs? Consider the case of shoes imported from low-wage developing countries. The owners of Canadian shoe factories and the workers often cry foul. They claim that the low-wage producers in the third world have an unfair advantage. Of course, the charge is untrue. If it were true, everything would be made in poor countries. Remember, it is comparative, not absolute, costs that determine trade. However, foreign shoes may still threaten the well-being of people involved in the Canadian shoe industry. Canadian workers' wages maybe lower, or they may even lose their jobs. The shareholders will find that their dividends drop as the shoe firms' profits fall. Some Canadian producers may even be forced into bankruptcy. The potential loss from removing import restrictions on shoes is very great for the relatively few individuals involved in the shoe industry. On the other hand, the gain for the millions of consumers, while very little individually, is collectively even greater than the losses to those in the industry.

A case study from the United States illustrates how restrictions can help a small number at a high price to society in general. In the early 1980s, in response to poor domestic auto sales, the Reagan administration was successful in getting Japan to voluntarily limit its auto exports to the United States. The Japanese probably agreed to the voluntary restriction to prevent even more damaging legislative restrictions. The major benefit of the import restriction was the significant number of jobs saved in the auto sector (at the expense of jobs lost in the export sector). The cost of the program was the increased price that car buyers had to pay for autos. Which effect is greater? One estimate suggests that the voluntary import restriction imposed a cost of US$160,000 per job saved.[5] That is, in an effort to save a job paying from US$30,000 to US$40,000, Americans spent US$160,000. Similar results would likely be found if we investigated a number of other cases in the United States, Canada, or elsewhere.

We noted that the jobs in the automobile industry were saved but likely at the cost of jobs in the export sector. When a country moves to restrict imports, jobs will be lost in the export sector for two reasons. The first is related to the supply and demand for foreign currency. If a country reduces its imports, it also reduces the supply of its currency available to foreigners to buy its exports. The second relates to the likely reaction of the country(ies) whose exports are restricted. If Canada restricts its imports from Brazil, Brazil is likely to retaliate and restrict its imports from Canada. This type of trade war developed in the 1930s as one country

---

[5]R. W. Crandell, "Import Quotas and the American Automobile Industry: The Costs of Protection," *Brookings Review*, Summer 1984, p. 8.

after another restricted imports in an effort to reduce domestic unemployment. Economists generally believe that these trade restrictions played an important role in increasing the length and severity of the Great Depression.

Even if society gains by moving toward freer trade, it also incurs real transitional costs. As we have seen, while society as a whole benefits, some individuals lose. Society could, but usually does not, compensate the losers. However, treaties to liberalize trade normally are phased in gradually over a number of years. The various GATT agreements, the FTA with United States, and the NAFTA all provided for a phased reduction in trade barriers. Phasing in tariff reductions over a number of years gives those in the affected industries time to adjust. Older workers can stay in the industry until they reach normal retirement age, and younger workers can retrain and relocate to better paying jobs.

Payments Problems

For a number of years, the United States has had an unfavourable balance on merchandise trade. At various times other countries have had similar problems. This situation can be difficult politically and often leads to demands for protectionist measures. The large American trade deficit with Japan has resulted in members of Congress pushing to restrict imports. This argument has also been applied to Canada, which generally has a favourable merchandise trade balance with the United States. The argument ignores the fact that overall payments must balance. While Canada exports more goods to the United States than we import from the United States, Americans earn more investment income in Canada than Canadians earn in the United States.

This argument also ignores international capital movements. Actually, as long as exchange rates are free to find their own value, foreign exchange rates should adjust to correct any long-term imbalance in trade and capital flows. If the quantity supplied of Canadian currency is greater than the amount demanded, then the value of the Canadian dollar will fall. If US$1.00 costs $1.33, then it will cost Canadians $1,330 to buy an American good that costs US$1,000 (1.33 × $1,000). However, if Canadians suddenly increase their demand for American goods, the supply of Canadian currency to pay for those goods will increase and the Canadian dollar will depreciate. Now assume that it costs $1.40 Canadian to buy US$1.00. The same US$1,000 American good will now cost Canadians $1,400. The higher price caused by the weaker Canadian dollar will reduce our imports of American goods and service and our willingness to invest in American assets. On the other hand, a depreciated Canadian dollar will make it more attractive for Americans to buy Canadian exports or invest in Canada. If it costs Canadians $1.33 to buy US$1.00, it costs Americans US$.75 to buy a Canadian dollar. It will cost an American only US$750

(1,000 ÷ 1.33) to import a $1,000 good from Canada. If the Canadian dollar depreciates so that it costs us $1.40 to buy US$1.00, then that $1,000 Canadian good will cost an American only US$714.29 ($1,000 ÷ 1.40). If the Canadian dollar depreciates, then Canadians will import less and invest less abroad and foreigners will buy more from Canada (our exports will increase) and purchase more assets from Canada. Naturally, if the American dollar depreciated, the opposite would happen.

Protection of Key Industries

It is often argued by protectionists that strategic industries must be protected for the security of a nation. Generally this argument has been used with respect to industries that produce goods that would be vital in the event of war—steel, energy, munitions, and staple foods. If a country is to be safe, it must be able to produce these goods domestically or run the risk it will be unable to defend itself. This argument has been extended to other industries. Canada has taken the view that certain cultural industries are important to our existence as an independent nation. To this end, Canada has enacted "Canadian content" rules for television and radio. Those who favour such restrictions argue that without content regulations Canadian broadcasters will buy much cheaper American programming and that we will slowly lose our identity. Certainly this contention is debatable, but at Canada's insistence both the FTA and the NAFTA exempt cultural industries from free trade.

Sometimes an industry will argue that it ought to be protected because it is an "infant industry." The case for an infant industry is based on the argument that a country may be able to develop a comparative advantage in the production of a good or service if it can get the new industry up and running. However, the industry may need protection while the industry is first starting for at least two reasons. The first is that workers and management need to gain experience. The only way to gain experience is to produce—learning by doing. However, until workers and management gain that experience, they may be less productive than the established firms in other countries and therefore unable to compete and gain the necessary experience without protection. The second reason that infant industries may need protection relates to many areas of heavy manufacturing. Many industries have attained significant economies of scale, but an infant domestic producer may lack the market to sell enough of its product to reach as low a cost as larger foreign firms have achieved. However, if it is protected until it grows large enough, the new producer can be an efficient competitor. Even in this case, some economists argue that such protection is not necessary because the domestic capital markets should be willing to finance the industry until it becomes efficient. The problem with the infant industry argument is that Canada (and many other countries) has some very old infants.

Those who favour free trade often cite the Auto Pact which came into effect in 1965 as proof of the gains that freer trade can bring. Clearly the Auto Pact brought a number of benefits to Canada. The price of cars fell while the wages and levels of employment in the Canadian auto industry rose.[6] These seemingly inconsistent outcomes were possible because of the improved efficiency in the industry. Prior to the Auto Pact, most cars manufactured in Canada were sold in Canada. Because of the relatively small Canadian market, producers were not able to realize economies of scale. Each plant produced several different models, but because of the small Canadian market, it could produce only a limited number of each type of vehicle at high cost. The Auto Pact allowed Canadian plants to specialize in a few models (or components) but produce them on a large scale because they now had unrestricted access to the American market. However, if it was not for the substantial tariff protection provided for Canadian car production, prior to the Auto Pact would there have been a Canadian industry to benefit from the Auto Pact?

Retaliation

A country might deem it appropriate to retaliate against the trading practice of another country or a foreign firm in a number of cases. If one country imposes a tariff on the exports of another country, the second country is likely to retaliate by imposing its own tariffs. For example, assume that the United States were to impose a tariff on Canadian beer. Canada might retaliate by imposing a tariff on American wine.

A second reason a country might wish to retaliate is that an exporting nation is paying subsidies to its producers. If a country pays subsidies to its exporters, it gives them a cost advantage in international markets. In recent years a number of countries have issued complaints about agricultural subsidies. The European Union (EU) pays particularly high agricultural subsidies. Both Canada and the United States claim to have been damaged by the EU subsidized exports. In this case the damage does not result from the EU increasing its exports to the United States and Canada, thereby displacing domestic production in local markets, but rather that American and Canadian farmers lose export markets to the cheaper EU product. If a satisfactory solution is not found, the United States and Canada may eventually retaliate, perhaps in the form of a countervailing duty.

Finally, most countries retaliate against dumping. *Dumping* is the practice of exporting goods at a very low price in order to sell off a surplus.

---

[6]A recent article indicates that cars are often substantially less expensive in Canada than in the United States. For example, a Chevy Lumina LS was $1,792 less in Canada than in the United States, a Ford Taurus LX wagon was $4,637 less, and a Chrysler Cirrus LXi was $2,094 less. See J. Cato,"Advantage: Canada Cars Often Cost Much Less Here Than in the U.S.," *Calgary Herald*, July 19, 1996, pp. E1 and E2.

Assume that a large foreign firm overproduces. It normally sells its product in its domestic market for the equivalent of $10. At that price the quantity demanded is 4 million so its total revenue would be $40 million. However, this year the firm has overproduced by 500,000 units. It could sell all the units in its domestic market by lowering its price to the equivalent of $9, for a total revenue of $40.5 million. However, it decides to sell the units in Canada at $6 each, even though that price is below its cost of production. The firm is willing to sell at this low price because it can then maintain a domestic price of $10. Only the units exported will be discounted. However, the firm will actually increase its profit. Its total revenue will now be $40 million from domestic sales plus $3 million from exports to Canada or a total of $43 million. Of course the Canadians who buy the discounted items are getting a good deal, however, the below cost price is unfair competition for Canadian producers. In a case like this the Canadian government could impose antidumping legislation to protect domestic producers.

FTA and NAFTA

The implementation of FTA and NAFTA was not nearly as significant as many supporters and opponents of these agreements would have us believe. Canada had been reducing trade barriers with the United States and the rest of the world for a number of years. Tariffs droped sharply in the later half of the 1930s, remained relatively constant during the 1940s and 1950s, and then began to decline steadily from the mid-1960s to the present. In a sense the FTA was simply part of an ongoing process of trade liberalization with our main trading partner, and NAFTA was just an extension of that policy to a third country. Still these agreements do represent important changes in Canadian commercial policy.

Many Canadians strongly opposed FTA and NAFTA. Much of the opposition was based on a lack of understanding of the issues. First, there was widespread fear of loss of jobs to larger and possibly more efficient American firms under FTA. Then there was the fear of the loss of jobs to low-wage workers in Mexico. As we have seen, neither of the fears was reasonable. Moreover, the postagreement events have failed to support these views. However, not all of the objections were based on ignorance. We have already seen that Canadians may have had a "good" reason to shun free trade in culture. Some Canadians believe that FTA and NAFTA in other ways as well threaten Canada's independence.

The most common barriers to trade are tariffs. It is relatively easy for countries to agree on tariff reductions or elimination. A tariff is easy to identify, and it is obvious if it is not removed. A subsidy may also be a barrier to trade. A subsidy reduces the cost of production and gives the seller an advantage. Unfortunately, it is not always clear what a subsidy is. For example, some Americans have claimed that Canadian social programs are unfair subsidies that give Canadian producers a cost advantage. Some American producers like to call almost every Canadian government payment a subsidy. This has led some Canadians to fear that FTA and NAFTA will lead to an end of programs such as Medicare and employment insurance. There have also been charges that Canadian agricultural programs and regional development programs are subsidies. In some sense Canadian Medicare *seems* like subsidy.

Canadian Medicare is considerably less costly than American medical care. It is mainly financed by the federal and provincial governments. American employers often, under collective agreements with their workers, provide private medical insurance, which represents a significant cost to American firms. Some Americans have claimed that Canadian Medicare is a subsidy. It is very unlikely that Americans will convince their own government that Canadian Medicare is really a subsidy, but their complaints are a cause for concern to some Canadians. This fear has been intensified by recent cuts to Medicare in a number of provinces and attempts by Alberta to create a private medical sector. There is some other evidence to support those who fear for Canadian Medicare. The 1995 debate in the American Congress demonstrated that some Americans strongly oppose a Canadian style health care system. Recent changes in Canadian drug patent laws were in part the result of multinational drug companies lobbying in Canada and American political pressure. American private insurers have indicated that they are willing to move into Canada should the the legal framework change to make it possible.

A second social program that has been alleged by some Americans to be a subsidy is employment insurance (EI). Canadian EI is more generous than the unemployment insurance plans that exist in most American states. In point of fact, EI is actually less generous than the program in New York State. Still EI has actually been raised as an issue in trade disputes. Of particular concern is the treatment of seasonal workers. The fact that EI is available to seasonal workers can be seen as a subsidy to those industries. Without EI those industries might have to pay higher wages to keep employees from leaving the industry. The reforms to EI announced in December 1995 should weaken the Americans claim. On the other hand, opponents of free trade may cite those changes as evidence that free trade has led to changes in Canadian social programs.

The fact that Canadian social programs are changing is quite likely more the result of fiscal problems in Canada than it is a result of free trade. Faced with large deficits, Alberta and Ontario have elected governments that are fiscally very conservative. Even Saskatchewan's NDP government has adopted far stricter budgets. While these changes are probably unrelated to free trade, some would argue that free trade has resulted in a more market-oriented approach to social programs.

In the 1960s and early 1970s, a number of Canadians became concerned with foreign ownership. The Canadian government passed legislation to control foreign takeovers. That legislation was already weakened before the FTA, but the agreement further reduced Canada's ability to limit foreign ownership and control. Many economists doubt that ownership is an important issue—companies maximize profits not political goals. However, foreign-owned companies are sometimes subject to foreign laws. In the past some Canadian subsidiaries have refused to trade with Cuba. In 1995 the American Congress passed legislation to increase the pressure on foreign subsidiaries of American firms and foreign-owned firms that do business with Cuba.

Similarly, free trade limited Canada's ability to control the export of its natural resources. Although we cannot be required to export Canadian water to a thirsty southern California, Canada does have less control over its resources as a result of the FTA and the NAFTA. (Of course the Americans also have less control over their resources.) Historically, Canada has developed economically by exporting staples such as fish, lumber, and grain in exchange for manufactured products. Although most of our exports are now manufactured goods, it is easy to see why many Canadians believe that free trade is just a way for foreigners to tap our vast natural resources.

Since the FTA went into effect, a number of trade disputes have erupted. One that is ongoing is the soft-wood lumber dispute. In spite of the fact that trade tribunals have repeatedly ruled in favour of Canada, the American lumber industry continues to claim that soft wood from British Columbia and Quebec is unfairly subsidized. The dispute highlights the problems with the definition of a subsidy. The government does not pay a subsidy to the Canadian producers. However, the fee that the Canadian producers pay the provincial government for the right to cut the trees is lower than the fee that American logging companies pay for the right to cut trees. As a result American lumber companies have complained that Canadian firms are subsidized. There have also been disputes over beer, beef, wheat, and a number of other goods and services. Some critics of free trade point to these disputes as evidence that the FTA and the NAFTA are not working. On the other hand, before the FTA a dispute-settling method did not exist. Canada has actually won most of the rulings under the FTA dispute mechanism.

Summary

The recessions of 1981–83 and 1990–91, along with the enactment of the FTA, NAFTA, and GATT, stepped up the controversy between protectionists and free traders. Protectionists argue that imports should be limited to reduce foreign competition with goods produced in Canada, to protect

Canadian jobs, and to encourage Canadian industries vital to national and economic welfare. Protectionists tend to see political and social goals as more important than economic goals while free traders emphasize economic goals. They maintain that the economic welfare of a country is enhanced by voluntary free exchange among countries.

A country's consumption possibilities are usually greater when it trades with other countries than when it does not. By concentrating on the production of goods in which it has a comparative advantage and trading for goods in which it has a comparative disadvantage, the population of the country will have a larger GDP to consume and/or invest.

International exchange markets arise from international transactions. A country's demands for foreign exchange are generated by imports of goods, investments in other countries, and any other transactions that result in payments made abroad. Supplies of foreign exchange are created by exports, foreign investments in the country, and by any other transactions that cause payments to be made to the country. Exchange rates are determined by the forces of demand for and supply of currencies used in international trade.

Checklist of Economic Concepts

Imports	Arbitrage
Exports	Current account transactions
Production possibilities curve	Capital account transactions
Consumption possibilities curve	Balance of trade (merchandise)
Comparative advantage	Balance of payments
Comparative disadvantage	Floating exchange rates
Absolute advantage	Gold standard
Terms of trade	Pegged exchange rates
Exchange rates	

Discussion Questions

1. Before the development of word processing, typewriter manufacturers hired highly skilled typists to give demonstrations to promote their products. These typists were highly paid for their demonstrations. Why did these typists usually hire a secretary, far less qualified, to type their letters?

2. Draw the production and consumption possibilities curves for the Alpha and Beta example given in this chapter.

3. Do you believe that Canada should use trade restrictions to protect Canadian television? Why or why not?

4. Why are trade restrictions not likely to be effective in lowering the unemployment rate in a country?

5. When might it be reasonable to protect a domestic industry from foreign competition?

6. Do you believe the NAFTA should be expanded to include other countries such as Chile and Brazil? Why or why not?

7. Assume the existence of only two countries, Canada and the United States, and only two goods, stereos and food. With 1,000 units of inputs, the United States can produce 100 units of food or two stereos. With 1,000 units of inputs, Canada can produce 900 units of food or 2.5 stereos. Determine the absolute and comparative advantage for food and of stereos.

Supplementary Reading

Bhagwati, J. "The Case for Free Trade." *Scientific American*, November 1993, pp. 42–49.

An excellent response to those who claim that trade agreements come at the expense of environmental standards.

Bowker, M. M. *On Guard for Thee*. Hull: Voyageur Publishing, 1988.

This book is now dated. It discusses Canada–United States trade from a Canadian nationalist viewpoint.

Carson, R. *Economic Issues Today*. 4th ed. New York: St. Martin's Press, 1987, chapter 15.

Provides conservative, liberal, and radical arguments on the question of free trade versus protectionism.

External Affairs and International Trade Canada, *NAFTA What's It All About?* Ottawa: Government of Canada, 1993.

Canadian government publication explaining NAFTA.

Shedd, M. S.; E. A. Wilman; and R. D. Burch, "An Economic Analysis of Canadian Content Regulations and a New Proposal." *Canadian Public Policy* 16, no. 1 (March 1990), pp. 60–72.

A discussion of Canadian television content regulations as a trade issue.

Smith, M. R. "A Sociological Appraisal of the Free Trade Agreement." *Canadian Public Policy*. 15, no. 1 (March 1989), pp. 57–71.

An alternative view of the FTA from a sociologist.

Stern, R. M., P. H. Trezise; and J. Whalley, ed. *Perspectives on US–Canadian Free Trade Agreement*. Ottawa: The Institute for Research on Public Policy 1987.

A somewhat dated selection of readings that cover a number of aspects of the FTA.

Watson, W. G. *North American Free Trade Area*. Kingston, ON: John Deutsch Institute for the Study of Economic Policy, 1991.

Another book of readings, this time covering the NAFTA.

Watson, W. G. "North American Free Trade: Lessons from Trade Data," *Canadian Public Policy* 18, no. 1 (March 1993), pp. 1–12.

A discussion of trade flows between Canada and Mexico, Canada and the United States, and Mexico and the United States. Provides an empirical background for understanding the likely effects of the NAFTA.

Young, R. A. "Political Scientists, Economists, and the Canada–US Free Trade Agreement," *Canadian Public Policy* 15, no. 1 (March 1989), pp. 49–56.

An alternative view of the FTA from a political scientist.

Chapter 13

Unemployment Issues
Why Do We Waste Our Labour Resources?

For a large and growing number of Canadians, unemployment poses a serious problem. In each decade since the 1940s, the average unemployment rate has ratcheted higher. . . . The economic and social costs of unemployment are extremely high. Unemployment represents a waste of economic resources and imposes considerable hardships on individuals and families.[1]

For most people fortunate to have sufficient skills and educational preparation, the challenge of finding a job should be manageable, although today's young graduates often have trouble landing a first job in their chosen field. . . . Increasingly, the hard core unemployed are those without the right skills and lacking flexibility, or opportunity, to acquire new skills.[2]

Our analysis of data does not indicate that Canada's economic problems have arisen because Canadian workers have demanded excessive wages. We find no evidence that the solution to the problems of increased economic inequality and poverty lies in decreasing the wages. . . . In thinking about public attitudes to Canada's economic problems, it is remarkable how successful the last fifteen years of bad economic performance have been in depressing the aspirations of many Canadians. . . .[3]

Some Effects of Unemployment

Both economic and social consequences are associated with unemployment. The economic effects are related to the impact of unemployment on the nation's production of goods and services, that is, the GDP. The social effects of unemployment are more difficult to pin down and measure, but they are just as real as the economic effects.

Effects on Gross Domestic Product

Idle human resources represent a waste, a loss of goods and services, and, therefore, a loss of real income. Unemployed resources could have contributed to society's well-being; the economic value of this lost contribution of goods and services is the economic cost of unemployment. The difference,

[1]S. Gera and K. McMullen, "Unemployment in Canada: Issues, Findings and Implications," in *Canadian Unemployment Lessons from the 1980s and Challenges for the 90s* (Ottawa: Economic Council of Canada, 1991), p. 1.

[2]Department of Finance, *Agenda: Jobs and Growth A New Framework for Economic Policy* (Ottawa: Government of Canada, October, 1994), p. 25.

[3]L. Osberg, F. Wien, and J. Grube, *Vanishing Jobs: Canada's Changing Workplaces* (Toronto: James Lorimer, 1995), p. xii.

then, between what may be produced at full employment and what is produced at less than full employment measures the economic cost of unemployment. In recent years some economists have estimated the opportunity cost of unemployment in Canada as approaching $57 billion per year worth of lost goods and services due to the idling of labour and other resources.[4]

Unemployment may affect not only current production of goods and services but also future production. During periods of unemployment, machines as well as workers are idle. Capital goods, plant and equipment, become obsolete and are not replaced. The productivity of labour and the overall ability of the economy to produce in the future are reduced during periods of unemployment.

Effects on Social Relations

Unemployment can threaten the mental health of individuals and the stability of households. Without income, or with a loss of income, household wants and needs are not fulfilled, and relationships among household members suffer. An unemployed person loses self-respect and influence among the employed, may be rejected by working companions, and loses pride and confidence. These effects are difficult to quantify but often have severe consequences on the individuals and households involved. Economic and social dependency and important ties among members of a household may be in jeopardy and may eventually be severed by prolonged unemployment.

The effects of prolonged unemployment may reach well beyond the individual and the household, threatening the viability of communities and regions and imposing increased costs on other members of society. Unemployed households in regions that experience prolonged high unemployment rates may find it necessary to relocate in search of work. This situation can lead to an exodus of population from high-unemployment regions, causing disruption to the social relations for relatives and friends of the households that must relocate. The loss of population can result in communities becoming too small to support a full range of social infrastructure, resulting in a general decay. In addition, the stress of prolonged unemployment and high rates of unemployment in specific regions is linked to increased rates of violence and health problems that result in the increased costs of combating illness and crime. All these effects are difficult to quantify, but in a modern market economy even a 1 percent rise in the unemployment rate is linked to significant increases in admissions to mental hospitals, domestic violence, property crimes, murder rates, the percentage of the population in prisons, higher rates of substance abuse, and a rise in the suicide rate.[5]

---

[4]Osberg. op. cit., p. 188.

[5]B. Bluestone and B. Harrison, *The Deindustrialization of America* (New York: Basic Books, 1982), chapter 3.

Although a few households may be economically and socially prepared for unemployment, it tends to strike households least capable of withstanding either its economic or its social effects. In recent Canadian experience, a minority of the labour force are increasingly bearing a disproportionately high burden of unemployment. A recent study revealed that while 20 percent of the labour force experienced some period of unemployment during a year, almost half the person-days spent unemployed were borne by 3.3 percent of the labour force whose individuals were out of work for at least six months each.[6] The incidence of longrun unemployment is also regionally biased, being much higher in the Atlantic region and Quebec than throughout the rest of Canada.

Measuring Unemployment

It would seem that unemployment could be easily defined. The first thought about unemployment may be that the unemployed are people without jobs. This definition may be true, but many people without jobs are not considered unemployed. What about a person who prefers leisure to work? Are individuals who have voluntarily retired considered unemployed? Is a full-time student attending a postsecondary institution included in the measurement of unemployment?

Our approach to unemployment in this section is, first, to give the official definition of the labour force, and, second, to elucidate the importance of the unemployment problem. The subsequent sections probe deeper into the sources of unemployment.

The Eligible Labour Force Population and the Labour Force

The **eligible labour force population** includes all individuals 15 years of age and older, excluding residents of the territories, residents of Indian reservations, and individuals who are institutionalized.

The **labour force** includes the portion of the eligible labour force population that is either employed for pay, actively seeking employment, or awaiting recall from a temporary layoff. It excludes those individuals in the eligible labour force population who are neither currently working nor seeking employment.

To understand how employment is defined and measured, we must first become familiar with two concepts: the eligible labour force population and the labour force. Canada defines its *eligible labour force population* as the sum of all individuals 15 years of age and older, excluding residents of the territories and Indian reservations and those who are institutionalized. Statistics Canada uses this measure to estimate the size and growth of the amount of labour that could be available to Canada under ideal conditions. Other nations use slightly different definitions, which sometimes make international comparisons difficult. By contrast, the *labour force* includes only that portion of the eligible labour force population that is presently employed or actively seeking employment. If an individual is part of the eligible labour force population but for some reason he or she is neither employed nor seeking employment, we do not count him or her as part of the labour force.

---

[6]M. Corak, "Canadian Unemployment in Retrospect," in Economic Council of Canada op. cit., pp. 65–77.

Several aspects of the definitions of the eligible labour force population and the labour force are important to understand. First, members of the eligible labour force population and the labour force must be at least 15 years of age. In Canada, children under the age of 15 are subject to child labour laws and are not legally available for most types of paid work outside the home. Second, individuals who are institutionalized are not considered part of either the eligible labour force population nor part of the labour force. Institutions include jails, prisons, mental hospitals, and long-term care facilities. Third, the labour force includes two identifiable groups from the eligible labour force population while excluding a third group. The labour force includes the members of the eligible labour force population who are employed and those who are unemployed but seeking employment. The employed members of the labour force consist of those who are working for pay. Unemployed members of the labour force include only those individuals legally eligible to work who are actively seeking employment and those waiting to be called back from a layoff. The labour force excludes those individuals in the eligible labour force population who are neither working nor actively seeking paid employment.

Someone who is actively seeking employment is undertaking the normal job search activities such as responding to want ads, submitting resumes and job applications, and taking interviews with prospective employers. If someone stops actively searching for a job, he or she no longer satisfies the definition of being part of the labour force. Individuals who give up searching for a job after a long period of unemployment are called *discouraged workers* and are not counted as part of the labour force even though they are still part of the eligible labour force population. Many economists believe that the failure to include discouraged workers in the official measures of the unemployment rate underestimates the amount of unemployment during downturns in the business cycle and in specific regions of the country.

The labour force in Canada is approaching 14.5 million members and constitutes over 60 percent of the eligible labour force population. The vast majority of the labour force is employed. Still for every year from 1982 to 1995, more than 1 million Canadians were counted as being unemployed. In some of these years the number of unemployed in Canada exceeded 1.5 million people—more than the population of any of the five smallest provinces. The percentage of the eligible labour force population that is in the labour force at any particular time is referred to as the *participation rate*. The participation rate varies over the course of the business cycle. It tends to increase when the economy is expanding and decrease when the economy enters a recession. In addition, the participation rate is affected by longrun demographic factors and changes to legal structures such as minimum wage laws and employment insurance benefits. Changes in the age distribution and cultural attitudes of society in the 1960s and 1970s increased the participation rate compared to previous periods.

The **participation rate** is the percentage of the eligible labour force population that is estimated to be in the labour force.

Participation rate

$$= \frac{\text{Labour force}}{\text{Eligible labour force population}} \times 100$$

The Official Unemployment Rate

The **unemployment rate** is the percentage of the labour force that is not working, but is actively engaged in seeking employment.

Unemployment rate

$$= \frac{\text{Unemployed}}{\text{Labour force}} \times 100$$

Although it is important to know how many people are eligible to work and how many of those are working or willing to work, an equally important question is, What is the portion of the labour force that is not working? The *unemployment rate* answers this question. The reliance on indicating the fraction of the labour force that is not working allows experts to focus on the efficiency of the economy. To say that 500,000 people are out of work gives no sense of the relative problem that having these people out of work creates for society. The idea that 500,000 people who want to work and are eligible to work but can not find work is obviously important but takes on a different context in a labour force of 14.5 million than it would in a labour force of 140 million. The unemployment rate is the percentage of the labour force that is not working, but is actively engaged in seeking employment.

The Natural Unemployment Rate

As the quotations at the beginning of the chapter indicate, there has been a rise in the unemployment rate over the years. The emergence of a persistent level of high unemployment in Canada and throughout the other industrialized countries has resulted in many analysts accepting that there is a difference between long term "core" unemployment and unemployment of a temporary nature. Many attempts have been made to create an estimate of the longrun unemployment rate to better study this emerging problem. Although economists use several different methods for measuring longrun unemployment, the most widely used measure is the *non-accelerating inflation rate of unemployment*, or NAIRU.[7]

The **non-accelerating inflation rate of unemployment** (NAIRU) or **natural unemployment rate** is the lowest rate of unemployment consistant with no acceleration of the inflation rate

The Non-Accelerating Inflation Rate of Unemployment (NAIRU).

For policy purposes, full employment is often defined as a situation in which the unemployment rate cannot be reduced further without accelerating inflation. In the 1950s and 1960s, the unemployment rate at which inflation began to accelerate was estimated at 2 to 3 percent. In the 1970s the estimate of this unemployment rate was increased to 6 percent, and in the early 1980s it was estimated to be in the 7 to 8 percent range.[8] The current consensus among economists is that the unemployment rate could be lowered to 7 or 7.5 percent without accelerating the inflation rate (although some estimates place it as high as 9 to 10 percent).

---

[7]There are several different ways of defining the natural unemployment rate, not all of which are based on NAIRU. For an excellent discussion of the different possible ways to measure the natural unemployment rate and the technical advantages and difficulties in using each, see A. Burns, "The Natural Rate of Unemployment: Canada and the Provinces," in Economic Council, op. cit., chapter 3.

[8]Economic Council of Canada, op. cit., chapters 3 and 4.

The basic reasons for defining full employment in reference to a particular measured unemployment rate are to account for the probability of increasing the inflation rate when the unemployment rate falls below a certain level, to account for structural changes in the labour force such as the increasing number of women and teenagers in the labour force, and to account for the changing industrial structure of Canada's economy in response to technological advances and changing demand.

The economy is considered to be operating at less than full employment if the unemployment rate exceeds NAIRU. If the unemployment rate exceeds this number, the difference is an estimate of the temporary type of unemployment that results from the fluctuations of the business cycle.

Who Are the Unemployed?

The unemployment rate hides the degree of unemployment confronted by certain persons in a given unemployment grouping. The groups that have a much higher poverty rate than the average are the same groups that have higher unemployment rates. In 1992, for example, when the overall unemployment rate was 11.3 percent, the rate for females between the ages of 15 and 24 was 15.2 percent, and for males between 15 and 24 it was 20.2 percent. By contrast, the unemployment rate for persons over the age of 25 was 9.9 percent. Females in this age group faced an unemployment rate of 9.3 percent, and males in this age group faced an unemployment rate of 10.4 percent.[9] The unemployment statistics from Statistics Canada do not highlight another disturbing trend in Canada's unemployment. While the disparities of unemployment rates remained roughly stable across genders and across age groups, there has been an increase in the amount of unemployment accounted for by those who are unemployed for six months or more. Some economists believe that the increase in the gap between temporary or shortrun unemployment and longrun unemployment reflects a growing trend in structural unemployment. The gap increases the burden of unemployment on a relatively small group of individuals who are geographically concentrated in the Atlantic provinces and Quebec.[10] Later in the chapter we will explore the differences between these two types of unemployment and the types of policies used to combat them.

Types of Unemployment

The meaning of unemployment may be elucidated further by distinguishing between different types of unemployment. Three major types are frictional, cyclical, and structural unemployment. As we discuss these three

---

[9]Statistics Canada, CANSIM, series D31252, D31253, D31254, and D41983.

[10]Miles Corak, op. cit., p. 71.

types of unemployment, we need to distinguish between the first two, which together make up shortrun unemployment, and the third, which is more closely linked to longrun unemployment, for two reasons. Shortrun unemployment is generally better understood and usually of less concern to policymakers than is longrun unemployment. Although frictional and cyclical unemployment can create severe problems for society, they tend to be spread across the social groups, are short term, and, at least since the 1930s, economists have created theories with effective policy instruments for combating shortrun unemployment. By contrast, longrun or natural unemployment has increasingly become concentrated in specific regions, industries, and demographic groups. Only recently have economists begun to develop strategies for alleviating longrun unemployment, and the relative effectiveness of the alternative emerging policy strategies is still being debated.

Frictional unemployment is transitional and is often in the form of people changing jobs and searching for new jobs.

Frictional Unemployment. *Frictional unemployment* is transitional or shortrun in nature. It may occur even in a healthy economy because people are changing jobs or searching for new jobs. People may be looking for new jobs for many reasons because the matching of job openings and job seekers does not always take place smoothly. Some frictional unemployment occurs if an employer fires an employee. The former employee will commence a search for a new position, often a job in the same geographic area that requires the worker's present skills. Alternatively, workers may resign from their present employment in order to increase the time they can devote to searching for positions that are either more pleasant or more financially rewarding in the same area. Thus workers, whether they quit or were fired, who are searching for jobs that require their present skills, in the region in which they were previously employed, and who are thought to have a good chance of finding such a job are referred to as frictionally unemployed.

The important thing about frictional unemployment is that it does not last very long. Frictional unemployment may exist at all times in the economy, but for any one person or family it is transitional. In addition, at least some of the frictional unemployment involves workers voluntarily leaving a job to find a better one. For these reasons, frictional unemployment is not considered a significant economic problem, and it can be reduced by improvements in the flow of information concerning job openings to the unemployed and labour skill availability to employers.

Cyclical unemployment is unemployment caused by a contraction in aggregate demand or total spending in the economy. The cyclical unemployment rate is often estimated as the unemployment rate minus NAIRU.

Cyclical Unemployment. Unemployment caused by economic fluctuations over the business cycle is called *cyclical unemployment*. Cyclical unemployment is caused by reductions in aggregate or total demand for goods and services in the economy overall. A decline in aggregate demand in the economy reduces total production and causes general unemployment throughout the economic system. Cyclical unemployment is usually the culprit when the unemployment rate goes above

NAIRU. If the unemployment rate is say 11 percent, and if NAIRU is 7.5 percent, we would say that the cyclical unemployment rate is 3.5 percent (11 percent minus 7.5 percent = 3.5 percent). A cautionary note: Although economists may talk about a natural unemployment rate of 7.5 percent on a national level, it is very important to realize that in Canada the geographic dispersion of the population and the different types of industrial structure from one region to another mean that the natural unemployment rate varies across the country with estimates as low as 6 percent in Ontario and a high of just over 13 percent in the Atlantic region.

Structural unemployment is unemployment that is caused by fundamental changes in demand for certain kinds of labour relative to supply. It is often caused by technological changes, changes in consumers' tastes and preferences, and changes to the structural mix of industrial production.

Structural Unemployment. *Structural unemployment* is usually longrun in nature. Structural unemployment results from changes in demand relative to supply for specific types of labour in whole industries and large regions of the country. The possible causes of prolonged low demand for labour in a specific industry or region are unlimited, but of particular importance are changes to the pattern of demand, technological progress, reduced mobility of factors of production between industries or geographically, and a loss of competitive productivity of resources in one region when compared to the resources of other countries. How these factors change the amount of structural unemployment will be explored later in the chapter.

Unemployment Rates over Time. Figure 13–1 shows the natural and measured unemployment rates in Canada from 1960 to 1994. Measured unemployment rates follow the ups and downs in the economy and are generally above the estimated natural unemployment rate officially targeted for policy purposes as full employment. The highest measured unemployment rate in the 1960s was in 1961 when the rate was 7.2 percent during the 1960–61 recession. After 1961 the unemployment rate declined steadily as the economy expanded, reaching a low rate of 3.4 percent in 1966. Unemployment increased after 1966, rising through the end of the decade to 4.4 percent by 1969. Over the decade of the 1960s, the average measured unemployment rate was 5 percent—only slightly higher than the estimated NAIRU for the decade. The measured unemployment rate rose during the early years of the 1970s, reaching 6.2 percent in 1972. It declined slightly in 1974 before beginning a rise to 8.3 percent by 1978. At the end of the decade, the measured unemployment rate declined to 7.4 percent in 1979. In comparison with the 1960s, the 1970s are characterized by generally higher unemployment rates. The average measured unemployment rate for the 1970s was 6.7 percent—above NAIRU for the period.

The 1980s began with measured unemployment at 7.5 percent. Then the recession of 1981 sent the measured unemployment rate soaring upward to peak at 11.8 percent in 1983, the highest since the Great Depression of the 1930s. Job opportunities began to improve in 1984 as the economy embarked on a rapid expansion. The result was impressive in terms of

Figure 13–1   **Comparison of the estimated natural unemployment rate 1963–86 and the measured unemployment rate**

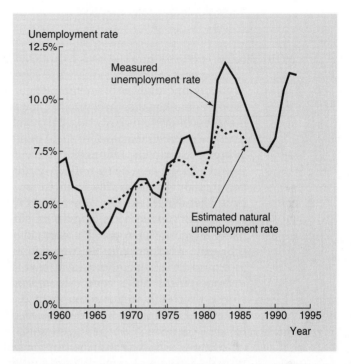

Source: For measured unemployment rates, Statistics Canada, CANSIM, series D31252, D31253, and D31254. For estimated natural unemployment rates, G. Surendra, *Canadian Unemployment Lessons from the 1980s and Challenges for the 90s* (Economic Council of Canada, 1991), p. 42.

growth in gross domestic product and stock market activity, but did not produce the expected decrease in the unemployment rate.

To emphasize the failure of the Canadian economy to create sufficient jobs for its growing labour force, it is interesting to compare the Canadian and American experiences. In the United States the unemployment rate fell from 10 to 5.6 percent between 1982 and 1990. In Canada the unemployment rate decreased from 11.8 percent to 7.5 percent between 1983 and 1989. Then the unemployment rate rose again as real GDP growth slowed and then declined by .2 percent in 1990 and 1.7 percent as the economy entered a recession.

The economy began to expand at the end of 1991, but the recovery was weak. The real GDP grew at only .7 percent in 1992. As a result, the unemployment rate continued to rise from 10.3 to 11.3 percent from 1991 to 1992, as shown in Figure 13–1. In fact, unlike the experience in the earlier recessions, the unemployment rate did not decrease until well into 1993 when the expansion of real GDP had been underway for more than a year.[11] This unique feature of the 1990–92 recession caused some people to name it "the jobless recovery."

Causes of Unemployment in a Market Economy

The economic analysis of unemployment originates with an application of supply and demand theory to the labour market. Unemployment in a market economy suggests that the quantity of labour supplied is greater than the quantity demanded. As in other markets that we have analyzed in previous chapters, failure of a market to reach equilibrium requires that the price of the item being traded—in this case the wage rate for labour—becomes stuck at some level other than equilibrium. Unemployment occurs when at the existing wage rate the number of workers willing and able to work exceeds the number of jobs. The theory of supply and demand suggests three possible behaviours that would reduce the unemployment. The first is to let competitive forces reduce the wage rate, in other words, rely on automatic market forces to provide a solution to the unemployment. The second is to expand demand so that the number of workers currently in the labour force at the existing wage can find jobs at that wage. The third is to reduce the supply of labour so that fewer workers are looking for the jobs that currently exist at the present wage rate.

Figure 13–2 illustrates how supply and demand theory can be used to provide a frame of reference for studying unemployment in a market economy. $D_{la}D_{la}$ and $S_{la}S_{la}$ are the demand and supply curves for labour. The index of the average wage rate across society is w_1. The amount of labour demanded at this wage rate is nd_1, and the amount supplied is ns_1. The difference between ns_1 and nd_1 is the unemployment at the wage rate of w_1. Unemployment will persist as long as the demand curve for labour does not shift to the right, the supply of labour does not shift left, or the wage rate does not decrease.

In a purely competitive situation, you might expect that the wage rate would be forced down to w_e and unemployment would disappear. Our discussion so far suggests that decreased wages might lead to increased employment, but several complications develop as we try to apply one isolated case where wages are above the equilibrium level in one purely competitive situation to unemployment across a whole market economy. First, there is good reason to believe that decreases in wages may not lead to reduced unemployment for an economy as a whole. If wages decrease in one industry or if one worker is willing to work for a lower wage, then supply and demand analysis may help explain why one

---

[11]Statistics Canada, *Canadian Economic Observer, Historical Supplement* (Ottawa: 1993–1994).

Figure 13–2   **Unemployment in a competitive market**

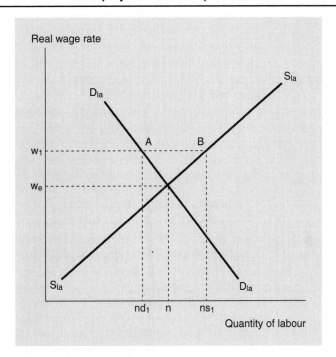

Demand curve for labour = $D_{la}D_{la}$.
Supply curve for labour = $S_{la}S_{la}$.
Amount of labour demanded at $w_1 = nd_1$.
Amount of labour supplied at $w_1 = ns_1$.
Unemployment = $ns_1 - nd_1$.

firm will increase employment or why a particular worker who will accept the lowest wage might get a job. Why then do falling wages not necessarily lead to increased employment for the economy as a whole? Part of the answer is that expecting falling wages to cure unemployment for the whole economy is an example of the fallacy of composition.

The **fallacy of composition** is the error in logic that occurs when we assume that because something is true for an individual, it is also true for the group to which the individual belongs.

The Fallacy of Composition. The *fallacy of composition* is the error in logic that occurs when we assume that because something is true for an individual, it is also true for the group to which the individual belongs. For the economy as a whole, workers in one industry are the consumers in other industries. If, on average, wages decrease throughout the economy, most workers in most industries will be paid lower wages and their incomes will be falling. As the incomes of the majority of the population decrease, the demands for most goods and services also decrease. The impact of reduced demand for most goods and services leads to firms reducing their production levels and consequently reducing the number of workers they are willing to employ. The reduced demand for goods and services shifts the demand for labour to the left and puts further downward pressure on wages and employment levels. Thus decreases in the average level of wages are likely to decrease the total spending levels and the total market for goods and services, which actually reduces employment opportunities.

Wage Rigidity. Experts studying unemployment and its cures have long observed that wages may not be flexible across the economy as a whole.[12] Most economists accept that while decreasing wages in a local market might help increase employment in that market, decreasing wage levels on average throughout the whole economy does not provide a solution to the unemployment problem.

Since the cure for unemployment on an economywide basis is not likely to be found through decreases in the average wage rate, we must look to other ways to reduce unemployment. To assist in this we shall accept the view that the wage rate is inflexible, that is wages, on average will not decrease. The reasons that wages are not completely flexible in the downward direction is not the focus of our investigation, but is used to prevent us from looking for a simplistic cure to society's chronic problem of high unemployment.[13] If we assume that wages will not fall when the supply of labour exceeds the demand for labour, the use of supply and demand analysis suggests at least two other ways unemployment could be reduced. If the wage rate remains at w_1, then the elimination of unemployment requires either a shift to the right in the position of $D_{la}D_{la}$ in Figure 13–2 or a shift to the left in the position of $S_{la}S_{la}$—or both. Some of the possible cures for Canada's unemployment problems discussed later in the chapter will result from attempts to use the power of the government to shift the demand curve for labour to the right.

By contrast, few economists or policy analysts would advocate shifting the supply curve of labour to the left as a cure for unemployment. Although it is technically possible to reduce unemployment by reducing labour supply, there is a complication that makes it generally unacceptable as a solution. Assuming that the labour market eventually does move to equilibrium, a shift left in the supply curve for labour would obviously lead to a reduction in the number of people employed. If the labour supply curve is shifted far enough to the left, then equilibrium could be es-

---

[12]The inflexibility of wages at least in the downward direction was first popularized as a theoretical tool by the British economist John Maynard Keynes in *The General Theory of Employment, Interest, and Money*, published during the Great Depression of the 1930s. Keynes also explored both the problems of inflexible wages and the possibility that falling wages may increase unemployment.

[13]Students interested in the study of why wages are inflexible in modern capitalist economies can find many good advanced works in the area. See particularly, G. Mankiw and D. Romer, *New Keynesian Economics* (Cambridge, MA: MIT Press, 1991), vol. 1 section II and vol. 2 section V.

tablished with a wage at w_1. While unemployment would be eliminated, such a shift would also lead to lower employment and production than if demand for labour were expanded. Thus, assuming the same population, the standard of living would decline as fewer people produced fewer goods and services for the same population.

The special characteristics of the labour force raise the need to explore why there may be more people looking for work than there are jobs available at the existing wage rate. In addition, the issues as to why this situation might occur in the shortrun and the likely pressures resulting from it must be considered separately from the study of why it might occur in the longrun.

Shortrun Unemployment

In the shortrun, unemployment is associated with the levels of frictional unemployment and cyclical unemployment. Most experts who have studied Canadian unemployment rates consider frictional unemployment to be a minor problem. The normal activities of people changing jobs, of new entrants to the labour market, and of workers leaving the labour force in a market economy imply that there will always be some frictional unemployment. In addition, a poorly managed firm will have low profits and will have to reduce production levels, releasing workers who will be out of work until they become reemployed in more financially successful enterprises. As the quotations at the beginning of the chapter indicated, workers moving from job to job under normal conditions or new workers entering the labour force for the first time who are temporarily unemployed are not usually regarded as a serious problem. By contrast, an unemployment rate that starts to increase indicates that something other than normal frictional unemployment may be developing. Because rises in unemployment imply some broader behaviour in the economy, most economists studying shortrun unemployment concentrate on investigating the behaviour of cyclical unemployment.

What Causes People to Lose Their Jobs?

To understand why people lose their jobs, we need to understand how jobs are created. In Chapter 2 we explained how equilibrium prices and quantities demanded for individual commodities, such as wheat, clothing, ice cream, and most other commodities are determined under competitive conditions. Although the demand and supply model for individual markets is of little use in explaining the behaviour of demand for the economy as a whole, there is a model that uses some of the features of demand and supply analysis that helps. We now change our focus from demand and supply curves for individual products to a demand and supply curve representing large aggregates—totals—for the economy. We will discuss the factors that might cause shifts in aggregate demand or aggregate supply and why those shifts can affect the level of unemployment.

Aggregate Demand

Aggregate demand is a schedule showing real output demanded at each general price level.

Aggregate demand is a schedule showing total output demanded by all sectors of the economy at different general price levels. Since we are concerned with the prices of all goods and services, we must use an index of the general price level—the GDP deflator, which was described in Chapter 1 and which we will discuss again in Chapter 14—as the indicator of the price of all goods and services. Similarly, we are measuring the quantities of all goods and services demanded by households, businesses, governments, and customers in foreign countries. Aggregate demand is an aggregation of things as diverse as clothes, petroleum reservoir accounting, ambulance service, and lumber exports. The practical way to measure this real output of the economy is to use something similar to real GDP, which was discussed in Chapter 1. Real GDP was the measure of the goods and services produced in the economy in one year. What we wish to measure here is not what the economy produced, but instead what the economy wanted to purchase in terms of final goods and services in one year.

Aggregate demand is illustrated in Figure 13–3. At the price level P_1, 200 units of goods and services are demanded, at the price level P, output demanded is 400 units, and so on. The output demanded at any general level of prices is the sum of the output of goods and services purchased by *consumers*, such as shoes and steaks; the output purchased by *firms*, such as new plants and equipment; the output purchased by *government*, such as highways and educational services; and *net exports*, that is, the difference between foreign purchases of goods and services produced in our country (exports) and Canadian purchases of goods and services produced by foreign countries (imports). A change in the output demanded at a given price level by these groups—consumers, investors, government, and foreign customers—will change aggregate demand. For example, if consumers begin to buy greater quantities of consumer goods at any specific price level than they did previously, aggregate demand will increase—shift to the right, indicating that greater output is demanded at each price level.

Aggregate demand equals consumption (C) plus investment (I) plus government expenditure on goods and services (G) plus net exports (X_n).[14] Households do not have the same aspirations as businesses or governments. Each of these major components of aggregate demand—consumption, investment, government spending, and net exports—behaves differently and is affected by many different determinants, which greatly complicates the detailed study of aggregate demand. It is not our intention to study each of the components of aggregate demand in depth. Although the study of aggregate demand and its impact on the economy is interesting, it is properly

---

[14]Net exports are equal to purchases of Canadian-made goods and services minus Canadian purchases of goods and service purchased from foreign countries.

Figure 13–3   **Aggregate demand**

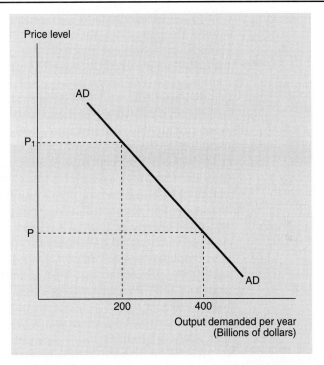

AD is an aggregate demand schedule that shows the real output demanded by households, businesses, governments, and foreign customers at different general price levels. For example, at price level P_1, $200 billion worth of goods and services are demanded per time period. At P, $400 billion worth of goods and services are demanded per time period.

the subject of a macroeconomic theory course and requires more detail and scope than we need at this point to gain an understanding of how the model can be used in analyzing unemployment.[15] For the purpose of understanding unemployment, we need to look only for the overall behaviour of aggregate demand considered by economists to be significant in affecting unemployment. Thus, even though the behaviour of consumption, investment, government spending, or net exports may be interesting or some determinant may be important in affecting their behaviour, unless that determinant is particularly relevant to causing unemployment, we will exclude it from discussion.

---

[15]Students wishing a complete detailed discussion of the full macroeconomic model of aggregate expenditure, aggregate demand, and aggregate supply can see C. M. Fellows, G. L. Flanagan, S. Shedd, and R. N. Waud, *Economics in a Canadian Setting* (New York: HarperCollins College Publishers, 1993), chapters 21–24.

Why Is Aggregate Quantity Demanded Inversely Affected by the Price Level?

Figure 13–3 indicates that as the general level of prices increases in Canada, other things being constant, the aggregate quantity demanded for Canadian products decreases. This inverse relationship between Canadian prices and the aggregate quantity demanded for goods and services is not simply "demand writ large"—it does not result from the same behaviour that caused the demand for an individual product to be downward sloping that was described in Chapter 2. As the general price level increases, it does not affect all markets or all individuals in the same way. An increase in the general price level causes three things to happen. The first, known as the *Pigou effect* is the inverse relationship between the general price level and consumption resulting from the change in the real purchasing power of money and Canadian dollar assets held by the public. When the general price level increases, those who have money and assets denoted in Canadian dollars experience a decrease in the real purchasing power of those assets. The decrease in their purchasing power will tend to make these people decrease their quantity demanded for Canadian products, and thus the aggregate quantity demanded decreases. Conversely, these people would experience an increase in real wealth whenever the general price level decreases and would increase the quantity demanded for Canadian products.

The Pigou effect is the inverse relationship between the general price level and consumption resulting from the change in the real purchasing power of wealth—money and Canadian dollar assets—when the general price level changes.

The second reason for the inverse relationship between the general price level and aggregate demand is usually referred to as the *Keynes effect*. If the general price level increases, the demand for money to pay the rising prices increases. The increase in the demand for money working through the financial markets tends to cause an increase in interest rates which results in decreases in investment and the portion of consumption spending that was financed with borrowed funds. The Keynes effect explains how a rise in the price level, working through the financial markets, causes a decrease in investment and other interest-sensitive expenditures, and results in a decrease in the aggregate quantity of goods and services demanded.

The Keynes effect is the inverse relationship between the general price level and the level of investment expenditure and other interest-rate-sensitive components of aggregate demand. An increase in the price level causes the demand for money to increase, which tends to increase interest rates and as a result causes decreases in all components of aggregate demand that are financed with credit.

The net foreign purchase effect is the inverse relationship between the general price level and net exports. As the general price level in Canada increases, other things being constant, Canadian products appear more expensive relative to foreign-made products and consequently the demand for net exports decreases.

The third explanation for the inverse behaviour of the aggregate quantity demanded curve is referred to as the *net foreign purchase effect*. Assume the general level of prices increases in Canada, but there is no change in the exchange rate or the level of prices in the countries with which we trade. As Canadian prices increase, Canadian goods will become more expensive relative to foreign-made goods and services. According to the net foreign purchase effect, as Canadian prices increase, Canadian exports decrease and Canadians purchase more foreign-made goods and services—net exports decrease—causing the aggregate quantity demanded to behave inversely to changes in the general level of prices in Canada.

The three effects always cause the aggregate quantity demanded to behave inversely to changes in the general price level. A rise in the general level of prices causes the Pigou effect, the Keynes effect, and the net foreign purchase effect to decrease separate components of aggregate demand, leading to an overall decrease in the aggregate quantity demanded for Canadian output. Conversely, a decrease in the general price level would cause all three effects to increase the aggregate quantity demanded for Canadian output.

Changes in the aggregate quantity demanded caused by changes in the general price level are shown as movements along the aggregate demand curve. In Figure 13–3 a rise in the general price level from P to P_1 resulted in a decrease in aggregate quantity demanded along the aggregate demand curve, shown by a move left along the line. Conversely, a decrease in the price level would cause a movement to the right along the curve as consumption, investment, and net exports increased because of the beneficial effects of the Pigou effect, the Keynes effect, and the net foreign purchase effect.

Does Aggregate Demand Shift—and How Far?

Although changes in the general level of prices in Canada will affect aggregate quantity demanded, by no means is the general price level the only determinant of aggregate demand. Any change in consumption, investment, government spending, or net exports that can not be attributed to a change in the general price level in Canada means that aggregate demand has changed at the same price level. If, for example, consumption increased because consumers became more optimistic about the future, aggregate demand would increase—the entire aggregate demand curve would shift to the right. Similarly, if the business community believed that future expected profits were likely to increase and increased investment, there would be an increase in aggregate demand. Aggregate demand would also increase if the government increased its expenditure on highway construction or if foreigners increased their purchases of Canadian-made goods. In short, anything that increased the size of the market at the same general level of prices would shift the aggregate demand curve to the right. The possible causes of such a change are many and varied, but history tells us that some causes are more likely to occur (and more likely to affect employment) than are some others. Among the more likely sources of a shift to the right in the aggregate demand are decreases in interest rates, changes in expectations that bring about increased consumer spending or investment by business, political decisions to expand the expenditure of government, and in Canada's case, increased export demand.

One of the most important features of aggregate demand analysis is the *multiplier effect*. John Maynard Keynes developed the theory of the multiplier in the 1930s.[16] Since that time the multiplier has been a central

---

[16]J. M. Keynes, *The General Theory of Employment, Interest, and Money* (New York: MacMillan, 1936).

The **marginal propensity to expend, (mpe)** is the ratio of extra expenditure on goods and services to the increase in current income that caused the increase in expenditure. On average, as real income rises by $1, it causes an increase in planned expenditure by the economy (households, businesses, and governments) that is less than one and greater than zero.

Marginal propensity to expend (MPE) =

Change in expenditure

Change in current income

$$MPE = \frac{\Delta C + \Delta I + \Delta G + \Delta X_n}{\Delta Y}$$

defining feature of all economic discussions of the behaviour of aggregate demand and is fundamental to the study of unemployment. According to Keynes's theory, consumption is the largest and most stable portion of aggregate demand. In addition, the most important determinant of consumption is the current level of real income. It follows that current real income is very important in predicting the behaviour of aggregate demand. As income increases, households spend more on consumption, and possibly some other elements in aggregate demand also increase in a predictable way. The relationship between current income and the economy's aggregate planned spending is direct and less than proportional. Thus a $1 increase in the total income of the economy—GDP—will bring about an increase in spending on goods and services of less than $1. The extra planned spending resulting from a $1 increase in income is known as the *marginal propensity to expend* (mpe). By knowing the marginal propensity to expend, we can predict by how much the economy's total planned spending will increase if income increases by a certain amount. Assume, for example, that the marginal propensity to expend is .6. Then an increase of income of $1 billion would cause the total of the planned purchases to increase by $600 million. Because we are focusing only on the marginal propensity to expend and not on the individual behaviour of households, businesses, governments, and foreign customers, we cannot predict what portion of the $600 million in spending would be for extra consumer spending and what portion would be on investment or government spending or changes in net exports. However, not knowing the exact distribution of the increased expenditure is not a major problem for our analysis of unemployment. In our example, if income increases by $1 billion, then it sets off a respending of $600 million. However, multiplier theory explains why the respending does not end here—at $600 million. Since the increased expenditure of $600 million creates an expanding market for goods and services, it causes producers in the business sector to expand production to sell to the increased market. As firms expand production to meet this increased market, they employ more resources. This expansion of employment causes a decrease in unemployment and also an increase in the incomes of resources suppliers whose labour or capital is now being used to produce for the expanding markets. Because the resource owners now have increased income, they in turn will increase their spending—the marginal propensity to expend comes into play again. In this example, as the incomes of the resource suppliers increase by $600 million, they will increase planned expenditure by the marginal propensity to expend times their increase in income—(mpe $\times$ ΔY). In effect, one person's expenditure becomes another person's income, and so as spending increases, it causes income to increase, which causes a portion of the income to get respent, forming another round of spending and repeating the cycle of spending. This respending behaviour is known as the multiplier effect.

In our example, the initial increase in income of $1 billion has now become $1.96 billion—the initial $1 billion plus the first round of respending $0.6 billion plus the second round of respending $0.36 billion. Notice that the additions to total demand decrease as each round of respending is added because the marginal propensity to expend is less than one. Therefore, only a portion of each increase in income is added to the spending stream.

The *multiplier* effect means that a $1 increase in expenditure by households, investors, governments, or foreign customers will set off a predictable respending pattern that causes aggregate demand to increase by more than $1. The mechanics of the multiplier and its mathematical derivation are more correctly the focus of a text on macroeconomic theory than a feature of an economic issues book, so we will not develop the complete mathematics of the model here.[17] For our purpose in studying unemployment, we need only to gain enough understanding of the implications of the role the multiplier can play in affecting employment. For technical reasons, the multiplier effect takes place only if an initial change in planned expenditure was caused by a change in a determinant of aggregate demand other than the general price level or current income—an exogenously caused change in aggregate demand.

The **multiplier (k),** is the number by which any exogenously caused increase in the economy's expenditure on final goods and services must be multiplied in order to estimate the resulting increase in aggregate demand. The multiplier also works in reverse; any exogenously caused decrease in planned spending on final goods and services will cause multiple decrease in aggregate demand. The multiplier is usually greater than one for economics with relatively stable price levels and a low risk of inflation.

$$k = \frac{1}{1 - mpe}$$

High Interest Rates as a Cause of Weak Aggregate Demand. Do high interest rates have an effect on aggregate demand and unemployment? Earlier in the chapter we pointed out that part of the key to understanding unemployment lay in understanding why aggregate demand might be insufficient to create a large enough market for goods and services to employ all the labour available. Because of the diverse nature of the components of aggregate demand, many factors could affect the total level of planned expenditure, but one is particularly important. Consumer spending on durables, such things as cars and household appliances, is often financed through credit with borrowed funds. Businesses usually finance the major portion of their purchases of plants and equipment using borrowed funds. As we will see in Chapter 15, the government has relied heavily on borrowed money to support a large portion of its expenditures since the 1970s. A common feature that affects households, businesses, and governments when they use borrowed funds to pay for part of their expenditure is the interest rate—the cost of paying for the credit. A rise in the interest rate makes the cost of carrying the debts incurred from financing the purchase of a new car or a new factory higher and tends to discourage some portion of expenditure. Thus a rise in the interest rate, other things constant, could cause aggregate

---

[17]For a detailed development of the multiplier and a discussion of the size of the multiplier under fixed-price and flexible-price assumptions, see C. M. Fellows, G. L. Flanagan, S. Shedd, and R. N. Waud, op. cit., p. 403.

demand to decrease. Consequently, increasing interest rates may help explain why aggregate demand may be weak and why unemployment may be a problem.

Aggregate demand does not operate in isolation in its effect on employment and unemployment. It interacts with the economy's aggregate supply behaviour—the business community's willingness and ability to produce final goods and services. Nevertheless, some implications of how aggregate demand theory causes unemployment are worth highlighting here. Any exogenously caused decrease in aggregate demand can create a decrease in the size of the total market for goods and services and may lead to a reduction in employment opportunities. In addition, part of any cure for short term unemployment can be found by policies aimed at shifting aggregate demand to the right. Finally, assuming that wages are not flexible in the downward direction, in an economy with a growing labour force, the unemployment rate will increase unless the aggregate demand curve shifts to the right fast enough to create jobs for the expanding labour force. Consequently, part of a possible solution to unemployment in an economy with a growing labour force involves developing government policies that encourage the aggregate demand to increase—to shift to the right. Later in this chapter and in Chapter 14, we will explore fiscal policy and monetary policy—two areas of public policy that can be used to influence aggregate demand. For now we will leave the discussion of aggregate demand by pointing out that if public policy can lead to the banking system lowering interest rates, the reduced cost of credit could help reduce unemployment. Alternatively, if some government action such as reductions in taxes or increases in government spending or subsidies were introduced, the resulting increases in expenditure could shift the aggregate demand curve to the right.

Aggregate Supply

Aggregate supply is a schedule showing the real output supplied by the business sector at different general price levels.

Aggregate supply is a schedule showing the output that the business sector will supply at each different general price level. Aggregate Supply is the real gross domestic product that the business sector is willing and able to produce at each price level and is shown in Figure 13–4. It is generally shown as an upward sloping curve, reflecting two distinct behaviours. First, as discussed in greater detail in Chapter 9, as any individual firm increases output in the shortrun, it faces increasing marginal costs. In the shortrun, competitive firms can only remain profitable while expanding production by increasing their prices to cover rising marginal costs. At the economywide level if marginal costs increase as output increases then it is profitable for the business sector to produce higher levels of output only if

Figure 13–4   **Aggregate supply**

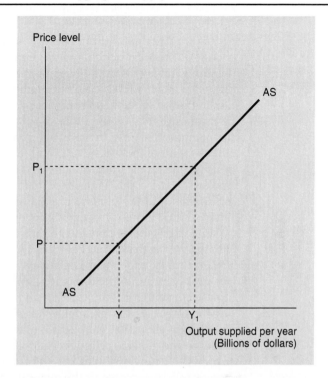

Aggregate supply shows the total output supplied by the business community at different general price levels. Given aggregate supply *ASAS*, at the price level *P* output supplied is *Y*, and at price level *P₁* the aggregate quantity supplied increases to *Y₁*.

the general price level increases. Second, any individual firm offering goods and services for sale must judge how much to offer for sale by making an educated guess about the relationship between the expected cost per unit of producing the product and the price it expects to receive for the product at the time of sale. In other words, the firm must use what economists refer to as *rational expectations* to judge in advance whether or not it is profitable to offer more of a good for sale. If most firms believe that an increase in the price of their product will be accompanied by a less than proportional rise in the cost of producing the good, they will increase their output in response to a price increase. If the majority of firms behave this way, output will increase if the deflator increases—the economy will have an upward sloping aggregate supply curve. In the short-run for most economies as the general price level increases, the increase in price will cause an increase in the level of production and consequently a need for more resources to be employed in producing the increased output. The aggregate supply behaviour includes a direct relationship between the general price level and the level of real output.[18]

The determinants of aggregate supply include some of the determinants of individual supply curves, but there are some important differences. All firms do not charge the same price or sell the same product in the same market. An understanding of the relationship between the change in a general level of prices—the deflator—and the level of production of the entire business community requires an exploration of the business community's expectations of inflation. It is important to realize that the aggregate supply curve is not simply the sum of individual supply curves for all of the individual firms in each market. Under normal conditions when there is unemployment, the aggregate supply curve will slope upward to the right. This shape reflects the direct relationship between production and the general price level, although the slope may be relatively shallow or fairly steep in a particular economy.

An aggregate supply curve that is relatively shallow, sloping up to the right only gently, indicates that a fairly small change in the general level of prices will cause a relatively large change in real output by the business community—an elastic relationship. Alternatively, an aggregate supply curve that is fairly steep as it rises to the right indicates that very large changes in the general level of prices are accompanied by only small changes in the real output level—an inelastic relationship. An increase in the general price level causes an increase in aggregate quantity supplied—a movement to the right along the aggregate supply curve. Conversely, a decrease in the general price level results in a decrease in aggregate quantity supplied—a movement to the left along the aggregate supply curve.

One interesting and controversial behaviour is that the price elasticity of shortrun aggregate supply varies inversely with the volatility of the inflation rate. When inflation increases, and especially if it becomes more volatile, it tends to disrupt the ability of firms to plan production and pricing behaviour in an orderly fashion. Thus as the volatility of inflation increases, firms are less likely to change production levels in response to changes in prices, and the aggregate supply curve becomes steeper.

Just as there were determinants that could shift the aggregate demand curve, there are determinants that can shift the aggregate supply. Some of the most important factors that can affect the position of the aggregate supply curve are longrun in nature, such as population growth, demographic changes, changes to the laws affecting the employment of workers, and changes to the size of the labour force. In this section our focus is

---

[18]Many discussions of aggregate supply curve use a horizontal curve or a segmented line with a horizontal section for low income, an upward sloping middle range, and a vertical line at full-employment output. These representations complicate a relatively straightforward relationship and restrict discussion to special cases.

still on cyclical and temporary unemployment, so we want to discuss the determinants that could affect the aggregate supply over a short period of time. The factors most likely to affect shortrun shifts in aggregate supply are technology, taxation, the price and availability of strategic resources, and the wage rate. Improvements in technology that increase the productivity of resources will generally increase aggregate supply. In addition, it is generally agreed that such improvements will increase employment overall as production levels increase, but there are important exceptions. We will see later in this chapter that the relationship between technology and employment is sometimes very complex. Lower taxation, especially lower taxation of the type that affects the employment of workers, will increase aggregate supply and increase the demand for labour. For example, if an employer must pay taxes to the government to insure workers against the possibly of becoming unemployed, then a reduction in that tax will increase the demand for labour compared to the demand for other

Figure 13–5   **An increase in aggregate supply**

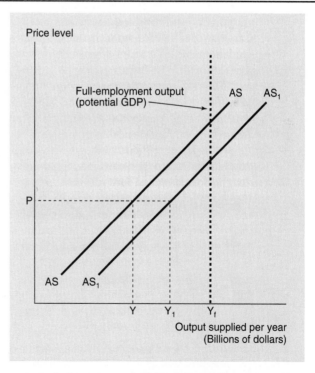

An increase in aggregate supply is represented by a shift to the right in the position of the entire aggregate supply curve. At price level P, output supplied is Y, given aggregate supply $ASAS$, and is Y_1, given aggregate AS_1AS_1. Aggregate supply AS_1AS_1 represents a greater aggregate supply than $ASAS$ represents.

factors of production. Higher resource prices decrease aggregate supply, and lower resource prices increase aggregate supply.

Two aggregate supply curves, $ASAS$ and AS_1AS_1, are shown in Figure 13–5. Both of these supply curves indicate the positive relationship between output supplied and the price level. At price level P, output supplied is Y, given $ASAS$, and Y_1, given AS_1AS_1. In reference to aggregate supply $ASAS$, aggregate supply AS_1AS_1 indicates an increase in aggregate supply. The output supplied at Y_f is the real output that would take place if the economy were operating at NAIRU. Therefore the highest output that can be produced without causing an acceleration of the inflation rate is Y_f and is often described as *potential GDP* or *full-employment GDP*.

Potential GDP, also called **full-employment GDP,** is the highest level of real output consistent with no acceleration of the inflation rate.

Figure 13–6   **Equilibrium output and price in the aggregate**

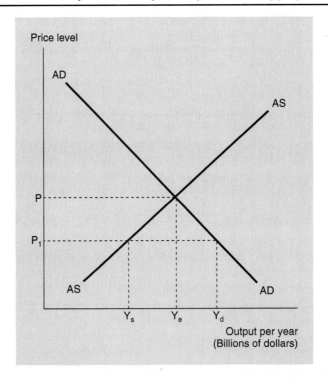

Given *AD* and *AS*, the equilibrium price level is *P* and the aggregate output is Y_e. If the price level were at P_1, then aggregate demand would exceed aggregate supply, as illustrated by the distance Y_d minus Y_s. This situation would cause shortages in the majority of markets leading to price increases in those markets. The result would be an increase in the general price level that would be accompanied by a decrease in aggregate quantity demanded and an increase in aggregate quantity supplied to return the economy to equilibrium.

Aggregate Demand and Supply

Employment and job opportunities depend on both aggregate demand and aggregate supply. In the shortrun, the economy moves toward an equilibrium between aggregate supply and aggregate demand. Figure 13–6 shows an aggregate demand curve *AD* and an aggregate supply curve *AS*. The economy represented should reach equilibrium at price level *P* and output Y_e. If the economy had a price level such as P_1, which is less than the equilibrium price level, aggregate demand would exceed aggregate supply as illustrated by the distance Y_a minus Y_s. This result is due to excess demand in the majority of markets because in general the level of prices is lower than equilibrium. Prices in each market experiencing excess demand will increase as described in Chapter 2. However, as the individual markets respond to the price increases, it causes the general price level to increase. As the price level increases, two behaviour patterns will alleviate the excess of aggregate demand. First, aggregate quantity demanded will decrease in response to the increase in the general price level as a result of the Pigou effect, the Keynes effect, and the net foreign purchase effect. Second, the rising price level will cause the aggregate quantity supplied to increase as described earlier in this chapter. Thus an increase in the general price level generates an equilibrating effect that brings aggregate supply into balance with aggregate demand. Once aggregate demand equals aggregate supply at price level *P* with output Y_e and there is no further pressure for the price level to increase or output to change. Conversely, if the general price level were above equilibrium, then aggregate quantity demanded would be less than aggregate quantity supplied. This situation should lead to a decrease in the general price level as firms respond to the insufficient demand conditions in the majority of markets.

The equilibrium illustrated in Figure 13–6 by the intersection of aggregate supply and aggregate demand indicates that the economy moves toward a state in which the pressure for changes to output and prices is self-eliminating. Unfortunately, at least in the shortrun, nothing in the economic model justifies that equilibrium must occur at full-employment.

Figure 13–7 shows three aggregate demand curves and two aggregate supply curves. Beginning with aggregate demand *AD* and aggregate supply *AS*, the equilibrium price level is *P*, and output demanded and supplied is Y_e. The economy is experiencing unemployment at this equilibrium level of gross domestic product, as indicated by the difference between Y_e and Y_f, the full-employment level of output. The distance from Y_f to Y_e is known as the *output gap* and represents the value of reduction in real output caused by having unemployment above the level of NAIRU.

Given aggregate supply *AS*, the economy could reach full-employment output only with a greater aggregate demand as represented by AD_2AD_2. At this level of aggregate demand, the equilibrium price level is P_2—much higher than it was at the lower level of aggregate demand. However,

---

The **output gap**, also called the **income gap**, is the value of the loss in real gross domestic product if unemployment is higher than NAIRU.

Output gap =
    Potential GDP
    − Actual GDP

Output gap = $Y_f - Y$

Figure 13–7   **Aggregate demand and supply and full employment**

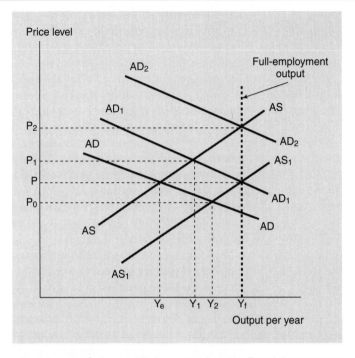

Starting with *AD* and *AS*, the equilibrium price level is *P* and the aggregate output is Y_e. Full-employment output Y_f can be reached by an increase in aggregate demand to AD_2AD_2. Full-employment output can be reached at a lower demand AD_1AD_1 if aggregate supply can be increased to AS_1AS_1.

given the higher level of aggregate supply AS_1AS_1, and the higher level of aggregate demand AD_1AD_1, full employment could be reached at price level *P*.

It can be said that at price level *P* and at output level Y_e, both aggregate demand and aggregate supply are deficient, for the economy is not operating at full employment when *AD* and *AS* represent the strength of aggregate demand and supply. What are some of the reasons for a relatively weak aggregate demand and supply?

Reasons for Deficient Aggregate Demand

Aggregate demand may not be high enough to provide for a full-employment economy for many reasons. A deficient aggregate demand may be the result of an inadequate level of output demanded by consumers. Consumers may reduce their rate of spending for many reasons that have been discussed, such as demographic factors, or increases in interest rates. The weakness in aggregate demand may be traced to the level of investment spending that falls short of the investment spending that would be required for a full-employment economy. This lack of investment may be the result of a fall in the expected profit rate, expectations of rising inflation in the future, an increase in the volatility of inflation, or a rise in interest rates. Alternatively, reductions in government purchases or increases in taxes that discourage private spending could cause deficient demand. Finally, aggregate demand may be deficient because of a high level of imports relative to exports. Any of these reasons may explain why the economy may not operate at its full potential.

Reasons for Weak Aggregate Supply

We have said that aggregate supply depends on expectations about inflation, expectations about profitability, resource prices and availability, and technology. Any exogenously caused increase in the price of the resources used with labour, increase in expected inflation rates, or reduction in labour productivity will cause weak aggregate supply. With a weakened aggregate supply, the demand for labour will be low and unemployment will be high. What events might really cause weak aggregate supply on a wide scale?

Suppose the price of a key resource, such as oil, increases, or the availability of a key resource is reduced. If the shortage of the key resource and its price increase is not offset by productivity increases in labour, the aggregate supply curve will shift to the left. In 1973 and again in 1979, the world price of fossil fuels rose to unprecedented levels as a result of political and technological factors. With high prices for fuel, the profits of many firms were reduced. In addition, the rise in fuel prices, as it was incorporated into the supply and demand for individual products, contributed to a rise in inflation rates. As we discussed earlier, a rise in inflation also tends to cause firms to reassess their expected future profits and can cause aggregate supply to shift left. In many cases low labour productivity may have less to do with the desire of the typical worker to deliver an honest day's work for an honest day's payment than it has to do with other factors, such as the availability of an inexpensive fuel to keep the capital machinery of the economy running.

Government action can also inadvertently weaken aggregate supply. If the government imposes taxes that specifically increase the cost of employing labour relative to employing other factors of production, the higher taxes will reduce the demand for labour relative to other resources and could cause unemployment. Because employment insurance premiums, premiums for workers' compensation, and employer contributions to Canada and Quebec Pension Plans apply only to labour and must be paid on a regular installment basis, they constitute taxes on labour. Increases in unemployment insurance premiums and pension premiums increase the cost of labour compared to other resources. In the 1980s and

Figure 13–8   **Real wages, productivity, and the labour market**

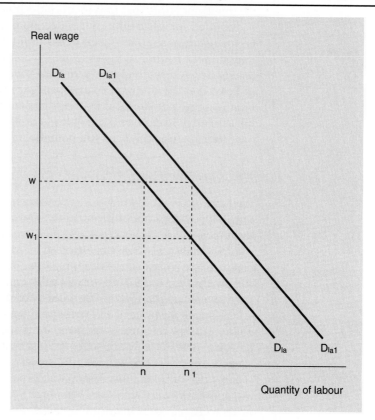

Given the demand or marginal product of labour $D_{la}D_{la}$ and the real wage w, the level of employment is n. One way to increase employment to n_1 is to reduce the real wage to w_1. A second way is to increase the marginal product of labour to $D_{la1}D_{la1}$.

1990s, governments have increased various taxes on labour as governments became increasingly concerned about deficits while seeking to ensure that employment insurance and the Canada and Quebec Pension Plans remain financially healthy. Finally, high interest rates reduce the incentive to firms to replace, modernize, and make additions to the economy's capital stock. As the stock of machinery ages, the productivity of labour falls. Decreasing labour productivity is particularly important in a country like Canada where such a large part of our aggregate demand comes from exports. If we fail to replace our capital equipment, our relative comparative advantages change. We may become less competitive internationally in industries in which we traditionally enjoy a high degree of competitiveness and high employment. For reasons that we will explore in

Chapter 14, Canada maintained high interest rates as part of its public policy to control inflation throughout the 1970s and 1980s. Many economists agree that these high interest rates reduced the demand for capital goods and resulted in weaker labour demand than would otherwise have been the case.

In a market economy the motivating force behind aggregate supply is the profit motive. Producers are not going to expand output if they do not believe that expanded output will generate increased profits. The relationship between employment and wages and productivity may be extended further. It is profitable to expand employment out to the point where the real wage equals the marginal productivity of labour. In Figure 13–8, with the demand or the marginal product of labour shown by $D_{la}D_{la}$ and the real wage equal to w, the equilibrium or profitable level of employment is equal to n. There are two ways that it would be profitable to expand output and increase employment to n_1. One way is for the real wage to decrease to w_1. The second way is for the marginal product of labour to increase to $D_{la1}D_{la1}$. Again, the weakness of aggregate supply is closely linked to wages and productivity.

The weakness of aggregate supply to create enough employment to keep the unemployment rate at NAIRU can be related to the factors that would shift the aggregate supply curve to the left. Among the more important factors that we have discussed above were high prices for other resources—particularly fossil fuels—taxes on labour, and high interest rates.

Changes to the Longrun Unemployment Rate

We identified structural unemployment as longrun unemployment. The factors that influence longrun unemployment tend to be different from the things that influence shortrun, cyclical unemployment. Changes in structural unemployment result in changes to the longrun persistent level of unemployment. Changes to structural unemployment can be brought about by shifts in the structure of demand for goods and services, technological change, change to the immobility of factors of production between industries and across regions, and changes in the relative productivity of resources in one region compared to those of another region or country.

Much of the longrun regional disparities in unemployment patterns have been attributed to differences in the industrial structure of the provinces and to differences in the demographic makeup of the labour force in different provinces.[19] Changes in the composition of demand by consumers and firms alter the mix and types of products demanded in the

[19]Andrew Burns, "Regional Disparity and Economic Structure," in Economic Council of Canada, op. cit., pp. 85–6.

economy. When demand patterns shift, production and employment expand in some industries and for some skills within industries but decrease for others. It might seem that the problem of unemployment resulting from changing demand patterns is avoidable by shifting resources no longer required to produce a product that is experiencing decreasing demand into producing a product with increasing demand. The discussion of the production possibility curve in Chapter 1 suggests that a properly working market economy will move resources from declining industries and reallocate them to expanding industries. This argument has some merit, but it overlooks two important factors. First, resources, whether these are labour or mineral deposits, may not be well suited to move from one industry to another within a given region. Second, even if an industry is experiencing growing demand for its products, the changing nature of the product in response to changing demand over time may reduce the employment opportunities for particular types of labour in specific regions.

The structure of an industry combined with shifts in the pattern of demand can affect structural unemployment in several ways. The rise in the demand for one industry may lead to a decrease in the demand for another and the resources may not be transferable. For example, assume that a rise in the demand for plastics in residential plumbing decreases the use of copper pipe. The regions of Canada that have the types of labour, mineral deposits, and infrastructure well suited to produce and distribute copper are not necessarily well suited to respond by using those resources to produce plastics. Even expanding demand for a product does not imply that the industry will not have increasing structural unemployment. Through time, as tastes have changed and as markets have become more global, products have generally become more complex, and selling them requires more careful geographic and demographic targeting. In a previous time it may have been fairly easy to find a local customer to purchase freshly landed halibut or the current wheat harvest. Today, Canadian producers must be sensitive to subtle differences in demand among different foreign markets. The difference in the nature of modern products often requires a bundling together of goods and services to provide a specialized and complex product that involves cooperative arrangements among a number of firms in separate industries and spread across several regions. For example, a firm wishing to sell halibut in a foreign market must be sensitive to whether the customer plans to use the fish as a raw material for the fast-food industry or whether the halibut is to be a featured food in restaurants specializing in healthy cuisine. The skills and co-operative corporate relationships required to ensure consistent performance in freshness, quality, portion sizes, packaging, delivery, inventory monitoring, financing, complementary product supply, customer service, and support advertising to supply halibut for the health-food markets in Japan or Europe are quite different than the skills needed to export salted fish a few decades ago.

Technological change is generally regarded as beneficial to the economy as a whole, but it may be devastating for employment opportunities in one region or one industry. Technological change can mean that one worker, using a new production method or machine, can do the work that previously required literally hundreds of workers. The analysis of technological progress helps to explain the behaviour of employment in the primary industries in Canada over the past 40 years. From 1951 to 1991 production of minerals and other products in the primary industries increased dramatically, but over the same period the number of Canadian workers employed in this sector decreased from just over 1.1 million workers in 1951 to under 869,000 in 1991.[20] When new technology is introduced, even in an industry with expanding demand, there is no guarantee that the expansion in output will be sufficient to increase the use of labour in the industry. Introduction of new technology often requires workers to have different and specialized skills to operate new equipment or participate in new procedures. Retraining at reduced income provides a barrier for experienced workers to upgrade skills if they are laid off because of technological change. In addition, workers may have little incentive to retrain if industry forecasts predict reductions in the number of job openings for that industry in the future.

Immobility of labour prolongs the period of unemployment that may have originated for some other reason. Immobility therefore increases the duration of unemployment and contributes to a rise in the permanent structural component of unemployment. Research suggests that the major factors that have affected the mobility of labour in Canada have been laws that inhibit the free movement of labour and demographic factors.[21] Changes to legislation, such as the broadening of employment insurance benefits for the unemployed, or increases in the disparity between minimum wage laws from one region to another can increase long-term unemployment. Adjustments to the former unemployment insurance system in the early 1970s, which increased the number of seasonal industry workers covered by unemployment insurance, increased the maximum weekly benefits, and lengthened the duration of benefits for the unemployed, may have accounted for some of increase in Canada's structural unemployment rate. More generous benefits allow unemployed, workers to stay in a given region and continue to look for work that makes use of their present skills for a longer period before relocating or seeking retraining. Some economists estimate that a significant portion of the increase in Canada's long-term unemployment, especially in seasonal industries, can be traced to these reforms.[22] Many of the changes to employment insurance that

---

[20]Osberg, op. cit., p. 1.

[21]M. Corak, "Unemployment Comes of Age: The Demographics of Labour Sector Adjustment in Canada," in Economic Council, op. cit., pp. 90–7.

[22]H. Grubel and J. Bronnici, "*Why Is Canada's Unemployment Rate So High*," *Focus* no. 19 (Vancouver: Fraser Institute, 1986).

could have accounted for permanently increased structural unemployment were reversed during the 1980s.[23]

Other types of legislation that can contribute to high structural unemployment, although regarded as less important, include barriers to the interprovincial movement of skilled labour and minimum wage laws. The immobility of the labour force is also affected by demographics. Older workers are generally less likely to become unemployed than younger workers—as indicated earlier, older workers have a lower unemployment rate than younger workers. However, if an older worker becomes unemployed, he or she is likely to be unemployed for a longer period than is a younger worker. In other words, although older unemployed workers are small in number, they are part of the reason that a small group accounts for a large portion of the structural unemployment problem. Older workers often face a relatively large drop in income from their last employment due to lost seniority when they get a new job. In addition, older workers may have to consider the employment of other members of the household and the best interests of dependents when contemplating a move to search for employment in another region. These factors contribute to older workers being less mobile than younger workers. Finally, prospective employers are sometimes less willing to provide retraining or share the cost of retraining for older workers. As one researcher put it, "Older workers are treated in a way similar to the way obsolete capital equipment is treated—they are scrapped."[24] Thus the aging of the labour force makes it more difficult for the nation to move workers from declining industries and regions to those that are experiencing expanding economic activity.

The last major contributor to higher structural unemployment is a lost competitiveness of labour in one region or throughout the country compared to labour in other regions or countries. Part of this discussion requires an understanding of the theory of comparative advantage, which was discussed in Chapter 12. There is, however, one aspect of international competitiveness that is worth including here. Labour is not employed in isolation from other factors. Labour works with capital and natural resources in production processes. Each factor is in a sense dependent on the others in a particular production process if it is to remain competitive. The structure of Canada's industry and the long distances separating the point of production from our end-use domestic and international markets have typically required high levels of petroleum and other fuels in Canadian production relative to other countries. Inexpensive fuels in the 1960s contributed to Canada's international competitiveness; by contrast, after fuel costs increased dramatically in the 1970s, many Canadian goods became less competitive on international markets.

---

[23]S. Gera, S. S. Rahman, and J. L. Arcand, "Unemployment and Job Vacancies," in Economic Council, op. cit., p. 58.

[24]Corak, op. cit., p. 89.

Combating Unemployment

Unemployment can be approached from either the aggregate demand or aggregate supply perspective. Generally the policies developed by economists for expanding aggregate demand work most effectively against cyclical unemployment—they are shortrun policies. In the 1950s, 1960s, and 1970s, an aggregate demand approach was taken to cope with unemployment. In a world made up of upward sloping aggregate supply curves, these aggregate demand approaches brought the unpleasant side effect of continually increasing price levels—demand-pull inflation. (Inflation and its consequences are the subject of the next chapter.) It is sufficient to point out that demand-expanding policies force society into a normative conflict between choosing lower inflation or lower unemployment. By contrast, with the aggregate demand approach to combating unemployment, the energy crisis of 1973 and 1979 revealed that unemployment could result from sudden leftward shifts in aggregate supply. Economists began to accept that more attention had to be paid to policies aimed at shifting the aggregate supply curve to the right—so-called supply-side theory. The focus of supply-side theory is to use government policy to create increased employment by shifting the aggregate supply curve to the right. Finally, it should be remembered that policies aimed at correcting cyclical unemployment may be of no use in correcting structural unemployment. Similarly, policies, whether aggregate demand based or aggregate supply based, that are aimed at correcting longrun structural unemployment may have little impact on cyclical or frictional unemployment.

Aggregate Demand Policies

Aggregate demand policies are used, by the government and/or the Bank of Canada, to shift the aggregate demand curve in order to influence aggregate production, employment, and the general price level. Two policy views have developed. The first view is known as *stabilization policy*, which includes changes in government spending, transfers, and taxes designed to smooth out fluctuations in the economy by stabilizing aggregate demand over the business cycle. To practise stabilization policy, government could increase government spending and transfers or decrease taxes when private spending is contracting and decrease government spending and transfers and/or increase taxes when private spending is expanding. This type of policy could be effective in combating cyclical unemployment. The second policy view is to stabilize aggregate demand at a high level of employment and production, say, at NAIRU. This policy would mean that government spending and possibly transfers would be increased and/or taxes decreased any time the economy was not operating at potential GDP. This latter view seems to have dominated the policy thinking during the 1960s and early part of the 1970s.

The aggregate demand approach to unemployment is to increase aggregate demand directly by increasing government purchases and to increase aggregate demand indirectly by some combination of increasing transfer payments and reducing taxes. Policies based on this approach are subgroups of two large categories of public policy that has been used to influence the position of the aggregate demand curve. The first is *discretionary fiscal policy*, which is the deliberate manipulation of government spending on goods and services, transfer payments, and taxes to influence unemployment or inflation. To combat cyclical unemployment discretionary fiscal policy would be used to shift the aggregate demand curve to the right. The government can shift aggregate demand to the right either directly, by increasing its own spending on goods and services, or indirectly, by putting more after tax income in the hands of the private sector by increasing transfers or reducing taxes.

The second form of public policy to influence aggregate demand is known as *monetary policy*. In Chapter 14 we will more fully examine the intricacies of monetary policy; for now it is sufficient to know that if the Bank of Canada increases the money supply, this action will tend to lower interest rates and cause increases in investment spending that shift the aggregate demand curve to the right. In either case, whether it comes from expansionary fiscal policy or through expansionary monetary policy, aggregate demand policy aimed at lowering cyclical unemployment tends to shift the aggregate demand curve to the right.

Many of the policies used to reduce unemployment rates by Canadian governments during the 1960s and the 1970s could be classified as demand approach policies. They were not an unqualified success. The economy did experience a long period of growth in real gross domestic product. Not surprisingly, unemployment was relatively low through the 1960s as shown earlier in the chapter in Figure 13–1. However, if the aggregate supply curve is upward sloping, then rightward shifts in the aggregate demand curve will cause an increase the general price level. In the shortrun, one side effect of expansionary fiscal policy or expansionary monetary policy that leads to higher output and decreased unemployment is an increase in the general price level. Consequently, while the economy is moving to the higher level of output and employment, it is also experiencing shortrun increases in the general price level—inflation. In addition, as the government attempted to expand aggregate demand using discretionary fiscal policy, it increased spending for goods and services and transfers while decreasing taxes. All of this activity tends to cause government expenditures to exceed government receipts. The expansionary fiscal policies of the 1970s brought with them deficits and increases to the public debt. Finally, expansionary monetary policy brings with it the risk of prolonged periods of inflation. To the extent that the

Discretionary fiscal policy is the deliberate manipulation of government spending, taxes, or transfer payments to combat unemployment of inflation

Monetary policy is the deliberate manipulation of interest rates and the money supply to influence unemployment, inflation, or the exchange rate.

fight against unemployment in the 1960s and 1970s involved expansionary monetary policy, it also increased the risk of higher inflation rates. Partly as a result of the expansionary fiscal and monetary policies of the late 1960s, the inflation rate increased and very little was done about it—and what was done was done too late.

Not all of the increased inflation of the 1970s can be attributed to the effects of public policy. In 1973 the western world was rocked by the Organization of Petroleum Exporting Countries (OPEC) oil embargo. OPEC, which controlled the major share of the petroleum production for western economies, restricted production. Petroleum is a strategic commodity of the type discussed under our aggregate supply model above. The nature of modern industrial economies is such that petroleum is used as fuel and input in most production processes. Therefore, when OPEC reduced the supply of petroleum, it in effect shifted the aggregate supply curve for Canada and most other economies to the left. The result, assuming a normal upward sloping aggregate supply and a normal downward sloping aggregate demand, was a rise in the general price level coupled with a reduction in output and a rise in unemployment. It is not surprising then that the unemployment rate rose from 5.3 percent in 1974 to more than 8.3 percent in 1978; the inflation rate (using the GDP deflator) also increased from 8.9 percent in 1973 to more than 14 percent for 1974 and remained higher than the previous decade throughout the rest of the 1970s. A second leftward shift in aggregate supply took place in 1979 when OPEC again restricted petroleum exports to other western economies. The result was again predictable. In 1980 the economy again entered a recession, and the growth rate slowed until real GDP actually decreased by 3.2 percent in 1982. During the same period both inflation and unemployment increased to more than 10 percent. The combination of rising unemployment combined with rising inflation presented policymakers with a serious problem. The aggregate demand expansion policies of the 1960s were clearly unacceptable as a cure for unemployment if they would make inflation even higher. This situation set the stage for the introduction of aggregate supply policies to cope with the problem of unemployment.

Aggregate Supply Policies and the Economy in the 1980s

Aggregate supply policy, sometimes called supply-side policy, is an approach to combating unemployment and inflation aimed at shifting the aggregate supply curve to the right. What sort of economic policy will reduce resource prices and increase productivity in the economy?

Almost any policy by the government that increases the return for hiring labour relative to the profits that can be expected from employing other factors will increase the demand for labour relative to the other factors. It should be stressed that to increase the demand for labour requires that the government policy must create circumstances that encourage businesses to seek to employ more workers at a given wage—the policy must shift the demand for labour to the right. The key to creating such a circumstance is not through reductions in the wage rate. Reductions in wages may simply set off competitive bidding for factors that causes the cost of capital and the cost of land to decrease—a fallacy of composition that leads to few or no extra jobs. Alternatively, reduced wages may result in labour being substituted for capital or land but with no increase in output. Thus there would be an increase in the number of people employed but there would be no increase in the real gross domestic product of the economy. In this situation the output gap would remain the same as before the increase in employment and the standard of living would not increase. In effect a policy that seeks to increase the level of employment without ensuring an increase in the level of output is rejected by most economists because it simply replaces unemployed people with underutilized capital or land and leaves the economy operating inside its production possibility curve.

The key to public policy that increases employment seems to lie in increasing the incentives for business to employ more labour without reducing the incentive for firms to utilize the other factors of production. The two most obvious strategies of supply-side policy are to increase the productivity of labour and to increase the incentives for firms to hire more of all factors. The government can use the tax system to increase the expected profits from investing in new capital and resource development as ways of expanding aggregate supply. In some situations the profit motive may not provide individual firms with sufficient incentive to make the investments in capital necessary to boost labour productivity. For example, if low productivity of labour were the result of low skill levels or of low mobility of labour between industries or regions, it might not be in the interests of any one firm to correct the situation. If a single firm were to invest in educating and training for prospective employees to raise their level of skill, very little would prevent other firms from hiring the workers once they had received the training. In effect, the other firms could act as free-riders and gain from the training provided by the first firm without having to pay for it. Similarly, if the problem of unemployment is associated with lack of mobility, a firm has little incentive to pay to increase workers' ability to relocate if those workers can then be hired away by competitors. Similar arguments apply to everything from the availability of low-cost health services, affordable day care, safety training in the operation of equipment, adequate sewage treatment, and clean drinking water. Yet it is fairly clear that if most members of the labour force have adequate skill levels and low rates of absenteeism, all firms will have generally higher productivity. This argument has often been used to support government programs to provide, at low cost, day care, education and training, clean water, health care, transportation systems, sewage treatment, and employment counselling services that contribute to higher labour productivity and mobility as a means of shifting the aggregate supply curve to the right.

In the early 1980s the governments of Great Britain and the United States attempted some supply-side policies with mixed results. In Canada the supply-side experiments really began with the 1987 budget of then Finance Minister Michael Wilson. Over the rest of the decade and into the 1990s, successive federal finance ministers in Progressive Conservative and Liberal governments have introduced changes to government policy that are in the ideological framework of supply-side theory. In 1987 the federal budget reduced the progressive nature of federal income tax rates from nine different rates based on the income of the taxpayer to just three and reduced the marginal tax rate faced by high income earners from 34 percent to 29 percent. Subsequent alterations included restructuring employment insurance to prevent people who quit their job or are fired for "just cause" from being able to collect the benefits of their insurance coverage. Employment insurance reform also reduced the maximum benefit that a recipient could receive and lengthened the period of time an employee had to work before qualifying for this reduced maximum benefit. The stated purpose of these changes was to reduce the relative attractiveness of not working and collecting employment insurance relative to living from earned income from participating in the employed labour force. Government representatives argued that these measures would increase aggregate supply by increasing incentives to save, work, and produce.

The economy's response to the above policy changes (and to other underlying forces in the market) was not encouraging. The real growth rate in GDP was running at 6.2 percent in 1984 but began to decline in the later part of the decade, reaching 2.4 percent by 1989. Throughout the decade, unemployment declined from 11.8 percent in 1982 to 7.5 percent by 1989. Unemployment did respond to the expansionary monetary and fiscal policies of the aggregate demand approach and to effects of expansionary supply-side policies. However, government policy is not the only cause of movements in the unemployment rate. During the 1980s many other factors were at work both domestically and internationally that had an impact on Canadian unemployment. In addition, the rise in the unemployment rate over the decade was not strictly a rise in cyclical unemployment. As economists compared the 1980s with the 1970s and the 1960s, they realized that even when unemployment did decrease, it failed to reach the low levels of previous expansionary periods. In other words, when cyclical unemployment was falling, it seemed to be accompanied by a rising trend in structural unemployment. It would be unfair to claim that government policies, whether demand approach or supply-side in nature, had not affected unemployment. However, most of these policies were aimed at cyclical unemployment. Expansionary discretionary fiscal policy and expansionary monetary policy were developed over a 50-year period from 1935 to 1985 when the focus of economic theory was on developing policies that were countercyclical. They are relatively well suited to deal with cyclical stabilization and shortrun behaviour of aggregate demand. Most economists agree that they were not developed to address the problems of structural unemployment and are not well suited to that task as indicated by the rising structural component of unemployment.

Beginning the Decade of the 90s: Recession, Recovery, and Expansion

1990–92 Recession and Recovery. During the 1990–91 recession, real GDP decreased by .2 percent in 1990 with a further 1.7 percent decrease in 1991. The recession ended in 1992 as real GDP managed to climb by .7 percent, reflecting a very weak and fragile recovery. During this contraction in the economy, the unemployment rate increased from 7.5 percent in 1989 to 11.3 percent by 1992. This recession probably did not seem so mild to the more than 1.5 million persons who were unemployed. The difference between this recession and the one that preceded it is very clear when we compare the declines in real GDP over the two recessions with the rises in unemployment for both recessions. In the 1980–81 recession, real GDP dropped by 3.2 percent and unemployment rose from 7.5 percent to 11.8 percent—a rise of 4.5 percent. Put another way, unemployment rose 1.4 percent for each 1 percent drop in real GDP in the 1980 recession. In the 1990 recession, real GDP dropped by 1.9 percent but unemployment rose from 7.5 percent to 11.3 percent—a rise of 3.8 percent. In the 1990 recession, unemployment rose by 2 percent for each 1 percent drop in real GDP. This increased sensitively of unemployment to changes in real GDP has some members of the public and some economists concerned that structural changes to the international markets and demographic changes to our labour market have increased Canada's vulnerability to rising unemployment. Another feature of the 1990–91 recession was the absence of an aggregate demand or supply policy to alleviate the recession and to stimulate the economy.

In the 1990–91 recession the policy belief was that the recession was mild and the economy would recover on its own. Some encouraging factors supported the belief that Canada's recession of the 1990s would be mild and short with a strong recovery. Generally, the duration of a recession is closely related to the size of the increase in inventories because of the depressing effects that a recession has on final sales. In the run up to the 1980 recession, inventories measured in real terms increased by almost $6 billion worth of goods. In the early stage of the 1990 recession, real inventories rose by only $3 billion. Canadian recessions frequently end when the United States economy begins to expand because a high portion of our exports flows to the United States. Two factors that affect Canada's net exports to the United States are the exchange rate on the Canadian dollar and our inflation rate relative to the inflation rate in the United States. During the recession of 1990, the Bank of Canada allowed the Canadian dollar to sink in value relative to the value of the American dollar. The Canadian inflation rate was below that of the United States. These factors made many business leaders and economists believe that once the United States started to recover, the improved competitiveness of Canadian goods in the United States would lead to a rapid expansion of our economy. Predictions from the United States were also encouraging for a short recession and sharp recovery, as indications were that consumer and business confidence in that country was expected to rise.

1991–94 Recovery and Expansion. As it turned out the 1991–92 recovery was among the weakest recoveries on record. After most recessions the economy bounces back with a real growth in the GDP of 4 to 5 percent in the first quarter. Instead, in 1992 the rate of growth in the nation's real income was only .7 percent. This slow pattern of growth continued into the beginning of 1993. During the last part of 1994 and into the beginning of 1995, the economy finally began to expand and did briefly reach a growth rate greater than 4 percent. As a result of the slow growth, the rate of unemployment not only did not decrease but increased from 1991 to 1992. The unemployment rate remained almost stable, peaking at 11.3 percent in 1993 before beginning to decline at the end of that year.

The expansion continued into 1994 but was plagued by two major political themes. Because of concern over the size of the public debt in Canada, governments at both the federal and provincial level began to reduce government expenditure and to increase user fees for services in an attempt to reduce their current deficits. This strategy is understandable. The economy was expected to be growing strongly, and the growth period would be the most favourable time to decrease government expenditure, as other components of aggregate demand were expected to be on the increase. The impact of these reductions in government expenditure was generally well received in the financial markets, but it resulted in thousands of layoffs among the civil service at both the federal and provincial levels. The federal government alone scheduled over 45,000 layoffs to the civil service between 1995 and 1996 as it reduced its support for everything from postsecondary education to employment counselling. The reductions in government expenditure also reduced the opportunities for private sector firms to sell goods and services directly to the government. Increased layoffs also had a chilling effect on consumer spending and was undoubtedly part of the reason that consumer spending remained weaker than expected during the recovery. A decrease in government spending and an increase in taxes or user fees will certainly tend to reduce aggregate demand. An equally rational argument for the expected effect of the government policy is that deficit reduction accompanied by lower long-term interest rates would stimulate private investment spending and increase employment. Under more normal political conditions many economists argue that reduced deficits by government will lead to a decline in long-term interest rates, which may be more than enough to neutralize the contractionary effects of reducing the budget deficit. Unfortunately for Canada, there was a second major political question that affected any positive lowering of the interest rates over the period from 1993 until late 1995. Political uncertainty escalated over the ability of the country to remain united as Quebec prepared for a referendum for its possible separation from the rest of the country. Investors, rather than rushing in to create capital in Canada, waited to see if they would be investing in one country or two. Nor did this political instability end with the Quebec referendum. The governor of the Bank of Canada, Gordon Theissen, made many public appearances in the aftermath of the 50.4 percent vote to keep Quebec in Canada to explain that such a narrow vote left much uncertainty in the financial market. The consensus seemed to be that Canada would have to pay higher interest rates in relation to other countries in order to get investors to overcome their reluctance to invest in Canada until the question of Quebec's role in confederation was decided more decisively.

Summary

There are economic and social effects of unemployment. The economic effect involves the waste and loss of goods and services when resources are unemployed—the output gap. The social effect involves the breaking up of human relationships within the family and the community.

The three types of unemployment are frictional, cyclical, and structural. Frictional unemployment is transitional in nature and is not a major economic issue. Cyclical and structural unemployment are major economic issues. Cyclical unemployment is associated with the expansion and contraction of aggregate demand and employment in the business cycle. Structural unemployment results from fundamental changes in demand and supply for products in specific sectors and regions of the economy.

Aggregate demand and supply theories are developed to explain why people lose their jobs. Aggregate demand is composed of the output demanded by consumers, investors, government, and the net demand for Canadian goods and services from foreign customers. The aggregate demand for Canadian made goods and services varies inversely with the general price level because of the Pigou effect, the Keynes effect, and the net foreign purchase effect. An increase in aggregate demand can create a larger market for Canadian products and lead to reduced unemployment.

The determinants that could cause an increase in aggregate demand include lower interest rates, higher expected profits, and increased export demand.

Unemployment may be caused by deficient aggregate demand or weak aggregate supply. An aggregate demand approach to unemployment is an attempt to use public policy to shift the aggregate demand curve to the right. The two types of policy using the demand approach are expansionary fiscal policy and monetary policy. Expansionary fiscal policy requires any combination of increases to government expenditures, increases in transfers, and decreases in taxes. Expansionary monetary policy involves the Bank of Canada increasing the money supply to lower interest rates. Both expansionary fiscal policy and expansionary monetary policy bring about controversial side effects, ranging from increased risk of inflation to increases in the size of the public debt. An aggregate supply approach to reduce unemployment attempts to shift the aggregate supply curve to the right. The determinants that can shift aggregate supply to the right include increasing the productivity of resources, decreasing the price of resources, reducing taxes that raise the cost of labour relative to other factors of production, and reducing the incentives to remain outside the labour force. Demand-based policies for combating unemployment originated in the 1930s and have a long and relatively successful history of reducing cyclical unemployment. By contrast, supply-side policy is a recent development, having originated in the 1980s, and is much more controversial.

The trend in Canadian unemployment over the last 30 years appears to have been to higher levels of structural unemployment. Studies suggest that some of these higher levels of structural unemployment can be attributed to higher participation rates, reduced labour mobility, rapid technological change, and changing patterns of demand that have led to an increased tendency to bundle goods and services together to create more sophisticated products prior to sale. Structural unemployment appears quite unresponsive to most of the demand approach public policies developed to counter cyclical unemployment. Theory suggests that in the longrun supply-side policies may be appropriate to reducing structural unemployment by improving the productivity and mobility of labour. Other possibilities that are being explored are changes in public policy that reduce the cost of labour relative to other factors of production.

The 1990s commenced with the economy in a recession. The economy started expanding in 1992 but the recovery was much slower and much weaker than previous recoveries since 1945. During the 1990–91 recession, the unemployment rate appeared much more sensitive to the decreases in real GDP than in previous recessions and continued to increase even after the economy began to expand. The slow recovery may have been exacerbated by two political events. The first was the change in policy direction by provincial and federal governments to reduce their deficits. The second was the political uncertainty that surrounded the Quebec referendum on national unity, which caused investment to remain sluggish. Because of these factors the Canadian economy entered the second half of the 1990s with unemployment much higher than their American counterparts. Unlike the United States, Canada failed to create enough jobs after the 1990–91 recession to get its unemployment rate down to its so-called natural rate.

Checklist of Economic Concepts

Eligible labour force population
Labour force
Participation rate
Unemployment rate
Discouraged workers
Non-accelerating inflation rate of unemployment, (NAIRU)
Frictional unemployment
Structural unemployment
Cyclical unemployment

Fallacy of composition
Aggregate demand
Marginal propensity to expend
Multiplier
Aggregate supply
Potential GDP
Output gap
Aggregate demand policies
Discretionary fiscal policy
Aggregate supply policies

Discussion Questions

1. Compare and contrast the eligible labour force population and the labour force. Is it possible for there to be an increase in the number of people who are not working in an economy at the same time that there is a decrease in the unemployment rate?

2. Is a full-time student attending a postsecondary institution and also working 35 hours a week at a retail store considered part of the labour force? If this student gets fired is he or she counted as unemployed? Explain your answer.

3. What are the three types of unemployment that economists refer to when studying unemployment? Briefly explain the differences between them.

4. Define the non-accelerating inflation rate of unemployment.

5. "The cure for unemployment is for people looking for work to accept lower wages—it's as simple as saying supply and demand." Give at least two reasons why most economists would disagree with the statement and why they argue that unemployment cannot be cured by lowering wages.

6. Define aggregate demand and give three reasons why it varies inversely with the general price index.

7. If the government engages in expansionary fiscal policy, explain why there is a multiplier effect to its increased spending.

8. Discuss some of the side effects of using demand approach policy to combat unemployment.

9. Explain why the current political desire to reduce government debt and ensure that governments at the provincial and federal level balance their budgets or run surplus budgets reduces the chance of using demand approach policies to fight cyclical unemployment.

10. Define aggregate supply. Give two reasons why economists believe aggregate supply is upward sloping in the shortrun.

11. Why might the energy crisis of 1973 or 1979 have caused an increase in unemployment and an increase in the inflation rate?

12. Explain the intent of supply-side policy for fighting unemployment. Why would reducing the average wage generally not be accepted by most economists as an efficient or desirable supply-side approach to curing unemployment?

Supplementary Reading

Colander, D. C. and P. S. Sephton. *Macroeconomics.* 1st Canadian edition. Toronto: Richard D. Irwin, 1996.

Chapters 8 through 10 provide a readable, logical presentation of the aggregate expenditure models and aggregate demand and aggregate supply models. The ways in which fiscal policy can be used to affect changes in the unemployment rate and the issues of timing and side effects from these policies are also discussed. This text is one of the few that integrates discussion of regional multipliers into a standard presentation of the multiplier model.

Fellows, C. M.; G. L. Flanagan; S. Shedd; and R. N. Waud. *Economics in a Canadian Setting.* New York: HarperCollins College Publishers, 1993.

Chapters 21 through 24 provide a detailed development of the aggregate demand and aggregate supply model of the economy with particular emphasis on the Canadian experience. This is one of the few introductory texts that includes a detailed discussion of the role of the information extraction problem as a factor influencing the shape of the shortrun aggregate supply curve.

Economic Council of Canada. *Canadian Unemployment, Lessons from the 1980s and Challenges for the 90s.* Ottawa: Minister of Supply and Services Canada, 1991.

A comprehensive study of the theoretical and empirical behaviour of unemployment in Canada. The authors provide an excellent discussion of the regional, legal, and demographic factors that may have affected the natural unemployment rate and non-cyclical rate of unemployment over a two-decade period. The collection of articles contains theoretical discussions comparing the merits of various measures of the natural unemployment rate, including NAIRU and NCRU.

McConnell, C. R.; S. L. Brue; and T. P. Barbiero. *Macroeconomics: Canada in the Global Economy*. Toronto: McGraw-Hill Ryerson, 1996.

This book provides a thorough presentation of the contemporary aggregate expenditure and aggregate demand models. For those wishing to use a three-segment aggregate supply model, the presentation is lucid. In addition, the issues surrounding the timing and effectiveness of demand approach policies to combating cyclical unemployment are clearly presented.

Osberg, L.; F. Wien; and J. Grube. *Vanishing Jobs: Canada's Changing Workplaces*. Toronto: James Lorimer, 1995.

The book provides a comprehensive review of the causes and anatomy of unemployment in Canada. Case studies investigate the impact of technological change and demographic shifting on employment opportunities. The authors focus primarily on the Atlantic provinces but point to the larger forces at work throughout the country.

Schiller, B. R. *The Macro Economy Today*. New York: Random House, 1983.

Supply-side policies are examined in Chapter 13. This chapter and Chapter 15, "Reagan Economics," are recommended.

Swartz, T. R.; F. J. Bonello; and Andrew F. Kozak. *The Supply Side*. Guilford, CT: Dushkin Publishing Group, 1983.

This book contains many essays on supply-side economics and on the philosophical thinking behind the supply-side approach.

Chapter 14

Inflation, Banking, and Money

Can Bankers Create Too Much Money?

We had sold out almost our entire inventory and, to our amazement, had nothing to show for it except a worthless bank account and a few suitcases full of currency not even good enough to paper our walls with. We tried at first to sell and then buy again as quickly as possible—but the inflation easily overtook us. The lag before we got paid was too long; while we waited, the value of money fell so fast that even our most profitable sale turned into a loss. Only after we began to pay with promissory notes could we maintain our position. Even so, we are making no real profit now, but at least we can live. Since every enterprise in Germany is financed in this fashion, the Reischsbank naturally has to keep on printing unsecured currency and so the mark falls faster and faster. The government apparently doesn't care; all it loses in this way is the national debt. Those who are ruined are the people who cannot pay with notes, the people who have property they are forced to sell, small shopkeepers, day laborers, people with small incomes who see their private savings and their bank accounts melting away, and government officials and employees who have to survive on salaries that no longer allow them to buy so much as a new pair of shoes. The ones who profit are the exchange kings, the profiteers, the foreigners who buy what they like with a few dollars, kronen, or zlotys, and the big entrepreneurs, the manufacturers, and the speculators on the exchange whose property and stocks increase without limit. For them practically everything is free. It is the great sellout of thrift, honest effort, and respectability. The vultures flock from all sides, and the only ones who come out on top are those who accumulate debts. The debts disappear of themselves.[1]

The opening quotation, written during the widespread rapid inflation in Germany in the 1920s, illustrates some of the social strains and economic problems that often accompany widespread rapid increases in the general level of prices. Inflation is considered by most people, along with unemployment and government debt, to rank among the nation's major aggregate economic problems. In almost every federal election, candidates call inflation a bad thing and vow to control it once elected. The rising cost of groceries, car repairs, pharmaceuticals, clothes, travel, and everything else is a main topic of conversation among consumers. Businesses realize that higher prices for materials, labour, equipment, and other things they buy may reduce their profits unless they are successful in passing these higher costs on to buyers in the form of higher prices. Inflation is a prime bargaining consideration in labour union negotiations. A stated national goal of government economic policy is to stabilize the

---

[1] E. M. Remarque, *The Black Obelisk* (New York: Harcourt Brace Jovanovich, 1957), pp. 54–55.

price level. Inflation affects all groups—households, businesses, governments, and foreign buyers of Canadian exports.

Meaning and Measurement of Inflation

Most people have a good idea of what is meant by inflation. They know that it causes the typical weekly basket of groceries to cost more money. They know that buying Christmas presents for their friends and relatives costs more. They know that it is more expensive to eat out, to go to a movie, to take a vacation, or to buy a car. They know they will be generally worse off in the future unless their income can keep up with inflation.

Inflation Defined

Inflation means that the general level of prices is rising.

Inflation means that the general level of prices is rising. That is, enough prices of goods and services are rising so that, on the average, prices in general are rising. During inflation some commodities may be falling in price and some may be rising, but the commodities rising in price are dominant, and they exert an upward force on the general price level.

Further Aspects of Inflation

Dynamic Aspects. Inflation has dynamic and self-sustaining properties. Increases in the price level induce economic groups to react to rising prices, causing further increases in prices. For example, consumers expecting increases in prices may increase current consumer spending, causing current market prices to rise. During periods of rising prices, producers are not inclined to resist increases in wages and other costs, since higher production costs may be shifted forward to consumers in the form of higher prices. These increases in prices, however, become the basis for further increases in production costs and still higher prices.

Inflation Without Rising Prices. Inflation is not always observable in the form of rising prices. It may be suppressed; market prices may not always reflect the inflationary forces operating in the economy. Suppressed inflation is usually associated with an attempt on the part of government to control prices. During the control period, market prices remain the same. Inflationary forces, however, continue to exist because the government is not doing anything to alter the underlying inflationary forces in the market. Under these circumstances, it is difficult to keep prices under control, and prices in general will rise rapidly when price controls are lifted.

Measurement of Inflation

Inflation is measured by price index numbers. Price index numbers indicate the general level of prices in reference to the base year. For example, the consumer price index in 1992 was 128.1, using 1986 as a base period. This means that consumer prices on the average increased 28.1 percent between the base period (1986 = 100) and 1992. The consumer price index was 130.7 in 1994. Therefore, the annual rate of inflation over the period from 1992 to 1994 was 1.01 percent. The inflation rate is the percentage change in the price index on a per annum basis.

$$\text{Inflation rate} = \frac{\left(\begin{array}{c}\text{Price index in} \\ \text{second year}\end{array}\right) - \left(\begin{array}{c}\text{Price index in} \\ \text{first year}\end{array}\right)}{\text{Price index in first year}} \times \frac{100}{\text{years}}$$

For example,

$$\text{Inflation rate per year} = \frac{(130.7 - 128.1)}{} \times \frac{100}{2} = 1.01$$

Price Indexes. The *consumer price index*, sometimes referred to as the cost-of-living index, includes goods and services that urban residents buy, such as food, housing, utilities, transportation, clothing, health services, and recreation. The wholesale price index includes hundreds of goods and services such as farm products and processed foods, as well as industrial commodities such as textiles, fuel, chemicals, rubber, lumber, paper, metals, machinery, furniture, non-metallic minerals, and transportation equipment. Another price index that is used often by economists is the implicit price deflator. The *implicit price deflator* includes the components of the gross domestic product—consumer services, durable and nondurable goods, residential and non-residential fixed investment, exports and imports, and goods and services purchased by governments.

> The **consumer price index,** sometimes referred to as the cost-of-living index, includes goods and services that urban residents buy, such as food, housing, utilities, transportation, clothing, health services, and recreation.

> The **implicit price deflator** includes the components of the gross domestic product—consumer services, durable and nondurable goods, residential and non-residential fixed investment, exports and imports, and goods and services purchased by governments.

Construction of a Price Index. Since inflation is measured by price index numbers, it is important to understand how price index numbers are derived. A simple illustration can point out the essential principles underlying the construction of the consumer price index. Suppose a family spends $20,000, $21,000, and $22,000 in 1994, 1995, and 1996, respectively, for an identical basket of goods and services. If 1994 is used as the base year, the index number for the goods for that year is 100. It is 105 for 1995, calculated by dividing the cost of the basket in the base year ($20,000) into the cost in 1995 ($21,000) and multiplying by 100 in order to remove the decimal. Using the same procedure, the index number in 1996 is 110, or

$$\text{Price index (1996)} = \frac{\text{Cost of market basket (1996)}}{\text{Cost of market basket (1994)}} \times 100$$

$$= \frac{\$22,000}{\$20,000} \times 100 = 110$$

The basket of goods used to compute price index numbers is a representative sample of the quantities of goods and services purchased by a typical urban household—the number of dresses, shirts, loaves of bread, litres of gasoline, movie tickets, television sets, autos, and so forth—bought during the year specified. The sum of the price times the quantity of each good in the basket gives the value of the basket. After the value of the basket is calculated, the final step in the construction of a price index is to select the base year and compute the index numbers as illustrated. A set of price index numbers is not a perfect measure of inflation. Only a sample of commodities is included in the basket. What constitutes a representative sample is difficult to determine, and it changes over time in response to changes in people's tastes and preferences. It is also difficult to account for changes in the quality of goods that occur over time; for some goods and services, higher index numbers reflect higher prices for a better commodity rather than a higher price for the same commodity. Despite these imperfections, price index numbers are still useful indicators of trends in the level of prices.

More specifically the equation for the consumer price index (CPI) can be written as

$$\text{Consumer price index} = \frac{P_C \times Q_B}{P_B \times Q_B} \times 100$$

In this equation Q_B represents a basket of goods with the weighting or amount of each good in the basket being set to reflect the actual consumption pattern of consumers in the base period—1994 in this example. The term P_C is the price for the basket containing the same items in the same amounts in the current period—1996. P_B is the price that would have to be paid for this same basket of goods and services in the base period—1994. While any year could be used as the base year, Statistics Canada uses the major census years 1981, 1986, 1991, and 1996 for calculating and updating the consumer price index.

Rate of Inflation

Figure 14–1 shows the average inflation rate from 1962 to 1994. The first half of the 1960s was a period when prices were almost stable, with consumer prices on the average increasing 1.7 percent each year. The infla-

Figure 14–1   **Average annual inflation rate in Canada 1962–1994**

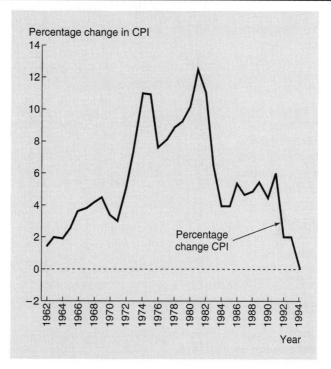

Source: Date combined from Canadian Economic Observer, Historical Statistical Supplement, and CANSIM.

tion scenario was different in the last half of the decade. The economy reduced unemployment below 4 percent in 1965 and inflationary forces began to mount. The result was an average annual inflation rate between 1965 and 1970 of over twice the rate of the earlier period (3.5 percent). The decade of the 1970s started with a high rate of inflation of about 4 percent and inflation rapidly accelerated to over 10 percent by the middle of the decade. What happened? How did the policy makers let inflation rise to such a high level? First, nothing was done to stem the inflationary forces in the late 1960s. An effective way to control a serious inflation is to not let it happen in the first place. Second, the rapid increases in energy prices after 1973 as a consequence of the energy crisis caused almost all costs to rise. In 1975 wage and price controls were enacted to control the inflationary pressures. From 1975 to 1977 the symptoms of inflation were suppressed, but the controls did not deal with the basic cause of inflation. The year controls were removed, 1978, the inflation rate jumped back up to over 8.5 percent and continued to climb. In 1979 there was a second energy shock. As the energy prices rose again, they pushed up the prices of other goods, taking inflation to more than 10.8 percent by the end of the decade. In part, then, the high annual rate of inflation of 9.8 percent between 1974 and 1982 reflects the higher costs of producing goods and services.

Inflationary forces were brought under control in the 1980s. It took a serious recession in 1981 and 1982 to do so. A recession after a long period of inflation can often be expected, for in the absence of a rapid growth in aggregate supply, in order for inflationary forces to be eliminated, the economy must slow down or decline. The average annual inflation rate was 7.3 percent between 1980 and 1985. However, this average rate of inflation was heavily influenced by the 12.4 percent inflation rate in 1981. The annual rate of inflation was reduced to 4.4 percent in the 1985–1990 period and fell further to 2.8 percent in 1990–1994. The lesson that can be learned from history is that very high inflation rates reflect the failure of resolving the problem of inflation when the problem first arises in the economy. Inflationary forces feed upon themselves and can cause people to expect inflation and behave in a way that causes inflation. The causes and cures of inflation will be discussed in subsequent sections.

Economic Effects of Inflation

The effects of inflation on the distribution of income are referred to as the **equity effects**

The effects on resource allocation and national output are called the **efficiency** and **output effects** of inflation, respectively

Inflation affects the distribution of income, the allocation of resources, and the national output. The effects of inflation on the distribution of income are referred to as the *equity effects,* and the effects on resource allocation and national output are called the *efficiency* and *output effects* of inflation, respectively.

Equity Effects

The impact of inflation is uneven. Some people benefit from inflation, and some suffer economic harm. Because inflation alters the distribution of income, a major concern is the degree of equity or fairness in the distribution of income. Anyone who is on a fixed income is hurt by inflation, since it reduces real income. For example, a person who earns $20,000 a year during an inflationary period in which there is a 25 percent increase in the price level suffers a cut in real income equivalent to the rate of inflation—approximately $5,000 in this illustration (20,000 × .25). Examples of people whose incomes often do not rise as fast as the price level are retired people on pensions, civil servants, people on public assistance, and workers in declining industries. People who hold assets in the form of money and who have fixed claims on money may be made worse off by inflation. Suppose a person deposits $1,000 in a savings account and receives 5 percent interest, or $50, during the year. If the rate of inflation is in excess of 5 percent, the real value of the original savings of $1,000 plus the $50 earned on the savings for a year is reduced to less than the original $1,000. Creditors and owners of mortgages and life insurance policies are hurt by inflation, since the real value of their fixed money claims is reduced. People who bought Canada Savings Bonds for $100.00 and were paid $133.33 at maturity 10 years later have sometimes discovered that the $133.33 would not buy the same quantity of goods and services that the $100.00 would have bought 10 years earlier. Inflation may cause the prices of some goods and resources to rise faster than the general level of prices. Wages and salaries of workers in rapidly growing industries are likely to rise faster than the price level. Strong unions are sometimes successful in bargaining for wage increases that are greater than the increases in the price level. People who depend on income in the form of profits—owners of stocks and business enterprises—may have increases in real income, depending upon the rate of increase in profits in comparison to prices. The value of land and improvements on land may rise during inflation; if they rise in value faster than the rate of inflation, landowners will be relatively better off. In summary, inflation alters the distribution of income and wealth.[2] Inflation is like a tax to some people and like a subsidy to others. People whose real incomes are reduced by inflation are those who have fixed incomes and hold assets in the form of money. People whose real incomes are increased by inflation are those who have money income that increases faster than prices and hold real assets that appreciate in value faster than inflation. The arbitrary manner in which inflation may change the pattern of income distribution supports the claim that inflation is inequitable.

Efficiency Effects

Inflation tends to change the pattern of resource allocation. In a competitive market, the prices of different goods and services reflect differences in consumer valuations of the quantities made available. Inflation causes demands for different goods and services to increase, but demands for some increase more rapidly than those for others. Increases in demands evoke supply responses, the extent of which varies from product to product. Thus inflation changes relative demands, relative supplies, and relative prices of different goods and services. The pattern of resource allocation, then, is not the same pattern that would exist in the absence of inflation. It is not certain that the pattern of resource allocation with inflation is less efficient (that is, results in lower economic welfare) than the pattern without

---

[2]In the analysis we assume that inflation is unanticipated. A fully anticipated inflation may not alter the distribution in the same way because those groups who expect the inflation and have the political and economic power to protect themselves from its negative effects will build inflation-compensating price and wage increases into their contractual relationships with others.

inflation.[3] However, many economists argue that inflation distorts the pattern of resource allocation, implying a less efficient allocation of resources. Inflation encourages economic agents to spend time and resources in an attempt to adjust to inflation. Since inflation reduces the purchasing power of money, it encourages people to economize or minimize their money balances, that is, assets held in the form of money. The time spent and the resources used in adjusting to inflation could have been used to produce goods and services. Inflation, by encouraging everyone to make adjustments and divert time and resources away from production, increases uncertainty and therefore reduces economic efficiency.

Output Effects

The preceding discussion of the equity and efficiency effects of inflation assumes that the levels of real output and production lie on the economy's production possibilities curve. This assumption is made in order to focus attention on how inflation may alter the distribution of real income among people (equity effects) and the allocation of resources (efficiency effects). Simply stated, a certain size pie is assumed in the previous discussion, and the concern is how inflation alters the slices of pie and affects the use of resources in making the pie. Now we consider the effects of inflation on the size of the pie. What are the effects of inflation on the level of output of goods and services?

Inflation may have a stimulating effect on production and employment in the economy. The argument in support of this proposition can be presented as follows. During inflation money wages often lag behind price increases. If this happens real profit income is increased. Under the stimulus of higher profits, producers expand production and employ more people. The argument that inflation may stimulate production and employment should be qualified. Runaway or hyperinflation may depreciate the value of money so drastically that it loses its acceptability as a medium of exchange. Under these circumstances, a barter economy develops, accompanied by lower production levels and higher unemployment. If the economy is operating at full capacity and full employment, then, of course, inflation cannot stimulate them further. Inflation at full employment is sometimes referred to as *pure inflation.*

Inflation at full employment is sometimes referred to as **pure inflation**

The impact of inflation depends on whether it is associated with increases in production and employment. As long as production is rising, there is a check on inflation because, although lagging behind demand, supply is increasing and inflationary forces are mitigated. Further, as long as production is increasing as quickly or more quickly than the growth rate in the population, then real income per capita is rising. The

---

[3]F. G. Steindl, "Money Illusion, Price Determinacy and Price Stability," *Nebraska Journal of Economics and Business,* Winter 1971, pp. 26–7.

equity effects of inflation are also minimized if production and employment are rising. However, as the economy approaches full employment, the seriousness of inflation increases. The possibility of an accelerated rate of inflation is nearer, and the possible beneficial effects of inflation on production and employment are diminished.

What Is Money?

It is sometimes stated that inflation is a situation in which "too much" money is chasing "too few" goods. As a first step to understanding inflation, we need to be able to answer the question, what is money?

Money is anything that is generally accepted as a means of payment for goods, services, and debt. Many diverse things have been used for money such as seashells, beaver pelts, playing cards, and even cigarettes. Money is much more than just cash. Economists measure money in several ways, and what is included in the money supply and the functions of money are the points of interest in this section.

Functions of Money

Money serves three basic functions: a medium of exchange, a measure of value, and a store of value. Goods and services are paid for in money, and debts are incurred and paid off in money. Without money, economic transactions would have to take place on a barter basis, that is, one good traded for another good. Thus the use of money as the *medium of exchange* simplifies and facilitates the exchange process. Second, the values of economic goods and services are measured in money. Money as a *measure of value* makes possible value comparisons of goods and services and the summation of quantities of goods and services on a value basis. It is not possible to add apples and computer services, but it is possible to add the values of apples and computer services. Third, wealth and assets may be held in the form of money. Money serves as a *store of value*.

The Money Supply (M1 and M2)

Money is an asset that is completely liquid; that is, you do not have to sell money in order to buy goods, services, and other assets. The money supply, then, is composed of assets that are 100 percent liquid or come so close to meeting this liquidity criterion that they are considered to be money. Several definitions of the money supply exist. The narrowest, called M1 for short, includes currency and coins in circulation and demand deposits at chartered banks. The second definition of the money supply, M2, is broader and includes M1 plus personal savings deposits and non-personal notice deposits. Technically, a demand deposit is an account in which the full balance may be withdrawn or transferred to a third party without prior notification, while a notice deposit is an account that may require the depositor to give advance notice before transacting activity on the account. In practice, we find very little difference between a demand deposit and a notice deposit, especially a notice deposit of a small denomination. Some savings accounts may have more stringent conditions placed on them, such as the loss of interest if they are withdrawn early, but in general, savings accounts are like money. Savings accounts are convenient, and depositors can earn more interest on them than on demand deposits.

Other broader definitions of money are referred to as M3 and $M2^+$. M3 is equal to M2 plus non-personal fixed-term deposits and foreign currency deposits held in Canada. $M2^+$ is a relatively recent development to measure the money supply that equals M2 plus deposits at trust companies, credit unions, the caisses populaires, the Ontario Savings Office, and the Alberta Treasury Branches. $M2^+$ is not used widely at the present time, but it is likely to become more important in the future because changing laws are reducing the distinction between the chartered banks and the other financial intermediaries.

The money supply M2 is the most widely used definition of the money supply, especially from a policy viewpoint. This definition of the money supply includes assets that are 100 percent liquid for all practical purposes and is a broader definition than the restrictive M1. For example, the dollar value of M2 in December 1994 was $364.3 billion, while the value of M1 was $57.3 billion.[4] The Bank of Canada keeps track of the growth rate of both M1 and the broader definitions of money because the growth of the amount of money in the economy is a major determinant of the inflation rate. Figure 14–2 shows the growth rate in the money supply over a 34-year period, 1960–1994. During the 1960s, the rate of growth in the money supply remained in the range of 4 to 10 percent for M1 and between 4.6 and 11.1 percent for M2. The growth rate pattern in the money supply in the decade of the 1970s tended to be in the upward direction with its most pronounced feature being wider swings from low to high and from high to low growth rates. For example, M1 increased from 2.2 percent in 1970 to percent 14.7 percent in 1973, then decreased to 9.8 percent in 1974, rising up to 14.4 percent in 1975, and falling to 7.8 percent for the next two years, before rising to 11.3 percent in 1978. In the 1980s the growth of M1 was lower overall than for the previous decade but still quite volatile. From 1980 to 1982 the growth of M1 decreased from 6.9 percent to .8 percent as the Bank of Canada restricted the growth of the money supply in an attempt to curb inflation. As the economy plunged into recession, the Bank of Canada reversed its policy and increased M1 by 8.2 percent in 1983. The growth rate moderated for the next

---

[4]Statistics Canada, *Canadian Economic Observer, Statistical Summary.* July 1995, Table 34.

Figure 14–2   **Percentage change in the money supply (M1 and M2)**
                         1962–1994

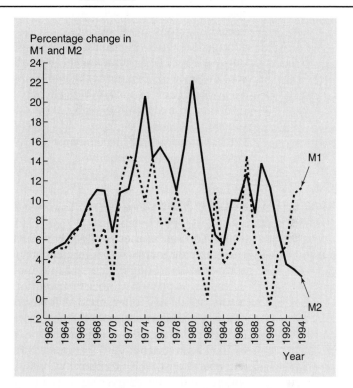

Source : Bank of Canada Review and Bank of Canada Review Supplement.

three years and then soared to 13.7 percent for 1987 only to decline to 4.8 percent for 1989. In 1990 the money supply actually decreased by 1.8 percent as the Bank of Canada again tried to restrict inflation, but the restrictions were short lived as the economy entered a recession again. As in the 1980 recession, the Bank of Canada reversed policy and allowed the money supply to expand. Over the next four years, the money supply was allowed to increase much more rapidly than the increase in real gross domestic product, with M1 rising by 11.9 percent in 1994 compared to an increase in real gross domestic product of only 4.2 percent.

The growth of the money supply using M2 as the measure was generally higher than the growth in M1 over the decade of the 1970s, although it was much less volatile than the growth in M1. M2 started the decade of the 1970s by growing at more than 10 percent in 1971 and rising to 20.9 percent by 1974. It decreased very slightly to between 14.5 and 15.8 percent for the last half of the 1970s. This high but stable rate of growth was replaced by a slightly more volatile growth over the first half of the 1980s. Between 1980 and 1981 M2 grew by 22.5 percent. This rate was followed by a volatile lower growth rate of 4.5 percent by 1984. During the later years of the 1980s, M2 grew more quickly, soaring to 13.1 percent in 1989. It then dropped to a growth rate of 10.7 percent in 1990—the same year that M1 declined by 1.8 percent. Since 1991, the growth of M2 has decreased steadily from 9.5 percent at the beginning to less than 2.5 percent by 1994. The volatility of the growth rates in M1 and M2 gives some preview of the difficulty in maintaining a stable growth in the money supply. The relationship between the growth in the money supply and inflation and how the Bank of Canada can control the growth in the money supply is discussed later in the chapter.[5]

The Process of Creating Money

The major part of the money supply is in the form of demand and other chequable deposits. Chequing deposits are held in chartered banks, trust companies, and other financial intermediaries. The 156 members of the Canadian Deposit Insurance Corporation are empowered to hold deposits of the public and offer various financial services, although only 14 are clearing members—meaning that they handle the settlement of accounts between the various members.[6] One hundred nineteen institutions— 63 banks and 56 trust and insurance companies—hold federal charters or incorporations, and another 36 institutions—trust companies, credit unions, and loans companies—are incorporated under provincial legislation.[7] In this section, the focus is on the way these deposits are created and destroyed.

Chartered Banks

Banks are private firms that are in business to make a profit by providing a full range of banking services, including chequing accounts, savings accounts, loans, automatic transfers from savings to chequing accounts, and electronic-banking services. Chartered banks are granted their charters by the federal government and are subject to the *Bank Act of Canada*, which is

---

[5]Data for this section is based on various issues of the *Canadian Economic Observer,* CANSIM, *The Bank of Canada Review,* and *Bank of Canada Review Supplement.*

[6]R. A. Shearer, J. F. Chant, and D. E. Bond, *Economics of the Canadian Financial System, Theory, Policy and Institutions* (Scarborough: Prentice Hall, 1995), chapters 1 and 12.

[7]B. Smith, and R. White, "The Deposit Insurance System in Canada: Problems and Policies for Change," *Canadian Public Policy,* December 1988, pp. 331–346.

federal government legislation because under the *Canada Act* banking is a federal responsibility. Depending on the degree of foreign ownership and the percentage of the common voting stock controlled by any one group, a bank is classified as either a Schedule I or Schedule II bank. The classification restricts some banking activities that can be performed only by Schedule I banks. At the present time Canada has 63 chartered banks, eight are Schedule I banks, which collectively are much more important in affecting the money supply than are the remaining 55 banks, which are classed as Schedule II banks.

Goldsmiths, the original bankers, provided the important service of a safe and convenient place to keep money or gold deposits, generally storing them in a vault. Depositors received a receipt for the gold deposited and used the receipt to buy goods and services. These receipts were the early form of paper money. Goldsmiths discovered early that it was not necessary to have a dollar in gold for each dollar issued in the form of receipts, since only a fraction of the gold deposited was required to meet gold withdrawals. This discovery led to two more important services. Loans were made to individuals and businesses, and paper money was created in the form of the issue of goldsmiths' receipts. The three main functions of banks today as then are (1) to provide a safe place for depositors to keep money and other assets, (2) to make loans, and (3) to create money as a group.

Other Financial Intermediaries

The traditional distinctions between chartered banks and other financial intermediaries are disappearing. The amendments to the *Bank Act* of 1991 allow more flexibility in providing a full range of banking services. Prior to this act, banks were restricted from certain trust and retail stock-trading activities, and insurance and trust companies were also restricted in the types and range of retail banking services that they could provide. Trust companies and insurance companies are now offering a wider range of chequing account services and are expanding other banking services. Conversely, the chartered banks are becoming financial supermarkets offering a wider range of trust activities and even venturing into telecommunication and electronic services that allow for retail stock trading. Historically, credit unions were used primarily as savings deposit firms that offered preferred consumer credit and home financing to members. Now, because of changes in the legislation, credit unions are offering chequing deposits, savings accounts, registered retirement savings plans, and other services in order to compete against the chartered banks who can now offer direct services in areas that they were formerly restricted from offering. This trend can be expected to continue in the future.

Balance Sheet of a Bank

A balance sheet of a bank shows the relationship among the bank's assets, liabilities, and net worth. The important feature of a balance sheet is:

$$\text{Assets} = \text{Liabilities} + \text{Net worth}$$

When there is a change on one side of the equation, there is an offsetting change either on the same side of the equation or on the other side of the equation. For example, if there is an increase in a liability of $10,000, there is a corresponding decrease of $10,000 in another liability or net worth, or an increase in an asset of $10,000.

The major assets of a bank are cash reserves, loans and investments, and fixed investments, such as a building and equipment. The major liabilities of banks are demand and notice deposits. The net worth of a bank is the shareholder's equity or the capital stock of the bank.

The balance sheet of a bank appears as follows:

Assets	Liabilities and Net Worth

Reserves:
            Desired reserves
            Excess reserves
Loans and investments
Fixed investments
	Liabilities:
	            Demand deposits
	            Time deposits
	
	Net Worth

In order to focus on the way money is created, we are concerned only with reserves and loans of banks on the asset side and demand or chequing deposits on the liability side.

The Fractional Reserve Banking System

Until the 1991 revisions to the *Bank Act* came into force in August 1994, chartered banks in Canada were required by law to keep a fraction of their deposits in reserves. These reserves were held primarily in the form of deposits at the Bank of Canada but also included the Bank of Canada Notes that chartered banks had on hand, sometimes referred to as *vault cash*. The legal reserve requirement was expressed in percentage terms and was called the *reserve ratio,* since it was the ratio of required reserves to bank deposits. For example, if the reserve ratio for a particular bank with demand deposits of $140 billion was 10 percent, this bank had to hold legal reserves equal to 10 percent of $140 billion, or $14 billion. Often banks held excess reserves, that is, reserves in addition to what was required to meet the legal reserve requirement. In 1994 the *Bank Act* amendments reduced the required reserve in Canada to zero. Therefore, today the chartered banks are not required by law to keep any cash on hand as a legal requirement to support their deposit liabilities. Although the banks are no longer legally bound to maintain reserves to support their liabilities, prudent banking necessitates that a bank keep sufficient reserves, either in vault cash or on deposit with the Bank of Canada, to provide for its clearing activities—the payments necessary to other financial intermediaries resulting from its depositors withdrawing funds and writing cheques against their accounts. In fact, since the change to a zero legal reserve requirement, the chartered banks have held desired reserves equal to approximately 2 percent of the deposits placed with them.[8]

Prudent banks will make new loans only when they have reserves in excess of the desired reserves they feel they need to cover their expected clearing activities. When banks, as a group, expand loans, they create demand deposits; and when banks, as a group, contract loans, they destroy demand deposits. Our discussion of M1 revealed that the money supply is made up of demand deposits in the chartered banks with only a small portion composed of actual coins and paper currency. This arrangement implies that the chartered banks can both create money and destroy it. Later in the chapter we will discuss some recent changes to the *Bank Act* that have increased the ability of the chartered banks to create money and have reduced the government's own authority over how much money exists in the economy at any given time. Now let's turn more specifically to the process of creating and destroying demand deposits or money.

Demand Deposit Creation

Suppose a bank receives a new demand deposit of $10,000, and that to meet either a legal requirement or to protect itself from a cash drain, the bank wishes to hold a desired cash-reserve ratio of 10 percent. The demand deposits of the bank increase $10,000, and reserves also increase $10,000. If the new deposit was made by withdrawing currency from circulation, the money supply does not change, since the money supply is composed of currency in circulation and demand deposits. Given a 10 percent cash-reserve ratio, the bank will need to keep $1,000 in reserves and has $9,000 in reserves in excess of its desired cash reserves. Now let's say you go to the bank and borrow $9,000 in order to buy a used car. You sign a piece of paper called a promissory note, agreeing to pay back the loan plus interest over a period of time in monthly installments. The car is used as collateral for the loan. After you sign the promissory note, the bank increases your chequing account by the amount of the loan, or $9,000. You write a cheque for $9,000 to pay for the used car. Your balance at the bank remains what it was prior to obtaining the loan. Demand deposits at another bank increase $9,000 when the car dealer deposits your cheque. A

---

[8]Shearer, op. cit., Chapter 12.

loan of $9,000 to pay for a used car has created new demand deposits of $9,000 in the banking system.

The process of demand deposit creation does not have to end after your loan of $9,000 creates new demand deposits of $9,000. With the assumed cash-reserve ratio of 10 percent, $900 ($9,000 × .10) is required to meet the banking system's desire to protect itself against unexpected withdrawals. Thus excess reserves of $8,100 remain in the system. By the same process as your loan, a new loan of $8,100 may be made that creates a new deposit of $8,100. This process may be repeated over and over again until excess reserves become zero.

The multiple expansion of demand deposits from a $10,000 deposit withdrawn from currency in circulation, assuming a cash reserve ratio of 10 percent, is shown through four stages in Table 14–1. Could you continue the stages through five, six, seven, and so on? In the final stage, demand deposits are $100,000, but the maximum demand deposit increase or money supply increase is $90,000, since $10,000 is currency withdrawn from circulation. Similarly, we may see a multiple contraction in demand deposits and the money supply when demand deposits are reduced in the banking system by a currency withdrawal of $10,000.

The maximum demand deposit creation possible from a given new demand deposit can be calculated from the following equation:

$$\text{Maximum deposits expansion} = \frac{1}{\text{Cash reserve ratio}} \times \text{Excess reserves}$$

$$D = \frac{1}{r} \times E$$

The deposit multiplier is a numerical coefficient derived from the cash-reserve ratio and equal to the reciprocal of the cash-reserve ratio. The deposit multiplier multiplied by a change in excess cash reserves of banks gives the maximum resulting change in the deposits. The deposit multiplier increases when the desired reserve ratio decreases.

where D = maximum deposit creation; E = excess reserves; and r = cash reserve ratio.

In our illustration the $10,000 new demand deposit increases the desired cash reserves $1,000 and excess reserves $9,000. The increase in excess reserves times the reciprocal of the cash-reserve ratio–deposit multiplier—equals the maximum deposit creation possible ($9,000 × 10 = $90,000).[9]

The *deposit multiplier* indicates the maximum amount that deposits could expand as a result of the banking system gaining new reserves

---

[9]A more detailed calculation of the money multiplier recognizes that when new Bank of Canada Notes are issued some of them remain in circulation outside the banking system. In this calculation the money multiplier (as distinct from the deposit multiplier) can be calculated with the equation $Ms = (1 + r)/(cr + r) \times H$, where Ms is the money supply = currency in circulation plus demand deposits, r = the cash ratio by the banks, cr = the currency-drain ratio (the ratio of cash circulating outside the banks to the total value of deposits), and H = high powered monetary base (the sum of the Bank of Canada Notes outside the Bank of Canada and the chartered banks' deposits with the Bank of Canada).

Table 14–1   **A $10,000 new deposit is made from currency in circulation (cash-reserve ratio = 10%)**

Assets			Liabilities	
Stage 1: Bank 1			Demand deposits	+$10,000
Reserves:				
Desired	+$1,000			
Excess	+$9,000			
		A $9,000 loan is made		
Stage 2: Bank 2			Demand deposits	+ $9,000
Reserves:				
Desired	+$900			
Excess	+$8,100			
		An $8,100 loan is made		
Stage 3: Bank 3			Demand deposits	+$8,100
Reserves:				
Desired	+$810			
Excess	+$7,290			
		A $7,290 loan is made		
Stage 4: Bank 4			Demand deposits	+$7,290
Reserves:				
Desired	+$729			
Excess	+$6,561			
At the end of Stage 4:				
Sum total of loans = $24,390				
Sum of			Sum of	
Reserves:			Demand deposits	+$34,390
Desired	+$3,439			
Excess	+$6,561			
Final stage: Sum total of all stages				
loans = $90,000				
Reserves:			Demand deposits	+$100,000
Desired	+$10,000			
Excess	$0			

under ideal conditions. It does not indicate what will be the most likely expansion of deposits as a result of new money being placed in circulation by the Bank of Canada. The difference lies in the fact that deposit creation is determined by the connection between the reserves that banks consider

A **currency drain** occurs if some portion of the money supply is not placed in circulation and is not used to support deposit expansion. It can result from hoarding by households, or it can be caused when banks are unable to find ways to lend out and invest a portion of their excess reserves.

excess to their need for financial security and the desire by businesses and households to borrow these excess reserves. If there is a difference between the amount of money that the Bank of Canada places into the economy and the amount that shows up in circulation or in reserves, there is said to be a *currency drain*. When a currency drains occurs, the deposit multiplier is smaller than predicted by the equation.

How does a currency drain come about? In order for the deposit multiplier to reflect the expansion of deposits that results from an increase in reserves, two conditions must be met when new money enters the economy. Banks must receive the money as a deposit and add it to their reserves before it can be considered excess reserves. If households decide to hold a larger portion of their money assets as cash outside the banking system, for instance as cash hoards in their homes, the banks do not receive some of the money that could have been added to reserves. Alternatively, assume that the banks did receive money, added it to their reserves, determined the amount excess to their needs, and wish to lend out the excess reserves to the public. In addition, assume that the economy is in a recession. During recessions, business prospects may look bleak and many households may be concerned that layoffs and wage rollbacks will cause their incomes to decrease in the future. In this situation, even though interest rates may be relatively low, businesses and households may be reluctant to borrow the funds that banks make available. If households and businesses are unwilling to increase their borrowing from the banks, the result is a smaller deposit multiplier than predicted by the deposit expansion equation.

The Issue of Monetary Control

It is apparent that with a fractional reserve banking system, the money supply can expand and contract rapidly. The system works well when money growth is controlled. The *Bank of Canada Act* of 1935 established the Bank of Canada. The main purpose of the Bank of Canada is to control the money supply.

The Bank of Canada

A central bank is a bank for private banks. Just as a private bank provides you with a full range of banking services, the Bank of Canada provides the chartered banks with many services. Among these services are the clearing of cheques, the holding of bank reserves or deposits, the providing of currency, and the making of loans—called *advances*—to chartered banks and some other members of the Canadian Payments Association. The Board of Governors is appointed by the Governor-General of Canada and is responsible for managing the Bank of Canada. The board consists of the Governor of the Bank of Canada and Deputy Governor, each appointed for a seven-year term, and twelve directors, each appointed for a three-year term. In addition, the deputy minister of finance sits as a non-voting member of the board. The Governor of the Bank of Canada, Gordon Thiessen, was appointed by the Governor-General in 1993. Thiessen replaced John Crow, who had been governor through the 1980s. Technically, the prime minister, acting on the advice of cabinet, can issue a directive to the governor of the Bank of Canada as to how to conduct monetary policy, and the governor must comply with that order. In practical terms, however, that power has not been exercised. The day-to-day operations of short-term monetary policy are determined by the professional staff of the Bank of Canada under the direction of the governor. Open market operations are the buying and selling of government securities in order to influence the level of bank reserves.

Controller of the Money Supply

Prior to 1967 the Bank of Canada had the legal ability to control the money supply either through changing the required reserve ratio or through changing the amount of Bank of Canada notes and reserve deposits that it made available to the chartered banks. In this period the Bank relied on changing the reserve base as the more efficient way of controlling the money supply. In 1967 Parliament amended the *Bank Act,* removing the Bank of Canada's power to change the required reserve rate. In the period between 1967 and 1994, the Bank of Canada relied on its ability to alter the reserve base, or so-called monetary base of Bank of Canada notes and reserve deposits available to the chartered banks, as the way to influence the money supply. In 1991 the *Bank Act* was further amended to reduce the required reserve ratio to zero percent. Technically this amendment means that the chartered banks can create money any time they find a borrower they believe will repay a loan. In other words, using the equation for deposit expansion, where the deposit multiplier $= \frac{1}{r}$ if $r = 0$, the deposit multiplier approaches infinity. However, in practical terms chartered banks need to keep cash and deposits at the Bank of Canada equal to approximately 2 percent of the value of their deposit liabilities in order to satisfy their liquidity needs for clearing activity. Therefore, many economists expect the reduction of the legal reserve ratio to zero percent to have little impact on the Bank of Canada's ability to control the nation's money supply.

The Bank of Canada uses three major policy instruments to influence the money supply and credit conditions: open market operations, the bank rate, and switching of government accounts. Each of these controls influences excess reserves and the lending ability of the chartered banks. Open market operations have a direct impact on the monetary base and on excess reserves and are the most important way that the Bank of Canada controls the money supply. The bank rate is not a powerful tool for control but is important because it may indicate the direction of the

Bank of Canada policy with respect to interest rates. Switching of government accounts is a powerful weapon that can be used like open market operations to affect the monetary base. However, switching has generally been used to balance and smooth the fluctuations of the money supply that result from such seasonal cyclical activities as the surge in the need for cash during the Christmas season and the decrease in the money supply that would result from the payment of income taxes in the spring.

Open market operations are the purchases and sales of government securities by the Bank of Canada in order to control the growth in the money supply.

Open Market Operations.

The Bank of Canada buys and sells government securities—usually 91-day treasury bills—in order to influence bank reserves, loans, and demand deposits. An open-market purchase means that the Bank of Canada is buying treasury bills from banks or from the non-bank public. In either case, the Bank of Canada pays for the treasury bills with a *draft* against itself. The draft is roughly equivalent to a certified cheque payable by the Bank of Canada to the holder of the draft. When the Bank of Canada purchases government securities from the chartered banks or the non-bank public, the seller receives the draft. Since the draft is not convenient to spend directly, the seller will likely deposit the draft into an account at a chartered bank. At the point that the draft is deposited in a chartered bank, the banking system has gained new reserves, some of which will be considered excess reserves. The primary impact of the purchase of government securities from banks is to increase excess reserves and to decrease government securities held by banks.

The primary impact of an open-market purchase from the non-bank public is to increase demand deposits and excess reserves of banks. The Bank of Canada makes the decision to buy government securities when it desires to expand the money supply. An open-market sale has the opposite effect. Excess reserves and the lending ability of banks are reduced by open-market sales. Thus the Bank of Canada makes the decision to sell government securities when it desires to contract growth in the money supply.

The **bank rate** is the rate of interest that the Bank of Canada charges when chartered banks and other members of the Canadian Payments Association borrow advances from the Bank of Canada to cover their short-term liquidity needs. Its primary function is to serve as a clear signal of the Bank of Canada's policy with respect to the level of interest rates.

Bank Rate.

The *bank rate* is the rate of interest that the Bank of Canada charges when banks or other members of the Canadian Payments Association borrow advances from the Bank of Canada. The amount that a bank borrows from the Bank of Canada counts as reserves for that bank. An increase in the bank rate increases the penalty to discourage chartered banks from borrowing from the Bank of Canada to meet any reserve deficiency. A rise in the bank rate encourages the chartered banks to be more cautious about becoming short of liquidity to meet clearing obligations. When the bank rate is increased, it tends to increase interest rates on bank loans generally. The Bank of Canada increases the bank rate when it desires to tighten credit and slow down growth in the money supply. In contrast, the Bank of Canada decreases the bank rate when it desires to ease money and credit. Because changes to the bank rate are viewed as signals indicating whether the Bank of Canada is pursuing or planning to pursue a policy of monetary ease or monetary tightness, the chartered banks and other members of society must get a clear signal of which way the Bank of Canada wants the interest rate to move.

Between 1956 and 1962 and again from 1980 to 1996, the Bank of Canada adopted the convention of setting the bank rate at one-quarter percent above the rate of return earned on 91-day treasury bills at the weekly auction of treasury bills.[10] Under this system, if the Bank of Canada wished to decrease the bank rate, it would engage in open-market purchases through the open market. If the Bank of Canada purchased treasury bills from the open market, it would increase the demand for treasury bills. As we explained using supply and demand theory in Chapter 2, when the demand for an item increases, all other things being constant, the price of that item also increases. Thus when the Bank of Canada bought treasury bills, it increased the demand for the bills and increased the market price of the treasury bills. Financial assets that have a predetermined value at maturity have an inverse relationship between the rate of return earned on the asset—its effective interest rate—and the market price of the asset. Thus when the Bank of Canada caused the market price of treasury bills to increase, it also caused the effective interest rate on the bills to decrease. The type of treasury bills that the Bank of Canada purchased were, and continue to be, important to the portfolio structure of many pension funds and financial intermediaries. When the effective interest rate that can be earned on treasury bills decreases, it lowers the opportunity for financial intermediaries to earn as high a return on their assets, which places downward pressure on other interest rates throughout the economy. Alternatively, if the Bank of Canada wants to increase the bank rate, it sells treasury bills in the open market.[11] Selling treasury bills has the opposite effect on the price of the treasury bills; it decreases their market price, and increases the effective interest rate on them.

During the 16-year period ending in 1996, the banking industry faced legislative changes to deregulate financial markets and technological innovations such as electronic trading. These changes resulted in some situations where the bank rate moved in response to short-term market forces in the international capital markets rather than as a reflection of the policy initiatives of the Bank of Canada. In February 1996 the Bank of Canada adopted its present policy of setting the bank rate based on the overnight lending rate that one chartered bank charges another chartered bank. The Bank of Canada has not chosen to set a specific premium to be added to

---

[10]Shearer, op. cit., pp. 653–7, and p. 661.

[11]For an excellent discussion of the relationship between the price of a financial asset and the effective rate of return on that asset see D. C. Colander and P. S. Sephton, *Macroeconomics, 1st Canadian ed.* (Toronto: Irwin, 1996), pp. 286–96.

the overnight lending rate in the way that it previously tied the bank rate to the yield on treasury bills, although it appears that the Bank of Canada clearly intends to maintain the bank rate at a level above the overnight lending rate. The new bank rate policy acts as a penalty rate that complements the change to the zero-reserve requirement mentioned earlier in the chapter.

Under the new system, chartered banks are required to pay the bank rate for any advances borrowed from the Bank of Canada to meet reserve deficiencies on both a daily or an average monthly basis. The first condition requires each chartered bank to maintain a zero-reserve balance at the end of each day. Banks may borrow from other institutions or from the Bank of Canada to cover any deficiency in their daily reserve. The rate of interest charged on the borrowing is the overnight loan rate if they borrow from a chartered bank or the bank rate if they borrow the funds from the Bank of Canada. The second condition is that, in addition to the daily zero balance, chartered banks must meet a reserve-averaging condition. The reserve-averaging condition requires that each direct-clearing financial intermediary must maintain an average monthly reserve at least equal to zero net of borrowings to meet its daily reserve position. The effect of this condition is that funds borrowed to meet shortages in the daily reserve balances are subtracted from an institution's positive daily balances over the averaging period in estimating its averaged reserve balance. Any chartered bank that held a zero-reserve position each day but met that condition by borrowing would be charged the bank rate on its averaged monthly deficiency. Under the new policy the bank rate has become more clearly a penalty fee that affects a bank in two ways if it fails to maintain its average reserve position at a zero balance without having to borrow.[12]

The change to the new bank rate policy allows the Bank of Canada to adjust the spread between the overnight rate and the bank rate only when the Bank of Canada wishes to indicate that a change in the interest rates was needed in consumer-lending and business-loan markets. It allows the bank rate to serve as a clearer signal to financial institutions and the public of the policy directions of the Bank of Canada without the distortions that occurred because of short-term capital market disruptions from the private sector. Economists also expect that the new system will, along with other revisions to the *Bank Act*, actually increase the penalty rate to any chartered bank for failing to meet its daily and monthly average liquidity obligations required to support its clearing activities with other members of the Canadian Payments Association. In this way the new system should give the Bank of Canada more power to influence interest rates than existed in the previous system. While the new system should reduce any distortions in the signal the Bank of Canada wants to send to markets and should enhance its direct influence to bring about the desired level of in-

---

[12]Shearer, op. cit., pp. 620–5.

terest rates, a change in the bank rate not supported by appropriate changes in other tools of monetary policy may not have much impact on the economy. To ensure that financial intermediaries and the public get a consistent signal of monetary policy, the Bank of Canada needs to coordinate the movements in the bank rate with its activities in the open market.

Switching Government Accounts. The Bank of Canada acts as the fiscal agent for the federal government of Canada. In its role as fiscal agent, the Bank of Canada is empowered to deposit and issue cheques or otherwise move the accounts of the federal government. When the Bank of Canada wishes to increase the monetary base, it can withdraw funds from a government of Canada account in the Bank of Canada and redeposit the funds in a chartered bank. The primary impact of switching government accounts into the chartered banks is to increase demand deposits and excess reserves of banks. The Bank of Canada makes the decision to switch government accounts into the chartered banks when it desires to expand the money supply. Conversely, if the Bank of Canada wishes to reduce the monetary base available to the chartered banks, it can withdraw funds from a government of Canada account in a chartered bank and redeposit those funds in a government of Canada account in the Bank of Canada. The monetary base and the lending ability of banks are reduced by switching government accounts out of the chartered banks and redepositing them in the Bank of Canada.

> **Switching government accounts** is the movement of government accounts out of the Bank of Canada and their redeposit into chartered banks to increase the money supply or the withdrawal of government accounts from chartered banks and their redeposit into the Bank of Canada to reduce the money supply.

Monetary Policy Targets

The three most often discussed monetary policy targets are the interest rate target, the exchange rate target, and the money growth rate target. Monetary policy has often focused on interest rates. When interest rates were believed to be "too high," the Bank of Canada pursued a policy of *easy money;* and when interest rates were believed to be "too low," the Bank of Canada pursued a policy of *tight money.* These policy actions are sometimes referred to as a policy of fine-tuning; that is, pursuing a policy that in effect changes the growth rate in the money supply in order to maintain interest rates at a level that will promote economic stability and growth. This focus on interest rates as the prime basis of monetary policy has at times led to serious inflationary problems. During periods of economic expansion, interest rates generally rise because of the increase in the demand for money and credit. To prevent interest rates from rising in these circumstances, the Bank of Canada may pursue a policy that increases the money growth rate. Also, political pressures on the Bank of Canada to keep interest rates low or to prevent interest rates from rising tend to increase inflationary expectations and eventually lead to a higher money growth rate and inflation. The major criticism of using interest rates as the main policy target is that the Bank of Canada would be relinquishing control over the growth in the money supply. The goal of targeting the exchange rate is important in a country like Canada where substantial numbers of jobs depend on exports and where many firms and individuals rely on imported goods as a matter of their normal routine. If the Bank of Canada views the value of the Canadian dollar as too low in relation to foreign currency, the bank can cause the dollar to increase in value by reducing the monetary base and forcing the interest rate to rise. The reason this action will cause the value of the Canadian dollar to increase in international markets is that the rise in the Canadian interest rate will entice foreigners to try to acquire Canadian dollars so that they can use them to earn the higher rate of interest being offered in Canada. Conversely, if the Bank of Canada feels that the Canadian dollar is being pushed too high on international markets and that this condition threatens to make Canadian products and services uncompetitive in international markets, the Bank of Canada can increase the monetary base. The resulting increase in the money supply will decrease the interest rate and cause foreigners to withdraw funds from Canada, putting a downward pressure on the value of the Canadian dollar on international markets.

In 1975 the Bank of Canada began to focus on money growth of M1 as the prime policy target in response to the high rate of inflation in early 1970s.[13] Money growth rates were established for the various measures of money supply. This policy of targetting the money supply growth rate in what was dubbed "monetary gradualism" continued until 1981 when it was formally abandoned. The abandonment occurred for two reasons. The governor of the Bank of Canada argued that targetting M1 as the monetary aggregate was not producing the results expected in terms of the rate of growth of GDP and the interest rate. In addition, the economy had begun to enter a recession in 1980, and pressure was growing to ease the growth of the money supply to counter the recessionary trend. From 1982 to 1985 the Bank of Canada achieved a stable inflation rate in the 4 to 5 percent range, but the governor of that period indicated that he felt a credible monetary policy required the Bank to adopt a target of zero inflation. In accordance with this policy and with the formal agreement by the finance minister, Michael Wilson, the Bank of Canada launched another attack on inflation by restricting monetary growth rates with the stated goal of reaching stable prices by 1995. The actual growth rate in M1 was 4.8 percent for 1989, followed by an actual decrease in the money supply of 1.8 percent in 1990 and by a rise to 3.1 percent for 1991. In response to this reduction in monetary growth the inflation rate fell from 5 percent in 1989 to 4.8 percent in 1990 and to 1.5 percent for 1991.

A fierce debate now rages in the economics discipline between economists supporting the money growth rate target and a growing number of economists who are expressing serious reservations over the efficacy of

---

[13]Ibid. pp. 832–9.

using the restrictions in the growth of the money supply and monetary rule as the tools to achieve stable prices. Most economists accept that the growth in the money supply ultimately determines the inflation rate over the long term. Second, they agree that erratic movements in the money growth rate are a major contributor to the instability in the economy. For these reasons, a Bank of Canada policy that concentrates on a stable money growth rate is generally seen as desirable by most economists. But to say that the Bank of Canada should attempt to stabilize the growth of the money supply is not to concede the point that the Bank of Canada should have no other responsibility than to keep prices from escalating. Critics of the Bank of Canada's policy of stable prices have pointed out that the Bank of Canada asserted early in its program that if slow growth in the money supply could establish stable prices, it should also strengthen the Canadian dollar on international exchange markets and reduce domestic inflation rates in Canada. It was argued by proponents of the bank's policy that both of these phenomena would create increased international competitiveness and job creation that would reduce the unemployment rate—shortrun pain of reduced monetary growth in return for longrun gain in competitiveness and job creation. The Bank of Canada has engaged in a policy of restricting monetary growth as a means of establishing price stability for most years since 1979; the policy has had almost sixteen years to work.

What are the obvious results of the Bank of Canada's policy? The Bank of Canada did manage to restrict the growth of the money supply to rates less than that of the growth of the money supply in the United States. The inflation rate in Canada has fallen from double-digit levels in the early 1980s to rates of less than 1 percent in recent years. Despite this and the fact that our price level grew more slowly than that of our trade partners, the Canadian interest rate remained very high in comparison with rates in the United States and other Western economies over most of the period. Although the Canadian dollar strengthened against the American dollar for part of the 1980s, it sank back in the 1990s, precisely when the Bank of Canada was enforcing its toughest campaign against inflation. Some supporters of the Bank of Canada strategy explain that the Canadian dollar would have been weaker still if it had not been for the Bank of Canada's resolve to control the growth of the money supply. They explain that the fall of the dollar is undoubtedly due to the high burden of the public debt and the continued federal and provincial government deficits or the political instability of the "Quebec question." While there is much truth to these claims, they can not detract from the point that the workings and the linkages between monetary growth and the price level, interest rates, exchange rates, and the unemployment rate are far more complex and slightly less predictable than the proponents of monetary rule thought they were a decade ago. In addition, the pursuit of restricted monetary growth as a means of controlling prices has brought with it much higher unemployment rates and slower economic growth than would otherwise have been the case.

Inflationary Causes and Cures

We will take two approaches to explain the causes of inflation and to present possible methods of stopping it. The quantity theory of money is the first approach. This theory stresses the importance of money in the inflationary process. Aggregate demand and aggregate supply analysis provides a framework for analyzing the causes of inflation.

Quantity Theory of Money

The starting point for the quantity theory of money is the *equation of exchange*

$$MV = PY$$

The **equation of exchange** is an identity. On the left side of the equation, the money supply times velocity equals total spending, and on the right side of the equation, the price level times the quantity of final goods and services produce equals the value of these goods and services produced—nominal GDP.

where M = the money supply; V = the income velocity of money or the number of times, on average, a dollar is used to buy final goods and services in a year; P = the price level or the average price of final goods and services; and Y = the quantity of final goods and services produced during the year—real GDP.

The left side of the equation, the money supply (M) times the velocity or turnover of money (V), measures total money spending in the economy. The right-hand side of the equation, the price level (P) times the real gross domestic output (Y), equals the money value of the output or nominal gross domestic product. The two sides of the equation are equal, since the total spending for goods and services is the same as the total sales value of goods and services. The quantity theory of money states that increases and decreases in M cause increases and decreases in P and Y, respectively. The assumption of this theory is that V is relatively constant or at least changes in a predictable way.[14] In Canada the evidence is clear that velocity is not constant, and some economists warn against the assumption of a constant V when using the quantity theory of money.[15] Although the warning is valid, the simplest review of the theory involves accepting a constant velocity as a starting point of exploration. If we further assume

---

[14]In Canada the evidence over the past 30 years reveals that neither has velocity been stable nor did it change in easily predictable ways. From 1960 to 1990 the velocity of M1 increased from approximately 7.5 to 17, and it varied by a larger percentage than the change in either the money supply or the real GDP over the past 30 years. For a discussion of this topic, see C. M. Fellows, G. Flanagan, S. Shedd and R. Waud, *Economics in a Canadian Setting* (New York: HarperCollins, 1993), pp. 804–15.

[15]P. L. Siklos, *Money, Banking, and Financial Institutions: Canada in the Global Environment* (Toronto: McGraw-Hill Ryerson, 1994), pp. 192–200.

that the real gross domestic output is fixed, then the price level will rise or fall at the same rate that M rises or falls. More relevant than this extreme assumption concerning output is that, given a constant or relatively constant V, the inflation rate is closely connected with the growth rate in the money supply as the economy expands and nears full employment.

An increase in the money supply will certainly increase prices unless either velocity of money decreases or output increases. In the event of no changes in V and Y, the price level is the equilibrating variable that moves the economy toward a new equilibrium where the increase in M is offset by an increase in P. That is to say, when an increase in M creates "excess money," the excess, assuming a constant V, flows into the final goods market, resulting in inflation. A decrease in V or an increase in Y could partially or wholly eliminate the excess money and, therefore, could partially or wholly offset the inflationary pressure. The quantity theory of money teaches, however, that growth in the money supply is the basic cause of inflation, and the cure for inflation is to control the growth in the money supply. The control can be achieved, of course, through the appropriate use of Bank of Canada controls over the money supply.

In view of the quantity theory of money, let's examine again the growth rates in inflation and the money supply. Figure 14–3 shows both the average inflation rate (CPI) and the money supply growth rate (M2) from 1962 to 1994. The rate of growth in the money supply exceeded the rate of inflation in almost every year from 1962 to 1980. In the 1981–1982 period, inflation exceeded the growth rate of the money supply. From 1983 to 1994 the growth rate of the money supply again exceeded the inflation rate. In observing the general direction of the movement of the money supply and the inflation rate, two separate patterns of behaviour between inflation and growth rates of the money supply emerge. In the years 1962–1975, 1979–1980, and 1981–1983, the growth rate of the money supply and the inflation rate moved in the same direction and with similar patterns of rates of growth. In other words, over these periods when the money supply grew more rapidly, the inflation rate increased; when the money supply growth rate decreased, the inflation rate decreased; and when the money supply decreased, the inflation rate either decreased or the price level actually fell. At the same time the link between the growth of the money supply and the inflation rate seems to become less well-defined in the later years than in the early years. There are, particularly in the later years, periods when the growth rate of the money supply and the inflation rate actually move in opposite directions. For example, when the money supply growth rate slowed between 1975–1978, 1980–1981, 1987–1988, and 1990–1991, the inflation rate actually increased. Some economists point out that the increases in the velocity in Canada coincide with technological innovations and changes to the legal and institutional structure of financial markets.[16] The changes in

---

[16]R. A. Shearer, op. cit., pp. 28–41 and pp. 725–8.

Figure 14–3   **Annual inflation rate and money supply growth rate 1962–1994**

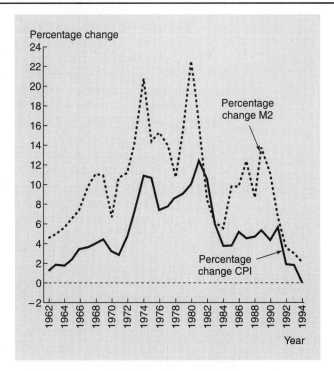

Sources: Canadian Economic Observer, Historical Statistical Supplement, CANSIM, Bank of Canada Review, and Bank of Canada Review Supplement.

technology and structure may have resulted in society being able to meet its needs for exchange and financial security without resorting to the use of money—causing velocity to increase. The data suggest a long-term link between the growth of the money supply and inflation, but the relationship is neither as tight and direct nor as simple as the quantity theory of money might suggest.

Demand-Pull Inflation

Demand-pull inflation stems from increases in total consumer, investment, government, and net export spending that cause rightward shifts in the aggregate-demand curve.

An alternative approach to the quantity theory of money is the aggregate-demand approach. This approach stresses excess demand as a major cause of inflation. The two approaches are similar in some respects, but have important differences in points of emphasis and in policy recommendations. The aggregate-demand approach places more emphasis on total consumer, investment, government, and net export spending in the economy and less emphasis on growth in the money supply. The money supply is viewed primarily as an accommodating variable instead of an initiating variable. According to aggregate-demand analysis, demand-pull inflation is initiated by an increase in aggregate demand and is self-enforcing by further increases in aggregate demand. A demand-pull inflation is associated with increasing production and decreasing unemployment at least until the economy approaches the non-accelerating inflation rate of unemployment, or NAIRU (discussed in Chapter 13). Once this functional full-employment ceiling is reached, further increases in aggregate demand will cause only accelerating increases in the general level of prices with no further increases in production.

Figure 14–4 depicts demand-pull inflation. Beginning at the price level p and production y, an increase in aggregate demand to AD_1 means that all demand cannot be satisfied at p. Thus the price level rises to p_1, and production rises to y_f. An increase in demand to AD_2 causes the price level to rise further to p_2. This inflationary process continues as long as aggregate demand increases, since all demand can be satisfied only at higher prices. Pure inflation, an increase in the price level without an increase in output, is shown when aggregate demand increases to AD_2.

Figure 14–4   Demand-pull inflation

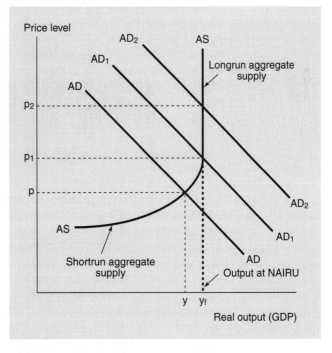

Demand-pull inflation results from increases in aggregate demand from *AD* to *AD₁* to *AD₂*.

The idea that aggregate demand shifts continuously to the right, tracing out increases in output and the general price level, raises at least one important question. What factors can cause the aggregate-demand curve to shift to the right continuously—or at least for long periods of time? To answer this question, we will briefly return to some of the ideas covered in Chapter 13. The aggregate-demand curve tells us the total combined spending by households, businesses, governments, and foreign customers for goods and services produced in the economy for each general price level. Because the curve involves all four sectors of the economy, including foreign customers for Canadian production, a vast array of possible causes can produce an increase in aggregate demand. We cannot deal with all the possible causes, but we can illustrate how the increase occurs.

Assume that the economy of a foreign country, to which Canada exports a large percentage of its output, begins to expand. The expansion could be caused by a demographic change to the foreign country's population that increases consumer spending. It could also result from increased investment, or it might result from a rise in the foreign government's deficit to pay for some national emergency. The reason for the expansion is not important to our discussion, but the expansion must be widespread and of long duration for our example to work. As the foreign economy expands, it will import more goods and services that are used as inputs to its own increasing production. In addition, as its citizens earn more income, they will respend some portion of their extra income, and some of it will likely be used to purchase consumer goods and services imported from Canada. Further, if we assume that the foreign economy had a large amount of unemployed resources at the beginning of the expansion, its growth could continue for a long time. Finally, if the foreign economy is very large relative to Canada, even if only a small proportion of the foreign income is used to purchase Canadian imports, it could be quite a large amount in relation to Canada's total output. As long as the foreign economy continues to grow, there is a growth in the aggregate demand for Canadian goods and services and the growth could be quite large in relation to what Canada is capable of producing at NAIRU. In this example, the growth in aggregate demand is not linked to causes that originated inside Canada and does not depend on whether Canada has the capacity to expand its production without experiencing an upward pressure on the general level of prices. Thus inflation in small economies with relatively high proportions of exports can be caused by growing demand in the foreign economies with which they trade.[17]

---

[17]Critics of this argument point out that increased foreign demand will likely cause an appreciation or increase in the value of the exporting economy's currency on international markets that will cause export demand to fall. This argument overlooks the fact that a change in the exchange rate depends on the international exchange rate system being flexible, and it occurs only in the long run. In effect, the change to the exchange rate is a response to the problem of inflation once it exists.

While our example concentrated on an increase in foreign demand as the factor that caused the demand-pull inflation, we stress that the causes are broad and varied. Our example specified that the foreign-caused demand-pull inflation required that the exporting country's economy had to be small compared to that of its trade partner. This example might be useful in some circumstances for Canada or the Netherlands to explain their inflation rates from time to time, but it is of little relevance to Germany, Japan, or the United States. Many economists believe that large, chronic government deficits run by most of the developed economies have been major contributing factors to widespread demand-pull inflations in the industrialized economies over the last 30 years.

Cures for Demand-Pull Inflation

Demand-pull inflation can be stopped by the appropriate use of monetary policy by the Bank of Canada and fiscal policy by the federal government. We know now that demand-pull inflation can be caused by excess money leading to excess spending or by excess demand accommodated by expansions in the money supply. In either case this type of inflation can be slowed down or stopped completely by monetary policy that slows down the growth in the money supply: namely, a tight monetary policy by the Bank of Canada to reduce the monetary base—the Bank of Canada notes and reserves available to the banking system. When the Bank of Canada practices a tight monetary policy, as the monetary base decreases, it creates a shortage of loanable funds that causes interest rates to increase. As interest rates rise, firms postpone investment spending and consumers reduce consumer spending on durable items that are typically financed through borrowing. Thus the tight monetary policy will lead to reductions in aggregate demand, which reduces the pressure for prices to increase. The appropriate federal fiscal policy to reduce demand-pull inflation is some combination of government expenditure cuts and tax increases; that is, federal budget deficits can be reduced or surpluses can be increased. A decrease in government purchases directly reduces total spending in the economy. A decrease in government transfer payments or an increase in taxes indirectly reduces aggregate demand by decreasing private spending. In addition, increases in the federal debt brought about by budget deficits should be financed in a way that does not create money.

Demand-pull inflation is difficult to stop without causing unemployment. The same economic forces causing inflation also increase production and employment. A popular view among economists for controlling demand-pull inflation is not to let it develop in the first place. Once inflation develops and is out of control, it seems almost inevitable that the opportunity cost to stop inflation is rising unemployment.

Supply-Shock Inflation

It is difficult to explain some of the inflationary periods in the 1970s and 1980s only on the basis of demand-pull inflation. The economy has experienced both inflation and recession together at certain times. How can this be? Demand-pull inflation is characterized by rising prices, rising production, and falling unemployment. Inflation and recession at the same time mean rising prices, falling production, and rising unemployment. The only way the theory can explain the economy experiencing simultaneous inflation and recession is for inflation to be initiated by a decrease in aggregate supply. This type of inflation is called supply-shock inflation. Increases in costs or increases in profit margins cause aggregate supply to shift left, reducing the quantity of goods produced and increasing prices.

Figure 14–5 illustrates supply-shock inflation. Beginning at price level p and production y_f, aggregate supply decreases to AS_1. Now all demand cannot be satisfied at p; that is, aggregate output demanded is greater than aggregate output supplied. As a consequence, the price level

Figure 14–5   Supply-shock inflation

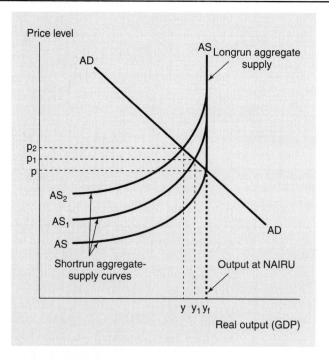

Supply-shock inflation results from a decrease in aggregate supply from AS to AS_1 and AS_2.

rises to p_1. Aggregate supply decreases further to AS_2. Again, all demand cannot be satisfied, and price rises to p_2. This inflationary process continues until there are no further decreases in aggregate supply. In Figure 14–5, supply-shock inflation is characterized by rising prices and falling production.

Supply-shock inflation occurs because of decreases in aggregate supply. But what causes aggregate supply to decrease? The answer is an increase in resource prices not offset by productivity increases. If a resource, such as energy, increases in price, it is not profitable to produce the same levels of output at the same price levels unless the higher energy costs are offset. For another illustration, an increase in the price of labour, unaccompanied by an increase in labour's productivity, increases labour unit costs and, therefore, decreases output supplied at every price level. Sometimes the blame for supply-shock inflation is placed on monopoly power in the labour market—the power of unions to negotiate successfully for wage gains in excess of productivity gains. Alternatively, the market power of monopoly firms to reduce output as a way of increasing prices can also cause supply-shock inflation. In the case of supply-shock inflation, most economists agree that the price increases and output reduction are relatively short lived; once the markets have adjusted to the increased cost of the resource or to the increased profit margin of the monopolist firms, the aggregate price adjustment will come to an end. The supply shock will have reached an equilibrium at a higher price level for goods and services and with a different distribution of purchasing power among the groups in society. In the absence of continuously increasing demand, supply pressures create only short-term inflation. In the absence of growing demand pressures, the monopoly powers of unions or producers to bring about supply-shock inflation are exaggerated. For inflation to be an ongoing problem for a society, it must be accompanied by growing aggregate demand. The major points to remember about supply-shock inflation are that it is caused by resource price increases, productivity decreases, or profit margin increases and that it is a short-term problem.

Demand-Pull and Then Supply-Shock Inflation

It may be misleading to look upon demand-pull and supply-shock as two separate inflationary processes. In fact, a single inflationary period may result from both demand-pull and supply-shock pressures. Suppose that increases in aggregate demand start the inflationary process. Prices, production, and employment rise in response to the pull of demand. Money wages rise but lag behind prices. Unions realize eventually that wages have lagged behind prices and begin to try to catch up by demanding wage increases in excess of productivity increases. Once this happens, supply-shock pressures begin to reinforce demand pressures. The end of an inflationary process may not coincide with the moment that demand-pull pressures no longer exist. Prices may continue to rise for a period because of supply-shock pressures. These pressures operating alone sustain the inflation temporarily, even though production and employment are falling. However, without demand-pull pressures, inflation eventually stops.

Can We Cure Supply-Shock Inflation?

Monetary and fiscal policies can deal, theoretically anyway, with demand-type problems. However, they are not well-suited to cope effectively with supply-shock inflationary pressures. Some economists have advocated certain other policies to deal with supply-shock inflationary pressures if these pressures stem from wage and price increases connected with monopoly power of unions or firms. These policies are often referred to as *incomes policies*.

Incomes policies are a set of government policies designed to deal with supply-shock inflationary pressures associated with imperfect labour and product markets by establishing wage and price ceilings and some mechanism for their enforcement.

An incomes policy can range from Parliament or the provincial legislatures publicizing voluntary guidelines that industry and unions are supposed to adhere to in their decisions to raise prices or wages, to the imposition of mandatory price and wage controls. Canada, like most Western economies, used wage and price programs during the mid-1970s to combat the supply-side inflationary pressures caused by the energy shortages at the time. In 1975 we created the Anti-Inflation Board (AIB) that had the power to limit wage increases and price increases for a three-year period. The AIB did manage to limit the symptoms of rising prices and wages, although there were technical difficulties with compliance. What the board failed to do was deal with the underlying causes of inflation. Once the board was eliminated in 1977, inflation increased rapidly over the next three years. The supply shocks that had resulted from the energy crisis of 1973 had been accommodated, and the increased demand pressures caused by increases in the money supply led to a pent-up aggregate demand. These pressures received further inflationary supply shock when the second energy shock hit in 1979. As indicated earlier in this chapter, beginning in 1981 the Bank of Canada greatly reduced the demand-side pressure for inflation by reducing the growth of the money supply. The effect was predictable and dramatic. Inflationary pressures were reduced and inflation was cut in half from previous levels. At the same time real output measured by gross domestic product actually decreased for the first time in 40 years, and unemployment rose by 50 percent of its own value. From 1983 to 1990 few supply-side forces were causing inflation during the economic expansion. The inflationary pressure in this period was characterized by growth on the demand side of the economy. Since 1990, as the economy entered the recession and the subsequent recovery, policymakers have been looking for policy that would shift the aggregate supply curve to the right.

The main criticism of almost any incomes policy is that it does not eliminate the cause of inflation. By contrast, the recent initiatives of the federal government have tried to address this problem.

The government, constrained by the fiscal burden of interest changes on the public debt and restricted by the political swing to the right so prevalent in the early 1990s, has been looking for policies that would cause firms and unions to increase output without this causing increases to the federal government deficit. The federal government's proposed reform of the unemployment insurance system introduced in the fall of 1995 was an example of policy designed to increase aggregate supply by using supply-side theory. The reforms were an attempt to transform the unemployment insurance system into an employment insurance program. Proponents of the change argued that the former program paid benefits to unemployed people in high-unemployment regions or from high-unemployment industries on more generous terms than it paid in regions and industries with lower unemployment. In the logic of supply-side theory, this situation implies that the system actually contributed to high levels of long-term unemployment in some regions and industries by reducing the relative benefits of being employed. To correct these perceived causes of unemployment, the new system will reduce benefits to individuals the longer they are unemployed as well as to individuals who are very active repeat claimants for unemployment benefits. It will provide progressive incentives to unemployed individuals to seek retraining the longer their duration of unemployment. It will allow individuals to use their benefits to start self-employed business ventures. In addition, the new system will increase the cost to workers and the industries that employ them if they have a record of above-average claims for unemployment insurance benefits. Proponents of these changes claim that the changes will do two things to shift the aggregate supply curve to the right. The first is that the measures will widen the gap between the income of being employed and being unemployed, which should make individuals more willing to work at lower wages. The result will be to reduce the costs to businesses and to increase the supply of goods and services that can be profitably offered for sale. Critics of this argument point out that if the plan works, it will cause a redistribution from the poor to the rich within Canada and will widen the gap between the haves and the have-nots, making us a less egalitarian society. The other measures that encourage the unemployed to seek training and education will work in a quite different way to increase the aggregate-supply curve. By increasing their skills at using the new technologies, unemployed workers increase their productivity and that of the country. This result, the proponents argue, will cause the aggregate-supply curve to shift to the right, allowing businesses to increase the employment levels while holding prices down.

Summary

Inflation means that the general level of prices is rising. It means that it takes more money to buy the same quantity of goods and services. Inflation may be suppressed when output demanded is greater than output supplied at the current price level, but the price level does not rise because of government price controls. The three effects of inflation are the equity, efficiency, and output effects. The equity effects are the results of inflation on income distribution. The people who lose during inflation are those who receive fixed incomes and have fixed money claims. The people who gain during inflation are those whose money incomes rise faster than prices and who hold assets that rise in value more than the increase in the average price of goods and services.

The efficiency effects of inflation are the results of inflation on the allocation of resources. Inflation changes the allocation of resources, since inflation alters relative commodity prices. It is not certain that this change in resource allocation is a less efficient allocation. Some economists argue that inflation distorts the allocation of resources and results in less efficient allocation.

The impact of inflation on the aggregate production of goods and services may be to encourage more production. Before the economy reaches full employment, rising prices tend to go hand-in-hand with rising production. The same forces that cause prices to rise cause production to rise. However, the continuation of inflationary forces once the economy is at full employment leads to pure inflation—that is, rising prices not associated with rising production.

Money plays an important role in the economy. Money is anything that is generally accepted as a means of payment for goods, services, and debt. Money serves three functions. First, money serves as a medium of exchange; second, the value of goods and services is measured in money; and third, money serves as a store of value. The supply of money in the economy includes currency and coins in circulation, demand deposits at banks, saving and notice deposits of small denominations, and other chequable deposits. Broader measures of the money supply include other near-money assets. The money supply expands when banks, as a group, expand loans, and it contracts when banks, as a group, contract loans. The Bank of Canada, which has the responsibility of controlling the money supply, attempts to fulfill its responsibility through the use of policy controls over the monetary base—Bank of Canada notes and the deposits of the chartered banks at the Bank of Canada. The three policy controls are open market operations, the bank rate, and switching government accounts. When the Bank of Canada wants to slow down growth in the money supply, the Bank can sell treasury bills or other government securities to the open markets, increase the bank rate, and withdraw government funds from accounts held in the chartered banks and redeposit them in the Bank of Canada. These policy actions decrease the cash reserves available to the chartered banks and reduce their lending ability. The Bank of Canada can take opposite policy actions if it wants to increase the growth in the money supply—namely, the Bank of Canada can buy treasury bills or other government securities from members of the private sector who had previously invested in them, decrease the bank rate, and withdraw government accounts from the Bank of Canada and redeposit them in the chartered banks. These actions increase the cash reserves available to the chartered banks and increase their lending ability.

Two approaches help explain the causes of inflation and the cures to inflation. The first approach is the quantity theory of money. This theory stresses the importance of money in the inflationary process. The second approach is an aggregate-demand and aggregate-supply approach. The central message of the quantity theory of money is that behind every long-term inflation is a growth in the money supply that exceeds the growth in real gross domestic product and that the way to stop inflation is to control the growth in the money supply. In a demand-pull inflation, excess aggregate demand initiates inflation. In a supply-shock inflation, aggregate supply decreases, resulting in upward pressures on prices. The cure for demand-pull inflation is the appropriate use of monetary and fiscal policies. The only likely solutions to supply-shock inflationary pressures are to increase factor productivity and to attempt to shift the aggregate supply curve to the right by other means. Incomes policy can be used to temporarily suppress the symptoms of either a demand-pull or supply-shock inflation, but it does not deal with the underlying causes of inflation.

Checklist of Economic Concepts

Inflation	Bank rate
Price index numbers	Open-market operation
Equity	Equation of exchange
Efficiency	Quantity theory of money
Money supply	Demand-pull inflation
Creating money	Supply-shock inflation
Deposit multiplier	Incomes policy
Reserve ratio	

Discussion Questions

1. Explain how the consumer price index is constructed. Why would the measured inflation rate from 1995 to 1997 be different if 1995 were used as the base year than if 1997 were used as the base year?

2. In 1962 Milton Friedman, a Nobel Prize–winning economist, wrote *Dollars and Deficits*, in which he postulated that "Inflation is always

and everywhere a monetary phenomenon." Explain why you agree or disagree with Friedman.

3. Norman Cameron, a professor at the University of Manitoba, once described money as one of humanity's finest inventions. Explain why money is more efficient than barter. Can you think of other reasons why Cameron would make such a claim?

4. Distinguish between M1, M2, M3, and M2+ as measures of the money supply. Why are cheques and credit cards not counted as money?

5. Critics of Canada's adoption of a zero required reserve ratio argue that it leaves the chartered banks free to create money out of thin air. Use a simplified balance sheet to investigate whether this allegation is true.

6. Write the equation for the deposit multiplier. What happens to the size of the deposit multiplier if the desired reserve ratio decreases?

7. Define the bank rate. How does the system for setting the bank rate adopted in February 1996 increase the Bank of Canada's flexibility in influencing interest rates?

8. Explain how the Bank of Canada can use open-market purchases to decrease the money supply. Why would a tight monetary policy combat a demand-pull type of inflation.

9. Use aggregate-supply and aggregate-demand graphs to illustrate a demand-pull inflation. What are some of the possible causes of a demand-pull inflation?

10. Use aggregate-supply and aggregate-demand graphs to illustrate and explain a supply-shock inflation. Briefly discuss some of the possible causes of a supply-shock inflation.

Supplementary Reading

Cameron, N. E. *Money Financial Markets and Economic Activity.* 2nd ed. Don Mills, ON: Addison-Wesley, 1992.
    Chapters 11 to 13 provide an excellent review of the chartered banks and other financial intermediaries in Canada. Chapters 16 and 17 use an aggregate-demand and aggregate-supply model to analyze the Canadian financial sector's links to unemployment and inflation.

Colander, D. C. and P. S. Sephton. *Macroeconomics. 1st Canadian ed.* Burr Ridge, IL: Richard D. Irwin, 1996.
    Chapters 11, 12, and 13 provide a thorough and up-to-date discussion of the linkages between interest rates, rates of return, and various financial assets; the

role of money in macroeconomic analysis, and the structure and exercise of monetary policy in Canada.

Fellows, C. M.; G. Flanagan; S. Shedd; and R. Waud. *Economics in a Canadian Setting*. New York: HarperCollins, 1993.

Chapters 24 and 26 create a thorough aggregate-demand/aggregate-supply model for examining inflation. Chapters 27 to 30 provide a thorough theoretical framework for analyzing the factors affecting the supply and demand for money in Canada. Chapters 27 and 30 also include investigations of Canada's relationship between changes to the money supply and the resulting changes to inflation and the velocity of circulation.

Mishkin, F. S. *The Economics of Money, Banking, and Financial Markets*. 3rd ed. New York: HarperCollins, 1992.

Chapter 27 includes an examination of the German hyperinflation from 1921 to 1923 and discusses different views of inflation.

Shearer, R. A.; J. K. Chant; and D. E. Bond. *Economics of the Canadian Financial System; Theory, Policy and Institutions*. Scarborough, ON: Prentice-Hall, 1995.

Chapters 1 and 12 provide a thorough review of the structure and workings of Canada's financial intermediaries. Chapter 17 is a thorough treatment of the quantity theory of money and behaviour of the velocity of circulation.

Siklos, P. L. *Money, Banking, and Financial Institutions: Canada in the Global Environment*. Toronto, ON: McGraw-Hill Ryerson, 1994.

Chapters 1, 2, and 3 provide a thorough review of money and its function in the modern Canadian economy, as well as a review of the structure and workings of Canada's financial intermediaries.

Chapter 15

Government Expenditure, Tax, and Debt Issues
Is Government Spending Too Much?

Seldom, in our history, have so many experienced such anxiety. Canadians feel our very way of life is at risk.

If there is one obligation before government today, it is to do its part to address these deep concerns. It is to do what we must so that confidence can overcome anxiety, and hope can replace despair. In short, we must act now to help Canadians secure their future.

Canadians know this can't be done by government alone. It will require the concerted efforts of individual Canadians, their governments, business and others for our country to tackle these challenges effectively. What Canadians want from their government is for it to set the goals, to have a plan and then to work as hard as it can—and as long as it must—to help get the job done.[1]

What Are People Concerned About?

The introductory quote from the Honourable Paul Martin, minister of finance, focusses on the concern people feel in the 1990s about their economic and social security in a rapidly changing socioeconomic environment. Canadians are raising questions about the appropriate role of government involvement in the economy in the form of government services, regulations, and controls and how this involvement is financed. Many people are questioning the distribution of government services and programs and the distribution and level of taxes needed to finance these services. On the whole Canadians have been generous in supporting programs that lessen income disparity and deliver services to all Canadians regardless of ability to pay. The overwhelming support for the government financed Medicare program is an example of this attitude. On the other hand there is increasing concern that many of the benefits of government are going to those least in need. Additionally, there is concern about the equity of the tax system, especially amid widespread reports that some millionaires and large corporations have paid no tax or are collecting unemployment insurance benefits. Canadians want government programs and taxes to be applied fairly, and of course, they want their governments to perform these functions efficiently.

On a broader, more philosophical plane, some people fear that the increasing scope of government narrows their individual choices and

---

[1]P. Martin, *Budget 1996, Budget in Brief* (Ottawa, Canada: Department of Finance, March 6, 1996).

reduces their individual rights. Many people are concerned with the sheer growth and size of government. The issues connected to the growth in government, the increasing tax burden and its distribution, and the growth in government debts are the focal points of this chapter.

Size of Government

Canada has three levels of government—federal, provincial, and local. The provincial level includes 10 provinces and two territories. However, the territories do not have the same level of autonomy as do the provinces. The local level of government includes municipalities, school boards, hospitals, special agencies, boards, and commissions. *The Constitution Act* determines the sharing of powers, including spending and taxation between the federal and provincial levels of government. Local governments are under the authority of provincial governments and obtain their powers only through provincial delegation. Therefore, these powers vary substantially across the nation.

There appears to be a growing feeling among many people that government is too big. If this is so, it could certainly be argued that government services and taxes should be cut. Is there a basis for this feeling? The answer almost certainly depends upon one's values. While sometimes there are positive questions relating to economic efficiency, much of any discussion of the size and role of government must be normative.

It is certainly true that we have big government. Government activities have extended into areas of society not deemed appropriate many decades ago. Personal taxes have risen to pay for these activities, and today most families have to pay a significant portion of their income in taxes. The worry that some people have about government waste and the abuse that is connected with government expenditures is not imaginary. People have found out about these things through the media. A month rarely passes without a report on unnecessary government expenditures or on abuse of some sort in the operation of one or more government expenditure programs.

Some fears of people concerning government size are not well-founded. Despite some inevitable waste, the government has implemented many successful expenditure programs, including the provision of benefits to many people and the fulfillment of the needs of people living in a changing society. For example, today Canada has one of the best educated and healthiest populations in the world. Rather than ask if government is too big, a more appropriate question might be, Why is government involved in our economy?

Government might be involved in the economy for a number of reasons, which we have discussed in various chapters throughout this book. For example, government might become involved in a regulatory role to prevent market failures that develop as a result of monopoly power. The government also gets involved with the provision of public goods, such as police and fire protection, or when externalities exist, as in the case of education and pollution. The government protects the public by prohibiting misleading or fraudulent information, by requiring proper product labelling, by testing certain goods such as meat and drugs, and by ensuring workplace safety. Finally, government may become involved to change the distribution of income as in the case of the provision of welfare payments to the poor or old-age supplements. Once again, although we can objectively investigate a number of areas with respect to the government's role in our economy, the question of whether the government is too big, just right, or too small ultimately is a normative one.

Part of the reason that the role of government has increased so rapidly is the nature of some of the services that we earlier chose to assign to government. The cost of health care has increased rapidly over the last three decades for two important reasons. First, we have an aging population. As the proportion of the elderly increases, the cost per capita of medical care increases. Second, health care is a normal good; therefore, as our incomes rise, we want more and better health care. As the needs and demand for health care increases, the cost to the government of providing Medicare also increases.[2] These aspects of health care were discussed in Chapter 6. Similarly, the government has historically provided education. Over the last three decades the proportion of Canadians undertaking postsecondary education has increased dramatically and so has the cost. The increase in demand for education is partly because education, like health care, is a normal good, but the main reason is the need to be better educated in today's technologically sophisticated society. In the 1980s the federal and provincial governments became involved in many projects that might have been left to the private sector. Projects such as the development of Hibernia oil reserves and the Alberta oil sands were often advanced as job creation endeavours. Government participation in such projects also increased the size of government. Finally, a substantial part of government spending today is the payment of interest on the government debt.

The source of some fears is not specific and concrete but more general and philosophical. Fear of too much government became a trend in many countries. This philosophy was central under Prime Ministers Thatcher and Major in Britain and under Presidents Reagan and Bush in the United States. In Canada the Mulroney Conservative government adopted this view, and it continued under the Chrétien Liberals. This position has also been strongly advocated by the Reform party, which although not the Official Opposition in parliament is an important player nonetheless. In a market-oriented economy, the supposition is

---

[2]The cost of health care in the United States, where it is mainly provided by the private sector, has risen even more rapidly than in Canada.

that the market will solve problems impersonally and efficiently, and this belief underlies the concerns of people when the government gets involved in the market economy.

Tax Inequities

A major concern of people involves the question of tax equity, that is, tax justice. Tax equity refers to the way taxes are distributed among people. Even if tax collections were exactly the right amount to pay for government goods and services demanded by people, there could be concern that the distribution of tax burden was not fair. Therefore, in addition to the fear that government is too big and taxes are too high in general, there is the fear that taxes are "too low" for certain taxpayers and "too high" for certain others.

Equity is a normative concept; there is little agreement on what would be fair. I may think my taxes are too high and your taxes are too low. You may think your taxes are too high and my taxes are too low. We might agree that "their" taxes are too low. We discuss the concept of equity and present illustrations of tax inequities later in the chapter. It may suffice here to point out that people's fears concerning the fairness of the distribution of the tax burden are an important dimension of the tax issue.

Deficits and Debts

A different but related concern to the size of government is the increasing concern with government deficits and debts. Government expenditures have been growing at a greater rate than government revenues. When a government spends more in a given year than it takes in in revenue, it incurs a *deficit*. The difference between its revenue and expenditures—the deficit—must be financed by borrowing. This new borrowing adds to the government's outstanding debt. Over the last 25 years most provincial governments and the federal government have been running annual deficits; therefore, their outstanding debts have been steadily growing. This accumulated government debt has become a major political issue as Canadians debate the size and financing of their governments. The issue of government debt is taken up in the last section of the chapter.

The Level of Government Spending

Our approach to the size of government is, first, to provide background information concerning this issue and, second, to analyze the issue of size in reference to the economic criteria of efficiency and equity.

Government **purchases of goods and services** are expenditures for currently produced goods and services and are a part of the nation's income.

Transfer payments are government expenditures in the form of money payments to households, firms, or other levels of government that do not contribute to the current production of goods and services because the government does not receive any good or service in return.

Government spending can be divided up into two broad categories called *purchases of goods and services* and *transfer payments*. When the government purchases goods or services, it receives value in exchange for the money it is spending. For example, the Canadian Armed Forces might buy a new fighter plane or a provincial government might pay to construct a new bridge. Alternatively, when a local government pays a worker a wage to work as a receptionist at city hall, the government (or those who come to city hall) receives a service in exchange for that wage. *Transfer payments* involve no *quid pro quo*. In the case of a transfer payment, no good or service is received in exchange for the transfer. Since nothing is produced in exchange for the payment, the transfer does not contribute to GDP.

The concern that some people have about the size of government becomes evident when certain indicators of the size of government (federal, provincial, and local) are examined. One way to indicate the size of government is to look at the expenditures of government. Later we will compare these expenditures to the nation's income or the GDP. Figure 15–1 shows the government expenditure by level since 1963. Certainly the level of government spending in Canada has increased substantially during that period. Figure 15–1 uses an area graph to show what has happened to spending at each of the three levels of government.[3] In most years expenditures by the federal government make up the largest component of total government spending. The combined spending of the provincial governments is second. Local government spending is clearly much lower than the other two levels. You should notice that the graph also contains a line marked total. That line indicates a lower level of spending than the aggregate of the three component parts. In this case the whole is less than the sum of its parts. The explanation for this seemingly impossible arithmetic is that the sum of the three levels includes some double counting.

Transfer Payments

Transfer payments are government expenditures in the form of money payments to households, firms, or other levels of government that do not contribute to the current production of goods and services because the government does not receive any good or service in return.

Governments make two types of transfer payments. Some transfers go to households and firms. At present these transfers need not concern us. Other transfers go to other levels of government. These transfers are of interest when discussing the total level of government spending. For

---

[3]Statistics Canada divides government spending into five different levels: federal, Canadian (Quebec) Pension Plan (C[Q]PP), provincial, hospital, and local. We will include CPP and QPP in federal and hospital in provincial.

Figure 15–1   **The growth of government expenditure in Canada**

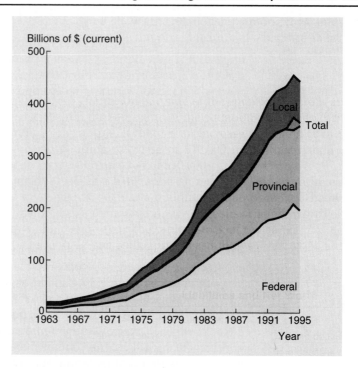

The growth in spending by the various levels of government since 1963 is illustrated. Note that the sum of spending by the three levels of government is greater than the total spending by all governments. This seeming inconsistency exists because of intergovernmental transfers. Some of the spending by provincial governments is financed by transfers from the federal government. Similarly, some of the spending by local government is funded by senior governments. In this graph C(Q)PP is included as federal spending, and hospitals are included as local spending.

Source: *Statistics Canada, National Income and Expenditure Accounts, Annual Estimates,* various years.

example, in 1995 the federal government transferred almost $32 billion to lower levels of government. Similarly, provincial governments transferred over $50 billion to local governments and hospitals. The governments that receive these transfers spend most of these funds on the purchase of goods and services. To count both the transfer and the spending financed by the transfer would be to count the same money twice. Therefore, total government spending is less than the sum of the spending by all levels of combined. The actual level of total spending in Figure 15–1 is indicated by the line labelled total spending.

Senior levels of government make transfers to lower levels of government for a number of reasons. The provinces in Canada have widely differing financial resources. Ontario, British Columbia, and Alberta have substantially greater ability to raise tax revenue than the other seven provinces do. To raise the same revenue per capita, the other provinces would have to have much higher tax rates than the three richest provinces. To partially offset the disadvantage of the poorer provinces, the federal government provides *equalization payments*. These transfers make up the largest proportion of general-purpose federal transfers. In addition, the federal government makes specific-purpose transfers. The provinces can use the revenue from general-purpose transfers as they see fit. The funds provided by specific-purpose transfers are restricted to designated uses. At one time the federal government made specific-purpose transfers to help fund health care, higher education, and the Canada Assistance Plan (CAP). In 1977 the health care and higher education grants were combined under a new program called Established Programs Financing (EPF). This left CAP as the only major specific purpose program. The 1995 federal budget announced that CAP too would be dropped and the federal transfer for all three would be combined in one block grant. When the federal government dropped specific transfers for postsecondary education and health care in 1977, part of their contribution was continued as EPF and part was through tax credits. That is, the federal government lowered its tax rates in order to allow the provincial governments to raise their tax rates without increasing the overall burden on taxpayers. Although a number of specific-purpose federal transfer programs still exist, none are very important in terms of the total money involved.

Provincial governments not only receive transfers from the federal government, they also make transfers to local governments and hospitals. The exact nature of these transfer programs varies from province to province, but they are generally made to fund specific programs like education. Local governments sometimes make very modest transfers to higher levels of government. Figure 15–2 shows how intergovernmental transfers have grown since 1963.

Government also makes transfer payments to households and business firms. Transfers to individuals include welfare payments and Old Age Security. Such transfers are generally intended to reduce disparities in the distribution of income and reduce poverty. They were discussed in Chapter 7. Transfer payments to businesses, called *subsidies*, are paid for

> Government transfers to business are called **subsidies**. They can be used to encourage production of goods and services that the government deems desirable or to change the distribution of income.

a variety of reasons. In some cases they are intended to increase production of a good or service that has external or spillover benefits. In other cases they may be made to encourage the development of new technologies and new industries. Often these transfers, like transfers to persons, are made in order to affect the distribution of income, for example, by bringing jobs to an area of high unemployment or by increasing the income of farmers. Often a subsidy to an employer is politically more acceptable than providing income support directly to the workers and their families. Figure 15–2 also shows how transfers to persons and businesses have grown since 1963.

Figure 15–2   **Program spending by three levels of government in Canada**

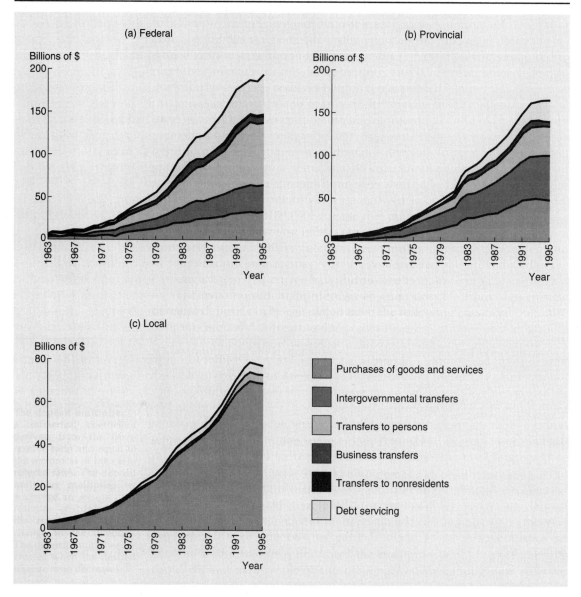

The categories of government spending are shown for the federal government (frame a), provincial governments (frame b), and local governments (frame c).

Source: Statistics Canada, *National Income and Expenditure Accounts, Annual Estimates*, various years.

Naturally not all government spending is on transfer payments. Government spending also goes to purchase goods and services. Service expenditures include spending on services produced by outside suppliers and also include the payments of wages for the services of government employees. Finally, a large portion of government spending is the payment of interest on government debt. Although these elements of government spending will be discussed later in the chapter, they are also illustrated in Figure 15–2 to show their respective growth and size.

The most obvious reason for the growth in government spending is the growth of the Canadian economy. As our population and our level of income have increased, the level of government spending has increased too. By tracking government spending as a percentage of GDP, Figure 15–3 shows that government spending has increased faster than the economy has grown. This trend, however, reversed for a short period during the late 1980s and again since 1992. Given current political attitudes, government spending will likely decrease as a percentage of GDP in the near future.

Government Receipts

Government obtains revenue to finance its expenditures. These monies are called **receipts**. These receipts include tax revenue from various sources; income from crown corporate activity, including sales of goods and services, and profits; resource rents; fines; licenses and permit sales; and in the case of lower levels of government —transfers.

The *receipts* of government are primarily derived from its various taxes: personal and corporate income taxes; consumption taxes such as the federal goods and services tax (GST), provincial sales taxes (PST), excise taxes, and property taxes; and health and social insurance levies (payroll taxes). "Income" includes revenue from crown corporate activity, including sales of goods and services and profits; natural resource rents; and income from fines and the sale of privileges, licences, and permits. The relative proportions of these sources of revenue are shown in Figure 15–4. The sources of each level of government's revenue is also shown in this figure. Transfers from a higher level of government are a large proportion of income for provincial and local governments. In addition to transfer income, local governments rely on property taxes and income from productive activity. Provincial government revenue is obtained largely from income and consumption taxes in addition to transfer revenue. The federal government, being the senior level, receives negligible transfer income. Its largest source of revenue is income tax, followed by consumption taxes, then payroll taxes. Of note is the declining importance of corporate income tax and the increasing proportion of personal income tax as total revenue sources.

The receipt side of the government expenditure–revenue system shows a pattern of growth similar to the expenditure side with respect to the GDP. However, as Figure 15–3 shows, the receipts have not kept up

Figure 15–3   **Consolidated government spending as a percentage of GDP**

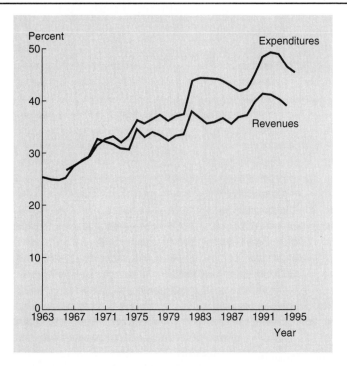

Government spending in Canada as a percentage of GDP has risen since the 1960s. However, spending did turn down in the later part of the 1980s and again the last three years. Government receipts have followed a similar pattern but since 1970 have not kept pace with spending. The divergence of expenditures and revenues has meant annual deficits and accumulating government debts.

Source: Derived from Statistics Canada *National Income and Expenditure Accounts, Annual Estimates*, various years and *Canadian Economic Observer*, various years.

A **balanced budget** means that government receipts are equal to government expenditures; a **deficit budget** means receipts are less than expenditures; and a **surplus budget** means that receipts are greater than expenditures.

with the expenditures. A government runs a *balanced budget* if its total receipts are equal to its total expenditures. Figure 15–3 indicates that all Canadian levels of government combined ran close to a balanced budget between 1967 and 1970. A *surplus budget* means that government receipts are greater than government expenditures. The year 1971 had a consolidated budget surplus. A *deficit budget* means that government receipts are less than government expenditures. Figure 15–3 indicates that Canadian government budgets (combined) have been in deficit for every year since 1971—over 25 years. An annual deficit must be financed by borrowing in order to pay for the expenditures in excess of revenue. The accumulation of these deficits constitutes the government debt.

Figure 15–4   **Government receipts for three levels of government in Canada**

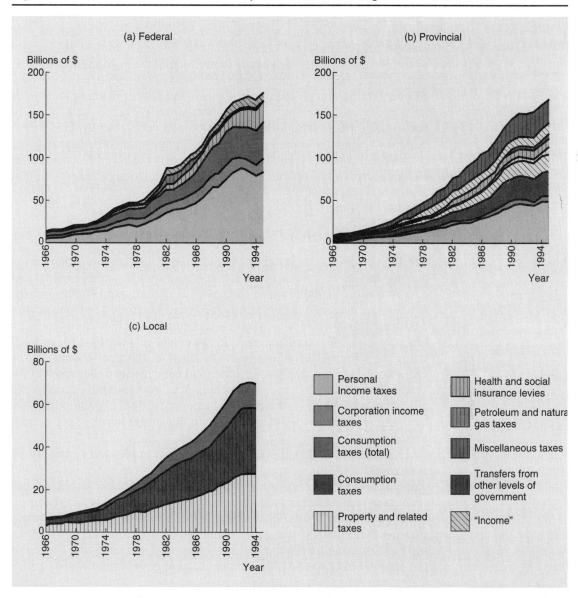

The categories of government revenues are shown for the federal government (frame a), provincial governments (frame b), and local governments (frame c).

Source: Statistics Canada, *National Income and Expenditure Accounts, Annual Estimates*, various years.

Economic Analysis of the Problem of Size

Economic efficiency and equity are two concepts that have been used to analyze many issues previously discussed. Efficiency in the use of scarce resources of society allows society to produce as many goods and services and satisfy as many human needs and wants as possible. Equity is concerned with the fair distribution of goods and services among all people. Both equity and efficiency considerations are involved in an analysis of the size of government, for the size of government is determined by expenditure programs aimed at redressing the unequal distribution of income and at providing goods and services that would not be provided at all, or at least would not be provided in efficient and equitable quantities, in the marketplace.

An Efficient Level of Government Expenditures

An efficient level of government expenditures is that level at which the net benefits to society are maximized, that is, the level at which benefits and costs are equal at the margin. The maximization of net benefits and the equation of marginal benefits and costs were illustrated in Chapter 4 in analyzing the efficient level of crime prevention activities. To move to an efficient level, government expenditures would be increased (decreased) when the marginal benefits per dollar spent in the public sector of the economy is greater (less) than the marginal benefits per dollar spent in the private sector. Finally, the efficient level of government expenditures would be reached when the marginal benefit per dollar spent in the public sector is equal to the marginal benefit per dollar spent in the private sector.

Although cost-benefit analysis has practical applications in many instances and is the guide to an efficient allocation of resources, benefits and costs of government expenditures can seldom be precisely quantified and often government programs are developed without any attempt to estimate benefits and costs. Thus there is no way of knowing for certain whether the present size of government is too big or too small. Further insight can be gained, however, into the question of efficiency and the size of government by discussing the proper scope of government.

Collective Goods and Services

As explained in Chapter 4, collective goods and services lie at the opposite pole from private goods and services because an individual is not able to isolate or identify a specific personal benefit. Let's take the meaning of collective goods and services a step further in the context of this chapter.

Collective goods and services, such as defence and crime prevention services, have two identifying characteristics: (1) demand for collective goods and services is not generally divisible on the basis of individual quantities demanded, and (2) supply of collective goods and services is not generally divisible into small units. These characteristics make it difficult, if not impossible, for these goods and services to be supplied and demanded in the marketplace. Thus, it is widely accepted that collective goods and services fall under the domain of government to provide.

The main issue in the supply of collective goods and services is for the government to provide these goods and services efficiently. For economic efficiency to be obtained, government has to provide collective goods and services at the lowest possible cost, and the output supplied has to equal output demanded. Even assuming collective goods and services are provided at the lowest possible costs, inefficiencies may arise if the output demanded is less than or greater than the output supplied. The only way people can reveal their preferences for collective goods and services is through the ballot box, which may not be a perfect indicator of the true preferences that people have for collective goods and services. However, assuming true preferences are revealed, the efficient amount of collective goods and services is the amount corresponding to the point where collective demand intersects the cost (marginal) of supplying collective goods and services.

External Benefits and Costs

The line of demarcation between what government should provide and what private producers should provide would be clear if all goods and services were either collective or private goods and services. However, as you learned in Chapter 3 on education and Chapter 6 on health care, the production of certain goods can generate social spillover costs, and the consumption of certain goods and services can generate social spillover benefits. The existence of *externalities*, that is, social spillovers in production and consumption, broadens the scope of government beyond collective goods and services.

Externalities are the social spillover benefits or costs that flow from the private consumption or production of a product.

Market demand indicates marginal private benefits (*MPB*), and market supply indicates marginal private costs (*MPC*). Assuming no externalities, marginal private benefits and costs equal marginal social benefits and costs. However, if either external benefits or costs are present, a divergence will exist between private and social benefits or between private and social costs. This divergence means that government action is required for resources to be used efficiently.

Figure 15–5 shows private demand and supply of good A. Assuming that no external benefits and costs exist, the efficient quantity would be q and the price would be p. Suppose now that in the consumption of good A, there are external benefits. In Figure 15–5, the demand curve $D_T D_T$ shows both marginal private and external benefits ($MPB + MEB$); that is, $D_T D_T$ shows the

Figure 15–5   **The efficient quantity assuming external benefits**
                         in consumption

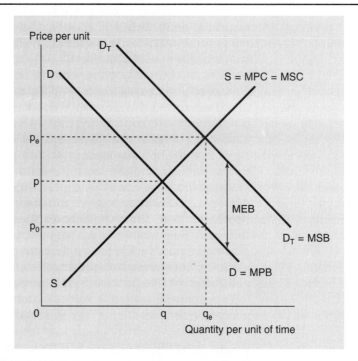

DD represents marginal private benefits (*MPB*), and D_TD_T represents *MPB* and marginal external benefits (*MEB*). Given the supply curve *SS*, the optimum or efficient quantity is at q_e where *MSB* equals *MSC*. The government could ensure that the efficient quantity would be demanded by giving a subsidy payment to consumers equal to $[(p_e - p_0) \times q_e]$.

total marginal social benefits. The demand curve that indicates all benefits is the relevant one. Thus the efficient quantity in Figure 15–5 is q_e, not q. What can government do to guarantee that the efficient quantity is provided?

The government could consider two choices. One choice would be for the government to produce good A and attempt to produce the efficient quantity. This type of action presumes that government will be an efficient supplier and can accurately estimate marginal social benefits. The second choice does not depend on government being an efficient supplier, but still depends on precise estimates of benefits. Government action could be in the form of subsidies to consumers of good A so that they would be willing to purchase the efficient quantity. In Figure 15–5 consumers would buy the correct amount at p_0. The total subsidy payment would be equal to $(p_e - p_0) \times q_e$. A subsidy payment greater than this amount would result in too much production of good A, and a subsidy payment smaller would mean that less than the efficient quantity is produced.

The case of external costs in production was examined in Chapter 5 and illustrated in the case of water pollution in the production of paper. In that instance the market price was too low and the production of paper was too high because external cost in the form of water pollution was not taken into account in the supply of paper. To correct the situation the government could levy a tax on each unit of paper supplied. The effect of the tax would be to increase the marginal cost of supplying paper and, therefore, decrease supply. Assuming the tax equals the marginal external costs, an efficient but lower quantity of paper will be supplied at a higher price. The price elasticity of demand for paper will determine how much the price of paper will rise as a result of the tax.

Income Distribution

Government actions thus far have been rationalized on economic efficiency grounds. The scope of government has been greatly extended and defended based on the belief that income inequality needs to be reduced. The distribution of income, and therefore consumption, would be largely based on the productivity of people in a highly competitive economy. Social problems arise because some people have no or low productivity. What should be done to alter the distribution of income so as to help people who cannot work and those who can work little?

Shifting income from those who are relatively productive to those who are relatively unproductive, say through taxes and subsidies, must be based on the values of people as to what constitutes a "fair" distribution. It is not surprising that government programs aimed directly or indirectly at altering the distribution of income are constantly debated. Evidently there is general support for programs aimed directly at helping low-income people, such as public assistance (welfare), and for programs that only indirectly help certain low-income groups, such as the Medicare program, for these programs have expanded relative to other government programs. Parallelling this growth has been the increased controversy concerning income transfer programs. Although the debate is not likely to end, the responsibility of government in the area of income redistribution is seemingly established. No private institutions could thoroughly cope with the problem.

Summary

The major ideas that have evolved from our discussion thus far are these: (1) collective goods and services must be supplied by government; (2) government actions are needed to improve the efficiency of the market system, especially where there are externalities; and (3) government may alter the distribution of income in order to move in the direction of an equitable distribution as determined by the beliefs of people in our society.

Tax Principles and Analysis

The first part of this section develops a theoretical framework based on the criteria of equity and efficiency. The second part examines tax principles pertaining to the shifting and incidence of taxes.

Tax Equity

Everyone agrees that taxes should be "just." The problem that arises, however, is over the exact meaning of justice or fairness in taxation. An idea that runs strongly through western thought is that tax justice means that taxpayers in equal economic circumstances should be treated equally. This is called the *equal tax treatment doctrine* and pertains to *horizontal equity;* that is, people in identical economic positions should pay equal taxes.

The **equal tax treatment doctrine** states that taxpayers in the same economic circumstances should be treated equally.

Horizontal equity is achieved when people in identical economic circumstances pay an equal amount of taxes.

In the application of the equal tax treatment doctrine, the best indicator or measure of economic circumstances has to be determined. Generally, economists interpret economic circumstances to mean a person's real income, which equals consumption plus changes in net wealth. Assuming real income is the best measure of economic circumstances, then horizontal equity is achieved when all taxpayers with the same income pay exactly the same amount in taxes.

Vertical equity is achieved when taxpayers in different economic circumstances are treated unequally based on either the ability to pay or the benefits received.

The relative tax treatment doctrine states that taxpayers in different economic circumstances should be treated unequally.

What about taxpayers in different economic circumstances? How should they be treated? These questions are related to the idea of *vertical equity*, that is, the tax treatment of taxpayers in different economic circumstances. The *relative tax treatment doctrine* now emerges. Taxpayers in different economic circumstances should be treated differently. But how differently? Two principles of taxation have been developed to shed light on this question—the ability-to-pay principle and the benefits-received principle.

Ability-to-Pay Principle

The **ability-to-pay principle** of taxation states that taxes should be distributed among taxpayers based on their ability to pay taxes.

The *ability-to-pay principle* of taxation supports the proposition that taxpayers with greater ability to pay taxes should pay more taxes. Again, using income as the measure of ability to pay, this principle means that taxpayers with more income should pay more taxes. But how much more? Progressive and proportional tax rates are always consistent with the ability-to-pay principle because if the rate of taxation (the percentage of income paid in taxes) is rising as income rises (progressive rates) or constant as income rises (proportional rates), the amount paid in taxes will always be higher as income is higher. On the other hand, regressive tax rates can violate the ability-to-pay principle, since the percentage of income paid in taxes decreases as income rises.

Benefits-Received Principle

The **benefits-received principle** of taxation equates taxes to marginal private benefits and is an attempt to apply the rule of market. This principle is a guide to an efficient allocation of taxes rather than to an equitable allocation.

Do you recall the way the market distributes the costs of producing private goods and services? The market distributes costs based on marginal private benefits. The *benefits-received principle* of taxation is an attempt to apply the rule of market; it is a guide to an efficient allocation of taxes rather than to an equitable allocation. However, efficient and equitable tax distributions are not always in conflict, and when equity in the distribution of income is not a concern, the benefits-received principle of taxation is an important tax standard. This principle is more limited than the ability-to-pay principle because private benefits received from government goods and services are usually more difficult to measure than the ability to pay. Illustrations of taxes that are defended on the benefits-received principle are the gasoline tax and local street assessments. The gasoline tax is used primarily to pay for highways. Thus the demander of highway services, the automobile user, pays for the benefits received from highway services through a tax levied on litres of gasoline consumed. The argument that well-maintained local streets benefit property owners by enhancing the value of property leads to the conclusion that property owners should pay for the benefits they receive from streets in the form of property taxes.

Tax Efficiency

Tax efficiency has two aspects. First, tax efficiency is concerned with the *administration* and *compliance* cost of taxes. Taxes should be economical to collect and to enforce. They should also be convenient and certain to the taxpayer.

The second and more important aspect of tax efficiency involves minimizing what economists call the excess burden from taxes. Suppose, for example, that the government transfers $10 billion worth of resources from the private sector to the public sector via taxes and provides marginal benefits equal to $10 billion. Further suppose that in the levy of taxes, tax rates are used that discourage incentives to work so that private production is less than what it would have been by $1 billion. This example shows a net loss of $1 billion, even though the government is using the resources transferred as efficiently as they would be used in the private sector. This net loss in production resulting from the disincentive effects of taxes is the *excess burden* that has arisen because of the imposition of taxes.

The **excess burden** of a tax is a measure of tax inefficiency; that is, it measures the non-neutral or the distortionary effects of the tax on relative prices and resource allocation.

If there is no excess burden or if the excess burden is small, then taxes have neutral effects or near-neutral effects on the operation of private economy. Unfortunately, taxes seldom have completely neutral effects. However, certain taxes adhere to the idea of neutrality better than others, and these are the taxes that we are searching for to put into an ideal tax scheme. Taxes that directly alter relative commodity prices or that do so indirectly through altering consumption and income patterns are taxes

Figure 15–6   Demand perfectly inelastic—complete forward shifting of an output tax

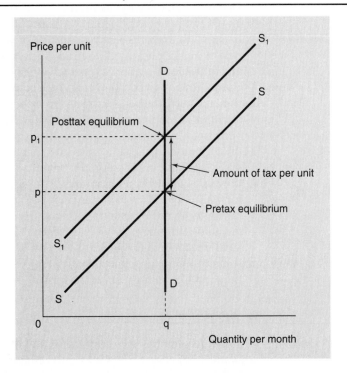

The pretax equilibrium is at price *p* and at quantity *q* where supply *SS* intersects demand *DD*. An output tax on each unit produced is levied with the amount of the tax shown above. The effect is to decrease supply to S_1S_1. Thus price rises to p_1 where S_1S_1 intersects *DD*. The full amount of the tax is shifted forward because the rise in price from *p* to p_1 equals the amount of the tax.

that have strong non-neutral effects and do not adhere to the concept of tax efficiency. For example, a tax levied on a specific commodity will increase the price of that commodity and result in a shift of spending away from the taxed commodity to non-taxed commodities. Progressive and regressive income tax rates change the pattern of income distribution as well as alter the price of work relative to the price of leisure.

Principles of Shifting and Incidence

Taxes may be levied on one taxpayer and shifted to another taxpayer. A tax that is shifted forward is a tax that is placed on a producer and then falls on the consumer in the form of higher prices; a tax that is shifted backward falls on the owners of resources in the form of lower resource prices. The incidence or burden of a tax that is not shifted, then, remains on the original taxpayer.

Forward shifting occurs when any part of the tax is paid for by consumers in the form of higher prices.

Backward shifting occurs when any part of the tax is paid for by the owners ofresources in the form of lower resource prices.

The **incidence of a tax** is the burden or the final resting place of the tax.

Two kinds of taxes are to be considered in the following analysis. The first is an output tax, and the second is a tax levied independent of output.

An Output Tax. An *output tax* is a tax that is levied on each unit of output produced, such as a tax on each pack of cigarettes or on each litre of gasoline. An output tax increases the cost of producing each unit and, therefore, decreases supply. Given the demand for the taxed commodity, a decrease in supply will increase the price of the commodity. How much of the tax will be shifted forward?

The extent of the forward shifting of an output tax depends essentially on the price elasticities of demand and supply. If demand is perfectly inelastic (Figure 15–6), the entire tax is shifted forward. The incidence of the tax, under these circumstances is completely on the consumer in the form of higher prices. If demand is perfectly elastic (Figure 15–7), none of the tax is shifted forward; in other words, all of the tax is shifted backward to

Figure 15–7   **Demand perfectly elastic—complete backward shifting of an output tax**

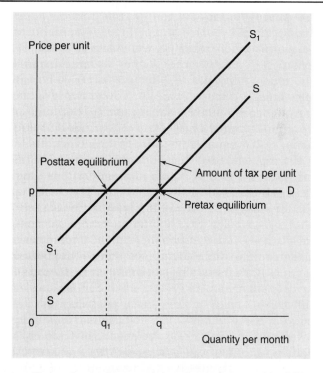

The pretax equilibrium is at price p and quantity q where supply SS intersects demand DD. An output tax decreases supply to $S_1 S_1$. The posttax equilibrium is at price p and quantity q_1 where supply $S_1 S_1$ intersects demand DD. There is no forward shifting of the tax because price does not change. Thus the entire tax is shifted backward to owners of resources, who receive only p_1 after paying the tax.

resources in the form of lower prices (lower wages, etc.). The elasticity of demand for most products will not be either of these two extremes. We can generalize, then, by saying that an output tax will normally be shifted forward and backward, with more forward shifting when demand is more inelastic and more backward shifting when demand is more elastic.

Independent of Output Tax. A tax levied on income, say the net income or profits of a business, is a good illustration of the tax we are to consider. Suppose a business has selected the best output, that is, the output where profits are maximized, before a 25 percent profits tax is imposed. Now, after the tax, is there a better output? The answer is no. If the best output is selected before the tax, it remains the best output after the tax. There is no shortrun shifting of a tax levied independently of output. The incidence of such a tax is on the owners of the business in the form of a reduction in profits. The difference between an output tax and a tax independent of output is that the former increases costs and decreases supply, whereas the latter does not. For taxes to be shifted, a change in supply has to occur.

Who Really Pays Taxes?

The question, who really pays taxes? is not easy to answer. A schedule of statutory tax rates by income classes is not necessarily the effective tax rates because of differences in tax deductions, credits, and exemptions. In addition, as you know now, the type of tax and the direction and degree of tax shifting are important in determining the incidence of taxes. An empirical study that was published in 1995 attempts to answer our question.[4] The study shows data on the incidence of taxes for selective years between 1951 and 1988 and attempts to measure the impact of all taxes on the relative well-being of families throughout the range of income distribution. This study also demonstrates the changing nature of tax incidence and the increase in average taxes in Canada over four decades. Some changes in the Canadian tax structure have occurred since the period considered in this study, especially with the replacement of the manufactures sales tax (MST) by the federal goods and services tax (GST). However, the data in this study remain the most recent available data on tax incidence.

Tax Incidence of the Canadian Tax System

Figure 15–8 documents the results of the tax incidence study. The tax system can best be described as proportional with ranges that are mildly progressive and ranges that are mildly regressive; that is, the tax rate or

---

[4]A. Vermaeten, W. I. Gillespie, and F. Vermaeten, "Who Paid the Taxes in Canada?" *Canadian Public Policy* 21, no. 2 (1995).

Figure 15–8   **Effective tax rates for all taxes and governments**

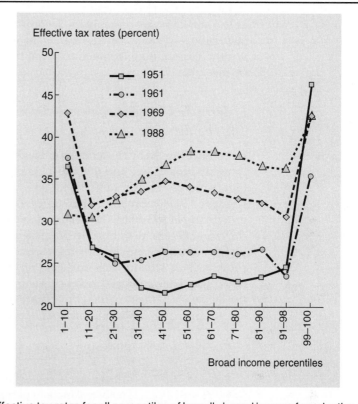

The effective tax rates for all percentiles of broadly based income for selective years are shown. All taxes collected by all government levels are included. Note that the last two percentile classes include a different (smaller) range than the rest.

Source: A. Vermaeten, W. I. Gillespie, and F. Vermaeten, "Who Paid the Taxes in Canada?" *Canadian Public Policy* 21, no. 2 (1995).

the ratio of taxes to income by income class is the same or rises and falls only slightly as you move from low-income classes to high-income classes. The study found that the effective tax rate of 1988 increased from only about 31 percent in the lowest income class (less than $10,523) to 42.5 percent in the very high income class ($174,852 and above). Most taxpayers pay a tax rate between 32 and 38 percent. Except for 1988 the tax rate on the lowest income class was significantly above the average tax rate on all income classes. This high tax on low income earners was due to the lower dependence on income tax in 1951, 1961, 1969 and the heavy burden that provincial and local regressive taxes placed on the lowest income group.

A tax system that is proportional will not alter the distribution of income. Under such a tax system, taxpayers in each income group will have proportionately less income after taxes than before taxes, but they will be in the same relative income position. The Canadian tax system, then, has only a small impact on reducing income inequality, since it is only moderately progressive at best. The statement sometimes made that taxes significantly redistribute income away from the rich to the poor is not verified by the data.

Federal Tax Incidence versus Provincial and Local Tax Incidence

It is often thought by the average citizen that the incidence of federal taxes is highly progressive and that the incidence of provincial and local taxes is highly regressive. Although the federal tax system became more progressive up to 1988 because it relied more heavily on income taxes, the relative growth in payroll taxes, the relative decline in corporate income taxes, and the recent flattening of tax rates in the federal tax code, have made the federal tax structure much less progressive than is generally believed. Also, provincial tax structures became less regressive by 1988 because of the relative growth in provincial income taxes and because of the assumption that the incidence of the provincial corporate income tax and the local property tax fall primarily on capital instead of consumption. Table 15–1 shows a

Table 15–1	Effective tax rates (federal, provincial, and local) by broad income percentile group, 1988				
Percentile	**Income**	**Federal**	**Provincial**	**Local**	**Total**
1–10	less than $10,524	9.0%	13.3%	8.5%	30.8%
11–20	10,524–16,628	10.9	12.6	6.9	30.4
21–30	16,629–23,102	13.5	13.2	6.0	32.7
31–40	23,103–30,419	15.7	13.9	5.4	35.0
41–50	30,420–38,184	17.4	14.4	4.8	36.6
51–60	38,185–47,413	18.8	15.1	4.4	38.3
61–70	47,414–58,404	19.2	15.1	4.0	38.3
71–80	58,405–73,223	19.3	14.7	3.8	37.8
81–90	73,224–97,217	19.0	14.1	3.4	36.5
91–98	97,218–174,851	19.4	13.7	3.1	36.2
99–100	174,852 and above	23.1	16.3	3.1	42.5
Average		18.8%	14.5%	4.0%	37.3%

Source: A. Vermaeten, W. I. Gillespie, and F. Vermaeten, "Who Paid the Taxes in Canada?" *Canadian Public Policy* 21, no. 2 (1995), appendix A, table 4, pp. 342–3.

slightly progressive incidence of between 13 and 15 percent for 1988. The incidence of local tax is quite regressive, as shown in Table 15–1. The burden on the lowest income class is 8.5 percent and then falls steadily over the income range to a low of about 3 percent on the highest income class.

Tax Rates by Type of Tax

The Vermaeten et al. study suggests that personal income taxes are the most progressive tax source. Corporate income taxes are very slightly progressive but have become a relatively insignificant source of government revenue. Property taxes, sales and excise taxes (commodity taxes), and payroll taxes are regressive taxes in all time periods except that payroll taxes are progressive up to the 61–70 percentile income group in 1988.

Personal income tax rates start at less than 1 percent on the lowest income group, steadily rising to 19 percent on incomes above $174,852. Corporate income tax rates are below 1 percent at each income class, with the exceptions of the four highest income groups, and are less progressive than individual income taxes but eventually reach about 12 percent on the highest income group.

Property taxes are highly regressive at the low end of the income range and largely proportional over other income groups with the effective tax rate about 8 percent at the lowest end of the income scale, falling to less than 2 percent at the top end (Table 15–2).

Table 15–2	Effective tax rates (federal, provincial, and local) by type of tax, 1988						
Percentile	**Income**	**Personal Income Tax**	**Corporate Income Tax**	**Commodity Taxes**	**Property Taxes**	**Payroll Taxes**	**Other Estate and Taxes**
1–10	less than $10,524	1.0%	0.4%	14.0%	8.0%	2.2%	5.2%
11–20	10,524–16,628	4.3	0.7	12.2	6.5	3.2	3.5
21–30	16,629–23,102	6.9	0.8	11.9	5.7	4.5	2.8
31–40	23,103–30,419	8.9	0.9	11.9	5.1	5.7	2.5
41–50	30,420–38,184	11.1	0.8	11.3	4.5	6.6	2.2
51–60	38,185–47,413	13.3	0.9	10.9	4.2	7.1	2.0
61–70	47,414–58,404	14.4	0.9	10.2	3.8	7.2	1.8
71–80	58,405–73,223	15.3	1.2	9.4	3.6	6.8	1.6
81–90	73,224–97,217	15.9	1.3	8.5	3.3	6.2	1.5
91–98	97,218–174,851	17.5	2.1	7.5	3.0	4.9	1.3
99–100	174,852 and above	19.0	11.6	5.9	3.0	1.7	1.4

Source: A. Vermaeten, W. I. Gillespie, and F. Vermaeten, "Who Paid the Taxes in Canada?" *Canadian Public Policy* 21, no. 2 (1995), appendix A, table 4, pp. 342–3.

The effective tax rates of commodity taxes decrease as you move from the low- to the high-income groups. Sales and excise taxes are very burdensome on the very lowest income groups, representing a tax rate of 14 percent (Table 15–2). In comparison, the tax rate of these taxes is only approximately 6 percent on the highest income class.

Payroll taxes also fall heavily on low- and middle-income groups. The rate of payroll taxes begins at about 2 percent, increases to just over 7 percent, and declines steadily to less than 2 percent on very high income groups.

Conclusions

The Vermaeten et al. study provides important insights as to who really pays taxes. First, the overall effective tax rates increased but not as much as government expenditures. Between 1951 and 1969 average effective tax rates increased from 27 percent to 34 percent. Between 1969 and 1988 the effective tax rates increased to 37 percent. The following conclusions may be drawn as to the incidence of taxes. First and foremost, the Canadian tax system had very little impact on the distribution of income. Most taxpayers pay a tax rate in the range of 32 to 38 percent. Second, over the period studied the federal tax system is relatively progressive, the provincial tax system is mildly progressive, and local tax system is regressive. The combination of these taxes makes for a generally proportional or very slightly progressive tax system overall. Third, individual income taxes are the most progressive taxes. Fourth, corporate and estate taxes have become relatively insignificant and have reduced the progressivity on the higher income groups. Finally, commodity taxes are the most regressive taxes, property taxes are also regressive, and the increased use of payroll taxes has contributed to the progressivity of taxes on the lower end of the income range.[5]

The Government Debt

The government debt is a subject of controversy and a source of concern to many people. Should we be concerned about it? Who owes what to whom? How can we tell whether the debt is too big or not? What are the burdens of the debt? And what are the implications of continually large deficits for budget policy given that deficits are the source of government debt growth?

---

[5]As the replacement of the MST with the GST comes after the period of this study and the GST incorporated a rebate system to low-income persons, the current progressivity (or regressivity) of that commodity tax incidence is uncertain.

What Is the National Debt?

Gross government debt includes all securities issued by the federal, provincial, and local governments—interest-bearing and non-interest-bearing securities, securities held by citizens of this country, securities held by citizens of other countries, securities held by government agencies and trust funds, those held privately by individuals, businesses, insurance companies, etc., securities held by the Bank of Canada, and those held by commercial banks. A government security is a promissory note stating that the government will pay the holder or the owner of the note the principal (the amount of money borrowed) plus interest over a specified period of time. The government is obligated to pay the holder so much money plus interest for the money borrowed. The government is the debtor or the borrower, and the owner of the government security is the creditor or lender.

The Absolute Growth in the National Debt

Since Confederation the federal public debt in Canada has increased almost every year in absolute terms. From a value of $76 million in 1867, the net federal debt (the gross public debt minus net recorded assets) increased to $541 billion by 1995, an increase of over 7,000 times.[6] Of course, this kind of comparison in absolute debt is not very enlightening given growth in GDP, inflation, and population growth over the history of Canada. Nonetheless, the consolidated national debt—the net debt of the federal, provincial, and local governments—is big. For every woman, man, and child, the national debt was about $25,311 in 1995. This total included $18,323 federal net debt; $6,160 average provincial net debt; and $828 average local debt (Table 15–3). The per capita debt varies across the country however, because of considerable differences between provincial and local debts.

Canadians probably became very concerned when the national debt topped 100 percent of GDP for the first time. It did this more than 50 years ago after we had finished with the massive deficits of the Great Depression of the 1930s and the huge spending made necessary by fighting World War II. During the 1950s, the national debt was actually reduced, distinguishing this period from the decades before and after as the decade to reduce the national debt. The federal debt shot upward 50 percent during the 1960s, going from $12 billion in 1960 to $18 billion by 1970. This growth rate seemed rapid at the time. As it happened, however, the federal debt growth rate in the 1960s was small compared to the growth rates in the 1970s and 1980s. During the 1970s the federal debt increased fourfold to $72 billion,

---

[6]Department of Finance, Statistics Canada, *Public Sector Finance 1995–1996*, catalogue no. 68-212-XPB (Ottawa: 1996), pp. 11–5.

Table 15–3		Net debt of federal, provincial, and local governments per capita			
Year	Federal	Provincial	Local	Consolidated	% of GDP
1977	$ 1,488	$ 367	$547	$ 2,402	28.78%
1978	1,903	420	589	2,912	32.03
1979	2,429	415	658	3,502	35.09
1980	2,953	434	656	4,043	35.87
1981	3,413	517	668	4,598	36.81
1982	3,889	445	675	5,009	35.35
1983	4,948	811	714	6,473	43.90
1984	6,330	1,108	723	8,161	51.56
1985	7,889	1,369	716	9,974	58.02
1986	9,183	1,873	728	11,784	64.40
1987	10,241	2,340	729	13,310	69.62
1988	11,130	2,615	755	14,500	70.41
1989	11,981	2,673	749	15,403	69.27
1990	12,825	2,750	707	16,282	69.23
1991	13,801	2,990	746	17,537	73.41
1992	14,824	3,835	776	19,435	81.65
1993	16,010	4,828	783	21,621	90.35
1994	17,266	5,694	786	23,746	97.19
1995	18,323	6,160	828	25,311	99.66
1996	19,415				

Source: Statistics Canada, *Public Sector Finance 1995–1996*, catalogue no. 68-212-XPB (Ottawa: 1996).

and during the 1980s it increased fivefold to $355 billion. Although the debt is still increasing, in the 1990s this high rate of increase has abated. However, consolidated government debt will again exceed 100 percent of GDP in 1996. Figure 15–9 shows the recent growth in consolidated net government debt.

The growth in debt in the past was generally associated with wars and economic slumps. The most recent upsurge in the national debt is a result of recessionary-induced budget deficits and high debt service costs. For the last eight years, the federal deficit, for example, has actually been lower than the debt servicing costs; that is, total program spending has been less than total revenue. The debt is growing because the cost of carrying the debt is so high due to the past high interest rate policies of the Bank of Canada.

The *net national debt* as referred to above includes all Canadian government securities outstanding—securities held by the public, including foreigners, less government financial assets. Some of the debt is held in

The **net national debt** is the debt held by the Bank of Canada and the public and excludes the debt held by government agencies and trust funds.

Figure 15–9   **The growth of consolidated government debt in Canada**

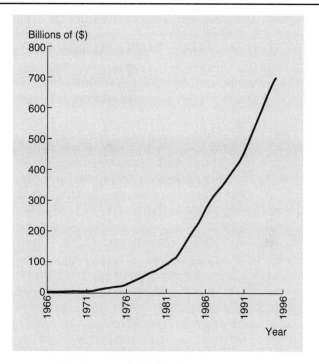

The growth in the consolidated debt of all levels of government since 1966 is illustrated in current dollars.

Source: Statistics Canada, *Public Sector Finance 1995–1996*, catalogue no. 68-212-XPB (Ottawa: 1996).

government accounts or issued to government trust funds, such as the Canada Pension Plan. Other debt is that incurred by government enterprises. This debt, which is usually about one-fourth to one-fifth of the gross federal debt, for example, does not have an economic impact like the debt that is issued to and held by the public. We will now examine the absolute and relative growth in the net debt held by the public.

The federal debt held by the public consists of federal debt held by the Bank of Canada and the public, including both domestic and foreign investors. The holdings of Canadian government securities by the Bank of Canada depends upon the policy of the Bank with respect to influencing the monetary base and controlling the growth in the money supply as was discussed in Chapter 14. The part of the federal debt held by the Bank of Canada varies. The Bank of Canada's share of the public-held federal debt was approximately 20 percent up to the late 1970s but has been progressively reduced to under 6 percent by 1993. This change reflects the increasing effort of the Bank of Canada to maintain a high interest rate policy aimed at controlling inflation.

Government Debt as a Percentage of the GDP

A better perspective of the growth in the government debt held by the public may be gained by comparing this growth to the growth of the economy's output and income as measured by the GDP. The public-held federal debt was very high compared to the GDP in 1946 (104 percent) mostly because of the rapid expansion in the federal debt during the Depression and World War II. However, after 1950 and until 1974, the public-held federal debt as a percentage of GDP was at its lowest at a little more than 20 percent. The public-held debt as a percentage of the GDP declined from more than 100 percent in the 1940s to 25 percent in the early 1970s. Figure 15–10 documents the consolidated government debt as a percentage of GDP. Since 1975 the debt has been growing as a percentage of GDP and was again approaching of 100 percent of GDP in 1995.

Figure 15–10   **The ratio of government debt to GDP in Canada**

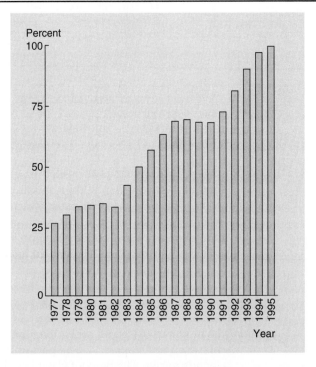

The rapid growth in the ratio of government debt to GDP of all levels of government since 1977.

Source: Statistics Canada, *Public Sector Finance 1995–1996*, catalogue no. 68-212-XPB (Ottawa: 1996).

Public-Held Government Debt as a Percentage of Total Credit Market Debt

Total **credit market debt** is the total government debt (federal, provincial, and local) and the total private debt outstanding in the economy.

Another way to understand the relative importance of government debt is to compare the growth in the federal and other levels of government debt held by the public to the growth in total *credit market debt*. The federal debt held by the public is the federal debt held by the Bank of Canada; private investors, such as individuals, businesses, commercial banks; and provincial and local governments. Total credit market debt is composed of government debt, persons and unincorporated business debt, and non-financial corporation debt. Figure 15–11 shows public-held government debt as a proportion of total credit market debt since 1960. Between 1960

Figure 15–11   **The ratio of public-held government debt to total credit market debt**

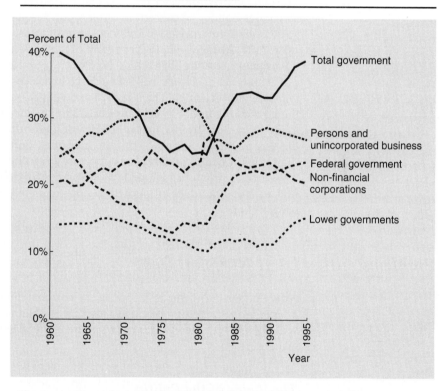

The percentage of total market debt held by the federal government, lower levels of government (provincial and local), persons and unincorporated businesses, and non-financial corporations. The solid line is the total for all government debt.

Source: Statistics Canada CANSIM, Financial flows, credit market Matrix 794.

and 1980 the total government debt fell from 40 percent to 25 percent and then climbed back up to 40 percent by 1995. The federal debt grew much more rapidly than credit market debt, increasing from 13 percent in 1976 to 24 percent in 1995. Lower governments' debt has been much more constant over the years.

Who Owns the National Debt?

Securities are held by government agencies and trust funds, the Bank of Canada, and private investors. Private investors include commercial banks, mutual funds, insurance companies, other corporations, provincial and local governments, and individuals. Private investors hold government securities because they represent a relatively safe income-yielding asset.

Of the $795 billion of gross consolidated government debt outstanding in 1993, 20 percent was in treasury bills, 47 percent in bonds and debentures, 14.5 percent in employees' pension plans, 5 percent in payables, 4.8 percent in savings bonds, 3.6 percent in other securities, 2 percent in deposits due government enterprises, 1.5 percent in advances, and 1 percent in bank overdrafts. Approximately 25 percent of this total gross debt is internal to government, leaving $596 billion held by the public.

A significant change has taken place in the composition of holders of government securities. The adage "we owe it to ourselves," meaning that the government debt is held by Canadian citizens and institutions, is no longer generally true. Foreign holders of government securities are now the second largest group of private investors. Foreign holdings of Canadian government securities have increased significantly in the 1980s and 1990s from a previous historic low of 5 percent of debt. Non-resident holdings of Canadian debt amounted to approximately 35 percent in 1995, or $209 billion.

Problems with a Large National Debt

Now that we know the definition of the national debt and who owns it, we are perhaps in a better position to identify problems associated with it. We will present two views—the views of the general public and the views of economists.

The Views of the Public

Why is the public aroused and alarmed about a large national debt? The public fears that a large national debt will bankrupt the economy and that future generations will have to bear the burden of the government debt. Are these fears justified?

The Bankruptcy Argument. The argument that a large government debt will lead to bankruptcy is primarily based on a false analogy. An individual or a business that has a large debt may go bankrupt. It happens all the time. By this reasoning, then, the government may become bankrupt if it has a large debt.

Unlike individuals and businesses, governments cannot go bankrupt in a legal sense, or indeed in any real sense. The federal government can always meet its debt obligations. It has the power to tax, and additionally the Bank of Canada has a legal obligation to act as lender of last resort. In the unlikely event that the government had difficulty in borrowing, then the Bank could increase the money supply and lend the government the necessary funds. Individuals and businesses do not have these sources of revenue and therefore are not like the federal government.

Shifting the Debt Burden. Many people are concerned about the government debt because they are worried about its burden on future generations. According to this argument, when the debt is incurred, the current generation is postponing paying for government goods and services and shifting the cost or burden to future generations. This reasoning is not entirely untrue as far as it goes. The difference between tax financing and debt financing is that in the former case individual taxpayers pay money today for government goods and services today, whereas in the latter case taxpayers pay money in the future for government goods and services today. However, is debt financing, which shifts money costs to the future, necessarily a bad deal for future taxpayers? Suppose the government develops an irrigation project for $1 billion and finances it from selling securities. In the future the government will have to service the debt by raising taxes to pay $1 billion plus interest. But what about the flow of benefits or income in the future? No net burden is shifted to the future if income from the irrigation project is in excess of the costs of servicing the debt. As a matter of fact, in this event future taxpayers incur a net gain. In a similar fashion investment in education and health care also provides a net gain to future generations.

The Views of Economists

Economists, like the public, are concerned about a large government debt. Economists don't think much of the argument that a large government debt will bankrupt the government and the economy; however, they have had a great deal to say about the primary burden of the national debt. Unlike the public, economists are generally more concerned about the secondary repercussions of a large government debt, that is, the economic impact of the debt on prices, output, and distribution of output. Additionally, the ability of governments to service debt is important. As the debt grows, a greater proportion of overall spending goes just to pay the annual interest on the debt. The growth in this proportion of spending is illustrated in Figure 15–2. Large debt-servicing obligations limit spending on other worthwhile programs.

The Primary Burden of an Internally Held Government Debt.

Two time periods should be distinguished in trying to locate the primary burden of government debt—the present, when the debt is incurred, and the future, when the debt is serviced. Most economists agree that the *primary burden* of an internally held federal debt is in the present in the form of a sacrifice in private production. Assuming full employment, deficit and tax-financed expenditures withdraw resources from private production. The value of goods and services that could have been produced is the primary burden or real cost. Since these goods are forgone in the present, the burden or real cost is in the present. What about the future, when the government debt is serviced, that is, when interest charges have to be paid? Economists have reasoned that no net primary burden exists in the future, since the reduced incomes of taxpayers having to pay higher taxes are offset by the increased incomes of bond holders who receive the interest payments. Private income does not decrease. Economists realize, of course, that paying interest charges on the debt may redistribute income. However, the income redistribution effects of servicing the national debt are considered a secondary effect, not a primary one.

The **primary burden** of government debt is in the form of the sacrifice in private production that may take place in the·present or in the future, depending upon whether the debt is held by institutions and citizens of this country or by foreign institutions and citizens.

The Primary Burden of an Externally Held National Debt.

Economists do agree that the primary burden of an externally held government debt is shifted to the future. The essential difference is that the sacrifice in private real income and production does not take place until the future in the case of an externally held debt. For example, suppose the government buys goods and services produced in another country and pays by selling government securities. There is no sacrifice in domestic private real income when the debt is incurred. However, in the future, when the government debt is serviced, a part of domestic private income is reduced, since taxes are increased to service the external debt. In this case the reduced incomes of taxpayers cannot be offset by the increased incomes of bond holders, for people outside the country hold the government securities.

Income Redistribution Effects.

The secondary effects of the national debt are the *income redistribution effects,* the output effects, and the inflationary effects. Servicing a government debt redistributes income and, therefore, alters the distribution of the nation's output among people. The income redistribution impact of servicing the debt depends on the distribution of taxes among people and the ownership pattern of the government debt. Suppose the tax system is less progressive than the ownership pattern of government securities; or, stated more extremely, suppose only poor people pay taxes and only rich people own government securities. What

Income redistribution effects are the effects that servicing the national debt has on the pattern of income distribution.

happens to the distribution of income if the government pays $10 billion in interest by increasing taxes by $10 billion? The answer is obvious: The distribution of income is shifted away from the poor to the rich. Economists generally believe that some shifting of income from lower- to upper-income groups occurs because of the national debt, although only a thorough examination of the relevant data can determine the actual degree of redistribution.

The **output effects** are the effects that creating and servicing the national debt has on productivity and the stock of real capital.

Output Effects. Our large national debt may reduce productivity and output. Taxes have to be increased in order to meet interest costs on the national debt. In this instance, the economy would be less efficient. It will not produce as much as it would if the national debt did not exist. The disincentive effects of taxes and other distortion effects that taxes may have are a worry.

Real output in the economy may be reduced in still another way by government debt financing and the ensuing national debt. In the process of creating and servicing the debt, governments compete for private saving and, in effect, reduce private saving and private capital formation, that is, the accumulation of real capital assets. The ability of the economy to produce goods and services depends on its stock of capital. A reduced stock of capital—machines, tools, and plants—associated with the national debt, lowers the level of national output or income. On the other hand, when the economy is operating below full employment, the government can borrow to create real capital expansion and the subsequent expansion in the economy will generate the increased taxes to pay for the cost of borrowing. In this case the output effect is positive.

The **inflationary effects** of the national debt are in the form of the inflationary pressures created when the debt is incurred and the increased difficulty that the Bank of Canada has in controlling inflation when banks and the public hold large amounts of short-term government securities.

Inflationary Effects. Inflationary woes may be associated with a large national debt if it is financed through monetary expansion. For one thing, government spending financed from debt is likely to be more inflationary than government spending financed from taxes. This point will be covered more carefully in the next section. In addition, a large national debt like ours gives the economy a great deal of liquidity, that is, assets that are near or like money. This liquidity aspect of the national debt means that people will tend to spend at a higher rate than they otherwise would. Government debt, then, may make inflation more difficult to control because of the liquidity effect.

Exchange Rate Effects. When government debt is financed through foreign borrowing, an exchange rate effect occurs. When foreigners buy Canadian government securities, the demand for Canadian dollars increases and the external value of the Canadian dollar rises, all other things being constant. This situation makes imports less expensive and Canadian products more expensive in foreign markets, and exports fall. The effect is to reduce Canadian production and employment.

Summary of Government Debt Problems

Government debt creates many problems, but some of the fears of the public are unfounded. They are often based on an analogy drawn between an individual and the government—an analogy that is often false. Economists also worry about the national debt, but their concerns tend to be related to the economic effects of government debt on the operation of the economy. The next section examines the economic effects of government debt financing more carefully.

Economic Analysis of Government Debt Financing

The following analysis starts with a discussion of the different methods of government finance, that is, the different ways in which the federal, provincial, and local governments can pay for goods and services. Second, the economic effects of government borrowing are presented; and third, the effects of tax and debt financing are compared and analyzed. The analysis draws upon the aggregate demand and supply framework presented in Chapter 13.

Methods of Finance

Governments have three primary ways of paying for goods and services. The government can pay for things out of current tax collections and other revenues, borrow, or the federal government can create money.

Tax Finance. The current income of the federal government is primarily derived from its various taxes, such as income taxes, payroll taxes, and commodity taxes. Taxes paid out of private income reduce private consumption and savings and, therefore, reduce private demand for goods and services. As previously discussed, a government runs a balanced budget when government revenues are equal to government expenditures, a budget surplus when government revenues are greater than expenditures, and a budget deficit when government revenues are less than government expenditures. The net effect of a balanced budget on aggregate demand tends to be neutral; the net effect of a budget surplus tends to reduce aggregate demand; and the net effect of a budget deficit tends to increase aggregate demand. With respect to a balanced budget, balancing the budget at higher levels of government purchases and taxes may not have a neutral impact on aggregate demand. The positive multiplier effects of an increase in government purchases may be greater than the negative multiplier effects of an increase in taxes, since the tax multiplier is the regular multiplier minus one. Figure 15–12 illustrates the net effect of a budget surplus and deficit on the price level and output.

Figure 15–12   **Net effect of a tax surplus and a budget deficit**

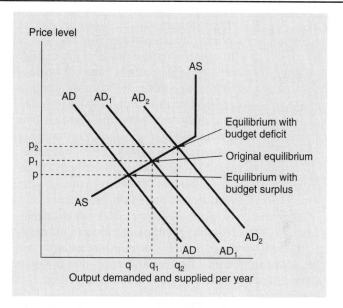

The original equilibrium is at price level p_1 where the output demanded and sup-plied is q_1. The net effect of a tax surplus is to reduce aggregate demand from AD_1AD_1 to $ADAD$. A tax surplus means that the government is taking more away from the income stream than it is putting into the income stream, thereby causing a reduction in the price level and output. The net effect of a budget deficit is to in-crease aggregate demand to AD_2AD_2. A budget deficit means that the government is putting more into than it is taking out of the income stream.

Debt Financing. The government incurs debt to finance budget deficits and to pay for goods and services over a period of time. Government debt is incurred by government borrowing, that is, by the government selling securities to private investors who desire to buy them. There are differ-ences between tax and debt financing. People have to pay taxes. People do not have to buy government securities. They do so because government securities are an alternative way of holding interest-yielding assets. Al-though tax and debt financing both may reduce private consumption and saving, debt financing does not change the total assets of people. It only changes the composition of assets, whereas tax financing reduces the as-sets of people. Last, tax financing is a way to pay for government goods and services today, and as mentioned previously, debt financing is a way to pay over a period of time.

Money Creation. The federal government may finance budget deficits and pay for goods and services and transfers by creating money. The process of money creation was discussed in Chapter 14. Government sales of securities to banks, assuming banks have excess cash reserves, is the modern way to create money or to *monetize the debt*. Let's illustrate how this process works. Suppose the government runs a $5 billion deficit and covers it by borrowing from banks. The initial effect of the deficit expenditure is to increase demand deposits and cash reserves of banks by $5 billion. The effect of government borrowing from banks is to reduce cash reserves and to increase government securities held by banks. Then the net effect of the whole fiscal operation is to increase demand deposits or the money supply by $5 billion. A budget deficit of $5 billion has generated an increase in the money supply of $5 billion. Thus in this instance, government debt has been monetized. Is the federal debt always monetized? The answer is no—only in the case when government securities are sold to banks. The money supply is not increased when the government borrows from non-bank sources such as individuals, businesses, and corporations. Thus increases in government debt may or may not lead to increases in the money supply. This method of finance will be referred to as *money creation* when the money supply increases. This terminology stresses the important fact that the debt is monetized.

Economic Effects of Government Debt Financing

Although government debt financing may reduce both private consumption and saving, it is likely to have its major impact on private saving. The part of the nation's income that is not consumed is saved. Savings may flow into low-interest-yielding assets such as demand deposits, interest-yielding assets such as private securities and government securities, and real investments. Government securities compete with private securities and all other alternative uses for savings. Thus when the government borrows, that is, sells securities to individuals, businesses, corporations, and the like, the government is tapping savings and reducing the amount of savings available for private borrowing and investment. In other words, government borrowing increases the demand for savings or loanable funds, which exerts upward pressure on the price paid for loanable funds or the rate of interest. This is shown in Figure 15–13. The effect of a higher rate of interest is to discourage private investment. Therefore, increases in government debt may directly reduce private debt and private investment and indirectly reduce private investment through exerting upward pressures on the rate of interest.

When the government creates money to finance budget deficits, private savings and investment may not be reduced. In this instance the money supply is increased and the rate of interest may remain unchanged (Figure 15–13). The difficulty here is that, especially at or near full employment, financing the deficit in this way may lead to a demand-pull inflation. The question as to the best way of financing a deficit depends on the state of the economy. Government debt financing is preferable during

Figure 15–13   **The effect of government borrowing and money creation on the interest rate**

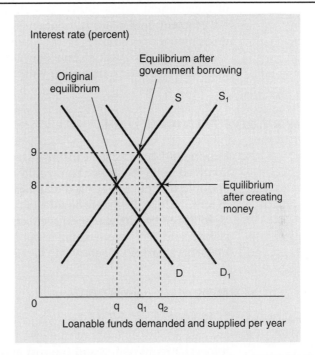

The original equilibrium is at 8 percent; that is, loanable funds (savings, etc.) demanded equal loanable funds supplied. Government borrowing increases the demand for loanable funds from DD to D_1D_1, causing the interest rate to rise to 9 percent. Money creation, that is, government borrowing from banks increases supply to S_1S_1. In this case the interest rate may remain at 8 percent as shown.

periods of high production and inflation, and creating money is preferable when the economy is in a deep recession or depression.

Differing Effects of Tax and Debt Financing

The differing effects of tax and debt financing may be known by now. However, several important points can still be stressed. Both tax and debt financing (borrowing from non-banks) will reduce private demand. Tax financing does it by reducing consumption and saving and leaving people with fewer assets. Debt financing does it by reducing primarily saving and increasing the rate of interest. Which has the greatest downward pull on the economy, tax or debt financing? Tax financing probably pulls the economy downward the most because taxes are a direct leakage from the private income stream, but both could have a similar downward impact.

Thus, excluding creating money, finance methods have a contractionary impact on the economy and partly offset the expansionary impact of government expenditures. Sometimes you may hear people say that government borrowing is inflationary. What they probably mean is that government expenditures may be inflationary and, as compared to tax financing, the net effect of financing budget deficits by incurring debt financed by monetary expansion will tend to be inflationary.

Managing a Large National Debt

How would you like to be the manager of the national debt? You would be involved in big business. You would have to determine the kinds of government securities to be used and the amounts of each. You would have to determine how they are to be sold and who is likely to buy them. You would be concerned with the economic effects on the securities market of your decisions, and you would desire to coordinate your decision with decisions made in regard to monetary and fiscal policy, which are closely related.

Debt Management Policy

Debt management policy is not concerned primarily with the size of the national debt or the cost and availability of credit, but with the types of government securities outstanding, the ownership pattern of the debt, and the maturity distribution of the national debt.

Debt management policy takes as a given the size of the national debt and the cost and availability of money. The size of the national debt is determined by fiscal policy, and the cost and availability of money and credit are in the domain of monetary policy. Debt management policy is essentially concerned with the structural characteristics of the national debt, namely, the types of securities, the ownership pattern, and the maturity distribution of the national debt.

Debt Management Principles

Stabilization Role. Economists differ as to what they believe should be the stabilization role of debt management policy. Some economists argue that debt management policy should be neutral; that is, it should be designed to have no appreciable effect on the economy. Others argue that debt management policy should play a positive role in stabilizing the economy. This type of policy would mean, during inflationary periods, that the debt coming due should be funded or refinanced into longer term government securities. The effect would be to put upward pressure on the long-term interest rate and thereby discourage private investment spending. The long-term interest rate, rather than the short-term rate, is the relevant rate in regard to investment decisions. An alternative to investment is to make loans, especially long-term loans. The long-term rate indicates the cost of acquiring long-term funds for investment.

During recessions and unemployment, the stabilization role of debt management policy would consist of funding the debt coming due into shorter term debt, or even into money. This action would reduce the government's demand for long-term funds, which would exert downward pressure on the long-term interest rate and encourage private investment.

Minimizing Interest Cost. The idea that debt management policy should be designed to minimize the interest cost of government debt seems reasonable. This principle means, essentially, funding the debt into short-term securities when the long-term interest rate is high and funding the debt into long-term debt when the long-term interest rate is low. The difficulty with this idea is that the effects of such a policy would tend to intensify ups and downs in the economy. The long-term interest rate is

Figure 15–14   **Refinancing short-term government debt into long-term debt**

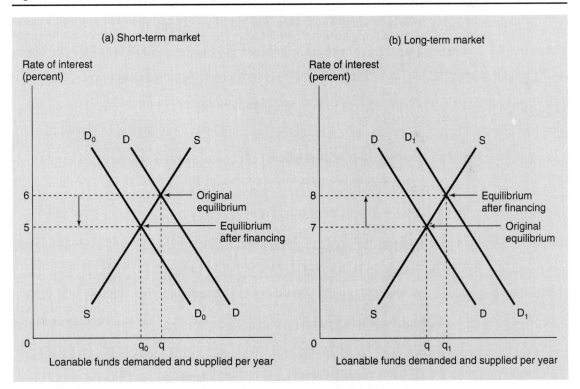

The effect of refinancing short-term government debt into long-term debt is to put upward pressures on the long-term interest rate and downward pressures on the short-term interest rate. The reason is that this debt management operation increases the demand for long-term loans and decreases the demand for short-term loans. Refinancing, that is, paying off long-term government securities, tends to have the opposite effect—it decreases the long-term interest rate and increases the short-term rate.

usually low during a recession. If the government increased the supply of long-term securities in a recession, this action would tend to drive up long-term interest rates and worsen the recession. Thus minimizing interest cost on the national debt is desirable only if it can be done without worsening recessionary and/or inflationary forces.

Lengthening the Debt. At present a major problem with the national debt is that it is concentrated at the short end of the market; that is, a high percentage of government securities outstanding is in the form of short-term securities such as treasury bills that come due within a year. For example, one-third of marketable public debt securities held by private investors matured within a year in 1994. The uncertainty and impact on the securities market of the government having to enter the market to fund a huge amount of the existing national debt in this brief time span can be significant. Treasury officials and economists agree that the maturity distribution of the national debt should be increased. This increase would enable the government to better manage and plan its debt management operations and would reduce the frequency and the amount of government securities that would have to be refinanced in a given year. Figure 15–14 shows the impact of refinancing short-term debt into long-term debt on short-term and long-term interest rates.

When Should the Government Borrow?

The economic effects of government borrowing, and problems associated with a large national debt, have been examined. An important question, however, still remains unanswered. When should the government borrow? Alternatively, when is government borrowing the best or most efficient method of government finance?

Public Investments

Government borrowing may be the efficient way to pay for investment or capital goods. These goods such as bridges, dams, schools, and hospitals provide benefits or real income to society over a period of time. Government borrowing, similar to private borrowing, permits the spreading of the cost of investment goods over a period of time. In this way costs and benefits can be related over a time span, avoiding the heavy tax claims on private income in a single year.

Government activity of any sort, regardless of how it is financed, should not be undertaken unless it is worthwhile to do so. In the case of public investments, therefore, the present value of the net benefits from the public investment should exceed the present value of the cost of the public investment. After this efficiency criterion is met, government borrowing is a legitimate way to distribute the costs of the investment over time.

If government debt is incurred only to pay for worthwhile public investments, the growth in the national debt would be limited to the growth in public investment goods. Government debt incurred to finance a given public investment project would be paid off over the lifetime of the project. Thus for the national debt to grow over time, the stock of public investment goods would have to grow.

Economic Instability

If the economy operated at full employment without inflation all the time, the only justification for government borrowing would be to finance public investments. However, this is not the case. The economy experiences ups and downs; that is, the economy experiences economic instability. A responsibility of the federal government is to pursue a fiscal policy that tends to stabilize the economy.

The stabilization responsibility of the federal government suggests three fiscal rules to be followed. First, assuming full or near-full employment and a stable or near-stable price level, policy designed to stabilize the economy would dictate a balanced budget. In this way the impact of fiscal operations on the level of aggregate demand would be largely neutral. Second, under the assumption of very high or full employment and inflation, the appropriate fiscal policy would be a budget surplus. The effect of the tax surplus would be to reduce the level of aggregate demand and, therefore, mitigate the inflation. Third, when the economy experiences low levels of production and employment and a decline in the price level, a budget deficit is the appropriate fiscal policy. The effect of the budget deficit would be to stimulate the economy.

Thus the stabilization responsibility of the federal government justifies government borrowing in times of economic recessions. Even if the government does not consciously plan budget deficits, they would likely occur anyway, since tax collections automatically decline during recessions. If this type of policy were adopted, the government would balance its budget over the business cycle but not every single year.

A Budget Proposal

A great deal of misunderstanding about budget deficits and the national debt could be clarified by dividing the federal budget into three major accounts—the current account, the investment account, and the stabilization account. The current account would always be kept in balance. This account would comprise all current costs, including interest costs on the national debt and current revenues exclusive of government borrowing. The investment account would include spending for investment goods and the debt incurred to finance these goods. The stabilization account would include spending programs designed to stabilize the economy and the methods used to finance these programs. The main reason for separating the budget into three major accounts is to make explicit the various responsibilities of government.

The current account recognizes the government's responsibility to manage its current operations based on principles of business and personal finance. Current costs should be met from current revenues. In the case of the government, this policy means, essentially, that tax revenues should pay for all current or recurrent expenditures such as expenditures for salaries, postal services, recreational services, supplies, interest on the national debt, medical services, and welfare services.

The investment account recognizes that a non-recurrent expenditure, that is, an investment expenditure, can be financed by government borrowing, which allows for the spreading out of the cost of the investment over a period of time. A $10 billion highway facility could be financed by the government incurring debt. However, the servicing of this debt, and operating and maintaining the highway facility, are current costs and would be paid from tax collections.

The stabilization account recognizes the government's responsibility for economic stabilization. Unemployment represents a waste of human and capital resources. Inflation has undesirable consequences; thus, on the stabilization account, a balanced budget, a tax surplus, or deficit spending would occur, depending upon the state of the economy. The fiscal rule would be (1) a balanced budget when the economy is at full employment without inflation, (2) a budget surplus when the economy is in a serious inflation, and (3) a budget deficit when the economy is in a recession.

With current federal budget procedures, it is difficult to evaluate government activities because all expenditures are lumped together. Budget position—a balanced budget, a surplus, or a deficit—is neither good nor bad in and of itself. It would be equally inappropriate for the government to incur debt to finance, say, increases in government employee salaries and not to incur debt to finance a profitable public investment or to promote employment when much unemployment exists.

A Final Look at the Deficit Issue

The issue of government budget deficits is a widely discussed and publicized issue. The major reason given for decreasing expenditures at both the federal and provincial levels was to reduce or eliminate deficits. The deficit issue was a focal point of discussion during the 1993 federal election campaign and in many provincial elections. All political parties generally agree that the deficit must be reduced or eliminated. It is even more important now than ever before to have a clear understanding of deficit budgetting, including the economic effects of reducing a deficit. The purpose of this last look at the deficit is to summarize some of the major points.

The real cost of increasing government spending is independent of the method of finance. This real cost, as you remember, takes the form of the subsequent decrease in private spending and production. The important economic consideration here is whether an increase in government spending is efficient. Assuming that such an increase is not efficient, then both tax financing and debt financing are undesirable from an economic perspective. Assuming that an increase in government spending is efficient, then the method of finance should depend on the type of expenditure. As explained in the previous section, a capital project such as a bridge should be financed by government borrowing. On the other hand, recurring expenditures such as interest on government debt and salaries of government employees should be financed by taxes.

A particular misunderstanding about budget deficits seems to be associated with confusing means and ends. An example of this confusion is balanced-budget legislation. This legislation suggests that balancing the budget is always desirable. A balanced budget is the end or goal under this proposal, but this goal contradicts the important stabilization role of the government. It is important for policy makers also, to understand the difference in a deficit due to the economy operating at less than full employment and a deficit due to a discretionary decision made by government. The former is called a *cyclical budget deficit* and the latter is referred to as a *structural budget deficit*. An attempt to reduce the cyclical budget deficit will tend to cause more unemployment and worsen the economy. In contrast, a reduction in a structural budget deficit will alleviate inflationary pressures caused by deficits when the economy is operating at full employment. Therefore, an important factor to consider before pursuing policies to reduce a deficit is the state of the economy.

Summary

Many concerns of people are related to the size of government, to inequities in the distribution of taxes, and to growing government debts. After discussing the concerns of people and concluding that some worries are well-founded and some are not, we approached the issues of government size, tax distributions, and growing government debt. For each issue relevant facts were presented first. Then an economic framework was developed based essentially on the concepts of efficiency and equity, and finally, policy proposals to deal with these issues were discussed.

In the economic analysis of the issue of size, efficiency considerations justify government expenditures in the form of provisions of collective goods and services, in the form of subsidies to encourage more consumption when external benefits in consumption are present, and in the form of taxes to discourage production when external costs in production are present. Equity considerations justify government programs designed to enhance the economic opportunities of people who do not earn an adequate income in the marketplace. The "adequacy" of income as well as the socially accepted distribution of income must be based on the beliefs of people.

In the development of tax principles, it was pointed out that an efficient tax is one that has neutral effects on the allocation of resources, and an equitable tax is one that can be defended on the ability-to-pay principle or the benefits-received principle. An equitable system would adhere to the equal tax treatment doctrine and to the relative tax treatment doctrine.

The incidence or burden of a tax is the final resting place of the tax. A tax may be shifted forward to consumers in the form of higher prices or backward to the owners of resources in the form of lower resource prices. The shifting of an output-type tax, such as the gasoline tax, depends on the price elasticity of demand. The more inelastic demand is, the more the tax will be shifted to consumers in the form of higher prices. A tax that is independent of output, such as an income tax, does not increase the cost of producing goods and services; therefore, this type of tax is not shifted, at least in the shortrun. For a tax to be shifted, supply has to decrease.

An empirical study of tax incidence was examined in order to answer the question, Who really pays taxes? This study discovered that the effective tax rate of combined federal, provincial, and local taxes is proportional or mildly progressive. In addition, it found that the tax rates of individual income taxes, corporate income taxes, and payroll taxes tend to be progressive, whereas the tax rates of commodity taxes and property taxes are regressive.

Do you now know the answer to the question, Is the national debt bad? You have read many pages to help you probe, understand, and possibly answer this question. The organization of your answer could be as follows: The size and growth of the national debt are closely connected to the way war was financed and the debt incurred during economic recessions.

The consolidated net national debt includes all the securities issued by the federal, provincial, and local governments minus government financial assets. Government securities are primarily purchased and owned by private investors, although federal securities are held also by government agencies and trust funds and the Bank of Canada. Most of the public debt is held by Canadian investors. However, in recent years foreign investors have increased the amount they own, and in 1995 held 35 percent of the national debt held by private investors.

Although problems are associated with a large national debt, not all the worries of the public are well-founded. Economists are troubled about a large national debt, especially with regard to the way the national debt may affect the operation of the economy. A large national debt may redistribute income away from low-income groups, reduce national output and the rate of capital formation, and increase prices.

The economic analysis of national debt financing focussed on the three methods of financing—tax finance, debt finance, and money creation—and the effects each method of finance has on aggregate demand. Taxes exert a strong downward pull on aggregate demand by reducing private consumption and saving. Government borrowing from non-banks tends to reduce aggregate demand by reducing saving and increasing the rate of interest. Government borrowing from banks (money creation) usually monetizes the national debt; that is, it increases the money supply.

Managing a large national debt is no easy task. Debt management policy uses the size of the national debt (fiscal policy) and the availability of money and credit (monetary policy) to determine the structural characteristics of the debt—types of securities, ownership pattern, and the maturity distribution of the national debt. Some economists believe that the debt management policy should play a positive role with regard to economic stabilization, while other economists visualize a neutral role. However, they generally agree that debt management policy designed to minimize the interest costs on the national debt is not always a desirable policy and that the maturity structure of the national debt should be lengthened. That is, the national debt should be composed of fewer short-term securities and more long-term securities.

Government borrowing is the appropriate method of financing in two circumstances—to finance profitable public investments and to finance programs designed to stimulate employment. Money creation, that is, government borrowing from banks, is the appropriate method of finance when there is much unemployment and no danger of inflation.

Some of the misunderstanding about budget deficits and the national debt could be lessened by dividing the federal budget into three accounts: the current account, the investment account, and the stabilization account. These accounts recognize the various responsibilities of the government, which are to pay for current expenditures out of tax collections, to pay for investment goods over a period of time, and to prevent both unemployment and inflation. Although not a panacea for government inefficiencies, these accounts would possibly provide a better understanding and a basis for evaluating government deficit spending and the ensuing growth in the national debt.

Checklist of Economic Concepts

Government purchases	Equal tax treatment doctrine
Transfer payments	Horizontal equity
Balanced budget	Vertical equity
Budget deficit	Relative tax treatment doctrine
Budget surplus	Ability-to-pay principle of taxation
Collective goods	Progressive tax rates
External benefits and costs	Proportional tax rates

Benefits-received principle of
  taxation

Tax efficiency

Forward and backward tax shifting

Tax incidence

Net debt

Public-held debt

Credit market debt

Primary burden

Secondary repercussions

Monetizing the debt

Debt management policy

Public investments

Recurrent expenditures

Fiscal rules

Current account

Investment account

Stabilization account

Discussion Questions

1. Explain the different effects to the economy of government expenditures on goods and services versus transfer payments to individuals and businesses.

2. Explain the difference between tax rates and tax incidence.

3. Define progressive, proportionate, and regressive tax structures. Discuss the different types of taxes in Canada and classify each as progressive, proportionate, or regressive.

4. Define horizontal equity and vertical equity. Consider each different type of tax in Canada with regard to these concepts. How well does each tax meet the criteria for horizontal equity and for vertical equity.

5. Compare and contrast the ability-to-pay principle of taxation with the benefits-received principle of taxation. Discuss the "fairness" of taxing seniors with no school-age children for public schooling (part of property taxes).

6. Outline the different roles for government in a modern mixed economy that this book has presented. Analyze and discuss the activities of the Canadian federal government in light of these roles. Then consider in the same way your provincial and local governments. Finally discuss which level of government you think is the most appropriate to serve each role.

7. Economists estimate that the implementation of the 7 percent federal goods and services tax (GST) raised prices on average only 3 to 4 percent. Use the elasticity concept to reconcile this apparent discrepancy.

8. Discuss the differences between the debt of governments and the debt of individuals and corporations.

9. Discuss the different effects on the domestic economy of financing government debt internally versus external (to the country) financing.

10. Apply the supply and demand model to the credit markets to show the changes to equilibrium interest rates in the shortrun and longrun markets when the government refinances short-term debt with long-term bonds.

11. Explain the effect of increased government spending on health care and education, which at the same time increases the participation rate and productivity of labour, on the government's budget. Discuss under what conditions the effect of this action increases debt; decreases debt. If GDP was initially $1,000 billion, debt was $500 billion, and this government action resulted in GDP growing by 5 percent, what is the maximum deficit that would keep the debt/GDP equal to 50 percent?

12. Use the aggregate demand and aggregate supply model to discuss when to use expansionary government policy (increased expenditures financed by a monetized deficit) and when to use contractionary government policy (surplus budget).

Supplementary Reading

Aaron, H. J. and M. J. Boskin, eds. *The Economics of Taxation.* Washington, DC: Brookings Institution, 1980.

A collection of essays on the economics, politics, and legal problems of taxation.

Boadway, R. W. and P. A. R. Hobson. *Intergovernmental Fiscal Relations.* Tax paper 96. Toronto: Canadian Tax Foundation, 1993.

A very thorough discussion of intergovernmental tax and transfer relations, including the constitutional issues of tax powers. Good discussion of the rationale (Chapter 3) for intergovernmental transfers.

Boadway R. W. and D. E. Wildasin. *Public Sector Economics.* Toronto: Little Brown, 1984.

This textbook is advanced theoretical treatment of government, its role, and financing.

Doern, G. B.; A. M. Maslove; and M. J. Prince. *Budgeting in Canada.* Ottawa: Carleton University Press, 1991.

Considers the budgeting process for a broad multidisciplinary perspective of politics, economics, and management with a balanced coverage of the spending and taxation sides of the budget.

Gore, A. *Creating a Government That Works Better and Costs Less.* New York: Plume, 1993.

Al Gore, the vice president of the United States, is also a journalist. This book is his report on the national performance review. Although an American perspective, this work has useful ideas for improving any government's performance.

Horray, I.; F. Palda; and M. Walker. *Tax Facts 9.* Vancouver, BC: Fraser Institute, 1994.

An easy-to-read introduction to tax incidence for the general reader with application to one's individual tax situation. The Fraser Institute's general philosophical bias opposing government is evident, and it confuses resource rent capture as taxation.

Ip, I. K. and J. M. Mintz. *Dividing the Spoils.* Toronto: C. D. Howe Institution, 1992. Discusses the federal–provincial allocation of taxing powers. Good coverage of the current legal structure of taxation. Significant recommendations for tax reform follow a detailed analysis of each type of tax.

Osberg, L. and P. Fortin, eds. *Unnecessary Debts.* Toronto: James Lorimer and Co., 1996.
A collection of papers on the deficit, debt history, and issues for Canada and the provinces. A common theme is that the Bank of Canada's effort to reach zero inflation was a major cause of the growth of debt as interest costs of debt servicing soared and became a major, if not the major, expenditure by governments.

School of Public Administration. *How Ottawa Spends.* Ottawa: Carleton University Press, various years.
This series is an annual publication that analyzes Canadian government and its finances. It is a useful reader for keeping up with current government issues in Canada.

Sharp, A. M. and C. A. Register. "Federal Budget Deficits: A Crisis or a Misunderstanding." *Journal of Business and Economic Perspectives* (Spring 1990), pp. 57–63.
This article presents a framework of discussion concerning federal budget deficits. The framework includes five propositions that lead to a better understanding of deficits.

Treff, K. and T. Cook. *1995 Finances of the Nation.* Toronto: Canadian Tax Foundation, 1995.
A comprehensive documentation of the current fiscal situation of each level of government and each specific government in Canada. Includes budgets and the principles behind them.

Vermaeten, A.; W. I. Gillespie; and F. Vermaeten, "Who Paid the Taxes in Canada?" *Canadian Public Policy* 21, no. 2 (1995).
The incidence of taxes by broad income groups is analyzed over four decades. The study compares tax by type and by jurisdiction. As it considers four time periods, the study sheds light on the changing burden of taxes as well. Although it extends only to 1988, this study is the best tax incidence study for Canada to date.

Chapter 16

Renewable and Non-Renewable Resources
Are Our Resources Running Out?

Vancouver—The federal government is expected to announce today that the West Coast salmon fleet will be reduced by at least one third. But even the unprecedented dry-docking of more than 1,500 fishing boats over the next few years, at a cost of at least $65-million to taxpayers, is unlikely to stave off the most disastrous salmon season in generations.

Years of poor management, overfishing and the unexpected warming of the ocean have combined to create a conservation crisis that threatens the livelihood of approximately 10,000 British Columbians who rely on the commercial fishery. Numbers of salmon returning from the Pacific Ocean this year will be so low, sources say, that much of the $450-million commercial fishery may simply have to be shut down to prevent an ecological disaster. . . .

One of the shutdowns is likely to be the Fraser River, a major artery for millions of West Coast salmon. Running through Vancouver, the Fraser has long been held up by the federal government as the symbol of a healthy fishery. But one confidential estimate by the department predicts that only about 1.5 million sockeye salmon will make it back to the river this year. This would mean most fishing will have to be curtailed to ensure enough fish make it up the river to lay eggs and replenish stocks.

Premier Glen Clark predicted yesterday that the commercial sockeye fishery on the Fraser River will in effect shut down this year.

Fearing a replication of the overfishing disaster that occurred on the East Coast, many West Coast fishermen have already agreed that the Fraser fishery should be shut down this year if fewer than two million sockeye salmon come from their four-year journey in the Pacific.[1]

Any number of different quotes could have been used to introduce this chapter. A discussion of the United States–Canada softwood lumber dispute, the Spanish–Canada turbot dispute, or oil royalties could have served the purpose equally well. Fish, forest, and oil are all natural resources. So are farmland, iron ore, water, or any naturally occurring ingredient we use to produce goods or services. In Chapter 1 we divided the resources (factors of production) available into three broad classifications—labour resources, capital resources, and land resources. It is often convenient to classify resources in this way. Labour refers to human resources, and capital refers to non-human resources, including all capital goods. *Land* refers to natural resources. In this chapter we will look at some elements of the economics

---

[1]M. Cernetig, "B. C. Fishery Faces Huge Shutdown—Ottawa expected to trim salmon fleet by at least one-third as conservation crisis worsens," *Globe and Mail*, March 29, 1996, p. A1. Reprinted with permission.

Economists refer to all natural resources as **land**. Land is the third factor of production.

of natural resources. For convenience, economists refer to all natural resources as land. Natural resources have played and continue to play an important role in the Canadian economy. Traditionally Canadian economic development has been explained in terms of the *staples thesis*. According to the staples thesis, as applied to Canada, the development of the Canadian economy through successive stages was based on the exploitation of key natural resources. At different times the staple good changed. The first staple was fish, then furs, lumber, and grain. While the staple thesis was first suggested by an American economic historian, a Canadian economist, H. A. Innis, became its main proponent.

Natural resources can be divided into two broad categories. Some natural resources are renewable. Lumber is an example of a *renewable resource*. Other resources are non-renewable. Oil is an example of a *non-renewable resource*. Obviously, there are some economic differences between renewable and non-renewable resources. It is possible to use a renewable resource and still never run out of it. On the other hand, if we use a non-renewable resource, we will eventually run out of it. It is true that given enough millions of years, we well may become oil just as the dinosaurs before us; however, from a practical standpoint we can treat oil as if it is finite and exhaustible in supply.

The way a society allocates its natural resources is important for a number of reasons. As is the case with labour and capital, the allocation of natural resources affects both the efficiency of the economy and the distribution of income. The issue of income distribution is important not only in context of the interpersonal distribution of income, which was discussed in Chapter 7, but also in the context of the intergenerational distribution of income. If we do not manage our resources optimally now, future generations will by poorer as a result. Such intertemporal issues are common in economics, but they are perhaps most obvious when discussing natural resources.

The Management of a Renewable Resource

The Allocation of a Renewable Resource at a Point in Time

Let us start our study of natural resources by considering a hypothetical lake fish industry. We will assume that the industry is purely competitive. (Purely competitive markets were discussed in Chapter 2.) There are a large number of small firms each one of which owns a lake from which it harvests fish. We will also assume that we are in a land in which there is no such thing as time. Economists often ignore time in their analysis; however, as we will see the assumption that time is irrelevent is not a reasonable assumption in this type of problem. However, this assumption is a useful starting point for the analysis so we will begin by making this assumption.

The market for fish is illustrated in Figure 16–1. The supply of fish is upward sloping because as each firm tries to catch more fish in a given time period, the fish become harder and harder to catch as their density in the lake becomes lower and lower. As a result it becomes more costly to catch the fish. Also as a firm tries to take more fish, it would be forced to catch smaller and smaller fish, so while the number of fish would increase, their total weight would increase much more slowly. The demand curve for fish slopes downward for the normal reasons.

Equilibrium in Figure 16–1 occurs at p_1 and q_1. That equilibrium exists at a given point in time. If you remember the discussion of supply and demand in Chapter 2, it was stated that both the supply and the

Figure 16–1   **The market for lake fish**

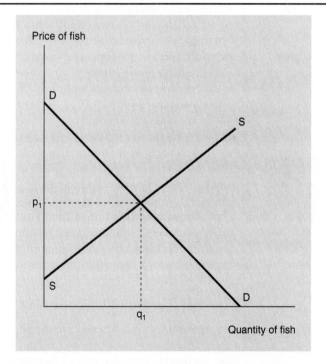

The market demand for fish slopes downward and to the right because as fish become cheaper, buyers choose to eat more fish. The supply curve slopes upward and to the right because as firms catch more fish, the remaining fish become harder to catch. At p_1 the quantity demanded and the quantity supplied of fish would be equal and the market would be in equilibrium.

demand relationships were based on the assumption *all other things being equal*. That is another way of saying that time does not matter. The equilibrium holds as long as nothing else changes. If there is no time, there can be no change.

The market for lake fish is purely competitive; therefore, any individual firm can not influence the price. Since an individual firm cannot influence the price of a good in a purely competitive market, economists say that such firms are *price takers*. If a firm is a price taker, it sees its own demand curve simply as a horizontal line at the market price. On the other hand, the individual firm's supply curve slopes upward and to the right. As the firm tries to catch more fish, its costs rise as the fish stock decreases. It can catch the extra fish only if it spends more time fishing or if it accepts smaller and smaller fish. Therefore, its costs rise as it tries to increase its catch, and it must receive higher prices to induce it to incur the higher costs. Figure 16–2 illustrates supply and demand for a single firm in the lake fish market.

> Individual firms in purely competitive markets are too small to influence the price. For this reason such firms are referred to as **price takers**.

We began by assuming that time was irrelevant. However, we warned that this assumption might not be appropriate for this type of issue. To introduce time into the analysis, we will assume that there are three different time periods. What happens in the initial time period may affect period 2 and what happens in period 2 may affect period 3. Of course, it is possible that nothing will happen in any one period time that will affect what happens in the other periods. If the economy has a large number of alternative food sources available and fish is not particularly popular, q_1 could represent a relatively small part of the total fish population in the fishery. Consequently, year after year the stock of fish would reproduce at a rate adequate to maintain its population. As long as nothing affected either the demand for fish, such as a decrease in the supply of alternative foods or the growth of human population, or the supply of fish, such as the technology for catching fish or a change in environment of the lakes, the equilibrium illustrated in Figure 16–1 could remain constant. The economy would be using its lake fish resource at a *sustainable* rate. Even if some of the circumstances changed from period to period, it is possible that the stock of fish would be large enough to absorb the changes.

> The level of exploitation of a resource is said to be at a **sustainable rate of use** if it is possible to maintain the rate of use into the indefinite future. Overall **sustainable economic growth** is that rate of growth for an economy that is possible for the indefinite future.

The Allocation of a Renewable Resource over Time

On the other hand, something could happen to disturb the equilibrium shown in Figure 16–1. For example, new technology could improve fishing methods, allowing fish to be caught more cheaply. The development of large factory ships and power winches to haul in huge nets are examples of such new technology in the ocean fishery. Such technology increases the supply of fish and lowers the price. The lower price would increase the quantity demanded of fish. If the new equilibrium quantity were great enough, the stock might no longer be able to reproduce fast enough to maintain itself.

Figure 16–2   **Supply and demand for an individual firm in the lake fish industry**

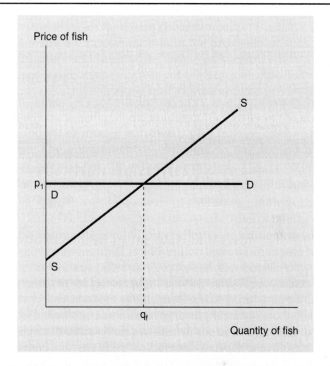

The individual firm does not see the demand curve as downward sloping because each firm is a price taker. Its production is too small to influence the price—it can sell all the fish it catches at the price determined in the market. The individual firm has a supply curve that slopes upward to the right for the same reason that the market supply curve slopes upward. As the firm tries to catch more fish, its costs increase. Therefore, the firm must realize a higher price if it is to sell fish. Given that the individual firm must accept p_1 as the price of fish, the only decision it has to make is how many fish to catch and sell. It does this by producing where the market price of fish cuts its supply curve for fish. In the case of the typical firm in Figure 16–2, this would occur at q_f.

An alternative possibility is that the population might grow between period one and period two. A one-time increase in population would cause the demand for fish to increase as illustrated in Figure 16–3. D_1D_1 represents the original demand curve for fish. D_2D_2 represents the demand for fish in time period 2 after the population has grown. The increase in demand caused by the population growth would result in a higher equilibrium price p_2 and a higher quantity of fish q_2. A large enough q_2 might affect the ability of the fish stock to reproduce itself. This might happen if a large number of smaller fish were caught before they became sexually mature and could mate. If q_2 was high enough, the stock could fall below the

Figure 16–3   **The possible effects of population growth on the lake fish industry**

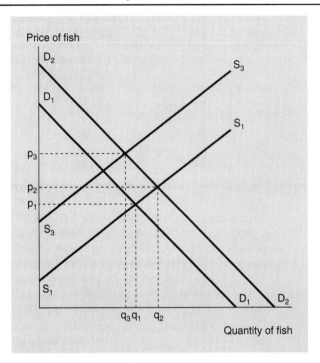

D_1D_1 and S_1S_1 represent demand and supply in period 1. Between period 1 and period 2 a one-time increase in population occurs. This increase in population causes the demand for lake fish to increase to D_2D_2. Supply in period 2 remains unchanged at S_1S_1; however, the quantity supplied increased to q_2 because of the shift in demand. Assume that the quantity supplied is beyond the sustainable level and the fish stock's ability to reproduce is affected. In that case the supply of fish will decrease in period 3. Supply in period 3 is represented by S_3S_3.

threshold where any fish would reproduce and the species would become extinct. The large catch could mean that the fish would become harder to catch in period 3, which would cause supply to shift in period 3 to S_3S_3. Since the growth in population was a one-time event, the demand for fish in period 3 would remain at D_2D_2. The market equilibrium in period 3 would be at p_3 and q_3.

The new higher price in itself leads to some conservation of the fish. The equilibrium quantity of fish is now lower than it was in period 1. The lower harvest might allow fish stocks to reproduce themselves in future time periods. The higher price will also cause an increase in the demand for other foods. Given sufficient time, the increase in demand for other foods in these substitute industries could lead to new technologies that would increase the supply of these alternative foods. However, the picture for the future may not be that bright. For one thing, our example assumes a one-time population increase, but the world's population is increasing continuously. Therefore, time period 3 would be characterized not only by a decrease in supply caused by the earlier overfishing but also by an increase in demand caused by new population growth. In fact, economists and many others have from time to time predicted dire consequences for human beings based on the growth of population and exhaustibility of natural resources.

In the first half of the 19th century, Thomas Malthus, an English clergyman and economist, believed that population growth would eventually overtake the world's ability to produce food. It was Malthus's pessimistic *Essay on the Principle of Population as It Affects the Future Improvement of Society* that led Thomas Carlyle to dub economics as the dismal science.

In the 1970s a group composed of academics, business and political leaders, and scientists which was known as the Club of Rome, raised the issue of the likelihood that population and economic growth would in the not-too-distant future be limited by the availability of natural resources.[2] Although a number of factors mitigate the consequences of population and economic growth, ultimately Malthus, the Club of Rome, and others who predict future problems cannot be dismissed. Economics is the study of the allocation of scarce resources. All we can do is look for ways in which society can adapt to the limitations caused by the scarcity of natural resources.

The Present Value of Future Resources

You learned in Chapter 1 that economists measure cost not in terms of simply the explicit costs that a firm must pay, but in terms of opportunity costs. The cost of producing anything is the alternatives that must be foregone in order for that production to take place. The opportunity cost concept means that the cost of catching fish in period 1 includes the costs of the use of boats, nets, and other fishing gear as well as the labour of the fishers. Those costs are explicit. However, when the fish caught in period 1 reduce the available catch in the future, that is an opportunity cost.

The opportunity cost of catching a fish now is the price that the firm could receive if it waited and caught the fish at a later time. Obviously this principle is applicable to any resource that can be stored and used later. It is not applicable to labour because labour cannot be stored. It is also not applicable to fresh fish that have already been caught, because they are perishable. It is applicable to live fish, but to a somewhat limited degree. Eventually the fish in the lake will die if not caught, so this natural event limits the application of this principle. If the fish are being caught at a sustainable rate, the future price of the fish will be the same as the present

---

[2] D. L. Meadows et al. *The Limits to Growth* (Washington, DC: Potomac Associates, 1972).

price, so it does not represent a cost. However, if current fishing is reducing the stock of fish, then the opportunity cost of catching a fish in period 1 is the price in the period with the highest future price for that fish. If we assume that a mature fish ceases to grow, then in the sustainable state its future price is the same as its present price. (The fact that mature fish do grow makes the problem a little more difficult, but it does not change the principle.) On the other hand, if the present level of exploitation is higher than the sustainable rate, the future price of fish will be higher than the present price, as was illustrated in Figure 16–3.

At first glance it might seem that the lake fish firms would never catch fish if the price is going to be higher in the future than it was at the present. Since the future price is an opportunity cost and it is higher than the present price, the cost of catching a fish now would also be higher than the revenue from catching a fish now and would be a money losing proposition for the firm. Therefore, the firm would just wait to catch the fish. This behaviour guarantees the conservation of natural resources. If the rate of utilization of fish rose above the sustainable rate, the future price would rise above the present price and the industry would stop catching fish until the supply replenished itself. Unfortunately, real life is not that simple.

The Present Value of a Future Payment

The **present value** or **discounted future value** of a future payment is equivalent to the amount of money that would have to be invested today at the current rate of interest to yield that payment at that future time.

The key to understanding how a market economy allocates resources over time lies in understanding the concept of *present value* or the *discounted future value* of future income. Assume that a distant, but rich, relative dies and leaves you a $1,000 guaranteed investment certificate (GIC) in trust. The certificate does not mature for three years and under the terms of the bequest you cannot touch the money, not even the interest, until the three years are up. This particular asset pays an interest rate of 7 percent compounded annually. When in three years time you cash in your GIC, you find that you have inherited considerable more than $1,000. At maturity your GIC will be worth $1,225.04. The reason it is worth more than $1,000 is that it earned interest over the three years. At the end of the first year it would be worth $1,070 ($1,000 plus $70 in interest). The second year you would earn an additional $70 in interest on the principle plus $4.90 interest on the first year's interest. Accordingly your GIC will be worth $1,144.90. In the third year you will earn interest on the balance at the end of the second year so the final value will be $1,144.90×1.07 or $1,225.04. What we have just done is to figure out the future value of a present asset. At 7 percent interest, $1,000 will be worth $1,225.04 in three years. Put another way, if the interest rate is 7 percent, $1,225.04 three years from now has a value at the present time, a present value (or a discounted future value) of $1,000. Future income is always worth a lesser amount than present income because if you have the money now you have the option of placing it in an interest-earning asset. If you do not get the money until some future date, you cannot earn interest on the funds until that date. When calculating the present value of a future payment, the interest rate is often referred to as the *discount rate*.

Many economic problems involve calculating the present value of a future payment. For example, if a firm is planning to buy a new machine, it knows that the new machine will enable the firm to produce and sell its product in the future. The firm must buy the machine now, but the income will flow in over time in the future. To make a rational decision, the firm must know the present value of that flow of expected future income. If its present value is greater than the cost of the machine, the machine is a good investment. Let us assume that your distant relative's will indicated not that you receive the $1,000 GIC, but that you will receive a payment of $1,225.04 in three years. Naturally you would be interested in knowing what your inheritance was really worth now. Again assuming a 7 percent interest rate, we can do the problem backward and solve for the present value of $1225.04 three years from now. If the GIC is only for one year, it will have a value at maturity of $1,070. To get the present value of $1,070, all that is required is to divide the future payment by one plus the interest rate: $1,070 ÷ 1.07 = $1,000. To work backward from a date three years in the future, you would have to divide the future payment by 1.07 three times: $1,225.04 ÷ 1.07 = $1,144.90 and $1,144.90 ÷ 1.07 = $1070.00 and $1.070 ÷ 1.07 = $1000.00.[3]

It is time to return to the lake fish industry. If the firms catch fish at a rate that reduces the future stocks of fish, we know that the higher future price is an opportunity cost of catching the fish now. However, the present value of the future price is the actual opportunity cost of catching the fish now. For example, let us assume the present price of fish delivered to the local fish market is $4.00 per kilogram. Let us also assume that the expected price one year from now is $4.25. If the interest rate is 7 percent, the present value of the future price is $4.25 ÷ 1.07 or $3.97. Therefore, it is better to catch the fish now. However, if the future price for next year was to rise to $4.30, the situation would change. At a 7 percent interest rate, the present value of $4.30 is $4.02. It would now be better to wait to catch the fish. The market for lake fish would avoid overfishing because if the firms caught too many fish in one time period, the price in the next time period would rise. Once the future price rose enough so that its present value was greater than the current market price of fish, the firms would reduce their catch. The market would provide an equilibrium both at any one point in time and also over time.

It is unlikely that real fishers would be able to make such precise calculation, but if they are rational, their behaviour should closely approximate the discussion above. There is one other limitation. Fishers must have the

---

[3]For students with a math background, the formula used to calculate present value is $PV = \sum_{t=1}^{n} \frac{R_t}{(1+i)^t}$ where PV is present value, t is the time period, n is the number of time periods, R_t is the payment in year t, and i is the interest (or discount) rate.

ability to support themselves until it is economically efficient to harvest the fish. If the fishers are very poor, they may not survive long enough to reap the higher price. Those of us in rich countries like Canada are often critical of people in poor countries because they do not conserve their resources. Faced with starvation, waiting can be fatal. Even the fisher in a Newfoundland outport may not have the means to delay catching cod or talbot until the stocks return to sustainable levels. Any policy to conserve fish stocks must recognize this limitation.

Common Property Rights and Resource Allocation over Time

In our example of the lake fishery industry, each firm owned its own lake. The fish are private property. While there are private lakes and ponds which produce fish, this situation is not the general case. Many lakes are very large and are not privately owned. Many fish are caught in the ocean. Who owns the fish in such cases? Often ownership is not clear. In a mixed economy such as Canada's, private property is part of an institutional set of rules about who can control the use of a resource. Alternative systems establish other rules for the control of the means of production. In the absence of such rules, everyone would have free access to a resource. In effect, everyone or no one would own the fish. Sometimes economists refer to such resources as *common property*. Normally common property rights apply to air. Sometimes common property rights apply to water. Note that common property is not the same as socialized ownership. In that case there is still an owner. There may be collective ownership but the government is an agent that can act on behalf of the society. Without a clear ownership claim on the fish, a market failure can occur.

Some resources do not have recognized ownership claims. No one can control these resources. There are **common property rights** for these resources.

When some agent has an ownership claim on a fish stock (or other resource), a market mechanism exists to prevent overfishing. If fish stocks drop below a sustainable level, the future price of fish will increase. The present value of that future price is an opportunity cost of catching the fish in the present time. If the cost of catching the fish now is higher than the revenue from catching the fish now, private firms will wait and catch the fish in a later time period. Even if the individual firm does not have the resources to wait to catch the fish later, it could borrow against the future income that the scarce fish will generate when they are caught.

The absence of property rights eliminates this mechanism. Without an ownership claim on the fish, possession becomes all 10 points of the law. Anyone can catch and sell the fish. The present value of the future price is no longer an opportunity cost, because if the firm does not catch the fish now, some other firm will almost certainly catch them. No firm can wait to catch the fish for fear that another firm will catch them first. The same applies to the national fishing fleets. The Spanish are worried that if they do not catch Atlantic ground fish now, the Canadians, the Portuguese, or someone else will catch them. Not catching does not mean conserving the stock—it is just giving the fish to someone else. The possible difference between a market that has specific property rights and one that has common property is illustrated in Figure 16–4. Specific property rights could be either private property rights or collective (government) property rights. However, a specific authority has the right to the use of the property. If that authority is government, it is assumed that it will operate so as to maximize the present value of the use of the property and not to maximize shortrun political goals such as maintaining employment until the next election. It is certainly possible to argue that governments have an interest in allowing overuse of a resource because the crisis of overuse will not become obvious until after they have long since ceased to be the government.

The existence of specific property rights reduces the supply of fish because the present opportunity cost of catching the fish includes the present value of the future price that the fishers could get if they waited to catch

Figure 16–4   **The market for fish with common and specific property rights**

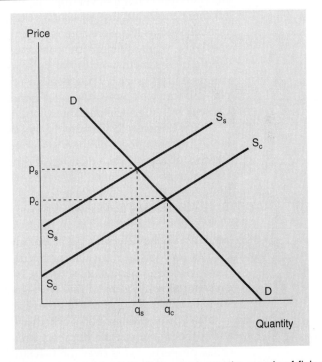

DD represents the demand for fish. S_cS_c represents the supply of fish with common property rights. S_sS_s represents the supply of fish with specific property rights. The existence of specific property rights reduces the supply of fish because the present value of the future catch is an opportunity cost of catching the fish now.

the fish in a later time period. With common property the equilibrium price would be p_c and the equilibrium quantity would be q_c. With specific property rights the equilibrium price would be p_s and the equilibrium quantity would be q_s. While it seems that the existence of specific property rights increases the price of fish, it is an illusion. The lower price with common property rights is less than the true cost of the fish. The extra cost will show up in the future when stocks decline because of overfishing. When that happens, the price will be higher than than p_s. In effect, S_cS_c represents the private cost of catching fish with common property. It understates the social cost of catching fish. The full cost to society is represented by S_sS_s.

The **Coase theorem** states that there must be a system of property rights if there is to be an efficient allocation of resources.

The idea that there must a system of property rights if there is to be an efficient allocation of resources is generally known as the *Coase theorem* after Ronald Coase. Moreover, that efficient solution can be achieved independently of who holds the ownership rights. In other words, there could be an efficient intertemporal allocation of fish in our example with a number of independent firms owning the fish. These firms could be absentee owners or the workers who actually did the fishing. An efficient allocation of resources could result if each lake were owned by an independent retail fish vendor. The fish even could be owned by the government provided the government did not exercise its monopoly power but behaved as if it were competitive. Even a monopoly that controlled all the lakes would benefit by conserving fish, though in that case there would be the inefficiencies normally associated with monopoly power as discussed in Chapter 9. Ownership of the resource will not affect its efficient allocation. Ownership is an important policy question, however, because it will affect the distribution of income.

Now it is easy to see why the stocks of cod and turbot in the North Atlantic are threatened. No one has a clear ownership claim on these fish. If the cod (or turbot) stayed entirely within recognized Canadian waters, the Canadian government could exercise ownership over the fish and allocate the catch within a market. For example, it could sell licences to catch fish. To be effective the licence would have to be quantitative. Simply issuing a licence that allowed a firm to catch fish would not be sufficient. The licence would have to set a quota on how much fish the firm could harvest. Fishers could bid on present or future rights to catch fish. If the government tried to maximize its revenue, it would not sell present rights if the present value of future rights were greater. Therefore, it would maintain sustainable stocks of cod and other fish.

This principle has not worked with regard to the North Atlantic cod and turbot fisheries for a number of reasons. First of all Canada cannot exercise property rights over the fish stock because fish swim in and out of Canadian territorial waters. Under international law there is no indisputable way that the Canadian government or individual Canadian fishers can make recognized ownership claims. Without an effective ownership claim on the fishery the resource becomes common property and it's first come first served. Not only is there no mechanism to conserve the fishery, there is an incentive to catch the fish before anyone else does.[4] Even if there was a clear and enforceable ownership claim to the Atlantic cod or the Pacific salmon, there would still be other problems. Even assuming that biological conditions are right, estimating the stock of cod in the North Atlantic is much harder than estimating this year's wheat crop. Moreover, just as an early snow can dramatically reduce the wheat harvest, unforeseen changes in ocean currents and temperatures make future fish stocks uncertain. If forecasts of stocks are not reliable, then forecasts of future prices may not be accurate. The cod fishery could appear to be sustainable when in fact it was being overfished. Such uncertainty with respect to the future is common to all business, but most industries face less uncertainty than exists in ocean fisheries.

There is another problem in determining the present value of the future price. Remember that the present value of a future payment is always less than the nominal value of the future payment. The payment of $1,225.04 in three years had a present value of $1,000 in the case cited above. The $1,000 was based on the fact that at 7 percent simple interest, $1,000 today would earn $225.04 interest over three years; therefore, $1,225.04 three years in the future has a present value of $1,000. What if the interest rate used for discounting was higher? For example, the present value of $1,225.04 at a 10 percent discount rate is only $920.39. At 15 percent, the present value would drop to $805.48. At 20 percent, the present value is only $708.94. Similarly, if the price of fish today is $4.00 a kilo, then the future price must be much higher for its present value to exceed the present price if interest rates are higher. At 7 percent, the present value of a $4.30 price a year hence is $4.02. At 15 percent the one-year future price must rise to more than $4.60 to make it worthwhile to wait to catch the fish. At 20 percent, the one-year future price would have to be more than $4.80 before it would be worth waiting to catch the fish next year. A GIC is a very safe asset. Even if the bank or trust company goes broke, its insurance would virtually guarantee that the owner of the GIC would get his or her money. While economists often talk about *the* interest rate, there is not a single interest rate. Different interest rates apply to different assets. One of the factors that determines the interest rate applicable for a particular purpose is the degree of risk or uncertainty associated with that asset.[5]

---

[4]An interesting variation of the problem of the fishery is presented by Garrett Hardin in "The Tragedy of the Commons." Professor Hardin discusses the problem in the context of cattle herders sharing a common grazing area. He concludes that viewed from the standpoint of individual self-interest, each herder will continue to increase the size of his or her herd. However, the commons has a finite ability to support cattle grazing and is soon over grazed with ruin for all. "The Tragedy of the Commons" is reprinted in R. Dorfman and N. S. Dorfman eds., *Economics of the Environment*. 3rd ed. New York: W. W. Norton, 1993.

[5]In economics *risk* and *uncertainty* have specific meanings. For our purposes we will use *uncertainty* to refer to both uncertainty and risks.

The greater the uncertainty, the higher the interest rate. The interest rate on government bonds and GICs issued by the chartered banks is relatively low because the uncertainty attached to owning such an asset is low. On the other hand, future fish stocks are very uncertain. Moreover, fishers faced with a loss of their livelihood and their whole way of life may have extremely high discount rates. What good is a healthy fish stock in five years if fishers are forced out of fishing this year? Many in Newfoundland cannot wait to see the cod return. Even with enforceable property rights that ensure that the Spanish will not catch "Canadian" cod or that the Americans will not catch "Canadian" salmon, there is no guarantee that the fish will be there in a year or two or into the indefinite future. Unless the expected future price is substantially higher than the current price, there is likely to be a bias toward taking the fish now. To paraphrase an old saying—a fish in the net is worth two in the ocean. Even government might yield to short-term political gain when faced with large numbers of potentially unemployed fishery workers now as opposed to diminished fish stocks in five years. Still a first (and vital) step in conserving many of the world's resources is to develop a workable set of property rules to cover all resources.

Resources and Rent

Buy Land—They Ain't Making It No More

The title for this subsection is roughly a quote of something the American humourist Will Rogers is supposed to have said. Whether or not he said it, it is true. Economists may be no more insightful than Will Rogers, but generally our grammar is better. Economists would say the supply of land is perfectly inelastic. Chapter 3 discussed the price elasticity of demand. As you recall, it was defined as a measure of the responsiveness of consumers to price changes. The *elasticity of supply* is the responsiveness of sellers to a change in price. If the supply of something is *perfectly inelastic,* sellers do not respond at all to a change in price. The supply of land is fixed. No matter how high the price, there will never be any more land. The supply curve is simply a vertical line, as is illustrated in Figure 16–5. Ultimately the supply of a non-renewable resource is perfectly inelastic. In practice however, many non-renewable resources have a normal upward sloping supply curve because we can extract more if we are prepared to pay higher costs. For example, some iron ore occurs near the surface and is easily (cheaply) recovered. Other iron ore is more difficult to recover, higher prices are required if that ore is to be recovered. To start with, we will consider land. (Here we use the term in its everyday meaning.)

In England in the early part of the 19th century, the price of grain rose substantially. Since much of the population depended upon bread as a

The **elasticity of supply** is the responsiveness of sellers to price changes and is equal to the percentage change in the quantity supplied divided by the percentage change in the price of the product. If the supply curve is vertical, supply is fixed or *perfectly (completely) inelastic.*

Figure 16–5   **The supply of land**

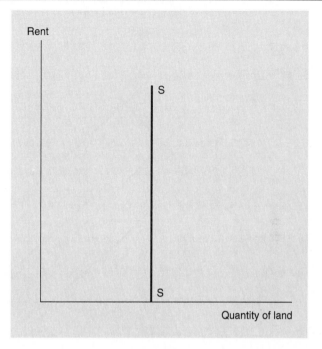

The supply curve for land is vertical because the supply of land is fixed. No matter how high the price of land goes, only a given amount of land is available.

staple food, the higher price became a matter of concern. The popular view was that the high rents that landlords charged for farmland caused the high price of grain. The great English economist David Ricardo argued that causality ran in the opposite direction. It was not the high cost of land that pushed up the price of grain; it was the high price of grain that pulled up the cost of land. You will recall from Chapter 8 that the demand for labour was derived from the demand for the output it produced. The same is true for land—the greater the price of grain, the greater the demand for land to produce grain and therefore the higher the rent that land commands. Consistent with this argument, Ricardo proposed that rather than impose controls on the rent on agricultural land, the English Parliament should repeal the Corn Laws.[6] The Corn Laws placed high duties on imported grain, thereby reducing the supply and raising the price. History has proven Ricardo correct.

Figure 16–6 illustrates what happens to the rent on land as the demand for land increases. If the demand for land is very low, land would be free.

---

[6]Corn referred to all grain.

Figure 16–6   **The effects of an increase in demand for land on rent**

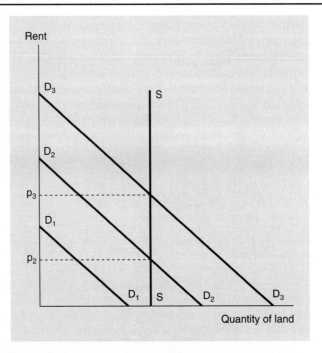

Initially the demand for land is D_1D_1. At that level there is more than enough land to go around and land is free. As the demand for land increases from D_1D_1 to D_2D_2, the land becomes scarce and the rent it receives increases to p_2. If the demand for land increases still more to D_3D_3, the rent will rise still further to p_3. No matter how high the demand for land goes, the supply will remain fixed at *SS*.

Assume that the demand for land is at D_1D_1. Even at a zero price, the quantity demanded is less than the available supply of land. That situation has existed in parts of Canada for much of our history. Many of those who live in the prairie provinces have ancestors who claimed essentially free land under the provisions of the *Homestead Act* of 1872. However, as the world's population grew, the demand for food grew and the demand for all farmland, including the Canadian prairies, grew. D_2D_2 and D_3D_3 show that as the demand for land increases, the rent on that land also increases.

You should notice that the vertical axis in Figure 16–6 is not labelled the price of land. It is labelled rent. Rent is not the the purchase price of land—it is the price for the use of the land. However, a relationship exists between the rent that is charged for the use of the land and the purchase price of the land. The purchase price of a piece of land is the present values of the rents it will earn in the future.

We have assumed that all land is the same. We have also assumed that land has only one use. Of course, this assumption is not true. Often land has many different uses. For example, a given piece of land might be used for grazing, for growing wheat, or for building a new residential subdivision. Obviously, a land rent will be determined by its best use. Equally clear is that not all land is equally productive. Some land is better than other land for any particular use. For example, some farmland is better for growing grain because it is more fertile, or its contour is better suited to the use of modern farm equipment or it is located in a region that has a more suitable climate. Urban land often varies in value because of its location. Downtown land is worth more than suburban land because running a business near banks, accountants, law offices, clients, and so forth is convenient. The higher value for downtown land is due to economies of agglomeration. Economies of agglomeration come about because of the cost savings associated with having a location near other businesses.

Let us assume that there are three different grades of farmland with the same supply of each grade. Grade 1 is poor land; it yields a relatively low output per hectare. Grade 2 is better land, and it yields a greater output per hectare. Grade 3 is the best land; it has the highest yield. Now assume that SS in Figure 16–6 represents the supply of any of the three grades of farmland. D_1D_1 represents the demand for grade 1 land. Just as the demand for labour in Chapter 8 was the marginal revenue product (MRP) of labour, the demand for land is its marginal revenue product. The rental price of grade 1 land would be zero. The land is so poor that at the present price of grain, this land cannot produce a great enough yield to earn a profit for the farmer; therefore, no one would want to use the land. In fact, millions of square kilometers of land in northern Canada fall into this category. Grade 2 land is better. Its demand is higher because its MRP is higher. It can be farmed at a profit. The demand for this land is represented by D_2D_2. Farmers would use this land as long as its rental price did not exceed p_2. D_3D_3 is the demand for the best farmland. It would earn a premium rent p_3 because its yield is even higher than grade 2 land.

While economists frequently assume that the supply of land is absolutely fixed, this assumption is not always exactly true from a practical point of view. Everyone knows that the Dutch have "created" land by building dikes and draining the seawater. Land for a particular purpose can often be created by shifting it from another use. For example, a woodlands can be cleared to grow crops, farmland can be converted to residential land, and residential land can become part of the downtown business core. Therefore, the supply of land for a particular purpose can be upward sloping. Nevertheless, the concept of land as having a fixed supply is extremely valuable in understanding many economic problems.

Economic rent is a payment for an asset that has a completely inelastic supply. Economists also use the term *rent* to refer to a payment that is not necessary to induce a unit to be supplied.

Clearly *rent* as we have been using the term is somewhat different from the everyday use of the word. *Economic rent* is a payment for an asset that has a fixed (completely inelastic) supply. Economic rent is different from other payments. Other payments provide incentives. If the tastes of Canadians change, the price system would work to match production to our new tastes.

For example, the station wagon used to be a very popular family vehicle, and every major car manufacturer produced several models. At some point Canadian tastes shifted. Vans and minivans became more popular with families, and station wagons became less popular. This change in tastes shifted the demand curves for station wagons and vans. The demand for station wagons decreased, causing their prices to fall and signalling to the manufacturers that they should produce fewer station wagons. On the other hand, the demand for vans and minivans increased, causing their prices to rise. The higher prices provided a signal (an incentive) for manufacturers to increase their production of vans and minivans, which was possible because the supply curve for most things is not fixed. A higher price will induce an increase in the quantity supplied. Economic rent does not provide any incentive to produce more because it is impossible to produce any more.

We have been using the term *rent* in a way that it is not usually used. A common use for the word rent is the payment to lease an apartment. Part of that payment is economic rent—the part of the payment that is for the land on which the apartment is located. The other part of the payment is for the building. If the demand for apartments were to increase, it would provide an incentive to build more apartments; however, it could not increase the amount of land available on which to build the apartments. Even though an increase in demand cannot induce an increase in the available land suitable for apartments, it can have an important allocative effect. As land prices rise, there is a trade-off between land and capital. If you cannot create more land you can build taller apartment and office buildings. High-rise buildings in the downtown core of large cities are the simple substitution of capital for land. They also illustrate an important economic point. As non-renewable resources become increasingly scarce, society can sometimes compensate by substituting other resources that are more widely available.

We started this chapter with a discussion about fish. The Atlantic cod and turbot fisheries and the Pacific salmon fishery have been a source of much controversy. We saw that at least some of that controversy was the result of a market failure that developed because there was no clear system of ownership rules. High rent on land has also been a source of much controversy. The high grain prices in England in the early nineteenth century prompted some to argue that the high rents landlords charged farmers were hurting the poor. Ricardo correctly identified the problem as being the high demand for grain caused by population growth and the restriction of grain imports. He proposed that England remove the duties on imported grain thereby increasing the supply of grain and lowering its price. Today there is still a debate between those who favour and those who oppose rent controls as a tool to help the poor. You will remember that rent controls were discussed in Chapter 7.

We just saw that as the demand for land increases in highly populated cities, its price increases. That increase in price can lead to the substitution of capital—tall buildings—for land. However, the issue is not that simple in practice. Cities have zoning requirements. If land is zoned for single-family homes or duplexes, it cannot be used for high-rise apartments or office towers. Therefore, the value of the land is limited to its *MRP* for the assigned low-density use. Much of the backroom politics at the local level takes place in the planning office. If a piece of land is rezoned from low-density use to high-density use, its value can skyrocket instantly. No wonder many planning decisions are so controversial; a favourable ruling on a block of land by a local planning commission can create instant millionaires.

Rent on Other Resources

While in a strict sense economic rent applies only in the case of a resource with a fixed supply, economists often broaden the definition to include certain other payments. Let us assume that Figure 16–7 represents the supply and demand curves of the market for oil. The demand

Figure 16–7   The rent generated in the market for oil

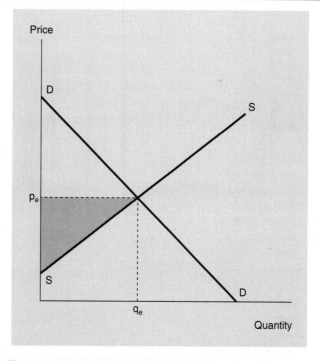

This figure illustrates the market for oil. The equilibrium price and quantity are determined by supply and demand. The shaded area is the producer surplus, or rent. The government attempts to capture this rent by charging the oil companies royalties.

curve *DD* slopes downward and to the right. The supply curve *SS* slopes upward and to the right. It is true that the world's supply of oil is fixed, and therefore the supply curve must ultimately be vertical. However, not all oil is equally easy to recover. Some high-quality oil is relatively close to the surface and therefore easy to recover and refine. Other oil is harder to get out of the ground and requires expensive recovery techniques. Some oil has impurities, such as sulfur, which must be removed. Other oil is located offshore, such as Hibirnia and the Arctic, and not only costs more to recover but also costs more to transport to market. If the price of oil is low, only the least expensive reserves will be exploited. As the price of oil increases, Alberta's oil sands and Newfoundland's offshore reserves become profitable. Therefore, the supply of oil is upward sloping, as is illustrated by *SS*. Given the supply and demand for oil, an equilibrium is reached at a price of p_e and a quantity of q_e. At that price the quantity of oil supplied is exactly equal to the quantity of oil demanded. If the price was a little lower, somewhat less oil would be produced. The oil that would not be produced at the lower price would be the oil that has a higher production cost than that price. In effect, the equilibrium price of oil has to be high enough so that it covers the cost of producing the last or most costly barrel of oil. However, that price is paid for all the barrels of oil produced, even though most of them had a much lower production cost. Assume that p_e was at $28 a barrel. It is quite likely that there will be conventional oil reserves in Alberta which can be recovered profitably at $15 a barrel. However, they will sell for the same price as the heavy oil in Saskatchewan that costs $20 to recover. Offshore Arctic oil that costs $25 a barrel will also fetch the full price. Once again the price is determined not by the cost of each barrel of oil, or the average price of all barrels of oil, but by the cost of the most costly barrel of oil sold. Can you imagine going to the gas station and having the attendant tell you that you only had to pay $.35 a liter because the particular gas you bought was made from oil that was cheap to recover and refine?

If most of the oil recovered would have been available at less than the price for which it is sold, substantial profits may be made from producing oil. If that is the case, who will receive those profits? In our earlier discussion of ocean fisheries, we indicated that the overfishing problem was at least in part due to the lack of a well-defined system of property rights. However, oil and other mineral resources have well-defined property rights. Generally mineral rights (including oil) are the property of the provincial governments. Even if you own your own home, you do not have a claim on the mineral under the land. The crown owns the minerals. One of the rights of ownership is the right of transfer. The crown can lease the mineral rights to the highest bidder. That is exactly what Alberta and Saskatchewan do with their rights to the oil. They earn royalties on the oil.

The area between the supply curve and the price line is the **producer surplus.** It is that part of the price not required as an incentive to induce production. The producer surplus is sometimes referred to as rent.

These royalties are possible because the oil companies earn a *producer surplus*. This surplus is sometimes referred to as rent. It is a rent in the sense that it is income not required in order to induce production. In Figure 16–7 notice the shaded triangular area between the supply curve and the equilibrium price. That area is the producer surplus or the rent that the oil companies receive. When the crown charges the oil company royalties, it is attempting to capture the rent. The government must be careful in establishing its royalty rates. If it overcharges, it will create a disincentive to produce. It is not simply the level of royalties that can create a disincentive to produce. If the royalties were charged on a per barrel basis, the payment would increase the cost of production and reduce the incentive to produce the oil. On the other hand, if the royalities were a lump sum that did not vary with the level of production, they would be a fixed cost and they would not affect the level of output. Such a tax could be collected by auctioning leases for mineral rights. Not surprisingly, the oil companies frequently claim that the royalties are too high. On the other hand, if the government undercharges, it will redistribute income from taxpayers in general to oil producers.

There is no objective reason that the rights to most natural resources rest with the crown. Any system of defined ownership rights would have worked as well to help establish an efficient utilization of resources. The decision to opt for public ownership of resources was a policy decision based on historical and normative grounds. The fact that most of Canada was "unowned" when the decision was made may well have led the government to claim the ownership. This method has since been adopted by Alaska for the development of its oil reserves.

Softwood lumber provides another example of a natural resource that earns rent. The American lumber producers have repeatedly sought protection from Canadian softwood exports because they claim that Canadian softwood lumber is unfairly subsidized. Normally a subsidy is a payment by the government to a producer. Certainly no such payment is made to Canadian lumber producers. The American softwood lumber industry claims that the "subsidy" exists because Canadian producers pay "too little" rent on the lumber they cut. Much of the softwood lumber in Canada and the western United States is harvested from government-owned land. The state or federal government in the United States auctions the right to cut lumber on its land. The fee that the lumber company pays to take the lumber is called a stumpage fee. Stumpage fees in the United States tend to be considerably higher than stumpage fees in Canada. While the Canadian practices have been repeatedly upheld by the dispute settlement procedure, Canada and the producing provinces have recently agreed to increase taxes on lumber exported to the United States—just another example of the controversy that surrounds the issue of resource use and rents.

Summary

This chapter has discussed the economics of natural resources. Economists refer to natural resources as land. Natural resources play a significant role on the economics of all countries. They have played a particularly important role in Canada's development as a major industrial power.

The way an economy uses its natural resources has important implications for both efficiency and the distribution of income. The inefficient allocation of resources will mean that society may have a lower standard of living. Moreover, it will also have important implications for the income of future generations.

Some natural resources have a finite supply. Once the supply is gone, the resource is used up. This reality has led many economists to make "doomsday" predictions about the future of civilization. Nineteenth-century economists feared that the human race would face a worldwide shortage of food as population outpaced the world's ability to produce. In the 1970s, the Club of Rome warned of limits to growth. While these predications have perhaps been overstated, the inevitable truth is that all resources are finite.

Certain market safeguards help society conserve natural resources. Most important is the fact that the future price that could be earned by waiting to sell a resource at a later time is one of the opportunity costs of selling that resource now. We saw how that mechanism could work to conserve fish stocks. The opportunity cost of the future price of fish can be discounted so that its present value is known. For a renewable resource used beyond its sustainable rate, the present value of its future price will represent a high opportunity cost that will provide an incentive to curtail its use. This mechanism requires a defined system of ownership rules to be effective, however, the system of ownership does not necessarily have to be one of private property.

Even the existence of a well-defined set of ownership rules does not guarantee that society will use its resources optimally over time. Uncertainty is always associated with the future. That uncertainty increases the discount rate used to calculate the present value of future income and creates a bias in favour of present use. Individuals faced with present disaster or governments faced with short-term political consequences may have very high discount rates when calculating present values.

Some natural resources such as agricultural land have a completely inelastic (fixed) supply. Consequently, an increase in the price of the resource cannot induce an increase in the quantity supplied. The payment for a resource that has a fixed supply is called economic rent. Even resources such as oil that do not have a completely inelastic supply can earn rent. The rent is a producer surplus that exists because the highest cost unit determines the price of the resource. Units that can be produced more cheaply still collect the market price. The extra revenue they receive is the producer surplus or rent. Governments often try to capture this surplus by charging royalties on the use of the resource.

Checklist of Economic Concepts

Land	Price takers
Staples thesis	Elasticity of supply
Coase theorem	Perfectly inelastic supply
Factors of production	Economic rent (rent)
Renewable resource	Producer surplus
Non-renewable resource	Present value (discounted future
Sustainable growth	value)

Discussion Questions

1. There are three factors of production—land, labour, and capital. In theory these factors seem quite distinct, but in practice they are not. Think about the following examples. How do the factors blend together in each case?

   a. Farmland that has been fertilized.

   b. A professional hockey player with unusual natural ability.

   c. A swamp that has been drained to use as farmland.

2. Large prizes awarded by lotteries are often paid in installments over a number of years. Are these prizes really as great as their promoters claim?

3. In some cases government permits to cut trees have a time limit. That is, the company that buys the permit must cut the trees within a specified period of time or the permit reverts back to the government. Why is such a permit not consistent with the efficient management of the forest?

4. Why do high-rise buildings tend to be in the downtown core of large cities?

5. Steel can be made from iron ore, or it can be made with scrap iron. As the world's supply of iron ore decreases, what will happen to the price of scrap iron? Explain your answer.

6. This question requires some ability with math. Assume that you are in charge of buying mineral rights for an oil company. You have a choice of bidding on two leases. Both will yield exactly 100,000

barrels of oil, which can be recovered and sold in exactly one year at a price of $23 a barrel. It will cost a constant $20 a barrel to recover and market the oil from lease A and $15 a barrel for the oil from lease B. In each case the cost includes a profit great enough to make the project worth undertaking. The current rate of interest is 10 percent. How much should you bid for lease A and how much for lease B?

Supplementary Reading

Anderson, F. J. *Natural Resources in Canada: Economic Theory and Policy.* 2nd ed. Scarborough, ON: Nelson Canada, 1991.

A good survey covering all aspects of natural resource economics for Canada. It is highly technical.

Anderson, F. J. and R. D. Cairns. "The Softwood Lumber Agreement and Resource Politics," *Canadian Public Policy* 14, no. 2 (June 1988), pp. 186–96.

Somewhat dated now but provides background into the issue of Canadian provincial stumpage fees as compared to American stumpage fees. Explains how stumpage is determined in the two countries.

Arai, A. B. "Enforcement in the Atlantic Fishery," *Canadian Public Policy* 20, no. 4 (December 1994), pp. 353–64.

Discusses practical difficulties in the enforcement of federal regulation in the Atlantic commercial fisheries.

Davis, A. and V. Thiessen. "Public Policy and Social Control in the Atlantic Fisheries," *Canadian Public Policy* 14, no. 1 (March 1988), pp. 66–77.

Discusses the use of licensing as a method of controlling fishing and the effect of government policies on entry into fishing and equity within the fishing industry.

Dorfman, R. and N. S. Dorfman. *Economics of the Environment.* 3rd ed. New York: W. W. Norton, 1993.

This book of readings includes "The Tragedy of the Commons" by Garrett Hardin. Many of the other selections are relevant to Chapter 5. Some readings are technical.

Heilbroner, R. L., *The Worldly Philosophers.* New York: Simon and Schuster, 1961

Chapter 4, "The Gloomy World of Parson Malthus and David Ricardo" is relevant to the problem at hand. The whole book is a wonderfully interesting way to learn economics.

Katz, M. L. and H. S. Rosen. *Microeconomics.* Burr Ridge, IL: Richard D. Irwin, 1994.

An intermediate microeconomics text that is quite readable for most students. Section 17.2 discusses the Coase theorem. Pages 141–142 discuss producer surplus, pages 364–365 discuss economic rent, and section 18.3 covers rent-seeking behaviour.

Marr, W. L. and D. G. Paterson. *Canada: An Economic History.* Toronto: Macmillan Co. of Canada, 1980.

Chapter 1 discusses the staples thesis. Chapter 2 looks at the role of the first staples—fish, furs, and timber—in Canadian economic development.

Pearse, P. H. "Property Rights and the Development of Natural Resources in Canada," *Canadian Public Policy* 14 no. 3 (September 1988), pp. 307–20.

This paper deals with resource property rights in Canada. The authors suggest that the form these rights takes leads to inefficiency and proposes changes in the system of property rights.

van Kooten, G. C. and A. Scott, "Constitutional Crisis, The Economics of Environment and Resource Development in Western Canada," *Canadian Public Policy* 21, no. 2 (June 1995), pp. 233–49.

A discussion of the division of functions relating to natural resources and the environment between the federal and provincial governments. Proposes an approach to determine what ought to be federally and provincially controlled.

Glossary

Ability-to-pay principle. The concept that taxes should be distributed among taxpayers based on their income, wealth, and dependents. (Chapter 15)

Absolute advantage. The ability to produce a good or service at a lower resource cost than one's trading partners. Absolute advantage does not determine trade. (Chapter 12)

Aggregate demand. The total quantities of goods and services that would be purchased in a given period of time by the economy at various general price levels, other things remaining constant. (Chapter 13)

Aggregate supply. The total quantities of goods and services that would be sold in a given period of time in the economy at various general price levels, other things remaining constant. (Chapter 13)

Arbitrage. The simultaneous buying and selling in two or more markets for the same good in order to profit from differing prices in these markets. It occurs in product markets such as wheat or gold, as well as in currency markets. (Chapter 12)

Average cost *(AC).* The ratio of total costs to units of output of a good or service. Also known as per unit cost. (Chapter 10)

Backward tax shifting. The transfer of any part of the burden of a tax to the owners of resources in the form of lower prices paid for their resources. (Chapter 15)

Balance of payments accounts. A statement showing a country's total monetary obligations per period of time to other countries and other countries' obligations to the home country. (Chapter 12)

Balance of trade. The difference in the value of a country's exports and the value of its imports per period of time. The balance of trade is in deficit when more is owed for imports than is earned by exports. It is in surplus when less is owed for imports than is earned by exports. (Chapter 12)

Balanced budget. Annual government receipts are equal to annual government expenditures. (Chapter 15)

Bank rate. The rate of interest that the Bank of Canada charges members of the Canadian Payments Association on advances from the Bank of Canada. Its primary function is to signal interest rate policy. (Chapter 14)

Barriers to entry. Means, such as product differentiation, economies of scale, and government licensing, to protect existing firms from competition from the establishment of new firms. (Chapter 9)

Benefits-received principle of taxation. The concept that taxpayers should pay taxes in accordance with the benefits they receive from the government. (Chapter 15)

Budget deficit. Annual government expenditures exceed annual government receipts. (Chapter 15)

Budget surplus. Annual government receipts exceed annual government expenditures. (Chapter 15)

Capital. Produced resources such as buildings, machinery and equipment, and semifinished materials used as inputs to produce goods and services. (Chapter 1)

Capital account transactions. International transactions in stocks, bonds, and real property. (Chapter 12)

Capture theory. The proposition that regulatory agencies, regardless of their intentions, eventually come to serve the interests of the firms being regulated rather than the general public. (Chapter 10)

Cartel. A group of firms that formally agree to coordinate their production or pricing decisions in a manner that maximizes their joint profits. (Chapter 11)

Ceiling price. A legislated maximum price. To have any effect, it must be set below the equilibrium price. (Chapter 7)

Change in demand. A shift in a demand curve, brought about by a change in one or more of the determinants of demand other than price. (Chapter 2)

Change in quantity demanded. A movement along a demand curve, brought about by a change in the price of the product. (Chapter 2)

Change in quantity supplied. A movement along a supply curve, brought about by a change in the price of the product. (Chapter 2)

Change in supply. A shift in a supply curve, brought about by a change in one or more of the determinants of supply other than price. (Chapter 2)

Coase Theorem. A proposition stating that an efficient allocation of resources cannot occur in the absence of a system of property rights. (Chapter 16)

Collectively consumed goods and services. See public goods.

Common property rights. Resources for which there are no recognized ownership claims. No one can be excluded from the use of such property. (Chapter 16)

Comparative advantage. The ability to produce a good or service with a smaller sacrifice of alternative goods and services than can one's trading partners. Comparative advantage determines trade. (Chapter 12)

Competitive market. A market in which there are many sellers and many buyers of a good or service. No one buyer or seller is large enough to be able to affect the price of the product. (Chapter 2)

Complementary goods. Two products for which an increase in the price of one leads to a decrease in the demand for the other. (Chapter 2)

Concentration ratio. An indicator of potential monopoly power, defined as the percentage of an industry's sales (or assets or output) controlled by the four (or eight) largest firms in the industry. (Chapter 9)

Consumption possibilities curve. A curve showing the maximum quantities of two goods or services that may be consumed in an economy, given the economy's resources and technology. In the absence of international trade, the consumption possibilities curve is identical to the production possibilities curve. (Chapter 12)

Contestable markets. The proposition that if a monopoly faces a credible threat of entry by new competitors, it will reduce its price and increase production until the price equals the average cost of production. (Chapter 10)

Cost-benefit analysis. A technique for determining the optimal level of an economic activity by considering the relationship between the costs and benefits of the activity. In general, an economic activity should be expanded as long as the resulting increase in benefits is at least as great as the resulting increase in costs. (Chapter 4)

Credit market debt. The total government debt (federal, provincial, and local) and the total private debt outstanding for the economy. (Chapter 15)

Currency drain. The portion of the money supply that is not placed in circulation and is not used to support deposit expansion. It can result from hoarding by households, or it can be caused by banks unable or unwilling to lend out and invest a portion of their excess reserves. (Chapter 14)

Current account transactions. International transactions that are more or less immediate or short term in character such as imports, exports, or the payment of investment income. (Chapter 12)

Cyclical unemployment. Unemployment caused by a contraction in aggregate demand or total spending in the economy. Cyclical unemployment is often estimated as the unemployment rate minus NAIRU. (Chapter 13)

Dead-weight welfare loss due to monopoly. The reduction in social welfare as a result of the exercise of monopoly power. (Chapter 9)

Debt management policy.   A policy to determine the structural characteristics of the national debt, that is, the types of securities, ownership pattern, and maturity distribution of the debt. (Chapter 15)

Deficit budget.   See budget deficit.

Deliberate discrimination.   A situation in which an individual has a preference to associate with a particular group or to avoid associating with a particular group. If necessary, such an individual will pay to discriminate. (Chapter 8)

Demand.   The quantities of a good or service per period of time that buyers would be willing and able to purchase at various alternative prices, other things remaining constant. (Chapter 2)

Demand-pull inflation.   Increases in the average price level initiated by and continued from increases in aggregate demand. (Chapter 14)

Deposit multiplier.   The number by which the reserves of the banking system are multiplied to determine the potential total money supply. (Chapter 14)

Derived demand.   The demand for a factor of production is determined by the demand for the product being produced by that factor. In this sense, the demand for labour is a derived demand. (Chapter 8)

Diminishing returns.   See Law of diminishing returns.

Discounted future value.   See present value.

Discouraged workers.   Those who have stopped actively searching for work are not considered to be part of the labour force. As such, they are classified as discouraged workers rather than unemployed. (Chapter 13)

Discrimination.   The situation that exists when equals are treated unequally or unequals are treated equally. (Chapter 8)

Diseconomies of scale.   The situation that occurs when beyond a certain production level, longrun average cost rises as output is increased. (Chapter 10)

Economic good.   A good or service that is both desirable and scarce. (Introduction)

Economic model.   An explanation of economic events that has been logically developed and empirically tested. (Introduction)

Economic policy.   The means society uses to accomplish subjective economic goals. To be effective it should be based on economic theory. (Introduction)

Economic rent.   The payment to a resource that has a completely inelastic supply. Economists also use the term *rent* to refer to a payment that is not necessary to induce a supply. (Chapter 16)

Economic theory.   The aggregation of the models that economists have developed to explain economic events. (Introduction)

Economics.   The study of how society allocates scarce resources among competing goals. (Introduction)

Economies of scale.   The situation that exists when longrun average costs fall as output increases. (Chapter 10)

Efficiency.   The production of the greatest desired output from the given resource base. (Chapter 1)

Elasticity of demand.   The responsiveness of the quantity demanded of a product to changes in its price. Measured by the percentage change in quantity divided by the percentage change in price. (Chapter 3)

Elasticity of supply.   The responsiveness of the quantity supplied of a product to changes in its price. Measured by the percentage change in quantity divided by the percentage change in price. (Chapter 16)

Equal tax treatment doctrine.   The concept that taxpayers in equal economic circumstances should be treated equally; that is, people in identical economic positions should pay the same amounts of taxes. (Chapter 15)

Equation of exchange, $MV = PY$.   An identity where the money supply (M) times the velocity of circulation (V) equals quantities of final goods and services sold (Y) times the average price level (P). (Chapter 14)

Equilibrium price.   The price at which the sellers of a product are willing and able to sell exactly the same amount as the consumers are willing and able to buy at that price. As such, the equilibrium price indicates when consumers feel that precisely the correct share of the economy's scarce resources are devoted to producing the product. (Chapter 2)

Equilibrium quantity.   The quantity of the product that is actually exchanged at the equilibrium price. (Chapter 2)

Equimarginal principle.   The allocation of spending among different inputs in such a way that the marginal benefits per dollar spent on any one input is the same as the marginal benefit per dollar spent on any other input. (Chapter 4)

Equity in distribution.   The normative notion of what constitutes fairness in the distribution of income and the output of the economy. (Chapter 7)

Erroneous discrimination. A situation in which individuals honestly believe untrue stereotypes that make it appear that the discrimination is based on objectively valid criteria. (Chapter 8)

Excess tax burden. The distortionary effects of a tax on relative prices and resource allocation. (Chapter 15)

Exchange rate. The cost of one country's currency in terms of the currency of another country. (Chapter 12)

Explicit costs. Costs of production incurred by the purchase or hire of resources by the producing unit paid out in money. (Chapter 3)

Exploitation. Circumstances in which either consumers pay a higher price for a product than its costs of production or resource owners receive a lower price for a resource than the value of marginal product of the resource. (Chapter 8)

Exports. Goods and services that firms in one country sell in other countries. (Chapter 12)

Externalities. The social spillover benefits or costs that flow from the private consumption or production of a product. (Chapter 15)

Fallacy of composition. The error in logic that occurs when we assume that because something is true for an individual it is also true for the group to which the individual belongs. (Chapter 13)

Fee-for-service principle. The concept that a seller is paid an amount based on the price and quantity of services provided. (Chapter 6)

Firm. A business enterprise. One of the three types of economic agents in society. (Introduction)

Fiscal policy. Government policy with respect to taxation, expenditures, and transfer payments. (Chapters 13 and 15)

Fixed exchange rate. A system of international exchange in which the value of each country's currency is defined in terms of an agreed currency (US$). Each country buys or sells its currency to maintain its pegged value. (Chapter 12)

Flexible exchange rate. A system of international exchange in which the value of each country's currency is determined by free markets. (Chapter 12)

Floor price. A legislated minimum price. To have any effect, it must be set above the equilibrium price. (Chapter 7)

Forward tax shifting. The transfer of any part of the burden of a tax to the consumers in the form of higher prices paid for the product. (Chapter 15)

Free good. A good or service that is not scarce. (Introduction)

Free riders.   Those who receive social spillover benefits without paying the costs of producing the goods or services that yield them. (Chapter 3 and 4)

Frictional unemployment.   Unemployment is transitional and often takes the form of people changing and searching for new jobs. (Chapter 13)

Full-cost pricing.   A situation in which the price of a product is equal to its average cost of production. (Chapter 6)

Full employment rate of unemployment.   See non-accelerating inflation rate of unemployment (NAIRU). (Chapter 13)

Full employment GDP.   See potential GDP.

Gold standard.   A system of international exchange in which the value of currency is set in terms of gold and is freely exchanged for gold. International payments deficits are paid in gold. (Chapter 12)

Government debt.   The total of the outstanding securities of all government, including interest-bearing and non-interest-bearing securities, Canadian and foreign held securities, privately and publicly held securities, and securities held by both the Bank of Canada and financial institutions. (Chapter 15)

Government purchases.   Government expenditures for currently produced goods and services. (Chapter 15)

Government receipts.   Tax revenue from various sources, income from crown corporate activity, resource rents, fines, licenses and permit sales, and in the case of lower levels of government—transfers. (Chapter 15)

Government transfer payments.   See transfer payments.

Gross domestic product (GDP).   The market value of all final goods and services produced within an economy during one year. GDP ignores the issue of whether the resources used for the production are domestically or foreign owned. (Chapter 1)

Gross national product (GNP).   The market value of all final goods and services produced by domestically owned resources during one year regardless of where the production takes place. (Chapter 1)

Horizontal equity.   The notion that people in the same economic circumstances should receive the same economic treatment. (Chapter 15)

Households.   Individuals and families. Households are one of the three types of economic agents in a society. (Introduction)

Human capital.   That part of the productive power of human or labour resources resulting from investment in education and training. (Chapter 3)

Imperfect competition.   Markets that fall between perfect competition and pure monopoly are said to be imperfectly competitive and may exhibit characteristics of either or both of those extremes. (Chapter 2)

Implicit costs.   Costs of production incurred by producing a unit from the use of self-owned, self-employed resources, without money exchanged. (Chapter 3)

Imports.   Goods and services that economic units in one country buy from other countries. (Chapter 12)

Income effect.   In general the effect of a change in income on the quantity of a good or service purchased. (Chapter 2) In a labour market, the change in the hours of work that occurs when there is a change in income, other things remaining constant. (Chapter 8)

Income gap.   See output gap.

Inferior good.   A good for which demand varies inversely with income, other things remaining constant. (Chapter 2)

Inflation.   A rising average price level of goods and services. (Chapter 14)

Investment.   The purchase by firms of real assets such as buildings, equipment, machinery, and raw and semifinished materials for the purpose of increasing output. (Chapter 13)

Keynes effect.   The inverse relationship between the general price level and the level of investment expenditure and other interest rate–sensitive components of aggregate demand. As the price level increases, it causes the demand for money to increase, which tends to increase interest rates and as a result causes decreases in all components of aggregate demand that are financed with credit. (Chapter 13)

Labour.   The physical and mental resources of an economy's people willingly offered as inputs to produce goods and services. (Chapter 1)

Labour force.   The portion of the eligible labour-force population that is either employed for pay, actively seeking employment, or awaiting recall from a temporary layoff. It excludes those individuals in the eligible labour-force population who are neither currently working nor seeking employment. (Chapter 13)

Labour union.   A formal organization of workers that bargains on behalf of its members over the terms and conditions of employment. (Chapter 11)

Land.   Naturally occurring resources used as inputs to produce goods and services. (Chapter 1)

Law of demand. The inverse relationship between the price and the quantity of a good or service that buyers are willing and able to take from the market. (Chapter 2)

Law of diminishing returns. The principle that additional increments of a variable input applied to a fixed input will eventually lead to smaller and smaller increments in additional product output. (Chapter 6)

Lockout. A work stoppage initiated by management. (Chapter 11)

Longrun. A period of time in which a firm can vary all factors of production. (Chapter 8)

Lorenz curve. A graphical representation of the distribution of income. It shows the cumulative percentage of total family (individual) income against the cumulative percentage of families (individuals). (Chapter 7)

Losses. The difference between a firm's total costs and its total revenues when total revenues are less than total costs, including as a part of total costs returns to investors in the firm sufficient to yield an average return on their investments. (Chapter 9)

Low income cut–offs. A Statistics Canada measurement widely used as a measure of poverty. (Chapter 7)

Macroeconomics. The study of the whole economy or large subdivisions of it. (Introduction)

Marginal benefit *(MB).* The change in total benefits due to a one-unit change in an economic activity. (Chapter 4)

Marginal cost *(MC).* The change in total costs due to a one-unit change in an economic activity. (Chapter 4)

Marginal cost of labour. The change that occurs in a firm's total costs due to a one-unit change in the number of workers. (Chapter 8 and 11)

Marginal product of labour *(MP$_l$).* The change in output due to a one-unit change in the number of workers. (Chapter 8)

Marginal propensity to expend *(mpe).* The ratio of extra expenditure on goods and services to the increase in current income that caused the increase in expenditure. On average, as real income rises by one dollar, an increase in planned expenditure by the economy (households, businesses, and governments) is less than one and greater than zero. (Chapter 13)

Marginal revenue *(MR).* The change in revenue due to a one-unit change in the sale of a product. (Chapters 8 and 9)

Marginal revenue product of labour *(MRP$_l$).* The change in revenue due to a one-unit change in the number of workers. (Chapters 7 and 8)

Marginal social benefit *(MSB)*. The change in satisfaction that society receives from a one-unit change in an activity. (Chapter 9)

Market. A mechanism by which individuals interact as buyers and sellers of a product to determine the price and quantity exchanged of the product. (Chapter 2)

Market failure. Certain factors such as monopoly power, social spillover costs, social spillover benefits, imperfect knowledge, or incomplete property rights can result in a market not working in accordance with the theoretical norm. (Chapters 4, 5, and 16)

Microeconomics. The study of individual economic agents and their interaction in the economy. (Introduction)

Minimum efficient scale (MES). The output level at which a firm's longrun average cost is at its lowest level. (Chapter 10)

Minimum wage. A legislated minimum wage rate. To have any effect it must be set above the equilibrium wage. (Chapter 7)

Mixed economic system. An economy that combines elements of both the pure-market and pure-command economies. (Chapter 2)

Money creation. The expansion of demand deposits when banks and other financial institutions, as a group, expand loans. (Chapter 14)

Money multiplier. A numerical coefficient equal to the reciprocal of the cash reserve ratio of the chartered banks. (Chapter 14)

Money supply (M_1). Currency held by the public plus demand accounts in chartered banks. (Chapter 14)

Monopoly. A single seller in a market. (Chapter 9)

Monopoly power. The degree to which sellers can control the supply and hence the price of what they sell. (Chapter 9)

Monopsony. A single buyer or employer in a market. (Chapters 8 and 11)

Monopsony power. The degree to which buyers can control the demand and hence the price of what they purchase. (Chapter 11)

Multiplier *(k)*. The number by which any exogenously caused change in the economy's expenditure on final goods and services must be multiplied in order to estimate the resulting change in aggregate demand. (Chapter 13)

NAIRU. See non-accelerating inflation rate of unemployment. (Chapter 13)

Natural monopoly. An industry in which the average cost of production is minimized by having only one firm produce the product. (Chapter 10)

Natural unemployment rate. See non-accelerating inflation rate of unemployment. (Chapter 13)

Near money.   Assets that are easily convertible to cash. These assets are similar to money because they are very liquid. (Chapter 14)

Negative income tax (NIT).   A transfer of income to all families and individuals whose income is below a guaranteed minimum level. As the family or individual earns income the transfer is taxed back at a predetermined rate. (Chapter 7)

Net foreign purchase effect.   The inverse relationship between the general price level and net exports. (Chapter 13)

Net national debt.   Includes the consolidated securities issued by the federal, provincial, and local governments minus the value of all government financial assets. It does not include the debt held by government agencies and trust funds. (Chapter 15)

Non-accelerating inflation rate of unemployment (NAIRU).   The lowest rate of unemployment consistent with no acceleration of the inflation rate. (Chapter 13)

Non-price competition.   Competition among firms in matters other than price. It usually takes the forms of advertising or changes in design and quality of the product. (Chapter 9)

Normal good.   A good for which demand varies directly with income, other things remaining constant. (Chapter 2)

Normative economics.   The study of what ought to be. Normative economic propositions can not be proven true or false. (Introduction)

Open-market operations.   The purchases and sales of government securities by the Bank of Canada in order to influence the growth in the money supply. (Chapter 14)

Opportunity costs.   The concept that the cost of an increment in the output of any good or service is measured by the value of the goods and services that must be given up to obtain it. (Chapter 1)

Output gap.   The loss in real gross domestic product if unemployment is greater than NAIRU. The output gap is equal to potential GDP minus actual GDP. (Chapter 13)

Participation rate.   The percentage of the eligible labour-force population that is in the labour force. (Chapter 13)

Pay equity.   Equal pay for work of equal value. Pay equity legislation is stronger than equal pay legislation, which only requires equal pay for the same work. (Chapter 8)

Pegged exchange rate.   See fixed exchange rate.

Pigou effect.   The inverse relationship between the general price level and consumption resulting from the change in the real purchasing of wealth—money and Canadian dollar assets—when the general price level changes. (Chapter 13)

Pollution rights market. A system by which firms are allowed to buy and sell government-issued licenses granting the holder the right to create a certain amount of pollution. (Chapter 5)

Positive economics. The study of what has been, what is, and what can be. Positive economics propositions can in theory be supported or refuted with evidence. (Introduction)

Potential GDP. The highest level of real output consistent with no acceleration of the inflation rate. (Chapter 13)

Poverty lines. See low income cut-offs. (Chapter 7)

Present value. The present value or discounted future value of a future payment is equivalent to the amount of money that would have to be invested today at the current rate of interest to yield that payment at the future time. (Chapter 16)

Price discrimination. The sale of the same product to different persons or groups of persons at different prices for reasons unrelated to cost. (Chapter 8)

Price elasticity of demand. See elasticity of demand.

Price index. A set of numbers showing price level changes relative to some base year. (Chapter 14)

Price takers. Individual buyers and sellers who are too small to influence the price. (Chapter 16)

Private good. Any good or service that benefits only the consumer of it. (Chapter 4).

Producer surplus. The part of the price not required as an incentive to induce production. It is represented by the area between the supply curve and the price line. It is sometimes referred to as rent. (Chapter 16)

Production. The process of using technology to combine and transform resources into goods and services. (Chapter 1)

Production possibilities curve. A representation of the maximum quantities of two goods or services that an economy can produce when its resources are used in the most efficient way possible given the available technology. (Chapter 1)

Profit. The difference between a firm's total revenue and total cost. (Chapter 9)

Profit-maximizing output. The output per period of time at which a firm's total revenue exceeds its total cost by the greatest possible amount.

It is the output at which the firm's marginal cost equals its marginal revenue. (Chapter 9)

Progressive tax rates.   A tax-rate schedule that results in an increase in the proportion of tax collections to income as income increases. (Chapter 15)

Proportional tax rates.   A tax-rate schedule that results in a constant proportion of tax collections to income as income changes. (Chapter 15)

Psychic costs.   A loss in personal satisfaction (disutility) rather than money costs. (Chapter 4)

Psychic income.   A gain in personal satisfaction rather than money income. (Chapter 4)

Public good.   Goods and services that yield benefits to each person within a group, and no one person in the group can identify the specific part of the benefit he or she receives. In addition, once provided, the benefits of a public good or service cannot be excluded from any member of the group. (Chapter 4)

Public investments.   Government spending for capital goods such as roads, bridges, dams, schools, and hospitals. (Chapter 15)

Pure command economy.   An economy characterized by state ownership and control of resources and centralized resource-use decision making. (Chapter 2)

Pure market economy.   An economy based on private ownership and control of resources, known as private property rights, and on coordination of resource-use decisions through markets. (Chapter 2)

Quantity theory of money.   The proposition that a change in the money supply will have a direct effect on the general price level. See also equation of exchange. (Chapter 14)

Quota.   A limit on the amount of a good that can be imported. (Chapter 12)

Rationing.   The allocation of given supplies of a good, service, or resource among its users. (Chapter 7)

Real GDP.   GDP in current dollars corrected for changes in the general price level. (Chapter 1)

Regressive tax rates.   A tax-rate schedule that results in a decrease in the proportion of tax collections to income as income increases. (Chapter 15)

Relative price.   The price of a good or service relative to the prices of all other goods and services. (Chapter 3)

Relative tax treatment doctrine.   The theory that taxpayers in different economic circumstances should pay different amounts of taxes. (Chapter 15)

Rent.   See producer surplus. Also see economic rent.

Resources.   The inputs that go into the production of goods and services. They consist of labour, capital, and land. (Chapter 1)

Risk and uncertainty.   Economic decisions normally must be made on the best information available to the agent. When unknown factors will affect the outcome, economists say that there is risk and/or uncertainty. (Chapter 4)

Scarcity.   The situation that exists when there is not enough of something so that everyone can have all they want. (Introduction)

Shortage.   The situation in which the quantity demanded exceeds the quantity supplied at the current price. (Chapter 2)

Shortrun.   The period of time during which a firm has at least one factor of production that cannot be varied. (Chapter 8)

Social overhead capital.   Capital used by the economy as a whole rather than being limited to use by specific firms. Examples include transportation and communications networks. (Chapter 1)

Social spillover benefits.   When the production or consumption of a good or service yields benefits to persons other than those doing the producing or consuming, such benefits are referred to as social spillover benefits or external benefits. (Chapter 3, 4, 5, and 6)

Social spillover costs.   When the production or consumption of a good or service imposes costs on persons other than those doing the producing or consuming, such costs are referred to as social spillover costs or external costs. (Chapter 3, 4, 5, and 6)

Standard of living.   The level of economic well-being of a population, usually measured in terms of its per capita real income. (Chapter 1)

Strike.   A work stoppage initiated by labour. (Chapter 11)

Structural unemployment.   Unemployment caused by fundamental changes in demand for certain kinds of labour relative to supply. Such changes are often the result of technological changes, changes in consumers' tastes and preferences, and changes to the structure and location of industrial production. (Chapter 13)

Subsidy.   Governments make transfers to business called subsidies to encourage production of goods and services that the government deems desirable or to change the distribution of income or to influence international trade. (Chapter 12 and 15)

Substitute goods.   Two goods or services for which an increase in the price of one leads to an increase in the demand for the other, other things remaining constant. (Chapter 2)

Substitution effect. In general, the effect of a change in relative price of a good or service on the quantity of it that is purchased. (Chapter 2) In a labour market, the change in the hours of work that occurs when there is a change in the relative wage rate, other things remaining constant. (Chapter 8)

Supply. The quantities of a good or service per period of time that sellers would be willing and able to sell at various alternative prices, other things remaining constant. (Chapter 2)

Supply-shock inflation. Increases in the general price level caused by increases in the costs of producing goods and services, or an increase in the profit margins of firms that shifts the aggregate supply curve leftward. (Chapter 14)

Surplus. The situation in which the quantity supplied exceeds the quantity demanded at the current price. (Chapter 2)

Sustainable economic growth. The rate of growth for an economy that is possible for the indefinite future. (Chapter 16)

Sustainable rate of use. The rate of exploitation of a resource that can be maintained into the indefinite future. (Chapter 16)

Switching operations. The withdrawal of government monetary deposits from the Bank of Canada and their redeposit in the chartered banks in order to increase the money supply; or the withdrawal of government deposits from the chartered banks and their redeposit in the Bank of Canada in order to reduce the money supply. (Chapter 14)

Tariff. A tax on imported goods. (Chapter 12)

Tastes and preferences. Buyers' psychological desires for goods and services. It is one of the determinants of demand for any one product. A change in consumers' tastes and preferences for a product will shift the demand curve for it. (Chapter 2)

Tax expenditure. The tax revenue lost to the government because of a tax credit or tax deduction. (Chapter 7)

Tax incidence. The burden of any given tax—who actually pays it. (Chapter 15)

Technology. The know-how or methods of production available within an economy. (Chapter 1)

Terms of trade. The cost, in terms of the home country's goods and services, of importing a unit of goods or services from other countries. (Chapter 12)

Transfer payments. Payments made to persons, firms, or other levels of government that are not for services currently performed. Transfers do not result in new output but simply transfer purchasing power from some persons or economic units to others. (Chapter 15)

Unemployment rate.   The unemployment rate is the percentage of the labour force that is not working but is actively engaged in seeking employment. (Chapter 13)

Vertical equity.   The notion that persons in different economic circumstances should receive different rewards from the economic system. (Chapter 15)

Wage discrimination.   Payment of unequal wage rates to persons with equal marginal revenue products. (Chapter 8)

Index